## Bash Shell

- Pipe:
  - `command1 | command2`

- Redirections:
  - `command > file` (output goes to file)
  - `command < file` (input from file)
  - `command > file` (append to file)
  - `command 2> file` (errors go to file)

- Commands:
  - `alias` (defines shortcut for a long command)
  - `apropos` (searches the man pages for keywords)

- `history` (displays most recent commands)
- `locate` (finds files)
- `whereis` (finds executable files for a command)
- `which` (shows full pathname for a command)
- `man` (displays online help)
- `printenv` (displays the environment variables)

- Environment variables:
  - `HOME` (user's home directory)
  - `PATH` (directories to search for commands)
  - `TERM` (name of terminal type)

## File System

- Key directories in the file system:
  - `/` Root directory (base of file system)
  - `/bin` (executable programs)
  - `/boot` (Linux kernel and boot loader)
  - `/dev` (special device files)
  - `/etc` (system configuration files)
  - `/home` (home directories of all users)
  - `/lib` (library files for programs)
  - `/mnt` (mount points for CD-ROM, floppy)
  - `/root` (home directory of the root user)
  - `/sbin` (system-administration commands)
  - `/tmp` (temporary directory)
  - `/usr` (many important programs)
  - `/var` (various system files, such as logs)

- Commands:
  - `cat`    Copies a file to the standard output
  - `cd`    Changes the current directory
  - `chmod`    Changes file permissions
  - `chown`    Changes file ownerships
  - `cp`    Copies files
  - `dd`    Copies blocks of data
  - `df`    Reports disk space usage by device
  - `diff`    Compares two text files
  - `du`    Reports disk space usage by directory
  - `file`    Displays the type of data in a file
  - `find`    Finds files based on specified criteria
  - `grep`    Searches for text in a file

- `ln`    Links a filename to a link name
- `ls`    Displays the contents of a directory
- `mkdir`    Creates a directory
- `more`    Displays a text file, one page at a time
- `mount`    Mounts a file system
- `mv`    Renames or moves file
- `pwd`    Displays the current directory
- `rm`    Deletes files
- `rmdir`    Deletes directories
- `sort`    Sorts lines in a text file
- `split`    Splits a file into smaller parts
- `umount`    Unmounts a file system
- `wc`    Counts words and lines in a file

- File permissions:
  - `rwxrwxrwx`: 3 groups of `rwx`, leftmost is for owner, middle for group, rightmost for others; `rwx` stands for read (`r`), write (`w`), execute (`x`); a dash (-) means no permission
  - `rwx------`: Only owner can read, write, execute
  - `rw--r--r--`: Everyone can read, owner can write
  - `rw-------`: Only owner can read and write
  - `r--r--r--`: Read-only file (everyone can read)

# Red Hat® Fedora™ Linux® 2 All-in-One Desk Reference For Dummies®

Cheat Sheet

## Fedora Core Installation

1. Resize the disk partition using a partitioning tool such as PartitionMagic or get a second hard disk.
2. Boot the PC from the DVD-ROM.
3. Go through the graphical installation steps.
4. Configure the other hardware when the system first boots up.

## Red Hat Linux Configuration

✔ Run the graphical system configuration tools from Main Menu⇨System Settings

✔ To configure the X Window System, run

`system-config-display`

✔ Printer setup: Main Menu⇨System Settings⇨Printing

✔ Sound card setup: Main Menu⇨System Settings⇨Soundcard Detection

## GNOME and KDE Desktops

✔ Click the Main Menu button in GNOME or KDE and then select the applications to run

✔ Always right-click for a pop-up menu of options

✔ Right-click the GNOME panel to add applets to the panel

✔ To run OpenOffice.org applications: Main Menu⇨Office

## System Administration

**Manage user accounts:** Main Menu⇨System Settings⇨Users and Groups

**Manage packages:** Main Menu⇨System Settings⇨Add/Remove Applications

**Configure services:** Main Menu⇨System Settings⇨Server Settings⇨Services

**Install RPM packages:** `rpm -ivh` *packagefile*

**Check if RPM is installed:** `rpm -q` *rpmname*

**Unpack compressed tar files:** `tar zxvf` *filename*`.tgz`

**Unpack bz2 compressed files:** `bzip2 -d` *filename*`.bz2`

## Network Configuration

✔ **Network configuration:** Main Menu⇨System Tools⇨Network Device Control

✔ **Internet connection:** Main Menu⇨System Tools⇨Internet Configuration Wizard

**Commands:**

| | |
|---|---|
| ✔ `ping` | Checks network connectivity |
| ✔ `ifconfig` | Configures network interface |
| ✔ `iwconfig` | Configures wireless network interface |
| ✔ `netstat` | Displays network status |

## For Dummies: Bestselling Book Series for Beginners

# Red Hat® Fedora™ Linux® 2
## ALL-IN-ONE DESK REFERENCE
# FOR
# DUMMIES®

## by Naba Barkakati

WILEY

Wiley Publishing, Inc.

**Red Hat® Fedora™ Linux® 2 All-in-One Desk Reference For Dummies®**

Published by
**Wiley Publishing, Inc.**
111 River Street
Hoboken, NJ 07030-5774

WILEY

# About the Author

**Naba Barkakati** is an electrical engineer and a successful computer-book author who has experience in a wide variety of systems, ranging from MS-DOS and Windows to UNIX and Linux. He bought his first personal computer — an IBM PC-AT — in 1984 after graduating with a PhD in electrical engineering from the University of Maryland at College Park. While pursuing a full-time career in engineering, Naba dreamed of writing software for the emerging PC software market. As luck would have it, instead of building a software empire like Microsoft, he ended up writing successful computer books. Currently, Naba is a Senior Level Technologist at the Center for Technology and Engineering in the U.S. General Accounting Office.

Over the past 15 years, Naba has written over 25 computer books on a number of topics ranging from Windows programming with C++ to Linux. He has authored several bestselling titles, such as The Waite Group's *Turbo C++ Bible*, *Object-Oriented Programming in C++*, *X Window System Programming*, *Visual C++ Developer's Guide*, *Borland C++ 4 Developer's Guide*, and *Linux Secrets*. His books have been translated into many languages, including Spanish, French, Polish, Greek, Italian, Chinese, Japanese, and Korean. Naba's most recent book is *Red Hat Linux 9 Professional Secrets*, also published by Wiley.

Naba lives in North Potomac, Maryland, with his wife Leha, and their children, Ivy, Emily, and Ashley.

# Dedication

I would like to dedicate this book to my wife Leha, and daughters Ivy, Emily, and Ashley.

# Author's Acknowledgments

I am grateful to Terri Varveris for getting me started on this book — a set of nine quick reference guides on all aspects of Red Hat Linux. As the project editor, Linda Morris guided me through the manuscript-submission process and kept everything moving. I appreciate the guidance and support that Terri and Linda gave me during this project.

I would like to thank Jason Luster for reviewing the manuscript for technical accuracy and providing many useful suggestions for improving the book's content.

Thanks to everyone at Wiley Publishing for transforming my raw manuscript into this well-edited and beautifully packaged book.

Of course, there would be no reason for this book if it were not for Linux. For this, we have Linus Torvalds and the legions of Linux developers around the world to thank. Thanks to Red Hat for providing beta copies of Red Hat Linux and the publisher's edition CDs that are bundled with this book.

Finally, and as always, my greatest thanks go to my wife, Leha, and our daughters, Ivy, Emily, and Ashley — it is their love and support that keeps me going. Thanks for being there!

## Publisher's Acknowledgments

We're proud of this book; please send us your comments through our online registration form located at www.dummies.com/register/.

Some of the people who helped bring this book to market include the following:

### Acquisitions, Editorial, and Media Development

**Project Editor:** Linda Morris

**Acquisitions Editor:** Terri Varveris

**Copy Editor:** Rebecca Senninger

**Technical Editor:** Jason Luster

**Editorial Manager:** Leah Cameron

**Permissions Editor:** Laura Moss

**Media Development Specialist:** Travis Silvers

**Media Development Manager:** Laura VanWinkle

**Media Development Supervisor:** Richard Graves

**Editorial Assistant:** Amanda Foxworth

**Cartoons:** Rich Tennant, www.the5thwave.com

### Composition

**Project Coordinator:** Courtney MacIntyre

**Layout and Graphics:** Amanda Carter, Andrea Dahl, Lauren Goddard, Denny Hager, Joyce Haughey, Stephanie D. Jumper, Michael Kruzil, Jacque Schneider

**Proofreaders:** Carl William Pierce, Sossity Smith, Brian H. Walls

**Indexer:** Lynnzee Elze

---

**Publishing and Editorial for Technology Dummies**

    **Richard Swadley,** Vice President and Executive Group Publisher

    **Andy Cummings,** Vice President and Publisher

    **Mary C. Corder,** Editorial Director

**Publishing for Consumer Dummies**

    **Diane Graves Steele,** Vice President and Publisher

    **Joyce Pepple,** Acquisitions Director

**Composition Services**

    **Gerry Fahey,** Vice President of Production Services

    **Debbie Stailey,** Director of Composition Services

# Contents at a Glance

**Introduction** .................................................. 1

**Book 1: Fedora Basics** ...................................... 7

Chapter 1: Introducing Fedora Core .................................9
Chapter 2: Installing Fedora Core .................................31
Chapter 3: Troubleshooting and Configuring Fedora Core ...................57
Chapter 4: Trying Out Fedora Core .................................75
Chapter 5: Cool Fedora Core Install Projects ...................99

**Book 11: Workstations and Applications** ...................... 109

Chapter 1: Exploring the GUI Desktops .................................111
Chapter 2: Learning the Shell .................................135
Chapter 3: Navigating the Linux File System .................................153
Chapter 4: Exploring Fedora Core Applications .................................169
Chapter 5: Using Text Editors .................................199

**Book 111: OpenOffice.org** .................................... 211

Chapter 1: Writing with OpenOffice.org Writer .................................213
Chapter 2: Preparing Spreadsheets with OpenOffice.org Calc .................................237
Chapter 3: Making Presentations with OpenOffice.org Impress .................................249
Chapter 4: Drawing with OpenOffice.org Draw .................................261

**Book 1V: Networking** ...................................... 269

Chapter 1: Connecting to the Internet .................................271
Chapter 2: Setting Up a Local Area Network .................................295
Chapter 3: Adding a Wireless Ethernet LAN .................................307
Chapter 4: Managing the Network .................................319
Chapter 5: Cool Networking Projects .................................329

**Book V: Internet** ........................................ 335

Chapter 1: Exchanging E-Mail and Instant Messages .................................337
Chapter 2: Using the Web .................................351
Chapter 3: Reading Newsgroups .................................371
Chapter 4: Transferring Files with FTP .................................383

## Book VI: Administration .............................391

Chapter 1: Performing Basic System Administration ...................................393
Chapter 2: Managing Users ............................................................425
Chapter 3: Managing the File System .................................................437
Chapter 4: Managing Applications ....................................................461
Chapter 5: Managing Devices and Printers ............................................479
Chapter 6: Upgrading and Customizing the Kernel .....................................493

## Book VII: Security .............................519

Chapter 1: Understanding Network and Host Security ..................................521
Chapter 2: Securing the Host ........................................................535
Chapter 3: Securing the Network .....................................................557
Chapter 4: Performing Security Audits ...............................................577

## Book VIII: Internet Servers .............................595

Chapter 1: Managing the Servers .....................................................597
Chapter 2: Running the Apache Web Server ............................................615
Chapter 3: Setting Up the FTP Server ................................................639
Chapter 4: Serving Up Mail and News .................................................647
Chapter 5: Setting Up DNS ...........................................................675
Chapter 6: Running Samba and NFS ....................................................695

## Book IX: Programming .............................707

Chapter 1: Fedora Core Programming Essentials .......................................709
Chapter 2: Programming in C .........................................................735
Chapter 3: Writing Shell Scripts ....................................................767
Chapter 4: Programming in Perl ......................................................779

## Appendix: About the DVD .............................807

## Index .............................811

# Table of Contents

*Introduction* ................................................................ *1*

About This Book ...............................................................1

Conventions Used in This Book ................................................2

What You Don't Have to Read ..................................................2

Who Are You? ..................................................................3

How This Book Is Organized ...................................................3

What's on the DVD? ...........................................................4

Icons Used in This Book ......................................................5

Where to Go from Here ........................................................5

*Book 1: Fedora Basics* ..................................................... *7*

## Chapter 1: Introducing Fedora Core ....................................9

What Is Fedora Core? .........................................................9

    Operating systems and Linux ............................................9

    Linux distributions ...................................................11

    Transitioning to the Fedora Project ...................................11

    Making sense of version numbers .......................................12

    Under the hood in Linux kernel 2.6 ....................................13

What Fedora Core Includes ...................................................16

    GNU software ...........................................................16

    GUIs and applications .................................................19

    Networks ...............................................................20

    Internet servers ......................................................21

    Software development ..................................................22

    Online documentation ..................................................23

What Fedora Core Helps You Manage ...........................................25

    Disks, CD-ROMs, and DVD-ROMs ..........................................25

    Peripheral devices ....................................................26

    File systems and sharing ..............................................27

    Network ................................................................27

How Do I Get Started? .......................................................28

    Install ................................................................28

    Configure ..............................................................28

    Explore ................................................................29

    Learn ..................................................................29

**Chapter 2: Installing Fedora Core** . . . . . . . . . . . . . . . . . . . . . . . . . .**31**

Following the Installation Steps . . . . . . . . . . . . . . . . . . . . . . . . . . . . . .31
Checking Your PC's Hardware . . . . . . . . . . . . . . . . . . . . . . . . . . . . . . .33
Setting Aside Space for Fedora Core . . . . . . . . . . . . . . . . . . . . . . . . . .34
Defragmenting your hard disk . . . . . . . . . . . . . . . . . . . . . . . . . .34
Resizing your hard disk partition . . . . . . . . . . . . . . . . . . . . . . . .36
Starting the Fedora Core Installation . . . . . . . . . . . . . . . . . . . . . . . . .39
Selecting Keyboard, Mouse, and Installation Type . . . . . . . . . . . . . . .40
Partitioning the Disk for Fedora Core . . . . . . . . . . . . . . . . . . . . . . . . .43
Setting Up Key System Parameters . . . . . . . . . . . . . . . . . . . . . . . . . . .47
Installing the boot loader . . . . . . . . . . . . . . . . . . . . . . . . . . . . . .47
Configuring the network . . . . . . . . . . . . . . . . . . . . . . . . . . . . . . .48
Configuring the firewall and SELinux . . . . . . . . . . . . . . . . . . . . .50
Selecting languages to support . . . . . . . . . . . . . . . . . . . . . . . . . .51
Setting the time zone . . . . . . . . . . . . . . . . . . . . . . . . . . . . . . . . .51
Setting the root password . . . . . . . . . . . . . . . . . . . . . . . . . . . . . .52
Selecting and Installing the Package Groups . . . . . . . . . . . . . . . . . . .53

**Chapter 3: Troubleshooting and Configuring Fedora Core** . . . . . . . .**57**

Using Text Mode Installation . . . . . . . . . . . . . . . . . . . . . . . . . . . . . . . .58
Using the linux noprobe Command . . . . . . . . . . . . . . . . . . . . . . . . . . .58
Troubleshooting X . . . . . . . . . . . . . . . . . . . . . . . . . . . . . . . . . . . . . . . .59
Resolving Other Installation Problems . . . . . . . . . . . . . . . . . . . . . . . .61
The fatal signal 11 error . . . . . . . . . . . . . . . . . . . . . . . . . . . . . . .61
Using kernel boot commands . . . . . . . . . . . . . . . . . . . . . . . . . . .62
Setting Up Printers . . . . . . . . . . . . . . . . . . . . . . . . . . . . . . . . . . . . . . .64
Turning On Sound . . . . . . . . . . . . . . . . . . . . . . . . . . . . . . . . . . . . . . . .68
Adding User Accounts . . . . . . . . . . . . . . . . . . . . . . . . . . . . . . . . . . . . .69
Managing DVDs and CD-ROMs . . . . . . . . . . . . . . . . . . . . . . . . . . . . . . .71
Installing RPM Packages . . . . . . . . . . . . . . . . . . . . . . . . . . . . . . . . . . .72

**Chapter 4: Trying Out Fedora Core** . . . . . . . . . . . . . . . . . . . . . . . . . .**75**

Booting Fedora Core . . . . . . . . . . . . . . . . . . . . . . . . . . . . . . . . . . . . . .75
Exploring GUI Desktops . . . . . . . . . . . . . . . . . . . . . . . . . . . . . . . . . . . .81
GNOME . . . . . . . . . . . . . . . . . . . . . . . . . . . . . . . . . . . . . . . . . . . .81
KDE . . . . . . . . . . . . . . . . . . . . . . . . . . . . . . . . . . . . . . . . . . . . . . .88
Playing with the Shell . . . . . . . . . . . . . . . . . . . . . . . . . . . . . . . . . . . . .94
Starting the Bash shell . . . . . . . . . . . . . . . . . . . . . . . . . . . . . . . .95
Understanding shell commands . . . . . . . . . . . . . . . . . . . . . . . . .95
Trying a few Linux commands . . . . . . . . . . . . . . . . . . . . . . . . . .96
Shutting Down . . . . . . . . . . . . . . . . . . . . . . . . . . . . . . . . . . . . . . . . . . .98

**Chapter 5: Cool Fedora Core Install Projects** . . . . . . . . . . . . . . . . . .**99**

Joining the BitTorrent . . . . . . . . . . . . . . . . . . . . . . . . . . . . . . . . . . . . .99
Things you need . . . . . . . . . . . . . . . . . . . . . . . . . . . . . . . . . . . . .100
Steps to follow . . . . . . . . . . . . . . . . . . . . . . . . . . . . . . . . . . . . . .100

Burning Fedora Core CDs .................................................103
    Things you need ...................................................103
    Steps to follow ..................................................103
Preparing a Fedora Core DVD ..........................................104
    Things you need ..................................................104
    Steps to follow ..................................................105
Doing an FTP Install .................................................107
    Things you need ..................................................107
    Steps to follow ..................................................107

## *Book II: Workstations and Applications* ......................*109*

### Chapter 1: Exploring the GUI Desktops .......................111

Learning the Common Features of the GUIs .............................111
    Desktop pop-up menus .............................................112
    Icon pop-up menus ................................................113
    The panel ........................................................114
    The Main Menu ....................................................116
Exploring GNOME ......................................................119
    Using the Nautilus shell .........................................120
    Configuring GNOME ................................................124
Exploring KDE ........................................................127
    Using Konqueror ..................................................128
    Configuring KDE ..................................................132

### Chapter 2: Learning the Shell ..............................135

Opening Terminal Windows and Virtual Consoles ........................135
Using the Bash Shell .................................................136
    Learning the syntax of shell commands ............................136
    Combining shell commands .........................................138
    Controlling command input and output ............................138
    Typing less with automatic command completion ...................140
    Going wild with asterisks and question marks ....................140
    Repeating previously typed commands .............................142
Learning Linux Commands ..............................................142
    Becoming root (superuser) .......................................146
    Managing processes ...............................................147
    Working with date and time ......................................147
    Processing files ................................................148
Writing Shell Scripts ................................................151

### Chapter 3: Navigating the Linux File System ................153

Understanding the Linux File System ..................................153
Navigating the File System with Linux Commands .......................157
    Commands for directory navigation ...............................158
    Commands for directory listings and permissions .................159

Commands for changing permissions and ownerships ..............162
Commands for working with files .....................................163
Commands for working with directories .........................164
Commands for finding files ............................................165
Commands for mounting and unmounting .....................166
Commands for checking disk-space usage ....................167

**Chapter 4: Exploring Fedora Core Applications** .................**169**

Taking Stock of the Fedora Core Applications ........................169
Office Applications and Tools .............................................171
Calculators .................................................................172
Commercially available office applications for Linux ...........173
aspell spelling checker ...............................................175
Databases ...................................................................176
Adding a database user ...............................................177
Reviewing the steps to build the database ....................178
Designing the database ...............................................179
Creating an empty database ........................................180
Using the PostgreSQL interactive terminal ...................180
Defining a table ..........................................................181
Inserting records into a table ......................................182
Querying the database ................................................182
Multimedia Applications ....................................................183
Using a digital camera ................................................183
Playing audio CDs ......................................................186
Playing sound files .....................................................187
Burning a CD ..............................................................188
Graphics and Imaging ........................................................193
The GIMP ...................................................................194
Gnome Ghostview ......................................................196

**Chapter 5: Using Text Editors** ...............................**199**

Using GUI Text Editors .......................................................199
Text Editing with ed and vi .................................................200
Using ed ....................................................................201
Using vi .....................................................................204

*Book III: OpenOffice.org* .................................*211*

**Chapter 1: Writing with OpenOffice.org Writer** .................**213**

Getting Documents from Others ..........................................214
Taking Stock of OpenOffice.org Writer ................................215

Getting Started with Writer ...........................................................216
    Examining the Writer main window ...............................217
    Setting up Writer ...............................................................218
Preparing Documents in Writer ...............................................221
    Editing and reviewing documents ...................................221
    Using styles and templates .............................................224
    Performing page layout .................................................228
    Creating and inserting graphics ......................................231
    Using fields ....................................................................233
    Working with large documents .......................................235

**Chapter 2: Preparing Spreadsheets with OpenOffice.org Calc ... .237**

Taking Stock of OpenOffice.org Calc .......................................237
Getting Started with Calc ........................................................238
    Examining the Calc main window ...................................239
    Setting up Calc ...............................................................240
Using Calc ...............................................................................241
    Entering and formatting data ..........................................241
    Calculating and charting data .........................................244

**Chapter 3: Making Presentations with OpenOffice.org Impress ...249**

Taking Stock of OpenOffice.org Impress ...................................249
Getting Started with Impress ...................................................250
Using Impress .........................................................................253
    Preparing presentations ................................................254
    Adding graphics and special effects ...............................257
    Delivering presentations .................................................260

**Chapter 4: Drawing with OpenOffice.org Draw .................261**

Taking Stock of OpenOffice.org Draw .......................................261
Getting Started with Draw ........................................................262
Using Draw .............................................................................264

*Book IV: Networking* ..................................................*269*

**Chapter 1: Connecting to the Internet ........................271**

Understanding the Internet .......................................................271
Deciding How to Connect to the Internet ...................................272
Connecting with DSL ...............................................................274
    How DSL works .............................................................274
    DSL alphabet soup: ADSL, IDSL, SDSL .........................275
    Typical DSL setup ..........................................................276

Connecting with a Cable Modem ...............................................279
How cable modem works ...........................................280
Typical cable modem setup .......................................282
Setting Up Dial-Up Networking ...........................................284
Connecting the modem ............................................286
Testing the modem ..................................................289
Setting up and activating a PPP connection ...............291
Configuring CHAP and PAP authentication ...............293

**Chapter 2: Setting Up a Local Area Network** ...................**295**

Understanding TCP/IP ......................................................295
TCP/IP and the Internet ...........................................297
IP addresses ............................................................297
Internet services and port numbers ...........................298
Setting Up an Ethernet LAN ...............................................299
How Ethernet works .................................................300
Ethernet cables .......................................................301
Configuring TCP/IP Networking ...........................................302
Connecting Your LAN to the Internet ...................................305

**Chapter 3: Adding a Wireless Ethernet LAN** ...................**307**

Understanding Wireless Ethernet Networks ...........................307
Understanding infrastructure and ad hoc modes .........308
Understanding wired equivalent privacy (WEP) ...........310
Setting Up the Wireless Hardware ......................................310
Configuring the wireless access point ........................312
Configuring Wireless Networking ........................................312

**Chapter 4: Managing the Network** ...........................**319**

Learning the TCP/IP Configuration Files ...............................319
/etc/hosts ...............................................................320
/etc/networks .........................................................320
/etc/host.conf ........................................................320
/etc/resolv.conf ......................................................321
/etc/hosts.allow ......................................................321
/etc/hosts.deny .......................................................322
/etc/nsswitch.conf ..................................................323
Checking Out TCP/IP Networks ...........................................323
Checking the network interfaces ...............................323
Checking the IP routing table ...................................324
Checking connectivity to a host ................................325
Checking network status ..........................................325
Sniffing network packets ..........................................327
Configuring Networks at Boot Time .....................................328

### Chapter 5: Cool Networking Projects . . . . . . . . . . . . . . . . . . . . . .329

Building Your Own Home Network . . . . . . . . . . . . . . . . . . . . . . . . . . . .329
    Things you need . . . . . . . . . . . . . . . . . . . . . . . . . . . . . .329
    Steps to follow . . . . . . . . . . . . . . . . . . . . . . . . . . . . . .330
Adding Wireless to Your Current Network . . . . . . . . . . . . . . . . . . . . . .331
    Things you need . . . . . . . . . . . . . . . . . . . . . . . . . . . . . .331
    Steps to follow . . . . . . . . . . . . . . . . . . . . . . . . . . . . . .331
Turning Your Fedora Core System into a NAT Router . . . . . . . . . . . . .332
    Things you need . . . . . . . . . . . . . . . . . . . . . . . . . . . . . .332
    Steps to follow . . . . . . . . . . . . . . . . . . . . . . . . . . . . . .333

## Book V: Internet . . . . . . . . . . . . . . . . . . . . . . . . . . . . . . . . . . .335

### Chapter 1: Exchanging E-Mail and Instant Messages . . . . . . . . . . .337

Understanding Electronic Mail . . . . . . . . . . . . . . . . . . . . . . . . . . . . . .338
    How MUA and MTA work . . . . . . . . . . . . . . . . . . . . . . . . .338
    Mail message enhancements . . . . . . . . . . . . . . . . . . . . . .339
Taking Stock of Mail Readers and IM Clients in Fedora Core . . . . . . .340
Using Ximian Evolution . . . . . . . . . . . . . . . . . . . . . . . . . . . . . . . . . . .340
Using Mozilla Mail . . . . . . . . . . . . . . . . . . . . . . . . . . . . . . . . . . . . . . .344
    Managing your Inbox . . . . . . . . . . . . . . . . . . . . . . . . . . . .347
    Composing and sending messages . . . . . . . . . . . . . . . . .348
Instant Messaging with Gaim . . . . . . . . . . . . . . . . . . . . . . . . . . . . . . .349

### Chapter 2: Using the Web . . . . . . . . . . . . . . . . . . . . . . . . . . . . .351

Discovering the World Wide Web . . . . . . . . . . . . . . . . . . . . . . . . . . . .351
    Like a giant spider's web . . . . . . . . . . . . . . . . . . . . . . . .352
    Links and URLs . . . . . . . . . . . . . . . . . . . . . . . . . . . . . . .353
    Web servers and Web browsers . . . . . . . . . . . . . . . . . . .355
Web Browsing in Fedora Core . . . . . . . . . . . . . . . . . . . . . . . . . . . . . .356
    Checking out the Web browsers in Fedora Core . . . . . . .357
    Starting Mozilla . . . . . . . . . . . . . . . . . . . . . . . . . . . . . . .357
    Learning Mozilla's user interface . . . . . . . . . . . . . . . . . .357
    Changing your home page . . . . . . . . . . . . . . . . . . . . . . .361
    Changing Mozilla's appearance . . . . . . . . . . . . . . . . . . .361
    Surfing the Net with Mozilla . . . . . . . . . . . . . . . . . . . . . .363
Creating Web Pages . . . . . . . . . . . . . . . . . . . . . . . . . . . . . . . . . . . . .364
    Introducing HTML . . . . . . . . . . . . . . . . . . . . . . . . . . . . .364
    Composing Web pages with Mozilla Composer . . . . . . . .366

## Chapter 3: Reading Newsgroups ............................ 371

Understanding Newsgroups ......................................................................371
    Newsgroup hierarchy ......................................................................372
    Top-level newsgroup categories ..................................................373
    Linux-related newsgroups ..............................................................374
Reading Newsgroups from Your ISP ....................................................375
    Reading newsgroups with Mozilla Mail ......................................376
    Newsgroup subscriptions ..............................................................378
    Posting news ....................................................................................379
Reading and Searching Newsgroups at Web Sites ............................380

## Chapter 4: Transferring Files with FTP ..................... 383

Using Graphical FTP Clients ..................................................................383
    Using gFTP ........................................................................................384
    Using a Web browser as an FTP client ........................................385
Using the Command-Line FTP Client ....................................................387

## *Book VI: Administration* ................................... *391*

### Chapter 1: Performing Basic System Administration ........... 393

Taking Stock of System-Administration Tasks ..................................393
How to Become root ................................................................................395
    Using the su - command ................................................................395
Becoming root for the GUI Utilities ....................................................395
    Recovering from a forgotten root password ..............................396
Understanding How Fedora Core Boots ..............................................397
    Understanding the init process ....................................................397
    Examining the /etc/inittab file ....................................................399
    Trying a new run level with the init command ..........................400
    Understanding the Fedora Core startup scripts ........................401
    Manually starting and stopping servers ....................................402
    Automatically starting servers at system startup ....................403
    Understanding the GUI startup ....................................................404
Taking Stock of Fedora Core System Configuration Files ................406
Monitoring System Performance ..........................................................408
    Using the top utility ......................................................................409
    Using the GNOME system monitor ..............................................411
    Using the uptime command ..........................................................412
    Using the vmstat utility ................................................................413
    Checking disk performance and disk usage ..............................414
Viewing System Information via the /proc File System ....................415
Scheduling Jobs in Fedora Core ............................................................418
    Scheduling one-time jobs ..............................................................419
    Scheduling recurring jobs ............................................................421

## Chapter 2: Managing Users ...............................425

Adding User Accounts ........................................425
    Using the User Manager to add user accounts ...............426
    Using commands to manage user accounts ...............428
Understanding the /etc/passwd File ........................429
Managing Groups ...........................................430
Exploring the User Environment ...........................431
Changing User and Group Ownership of Files ...............434

## Chapter 3: Managing the File System .......................437

Learning the Linux File System ..............................437
    Understanding the file-system hierarchy ...............438
    Mounting a device on the file system ...............440
    Examining the /etc/fstab file ...............442
Sharing Files with NFS .......................................443
    Exporting a file system with NFS ...............444
    Mounting an NFS file system ...............445
Backing Up and Restoring Files ..............................445
    Selecting a backup strategy and media ...............445
    Commercial backup utilities for Linux ...............447
    Using the tape archiver — tar ...............447
Accessing DOS/Windows File Systems ........................452
    Mounting a DOS disk partition ...............452
    Mounting DOS floppy disks ...............453
    Mounting an NTFS Partition ...............455
Using mtools ...............................................455
    Trying mtools ...............456
    Understanding the /etc/mtools.conf file ...............456
    Learning the mtools commands ...............457
    Formatting a DOS floppy ...............459

## Chapter 4: Managing Applications ..........................461

Working with Red Hat Package Manager .......................461
    Using the RPM commands ...............461
    Understanding RPM filenames ...............462
    Finding out about RPMs ...............463
    Installing an RPM ...............466
    Removing an RPM ...............467
    Upgrading an RPM ...............467
    Verifying an RPM ...............468
Building Software Packages from Source Files ...............469
    Downloading and unpacking the software ...............469
    Building the software from source files ...............471
    Installing SRPMS ...............474
Updating Fedora Core Applications with Up2date ...............474
Using Yellow dog Updater, Modified (Yum) ...............475

### Chapter 5: Managing Devices and Printers . . . . . . . . . . . . . . . . . . . .479

Understanding Linux Devices ............................................................479
    Device files ....................................................................................480
    Persistent device naming with udev ..........................................482
Managing Loadable Driver Modules ..................................................482
    Loading and unloading modules .................................................483
    Using the /etc/modprobe.conf file ..............................................485
Managing USB Devices ........................................................................486
Managing Print Queues in Fedora Core ............................................488
    Spooling and print jobs ................................................................488
    Printing with the lp command .....................................................490
    Checking the print queue using lpq ............................................490
    Canceling the print job using cancel ..........................................490
    Checking the printer status using lpstat ....................................491
    Controlling the print queue ........................................................491

### Chapter 6: Upgrading and Customizing the Kernel . . . . . . . . . . . . .493

Upgrading with a Kernel RPM ............................................................494
    Downloading new kernel RPMs ...................................................494
    Installing the kernel RPMs ...........................................................494
    Trying out the new kernel ............................................................495
Rebuilding the Kernel ..........................................................................496
    Creating a monolithic versus a modular kernel ........................497
    Configuring the kernel .................................................................498
    Running the kernel configuration tool ......................................499
Building the Kernel and the Modules ................................................513
Installing the Modules ........................................................................514
Creating the Initial RAM Disk File .....................................................514
Installing the New Kernel and Setting Up GRUB .............................515
Rebooting the System .........................................................................517

## Book VII: Security ...............................................519

### Chapter 1: Understanding Network and Host Security . . . . . . . . . .521

Why Worry About Security? ................................................................521
Establishing a Security Framework ...................................................522
    Determine business requirements for security .........................523
    Perform risk analysis ...................................................................524
    Establish security policy ..............................................................525
    Implement security solutions (mitigation) ................................526
    Manage security ............................................................................526

Securing Linux ........................................................................527
    Understanding the host security issues .......................527
    Understanding network security issues .......................528
Learning Computer Security Terminology ........................529
Keeping Up with Security News and Updates ..................532

## Chapter 2: Securing the Host ...............................535

Installing Operating System Updates .............................535
Securing Passwords ........................................................536
    Shadow passwords .......................................................536
    Pluggable authentication modules (PAMs) .................537
Protecting Files and Directories ......................................540
    Viewing ownerships and permissions .........................540
    Changing file ownerships ............................................541
    Changing file permissions ...........................................541
    Setting default permission ..........................................542
    Checking for set user ID permission ..........................543
Using exec-shield ............................................................544
Using SELinux .................................................................545
Encrypting and Signing Files with GnuPG ......................547
    Understanding public-key encryption .........................547
    Understanding digital signatures ...............................548
    Using GPG ...................................................................550
Monitoring System Security .............................................554

## Chapter 3: Securing the Network ...........................557

Securing Internet Services ..............................................557
    Using chkconfig to disable standalone services ..........558
    Configuring the xinetd server to disable services ........558
Using Secure Shell (SSH) for Remote Logins .................561
Setting Up Simple Firewalls ............................................563
    Screening the router with packet filtering ..................565
    Dual-homed host .........................................................567
    Perimeter network with bastion host ..........................568
    Application gateway .....................................................570
Enabling Packet Filtering on Your Fedora Core System .........571
    Using the security level configuration tool .................572
    Using the iptables command .......................................573

## Chapter 4: Performing Security Audits ....................577

Understanding Security Audits ........................................577
    Nontechnical aspects of security audits ......................578
    Technical aspects of security audits ...........................579

Learning a Security Test Methodology .................................................579
  Some common computer vulnerabilities ...........................580
  Host security review ..............................................................582
  Network-security review .......................................................585
Exploring Security Testing Tools .....................................................588
  Nmap ..........................................................................................589
  Nessus ........................................................................................590
  SAINT .........................................................................................593
  SARA ...........................................................................................594

## *Book VIII: Internet Servers ...........................................595*

### Chapter 1: Managing the Servers ...........................597

Understanding Internet Services ....................................................597
  TCP/IP and sockets ................................................................598
  Internet services and port numbers ..................................601
Using the xinetd Super Server .......................................................603
Running Standalone Servers ............................................................606
  Starting and stopping servers manually ...........................606
  Starting servers automatically at boot time ....................607

### Chapter 2: Running the Apache Web Server ..............615

Exploring HTTP ....................................................................................615
Exploring the Apache Web Server ..................................................618
  Installing the Apache Web server .......................................619
  Starting the Apache Web server .........................................620
Configuring the Apache Web Server ..............................................621
  Using Apache configuration tools ......................................622
  Apache configuration files ...................................................623
  The httpd.conf configuration file .......................................624
  Virtual host setup ...................................................................634

### Chapter 3: Setting Up the FTP Server ......................639

Installing the FTP Server ..................................................................639
Configuring the FTP Server ..............................................................640
  vsftpd configuration files .....................................................640
  /etc/vsftpd/vsftpd.conf file ..................................................641
  /etc/vsftpd.ftpusers file ........................................................643
  /etc/vsftpd.user_list file ........................................................644
Setting Up Secure Anonymous FTP ................................................644
Trying Anonymous FTP .......................................................................645
  Key features of anonymous FTP ..........................................645

**Chapter 4: Serving Up Mail and News** . . . . . . . . . . . . . . . . . . . . . . .647

Installing the Mail Server . . . . . . . . . . . . . . . . . . . . . . . . . . . . . . . . . . . . . . . . . . . . . .647
    Using sendmail . . . . . . . . . . . . . . . . . . . . . . . . . . . . . . . . . . . . . . . . . . . . . . . . . . . . .648
    A mail-delivery test . . . . . . . . . . . . . . . . . . . . . . . . . . . . . . . . . . . . . . . . . . . . . . . . .649
    The mail-delivery mechanism . . . . . . . . . . . . . . . . . . . . . . . . . . . . . . . . . . . . .649
    The sendmail configuration file . . . . . . . . . . . . . . . . . . . . . . . . . . . . . . 651
    sendmail.cf file syntax . . . . . . . . . . . . . . . . . . . . . . . . . . . . . . . . . . . . . . . . . . . . .659
    Other sendmail files . . . . . . . . . . . . . . . . . . . . . . . . . . . . . . . . . . . . . . . . . . . . . .661
    The .forward file . . . . . . . . . . . . . . . . . . . . . . . . . . . . . . . . . . . . . . . . . . . . . . . . . . .662
    Invoking procmail in the .forward file . . . . . . . . . . . . . . . . . . . . . . . .663
    The sendmail alias file . . . . . . . . . . . . . . . . . . . . . . . . . . . . . . . . . . . . . . . . . . . .664
Installing the News Server . . . . . . . . . . . . . . . . . . . . . . . . . . . . . . . . . . . . . . . . . .665
Configuring and Starting the INN Server . . . . . . . . . . . . . . . . . . . . . . . . . . .665
    InterNetNews components . . . . . . . . . . . . . . . . . . . . . . . . . . . . . . . . . . . . . . .666
    The incoming.conf file . . . . . . . . . . . . . . . . . . . . . . . . . . . . . . . . . . . . . . . . . . . .670
    The readers.conf file . . . . . . . . . . . . . . . . . . . . . . . . . . . . . . . . . . . . . . . . . . . . . .671
    InterNetNews startup . . . . . . . . . . . . . . . . . . . . . . . . . . . . . . . . . . . . . . . . . . . . .671
Setting Up Local Newsgroups . . . . . . . . . . . . . . . . . . . . . . . . . . . . . . . . . . . . . . .672
    Defining a newsgroup hierarchy . . . . . . . . . . . . . . . . . . . . . . . . . . . . . . . .673
    Updating configuration files . . . . . . . . . . . . . . . . . . . . . . . . . . . . . . . . . . . .673
    Adding the newsgroups . . . . . . . . . . . . . . . . . . . . . . . . . . . . . . . . . . . . . . . . . .674
    Testing your newsgroups . . . . . . . . . . . . . . . . . . . . . . . . . . . . . . . . . . . . . . . .674

**Chapter 5: Setting Up DNS** . . . . . . . . . . . . . . . . . . . . . . . . . . . . .675

Understanding Domain Name System (DNS) . . . . . . . . . . . . . . . . . . . . . . . .675
    What is DNS? . . . . . . . . . . . . . . . . . . . . . . . . . . . . . . . . . . . . . . . . . . . . . . . . . . . . . .676
    Learning hierarchical domain names . . . . . . . . . . . . . . . . . . . . . . . . . . .677
    Exploring Berkeley Internet Name Domain (BIND) . . . . . . . . . . . . . .678
Configuring DNS . . . . . . . . . . . . . . . . . . . . . . . . . . . . . . . . . . . . . . . . . . . . . . . . . . . . .682
    Configuring the resolver . . . . . . . . . . . . . . . . . . . . . . . . . . . . . . . . . . . . . . . .682
    Configuring a caching name server . . . . . . . . . . . . . . . . . . . . . . . . . . . . .683
    Configuring a primary name server . . . . . . . . . . . . . . . . . . . . . . . . . . . .692

**Chapter 6: Running Samba and NFS** . . . . . . . . . . . . . . . . . . . . . . .695

Sharing Files with NFS . . . . . . . . . . . . . . . . . . . . . . . . . . . . . . . . . . . . . . . . . . . . . . .695
    Exporting a file system with NFS . . . . . . . . . . . . . . . . . . . . . . . . . . . . . . . .696
    Mounting an NFS file system . . . . . . . . . . . . . . . . . . . . . . . . . . . . . . . . . . . .698
    Using the NFS Server Configuration tool . . . . . . . . . . . . . . . . . . . . . . .699
Setting Up a Windows Server Using Samba . . . . . . . . . . . . . . . . . . . . . . . . . .700
    Checking whether Samba is installed . . . . . . . . . . . . . . . . . . . . . . . . . . .702
    Configuring Samba . . . . . . . . . . . . . . . . . . . . . . . . . . . . . . . . . . . . . . . . . . . . . . .703
    Trying out Samba . . . . . . . . . . . . . . . . . . . . . . . . . . . . . . . . . . . . . . . . . . . . . . . . .705

## Book IX: Programming ................................................. 707

### Chapter 1: Fedora Core Programming Essentials ................ 709

Learning Programming ............................................................ 709
    A simplified view of a computer ...................................... 710
    Role of the operating system .......................................... 711
    Basics of computer programming ................................... 712
Exploring the Software Development Tools in Fedora Core ......... 713
    GNU C and C++ compilers .............................................. 714
    The GNU make utility ..................................................... 718
    The GNU debugger .......................................................... 725
Understanding the Implications of GNU Licenses .................... 732
    The GNU General Public License ..................................... 732
    The GNU Library General Public License ......................... 733

### Chapter 2: Programming in C ................................. 735

The Structure of a C Program ................................................ 735
Preprocessor Directives ........................................................ 737
    Including files ................................................................ 738
    Defining macros ............................................................. 738
Declaration and Definition of Variables ................................. 741
    Basic data types ............................................................ 741
    Enumerations ................................................................. 742
Structures, Unions, and Bit Fields ......................................... 743
    Arrays ........................................................................... 743
    Pointers ......................................................................... 744
    Type definitions ............................................................. 745
    Type qualifiers: const and volatile ................................. 746
Expressions ......................................................................... 747
Operator Precedence ............................................................ 749
Statements ........................................................................... 751
    The break statement ...................................................... 751
    The case statement ........................................................ 752
    A compound statement or block ..................................... 752
    The continue statement .................................................. 752
    The default label ............................................................ 753
    The do statement ........................................................... 753
    Expression statements ................................................... 753
    The for statement .......................................................... 753
    The goto statement ........................................................ 754
    The if statement ............................................................ 754
    The if-else statement ..................................................... 754
    The null statement ......................................................... 755
    The return statement ..................................................... 755

The switch statement ................................................... 755
The while statement .................................................... 756
Functions .......................................................................... 757
Function prototypes ................................................... 757
The void type ............................................................. 758
Functions with a variable number of arguments ...... 758
The C Library ..................................................................... 758
Shared Libraries in Linux Applications ............................ 760
Examining shared libraries that a program uses ...... 760
Creating a shared library .......................................... 762
Dynamically loading a shared library ....................... 764

## Chapter 3: Writing Shell Scripts . . . . . . . . . . . . . . . . . . . . . . . . . . . . . 767

Trying Out Simple Shell Scripts ....................................... 767
Learning the Basics of Shell Scripting ............................. 770
Storing stuff ............................................................... 770
Calling shell functions ............................................... 771
Controlling the flow .................................................. 772
Exploring Bash's built-in commands ......................... 775

## Chapter 4: Programming in Perl . . . . . . . . . . . . . . . . . . . . . . . . . . . . . . 779

Understanding Perl ............................................................ 779
Determining Whether You Have Perl ............................... 780
Writing Your First Perl Script .......................................... 782
Getting an Overview of Perl ............................................. 783
Basic Perl syntax ....................................................... 783
Variables .................................................................... 784
Operators and expressions ........................................ 787
Regular expressions ................................................... 789
Flow-control statements ............................................ 791
Accessing Linux commands ....................................... 795
File access .................................................................. 797
Filename with pipe prefix .......................................... 798
Subroutines ................................................................ 799
Built-in functions in Perl ........................................... 800
Understanding Perl Packages and Modules .................... 800
Perl packages ............................................................. 801
Perl modules .............................................................. 802
Using a module .......................................................... 803
Using Objects in Perl ....................................................... 804
Understanding Perl Objects .............................................. 804
Creating and accessing Perl objects .......................... 805
Using the English module ......................................... 806

Appendix: About the DVD ..............................................807
    DVD Installation Instructions ...................................807
    What You Can Find on the DVD ...............................809
    Troubleshooting ......................................................810

Index.....................................................................811

# Introduction

**R**ed Hat has recently decided to discontinue the Red Hat Linux product line and instead focus on the commercial Red Hat Enterprise Linux — RHEL — product line. The evolution of the now-defunct Red Hat Linux product line continues on as the Fedora Project, a Red Hat-sponsored and community-supported open source project that continues to evolve what once was Red Hat Linux. What comes out of the Fedora Project is a Fedora Core release every six months or so. (For example, Fedora Core 1 came out in November 2003 and Fedora Core 2 was released in May 2004.) In contrast to the rapid Fedora Core release cycles, RHEL is a stable product line with a 12 to 18 month release cycle and five years of support for every version. New technologies that first appear in Fedora Core will eventually find their way into the next-generation Red Hat Enterprise Linux (RHEL) product. Thus, Fedora Core releases are a precursor to what's coming in RHEL in the future.

The recently released Fedora Core 2 comes with many new system components including the Linux 2.6.5 kernel, X.Org X11 6.7.0, GNOME 2.6, KDE 3.2.2, GCC 3.3 compiler, and the glibc 2.3.3 system libraries. This version supports many new features such as Advanced Configuration and Power Interface (ACPI), Bluetooth wireless connections, and a graphical boot screen that shows system startup messages in a user-friendly screen.

Fedora Core 2 also includes the OpenOffice.org 1.1.1 office suite. To top it off, Fedora Core continues to come with a graphical installation program that makes installation easy!

## About This Book

*Red Hat Fedora Linux 2 All-in-One Desk Reference For Dummies* gives you nine different quick-reference guides in a single book. Taken together, these nine books provide detailed information on installing, configuring, and using Fedora Core.

What you'll like most about this book is that you don't have to read it sequentially chapter by chapter, or, for that matter, even the sections in a chapter. You can pretty much turn to the topic you want and quickly get the answer to your pressing questions about Fedora Core, be it about using the OpenOffice.org word processor or setting up the Apache Web server.

Here are some of the things you can do with this book:

✦ Install and configure Fedora Core from the DVD-ROM included with the book.

✦ Connect the Fedora Core PC to the Internet through a DSL or cable modem.

✦ Set up dial-up networking with PPP.

✦ Get tips, techniques, and shortcuts for specific uses of Fedora Core, such as

  • Setting up and using Internet services such as Web, Mail, News, FTP, NFS, and DNS.

  • Setting up a Windows server using Samba.

  • Using Linux commands.

  • Using Perl, shell, and C programming on Linux.

  • Using the OpenOffice.org office suite and other applications that come with Fedora Core.

✦ Understand the basics of system and network security.

✦ Perform system administration tasks.

## Conventions Used in This Book

I use a simple notational style in this book. All listings, filenames, function names, variable names, and keywords are typeset in a `monospace` font for ease of reading. I italicize the first occurrences of new terms and concepts and then provide a definition right there. The output of commands follows the typed command and the output is shown in a monospace font.

## What You Don't Have to Read

Each mini reference book zeros in on a specific task area such as using the Internet or running Internet servers and then provides hands-on instructions on how to perform a series of related tasks. You can jump right to a section and read about a specific task. You don't have to read anything but the few paragraphs or the list of steps that relate to your question. Use the Table of Contents or the Index to locate the pages relevant to your question.

You can safely ignore text next to the Technical Stuff icons as well as the sidebars.

# Who Are You?

I assume that you are somewhat familiar with a PC — you know how to turn it on and off and you have dabbled a bit with Windows. Considering that most new PCs come preloaded with Windows, this assumption is safe, right?

When installing Fedora Core on your PC, you may want to retain your Windows 2000 or Windows XP installations intact. I assume you don't mind investing in a good disk-partitioning tool such as PowerQuest's PartitionMagic, available at `www.powerquest.com/partitionmagic` (no, I don't have any connections with PowerQuest).

I also assume that you are willing to accept the risk that when you try to install Fedora Core, some things may not quite work. Problems can happen if you have some uncommon types of hardware. If you are afraid of ruining your system, try finding a slightly older spare Pentium PC that you can sacrifice and then install Fedora Core on that PC.

# How This Book Is Organized

*Red Hat Fedora Linux 2 All-in-One Desk Reference For Dummies* has nine books, each of which focuses on a small set of related topics. If you are looking for information on a specific topic, check the book names on the spine or consult the Table of Contents.

This desk reference starts with a minibook that explains the basics of Fedora Core and guides you through the installation process (a unique aspect of this book because you typically do not purchase a PC with Fedora Core pre-installed). The second minibook serves as a user's guide to Fedora Core — it focuses on exploring various aspects of a Fedora Core workstation, including the GNOME and KDE GUIs and many of the applications that come bundled with Fedora Core. The third minibook is a user's guide to the OpenOffice.org office applications. The fourth minibook covers networking and Book V goes into using the Internet. Book VI introduces system administration. The seventh minibook turns to the important subject of securing a Fedora Core system and its associated network. Book VIII shows you how to run a variety of Internet servers from mail to a Web server. The ninth and final minibook introduces you to programming.

Here's a quick overview of the nine books and what they contain:

**Book I: Fedora Basics:** What is Fedora Core? Understanding what's new in the Linux 2.6 kernel. Installing, configuring, and troubleshooting Fedora Core. Taking Fedora Core for a test drive.

**Book II: Workstations and Applications:** Exploring GNOME and KDE. Using the shell (what's a shell anyway?). Navigating the Fedora Core file system. Exploring the applications such as multimedia software as well as the text editors (`vi` and `ed`).

**Book III: OpenOffice.org:** Writing with OpenOffice.org Writer. Preparing spreadsheets with OpenOffice.org Calc. Making presentations with OpenOffice.org Impress. Preparing drawings with OpenOffice.org Draw.

**Book IV: Networking:** Connecting the Fedora Core PC to the Internet through a dial-up connection or a high-speed always-on connection such as DSL or cable modem. Configuring and managing TCP/IP networks, including wireless networks.

**Book V: Internet:** Using various Internet services such as e-mail, Web surfing, and reading newsgroups. Transferring files with FTP.

**Book VI: Administration:** Performing basic system administration. Managing user accounts and the file system. Installing applications. Working with devices and printers. Using USB devices. Upgrading and customizing the Linux kernel.

**Book VII: Security:** Understanding network and host security. Securing the host and the network. Performing security audits.

**Book VIII: Internet Servers:** Managing the Internet services. Configuring the Apache Web server. Setting up the FTP server (including anonymous FTP). Configuring the mail and news servers. Providing DNS. File sharing with NFS. Using Samba to set up a Windows server.

**Book IX: Programming:** Finding out the basics of programming. Exploring the software development tools in Fedora Core. Writing shell scripts. Learning C and Perl programming.

**Appendix: About the DVD:** Summarizes the contents of the book's companion DVD-ROM.

## What's on the DVD?

The DVD contains Fedora Core 2 from the Fedora Project (`fedora.redhat.com`). You may use the DVD in accordance with the license agreements accompanying the software. To discover more about the contents of the DVD, please consult the appendix.

---

## Sidebars

I use sidebars throughout the book to highlight interesting, but not critical, information. Sidebars explain concepts you may not have encountered before or give a little insight into a related topic. If you're in a hurry, you can safely skip the sidebars.

---

## Icons Used in This Book

Following the time-honored tradition of the *All-in-One Desk Reference For Dummies* series, I use icons to help you quickly pinpoint useful information. The icons include the following:

The Remember icon marks a general interesting fact — something that I thought you want to know and remember.

The Tip icon marks things that you can do to make your job easier.

The Warning icon highlights potential pitfalls. With this icon, I'm telling you: "Watch out! This could hurt your system!"

The Technical Stuff icon marks technical information that could be of interest to an advanced user (or those of us aspiring to be advanced users).

## Where to Go from Here

It's time to get started on your Fedora Core adventure. Take out the DVD and install Fedora Core. Then, turn to a relevant chapter and let the fun begin. Use the Table of Contents and the Index to figure out where you want to go. Before you know it, you'll become an expert at Fedora Core!

If you want to participate in the Fedora Core project, visit the project's Web site at fedora.redhat.com for more information.

I hope you enjoy consulting this book as much as I enjoyed writing it!

# Book I

# Fedora Basics

The 5th Wave    By Rich Tennant

"It's called Linux Poker. Everyone gets to see everyone else's cards, everything's wild, you can play off your opponents' hands, and everyone wins except Bill Gates whose face appears on the Jokers."

# Contents at a Glance

Chapter 1: Introducing Fedora Core .................................................................9

Chapter 2: Installing Fedora .........................................................................31

Chapter 3: Troubleshooting and Configuring Fedora Core ...............................57

Chapter 4: Trying Out Fedora Core ...............................................................75

Chapter 5: Cool Fedora Install Projects .........................................................99

# Chapter 1: Introducing Fedora Core

## In This Chapter

✓ **Explaining what Fedora Core is**

✓ **Going over what Fedora Core includes**

✓ **Discovering what Fedora Core helps you manage**

✓ **Getting started**

*1* bet you've heard about Linux and you probably know about Red Hat Linux as well, but chances are Fedora Core is new to you. If you're wondering what exactly Fedora Core is and what it can help you do, this chapter is all about answering those questions. Here I provide a broad-brushstroke picture of Fedora Core and tell you how you can start using it right away.

By the way, this book covers Fedora Core for Intel 80x86 and Pentium processors (basically any PC that can run any flavor of Windows).

## What Is Fedora Core?

Fedora Core is what used to be Red Hat Linux — the Linux distribution from Red Hat that used to be available free of charge. If you never knew Red Hat Linux, think of Fedora Core as another Linux distribution. That leaves you with the question: What is a Linux distribution anyway?

Trying to describe a Linux distribution is a bit like that story of six blind men trying to describe an elephant. You know the one — one blind man touches the elephant's side and says the elephant is like a wall, another checks out the tusk and concludes that an elephant is like a spear, and so on. Along those lines, a Linux distribution appears to be many different things, depending on what you experience. You can think of it as the graphical user interface or just a PC to run your e-mail program, but, at its heart, it's an operating system. The following sections explain what I mean by this statement.

### Operating systems and Linux

You know that your PC is a bunch of *hardware* — things you can touch, like the system box, monitor, keyboard, and mouse. The system box contains the most important hardware of all — the *central processing unit* (CPU), the microchip that runs the *software* (any program that tells the computer how to do your bidding) — which you actually *can't* touch. In a typical Pentium 4 PC, the Pentium 4 microprocessor is the CPU. Other important hardware in the system box includes the memory (RAM chips) and the hard drive — and one program has to run all this stuff and get it to play nice: the operating system.

The *operating system* is software that manages all the hardware and runs other software at your command. You, the user, provide those commands by clicking menus and icons or by typing some cryptic text. Linux is an operating system — as are UNIX, Windows 98, Windows 2000, and Windows XP. The Linux operating system is modeled after UNIX; in its most basic, no-frills form, it also goes by the name *Linux kernel*.

The operating system is what gives a computer — any computer — its personality. For example, you can run Windows 98 or Windows XP on a PC — and on that same PC, you can *also* install and run Linux. That means, depending on which operating system is installed and running, *the same PC* can be a Windows 98, Windows XP, or Linux system.

The primary job of an operating system is to load software (computer programs) from the hard disk (or other permanent storage) into the memory and get the CPU to run those programs. Everything you do with your computer is possible because of the operating system — so if the operating system somehow messes up, the whole system freezes up. You know how infuriating it is when your favorite operating system — maybe even the one that came with your PC — suddenly calls it quits just as you are about to click the Send button after composing that long e-mail to your friend. You try the three-finger salute (pressing Ctrl+Alt+Del), but nothing happens. Then it's time for the Reset button (provided your computer's builders were wise enough to include one). Luckily, that sort of thing almost never happens with Linux — it has a reputation for being a very reliable operating system.

## Does Linux really run on any computer?

Linux runs on many different types of computer systems — and it does seem able to run on nearly any type of computer. Linus Torvalds and other programmers originally developed Linux for the Intel 80x86 (and compatible) line of processors. Nowadays, Linux is also available for systems based on other processors — such as those with AMD's 64-bit AMD64 processors, the Motorola 68000 family; Alpha AXPs; Sun SPARCs and UltraSPARCs; Hewlett-Packard's HP PA-RISC; the PowerPC and PowerPC64 processors; and the MIPS R4x00 and R5x00. More recently, IBM has released its own version of Linux for its S/390 mainframe. This book covers Linux for Intel 80x86 and Pentium processors (these have in common a basic physical structure known as *IA-32 architecture*).

In technical mumbo jumbo, Linux is a *multiuser, multitasking operating system.* All this means is that Linux enables multiple users to log in, and Linux can run more than one program at the same time. Nearly all operating systems are multiuser and multitasking these days, but when Linux first started in 1994, *multiuser* and *multitasking* were big selling points.

## Linux distributions

Fedora Core is a specific *Linux distribution* — essentially a package of features. Fedora Core consists of the Linux *kernel* (the operating system) and a collection of applications, together with an easy-to-use GUI installation program, called Anaconda.

You find many Linux distributions, and each includes the standard Linux operating system:

✦ **The X.Org X Window System:** The graphical user interface.

✦ **One or more graphical desktops:** Among the most popular are GNOME and KDE.

✦ **A selection of applications:** Linux programs come in the form of ready-to-run software, but the *source code* (the commands we humans use to tell the computer what to do, but you don't need the source code to run the operating system or any applications) is included, as is its documentation.

Current Linux distributions include a huge selection of software — so much that it requires multiple CD-ROMs or a single DVD-ROM (which this book includes).

Many Linux distributions are commercial products that you can buy in computer stores and bookstores. If you have heard about Open Source and the GNU (*GNU's Not UNIX*) license, you may assume that no one can sell Linux for profit. Luckily for companies that sell Linux distributions, the GNU license — also called the GNU General Public License (GPL) — does allow commercial, for-profit distribution, but requires that the software be distributed in source-code form, and stipulates that anyone may copy and distribute the software in source-code form to anyone else. Fedora Core is available free of charge under the GPL, which means that my publisher may include the Fedora Core DVD-ROM with this book and you may make as many copies of the DVD as you like.

## Transitioning to the Fedora Project

In late September 2003, Red Hat announced the Fedora Project — an open-source project sponsored by Red Hat where the developer community can participate and continue to evolve what used to be the Red Hat Linux product. The new product goes by the name *Fedora Core* and the project is expected to have Fedora Core releases every four to six months. Red Hat continues to participate in the Fedora Project and help prepare the Fedora Core releases, but everything is done with involvement of the open source community under a public release schedule. As you may expect, Fedora Core is available freely, just as Red Hat Linux used to be, and you can expect books such as this one to include Fedora Core on DVD or CDs.

Red Hat continues to sell its commercial Linux distribution — called Red Hat Enterprise Linux. Red Hat anticipates that new technologies and enhancements that first appear in Fedora Core will eventually find their way into Red Hat Enterprise Linux. In this way, the Fedora Project serves as an incubator and testing ground for future Linux development.

To find out more about the Fedora Project, visit `fedora.redhat.com`.

## Making sense of version numbers

Both the Linux kernel and Fedora Core have their own version numbers, not to mention the many other software programs (such as GNOME and KDE) that come with Fedora Core. The version numbers for the Linux kernel and Fedora Core are unrelated, but each has particular significance.

### Linux-kernel version numbers

After Linux kernel version 1.0 was released on March 14, 1994, the loosely knit Linux development community adopted a version-numbering scheme. Version numbers such as 1.*X.Y* and 2.*X.Y,* where *X* is an even number, are considered the stable versions. The last number, *Y,* is the patch level, which is incremented as problems are fixed. For example, 2.6.5 is a typical, stable version of the Linux kernel. Notice that these version numbers are in the form of three integers separated by periods — *Major.Minor.Patch* — where *Major* and *Minor* are numbers denoting the major and minor version numbers, and *Patch* is another number representing the patch level.

Version numbers of the form 2.*X.Y* with an odd *X* number are beta releases for developers only; they may be unstable, so you should not adopt such versions for day-to-day use. For example, when you look at version 2.5.75 of the Linux kernel, notice the *5* — that tells you it's a beta release. Developers add new features to these odd-numbered versions of Linux.

You can find out about the latest version of the Linux kernel online at `www.kernel.org`.

### Fedora Core version numbers

The Fedora Core development community, led by Red Hat, assigns the Fedora Core version numbers, such as 1 or 2. They are of the form *X.Y,* where *X* is the major version and *Y* the minor version. Nowadays if the minor version number is zero, it's simply dropped — as in Fedora Core 1 and Fedora Core 2.

Unlike with the Linux-kernel version numbers, no special meaning is associated with odd and even minor versions. Each version of Fedora Core includes specific versions of the Linux kernel and other major components, such as GNOME, KDE, and various applications.

The Fedora Project releases new versions of Fedora Core on a regular basis — every six months or so. For example, Fedora Core 1 came out in November 2003 and Fedora Core 2 in May 2004. Typically, each new major version of Fedora Core provides significant new features.

## Under the hood in Linux kernel 2.6

Linux kernel 2.6 includes many new features and improvements when compared to its predecessor — the 2.4 kernel. I highlight some of these improvements in this section. You may not notice many of these improvements because they work behind the scenes. All you see is a Linux system that simply works great!

### Support for wider range of computer hardware

For starters, the 2.6 kernel has been redesigned to support computers spanning a wider range of hardware than before — from bare-bones embedded microcontrollers to larger-scale servers with multiple processors.

To support distinct hardware architectures of the same processor family (such as x86), Linux 2.6 uses the concept of a *subarchitecture,* which refers to the processor and the associated bus and other hardware that defines a unique type of computer. For example, most of today's PCs are based on what is called the PC/AT subarchitecture because these PCs are based on the original IBM PC/AT. The 2.6 kernel supports PC/AT machines as well as other x86 subarchitectures, such as the NEC Voyager and the PC-9800 machines. The bottom line is that the 2.6 kernel can run on many variations of the x86-based machines.

Linux 2.6 also supports advanced features of processors such as hyperthreading, which enables a single processor to act as multiple virtual processors at the hardware level.

### Better scalability

The 2.6 kernel provides better scalability for Intel x86 hardware by supporting advanced features such as Intel's Physical Address Extension (PAE), which enables many newer 32-bit x86 systems to access up to 64GB of memory. Linux 2.6 also provides better handling of interrupts for multiprocessor systems through improved support for Intel's Input/Output (I/O) Advanced Programmable Interrupt Controller (APIC).

Internally, the 2.6 kernel raises many internal limits from number of users to the maximum number of open files. For example, the number of unique users and groups has been increased from 65,536 to over 4 billion. The maximum number of open files can now grow as needed. File systems can be as large as 16TB (that's about 16,000 gigabytes!).

Linux 2.6 also increases the limits on the major and minor device numbers, which used to be a maximum of 255 in earlier kernels. These device numbers translate to 255 device types and 255 devices of a single type. In kernel version 2.6, the major device numbers can be up to 4,095 and minor device numbers can be more than a million. The upshot is that Linux 2.6 can support many more device types and many devices of a single type.

### Improved device handling

Linux 2.6 has a number of new features for handling devices — especially hot plug devices such as the ones that connect to USB and Firewire interfaces common in today's PCs. First, the kernel uses a new virtual file system called *sysfs* that is meant to hold information about the devices on the system. The sysfs file system mounts on /sys and it presents a hierarchical view of all the devices organized by device type, bus, and so on. Through sysfs, the 2.6 kernel makes available to other applications a lot of information about devices, including the name of a device, resources such as interrupts and I/O ports used by the device, the power status of the device, and so on.

By using the sysfs capabilities available in the 2.6 kernel, a separate device-handling program called udev can now dynamically add device files when a device is added to a system. The udev program is invoked by the /sbin/hotplug shell script that runs when any hot plug device such as a USB device is plugged into the computer. udev gives each device a name that stays the same every time that device connects to the system. In Fedora Core, udev is not configured by default to manage the device files in the /dev directory. Instead udev manages device files in the /udev directory. However, you can easily configure udev (through the /etc/udev/udev.conf file) to manage the device files in /dev directory.

Other device-handling improvements in Linux 2.6 include ensuring that device driver modules are not unloaded while still in use and standardizing the way in which device drivers make available information about devices they support. All device driver module filenames now use the .ko extension — for *kernel object* — instead of the generic .o extension commonly used for object files.

Linux 2.6 also has improved support for many devices such as USB 2.0 and wireless devices. As for storage devices, the Integrated Drive Electronics (IDE) — also called AT Attachment (ATA) — and Small Computer System Interface (SCSI) support was updated in Linux 2.6. For example, IDE

CD-recorders are now accessed through the IDE driver instead of a special SCSI-emulation driver that was used in earlier versions of the kernel. The 2.6 kernel also supports the new Serial ATA (SATA) interface that can support data transfer rates of 150MB per second.

### Mandatory access control with Security Enhanced Linux (SELinux)

Linux kernel 2.6 includes the mandatory access control framework provided by Security Enhanced Linux (SELinux), which was developed by the National Security Agency (NSA), a U.S. government agency. SELinux is implemented as a Linux Security Module (LSM) — an extension of the Linux kernel that allows security mechanisms to be easily added to the kernel. You can find more about SELinux at the NSA's Web site, `www.nsa.gov/selinux/`.

Without SELinux, access control in Linux is based on the user and group ID that owns a process or a file. In this discretionary access control approach, the superuser (`root`) has absolute discretion to access and do anything on the system. In contrast to this approach, SELinux views the system in terms of *subjects* (users or processes) and *objects* (files, devices, any system resources). Subjects can take on different *roles* such as normal user or system administrator. Each subject also has a *domain* and each object has a *type*. SELinux provides fine-grained control over who can access what in a Linux system by defining what domains can access what types and how one domain can transition into another when programs execute.

The mandatory access control rules are defined in the SELinux *security policy*. To support the fine-grained access control, all files need additional attributes called *contexts* that are stored in labels added to the files. Think of the contexts as information on which roles can access and do what with the file. When SELinux is enabled, all files in the file system have to be labeled with the security contexts. Only then can SELinux manage the fine-grained access control.

When you install Fedora Core, you can type **selinux** at the installer's `boot:` prompt to install SELinux and select the level of access control you want SELinux to enforce. This option appears in the screen where you configure the firewall.

*Note:* SELinux can be very helpful in securing your organization's external Web and e-mail servers that are exposed to the Internet and, therefore, subject to attacks. With a well-designed security policy, SELinux can make such Internet-facing servers resistant to damage from attacks, even if an attacker manages to gain superuser privileges. However, the additional effort involved in setting up and running SELinux may not be worthwhile for internal servers not directly connected to the Internet.

# What Fedora Core Includes

Fedora Core comes with the Linux kernel and a whole lot more software. These software packages include everything from the graphical desktops to Internet servers and programming tools to create new software. In this section, I briefly describe some major software packages that come bundled with Fedora Core. Without this bundled software, Fedora Core wouldn't be as popular as it is today.

## GNU software

I start with a collection of software that came from the GNU Project. You get to know these GNU utilities only if you use your Fedora Core system through a text terminal (or a graphical window that mimics one) — a basic *command-line interface* that puts nothing much on-screen but a prompt at which you type in your commands. The GNU software is one of the basic parts of Fedora Core.

As a Fedora Core user, you may not realize the extent to which Fedora Core (and, for that matter, all Linux distributions) relies on GNU software. Nearly all tasks you perform in a Fedora Core system involve one or more GNU software packages. For example, the GNOME graphical user interface (GUI) and the command interpreter (that is, the Bash shell) are both GNU software programs. By the way, the *shell* is the command-interpreter application that accepts the commands you type and runs programs in response to those commands. If you rebuild the kernel or develop software, you do so with the GNU C and C++ compiler (which is part of the GNU software that accompanies Fedora Core). If you edit text files with the `ed` or emacs editor, you're again using a GNU software package. The list goes on and on.

## What is the GNU Project?

GNU is a recursive acronym that stands for *GNU's Not UNIX*. The GNU Project was launched in 1984 by Richard Stallman to develop a complete UNIX-like operating system. The GNU Project developed nearly everything needed for a complete operating system except for the operating system kernel. All GNU software was distributed under the GNU General Public License (GPL). GPL essentially requires that the software is distributed in source-code form and stipulates that any user may copy, modify, and distribute the software to anyone else in source-code form. Users may, however, have to pay for their individual copies of GNU software.

The Free Software Foundation (FSF) is a tax-exempt charity that raises funds for work on the GNU Project. To find out more about the GNU Project, visit its home page at www.gnu.org. You can find information about how to contact the Free Software Foundation and how to help the GNU Project.

Table 1-1 lists some of the well-known GNU software packages that come with Fedora Core. I show this table only to give you a feel for all the different kinds of things you can do with GNU software. Depending on your interests, you may never need to use many of these packages, but knowing they are there in case you ever need them is good.

| Table 1-1 | Well-Known GNU Software Packages |
|---|---|
| *Software Package* | *Description* |
| Autoconf | Generates shell scripts that automatically configure source-code packages |
| Automake | Generates `Makefile.in` files for use with Autoconf |
| Bash | The default shell — command interpreter — in Fedora Core |
| Bc | An interactive calculator with arbitrary precision numbers |
| Binutils | A package that includes several utilities for working with binary files: `ar`, `as`, `gasp`, `gprof`, `ld`, `nm`, `objcopy`, `objdump`, `ranlib`, `readelf`, `size`, `strings`, and `strip` |
| Coreutils | A package that combines three individual packages called Fileutils, Shellutils, and Textutils and implements utilities such as `chgrp`, `chmod`, `chown`, `cp`, `dd`, `df`, `dir`, `dircolors`, `du`, `install`, `ln`, `ls`, `mkdir`, `mkfifo`, `mknod`, `mv`, `rm`, `rmdir`, `sync`, `touch`, `vdir`, `basename`, `chroot`, `date`, `dirname`, `echo`, `env`, `expr`, `factor`, `false`, `groups`, `hostname`, `id`, `logname`, `nice`, `nohup`, `pathchk`, `printenv`, `printf`, `pwd`, `seq`, `sleep`, `stty`, `su`, `tee`, `test`, `true`, `tty`, `uname`, `uptime`, `users`, `who`, `whoami`, `yes`, `cut`, `join`, `nl`, `split`, `tail`, `wc`, and so on |
| Gnuchess | A chess-playing program |
| GNU C Library | For use with all Linux programs |
| Cpio | Copies file archives to and from a disk or to another part of the file system |
| Diff | Compares files, showing line-by-line changes in several different formats |
| ed | A line-oriented text editor |
| emacs | An extensible, customizable full-screen text editor and computing environment |
| Findutils | A package that includes the `find`, `locate`, and `xargs` utilities |
| Finger | A utility program designed to enable users on the Internet to get information about one another |
| Gawk | The GNU Project's implementation of the AWK programming language |
| GCC | Compilers for C, C++, Objective C, and other languages |

*(continued)*

**Table 1-1** *(continued)*

| Software Package | Description |
|---|---|
| Gdb | Source-level debugger for C, C++, and Fortran |
| Gdbm | A replacement for the traditional dbm and ndbm database libraries |
| Gettext | A set of utilities that enables software maintainers to internationalize (that means make the software work with different languages such as English, French, Spanish, and so on) a software package's user messages |
| Ghostscript | An interpreter for the Postscript and Portable Document Format (PDF) languages |
| Ghostview | An X Window System application that makes Ghostscript accessible from the GUI, enabling users to view Postscript or PDF files in a window |
| The GIMP | The GNU Image Manipulation Program is an Adobe Photoshop-like image-processing program |
| GNOME | Provides a graphical user interface (GUI) for a wide variety of tasks that a Linux user may perform |
| Gnumeric | A graphical spreadsheet (similar to Microsoft Excel) that works in GNOME |
| grep package | Includes the grep, egrep, and fgrep commands that are used to find lines that match a specified text pattern |
| Groff | A document-formatting system similar to troff |
| GTK+ | A GUI toolkit for the X Window System (used to develop GNOME applications) |
| Gzip | A GNU utility for compressing and decompressing files |
| Indent | Formats C source code by indenting it in one of several different styles |
| Less | A page-by-page display program similar to more, but with additional capabilities |
| Libpng | A library for image files in the Portable Network Graphics (PNG) format |
| m4 | An implementation of the traditional UNIX macro processor |
| Make | A utility that determines which files of a large software package need to be recompiled, and issues the commands to recompile them |
| Mtools | A set of programs that enables users to read, write, and manipulate files on a DOS file system (typically a floppy disk) |
| Ncurses | A package for displaying and updating text on text-only terminals |
| Patch | A GNU version of Larry Wall's program to take the output of diff and apply those differences to an original file to generate the modified version |

| Software Package | Description |
| --- | --- |
| RCS | The Revision Control System is used for version control and management of source files in software projects |
| Sed | A stream-oriented version of the ed text editor |
| Sharutils | A package that includes shar (used to make shell archives out of many files) and unshar (to unpack these shell archives) |
| Tar | A tape archiving program that includes multivolume support; the capability to archive sparse files, handle compression and decompression, and create remote archives; and other special features for incremental and full backups |
| Texinfo | A set of utilities that generates printed manuals, plain ASCII text, and online hypertext documentation (called Info), and enables users to view and read online Info documents |
| Time | A utility that reports the user, system, and actual time that a process uses |

## GUIs and applications

Face it — typing cryptic Linux commands on a terminal is boring. For average users like us, using the system through a *graphical user interface* (*GUI,* pronounced "gooey") that gives us pictures to click and windows (small *w*) to open is much easier. This is where the X Window System, or X, comes to the rescue.

X is kind of like Microsoft Windows, but the underlying details of how X works is completely different from Windows. Unlike Windows, X provides the basic features of displaying windows on-screen, but it does not come with any specific look or feel for graphical applications. That look and feel comes from GUIs, such as GNOME and KDE, which make use of the X Window System.

Fedora Core comes with the X Window System in the form of X.Org X11 — an implementation of X Window System for 80x86 systems. X.Org X11 works with a wide variety of video cards available for today's PCs.

Until recently XFree86 from the XFree86 Project (www.xfree86.org) was the commonly used X Window System implementation for x86 systems. However, around version 4.4, some changes to the XFree86 licensing terms caused concerns to many Linux and UNIX vendors — they felt that the licensing terms were no longer compatible with the GNU General Public License (GPL). In January 2004, several vendors formed the X.Org Foundation (www.x.org) to promote continued development of an open source X Window System and graphical desktop. The first release of X.Org X11 uses the same code as that used by XFree86 4.4, up until the time when the XFree86 license changes precipitated the creation of X.Org Foundation.

As for the GUI, Fedora Core includes two powerful GUI desktops: KDE (K Desktop Environment) and GNOME (GNU Object Model Environment). If both GNOME and KDE are installed on a PC, you can choose which desktop you want as the default — or switch between the two. KDE and GNOME provide desktops similar to those of Microsoft Windows and the Macintosh OS. GNOME also comes with the Nautilus graphical shell that makes finding files, running applications, and configuring your Fedora Core system easy. With GNOME or KDE, you can begin using your Fedora Core workstation without having to know cryptic Linux commands. However, if you ever need to use those commands directly, all you have to do is open a terminal window and type them at the prompt.

Fedora Core also comes with many graphical applications. The most noteworthy program is the GIMP (GNU Image Manipulation Program), a program for working with photos and other images. The GIMP's capabilities are on a par with Adobe Photoshop.

Providing common productivity software — such as word-processing, spreadsheet, and database applications — is an area in which Linux used to be lacking. This situation has changed, though. Fedora Core comes with the OpenOffice.org office-productivity applications. In addition, you may want to check out these prominent, commercially available office-productivity applications for Linux that are not included on the companion DVD-ROMs:

✦ **Applixware Office:** Now called Anyware Desktop for Linux, this office package is a good example of productivity software for Linux. You can find it at www.vistasource.com.

✦ **StarOffice:** From Sun Microsystems (www.sun.com/staroffice), StarOffice is another well-known productivity software package.

✦ **CrossOver Office:** From CodeWeavers (www.codeweavers.com/products/office/), you can install your Microsoft Office applications (Office 97, Office 2000, and Office XP) in Linux. Note that only the Office 2000 versions of two Office applications — Microsoft Access and Outlook — are supported.

As you can see, there's no shortage of Microsoft Office-compatible office applications for Linux.

## Networks

Fedora Core comes with everything needed to use the system in networks so that the system can exchange data with other systems. On networks, computers that exchange data have to follow well-defined rules or protocols. A *network protocol* is a method that the sender and receiver agree upon for exchanging data across a network. Such a protocol is similar to the rules you might follow when you're having a polite conversation with someone at a party. You typically start by saying hello, exchanging names, and then taking turns talking. That's about the same way network protocols work. The two computers use the protocol to send bits and bytes back and forth across the network.

One of the most well-known and popular network protocols is Transmission Control Protocol/Internet Protocol (*TCP/IP*). TCP/IP is the protocol of choice on the Internet — the "network of networks" that now spans the globe. Fedora Core supports the TCP/IP protocol and any network applications that make use of TCP/IP.

## Internet servers

Some popular network applications are specifically designed to deliver information from one system to another. When you send electronic mail (e-mail) or visit Web sites using a Web browser, you use these network applications (also called Internet services). Here are some common Internet services:

✦ Electronic mail (e-mail) that you use to send messages to any other person on the Internet using addresses like `joe@someplace.com`.

✦ World Wide Web (or simply, Web) that you browse using a Web browser.

✦ News services, where you can read newsgroups and post news items to newsgroups with names such as `comp.os.linux.networking` or `comp.os.linux.setup`.

✦ File-transfer utilities that you can use to download files.

✦ Remote login that you can use to connect to and work with another computer (the remote computer) on the Internet — assuming you have the required username and password to access that remote computer.

Any Fedora Core PC can offer these Internet services. To do so, the PC must be connected to the Internet and it must run special server software called *Internet servers*. Each of the servers uses a specific protocol for transferring information. For example, here are some common Internet servers that you find in Fedora Core:

✦ `sendmail` is the mail server for exchanging e-mail messages between systems using SMTP *(Simple Mail Transfer Protocol)*.

✦ Apache `httpd` is the Web server for sending documents from one system to another using HTTP *(Hypertext Transfer Protocol)*.

✦ `vsftpd` is the server for transferring files between computers on the Internet using FTP *(File Transfer Protocol)*.

✦ `innd` is the news server for distribution of news articles in a store-and-forward fashion across the Internet using NNTP *(Network News Transfer Protocol)*.

✦ `in.telnetd` allows a user on one system to log in to another system on the Internet using the TELNET protocol.

✦ `sshd` allows a user on one system to securely log in to another system on the Internet using the SSH (Secure Shell) protocol.

## Software development

Fedora Core is particularly well suited to software development. Straight out of the box, it's chock-full of software-development tools such as the compiler and libraries of code needed to build programs. If you happen to know UNIX and the C programming language, you will feel right at home programming in Fedora Core.

As far as the development environment goes, Fedora Core has the same basic tools (such as an editor, a compiler, and a debugger) that you might use on other UNIX workstations, such as those from IBM, Sun Microsystems, and Hewlett-Packard (HP). What this means is that if you work by day on one of these UNIX workstations, you can use a Fedora Core PC in the evening at home to duplicate that development environment at a fraction of the cost. Then you can either complete work projects at home or devote your time to software you write for fun and to share on the Internet.

Just to give you a sense of Linux's software-development support, here's a list of various features that make Linux a productive software-development environment:

✦ GNU C compiler, `gcc`, can compile ANSI-standard C programs.

✦ GNU C++ compiler (`g++`) supports ANSI-standard C++ features.

✦ The GNU Java compiler (`gcj`) can compile programs written in the Java programming language.

✦ The GNU `make` utility enables you to compile and link large programs.

✦ The GNU debugger, `gdb`, enables you to step through your program to find problems and to determine where and how a program failed. (The failed program's memory image is saved in a file named core; `gdb` can examine this file.)

✦ The GNU profiling utility, `gprof`, enables you to determine the degree to which a piece of software uses your computer's processor time.

✦ Subversion, Concurrent Versions System (CVS), and Revision Control System (RCS) maintain version information and control access to the source files so two programmers don't modify the same source file inadvertently.

✦ The GNU emacs editor prepares source files and even launches a compile-link process to build the program.

✦ Perl is a scripting language you can use to write scripts to accomplish a specific task, tying together many smaller programs with Linux commands.

✦ The Tool Command Language and its graphical toolkit (Tcl/Tk) enable you to build graphical applications rapidly.

✦ Python is an interpreted programming language comparable to Perl and Tcl (the Fedora Core installation program, called `anaconda`, is written in Python).

✦ Dynamically linked shared libraries allow your actual program files to be much smaller because all the library code that several programs may need is shared — with only one copy loaded in the system's memory.

## Online documentation

As you become more adept at using Fedora Core, you may want to look up information quickly — without having to turn the pages of (ahem) this great book, for example. Luckily, Fedora Core comes with enough online information to jog your memory in those situations when you vaguely recall a command's name, but can't remember the exact syntax of what you're supposed to type.

If you use Linux commands, you can view the manual page — commonly referred to as the *man page* — for a command by using the `man` command. (You do have to remember that command in order to access online help.)

You can also get help from the GUI desktops. Both GNOME and KDE desktops come with help viewers to view online help information. In GNOME, select Main Menu➪Help. You then see two broad categories of information:

✦ **GNOME - Desktop** is information on how to use the GNOME desktop and some GNOME applications.

✦ **Additional documents** include online documentation for the GNU software (primarily for the applications and the software development tools).

You can then browse the information by clicking the links on the initial help window. Figure 1-1 shows a typical help file in GNOME.

In KDE desktop, you can start KDE Help by choosing Main Menu➪Help. The KDE Help application looks similar to the GNOME help browser (see Figure 1-2).

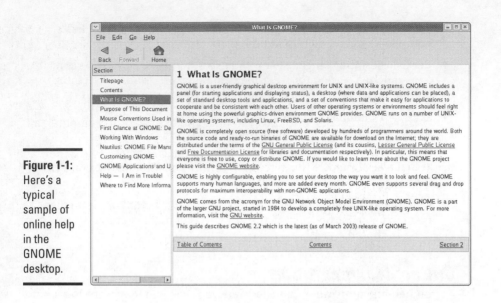

**Figure 1-1:**
Here's a typical sample of online help in the GNOME desktop.

**Figure 1-2:**
The KDE Help Center provides online help in the KDE desktop.

You can then click the links to view specific online help information. You can follow links to discover how to use KDE and obtain information about the KDE Project. Another set of links provides access to the man pages and GNU info pages, just as the GNOME help browser does.

# What Fedora Core Helps You Manage

As an operating system, Fedora Core acts as the intermediary through which you, as the "lord of the system," manage all the hardware. The hardware includes the system box, the monitor, the keyboard, the mouse, and anything else connected to the system box. The catchall term *peripheral* refers to any equipment attached to the system. If you use a laptop computer, all your hardware is packaged into the laptop.

Inside that system box is the system's brain — the microprocessor (Intel Pentium 4, for example) or the central processing unit (CPU) — that performs the instructions contained in a computer program. When the microprocessor is running a computer program, that program's instructions are stored in the memory or RAM. RAM stands for *Random Access Memory* (that means any part of the memory can be accessed randomly — in arbitrary order).

The system box has another crucial component — the hard disk or hard drive, as it is sometimes called. The hard disk is the permanent storage space for computer programs and data. It's permanent in the sense that the contents don't disappear when you power off the PC. The hard disk is organized into files, which are in turn organized in a hierarchical fashion into directories and subdirectories (somewhat like organizing paper folders into the drawers in a file cabinet).

To keep a Fedora Core system running properly, you or someone else has to make sure the hardware is working properly and the files are backed up regularly. There is also the matter of security — making sure only legitimate people can access and use the system. These tasks are called *system administration*.

If you are using Fedora Core at a big facility with many computers, a full-time system administrator probably takes care of all system administration tasks. On the other hand, if you are running Fedora Core on a home PC, you are the system administrator. Don't let the thought frighten you. You don't have to know any magic incantations or prepare cryptic configuration files to be a system administrator. Fedora Core includes many graphical tools such as GNOME's Nautilus graphical shell that makes system administration a "point-and-click" job just like running any other application.

## Disks, CD-ROMs, and DVD-ROMs

Fedora Core comes on a single DVD-ROM. After installation, the Linux kernel and all the applications are stored on your hard drive — which is where your PC looks first when you tell it to do something.

Typically, the hard drive is prepared to use Fedora Core during the installation process. After that, you usually leave the hard drive alone except to back up the data stored there or (occasionally) to install new applications.

Using CD-ROMs or DVD-ROMs in Fedora Core is easy. While you are logged in at the GNOME or KDE desktop, just pop in a CD or DVD in the drive and a DVD/CD-ROM icon appears on the desktop. You can then double-click that DVD/CD-ROM icon and the CD or DVD's contents appears in a window. This whole process of accessing the files on a CD or a DVD from Fedora Core is called *mounting the CD or the DVD*.

Besides the hard drive and DVD/CD-ROM drive, of course, your PC may have other drives, such as a floppy disk or Zip drive, and using those disks in Fedora Core is also simple: You insert a disk and double-click the icon that represents the disk drive on the GUI desktop. Doing so mounts the disk so you can begin using it.

## Peripheral devices

Anything connected to your PC is a peripheral device, and so are some components like sound cards that are installed inside the system box. You can configure and manage these peripheral devices in Fedora Core.

One of the common peripherals is a printer, typically hooked up to the parallel port of your PC. (Fedora Core comes with a graphical Printer Configuration tool that you can use to configure the printer.)

Another peripheral device that needs configuration is the sound card. Unlike Windows, Fedora Core requires you to perform a configuration step before the sound works. Again, you can run a graphical sound-card detection utility to test the sound card (choose Main Menu⇨System Settings⇨Soundcard Detection from the graphical desktop).

Fedora Core configures other peripheral devices such as the mouse and keyboard at the time of installation. You can pretty much leave them alone after installation.

Nowadays PCs come with the USB (Universal Serial Bus) interface and many devices, such as printers and scanners, plug into a PC's USB port. One nice feature of USB devices is that you can plug them into the USB port and unplug them at any time — the device does not have to be connected when you power up the system. These devices are called *hot plug* because you can plug in a device when the system is hot, meaning while it's running. Fedora Core supports many hot plug USB devices. When you plug in a device into the USB port, Fedora Core loads the correct driver and makes the device available to applications.

## File systems and sharing

The whole organization of directories and files is called the *file system*. You can, of course, manage the file system using Fedora Core. When you browse the files from the GNOME or KDE graphical desktop, you work with the familiar folder icons.

A key task in caring for a file system is to back up important files. In Fedora Core you can use the tar program to archive one or more directories on a floppy or a Zip drive. You can even back up files on a tape (if you have a tape drive). If you have a CD burner, you can also burn a CD with the files you want to back up or save for posterity.

Fedora Core can also share parts of the file system with other systems on a network. For example, you can use the Network File System (NFS) to share files with other systems on the network. To a user on the system, the remote system's files appear to be in a directory on the local system.

Fedora Core also comes with the Samba package, which supports file sharing with Microsoft Windows systems. Samba makes a Fedora Core system work just like a Windows file or print server.

## Network

Now that most PCs are either in a local area network or connected to the Internet, you need to manage the network as well. Fedora Core comes with a Network Configuration tool to set up the local area network. For connecting to the Internet using a modem, you use the Internet Configuration Wizard (choose Main Menu⇨System Tools⇨Internet Configuration Wizard).

If you connect to the Internet using DSL (that's the fast Internet connection from the phone company) or cable modem, you need a PC with an Ethernet card that connects to the cable or DSL. It also means you have to set up a local area network and configure the Ethernet card. But fortunately, these steps are typically a part of Fedora Core installation. If you want to do the configurations later, you can — by using the Network Configuration tool (choose Main Menu⇨System Settings⇨Network).

Fedora Core also includes tools for configuring a *firewall,* a protective buffer that helps keep your system relatively secure from anyone trying to snoop over your Internet connection. You can configure the firewall by running the Firewall Configuration tool (choose Main Menu⇨System Settings⇨ Security Level from the graphical desktop).

# How Do I Get Started?

Based on my personal experience in learning new subjects, I prescribe a four-step process to get started with Fedora Core:

1. Install Fedora Core on your PC.
2. Configure Fedora Core so that everything works to your liking.
3. Explore the GUI desktops and the applications.
4. Learn the details of specific subjects such as Internet servers.

In the following sections, I explain this prescription a bit more.

## Install

Microsoft Windows comes installed on your new PC, but Fedora Core usually doesn't. So your first hurdle is to get Fedora Core onto your PC.

After you overcome that initial human fear of the unknown, I'll bet you find Fedora Core fairly easy to install — but where do you *get* it in the first place? Well, the good news is that it's free — available just for the downloading. For example, you can visit the Linux Online Web site at www.linux.org and click the Download button.

Because the complete distribution is HUGE — it takes up several CDs or a single DVD — your best bet is to buy a book (such as this one) that comes with Fedora Core on a DVD-ROM. You can then do the installation by following the instructions in the book.

Just to pique your curiosity, installation involves creating space on the hard disk for both Windows and Linux. Then a step creates the Linux partitions and installs Fedora Core from the DVD. Along the way, you configure many items from the Ethernet card (if any) to the X Window System.

## Configure

When you finish installing Fedora Core, the next step is to configure individual system components (for example, the sound card and the printer) and tweak any needed settings that aren't configured during installation.

If you aren't getting a graphical login screen, for example, Fedora Core comes with tools that help you troubleshoot that problem (typically by configuring the X Window System).

You also want to configure your GUI desktop of choice — GNOME or KDE. Each has configuration tools. You can use these tools to adjust the look and feel of the desktop (background, title fonts, even the entire color scheme).

After you're through with the configuration step, all the hardware on your system and the applications run to your liking.

## Explore

With a properly configured Fedora Core PC at your disposal, you are ready to explore Fedora Core itself. You can begin the exploration from the GUI desktop that you get after logging in.

Explore the GUI desktops — GNOME and KDE — and the folders and files that make up the Linux file system. You can also try out the applications from the desktop. You find office and multimedia applications and databases to explore.

Also try out the shell — open up a terminal window and type some Linux commands in that window. You can also explore the text editors that work in text mode. Knowing how to edit text files without the GUI just in case the GUI is not available is good. At least you won't be helpless.

## Learn

After you explore the Fedora Core landscape and know what is what, you can then dig in deeper and learn specific subject areas. For example, you may be interested in setting up Internet servers. You can then learn the details of setting up individual servers such as sendmail for e-mail, Apache for a Web server, and the INN server for news.

You can choose to find out about many more areas, such as security, programming, and system administration.

Of course, you can expect this step to go on and on, even after you have your system running the way you want it — for now. After all, learning is a lifelong journey.

Bon voyage!

# Chapter 2: Installing Fedora Core

## In This Chapter

✔ **Making a list of your PC's hardware**

✔ **Setting aside disk space for Fedora Core**

✔ **Starting the Fedora Core installation**

✔ **Creating hard disk partitions for Fedora Core**

✔ **Setting up key system parameters**

✔ **Selecting packages to install**

*P*Cs come with Microsoft Windows preinstalled. If you want to use Fedora Core, first you have to install it. This book comes with the Fedora Core DVD-ROM — all you have to do to install it is follow the steps in this chapter.

You may feel worried about installing a new operating system on your PC. You may feel that it's like brain surgery — or, rather, more like grafting on a new brain because you can install Fedora Core in addition to Microsoft Windows. When you install two operating systems like that, you can choose to start one or the other as you power up the PC. The biggest headache in adding Fedora Core to a PC with Windows is creating a new *disk partition* — basically setting aside a part of the disk — for Fedora Core. The rest of the installation is fairly routine — just a matter of following the instructions. I explain everything in this chapter.

## Following the Installation Steps

Installing Fedora Core involves a number of steps — and I want to walk you through them briefly, without the details. Then you can follow the detailed steps and install Fedora Core from this book's companion DVD-ROM.

The very first step is to make sure that your PC and its peripheral components are Linux-friendly and you can successfully install Fedora Core on the PC. Linux installation has come a long way from the old days when you had to manually load drivers for your specific brand of components such as CD-ROM drive and network card. Nowadays the Fedora Core installation program (called Anaconda) can detect and work with most PC peripherals.

If you run into a problem installing Fedora Core, go to the Fedora Core mailing lists at Red Hat's Web site (www.redhat.com/mailman/listinfo) and look through the archives. Chances are someone else has had the same problem and a solution has been suggested in the mailing list. You may also get good results by searching Google (www.google.com) with the words **Fedora Core** and the make and model of the peripheral that's giving you a problem.

The second step is to make sure that your PC can boot from the DVD/CD-ROM drive. This book comes with Fedora Core on a DVD. If you don't have a DVD-ROM drive, you can order the CDs by using the coupon at the back of the book.

Prior to Fedora Core 2, you could prepare a Fedora Core *installer boot disk* — a floppy disk you could use to boot the PC when you start the installation. Unfortunately, the latest Linux kernel used during the Fedora Core installation is too big to fit on a 1.44MB floppy disk. Therefore, in order to install Fedora Core, you need a PC with a DVD/CD drive and the ability to boot from that DVD/CD drive. If your PC has a CD drive only (no DVD drive), you have to get the Fedora Core CDs (see the back page of this book for more information).

The third step is to make room for Fedora Core on your PC's hard disk. If you're running Microsoft Windows, this step can be easy or hard, depending on whether you want to *replace* Windows with Fedora Core or keep *both* Windows and Fedora Core.

If you want to install Fedora Core without removing (or disturbing) Windows, remember that your existing operating system — which is, I assume, Windows 95, 98, Me, NT, 2000, or XP — is currently using the entire hard disk. That means you have to *partition* (divide) the hard disk so Windows can live on one part of it and Fedora Core can live on the other. Doing so can be a scary step because you run the risk of ruining the hard disk and wiping out whatever is on the disk.

Before you create a new place on your hard drive that the Fedora Core installation program can use, you may want to preserve your peace of mind by using a program to help you create the partition. If your version of Windows is NT, 2000, or XP, consider investing in a commercial hard-drive partitioning product such as PartitionMagic. For Windows 95/98/Me systems, you can use a program called FIPS (included on this book's DVD-ROM).

After you set aside a hard-drive partition for Fedora Core, you can begin the final step — boot the PC from your Fedora Core installer boot disk and start the Fedora Core installation. Quite a few steps occur during installation, but, when you've come this far, it should be smooth sailing. Just go through the installation screens and you are done in an hour or two. The Fedora Core installer brings up a graphical user interface (GUI) and guides you through all the steps. One key step involves partitioning the hard disk again, but this time you simply split the extra partition you created earlier. After a few configuration steps, such as setting up the network and the time zone, you select the software packages to install and then let the installer complete the remaining installation chores.

**Book I**
**Chapter 2**

Installing
Fedora Core

# Checking Your PC's Hardware

When you are thinking about Linux-compatible hardware, here are some of the key components in your PC that you need to consider before you start the Fedora Core installation:

+ **Processor:** A 400 MHz Pentium II or better is best. The processor speed, expressed in MHz (megahertz) or GHz (gigahertz), is not that important as long as it's over 400 MHz, but the faster the better. Fedora Core can run on other Intel-compatible processors such as AMD, Cyrix, and VIA processors.

+ **RAM:** RAM is the amount of memory your system has. As with processing speed, the more RAM, the better. You need 256MB to install Fedora Core and comfortably run a GUI desktop.

+ **DVD/CD-ROM:** You must have a DVD/CD-ROM drive and the PC must be able to boot from that drive. The exact model doesn't matter. What matters is how the DVD/CD-ROM drive connects to the PC. Most new PCs have DVD/CD-ROM drives that connect to the hard disk controller (called IDE for *integrated drive electronics* or ATA for *AT Attachment*). If you add an external DVD/CD drive, it most likely connects to the USB port. Any IDE/ATA or USB DVD/CD-ROM works in Fedora Core.

+ **Hard drives:** Any IDE disk drive works in Fedora Core. Another type of hard disk controller is SCSI (Small Computer System Interface), which Fedora Core also supports. To comfortably install and play with Fedora Core, you need about 5GB of disk space.

+ **Keyboard:** All keyboards work with Fedora Core and X Window System.

+ **Mouse:** The installation program can detect the mouse. All types of mouse (such as PS/2 or USB) work with Fedora Core and X Window System.

+ **Video card:** Fedora Core works fine with all video cards (also known as display adapters) in text mode, but if you want the GUI, you need a video card that works with the X Window System. The installer can detect a supported video card and configure X Window System correctly.

✦ **Monitor:** The kind of monitor is not particularly critical except that it must be capable of displaying the screen resolutions that the video card uses. The screen resolution is expressed in terms of the number of picture elements (pixels), horizontally and vertically (for example, *1024 x 768*). The installer can detect most modern monitors. If it does not detect, you can select a generic monitor type with a specific resolution such as *1024 x 768*. You can also specify the monitor by its make and model (which you can find on the back of the monitor).

✦ **Network card:** Not all PCs have network cards, but if yours does, the installer can probably detect and use it. If you have problems, try to find the make and model (such as *Linksys LNE100TX Fast Ethernet Adapter*) so that you can search for information on whether Linux supports that card or not.

✦ **SCSI controller:** Some high-performance PCs have SCSI controllers that connect disk drives and other peripherals to a PC. If your PC happens to have a SCSI controller, you might want to find out the make and model of the controller.

✦ **Sound card:** If your PC has a sound card and you want to have sound in Fedora Core, you have to make sure it's compatible. You can configure the sound card after successfully installing Fedora Core.

✦ **Modem:** If you plan to dial out to the Internet, you need a modem that Linux supports. For software-based modems, called soft modems or win-modems, you may have to download a driver from the manufacturer (it may or may not be freely available).

In addition to this hardware, you need to also find out the make and model of any printer you plan to use in Fedora Core.

# Setting Aside Space for Fedora Core

In a typical Windows PC, Windows is sitting on a big partition, taking over the whole disk. You want to shrink that partition and create room for Linux. During Linux installation, the installation program uses that free space for the Linux partitions.

The challenge is to resize the current partition without destroying anything on the hard disk. I cover tools that help you resize the partition, but first you have to make sure that all used areas of the disk are *contiguous,* or as tightly packed as possible. This is where defragmenting comes in.

## Defragmenting your hard disk

"Defrag your disk" is the magic chant of many a help desk. It's the help desk's prescription for all PC ailments. Well, for once they're right —

you *do* need to defragment your hard disk to make room for Fedora Core. What defragmenting does is move all the files to the beginning of the partition and pack them tight. The result is free space at the end of the partition, so the partition can be shrunk without destroying any data.

To defragment the hard disk, follow these steps:

1. **Double-click My Computer from the desktop, right-click the disk icon, and then select Properties from the pop-up menu.**

2. **In the Properties window, click the Tools tab and then click the Defragment Now button.**

3. **Wait. And wait. And wait.**

   You hear lots of noise from the disk drive while it moves files around. After a couple of hours, the defragmenting completes.

There are some *gotchas* with these instructions. First, don't use your PC or other programs while defragmenting the hard disk. Close all programs, including the ones in the system tray. One good way to do so is to press Ctrl+Alt+Del (which calls up the Task Manager), select which program you want to stop, and then click the End Task button.

The second *gotcha* is that the defragmenter does not move hidden files — and plenty of such files are in your system. You don't see them in the folders because (guess what) they're hidden. You may have to manually find the hidden files and see whether you can delete the ones that seem to be junk. (Don't worry; a how-to is coming right up.)

You can find all the hidden files in your PC with a simple command. Open a Command Prompt window and then type the following commands:

```
cd \
dir /a:h /s > hidden.txt
```

After the command finishes, you have a list of all hidden files in the text file called `hidden.txt`. Open the file in Microsoft Word or just type **edit hidden. txt** to browse that file in a text editor. When I tried this, I noticed a whole lot of files with names like `~WRL0004.TMP` — and they clearly seemed to be temporary files, created by some Microsoft software (probably Word). Who knows why they are hidden? Anyway, I had to change the file attribute by using MS-DOS incantations like `ATTRIB -H ~WRL0004.TMP` and then typing **ERASE ~WRL0004.TMP** to finally delete the file. I had to repeat this command for many more junk files. What a bummer — but it's worth taking your time and doing it carefully!

Another option for dealing with the hidden files is to just unhide them and then run the defragmenter. To unhide all files in the PC, type the following command in an MS-DOS window:

```
attrib -h *.* /s
```

Sit back. After a long time, this command unhides all files. *Then* you can run the defragmenter.

## Resizing your hard disk partition

After defragmenting the hard disk, you're ready to shrink the existing hard disk partition. You want to partition without damaging the current contents of the hard disk. You have two choices:

✦ **PartitionMagic:** This commercial product can resize hard-drive partitions and create new partitions for any version of Microsoft Windows.

✦ **FIPS:** This free program runs in MS-DOS mode and can split an existing partition into two. FIPS works only with Windows 95/98/Me systems. More accurately, FIPS does not work with the NTFS file system that's often used in Windows NT/2000/XP systems. For those systems, your best bet is PartitionMagic.

I quickly go over repartitioning with both PartitionMagic and FIPS.

### Repartitioning with PartitionMagic

PartitionMagic, from PowerQuest, can resize and split disk partitions in all Microsoft operating systems from Windows 95/98/Me to Windows NT/2000/XP. It's a commercial product, so you have to buy it to use it. At the time I'm writing this, the list price of PartitionMagic 8.0 is $69.95. You can read about it and buy it at `www.powerquest.com/partitionmagic`.

Resizing the disk partition always involves the risk of losing all data on the hard disk. Therefore, before you resize hard disk partitions using a disk-partitioning tool such as PartitionMagic, *back up your hard drive*. After making your backup — and before you do *anything* to the partitions — please make sure that you can restore your files from the backup.

When you run PartitionMagic, it shows the current partitions in a window. If you're running Windows XP, your hard disk typically has two partitions: one small, hidden partition that contains Windows XP installation files, and a huge second NTFS partition that serves as the C drive. You have to reduce the size of the existing C drive. Doing so creates unused space following that partition. Then, during Fedora Core installation, the installation program can create new Linux partitions in the unused space.

To reduce the size of the Windows partition, follow these steps:

1. **In the partition map in PartitionMagic's main window, right-click the partition and select Resize/Move from the menu.**

   The Resize Partition dialog box appears.

2. **In the Resize Partition dialog box, click and drag the right edge of the partition to a smaller size.**

   For a large hard disk (anything over 10GB), reduce the Windows partition to 5GB and leave the rest for Fedora Core.

3. **Click OK and then Apply to apply the changes. After PartitionMagic has made the changes, click OK.**

4. **Reboot the PC.**

5. **Choose Start⇨Programs⇨Accessories⇨System Tools⇨ScanDisk to run ScanDisk.**

You don't have to do anything with the disk space left over after shrinking the partition that used to be the C drive. During installation, the Fedora Core installer uses that free space to install Fedora Core.

## Repartitioning with FIPS

The DVD-ROM includes a utility program called FIPS (*First Nondestructive Interactive Partition Splitting Program*) that can split an existing disk partition into two partitions. FIPS cordons off the unused part of a hard disk and makes a new partition out of that unused part without destroying any existing data. FIPS cannot split partitions with the NTFS file system that's often used in Windows NT/2000/XP systems.

Some words of caution before you proceed to repartition your hard disk with FIPS. In the words of FIPS author Arno Schaefer, "FIPS is still somewhat experimental, although it has been used by many people successfully and without serious problems." That tells you in a nutshell that you're on your own when it comes to using FIPS. Neither the publisher nor I can accept responsibility or liability for damages resulting from the use or misuse of FIPS. There is a chance that FIPS could damage your hard disk, making it unusable. Try FIPS only after making sure that you backed up everything on the hard drive and that your backup is usable. Also, before you use FIPS, check your hard disk to make sure it's ready:

✦ Your hard drive has only a FAT or FAT32 partition to start with.

✦ The drive has enough free space available for a useful Fedora Core installation — and that means 3 to 4 gigabytes (3–4GB) of free space.

✦ The drive must be defragmented before you can use FIPS.

✦ The drive must not be in use. You can't partition the hard drive while you're using it, which means (among other things) that you can't run FIPS from inside Windows. You have to shut down Windows, boot from a startup disk, and run FIPS by itself.

When you're ready to use FIPS, follow these steps (use FIPS only if you are running Windows 95/98/Me):

*1.* **Open the Control Panel by choosing Start⇨Settings⇨Control Panel.**

*2.* **Double-click the Add/Remove Programs icon in the Control Panel window.**

*3.* **Click the Startup Disk tab, click the Create Disk button, and follow the instructions.**

*4.* **Insert this book's DVD-ROM in the DVD-ROM drive.**

*5.* **Use Explorer to view the contents of the DOSUTILS folder. Then copy FIPS.EXE and RESTORRB.EXE to the startup disk in the A drive.**

FIPS.EXE is the program that splits partitions. RESTORRB.EXE is a program that can restore parts of your hard drive from a backup of the areas created by FIPS (you use RESTORRB if something goes wrong).

*6.* **Go to the FIPSDOCS folder that's inside the DOSUTILS folder in the DVD. Copy the ERRORS.TXT file to the startup disk.**

ERRORS.TXT is a list of FIPS error messages. Consult this list for an explanation of any error messages displayed by FIPS.

*7.* **Leave the startup disk in the A drive, and restart the PC.**

The PC boots from the A drive and displays the A:\> prompt.

*8.* **Type FIPS.**

The FIPS program runs, showing you information about your hard disk. FIPS gives you an opportunity to save a backup copy of important disk areas before you proceed. After that, FIPS displays the first free *cylinder* (section of the disk) where a new partition can start — as well as the size of the partition, in megabytes. Ignore the cylinder number and focus on the number of megabytes. You need 4 to 5 thousand of them (that is, 4 to 5 gigabytes).

*9.* **Use the left and right arrow keys to adjust the size of the new partition — the one that results from splitting the existing partition.**

Pressing the left arrow shrinks the existing partition; pressing the right arrow leaves more room in the existing partition, but reduces the size of the new partition you are creating.

*10.* **When you're satisfied with the size of the new partition, press Enter.**

FIPS displays the modified partition table and prompts you to press the C key to continue or the R key to reedit the partition table.

*11.* **Press C to continue.**

FIPS displays some information about the disk and asks whether you want to write the new partition information to the disk.

*12.* **Press the Y key.**

FIPS writes the new partition table to the hard disk and then exits.

*13.* **Remove the disk from the A drive and reboot the PC.**

When the system comes back up, everything on your hard drive is intact, but the C drive is smaller. That's because you created a new partition from the unused parts of the old C drive.

*14.* **Choose Start⇨Programs⇨Accessories⇨System Tools⇨ScanDisk to run ScanDisk.**

Running this program ensures that Windows gets adjusted to the new size of the C drive.

You needn't do anything with the newly created partition under DOS. Later, during Fedora Core installation, you create two or more Linux partitions out of this new partition.

After you use FIPS, Windows may assign different drive letters to other disk and DVD-ROM drives on your PC. (For example, your D drive may become E.) FIPS does make sure, however, that the C drive remains C, so you can boot your system after FIPS splits the partitions. Remember those different drive names (for example, E instead of D) when you want to get to programs and files on drives other than C. Keeping a list of them couldn't hurt, at least until you get used to them.

## Starting the Fedora Core Installation

To install Linux, insert the DVD in the DVD drive and restart your PC (in Windows choose Start⇨Shutdown and then select Restart from the dialog box). If you are using CDs, the installation steps are the same as that for the DVD except that you have to swap CDs when prompted by the installation program.

Most new PCs can boot directly from the DVD drive, but some PCs may require intervention from you. Typically, the PC may be set to boot from the hard drive before the DVD/CD drive and you have to get into SETUP to change the order of boot devices. To set up a PC to boot from the DVD drive, you have to go into SETUP as the PC powers up. The exact steps for entering SETUP and setting the boot device vary from one PC to the next, but typically they involve pressing a key such as F2. As the PC powers up, a brief message tells you what key to press to enter SETUP. When you're in SETUP, you can designate the DVD drive as the boot device. After your PC is set up to boot from the DVD drive, simply put the DVD in the DVD drive and restart your PC.

After your PC powers up, it loads the Linux kernel from the DVD and the Linux kernel starts running the Fedora Core installation program. For the rest of the installation, you work with the installation program's GUI screens.

After a few moments, the text screen displays a welcome message and a boot: prompt. The welcome message tells you that help is available by pressing one of the function keys F1 through F5. To start installing Fedora Core immediately, press Enter. You can also enter other options at the boot: prompt. For example, type **linux mediacheck** to test the DVD media for any problems. Press Enter to perform the media check. After the media check, you can continue with the installation. If you want to install Fedora Core with the new Security Enhanced Linux (SELinux) extensions enabled, type **selinux** at the boot: prompt.

Installing Fedora Core from the companion DVD-ROM on a fast (400MHz or better) Pentium PC takes about an hour or so, if you install nearly all packages.

The Fedora Core installation program *probes* — attempts to determine the presence of — specific hardware and tailors the installation steps accordingly. For example, if the installation program detects a network card, the program automatically displays the screens needed to configure your PC to work with the network in Linux. You may see a different sequence of screens from what I show in this chapter; the exact sequence depends on your PC's specific hardware configuration.

If you run into any problems during the installation, turn to Chapter 3 of this minibook. That chapter shows how to troubleshoot common installation problems.

## Selecting Keyboard, Mouse, and Installation Type

This first phase of the installation is where you go through a number of steps before moving on to create the disk partitions for Fedora Core. Here are the steps in the first phase:

*1.* **The installation program displays a list of languages that you can use for the rest of the installation. Use your mouse to select the language you want from the list displayed and then click Next to proceed to the next step.**

Each screen has online help available on the left side of the screen. You can read the help message to find out more about what you're supposed to do in a specific screen.

*2.* **The installation program displays a list of keyboard layouts, as shown in Figure 2-1.**

Select a keyboard layout suitable for your language's character set (for example, U.S. English in the United States) and then click Next to continue.

*3.* **The installation program displays a screen from which you can configure the mouse in your system.**

A treelike list shows the mouse types, organized alphabetically by manufacturer. You need to know your mouse type and whether it's connected to the PC's serial port or the PS/2 port (the small, round connector). If the name of your mouse appears in the list, select it. Otherwise select a generic mouse type. Most new PCs have a PS/2 mouse. For a two-button mouse, select the Emulate 3 Buttons option. Because many X applications assume you're using a three-button mouse, select this option. (On a typical two-button mouse, you can simulate a middle-button click by pressing both buttons simultaneously. On a Microsoft Intellimouse, the wheel acts as the middle button.) Click Next after selecting the mouse.

The installer tries to detect the monitor and displays a screen with the results, whether or not it detects the monitor correctly (see Figure 2-2).

*4.* **If the Fedora Core installer displays a wrong monitor or a generic one as the choice, scroll through the list and pick the correct name of your monitor from the list.**

(One good thing about monitors is that you can always easily look up the make and model number on the back of the monitor.)

*5.* **The installation program displays a screen asking whether you want to install a new system or upgrade an older Fedora Core installation. For a new Fedora Core installation, click Install. Then a screen (see Figure 2-3) prompts you for the installation type.**

For a new installation, you have to select the installation type — Personal Desktop, Workstation, Server, or Custom. The Personal Desktop, Workstation, and Server installations simplify the installation process by partitioning the disk in a predefined manner. The Personal Desktop installation creates a Fedora Core system for home, laptop, or desktop use. A graphical environment is installed along with productivity applications.

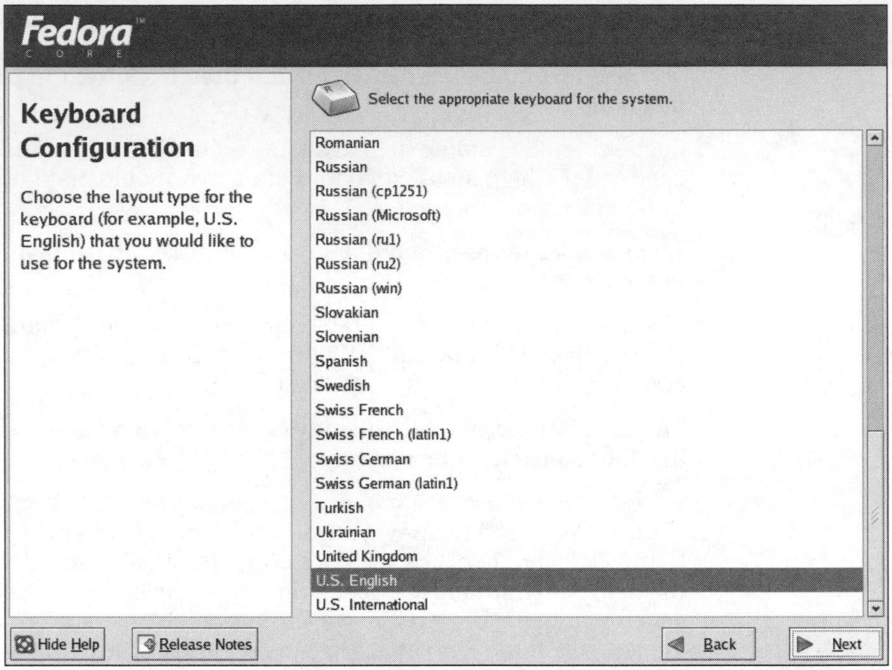

**Figure 2-1:**
Select a keyboard configuration from this screen.

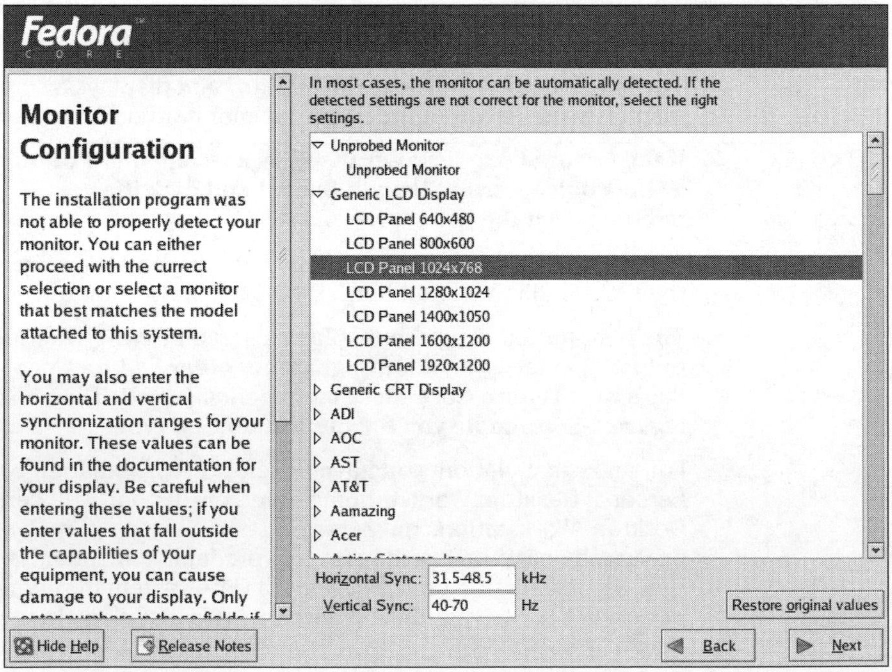

**Figure 2-2:**
Select your monitor type from this screen.

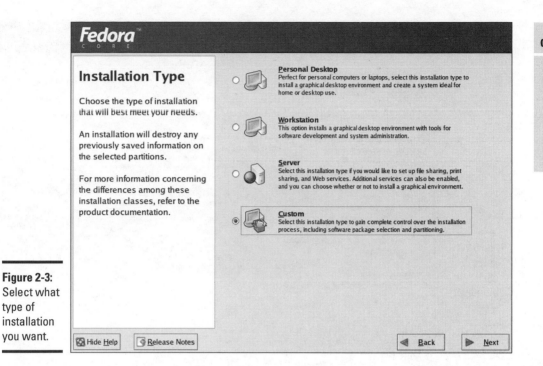

**Figure 2-3:**
Select what
type of
installation
you want.

A Workstation-class installation installs a graphical environment as well
as software development tools. This type of installation also deletes all
currently existing Linux-related partitions, creating a set of new partitions for Linux.

A Server-class installation deletes *all* existing disk partitions, including
any existing Windows partitions, and creates a whole slew of Linux partitions. Server-class installation does not install the graphical environment.

For maximum flexibility, select the Custom installation. That way you
can select only the packages you want to try out.

The next major phase of installation involves partitioning the hard disk for
use in Fedora Core.

## Partitioning the Disk for Fedora Core

The Fedora Core installer displays a screen (see Figure 2-4) from which you
can select a partitioning strategy.

**Figure 2-4:**
Select
a disk-
partitioning
strategy
from this
screen.

**Fedora™**
CORE

**Disk Partitioning Setup**

One of the largest obstacles for a new user during a Linux installation is partitioning. This process is made easier by providing automatic partitioning.

By selecting automatic partitioning, you will not have to use partitioning tools to assign mount points, create partitions, or allocate space for your installation.

To partition manually, choose the **Disk Druid** partitioning tool.

Use the **Back** button to choose

Automatic Partitioning sets partitions based on the selected installation type. You also can customize the partitions once they have been created.

The manual disk partitioning tool, Disk Druid, allows you to create partitions in an interactive environment. You can set the file system types, mount points, partition sizes, and more.

- ● Automatically partition
- ○ Manually partition with Disk Druid

Hide Help     Release Notes     Back     Next

The screen gives you the following options for partitioning and using the hard disk:

✦ **Automatically Partition:** This option (the one most users choose) causes the Fedora Core installation program to create new partitions for installing Linux according to your chosen installation type, such as workstation or server. After the automatic partitioning, you get a chance to customize the partitions.

✦ **Manually Partition with Disk Druid:** With this option, you can use the Disk Druid program that lets you partition the disk and, at the same time, specify which parts of the Linux file system to load, and on which partition(s).

**TIP**

From the disk-partitioning strategy screen (refer to Figure 2-4), select the first option to have the installer automatically partition the disk for you. The Fedora Core installer then displays another screen (see Figure 2-5) that asks you how you want the automatic partitioning to be done.

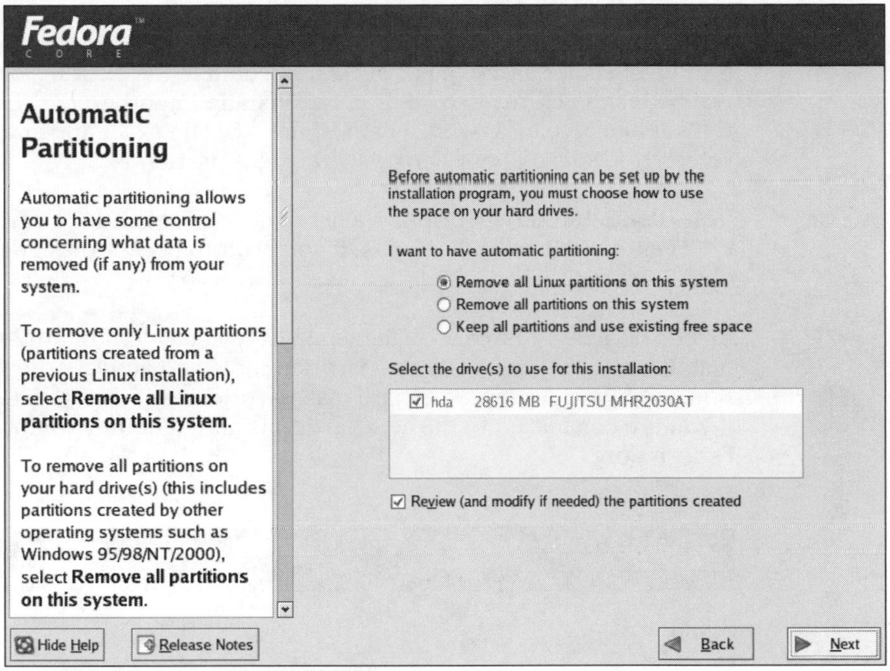

**Figure 2-5:**
Select an automatic partitioning option from this screen.

You can select from three options:

✦ **Remove All Linux Partitions on This System:** This option causes the Fedora Core installer to remove all existing Linux partitions and to create new partitions for installing Fedora Core. You can use this option if you already have any version of Linux installed on your PC and want to wipe it out and install the latest version of Fedora Core.

✦ **Remove All Partitions on This System:** This option is similar to the first option, except that the installation program removes all partitions, including those used by other operating systems such as Microsoft Windows. *Use this only if you want Fedora Core as the only operating system for your PC.*

✦ **Keep All Partitions and Use Existing Free Space:** If you created space for Linux by using PartitionMagic or the FIPS utility, select this option to create the Linux partitions using the free space on the hard disk. If you are installing Fedora Core on a new PC after resizing the partition, this option is the right one to choose.

Select the appropriate option and click Next. For example, if you select the first option, the Fedora Core installation program displays a dialog box to confirm your choice and to point out that all data in the existing Linux partitions will be lost. Click Yes to continue. The installation program shows the partitions it has prepared, as shown in Figure 2-6. The exact appearance of this screen depends on your hard disk's current partitions.

This Disk Setup screen displays a list of disk drives and the current partition information for one of the drives. If you want to accept these partitions as is, click Next to proceed.

If your PC doesn't have enough memory (typically less than 128MB), the installer asks if it can write the partition table and activate the swap partition. After you do this, your hard disk partitions are changed. Click Yes *only* if you are committed to the new partitions and definitely want to install Fedora Core.

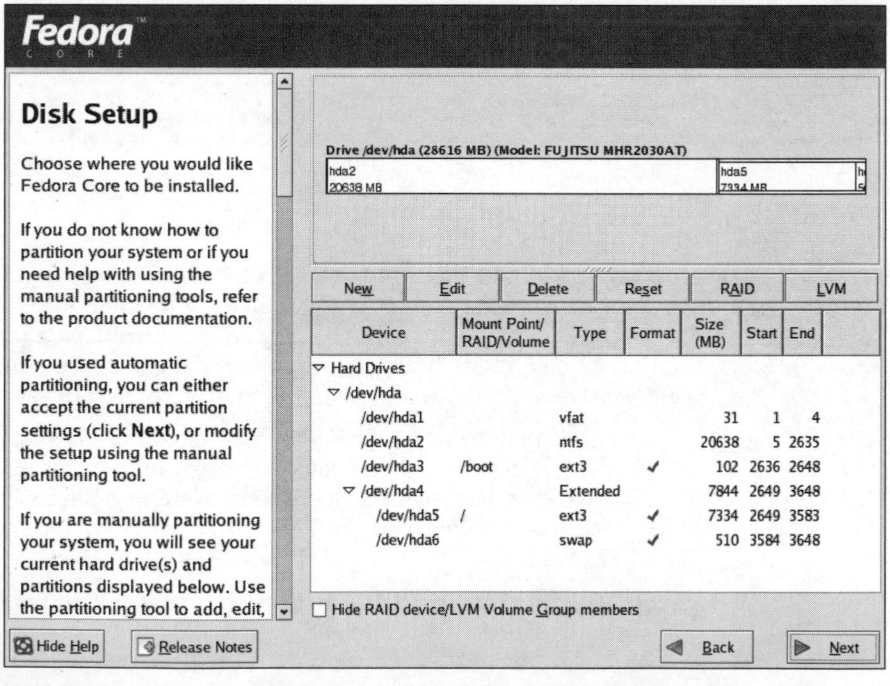

**Figure 2-6:**
Disk partitions created by the Fedora Core installer.

### Fedora CORE

## Disk Setup

Choose where you would like Fedora Core to be installed.

If you do not know how to partition your system or if you need help with using the manual partitioning tools, refer to the product documentation.

If you used automatic partitioning, you can either accept the current partition settings (click **Next**), or modify the setup using the manual partitioning tool.

If you are manually partitioning your system, you will see your current hard drive(s) and partitions displayed below. Use the partitioning tool to add, edit,

Drive /dev/hda (28616 MB) (Model: FUJITSU MHR2030AT)

| hda2 | hda5 | h |
| 20638 MB | 7334 MB | s |

| New | Edit | Delete | Reset | RAID | LVM |

| Device | Mount Point/ RAID/Volume | Type | Format | Size (MB) | Start | End |
|---|---|---|---|---|---|---|
| ▽ Hard Drives | | | | | | |
| ▽ /dev/hda | | | | | | |
| /dev/hda1 | | vfat | | 31 | 1 | 4 |
| /dev/hda2 | | ntfs | | 20638 | 5 | 2635 |
| /dev/hda3 | /boot | ext3 | ✓ | 102 | 2636 | 2648 |
| ▽ /dev/hda4 | | Extended | | 7844 | 2649 | 3648 |
| /dev/hda5 | / | ext3 | ✓ | 7334 | 2649 | 3583 |
| /dev/hda6 | | swap | ✓ | 510 | 3584 | 3648 |

☐ Hide RAID device/LVM Volume Group members

| 🖁 Hide Help | 🔄 Release Notes | | ◀ Back | ▶ Next |

# Setting Up Key System Parameters

With the disk partitioning out of the way, you're almost ready to begin installing the software packages. First, the Fedora Core installer prompts you to set up some key system parameters. Specifically, you have to do the following:

+ Install the boot loader
+ Configure the network
+ Configure the firewall and SELinux
+ Select languages to support
+ Set the time zone
+ Set the root password

You can go through these steps fairly quickly.

## Installing the boot loader

You can install one of two boot loaders — GRUB or LILO. GRUB stands for *GRand Unified Bootloader*, and LILO stands for *Linux Loader*. The *boot loader* is a tiny program that resides on the hard disk and starts an operating system when you power up your PC. If you have Windows on your hard disk, you can configure the boot loader to load any other installed operating systems as well.

The Fedora Core installer displays the boot loader installation screen (shown in Figure 2-7) that prompts you to select the boot loader you want to install — and where to install it.

The top part of the screen explains that GRUB is the default boot loader and that it's installed by default. If you want, click the Change Boot Loader button to select the older LILO boot loader. You can also skip the boot loader installation entirely. If you choose not to install any boot loader, definitely create a boot disk later on. Otherwise, you aren't able to start Fedora Core when you reboot the PC. You get a chance to create the boot disk at the very end of the installation.

The middle of the boot loader installation screen lists the disk partitions from which you can boot the PC. A table lists the Linux partition and any other partitions that may contain another operating system (such as Windows XP or 2000). Each entry in that table is an operating system that the boot loader can load and start. Any Windows operating system appears with an Other label. The default operating system is the one with a check mark in the Default column shown in Figure 2-7 (in this case, Fedora Core is the default operating system).

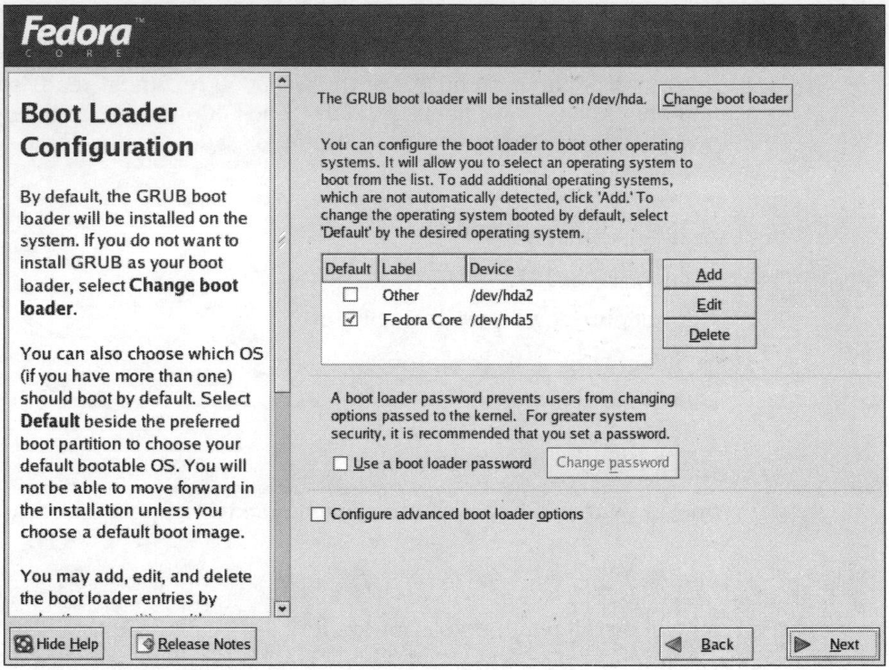

**Figure 2-7:**
Indicate whether to install a boot loader and where to install it.

For greater security (so no one can boot your system without a password), select the Use a Boot Loader Password check box. The installer displays a dialog box in which you can specify a password for GRUB.

If you select the Configure Advanced Boot Loader Options check box (refer to Figure 2-7) and click Next, the next screen gives you the option to install the boot loader in one of two locations:

✦ *Master Boot Record* (MBR), which is located in the first sector of your PC's hard drive (the C drive)

✦ First sector of the Linux boot partition

Install the boot loader in the Master Boot Record unless you are using another operating system loader, such as BootMagic or Windows NT/2000/XP Boot Manager. After making your selections, click Next to continue.

## Configuring the network

Assuming the Linux kernel detects a network card, the Fedora Core installer displays the network configuration screen (as in Figure 2-8).

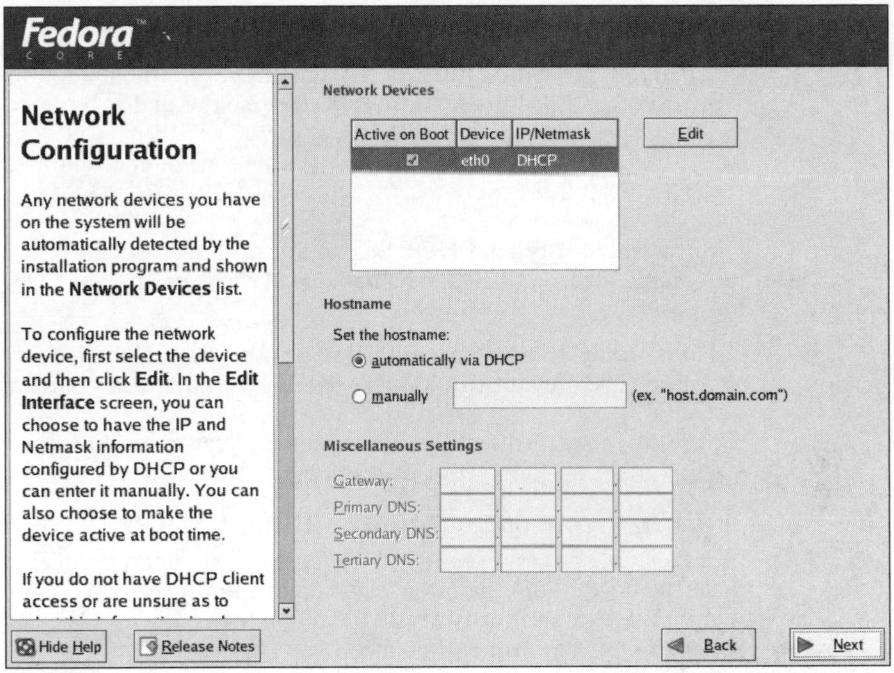

**Figure 2-8:**
Configure
the network
options from
this screen.

From this screen, you can set up your network card's IP address (so other PCs in the network can talk to your PC). This screen displays a list of the network devices (for example, Ethernet cards) installed in your PC. For each network device, you can indicate how the IP address is set. Click the Edit button next to the list and a dialog box appears; there you can specify the options.

You have two choices for specifying the IP (Internet Protocol) address for the network card:

✦ **Configure Using DHCP:** Enable this option if your PC gets its IP address and other network information from a *Dynamic Host Configuration Protocol* (DHCP) server. This is often the case if your PC is connected to a DSL or cable modem router.

✦ **Activate on Boot:** Enable this option to turn on the network when your system boots.

Select DHCP only if a DHCP server is running on your local area network. If you choose DHCP, your network configuration is set automatically, and you can skip the rest of this section.

If you do not select the Configure Using DHCP option, you have to provide an IP address and other network information. Do so by entering the requested parameters in the text-input fields that appear in the dialog box. Make the appropriate selections and click OK to close the dialog box.

In the rest of the Network Configuration screen (refer to Figure 2-8), you specify how to set the host name. You have two options:

✦ **Automatically via DHCP:** Enable this option to assign a host name automatically using DHCP (the name is of the form dhcppc1, dhcppc2, and so on).

✦ **Manually:** Use this option if you want to manually specify a host name and type the name in the text field next to the radio button.

Enter the requested parameters and click Next to continue.

## Configuring the firewall and SELinux

In this step, select a predefined level of security and the level of SELinux access control from the Firewall Configuration screen (see Figure 2-9) and customize these security levels to suit your needs. Note that you get the SELinux configuration option only if you type **selinux** at the `boot:` prompt.

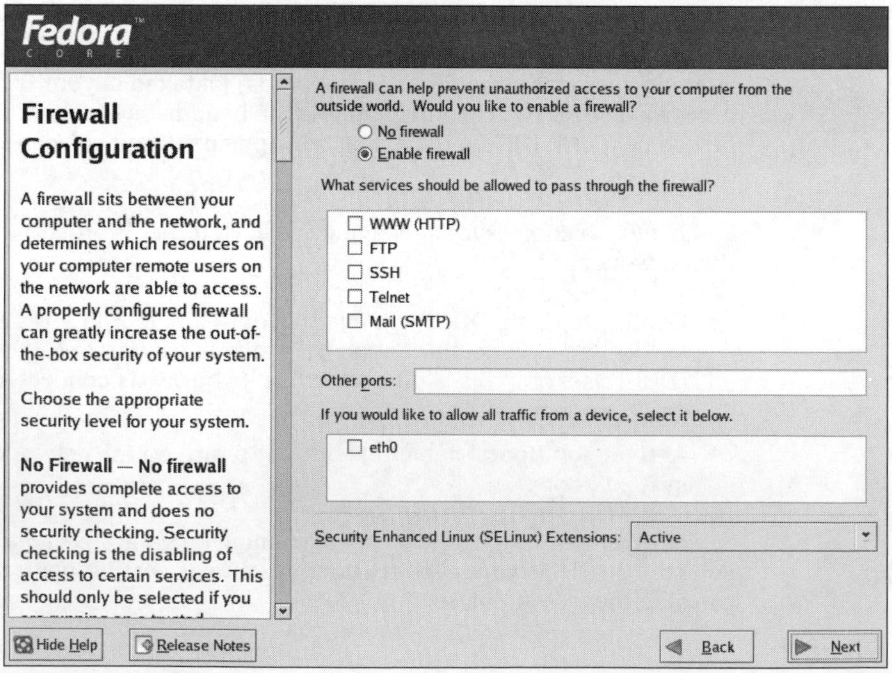

**Figure 2-9:** Select a security level and SELinux access control from this screen.

From this screen, you can set the security levels of your Fedora Core PC. You have to select from one of the following options:

✦ **No firewall** means your system accepts all types of connections and does not perform any security checking. Use this option only if your system runs in a trusted network or if you plan to set up a firewall configuration later on (the sooner the better).

✦ **Enable firewall** means you want to set up a firewall. You can then select the services such as Mail and FTP that are allowed to pass through the firewall. You can also enter port numbers that are allowed through the firewall. You can also allow all traffic from a specific network interface card.

Additionally, you can also enable selected services to pass through the firewall.

For the SELinux access control configuration, you can choose from a drop-down list one of the following options:

✦ **Active** means SELinux enforces mandatory access control.

✦ **Warn** means SELinux prints warning messages, but does not actually enforce the access control policies.

✦ **Disable** means SELinux is turned off.

If you want to try out SELinux, leave the SELinux access control set at its default setting of Active. When you're done configuring the firewall and setting SELinux, click Next to continue.

## Selecting languages to support

In this step, select one or more languages that your Fedora Core system must support when the installation is complete. These are the languages that the system supports when you reboot the PC after completing your Fedora Core installation. From the Language Support Selection screen, select one or more languages to support. You must also select a default language. Then click Next to continue.

## Setting the time zone

After completing the network configuration, select the time zone — the difference between the local time and the current time in Greenwich, England, which is the standard reference time (also known as *Greenwich Mean Time* or GMT as well as UTC or *Universal Coordinated Time*). The installer shows you a screen (as in Figure 2-10) from which you can select the time zone, in terms of a geographic location.

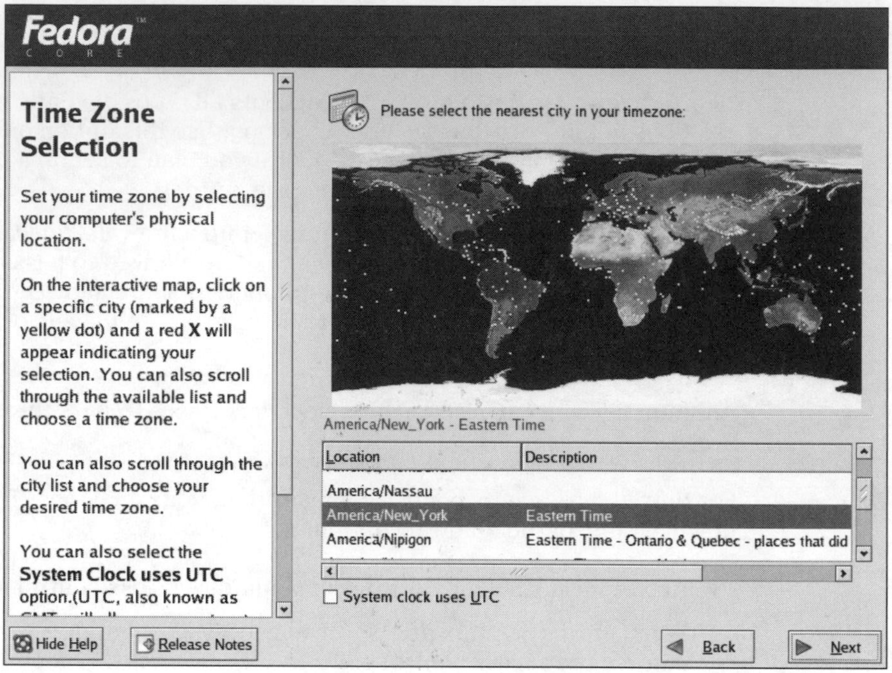

**Figure 2-10:**
Select your
time zone in
terms of a
geographic
location.

As you move the mouse over the map, the currently selected location's name appears in a text field. If you want, you can also select your location from a long list of countries and regions. If you live on the East Coast of the United States, for example, select America/New_York. (Of course, the easiest way is to simply click a location nearest to your city in the eastern United States on the map.)

After you select your time zone, click Next to continue.

## Setting the root password

The installer displays the Set Root Password screen (see Figure 2-11) from which you can set the root password. Earlier versions of the Fedora Core installer enabled you to add one or more user accounts at this step, but now you get a chance to add user accounts when the system boots for the first time (see Chapter 4 of this minibook).

The *root user* is the *superuser* in Linux — the one who can do anything in the system. You're better off reserving that account for your own exclusive use. You need to assign a password that you can remember but that others cannot guess easily. Make the password at least eight characters long, include a mix of letters and numbers, and (for good measure) throw in some special characters, such as + or *.

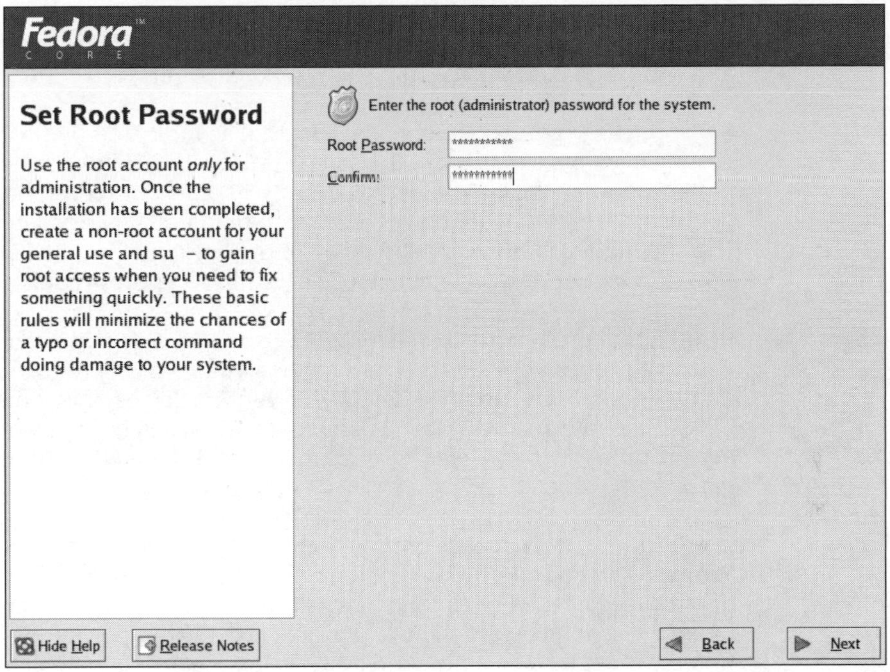

## Set Root Password

**Fedora**
C O R E

Use the root account *only* for administration. Once the installation has been completed, create a non-root account for your general use and su  – to gain root access when you need to fix something quickly. These basic rules will minimize the chances of a typo or incorrect command doing damage to your system.

Enter the root (administrator) password for the system.

Root Password:  ***********

Confirm:  ************

Hide Help     Release Notes                                      ◀ Back     ▶ Next

**Figure 2-11:**
Set the root password from this screen.

Type the password on the first line and re-enter the password on the next line. Each character in the password appears as an asterisk (*) on-screen. You have to type the password twice, and both entries must match before the installation program accepts it. This feature ensures that a mistyped (or guessed) password doesn't work.

You must enter the root password before you can proceed with the rest of the installation. After you have done so, click the Next button to continue with the installation.

## Selecting and Installing the Package Groups

After you set up the key system parameters, the installer displays a screen from which you can select Fedora Core package groups to install. After you select the package groups, you can take a coffee break and let the Fedora Core installation program get busy formatting the disk partitions and copying all your selected files to those partitions.

A *package group* is made up of several Fedora Core packages. Each Fedora Core package, in turn, includes many files that make up specific software.

Figure 2-12 shows the screen with the list of package groups (in effect the software components) you can choose to install. An icon, a descriptive label, and a check-box prefix identify each package group.

Some package groups are already selected, as indicated by the check marks in the check boxes. Think of the selected package groups as the minimal set of packages for the class of installation (workstation, server, or custom) you've chosen. You can, however, choose to install any or all components. Use the mouse to move up and down in the scrolling list, clicking a check box to select or deselect each package group as appropriate.

**TIP**

In an actual production installation of Fedora Core, you install exactly the package groups you need. However, when you're trying to learn everything about Fedora Core, you need many different packages. If you have enough disk space (at least 6GB) for the Linux partition, select the Everything package group — all the package groups install so you can try out the whole nine yards.

In addition to the package groups that you select from the screen shown in Figure 2-12, the Fedora Core installer automatically installs a large number of packages needed to run the Linux kernel and the applications you select. Even if you don't select a single package group from this screen, the installation program installs a plethora of packages — and they're all needed simply to run the core Linux operating system and a minimal set of utilities.

**Figure 2-12:**
Select the
package
groups to
install from
this screen.

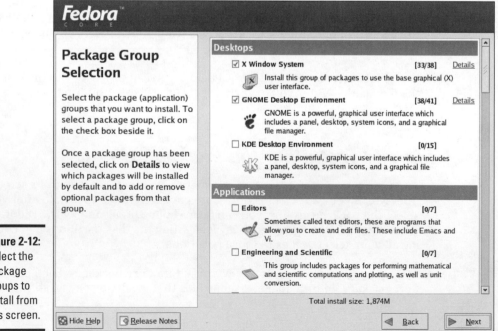

Each package group requires specific packages to run. The Fedora Core installation program automatically checks for any package dependencies and shows you a list of any required packages you haven't selected. In this case, install the required packages.

After you select the package groups you want to install, click Next to continue.

The installer then displays a screen informing you that installation is about to begin. Click Next to proceed with the installation. The Fedora Core installer formats the disk partitions and installs the packages. As it installs packages, the installation program displays a status screen to show the progress of the installation, including information such as total number of packages to install, number installed so far, estimated amount of disk space needed, and estimated time remaining until the installation is complete.

The hard disk formatting and installation can take quite a bit of time — so you can take a break and check back in 15 minutes or so. When you come back, you can get a sense of the time remaining from the status screen, which updates continuously.

After all the packages install, the installer displays a message informing you that installation is complete. Eject the Fedora Core DVD or CD and click the Exit button to reboot your PC.

Congratulations! You're now the owner of a brand-new Fedora Core system!

# Chapter 3: Troubleshooting and Configuring Fedora Core

## In This Chapter

✔ **Troubleshooting the installation**

✔ **Configuring X**

✔ **Setting up printers**

✔ **Turning on sound**

✔ **Adding user accounts**

✔ **Managing DVDs and CD-ROMs**

✔ **Installing RPM packages**

**D**uring Fedora Core installation, the installer attempts to detect key hardware components, such as the SCSI controller and network card. According to what it detects, the program takes you through a sequence of installation steps. For example, if the installer cannot detect the network card, it skips the network configuration step.

Another installation problem crops up when you restart the PC and, instead of a graphical login screen, you get a text terminal — which means something is wrong with the X Window System (or X) configuration.

Also, the Fedora Core installation doesn't include configuration procedures for every piece of hardware in your PC system. For example, the installation does not set up printers or configure the sound card.

In this chapter, I show you some alternative ways to install Fedora Core so that you can force it to configure some key hardware, such as the network card and the SCSI controller (if you have one). I show you how to reconfigure X and do a few other configuration steps, such as adding a user account, setting up a printer, and configuring the sound card.

You may also have to install additional software packages from the companion DVD-ROM. I show you how to install Red Hat Packages (RPMs) — the format in which you get the most from this software.

## Using Text Mode Installation

The Fedora Core installer attempts to use an X Window System (X) to display the graphical user installation screens. If the installer fails to detect a video card, X does not start. If — for this reason or any other reason — it fails to start X, you can always fall back on a text-mode installation. Then you can specify the video card manually.

To use text-mode installation, type **text** at the boot: prompt after you start the PC from the Fedora Core installer boot floppy. From then on, the basic sequence of installation is similar to that of the graphical installation that I describe in Chapter 2 of this minibook. You respond to the prompts and perform the installation.

In text mode, if the installer fails to detect the video card, it displays a list of video cards from which you can select one. By selecting the video card, you make X likelier to work when you reboot the PC. If it doesn't, you can configure X by using the Xconfigurator program (which I show later in this chapter).

## Using the linux noprobe Command

If the Fedora Core installer does not detect the SCSI controller or network card, you can specify these devices manually by typing **linux noprobe** at the boot: prompt.

To see whether the installer deleted the hardware, look for any indication of SCSI or network devices in the messages the Linux kernel displays as it boots. To view these messages during installation, press Ctrl+Alt+F4. The display switches to a text-mode virtual console on which the messages appear. (A *virtual console* is a screen of text or graphical information stored in memory that you can view on the physical screen by pressing a specific key sequence.)

Another sign of undetected hardware is when the installation program skips a step. For example, if the Linux kernel does not detect the network card, the installation program skips the network configuration step.

To manually install devices, follow these steps:

*1.* **Type** linux noprobe **at the** boot: **prompt in the initial text screen.**

The installer then displays a dialog box that shows you the devices that are detected and gives you the opportunity to add other devices.

*2.* **Press Tab to highlight the Add Device button; then press Enter.**

The installer displays a dialog box that prompts you for the type of device — SCSI or Network.

3. **If you have any SCSI device, such as a SCSI hard drive, select SCSI and press Enter.**

   The installer displays a list of SCSI controllers. When you select the one on your system and press Enter, the installer then loads the appropriate driver module. The SCSI driver automatically probes and determines the SCSI controller's settings.

   After you add any SCSI controllers, you're back at the initial dialog box — and from there you can add network cards.

4. **If you select Network from the list and press Enter, the installation program displays a list of network cards from which you can select your network card.**

   When you press Enter, the installation program loads the driver module for the selected network card. That driver then probes and determines the network card settings.

5. **[Optional] If you need a Linux device driver that does not come with Fedora Core, try checking the vendor's Web site or a search engine (such as Google —** www.google.com**).**

   Many hardware vendors provide Linux device drivers for download, just as they do Windows drivers.

   After you finish adding the SCSI controllers and network cards, the installer switches to graphics mode and guides you through the rest of the installation.

# Troubleshooting X

I have this problem on an older PC every time I install Fedora Core: During installation, the GUI installation works fine — but when I reboot the PC for the first time after installation, the graphical login screen does not appear. Instead, the boot process seems to hang just as it starts firstboot. If this problem happens to you, here's how you can troubleshoot the problem.

That firstboot process happens to be a special step where, if all went well, the Red Hat Setup agent starts and enables you to perform one-time setups (such as date and time configuration) and install programs from any other CDs. The reason firstboot may get stuck is because the graphical X environment isn't working on your system. You have to get around the firstboot process and configure X again before you can continue. Here's what you do:

1. **Press Ctrl+Alt+F1 to get back to the boot screen.**

   You see the text display with the boot messages that stop at a line displaying information about firstboot.

2. **Press Ctrl+Alt+Del to reboot the PC.**

   The PC starts to boot and you get to a screen where the GRUB boot loader prompts you to press Enter to boot Fedora Core.

3. **Press the A key to add an option for use by the Linux kernel.**

   The GRUB boot loader then displays a command line for the Linux kernel and prompts you to add what you want.

4. **Type a space followed by the word** single **and then press Enter.**

   The Linux kernel boots in a single-user mode and displays a prompt that looks like the following:

   ```
   sh-2.05b#
   ```

   Now you're ready to configure X.

X uses a configuration file, called `Xorg.conf`, to figure out the type of display card, monitor, and the kind of screen resolution you want. The Fedora Core installer prepares the configuration file, but sometimes the configuration isn't correct.

To quickly create a working `Xorg.conf` file, follow these steps:

1. **Type the following command:**

   ```
   /usr/X11R6/bin/Xorg -configure
   ```

   The screen goes blank and then Xorg exits after displaying some messages. The last line of the message says the following:

   ```
   To test the server, run 'X -xf86config //Xorg.conf.new'
   ```

2. **Use a text editor such as** vi **to edit the** Xorg.conf.new **file and change** /dev/mouse **to** /dev/input/mice.

3. **Try the new configuration file by typing the following command:**

   ```
   /usr/X11R6/bin/Xorg -xf86config //Xorg.conf.new
   ```

   If you see a blank screen with an X-shaped cursor, the configuration file is working fine.

4. **Press Ctrl+Alt+Backspace to kill the X server.**

5. **Copy the new** Xorg.con **file to the** /etc/X11 **directory with the following command:**

   ```
   cp //Xorg.conf.new /etc/X11/Xorg.conf
   ```

   You now have a working X configuration file.

6. **Reboot the PC by pressing Ctrl+Alt+Del or typing** reboot.

   If all goes well, you go through the normal Fedora Core initial setup screens and (finally) get the graphical login screen.

The `Xorg.conf` file created by using the `-configure` option of the X server does not display at the best resolution possible. To fine-tune the configuration file, run the Display Settings utility (choose Main Menu⇨System Settings⇨ Display) after you reboot the system. By using that utility, you can config-ure the video card, monitor, and display settings through a graphical user interface.

# Resolving Other Installation Problems

I'm sure I haven't exhausted all the installation problems that are lurking out there. Nobody can. There are so many different combinations of compo-nents in Intel x86 PCs that Murphy's Law practically requires some combina-tion of hardware to exist that the installation program can't handle. This section lists a few known problems. For others, I advise you to go to Google Groups (`groups.google.com`) and type in some of the symptoms of the trouble. Assuming that others are running into similar problems, you can get some indication of how to troubleshoot your way out of your particular predicament.

## The fatal signal 11 error

Some people get a fatal `signal 11 error` message during installation — and it stops the process cold. This error usually happens past the initial boot screen as the `anaconda` installer is starting its GUI or text interface. The most likely cause of a `signal 11 error` during installation is a hard-ware error related to memory or the cache associated with the CPU (micro-processor).

Signal 11, also known as SIGSEGV (short for Segment Violation Signal), can occur in other Linux applications. A *segment violation* occurs when a process tries to access a memory location that it's not supposed to access. The oper-ating system catches the problem before it happens and stops the offending process by sending it a signal 11. When that happens during installation, it means `anaconda` made an error while accessing memory, and the most likely reason is some hardware problem. A commonly suggested cure for the signal 11 problem is to turn off the CPU cache in the BIOS. To do so, you have to enter SETUP while the PC boots (by pressing a function key such as F2) and then turn off the CPU cache from the BIOS setup menus.

If the problem is due to a hardware error in memory (in other words, the result of bad memory chips), you could try swapping the memory modules around in their slots. You may also consider replacing an existing memory module with another memory module, if you have one handy.

You can read more about the signal 11 problem at `www.bitwizard.nl/ sig11/`.

## Using kernel boot commands

When you boot the PC for installation, either from the DVD or the first CD-ROM, you get a text screen with the boot: prompt. Typically, you press Enter at that prompt or do nothing and the installation begins shortly. You can, however, type quite a variety of commands at the boot prompt. The commands can provide options to the Linux kernel that takes care of the installation and controls various aspects of the installation such as whether the kernel should probe for hardware or whether to use GUI screens for the installation. Some of these commands can be helpful in bypassing problems that you may encounter during installation.

To use these boot commands, type **linux** followed by the boot command. For example, to perform text-mode installation and tell the kernel that your PC has 256MB of memory, you type the following at the boot prompt:

```
linux text mem=256M
```

Consult Table 3-1 for a brief summary of some of the Linux boot commands. You can use these commands to turn certain features on or off.

Although I mention these Linux kernel boot commands in the context of troubleshooting installation problems, you can use many of these commands any time you boot a PC with any Linux distribution and you want to turn specific features on or off.

| Table 3-1 | Some Common Linux Kernel Boot Commands |
|---|---|
| *Command* | *Description* |
| askmethod | Prompts you for other installation methods such as installing over the network using NFS, FTP, or HTTP. |
| apic | Works around a bug commonly encountered in the Intel 440GX chipset BIOS and only executes with the installation program kernel. |
| acpi=off | Disables ACPI (Advanced Configuration and Power Interface) in case there are problems with ACPI. |
| dd | Prompts for a driver disk during the installation of Red Hat Linux. |
| display=IP_address:0 | Causes installer GUI to appear on the remote system identified by the IP address. (Make sure that you run the command xhost +hostname on the remote system where *hostname* is the host where you are running the installer.) |
| driverdisk | Performs the same function as the dd command. |
| enforcing=0 | Turns off Security Enhanced Linux (SELinux) mandatory access control. |

| Command | Description |
|---|---|
| expert | Enables you to partition removable media and prompts for a driver disk. |
| ide=nodma | Disables DMA (direct memory access) on all IDE devices and can be useful when you are having IDE-related problems. |
| ks | Configures the Ethernet card using DHCP and then runs a kickstart installation by using a *kickstart* file from an NFS server identified by the bootServer parameters provided by the DHCP server. |
| ks=*kickstartfile* | Runs a kickstart installation by using the kickstart file specified by *kickstartfile*. (The idea behind kickstart is to create a text file with all the installation options and then "kick start" the installation by booting and then providing the kickstart file as input.) |
| lowres | Forces the installer GUI to run at a lower resolution (640x480). |
| mediacheck | Prompts you if you want to check the integrity of the CD image (also called the ISO image). Checking the image is done by computing the MD5 checksum and comparing that with the official Fedora Core value. It can take a few minutes to check a CD-ROM. |
| mem=*xxx*M | Overrides the amount of memory the kernel detects in the PC (some older machines could detect only 16MB of memory, and on some new machines the video card may use a portion of the main memory). Replace *xxx* with the number representing the megabytes of memory in your PC. |
| nmi_watchdog=1 | Enables the built-in kernel deadlock detector that makes use of Non Maskable Interrupt (NMI). |
| noapic | Prevents the kernel from using the Advanced Programmable Interrupt Controller (APIC) chip. (Use this command on motherboards known to have a bad APIC.) |
| nofirewire | Does not load support for FireWire. |
| noht | Disables *hyperthreading* (a feature that enables a single processor to act as multiple virtual processors at the hardware level). |
| nomce | Disables self-diagnosis checks performed on the CPU by using Machine Check Exception (MCE). On some machines, these checks are performed too often and need to be disabled. |
| nomount | Does not automatically mount any installed Linux partitions in rescue mode. |
| nopass | Does not pass the keyboard and mouse information to stage 2 of the installation program. |

*(continued)*

**Table 3-1** *(continued)*

| Command | Description |
|---|---|
| nopcmcia | Ignores any PCMCIA controllers in system. |
| noprobe | Disables automatic hardware detection and instead prompts the user for information about SCSI and network hardware installed on the PC. You can pass parameters to modules by using this approach. |
| noshell | Disables shell access on virtual console 2 (the one you get by pressing Ctrl+Alt+F2) during installation. |
| nousb | Disables the loading of USB support during the installation (may be useful if the installation program hangs early in the process). |
| nousbstorage | Disables the loading of the usbstorage module in the installation program's loader. It may help with device ordering on SCSI systems. |
| reboot=b | Changes the way the kernel tries to reboot the PC so that it can reboot even if the kernel hangs during system shutdown. |
| pci=noacpi | Causes the kernel to not use ACPI to route interrupt requests (IRQs). |
| rescue | Starts the kernel in rescue mode where you get a shell prompt and can try to fix problems. |
| resolution=*HHH*x*VVV* | Causes the installer GUI to run in the specified video mode (replace *HHH* and *VVV* with standard resolution numbers, such as 640x480, 800x600, 1024x768, and so on). |
| selinux=0 | Disables the SELinux kernel extensions. |
| serial | Turns on serial console support during installation. |
| skipddc | Skips the Display Data Channel (DDC) probe of monitors (useful if the probing causes problems). |
| text | Runs the installation program in text mode. |

# Setting Up Printers

The Fedora Core installer does not include a printer configuration step, but you can easily configure a printer from a graphical utility program. To set up printers, follow these steps:

*1.* **From the graphical login screen, log in as** root.

If you're not logged in as root, proceed to the next step and the printer configuration tool prompts you for the root password.

2. **From the GNOME or KDE desktop, choose Main Menu⇨ System Settings⇨Printing.**

   The printer configuration tool is called `system-config-printer`. Figure 3-1 shows its main window.

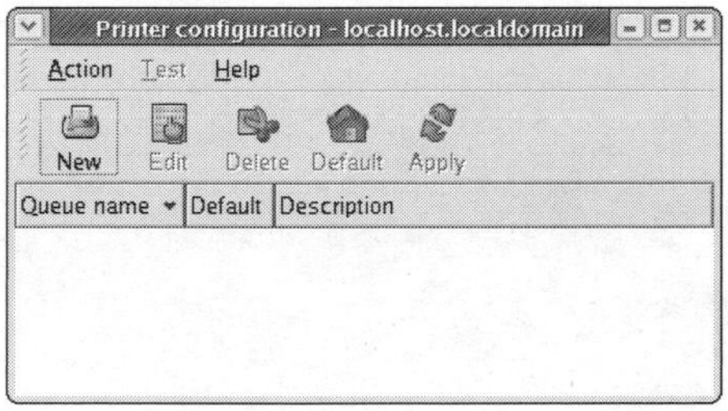

**Figure 3-1:**
Configure
and manage
printers
from the
Printer
Configura-
tion tool.

3. **Click the New button to configure a new printer.**

   The Fedora Core's Printer Configuration Wizard starts. The initial window displays a message that assures you that nothing changes until you click the Apply button at the end of all the steps. Click Forward to continue.

4. **In the next screen (see Figure 3-2), enter the name for the print queue and a short description of the print queue; then click Forward.**

   Use some systematic approach when naming the print queue. For example, if I have a HP Laserjet 5000 printer on the second floor in Room 210, I might name the queue `Room210HPLJ5000` because this name makes finding the printer easier. Sometimes systems administrators choose cute names such as `kermit`, `piggy`, `elmo`, `cookiemonster`, and so on, but after you have too many printers, such cute schemes don't work well. Providing a clue about the printer's location as well as the make and model in the print queue's name is best.

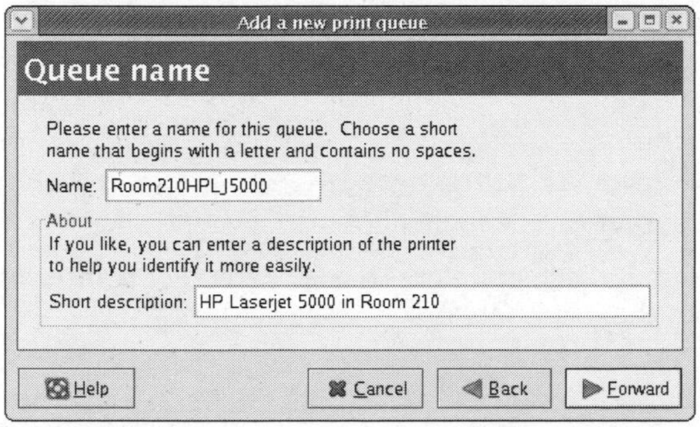

**Figure 3-2:**
Enter the
print queue
name and
description.

5. **In the next screen (see Figure 3-3), select a queue type from the drop-down selection box; then click Forward.**

Select the print-queue type that applies to your situation. For example, if you want to print on a shared Windows printer, select the Windows Printer check box.

To set up a printer connected to your PC's parallel port, select Locally-connected.

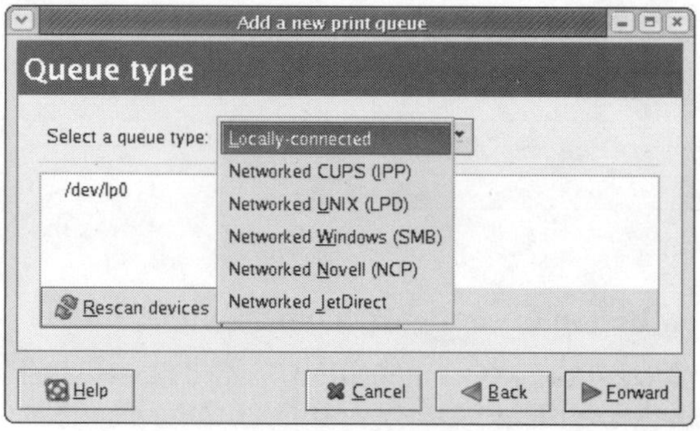

**Figure 3-3:**
Select the
print queue
type from
this window.

The following types of print queues are available:

- **Locally-connected:** Refers to a printer connected directly to the serial, parallel, or USB port of your PC.

- **Networked CUPS (IPP):** Refers to a Common UNIX Printing System (CUPS) print queue at another server on the network (IPP refers to the Internet Printing Protocol used to communicate with the remote CUPS server).

- **Networked UNIX (LPD):** Refers to a print queue managed by the LPD server on another UNIX system on the local network (LPD refers to Line Printer Daemon — another print spooler for UNIX systems).

- **Networked Windows (SMB):** Refers to a printer connected to another PC on the local network and that uses the Server Message Block (SMB) protocol, the underlying protocol in Windows file and print sharing.

- **Networked Novell (NCP):** Refers to a printer connected to a Novell Netware server on the local network.

- **Networked JetDirect:** Refers to a HP JetDirect printer connected directly to the local network.

6. **If you select the Local Printer, the next screen displays information about the detected parallel port; click Forward to continue.**

   For other options, you get a screen that prompts you to identify the network printer. The way you specify a network printer depends on the network type. For example, to use a networked CUPS printer on a host with the IP address 192.168.0.8 on your local area network, you have to type a name such as **http://192.168.0.8:631/printers/HPLaserjetRoom210** where *HPLaserjetRoom210* is the name of the networked printer.

7. **Select the make and model of your printer from the screen shown in Figure 3-4 and then click Forward.**

   Click the drop-down list (above the scrolling list) to display a list of printer manufacturers. When you choose a printer manufacturer from this list, the scrolling list displays the names of different printer models from that manufacturer, as shown in Figure 3-4 (for HP). If you have a PostScript printer, you can simply go to the Generic list (Generic is one of the choices in the manufacturer list) and select PostScript printer.

   The last screen shows information about the new print queue.

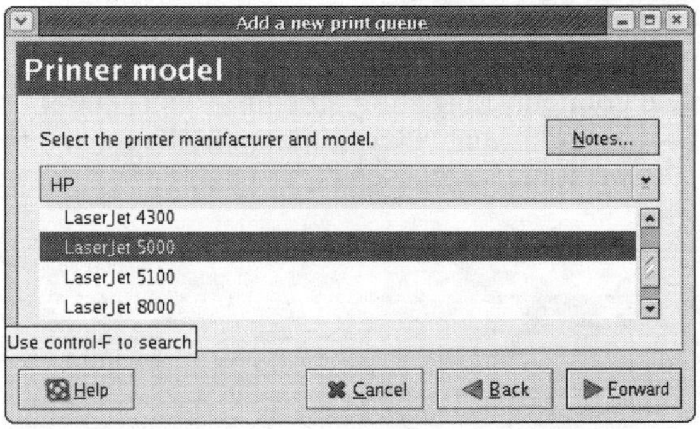

**Figure 3-4:**
Select your
printer's
make and
model from
this window.

8. **Review all information to make sure it's correct and then click Finish to create the print queue.**

9. **When a dialog box appears, asking whether you want to print a test page, click Yes.**

   Doing so applies all changes and restarts the print-scheduler program that takes care of printing. The printer now prints a test page, after which a message box appears and asks you to check the test page.

10. **Click OK to dismiss the message box.**

    The new print queue appears in the printer configuration window, and you can submit print jobs to this queue.

**11. Quit the printer configuration tool.**

You can do so by choosing Action⇨Quit, or by closing the printer configuration window (click the X button in the upper-right corner of the window's frame). You are prompted to save the printer information.

## *Turning On Sound*

Your PC must have a sound card and speakers to play audio CDs. If your PC has a sound card, hook up the speakers according to the instructions from the PC's manufacturer.

When you first boot your PC with Fedora Core, a utility called Kudzu detects the sound card and installs the driver. If you've gone through that step, you're set to try out the sound card. Otherwise, you can set up the sound card by following these steps:

**1. At the graphics login screen, log in as** root.

**2. When you get to the GNOME desktop, choose Main Menu⇨System Settings⇨Soundcard Detection.**

The sound card configuration utility runs.

The sound card configuration utility gets information about the sound cards from another program called Kudzu and displays information about the detected sound card (see Figure 3-5).

**Figure 3-5:** The sound card configuration utility displays information about the sound card.

**3. Click the Play Test Sound button to play a test sound clip.**

If all goes well, you hear the sound.

**4. Click OK to quit the sound card configuration utility.**

After you configure the sound card, you can play audio CDs and other sound files in Fedora Core.

# Adding User Accounts

When you start Fedora Core for the first time, you get the chance to add a personal user account. If you didn't add a user account during the first boot as described in Chapter 4 of this minibook (or if you want to add more user accounts for family members or coworkers), you can do so at any time by using the Red Hat User Manager.

Setting up a personal user account other than root is a good idea. The problem with root is the absolute power of that superuser account — you can literally do anything, even destroy critical system files, with ease. Logging in as an ordinary user is better. When you must do something as root, simply type the su - command. You're prompted for the root password and after you enter that password, you become root. When you finish with your superuser duties, type **exit** to return to your mere mortal self.

To add user accounts with the User Manager, follow these steps:

*1.* **Choose Main Menu⇨System Settings⇨Users and Groups from the GNOME desktop.**

   If you're not logged in as root, the User Manager prompts you for the root password (see Figure 3-6), which you have to enter to run the manager.

**Figure 3-6:**
Enter the
root
password
here.

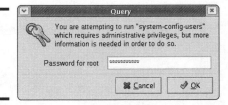

*2.* **Enter the password and click OK.**

   The User Manager window (shown in Figure 3-7) features two tabs: Users and Groups. The Users tab displays the current list of user accounts. The Groups tab lists your current groups. Figure 3-7, for example, lists the users on my Fedora Core system; the list is different on your system.

*3.* **To add a new user, click the Add User button on the toolbar.**

   The Create New User dialog box appears, as shown in Figure 3-8.

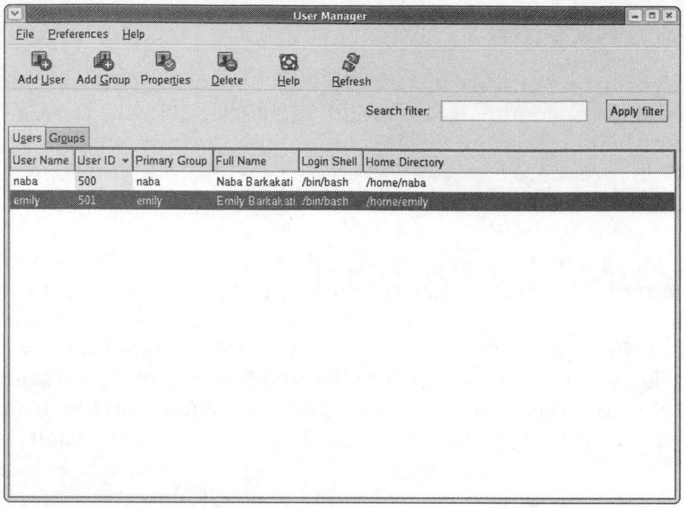

**Figure 3-7:**
The User
Manager
window
shows the
current user
accounts.

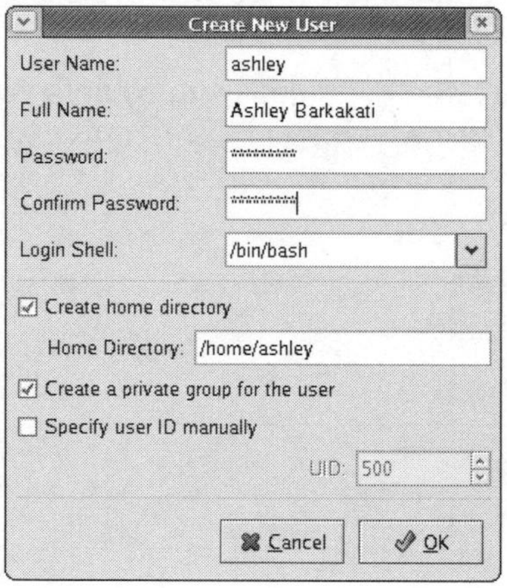

**Figure 3-8:**
Entering
information
about a
new user
account.

4. **Fill in the requested information, and then click OK.**

   The new user now appears in the list on the Users tab in the User
   Manager window.

5. **Repeat Steps 3 and 4 to add as many user accounts as you want.**

6. **When you're done, choose File⊅Exit to quit the User Manager.**

To edit existing user-account information, select the username from the list in the Users tab and then click the Properties button on the toolbar. The selected user's information appears in a User Properties dialog box, where you can then edit it; click OK to make the changes.

If you want to remove a user account, select the username on the Users tab. Then click the Delete button on the toolbar.

## Managing DVDs and CD-ROMs

The GNOME desktop makes using DVDs and CD-ROMs in Fedora Core easy. Just place a DVD or a CD-ROM in the drive, and an icon appears on the desktop. Behind the scenes, a special utility called Magicdev is always running, waiting to detect when a CD-ROM is inserted or removed. Magicdev puts a DVD/CD-ROM icon on the GNOME desktop when it detects a CD or DVD in the drive. You can then access the CD or DVD by double-clicking the icon on the desktop. To access the files and folders, you simply double-click the icons that appear in the Nautilus window.

The DVD/CD-ROM icon is your best bet for certain tasks such as ejecting the CD when you're done with it. If you right-click the DVD/CD-ROM icon, a pop-up menu appears, listing the things you can do with the DVD/CD-ROM (as in Figure 3-9).

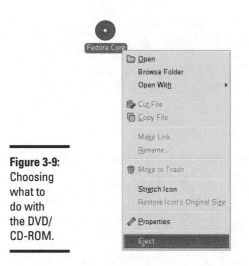

**Figure 3-9:**
Choosing
what to
do with
the DVD/
CD-ROM.

When you're done with the DVD or CD, choose Eject from the pop-up menu to eject the DVD/CD-ROM from the drive. Doing so automatically removes the icon.

If a DVD or CD is in the DVD/CD-ROM drive and you don't see a DVD/CD-ROM icon on the GNOME desktop, just eject the DVD or CD (by pressing the Eject button on the DVD/CD-ROM drive). Insert the DVD or CD again and Magicdev recognizes the DVD or CD.

The KDE desktop has a DVD/CD-ROM icon. You can access the contents of a DVD or CD by inserting the DVD/CD into the drive and double-clicking the DVD/CD-ROM icon. The contents then appear in a file manager called Konqueror. For example, Figure 3-10 shows the result of inserting a DVD and then double-clicking the DVD/CD-ROM icon on the KDE desktop.

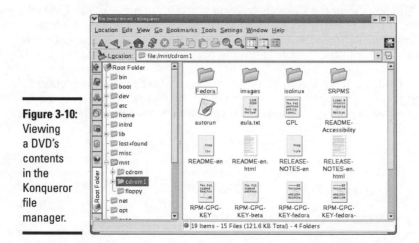

**Figure 3-10:** Viewing a DVD's contents in the Konqueror file manager.

# Installing RPM Packages

Sometimes you have to install or remove software to troubleshoot or config-ure your Fedora Core system. Most Fedora Core software comes in the form of Red Hat Package Manager (RPM) files. An RPM file is basically a single pack-age that contains everything — all the files and configuration information — needed to install a software product. This section shows you how to install RPM packages.

From the GNOME desktop, use the Add or Remove Packages utility — a graphical utility for installing and uninstalling RPMs. Follow these steps:

1. **Choose Main Menu⇨System Settings⇨Add/Remove Applications.**

   If you're not logged in as root, a dialog box prompts you for the root password.

2. **Type in the root password and press Enter.**

   The Add or Remove Packages utility starts and gathers information about the status of packages installed on your system. After it sorts through the information about all the installed packages, the utility displays a list of all the packages (see Figure 3-11).

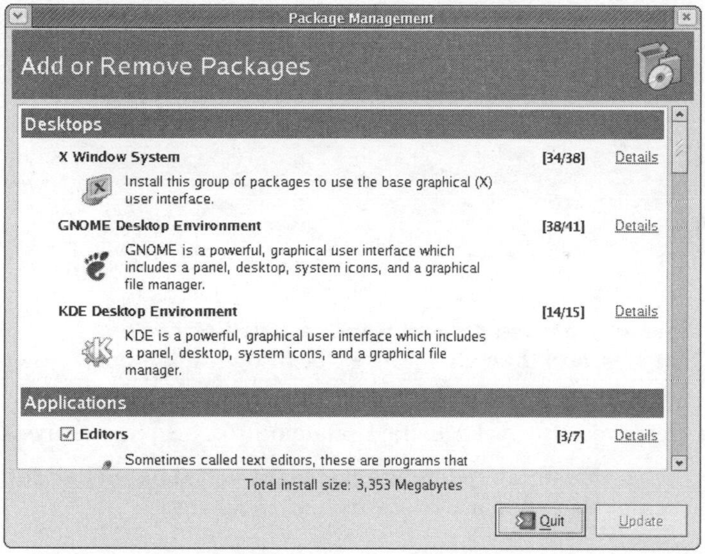

**Figure 3-11:** The Add or Remove Packages utility shows information about the package groups.

The utility displays information about the packages organized into package groups such as Desktops and Applications (a *package group* is a collection of related RPMs). Each package group has a graphical icon, a label such as X Window System or GNOME Desktop Environment, and a brief description as well. For each package group, the utility displays how many packages are installed. If a package group has any uninstalled packages, the utility displays a Details hyperlink. For an uninstalled package group, you see an unchecked box to the left of the package group's name.

3. **To install an uninstalled package group, click the check box to the left of that package group's name. For partially uninstalled package groups, click the Details hyperlink next to that package.**

   A dialog box appears with details of the packages in the package group. Figure 3-12 shows the result of clicking the Details link next to the X Window System package group in Figure 3-11.

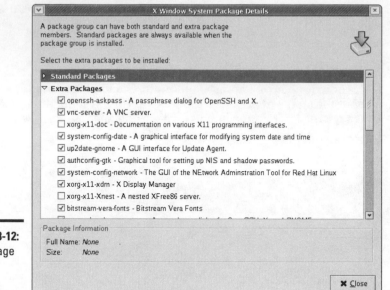

**Figure 3-12:**
A package
group's
details.

4. **Select the packages you want to install or remove by clicking the names, and then click Close to exit the dialog box.**

   You return to the Package Management dialog box and, if you added or removed any package, the Update button becomes active.

5. **Click Update to update the packages based on any additions or removals you made in the lists of packages.**

# Chapter 4: Trying Out Fedora Core

## In This Chapter

✔ Booting Fedora Core

✔ Logging in

✔ Checking out the GUI desktops

✔ Playing with the shell

✔ Shutting down

You're sitting in front of your PC about to turn it on. You know that the PC has Fedora Core installed (maybe you did the installing yourself, but who's keeping track?). You're wondering what to expect when you turn it on and what you do afterward. Not to worry. If you're using Fedora Core for the first time, this chapter shows you how to log in, check out the graphical desktops, try out some cryptic Linux commands, and finally, shut down the PC.

Those of you who already know something about Fedora Core, flip through the pages to see if anything here looks new. You never know what you may not know!

## Booting Fedora Core

When you power up the PC, it goes through the normal power-up sequence and loads the boot loader — GRUB or LILO, depending on which one you selected during Fedora Core installation. The *boot loader* (once known as bootstrap loader) is a tiny computer program that loads the rest of the operating system from disk into the computer's memory. The whole process of starting up a computer is called *booting*.

Whether the boot loader is LILO or GRUB doesn't matter much. In either case, a graphical screen appears with the names of operating systems that the boot loader can load. For example, if your PC has Windows and Fedora Core, you see both names listed. You can then use the Up and Down arrow keys to select the operating system you want to use. If the PC is set up to load Fedora Core by default, wait a few seconds and then the boot loader starts Fedora Core. To be more precise, the boot loader loads the *Linux kernel* — the core of the Linux operating system — into the PC's memory.

As the Linux kernel starts, you see a long list of opening messages often referred to as the *boot messages* (you can see these messages at any time by typing the `dmesg` command in a terminal window). These messages include the names of the devices that Linux detects. One of the first lines in the boot messages reads

```
Calibrating delay loop... 2957.31 BogoMIPS
```

*BogoMIPS* is Linux jargon (explained in this chapter in a handy sidebar) for a measure of time. The number that precedes `BogoMIPS` depends on your PC's processor speed, whether it's an old 200MHz Pentium or a new 4GHz Pentium 4. The kernel uses the BogoMIPS measurement when it has to wait a small amount of time for some event to occur (like getting a response back from a disk controller when it's ready).

After the boot messages, Fedora Core switches to a graphical boot screen that shows information about the progress of system startup. Specifically, you see information such as servers being started and hardware being probed.

When you boot Fedora Core for the first time after installation, you get the Firstboot program that displays a welcome screen and asks you to agree to the Fedora Core license agreement (it's the GNU General Public License). Click the Yes radio button and then click Next. After that Firstboot takes you through date and time setup (see Figure 4-1), display setup, user account setup, sound card check, and, finally, gives you a chance to install programs from any additional CDs.

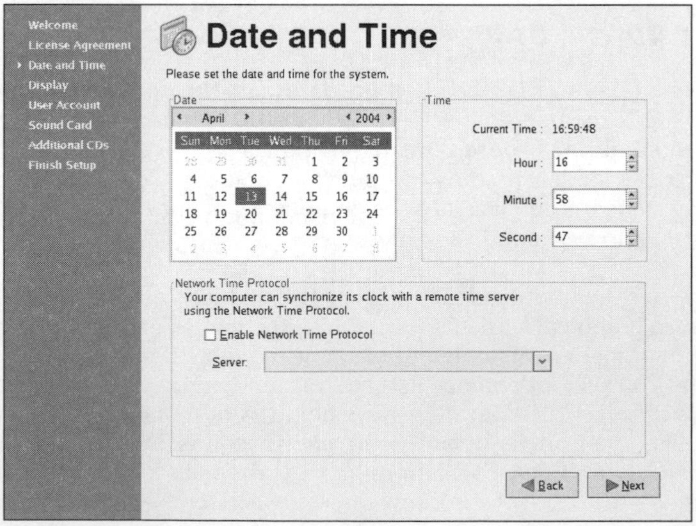

**Figure 4-1:** Configure date and time from this screen in Firstboot.

# What is BogoMIPS?

As Fedora Core boots, you get a message that says `Calibrating delay loop... 421.23 BogoMIPS.` with some number before the word *BogoMIPS*. BogoMIPS is one of those words that confounds new Linux users, but it's just jargon with a simple meaning.

BogoMIPS is Linus's invention (yes, the same Linus Torvalds who started Linux), and it means *bogus MIPS*. As you may know, MIPS is an acronym for *millions of instructions per second* — a measure of how fast your computer runs programs. Unfortunately, MIPS isn't

a very good measure of performance; the MIPS measurements of different types of computers are difficult to compare accurately. BogoMIPS is basically a way to measure the computer's speed that's independent of the exact processor type. Linux uses the BogoMIPS number to calibrate a *delay loop,* in which the computer keeps running some useless instructions until a specified amount of time passes. Of course, the reason for killing valuable processor time like this is to wait for some slowpoke device to get ready for work.

If the screen goes dark and you see no activity, the first-time configuration utility may be having trouble starting the X Window System. Unfortunately, you cannot try out Fedora Core without fixing this problem. Sometimes the graphical environment fails even though the graphical interface seems to work fine during installation. There are ways to fix this problem. Go to Chapter 3 of this minibook for more information on how to troubleshoot this problem.

Firstboot's first configuration step is for date and time setup. You can set the date and time from the Date and Time window (refer to Figure 4-1) and then click Next.

If your system is connected to the Internet, select the Enable Network Time Protocol check box and then select a server from the Server drop-down list. That way, the system gets its time values directly from one of the super-accurate time servers on the Net. Firstboot's second configuration step enables you to set up the resolution and number of colors for your display, as shown in Figure 4-2.

You can change the display settings to your liking (or accept the default) and click Next. Firstboot then displays a screen (see Figure 4-3) from which you can set up a user account.

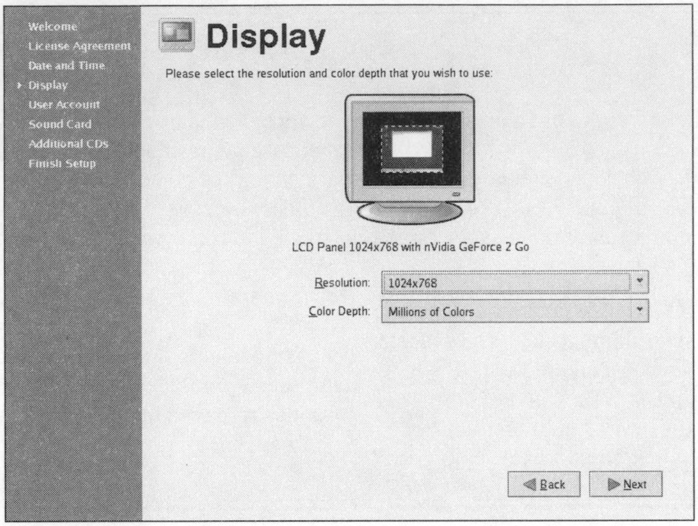

**Figure 4-2:**
Configure
the display
from this
window.

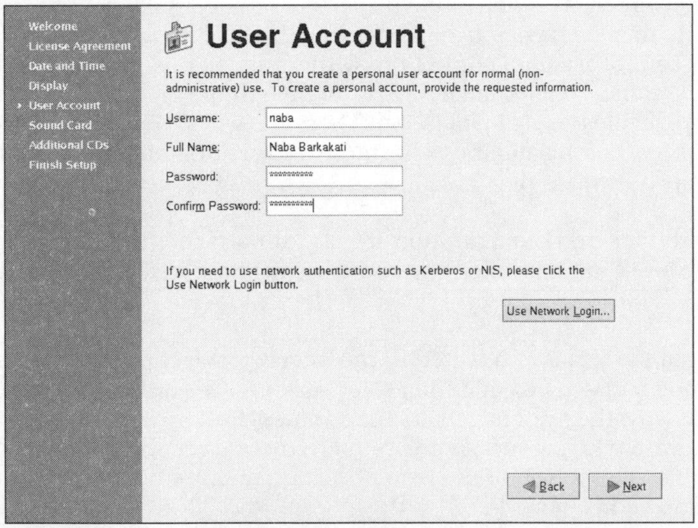

**Figure 4-3:**
Set up a
user
account
from this
window.

Enter the account information in the screen. After entering the user account information, click Next. Firstboot then displays information about the sound card and gives you an opportunity to play a test sound. Click Next to continue. Firstboot then displays a window from which you can install programs from additional CDs (see Figure 4-4). If you have additional CDs to install, click the appropriate icon. Otherwise, click Next.

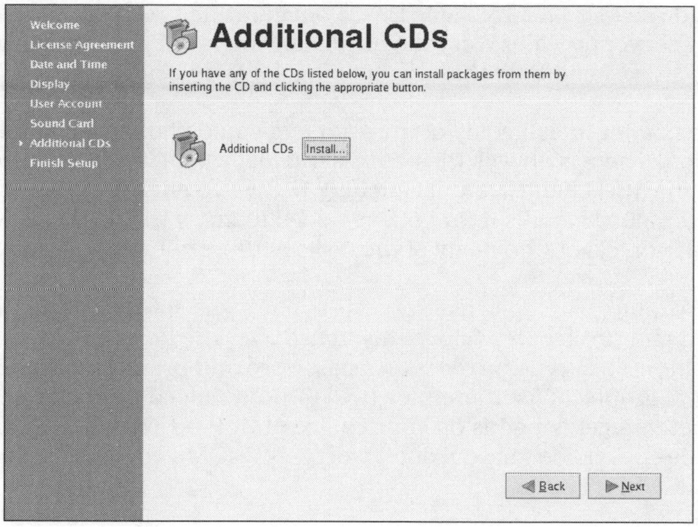

**Additional CDs**

If you have any of the CDs listed below, you can install packages from them by inserting the CD and clicking the appropriate button.

Additional CDs [Install...]

Welcome
License Agreement
Date and Time
Display
User Account
Sound Card
▸ Additional CDs
Finish Setup

◁ Back   ▷ Next

**Figure 4-4:**
You can
install any
other CDs
you may
have.

When you're done with Firstboot, you're really done for good because it runs only once when you boot for the first time. If, for some reason, you want to go through these steps again, here's the scoop on how to run Firstboot again:

Log in as `root` and type the following commands in a terminal window (to open a terminal window, choose Main Menu⇨System Tools⇨Terminal):

```
rm /etc/sysconfig/firstboot
chkconfig --level 5 firstboot on
```

That's it! Next time you reboot the PC, you have the pleasure of meeting Firstboot again. If you want to run Firstboot interactively from GNOME or KDE, you can do so by logging in as `root` and typing the following commands in a terminal window:

```
rm /etc/sysconfig/firstboot
firstboot
```

When you're through with Firstboot, you get the graphical login screen (shown in Figure 4-5).

The login window in the middle of the screen displays a welcome message with your PC's name — it's called the *host name*. The name is assigned when the network is configured. If the network isn't configured, `localhost.localdomain` is the host name. If your PC gets its network address (the

IP address) from a Dynamic Host Configuration Protocol (DHCP) server, that server provides a cryptic host name for your PC. The login window also has a text input field that prompts you for your username.

You can log in using any of the accounts you define during or after the installation. There is always the root username, which happens to be the superuser or the administrator account. Whether you install Fedora Core yourself or someone installs it for you, you need to know the root password. Without that, you cannot do many of the tasks necessary to learn how Linux works.

For example, to log in as user spiderman, type **spiderman** in the first text field and press Enter (move the mouse over the login box before you begin typing). Then type spiderman's password and press Enter. You then see the initial graphical user interface (GUI — pronounced *gooey* for short) appear. What you get depends on your choice of GUI — GNOME or KDE. If someone made the choice for you, don't worry — GNOME and KDE are both quite good and versatile.

**Figure 4-5:**
The Welcome screen is where you log in as a user.

# Exploring GUI Desktops

Fedora Core comes with two GUI desktops — GNOME and KDE. If you installed both, you can try them out one by one. Selecting one of these desktops just before you log in to the system is easy — and here's where I show you how.

GNOME is typically the default GUI in Fedora Core, so you can start with GNOME. Then log out and log back in, but select KDE as the GUI. That way, you can try out both desktops.

## GNOME

GNOME stands for *GNU Network Object Model Environment* (and GNU, as you probably know, stands for *GNU's Not UNIX*). GNOME is a graphical user interface (GUI) and a programming environment. From the user's perspective, GNOME is like Microsoft Windows. Behind the scenes, GNOME has many features that allow programmers to write graphical applications that can work together well. In this chapter, I point out only some key features of the GNOME GUI, leaving the details to you to explore on your own at your leisure.

If you're curious, you can always find out the latest information about GNOME by visiting the GNOME home page at `www.gnome.org`.

Typically, GNOME is the default desktop in Fedora Core. After you log in, you see the GNOME GUI desktop. Figure 4-6 shows the GNOME desktop for user-name `emily`.

When you log in as `root`, you can accidentally damage your system because you can do anything when you're `root`. Always log in as a normal user.

The exact appearance of the GNOME desktop depends on the current *session* (the set of applications running at that time). As you can see, the initial GNOME desktop, shown in Figure 4-6, is very similar to the Windows desktop. It has the GNOME panel, or simply the panel (similar to the Windows taskbar) along the bottom and icons for folders and applications appear directly on the desktop. You can place icons directly on the Windows desktop in a similar way.

**Figure 4-6:**
The initial
GNOME GUI
desktop
after
logging in.

You can move and resize the windows just as you do in Microsoft Windows. Also, as in the window frames in Microsoft Windows, the right-hand corner of the window's title bar includes three buttons. The leftmost button reduces the window to an icon, the middle button maximizes the window to fill up the entire screen, and the rightmost button closes the window.

### The GNOME panel

The GNOME panel is a key feature of the GNOME desktop. The panel is a separate GNOME application. As Figure 4-7 shows, it provides a display area for menus and small panel applets. Each panel applet is a small program designed to work inside the panel. For example, the clock applet on the panel's far right displays the current date and time.

**Figure 4-7:**
The GNOME
panel.

The panel includes several other applets besides the clock applet at the far right edge:

✦ **The GNOME Pager applet:** Provides a virtual desktop that's larger than the physical dimensions of your system's screen. In Figure 4-7, the pager displays four pages in a small display area. Each page represents an area equal to the size of the display screen. To go to a specific page, click that page in the pager window. The GNOME Pager applet displays buttons for each window being displayed in the current virtual page.

✦ **Launcher applets:** The buttons to the right of the Main Menu icon are launcher applets. Each of these applets displays a button with the icon of an application. Clicking a button starts (launches) that application. Try clicking each of these buttons to see what happens. The mouse and earth button launches the Mozilla Web browser, whereas clicking the pen and paper icon opens the OpenOffice.org Writer word processor. Move the mouse over an icon and a small help message appears with information about that icon.

✦ **The GNOME weather applet:** Displays the local weather. You don't see this applet until you start it. You can start it from the menu that appears when you right-click an empty area of the panel.

### The Main Menu button, or the "Red Hat Logo"

In Figure 4-8, the leftmost edge of the panel shows a button with the familiar Red Hat logo. That "red hat" is the Main Menu button — the most important part of the GNOME panel. Just like the Start button in Microsoft Windows, you can launch applications from the menu that pops up when you click the red hat. Figure 4-8 shows a typical view of the Main Menu on a Fedora Core PC.

Typically, the Main Menu and its submenus list items that start an application. Some menu items have an arrow; move the mouse pointer on an item with an arrow and another menu pops up. In Figure 4-8, the menu selection is Main Menu➪System Settings➪Server Settings➪Services. Notice that when you point to a menu selection, a balloon help pops up with information about that selection.

You can start applets such as the weather applet from the menu that appears when you right-click the GNOME panel. To start the weather applet, right-click the panel and select Add to Panel➪Accessories➪Weather Report (see Figure 4-9). In the Add to Panel menu, you find many more categories of applets you can try.

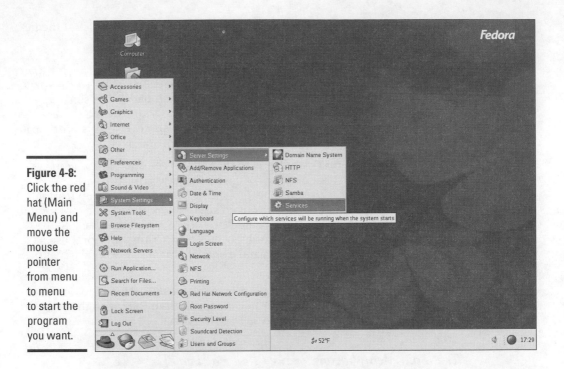

**Figure 4-8:**
Click the red
hat (Main
Menu) and
move the
mouse
pointer
from menu
to menu
to start the
program
you want.

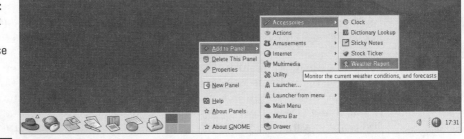

**Figure 4-9:**
Right click
the panel
and choose
Add to
Panel to
see the
available
applets.

Explore all the items on the Main Menu to see all the tasks you can perform
from this menu. In particular, move the mouse pointer over the Main Menu⇨
Preferences item to see your options (see Figure 4-10) for changing the
appearance of the desktop. For example, you can change the desktop's
background from this menu.

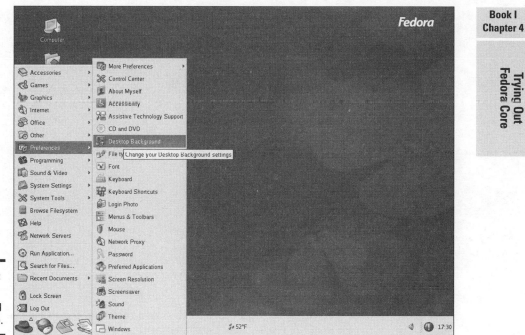

**Figure 4-10:**
Options for
customizing
the desktop.

## Customizing GNOME

By now, you may be itching to do a bit of decorating. No one likes to stick
to the plain blue GNOME desktop. After all, it's your desktop. You can set it
up any way you want it. You can configure most aspects of the GNOME desktop's *look and feel* — the appearance and behavior — by choosing various
options from the Main Menu⇨Preferences menu.

### Changing the background

To see how the desktop decorating business works, start by choosing
Main Menu⇨Preferences⇨Desktop Background and a dialog box appears,
as shown in Figure 4-11.

From this dialog box, you can select a background of solid color or color
gradient background or pick *wallpaper* (an image used as the background).
A *color gradient* background starts with one color and gradually changes to
another color. The gradient can be in the vertical direction (top to bottom)
or horizontal (left to right).

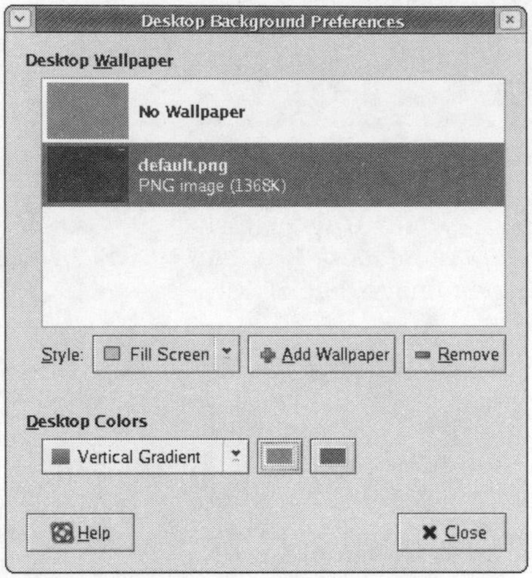

**Figure 4-11:**
Changing
the GNOME
desktop's
background.

To select a horizontal color gradient, try these steps:

*1.* **From the Desktop Colors drop-down menu (refer to Figure 4-11), choose the Horizontal Gradient option.**

*2.* **Click the left color button next to the drop-down menu.**

   A color selection dialog box comes up (shown in Figure 4-12) from which you can pick a color.

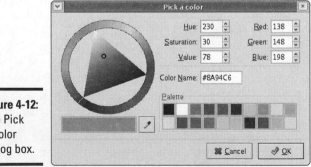

**Figure 4-12:**
The Pick
a Color
dialog box.

*3.* **Repeat the same process to select the right color.**

After you complete these steps, the image of the monitor in the dialog box shows you a preview of the new background color.

If you want to use an image as wallpaper, click the Add Wallpaper button in the middle of the dialog box. The Add Wallpapers dialog box appears from which you can select an image to use as wallpaper. By clicking the folder names in the Add Wallpapers dialog box, go to the /usr/share/ backgrounds/images directory. That directory has the default.png file with the default wallpaper you see on the GNOME desktop. To change the wallpaper, select an image you want. You can select any *Joint Photographic Experts Group* (JPEG) or *Portable Network Graphics* (PNG) format image file as wallpaper. After selecting an image, click OK.

The new wallpaper immediately appears on the desktop (as in Figure 4-13). When you're done making the changes, click the Close button (refer to Figure 4-11) to close the dialog box and apply the changes.

### Selecting a theme

Another more exciting customization is to select a new theme for the entire user interface. A *theme* refers to a collection of an appearance and a behavior (look and feel) for all the user interface components: buttons, check boxes, scrollbars, and so on.

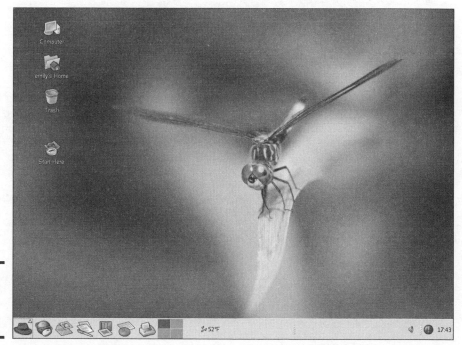

**Figure 4-13:**
The newly selected wallpaper.

To try out some new themes, choose Main Menu⇨Preferences⇨Theme. From the Theme Preferences dialog box (see Figure 4-14), you can try different themes and select one that you like. The default theme is called Bluecurve. To try another theme, select the theme from the list and the desktop's appearance changes to match the theme.

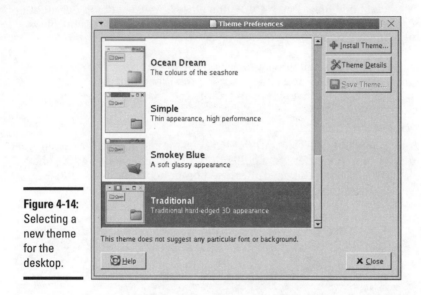

**Figure 4-14:** Selecting a new theme for the desktop.

Go ahead and try some of the available themes. When you select a theme, you can see the results in the desktop and the Theme Preference window itself. As you can see from Figure 4-14, even the panel icons change with the theme. If you like a theme, click the Close button to use that theme. Otherwise, select the Bluecurve theme before clicking Close.

### Logging out of GNOME

If you want to try the KDE GUI, you have to log out first. Choose Main Menu⇨ Log Out. Click Yes when a dialog box asks whether you really want to log out.

## KDE

KDE stands for the *K Desktop Environment*. The KDE project started in October 1996 with an intent to develop a common GUI for UNIX systems that use the X Window System. The first beta version of KDE version was released a year later in October 1997. KDE version 1.0 was released in July 1998; KDE 2.0 on October 23, 2000; KDE 3.0 was released on April 3, 2002; and the latest version — KDE 3.2.2 — was released on April 19, 2004.

From the user's perspective, KDE provides a graphical desktop environment that includes a window manager, the Konqueror Web browser and file manager, a panel for starting applications, a help system, configuration tools, and many applications, including the OpenOffice.org office suite, image viewer, PostScript viewer, and mail and news programs.

From the developer's perspective, KDE has class libraries and object models for easy application development in C++. KDE is a large development project with many collaborators.

You can always find out the latest information about KDE by visiting the KDE home page at `www.kde.org`.

To try the KDE GUI, you have to install KDE on your system. If you don't have KDE installed, you probably did not want the KDE GUI in the first place. If your system has only KDE installed, you get the KDE GUI as soon as you log in.

If you have both GNOME and KDE installed on your system, you can select the GUI just before you log in. From the login window, click Session and from the pop-up dialog box (see Figure 4-15), choose KDE for a KDE session and then log in as usual. A dialog box asks whether you want to make KDE the default for future sessions. Click Yes or No depending on what you prefer.

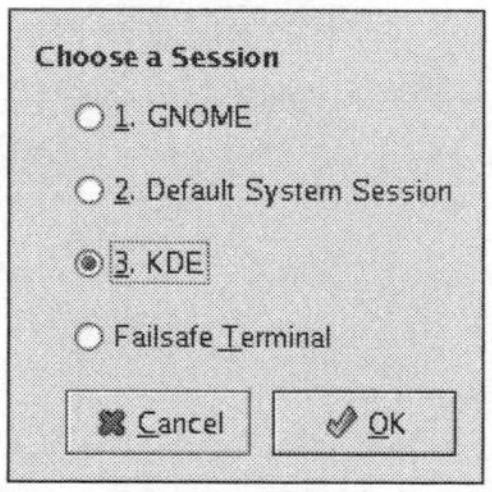

**Figure 4-15:**
Choosing
a KDE
session.

**Choose a Session**

○ 1. GNOME

○ 2. Default System Session

◉ 3. KDE

○ Failsafe Terminal

✖ Cancel    ✓ OK

When you log in after selecting a KDE session, you get the KDE desktop for this session. The next time you log in, the system continues to use KDE until you switch back to GNOME.

After you select KDE as the GUI for the session and then log in, you see an initial KDE desktop similar to the one shown in Figure 4-16. The initial KDE session includes a window showing a helpful tip. That's the only part that makes this desktop look different from the one you get in GNOME.

**Figure 4-16:**
The initial
KDE
desktop for
a typical
user.

You will find that KDE is very easy to use and is similar in many ways to the Windows GUI. You can start applications from a menu that's similar to the Start menu in Windows. As in Windows, you can place folders and applications directly on the KDE desktop.

### KDE panel

The KDE panel appearing along the bottom edge of the screen is meant for starting applications. The most important component of the panel is the Main Menu button on the left-hand side of the panel. That button is like the Start button in Windows. When you click the Main Menu button, a pop-up menu appears. From this menu, you can get to other menus by moving the mouse pointer over items that display a rightward-pointing arrow. For example, Figure 4-17 shows a typical menu selection for configuring various services.

You can start applications from this menu. That's why the KDE documentation calls the Main Menu button (of course, the KDE documentation refers to the button as the K button) the *Application Starter*.

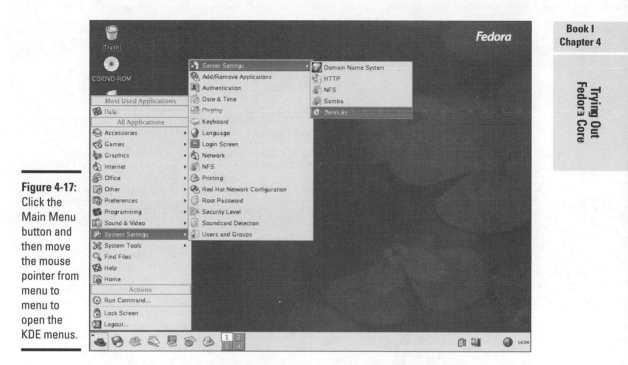

**Figure 4-17:**
Click the
Main Menu
button and
then move
the mouse
pointer from
menu to
menu to
open the
KDE menus.

Next to the Main Menu button, the panel includes many more buttons. If you
don't know what a button does, simply move the mouse pointer over the
button; a small pop-up window displays a brief message about that button.

Table 4-1 gives you an idea of what happens when you click each of the
major buttons on the KDE panel. When you have some time, try these
buttons one by one to get a feel for what you can do in KDE.

| Table 4-1 | KDE Panel Buttons |
|---|---|
| *When You Click* | *It Does This* |
| | Shows the application menu from which you can start any application. |
| | Starts the Mozilla Web browser. |
| | Starts the Ximian Evolution e-mail and calendaring software. |

*(continued)*

**Table 4-1** *(continued)*

| When You Click | It Does This |
| --- | --- |
|  | Runs OpenOffice.org Writer, a Microsoft Word-like word processor. |
|  | Runs the OpenOffice.org Impress slide presentation program that's similar to Microsoft PowerPoint. |
|  | Runs OpenOffice.org Calc, a Microsoft Excel-like spreadsheet program. |
|  | Runs Print Manager, a utility that enables you to set up and monitor print queues. |
|  | Switches to the desktop whose number you have clicked. |
|  | Runs Klipper, the KDE clipboard utility for cutting and pasting information. |
| 20:42 | Displays the current time. Click to view the current month's calendar. Right click for the menu to adjust the date and time. |

### Customizing the KDE desktop

KDE makes customizing the look and feel of the KDE desktop easy. Everything you have to decorate the desktop is in one place: the KDE Control Center. To start the KDE Control Center, choose Main Menu⇨Preferences⇨More Preferences⇨Control Center.

When the KDE Control Center starts, it displays the main window with a tree menu on the left side and some summary information about your system in the workspace to the right, as shown in Figure 4-18.

The KDE Control Center's tree menu shows the items that you can customize with this program. The tree menu is organized into categories such as Appearance & Themes, Internet & Network, Peripherals, Security & Privacy, and so on. Click the plus sign (+) to the left of an item to view the subcategories for that item. To change an item, go through the tree menu to locate the item and then click it. That item's configuration options then appear in a tabbed dialog box on the right side of the window.

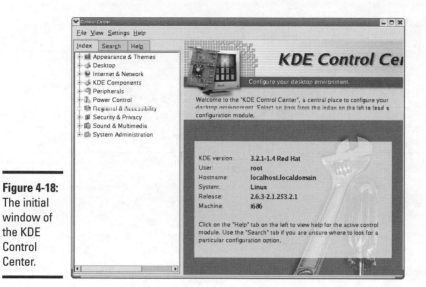

**Figure 4-18:**
The initial
window of
the KDE
Control
Center.

### Changing the background

To change the desktop's background, choose Appearance & Themes↔
Background. A tab appears (as in Figure 4-19) that shows the options for
customizing the desktop's background.

If you want to change the background of a specific desktop, click the Setting
for Desktop drop-down menu. From the list of desktops, you can select the
desktop whose background you want to change.

For a colored background, select the No Picture radio button. From the
Colors drop-down menu, you can select either a single color background
or a variety of color gradients (meaning the color changes gradually from
one color to another) or a picture (an image used as a background). You can
then pick the two colors by clicking the color buttons that appear under the
Colors drop-down menu. After making your selections, click Apply to try out
the background. (If you don't like what you get, click Reset to revert to the
previous background.)

If you want to use a picture as background, select the Picture radio button
and then click the folder icon next to that radio button. A dialog box comes
up, showing the JPEG images in the /usr/share/backgrounds/images
directory. You can select any one of these images and click OK. Then click
the Apply button in the KDE Control Center to apply this wallpaper to the
desktop. If you don't like the appearance, click Reset.

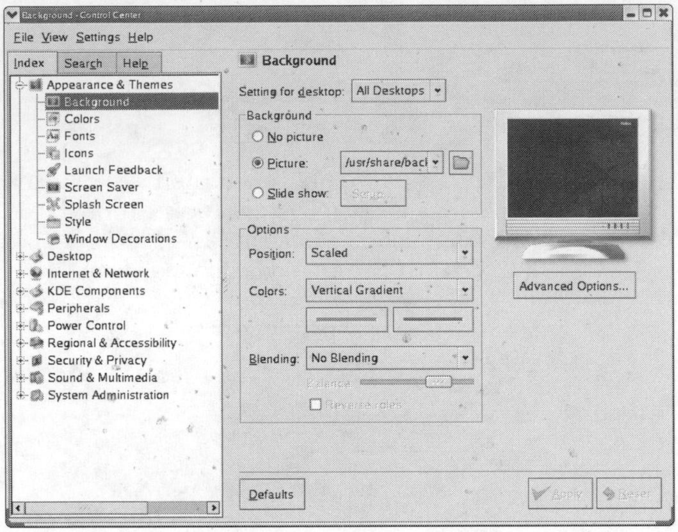

**Figure 4-19:** Changing the desktop background with KDE Control Center.

### Logging out of KDE

When you're done exploring KDE, log out. To log out of KDE, choose Main Menu⊅Logout. You can also right-click empty areas of the desktop and choose Logout from the pop-up menu that appears.

## Playing with the Shell

Fedora Core is basically UNIX, and UNIX just doesn't feel like UNIX unless you can type cryptic commands in a text terminal. Although GNOME and KDE have done a lot to bring us into the world of *w*indows, *i*cons, *m*ouse, and *p*ointer (affectionately known as *WIMP* :-), sometimes you're stuck with nothing but a plain text screen with a prompt that looks like this (when you log in as root):

```
[root@localhost etc]#
```

You see the text screen most often when something is *wrong* with the X Window System, which is essentially the machinery that runs the windows and menus you normally see. In those cases, you have to work with the shell and learn some of the cryptic Linux commands.

You can prepare for unexpected encounters with the shell by trying out some Linux commands in a terminal window while you're in the GNOME or KDE GUI. After you get the hang of it, you might even keep a terminal window open, just so you can use one of those cryptic commands simply because it's faster than trying to point and click (those two-letter commands do pack some punch!).

## Starting the Bash shell

Simply put, the *shell* is the Linux *command interpreter* — a program that reads what you type, interprets that text as a command, and does what the command is supposed to do.

Before you start playing with the shell, open a terminal window. In either GNOME or KDE, select Main Menu⇨System Tools⇨Terminal. What appears is a window with a prompt, like the one shown in Figure 4-20. That's a terminal window, and it works just like an old-fashioned terminal. A shell program is running and ready to accept any text that you type. You type text, press Enter, and something happens (depending on what you typed).

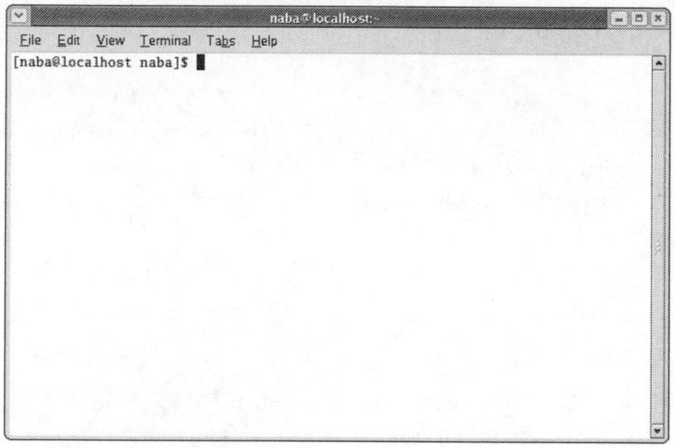

**Figure 4-20:**
You can type Linux commands at the shell prompt in a terminal window.

The prompt that you see depends on the shell that runs in that terminal window. The default Linux shell is called *Bash.*

Bash understands a whole host of standard Linux commands with which you can look at files, go from one directory to another, see what programs are running (and who else is logged in), and a whole lot more.

In addition to the Linux commands, Bash can run any program stored in an executable file. Bash can also execute *shell scripts,* text files that contain Linux commands.

## Understanding shell commands

Because a shell interprets what you type, knowing how the shell figures out the text that you enter is important. All shell commands have this general format:

```
command option1 option2 ... optionN
```

Such a single line of commands is commonly called as a *command line*. On a command line, you enter a command followed by one or more optional parameters (or *arguments*). Such *command-line options* (or command-line arguments) help you specify what you want the command to do.

One basic rule is that you have to use a space or a tab to separate the command from the options. You also must separate options with a space or a tab. If you want to use an option that contains embedded spaces, you have to put that option inside quotation marks. For example, to search for two words of text in the password file, I enter the following `grep` command (`grep` is one of those cryptic commands that searches for text in files):

```
grep "Font Server" /etc/passwd
```

When `grep` prints the line with those words, it looks like this:

```
xfs:x:43:43:X Font Server:/etc/X11/fs:/sbin/nologin
```

If you created a user account in your name, go ahead and type the `grep` command with your name as an argument, but remember to enclose the name in quotes.

## Trying a few Linux commands

While you have the terminal window open, try a few Linux commands just for fun. I guide you through some random examples to give you a feel for what you can do at the shell prompt.

To see how long the Fedora Core PC has been up since you last powered it up, type the following command. (*Note:* I show the typed command in bold, followed by the output from that command.)

```
uptime
```

```
 21:19:01 up 29 days, 55 min,  3 users,  load average: 0.04,
   0.32, 0.38
```

The part `up 29 days, 55 min` tells you that this particular PC has been up for nearly a month. Hmmm . . . can Windows do that?

To see what version of Linux kernel your system is running, use the `uname` command like this:

```
uname -srv
```

```
Linux 2.6.5-1.358 #1 Sat May 8 09:04:50 EDT 2004
```

In this case, the system is running Linux kernel version 2.6.5.

To read a file, use the `more` command. Here's an example:

```
more /etc/passwd
```

```
root:x:0:0:root:/root:/bin/bash
bin:x:1:1:bin:/bin:/sbin/nologin
daemon:x:2:2:daemon:/sbin:/sbin/nologin
adm:x:3:4:adm:/var/adm:/sbin/nologin
... lines deleted ...
```

To see a list of all the programs currently running on the system, use the `ps` command, like this:

```
ps ax
```

```
 PID TTY       STAT    TIME COMMAND
   1 ?         S       0:05 init [5]
   2 ?         SWN     0:00 [ksoftirqd/0]
   3 ?         SW<     0:00 [events/0]
   4 ?         SW<     0:00 [kblockd/0]
   5 ?         SW<     0:00 [pdflush]
   6 ?         SW<     0:00 [pdflush]
   8 ?         SW<     0:00 [aio/0]
   7 ?         SW      0:00 [kswapd0]
   9 ?         SW      0:00 [kseriod]
  13 ?         SW      0:00 [kjournald]
  98 ?         SW      0:00 [khubd]
 222 ?         SW      0:00 [usb-storage]
 223 ?         SW      0:00 [scsi_eh_0]
 759 ?         SW      0:00 [kjournald]
2177 ?         S       0:00 /sbin/dhclient -1 -q -lf
   /var/lib/dhcp/dhclient-eth0.leases -pf /var/run/dhclient-
   eth0.pid -cf /etc/dhclient-eth0.conf eth0
2226 ?         S       0:00 syslogd -m 0
2230 ?         S       0:00 klogd -x
2258 ?         S       0:00 portmap
2278 ?         S       0:00 rpc.statd
... lines deleted ...
```

Amazing how many programs that can run on a system even when only you are logged in as a user, isn't it?

As you can guess, you can do everything from a shell prompt, but it does take some getting used to.

# Shutting Down

When you're ready to shut down Fedora Core, you must do so in an orderly manner. Even if you're the sole user of a Fedora Core PC, several other programs are usually running in the background. Also, operating systems such as Linux try to optimize the way that they write data to the disk. Because disk access is relatively slow (compared with the time needed to access memory locations), data generally is held in memory and written to the disk in large chunks. Therefore, if you simply turn off the power, you run the risk that some files aren't updated properly.

Any user (you don't even have to be logged in) can shut down the system from the desktop or from the graphical login screen. Choose Main Menu⇨Log Out. A Logout dialog box appears and it provides the options for rebooting or halting the system or simply logging out. To shut down the system, simply select Shutdown, and click OK. The system then shuts down in an orderly manner.

If you're at the graphical login screen, click the Shutdown label in the bottom part of the screen. Then another dialog box asks you to confirm that you really want to halt the system. Click the Yes button. The system then shuts down in an orderly manner.

As the system shuts down, you see messages about processes being shut down. You may be surprised at how many processes there are, even when no one is explicitly running any programs on the system. If your system does not automatically power off on shutdown, you can manually turn off the power.

Note that shutting down or rebooting the system does *not* require `root` access. Make sure that physical access to the console is protected adequately.

# Chapter 5: Cool Fedora Core Install Projects

## In This Chapter

✔ Joining the BitTorrent

✔ Burning Fedora Core CDs

✔ Preparing a Fedora Core DVD

✔ Doing an FTP install over the network

**H**ave you ever wished you could burn your own Fedora Core CDs? What about a Fedora Core DVD? Do you wonder how the hip crowd downloads Fedora Core? Well, wonder no more! Here are a few cool projects to help you master the Fedora Core download and install process.

The first project shows you how to join BitTorrent and help the community get their Fedora Core while you get yours as well. In the second project, you find out how to burn CDs from the downloaded ISO images. If you have a DVD burner as well, the third project gives you the recipe for burning a Fedora Core DVD. Finally, the fourth project is all about installing Fedora Core over the network, which can be handy if you are installing on a CD-less laptop.

## Joining the BitTorrent

BitTorrent is a protocol for distributing files. You don't really need to understand the protocol to use BitTorrent. All you need to know is that as you download a file, your machine also uploads the file to others who want the same file. So you are not just taking something, you are also giving something back — you are helping others get that file without overloading the server from which you started getting the file. That communal spirit of sharing in an equitable manner is what makes BitTorrent an appealing way to distribute software such as Fedora Core. In fact, once you try it, you'll find that downloading Fedora Core is easier by joining the BitTorrent than getting it through FTP from a central server. You do have to do a few things before you can start using BitTorrent. It's a neat little project to download the CD- or DVD-image of Fedora Core and burn the CD (or DVD). The first project is to join the BitTorrent and download the necessary files.

## Things you need

Here's what you need to join the BitTorrent:

✦ A PC running Red Hat Linux or Fedora Core — you use this system to run the BitTorrent client and download Fedora Core. If you are running Microsoft Windows on your PC, you can still use BitTorrent; just check out the information at bitconjurer.org/BitTorrent/download.html.

✦ Make sure that Python version 2 is already installed on your Linux system. If not, insert the companion DVD into the DVD drive, mount it, and type **rpm -ivh /mnt/cdrom/Fedora/RPMS/python-2*.rpm** to install Python 2.

✦ A connection to the Internet, the higher the bandwidth the better.

## Steps to follow

You have three high-level steps to complete:

*1.* **Download and install the BitTorrent client software on your system.**

*2.* **Adjust your system's firewall settings to open up TCP ports 6881 through 6999 that are used by BitTorrent to send files to others.**

*3.* **Run the BitTorrent client to start the file transfers.**

I describe these three high-level steps in detail in the following sections.

### Download and install BitTorrent software

Make sure your system's Internet connection is up. Then follow these steps:

*1.* **Run the Mozilla Web browser and visit** torrent.dulug.duke.edu/ btrpms/ **and click one of the RPM files to download the BitTorrent software for your version of Red Hat Linux or Fedora Core.**

For Fedora Core, download the version with fc1 (that means Fedora Core 1) or rh90 (that means Red Hat 9.0) in the name — these versions run on Fedora Core. Save the downloaded RPM file in a directory on your system and make note of where you saved it.

*2.* **Open a terminal window and change the directory to where you saved the BitTorrent RPM file and then install the BitTorrent software.**

Type the following command to install BitTorrent:

```
rpm -ivh bittorrent*.rpm
```

If you don't find the correct BitTorrent RPM file at `torrent.dulug.duke.edu/btrpms/`, you can always download the files from the official BitTorrent home page at `bitconjurer.org/BitTorrent/`. For example, to download and install BitTorrent 3.3, open a terminal window and type the following commands:

```
wget http://bitconjurer.org/BitTorrent/BitTorrent 3.3.tar.gz
tar -xzf BitTorrent-3.3.tar.gz
```

In this case, the BitTorrent software is installed in the BitTorrent-3.3 subdirectory of the current directory and you have to run the BitTorrent client from that subdirectory.

### Open incoming TCP ports used by BitTorrent

Typically, your system runs a firewall that restricts access to many of the ports. BitTorrent, however, requires that you open up the TCP ports numbered 6881 through 6999 so that other BitTorrent clients can contact your system and request uploads. To open TCP ports 6881 through 6999, type the following command in a terminal window:

```
iptables -I RH-Firewall-1-INPUT --protocol tcp --dport
    6881:6899 -i eth0 -j ACCEPT
```

This command assumes that your system connects to the Internet through its Ethernet interface and that interface is `eth0` (the first Ethernet card). Change `eth0` to the name of the external network interface of your system. For example, if it's the second Ethernet card, the interface is `eth1`. For a dial-up PPP connection, the interface is `ppp0`.

### Start BitTorrent transfers

To download using BitTorrent, you have to run the BitTorrent client. You use a URL to identify the *torrent,* which refers to the collection of files that you want to download. The URL also identifies the tracker — the server that hooks up your system's BitTorrent client with others that can provide parts of the files you want. In turn, the tracker also lets other clients begin requesting the torrent from your system.

Follow these steps to download one of the Fedora Core torrents:

*1.* **Visit the Fedora Core tracker at** `torrent.dulug.duke.edu.`

You find a list of different torrent files listed at this site. Locate the file that you want. For example, if you are planning to burn Fedora Core CDs, you want the torrent for the Fedora Core binary ISO images.

2. **Open a terminal window and change to the directory where you want to store the files that you plan to download.**

3. **Run the BitTorrent client.**

   Type the following command where *tfile* is the name of the torrent file that you want:

   ```
   btdownloadcurses.py --url http://torrent.dulug.duke.
      edu/tfile
   ```

   For example, to download the CD ISO images for Fedora Core 1 — provided in a torrent named `yarrow-binary-i386-iso.torrent` — you type:

   ```
   btdownloadcurses.py --url http://torrent.dulug.duke.
      edu/yarrow-binary-i386-iso.torrent
   ```

   The text screen (shown in Figure 5-1) shows you the status of the BitTorrent download as well as any uploads going on at the same time.

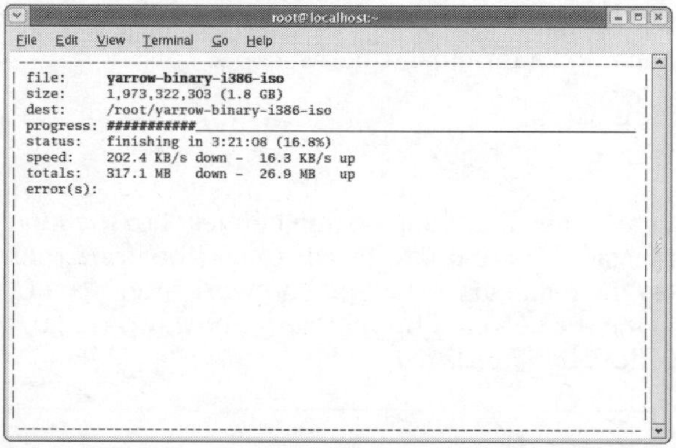

```
 root@localhost:~                                     _ ▢ □ ✕
File   Edit   View   Terminal   Go   Help
 ────────────────────────────────────────────────────────
| file:     yarrow-binary-i386-iso                        |
| size:     1,973,322,303 (1.8 GB)                        |
| dest:     /root/yarrow-binary-i386-iso                  |
| progress: ###########                                   |
| status:   finishing in 3:21:08 (16.8%)                  |
| speed:    202.4 KB/s down -  16.3 KB/s up               |
| totals:   317.1 MB   down -  26.9 MB   up               |
| error(s):                                               |
|                                                         |
|                                                         |
```

**Figure 5-1:** Downloading Fedora Core distribution using BitTorrent.

If you install the BitTorrent software from a `tar.gz` file that you downloaded from `bitconjurer.org/BitTorrent/`, you have to change the directory to where the BitTorrent software is installed and then run the BitTorrent client with a command-line of the following form:

```
./btdownloadcurses.py  --url torrentname
```

where *torrentname* is the URL of the torrent you want to access.

After BitTorrent finishes the download, leave the BitTorrent client running for as long as possible. This time enables your system to provide the file to others who are also joining BitTorrent. After all, this sharing is what makes BitTorrent such an efficient way to distribute files.

# Burning Fedora Core CDs

Linux distributions, including Fedora Core, are available for download from various Internet sites in the form of ISO images — an *ISO image* is an exact copy of an entire CD-ROM in a single, huge file (typically around 650MB). These files usually have the .iso extension. The *ISO* part of the name comes from the fact that the CD-ROM uses the ISO 9660 file system and *image* means the file is an exact replica of every bit of data on the CD-ROM.

In this project, I show you how to burn Fedora Core CDs from the ISO images by using the GnomeToaster application.

## Things you need

Here's what you need to burn the Fedora Core CDs:

✦ A PC running Red Hat Linux or Fedora Core with the X-CD-Roast application installed (consult Book II, Chapter 4 for more information on how to install X-CD-Roast).

✦ An internal or external CD recorder.

✦ Blank CD-R media — you need four blanks for the four-CD Fedora Core.

✦ The downloaded Fedora Core ISO files. If you have not done so already, complete the BitTorrent project and download the four-CD Fedora Core ISO files.

## Steps to follow

Follow these steps to use X-CD-Roast to burn the Fedora Core CDs:

*1.* **Copy the Fedora Core ISO files to the directory specified in X-CD-Roast as the temporary image storage directory.**

For example, if you use /tmp as the image storage directory, copy the ISO files to the /tmp directory by using the cp or mv command.

*2.* **Choose Main Menu⇨System Tools⇨CD Writer from the GNOME or KDE desktop.**

If you aren't logged in as root, you're prompted for the root password. Then the X-CD-Roast main window appears.

*3.* **Click Create CD.**

X-CD-Roast displays the Create CD window.

*4.* **Click Write Tracks.**

X-CD-Roast displays two side-by-side panes: The right pane shows the names of the ISO image files, and the left pane shows what you want to burn on the CD. Initially, the left pane is empty.

5. **Select an ISO file on the right pane and click Add.**

   X-CD-Roast shows the selected ISO file in the left pane as an item to be written to a CD-R.

6. **Click the Accept Track Layout button below the panes.**

   X-CD-Roast changes the button to Write Tracks (and displays a few other buttons for performing other tasks).

7. **Insert a blank CD-R into the CD burner and click Write Tracks.**

   X-CD-Roast then begins to burn the CD and shows the progress in a window. When the CD is done, X-CD-Roast ejects the CD.

8. **Repeat Steps 3 through 6 for the remaining Fedora Core ISO images.**

## Preparing a Fedora Core DVD

Typically, the binary Fedora Core distribution takes four CDs and the source RPM files take another four CDs (there is also a rescue CD that lets you boot the system and fix problems). On the other hand, a DVD with its 4.7GB capacity can easily hold all the binary and source files for the complete Fedora Core distribution. (By the way, that's why my publisher bundles a Fedora Core DVD with this book.)

A word of caution about DVD capacity — when marketing people talk about the 4.7GB capacity of a DVD, they mean 4,700,000,000 bytes. However, for technology purists, that number translates to about 4,482MB or only 4.377GB because 1,024 bytes are in each KB and 1,024 x 1,024 = 1,048,576 bytes in a MB, and so on. The bottom line is that you can only fit about 4,482MB of data onto a DVD.

If you want to burn your own Fedora Core DVD, doing so is easy enough, provided you have a DVD recorder. This project guides you through the steps in burning a Fedora Core DVD.

### Things you need

Here's what you need to burn the Fedora Core DVD:

✦ A PC running Red Hat Linux or Fedora Core. Note that you need Linux kernel version 2.4 or higher so that you can create a DVD ISO file that's larger than 2GB.

✦ At least 10GB of available space on the hard drive (you need room for all the CD ISO files and the DVD ISO file you are about to create).

✦ An internal or external DVD recorder.

+ Blank DVD recordable media in a format compatible with your DVD recorder — the media can be one of DVD-R, DVD-RW, DVD+R, or DVD+RW.

+ The downloaded Fedora Core CD ISO files or, even better, the DVD ISO file. If you have not done so already, complete the BitTorrent project and download the four-CD Fedora Core ISO files or, if available, download the larger DVD ISO file.

## Steps to follow

The steps you follow to burn a Fedora Core DVD depend on whether you downloaded the Fedora Core CD ISO files or the DVD ISO file. If you download the CD ISO files, you have to first prepare a DVD ISO file from those CD images. After that, you can burn the DVD ISO file onto a DVD. I explain both steps.

If you have already downloaded the DVD ISO file, you can go right to burning the DVD.

### Create DVD ISO file from CD ISO files

Follow these steps to create a single DVD ISO file out of the four CD ISO files:

*1.* **Move the four ISO files to the** /tmp **directory using commands of the following form:**

```
mv /full/path/ISOfilename.iso /tmp
```

Replace the part /full/path/ISOfilename.iso with the full pathname of the ISO file. Repeat the copy command for all four CD ISO files.

*2.* **Create four directories that you can use as mount points for the four CD ISO images.**

Assuming that you want these four directories in the /tmp directory, log in as root and type the following commands in a terminal window:

```
cd /tmp
mkdir ISO1
mkdir ISO2
mkdir ISO3
mkdir ISO4
```

*3.* **Mount the four ISO files on the four mount points.**

Assuming that the filenames for the four CD ISO image files are ISOfilename1.iso, ISOfilename2.iso, ISOfilename3.iso, and ISOfilename4.iso, type the following commands to mount them:

```
mount -o ro,loop ISOfilename1.iso ISO1
mount -o ro,loop ISOfilename2.iso ISO2
mount -o ro,loop ISOfilename3.iso ISO3
mount -o ro,loop ISOfilename4.iso ISO4
```

Remember to replace the filenames with the actual filenames.

4. **Copy the** `isolinux` **directory and the** `.discinfo` **file from the first CD ISO file to the** `/tmp` **directory (which happens to be the current directory).**

   Type the following command to copy the files:

   ```
   cp -af ISO1/isolinux ISO1/.discinfo .
   ```

   Don't miss that single period at the end of the command!

5. **Open the** `.discinfo` **file in a text editor and edit the fourth line as follows:**

   ```
   1,2,3,4
   ```

   That line lists the numbers of CD ISO images that are being included on the DVD ISO image. Save the `.discinfo` file after editing that line.

6. **Create the DVD ISO file out of the four CD ISO files.**

   Type the following long `mkisofs` command to create a new ISO file named `fedora-core-dvd.iso`:

   ```
   mkisofs -o fedora-core-dvd.iso \
           -V 'Fedora Core DVD' \
           -b isolinux/isolinux.bin -c isolinux/boot.cat \
           -no-emul-boot -boot-load-size 4 -boot-info-
   table \
           -R -m TRANS.TBL \
           -x ISO1/.discinfo \
           -x ISO1/isolinux \
           -graft-points ISO1 \
           .discinfo=.discinfo isolinux/=isolinux \
           Fedora/=ISO2/Fedora \
           Fedora/=ISO3/Fedora \
           Fedora/=ISO4/Fedora
   ```

Now you can burn the DVD ISO file onto DVD media.

### Burn DVD ISO file onto DVD media

Assuming that the DVD ISO file is named `fedora-core-dvd.iso`, follow these steps to burn the DVD ISO file onto the DVD:

1. **Use the** `cd` **command to change the current directory to where the DVD ISO file is located.**

2. **Place a blank DVD media into the DVD recorder.**

3. **Type the following** `growisofs` **command to start burning the DVD:**

   ```
   growisofs -Z /dev/scd0=fedora-core-dvd.iso
   ```

Remember to change the DVD recorder device name from /dev/scd0 to whatever is appropriate for your PC's DVD recorder. Use the /dev/scd0 device name for an external DVD recorder. For internal DVD recorders, use /dev/cdrom as the device name.

# Doing an FTP Install

If you want to install Fedora Core on a laptop or desktop PC that has a CD drive, you can do an FTP installation from another system that has the Fedora Core distribution files. Even if you have a CD drive, FTP installation makes sense if you are installing Fedora Core on PCs in a network and you don't want to go around feeding CDs on each PC. This project walks you through an FTP install.

## Things you need

Here's what you need to burn the Fedora Core CDs:

✦ A Fedora boot CD to boot the PC. The current Fedora Core installation kernel is too big to fit on a floppy disk, so you can only boot from a CD.

✦ A local area network with another Fedora Core or Red Hat Linux system with the Fedora Core CD ISO files.

✦ A network-connected PC on which you want to install Fedora Core via FTP.

## Steps to follow

Follow these steps to do an FTP install from the Fedora Core ISO files over the network:

*1.* **On the Linux system where you have the Fedora Core ISO files, mount the four ISO files on four mount points.**

I assume that the four ISO files are in /usr/local directory and the files are named disc1.iso, disc2.iso, disc3.iso, and disc4.iso. Log in as root and type the following commands in a terminal window:

```
mkdir /var/ftp/pub/fedora
cd /var/ftp/pub/fedora
mkdir disc1
mkdir disc2
mkdir disc3
mkdir disc4
mount -o loop,ro /usr/local/disc1.iso disc1
mount -o loop,ro /usr/local/disc2.iso disc2
mount -o loop,ro /usr/local/disc3.iso disc3
mount -o loop,ro /usr/local/disc4.iso disc4
```

Remember to replace the pathname of the Fedora Core ISO files with the correct directory and filenames.

2. **Make sure the FTP server is running on the Linux system from where you mounted the Fedora Core ISO files.**

Type the following command in the terminal window:

```
service vsftpd restart
```

3. **Create a Fedora Core boot CD.**

Use a CD burner to burn the ISO image named boot.iso — located in the /usr/local/disc1.iso/images directory. See the "Burning Fedora Core CDs" section for instructions on how to burn a CD from an ISO image.

4. **Go to the PC on which you want to do the FTP install, insert the boot CD, and restart the PC.**

The PC reboots and after a few moments, a text screen displays a welcome message and a boot: prompt.

5. **Type** linux askmethod **and press Enter.**

A text menu displays various installation methods.

6. **Select FTP as the installation method and press Enter.**

You are prompted to configure TCP/IP network for the PC.

7. **Select Dynamic IP Configuration and select OK.**

If your network does not support dynamic IP addresses, enter a valid IP address for the PC. The FTP setup screen appears after you configure TCP/IP the network.

8. **Enter the IP address or the name of the FTP server where the Fedora Core ISO files are mounted.**

For an Internet-connected PC, you can even specify any server on the Internet that has the Fedora Core distribution available. For a list of such servers, consult fedora.redhat.com/download/mirrors.html.

9. **Specify the directory where the Fedora Core ISO files are located and press OK.**

For the example in Step 1, enter /pub/fedora as the directory. The normal graphical installation begins after this step.

10. **Respond to the prompts from the graphical installation steps and proceed with the installation as usual.**

# Book II

# Workstations and Applications

The 5th Wave          By Rich Tennant

"You the guy having trouble staying connected to the network?"

# Contents at a Glance

**Chapter 1: Exploring the GUI Desktops** ...............................................................111

**Chapter 2: Learning the Shell** ..........................................................................135

**Chapter 3: Navigating the Linux File System** ...................................................153

**Chapter 4: Exploring Fedora Core Applications** ..............................................169

**Chapter 5: Using Text Editors** .........................................................................199

# Chapter 1: Exploring the GUI Desktops

## In This Chapter

✔ Learning common features of the GUIs

✔ Using the Nautilus shell in GNOME

✔ Configuring GNOME

✔ Using Konqueror in KDE

✔ Configuring KDE

---

**F**edora Core comes with two graphical user interfaces (GUIs) — GNOME and KDE. GNOME and KDE are similar to Microsoft Windows, but they are unique in one respect. Unlike Microsoft Windows, you can pick your GUI in Fedora Core. If you don't like GNOME, just log out and log back in with KDE, the other GUI. Try doing that with Microsoft Windows!

GNOME and KDE were developed independent of Linux. In fact, GNOME and KDE run on other UNIX operating systems besides Linux. You also have the option to install other GUIs on Fedora Core. For example, you can download and install Ximian Desktop 2 (XD2) — a GUI desktop from Ximian, available from www.ximian.com/products/desktop/download.html.

This chapter explores the major features of GNOME and KDE. You can best learn these GUIs by simply starting to use them. By the way, you can try both GNOME and KDE, provided you installed both when you installed Fedora Core. Otherwise, GNOME is the default GUI in Fedora Core.

## Learning the Common Features of the GUIs

From your perspective as a user, both GNOME and KDE probably seem similar because many features work similarly. Becoming familiar with these common features is helpful so you can rely on them no matter which GUI you choose to use for your daily work.

For starters, the initial desktop for both GNOME and KDE looks like any other popular GUI, such as Microsoft Windows or the Apple desktop on a Mac. For example, Figure 1-1 shows the initial GNOME desktop.

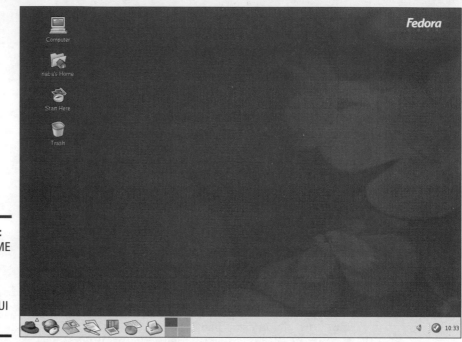

**Figure 1-1:**
The GNOME desktop looks like other popular GUI desktops.

The desktop initially shows icons for your computer, your home folder, and the trash can for deleted files. The other major feature of both GNOME and KDE desktops is the bar along the bottom, which is called the *panel*. The panel is similar to the Windows taskbar. It has buttons on the left (shortcuts to various programs) and a sound volume control, an icon for available updates, and a time display to the right. The middle part of the panel shows buttons for any applications you've started (or were automatically started).

Move the mouse over any icon on the panel and a small pop-up window displays the name of that icon. The pop-up window also gives a hint about what you can do with that icon.

## Desktop pop-up menus

Both GNOME and KDE desktops display a pop-up menu when you right-click a clear area on the desktop. The exact contents of that menu depends on the desktop, but it typically offers menu options that enable you to perform the following types of tasks:

✦ Open a terminal window where you can type Linux commands.

✦ Create a new folder.

✦ Configure the desktop background.

✦ Rearrange the icons on the desktop.

For example, Figures 1-2 and 1-3 respectively show the desktop pop-up menus in GNOME and KDE. Desktop menu options with a right-pointing arrow have other menus that appear when you put the mouse pointer over the arrow.

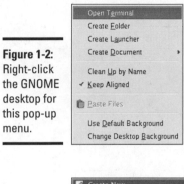

**Figure 1-2:**
Right-click
the GNOME
desktop for
this pop-up
menu.

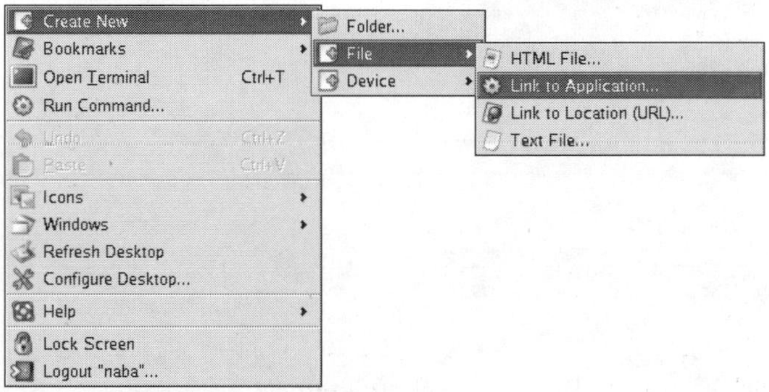

**Figure 1-3:**
Right-click
the KDE
desktop for
this pop-up
menu.

## Icon pop-up menus

Right-clicking any desktop icon in GNOME or KDE causes another menu to appear (see Figures 1-4 and 1-5). Many items on this pop-up menu are the same no matter what icon you click — but right-clicking certain icons (for example, the Trash icon) produces a somewhat different menu. You can perform the following typical tasks from icon pop-up menus:

✦ Open a folder in a file manager.

✦ Open a file with an application that you choose.

✦ Rename the icon.

✦ Move the icon to the trash.

✦ View the properties of that icon.

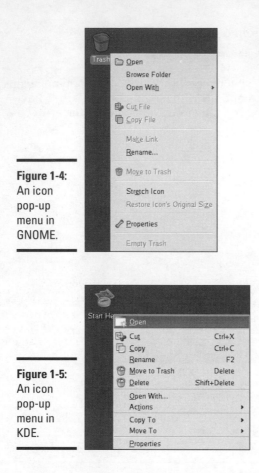

**Figure 1-4:**
An icon
pop-up
menu in
GNOME.

**Figure 1-5:**
An icon
pop-up
menu in
KDE.

For the Trash icon, the icon pop-up menu also provides an option to permanently delete the items in the trash (you get a chance to say yes or no).

I bet you see a pattern here. It's the right-click. No matter where you are in GNOME or KDE, *always right-click before you pick.* You're bound to find something useful when you right-click!

## The panel

The panel is the long bar that stretches across the bottom of the desktop. Figures 1-6 and 1-7 show typical views of the GNOME and KDE panels, respectively.

The panel is a parking place for icons. Some icons start programs when you click them. Some show status (such as what programs are currently running), as well as information such as the date and time.

Figure 1-6:
A typical
view of
the GNOME
panel.

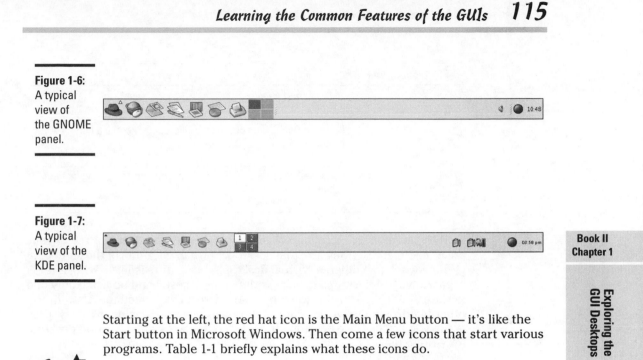

Figure 1-7:
A typical
view of the
KDE panel.

Starting at the left, the red hat icon is the Main Menu button — it's like the Start button in Microsoft Windows. Then come a few icons that start various programs. Table 1-1 briefly explains what these icons do.

By the way, if you move the mouse pointer on top of an icon, a small help balloon pops up and gives you a helpful hint about the icon.

| Table 1-1 | Some Common Icons on the Panel |
|---|---|
| *When You Click This Icon* | *It Does the Following* |
|   | Brings up the Main Menu from which you can select applications to run. |
|   | Runs the Mozilla Web browser. |
|   | Starts the Ximian Evolution e-mail and calendar software. |
|   | Runs OpenOffice.org Writer, a Microsoft Word-like word processor. |
|   | Runs the OpenOffice.org Impress slide-presentation program (which is similar to Microsoft PowerPoint). |

*(continued)*

**Table 1-1** *(continued)*

| When You Click This Icon | It Does the Following |
|---|---|
| | Runs the OpenOffice.org Calc, a Microsoft Excel-like spreadsheet program. |
| | Runs the Print Manager, from which you can set up and monitor printers. |

To the right of these icons, a workspace-switcher icon shows four rectangular areas, each representing a virtual desktop. You can click one of these rectangles to switch to a different virtual desktop. This feature is like having four separate virtual desktops to work with. To be honest, I end up using only one desktop, but I like knowing the others are there if I ever need them. On the other hand, if you're writing code and preparing a user's guide for a new program, you can use one desktop for all the coding work and a second desktop for writing the user's guide. You can, of course, switch from one desktop to the other with a single mouse click.

The area to the right of the pager icon displays buttons for the programs you have started so far. This area is blank if you have not yet started any programs.

Other icons may be next to the pager, but the date and time always appear at the far right edge of the panel.

Now for a little bit of technical detail about these icons on the panel. The panel itself is a separate application; each icon is a button or a program called an *applet*. The applets are little applications (also called *plugins*). These panel applets can do things such as launching other programs or displaying the date and time. To run an applet, right-click an empty area of the panel and select the appropriate menu item to add an applet to the panel. After adding the applet, you can right-click the applet's icon to configure it or perform some task that the applet supports.

If you right-click any icon — or right-click anywhere on the panel — you get a pop-up menu where you can do something relevant to that icon (such as move it or remove it entirely). You can also set some preferences and add more buttons and applets to the panel.

## The Main Menu

The leftmost icon on the panel is the *Main Menu* button. That's where you find everything you want to run in Fedora Core. In this section, I provide an overview of the Main Menu and point out some interesting items. You can then do further exploration yourself.

Click the Main Menu button to bring up the first level menu. Then mouse over any menu item with an arrow to bring the next level menu and so on. You can go through a menu hierarchy and make selections from the final menu.

A word about the way I refer to a menu selection: I use the notation Main Menu⇨Internet⇨Evolution Email to indicate the menu selection sequence that you use to select the mail reader. Similarly, I say choose Main Menu⇨Internet⇨Mozilla Web Browser to start the Mozilla Web browser (see Figure 1-8). You get the idea.

In GNOME, the top-level main menu has the following menu categories:

✦ **Accessories:** This menu has a host of utility programs, such as a scientific calculator, character selector, floppy formatter, dictionary, Palm Pilot or Handspring sync, and so on.

✦ **Games:** This menu brings up a menu of what else, games (and a whole lot of them at that).

✦ **Graphics:** This menu has programs such as the GIMP (an Adobe Photoshop-like program), a digital camera interface, a scanner interface, a screen capture program, and an Adobe Acrobat viewer.

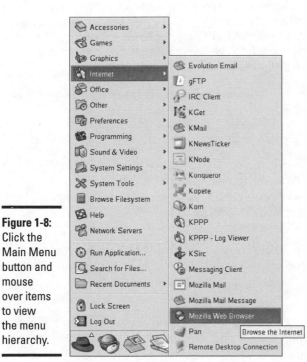

**Figure 1-8:**
Click the
Main Menu
button and
mouse
over items
to view
the menu
hierarchy.

✦ **Internet:** This menu (refer to Figure 1-8) is for Internet applications, such as the Web browser, e-mail reader, and Instant Messenger.

✦ **Office:** This menu brings up a menu of applications from the OpenOffice.org office suite (includes Writer word processor, Calc spreadsheet, Impress slide presentation program, Draw drawing program, and much more).

✦ **Preferences:** This menu brings up another menu from which you can configure many aspects of the system including the appearance and the behavior of the desktop.

✦ **Programming:** This menu lets you run software development tools, such as the emacs editor.

✦ **Sound & Video:** This menu has multimedia applications such as CD player, sound mixer, sound recorder, and volume control.

✦ **System Settings:** This menu lists many tools for setting up your Fedora Core system. It includes tools for managing user accounts, configuring printers, and changing the root password. The Server Settings submenu provides access to tools for configuring the Web server, Domain Name System (DNS) server, and Network File System (NFS) server. You can also turn various services on or off from this menu.

✦ **System Tools:** This menu has a number of tools for performing tasks such as configuring the Internet connection, viewing the system logs, and opening a terminal window where you can type Linux commands. This menu also enables you to run many more tools, including a CD Writer (provided you install the X-CD-Roast CD writer).

The Main Menu also has the following menu items for some commonly performed tasks:

✦ Main Menu⇨Browse Filesystem opens your home directory in the Nautilus file manager.

✦ Main Menu⇨Help brings up the GNOME help browser.

✦ Main Menu⇨Network Servers displays your network servers in the Nautilus file manager. You can access any Windows servers on your network from this Nautilus window.

✦ Main Menu⇨Run Application displays a dialog box where you can enter the name of a program to run and then click Run to start that program.

✦ Main Menu⇨Search for Files runs a search tool from which you can search for files.

✦ Main Menu⇨Recent Documents shows a submenu with a list of documents that you have recently opened. You can then select a document to open it again.

✦ Main Menu➪Lock Screen starts the screen saver and locks the screen. When you want to return to the desktop, the system prompts you for your password.

✦ Main Menu➪Logout logs you out (you get a chance to confirm whether you really want to log out or not).

The Main Menu in KDE has a few different categories, but it has enough similar items that you can easily find what you need.

Okay. That's all I'm telling you about the Main Menu. You'll use the Main Menu a lot as you use GNOME or KDE. Even if it seems too much initially, it'll all become very familiar as you spend more time with Fedora Core.

**Book II
Chapter 1**

Exploring the
GUI Desktops

# Exploring GNOME

GNOME (pronounced *Guh-NOME*) is the default GUI for Fedora Core. When you use GNOME, all that you see and experience is the GUI desktop. You find, however, much more to GNOME than the GUI desktop. For example, here are some key facts about GNOME:

✦ GNOME provides a development environment for GUI applications. It comes with a programming toolkit that programmers can use to create GUI applications.

✦ GNOME supports an object model — it defines the structure of software components so that they can communicate with one another.

✦ The GNOME GUI is modular, so it works with any window manager designed for the X Window System. For example, Fedora Core comes with several window managers such as Metacity, MWM, and TWM. Each window manager has its own look and feel. GNOME works with any of these window managers.

✦ All GNOME documentation is written using the *Standard Generalized Markup Language* (SGML). You can view the manual for a GNOME application on any Web browser.

✦ GNOME comes with a set of office applications called OpenOffice.org. It includes the Writer word processor, the Calc spreadsheet, the Impress presentation program, and the Draw drawing program. See Book III for more about OpenOffice.org.

Okay, I think you get the idea. GNOME is a mighty workhorse underneath that pretty exterior. If you want to find out more about GNOME, visit the GNOME home page at `www.gnome.org`.

If you have both GNOME and KDE installed on your system, you can select which GUI you want just before you log in. From the graphical login window, select Session➪GNOME to select a GNOME session and then log in as usual.

## Using the Nautilus shell

The Nautilus file manager, or more accurately *graphical shell*, comes with GNOME. Nautilus is intuitive to use — it's similar to the Windows Active Desktop. You can manage files and folders and also manage your system with Nautilus.

The current version of Nautilus has changed from what you may have known in previous versions of Red Hat Linux or Fedora Core. Nautilus now provides a new *object window* view in addition to the navigation window that you know from the past. When you double-click any object on the desktop, Nautilus opens an object window that shows that object's contents. If you want the older navigation window with its Web browser-like user interface, right-click a folder and select Open➪Browse Folder from the pop-up menu.

### Viewing files and folders in object windows

When you double-click a file or a folder, Nautilus opens that object in what it calls an object window. Unlike the Nautilus windows of past that enabled you to navigate the directory hierarchy, the object window does not have any back and forward buttons, toolbar, or side pane. For example, double-click the Start Here icon on the left side of the GNOME desktop. Nautilus opens an object window where it displays the contents of the Start Here object. If you double-click an object inside that window, Nautilus opens another object window where that object's contents appear. Figure 1-9 shows the result of double-clicking two objects in the Start Here window.

The Nautilus object window has a sparse user interface that has just the menu bar. You can perform various operations from the menu bar such as open an object using an application, create folders and documents, and close the object window.

### Burning data CDs from Nautilus

If you have a CD recorder attached to your system (it can be a built-in ATAPI CD recorder or an external one attached to the USB port), you can use Nautilus to burn data CDs. From a Nautilus object window, you can access the CD Creator built into Nautilus. Just follow these simple steps:

*1.* **In any Nautilus object window, select Places➪CD Creator.**

Nautilus opens a CD Creator object window. If you don't have any Nautilus object windows open, just double-click the computer icon on the desktop.

**Figure 1-9:**
By default,
Nautilus
opens a
new object
window for
each object.

**2. From other Nautilus windows, drag and drop into the CD Creator window whatever files and folders you want to put on the CD.**

To get to files on your computer, open the Computer icon in Nautilus and find the files you want. Then drag and drop those file or folder icons into the CD Creator window.

**3. From the CD Creator window, select File⇨Write to CD.**

Nautilus displays a dialog box where you can select the CD recorder, the write speed, and several other options, such as whether to eject the CD when done. You can also specify the CD title.

**4. Click Write Files to CD.**

Nautilus burns the CD.

### Browsing folders in a navigation window

If you prefer to use the familiar navigation window for browsing folders, you have to do a bit of extra work. Instead of double-clicking an icon, right-click the icon and select Browse Folder from the pop-up menu. Nautilus then opens a navigation window with the contents of the object represented by the icon. For example, double-click the home folder icon in the upper-left corner of the GNOME desktop. Nautilus opens a navigation window where it displays the contents of your home directory (think of a *directory* as a folder that can contain other files and folders). Figure 1-10 shows a typical user's home directory in a Nautilus navigation window.

The navigation window is vertically divided into two parts. The left window shows different views of the file system and other objects that you can browse with Nautilus. The right window shows the files and folders in the currently selected folder in the left window. Nautilus displays icons for files and folders. For image files, it shows a thumbnail of the image.

The navigation window's user interface is similar to that of a Web browser. The window's title bar shows the name of the currently selected folder. The Location text box along the top of the window shows the full name of the directory in Linuxspeak — for example, Figure 1-10 shows the contents of the /home/naba directory.

If you have used Windows Explorer, you can use the Nautilus navigation window in a similar manner. To view the contents of another directory, do the following:

1. **Choose Tree from the Information drop-down menu (located in the left-window).**

   A tree menu of directories appears in that window. Initially the tree shows the Home folder and the file system's root directory as a Filesystem folder.

**Figure 1-10:**
You can view files and folders in the Nautilus navigation window.

2. **Click the right arrow next to the Filesystem folder; in the resulting tree view, locate the directory you want to browse.**

   For example, to look at the /etc directory, click the right arrow next to the etc directory. Nautilus displays the subdirectories in /etc and to change the right arrow to a down arrow. X11 is one of the subdirectories in /etc that you view in the next step.

3. **To view the contents of the X11 subdirectory, click X11.**

   The window on the right now shows the contents of the /etc/X11 directory.

Nautilus displays the contents of the selected directory using different types of icons. Each directory appears as a folder, with the name of the directory shown underneath the folder icon. Ordinary files, such as xorg.conf, appear as a sheet of paper. The X file is a link to an executable file. The prefdm file is another executable file.

The Nautilus navigation window has the usual menu bar and a toolbar. Notice the View as Icons button in Figure 1-10 on the right side of the toolbar. This button shows Nautilus is displaying the directory contents using large icons. Click the button, and a drop-down list appears. Select View as List from the list; Nautilus displays the contents by using smaller icons in a list format, along with detailed information, such as the size of each file or directory and the time when each was last modified, as shown in Figure 1-11.

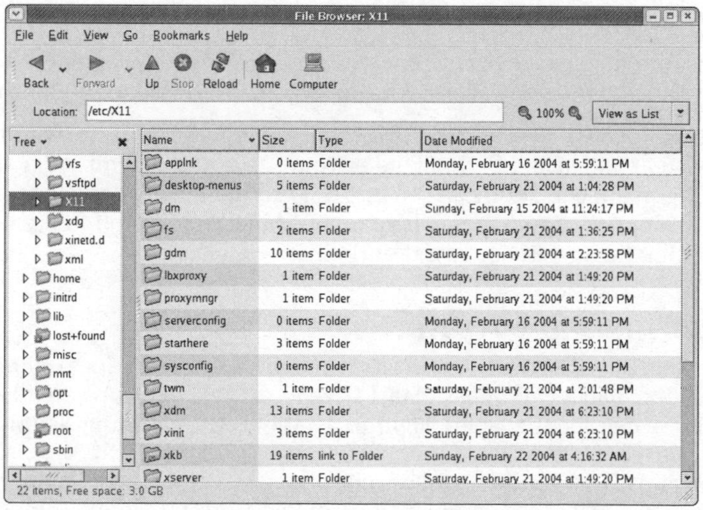

**Book II Chapter 1**

Exploring the GUI Desktops

**Figure 1-11:** The Nautilus navigation window with a list view of the /etc/X11 directory.

If you click any of the column headings — Name, Size, Type, or Date Modified — along the top of the list view, Nautilus sorts the list according to that column. For example, click the Date Modified column heading. Nautilus now displays the list of files and directories sorted according to the time of their last modification. Clicking the Name column heading sorts the files and folders alphabetically.

Not only can you move around different folders using the Nautilus navigation window, you can also do things such as move a file from one folder to another or delete a file. I don't outline each step, because they are intuitive and similar to what you do in any GUI, such as Windows or the Mac OS. Here are some of the things you can do in Nautilus:

✦ To move a file to a different folder, drag and drop the file's icon on the folder where you want the file.

✦ To copy a file to a new location, select the file's icon and choose Edit⇨ Copy File from the Nautilus menu. You can also right-click the file's icon and select Copy File from the pop-up menu. Then move to the folder where you want to copy the file and choose Edit⇨Paste Files.

✦ To delete a file or directory, right-click the icon, and select Move to Trash from the pop-up menu (you can do this only if you have permission to delete the file). To permanently delete the file, right-click the Trash icon on the desktop, and select Empty Trash from the pop-up menu. Of course, do this only if you really want to delete the file. If you have to retrieve a file from the trash, double-click the Trash icon and then drag the file's icon back to the folder where you want to save it. You can retrieve a file from the trash until you empty it.

✦ To rename a file or a directory, right-click the icon and select Rename from the pop-up menu. Then you can type the new name or edit the name.

✦ To create a new folder, right-click an empty area of the window on the right and select Create Folder from the pop-up menu. After the new folder icon appears, you can rename it by right-clicking and selecting Rename from the pop-up menu. If you don't have permission to create a folder, that menu item is grayed out.

## Configuring GNOME

To configure GNOME (as well as other parts of Fedora Core), simply double-click the map and compass Start Here icon (yes, the icons are hard to identify, but you can see the label). Figure 1-12 shows the resulting Nautilus window.

The Start Here window looks somewhat like the Control Panel in Microsoft Windows. As in the Windows Control Panel, you do many things from the Start Here window.

To configure the GNOME desktop from the window shown in Figure 1-12, do the following:

*1.* **Double-click the Preferences icon.**

Nautilus displays the Preferences window, as shown in Figure 1-13.

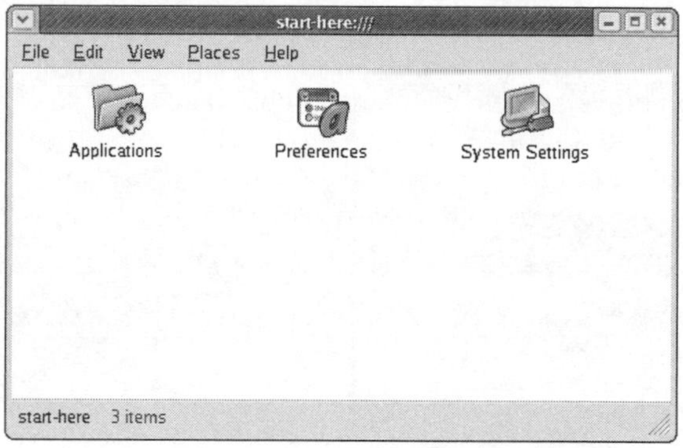

**Figure 1-12:**
You can
configure
the desktop
and the
system from
the Start
Here
window.

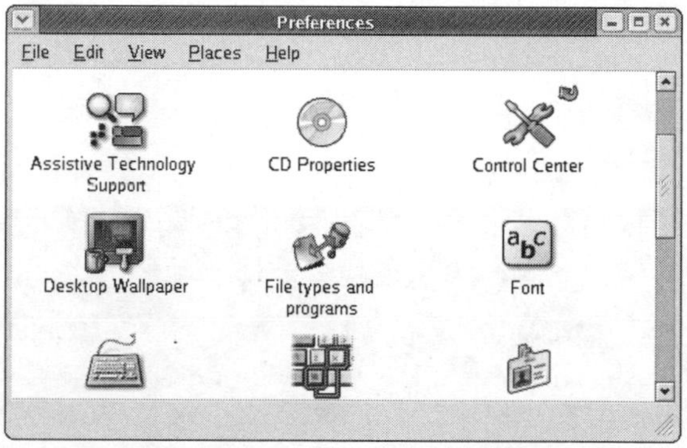

**Book II
Chapter 1**

**Exploring the
GUI Desktops**

**Figure 1-13:**
Indicate
your
preferences
from this
window.

*2.* **You can configure many different items from the Control Center. To select a background, double-click the Desktop Wallpaper icon.**

Nautilus launches the Desktop Wallpaper Preferences dialog box (see Figure 1-14).

In this dialog box, you can now select a desktop color or wallpaper (an image used as background) for the desktop:

a. **To pick wallpaper, click the Add Wallpaper button in the lower-middle part of the window (see Figure 1-14) and go through the directories to select any JPEG file as the wallpaper.**

b. **Pick one of the images in the** /usr/share/wallpaper **directory, and then click OK. That image filename appears in the Desktop Wallpaper Preferences dialog box.**

c. **Click to select the new wallpaper; then click Close to exit out of the dialog box.**

Figure 1-15 shows the GNOME desktop after I selected the `alien-night.jpg` file as the wallpaper.

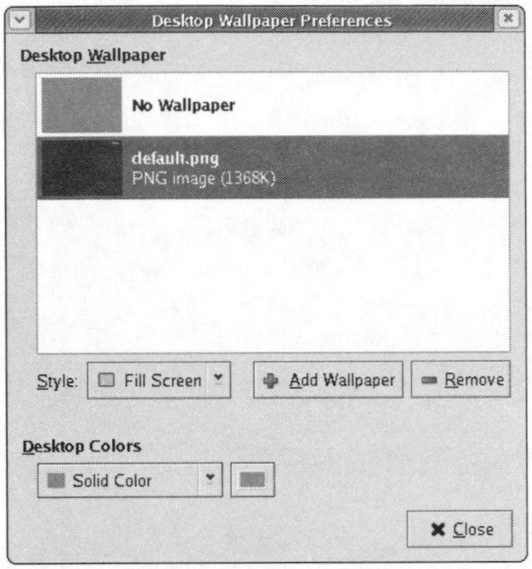

**Figure 1-14:**
Select a desktop color or wallpaper from this dialog box.

**Figure 1-15:**
The GNOME desktop looks more appealing with a new wallpaper.

3. **If you want to configure other aspects of the GNOME desktop or Fedora Core, simply double-click one of the icons in Figure 1-13 and give it a try. When you're done, click the X button in the upper-right corner of the Preferences window to close the window.**

## Exploring KDE

KDE (pronounced *kay-dee-ee*) is another GUI for Fedora Core. KDE is similar to Microsoft Windows, but it plays a different role: Unlike Microsoft Windows, which is also the operating system, KDE is just a GUI that runs on the Linux operating system. From your perspective, if you don't like KDE, all you have to do is log out and then log back in with the other GUI — GNOME. If you wonder why there are two GUIs to begin with, just remember that no single person or corporation decides what open-source software to develop. When it comes to GUIs, having choices makes sense because different people like different things, so the GNOME and KDE teams give you the choice. All you have to do as a user is to explore the two GUIs and take your pick. You can even pick a different GUI each time you log in to your Fedora Core system!

KDE is a complete desktop environment for users, but it is also a programming environment for developers. Here are some key facts about KDE:

✦ KDE is written in C++ and uses object-oriented development.

✦ KDE includes a GUI toolkit so that developers can write GUI applications using the toolkit.

✦ KDE supports an *object model* — software components that can interact with each other.

✦ KDE includes an office application suite. The office suite, KOffice, includes a spreadsheet (KSpread), a FrameMaker-like word processor (KWord), a presentation application (KPresenter), and a drawing program (KIllustrator). Fedora Core, however, includes only the OpenOffice.org applications.

✦ KDE supports internationalization, and most KDE applications have been translated into over 25 languages.

Okay, you get the idea. KDE is not just a pretty face — some pretty powerful machinery is underneath that polished exterior. To keep up with KDE news, visit the KDE home page at www.kde.org.

To start a KDE session, click Session at the bottom of the graphical login screen. A dialog box appears with a list of sessions (shown in Figure 1-16). Select the KDE radio button in the dialog box, and then click OK to continue.

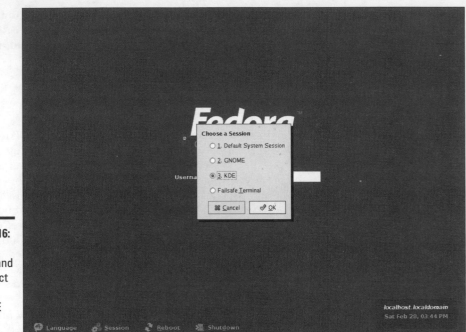

**Figure 1-16:**
Click
Session and
then select
KDE to
get a KDE
desktop.

Type your username and password in the GUI login screen and log in as usual. A dialog box informs you that if you want to make KDE your default desktop, you need to run the switchdesk utility (you can start it by selecting Main Menu➪Settings➪Desktop Switching Tool from the GNOME desktop).

After that KDE starts up. If you're using KDE for the first time, a personalization window appears and you have to specify a number of preferences, such as the default GUI style. If you select the default Bluecurve style, your KDE desktop (shown in Figure 1-17) looks similar to the GNOME desktop.

## Using Konqueror

Konqueror is a file manager as well as a Web browser that comes with KDE. It's intuitive to use — somewhat similar to the Windows Active Desktop. You can manage files and folders (and also view Web pages) with Konqueror.

### Viewing files and folders

When you double-click a folder icon on the desktop, Konqueror starts automatically. For example, double-click the home icon in the upper-left corner of the KDE desktop. Konqueror runs and displays the contents of your home directory (think of a *directory* as a folder that can contain other files and folders). Figure 1-18 shows a typical user's home directory in Konqueror.

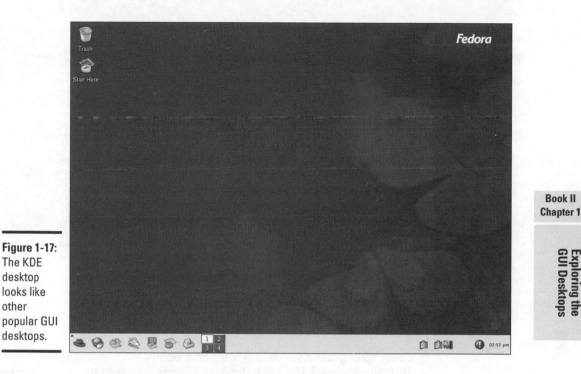

**Figure 1-17:**
The KDE desktop looks like other popular GUI desktops.

If you have used Windows Explorer, you can use Konqueror in a similar manner.

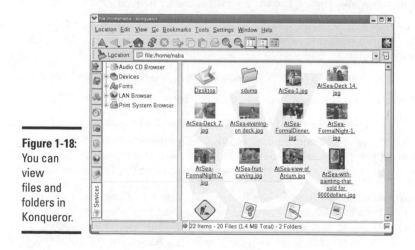

**Figure 1-18:**
You can view files and folders in Konqueror.

The Konqueror window is vertically divided into three parts:

✦ A narrow left window shows icons you can click to perform various tasks in Konqueror.

✦ The wider middle window shows a tree view of the current folder.

✦ The widest window (at the right) uses icons to show the files and folders in the current folder.

Konqueror uses different types of icons for different files and shows a preview of each file's contents. For image files, the preview is a thumbnail version of the image.

The Konqueror window's title bar shows the name of the currently selected directory. The Location text box (along the top of the window) shows the full name of the directory, using Konqueror terminology — in this case, Figure 1-18 shows the contents of the /home/naba directory.

Use the leftmost vertical row of buttons to select other things to browse. When you click one of these buttons, the middle window displays a tree menu of items you can browse. For example, to browse other parts of the file system, do the following:

*1.* **From the leftmost vertical column of icons in the Konqueror window (refer to Figure 1-18), click the Root Folder icon (the one that appears just above the Services icon).**

A tree menu of directories appears in the middle window.

*2.* **In the tree view, locate the folder you want to browse.**

For example, to look at the etc folder, click the plus sign next to the etc folder. Konqueror displays the other folders and changes the plus sign to a minus sign.

*3.* **To view the contents of the X11 subdirectory, scroll down and click X11.**

The window on the right now shows the contents of the /etc/X11 directory.

Konqueror displays the contents of a folder using different types of icons. Each directory appears as a folder, with the name of the directory shown underneath the folder icon. Ordinary files appear as a sheet of paper.

The Konqueror window has the usual menu bar and a toolbar. You can view the files and folders in other formats as well. For example, choose View➪ View Mode➪Detailed List View to see the folder's contents using smaller icons in a list format (see Figure 1-19), along with detailed information (such as the size of each file or directory, and at what time each was last modified).

If you click any of the column headings — Name, Size, File Type, or Modified — along the top of the list view, Konqueror sorts the list according to that column.

For example, click the Modified column heading, and Konqueror displays the list of files and folders sorted according to the time of the last modification. Clicking the Name column heading sorts the files and directories alphabetically by name.

Not only can you move around different folders using Konqueror, you can also do things such as move a file from one folder to another or delete a file. I don't outline each step because the steps are intuitive and similar to what you do in any GUI (such as Windows or the Mac interface). Here are some things you can do in Konqueror:

**Book II
Chapter 1**

Exploring the
GUI Desktops

✦ **View a text file:** Click the filename and Konqueror runs the KWrite word processor, displaying the file in a new window.

✦ **Copy or move a file to a different folder:** Drag and drop the file's icon on the folder where you want the file to go. A menu pops up and asks you whether you want to copy, move, or simply link the file to that directory.

✦ **Delete a file or directory:** Right-click the icon, and select Move to Trash from the pop-up menu. To permanently delete the file, right-click the Trash icon on the desktop, and choose Empty Trash from the pop-up menu. Of course, do this only if you really want to delete the file. If you want to recover a file from the trash, double click the Trash icon on the desktop and from that window drag and drop the file icon into the folder where you want to save the file. When asked whether you want to copy or move, select Move. You can recover files from the trash until the moment you empty the trash.

✦ **Rename a file or a directory:** Right-click the icon, and select Rename from the pop-up menu. Then you can type the new name or edit the old name.

**Figure 1-19:**
Konqueror
shows a
detailed list
view of the
/etc/X11
directory.

| Name ▼ | Size | File Type | Modified | Permissions | Owner | Group |
|---|---|---|---|---|---|---|
| applnk | 4.0 KB | Folder | 02/16/2004 05:59 pm | rwxr-xr-x | root | root |
| desktop-menus | 4.0 KB | Folder | 02/21/2004 01:04 pm | rwxr-xr-x | root | root |
| dm | 4.0 KB | Folder | 02/15/2004 11:24 pm | rwxr-xr-x | root | root |
| fs | 4.0 KB | Folder | 02/21/2004 01:36 pm | rwxr-xr-x | root | root |
| gdm | 4.0 KB | Folder | 02/21/2004 02:23 pm | rwxr-xr-x | root | root |
| lbxproxy | 4.0 KB | Folder | 02/21/2004 01:49 pm | rwxr-xr-x | root | root |
| proxymngr | 4.0 KB | Folder | 02/21/2004 01:49 pm | rwxr-xr-x | root | root |
| serverconfig | 4.0 KB | Folder | 02/16/2004 05:59 pm | rwxr-xr-x | root | root |
| starthere | 4.0 KB | Folder | 02/16/2004 05:59 pm | rwxr-xr-x | root | root |
| sysconfig | 4.0 KB | Folder | 02/16/2004 05:59 pm | rwxr-xr-x | root | root |
| twm | 4.0 KB | Folder | 02/21/2004 02:01 pm | rwxr-xr-x | root | root |
| xdm | 4.0 KB | Folder | 02/21/2004 06:23 pm | rwxr-xr-x | root | root |
| xinit | 4.0 KB | Folder | 02/21/2004 06:23 pm | rwxr-xr-x | root | root |
| xkb | 4.0 KB | Folder | 02/22/2004 04:16 am | rwxr-xr-x | root | root |
| xserver | 4.0 KB | Folder | 02/21/2004 01:49 pm | rwxr-xr-x | root | root |
| xsm | 4.0 KB | Folder | 02/21/2004 01:49 pm | rwxr-xr-x | root | root |

22 Items - 6 Files (5.9 KB Total) - 16 Folders

✦ **Create a new folder:** Choose View⌐View Mode⌐Icon View. Then right-click an empty area of the rightmost window and choose Create New⇨Directory from the pop-up menu. Then type the name of the new directory and click OK. (If you don't have permission to create a directory, you get an error message.)

### Viewing Web pages

Konqueror is much more than a file manager. With it, you can view a Web page as easily as you can view a folder. Just type a Web address in the Location box and see what happens. For example, Figure 1-20 shows the Konqueror window after I typed `www.irs.gov` in the Location text box on the toolbar and pressed Enter.

Konqueror displays the Web site in the window on the right. The left window still shows whatever it was displaying earlier.

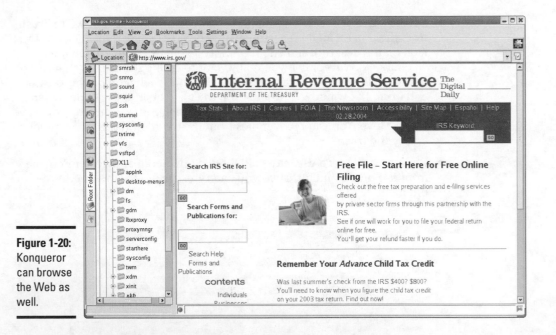

**Figure 1-20:** Konqueror can browse the Web as well.

## Configuring KDE

You can configure the KDE desktop in many ways, but I use the KDE Control Center for one-stop-shopping KDE configuration. Choose Main Menu⇨ Settings⇨Control Center. The Control Center starts and shows summary information about the Fedora Core system in a window (see Figure 1-21).

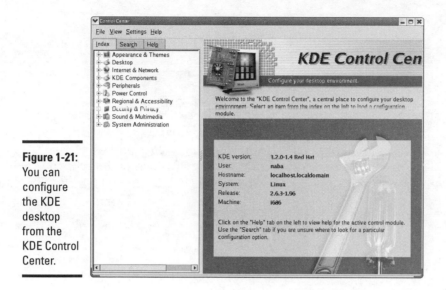

**Figure 1-21:**
You can
configure
the KDE
desktop
from the
KDE Control
Center.

The Control Center window is vertically divided into two parts:

✦ The narrower left window shows a tree menu with 10 or so top-level categories of customization that you can perform.

✦ The wider right window is where you enter information.

To customize a specific category such as Appearance & Themes, click the
plus sign (+) to the left of the label. The plus sign changes to a minus sign
(–), and you get a list of all the items that you can specify. For example, to
change the KDE desktop's background from the window shown in Figure
1-21, do the following:

*1.* **Click the plus sign next to Appearance & Themes; from the new items
that appear, click Background.**

The Control Center displays the choices for desktop background, using
the right window as shown in Figure 1-22. You can select a background
color or *wallpaper* (an image used as background) for your desktop here.

*2.* **To select a picture as background, select Picture and then click the
button with the folder icon, next to the name of the current picture.**

The Control Center brings up a dialog box (shown in Figure 1-23) showing the contents of the /usr/share/backgrounds/images directory.

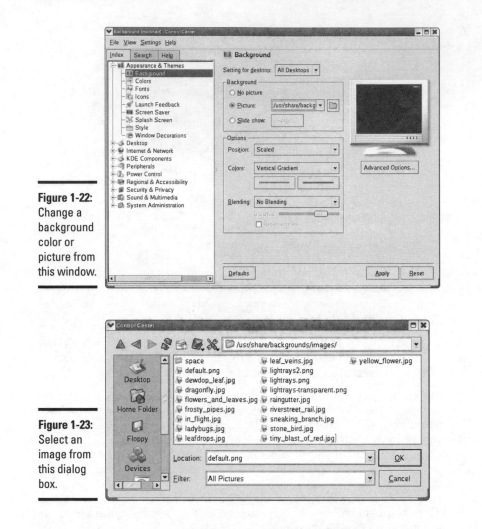

**Figure 1-22:**
Change a
background
color or
picture from
this window.

**Figure 1-23:**
Select an
image from
this dialog
box.

*3.* **Pick one of the image files from the list of files, and then click OK.**

*4.* **When you get back to the Control Center window, click Apply to put the new change into effect.**

*5.* **If you want to configure other aspects of the KDE desktop, select another item in the Appearance & Themes list (refer to Figure 1-22) and give it a try.**

Click Apply to try a new configuration; if you don't like the result, click Reset to revert to the old settings.

# Chapter 2: Learning the Shell

## In This Chapter

✔ Opening terminal windows and virtual consoles

✔ Using the Bash shell

✔ Learning some Linux commands

✔ Writing shell scripts

Sometimes things just don't work. What do you do if the GUI desktop stops responding to your mouse clicks? What if the GUI doesn't start at all? You can still tell your Fedora Core system what to do, but you have to do it by typing commands into a text screen. In these situations, you work with the *shell* — the Linux command interpreter. I introduce the Bash shell (the default shell in Fedora Core) in this chapter.

After you learn to work with the shell, you may even begin to like the simplicity and power of the Linux commands. And then, even if you're a GUI aficionado, someday soon you may find yourself firing up a terminal window and making the system sing and dance with two- or three-letter commands strung together by strange punctuation characters. (Hey, I can dream, can't I?)

## Opening Terminal Windows and Virtual Consoles

First things first. If you're working in GNOME or KDE, where do you type commands for the shell? Good question.

The easiest way to get to the shell is to open a *terminal* (also called *console*) window. Both GNOME and KDE panels have an icon to open a terminal window, which looks like a monitor. Click that icon to get a terminal window. Now you can type commands to your heart's content.

If, for some reason, the GUI seems to be *hung* (you click and type but nothing happens), you can turn to the *virtual consoles*. (The *physical* console is the monitor-and-keyboard combination.) The idea of virtual consoles is to give the ability to switch between several text consoles even though you have only one physical console. Whether you are running a GUI or not, you can then use different text consoles to type different commands.

To get to the first virtual console from the GNOME or KDE desktop, press Ctrl+Alt+F1. Press Ctrl+Alt+F2 for the second virtual console, and so on. Each of these virtual consoles is a text screen where you can log in and type Linux commands to perform various tasks. When you're done, type **exit** to log out.

You can use up to six virtual consoles. The seventh one is used for the GUI desktop. To get back to the GUI desktop, press Ctrl+Alt+F7.

# Using the Bash Shell

If you've used MS-DOS, you may be familiar with COMMAND.COM, the DOS command interpreter. That program displays the infamous C:\> prompt. In Windows, you can see this prompt if you open a command window. (To open a command window in Microsoft Windows, choose Start⇨Run, type **command** in the text box, and then click OK.)

Fedora Core comes with a command interpreter that resembles COMMAND. COM in DOS, but can do a whole lot more. The Fedora Core command interpreter is called a *shell*.

The default shell in Fedora Core is Bash. When you open a terminal window or log in at a text console, the Bash shell is what prompts you for commands. Then, when you type a command, the shell executes your command. By the way, just as there are multiple GUIs (GNOME or KDE) for Fedora Core, you have the choice of shells besides Bash. For example, the C Shell is an alternate shell that some people prefer. You can easily change your default shell by typing the **chsh** command.

In addition to the standard Linux commands, Bash can execute any computer program. So you can type the name of an application (the name is usually more cryptic than what you see in GNOME or KDE menus) at the shell prompt, and the shell starts that application.

## Learning the syntax of shell commands

Because a shell interprets what you type, knowing how the shell processes the text you enter is important. All shell commands have this general format that starts with a command followed by options (some commands have no options):

```
command option1 option2 ... optionN
```

Such a single on-screen line of command is commonly referred to as a *command line*. On a command line, you enter a command, followed by zero or more options (or *arguments*). These strings of options — the *command-line options* (or command-line arguments) — modify the way the command works so you can get it to do specific tasks.

The shell uses a blank space or tab to distinguish between the command and options. Naturally, you help it by using a space or a tab to separate the command from the options and the options from one another.

An option can contains spaces — all you have to do is put that option inside quotation marks so the spaces are included. For example, to search for my name in the password file, I enter the following grep command (grep is used for searching for text in files):

```
grep "Naba Barkakati" /etc/passwd
```

When grep prints the line with my name, it looks like this:

```
naba:x:500:500:Naba Barkakati:/home/naba:/bin/bash
```

If you created a user account with your username, type the grep command with your username as an argument.

In the output from the grep command, you can see the name of the shell (/bin/bash) following the last colon (:).

The number of command-line options and their format, of course, depends on the actual command. Typically, these options look like -X, where X is a single character. For example, the ls command lists the contents of a directory. You can use the -l option to see more details, such as this:

```
[ashley@dhcppc4 ashley]$ ls -l
total 8
drwxrwxr-x   2 ashley   ashley   4096 Jun 29 13:35 Directory
drwx------   7 ashley   ashley   4096 Jun 29 11:44 Mail
```

The [ashley@dhcppc4 ashley]$ part is the shell prompt for the user named ashley. On your system, the prompt depends on your username. When showing examples, I omit the prompt.

If a command is too long to fit on a single line, type a backslash followed by Enter. Then, continue typing the command on the next line. For example, type the following command (press Enter after each line):

```
cat \
/etc/passwd
```

The cat command then displays the contents of the /etc/passwd file.

You can concatenate several shorter commands on a single line. Just separate the commands by semicolons (;). For example, the following command

```
cd; ls -l; pwd
```

changes the current directory to your home directory, lists the contents of that directory, and then shows the name of that directory.

## Combining shell commands

You can combine simple shell commands to create a more sophisticated command. Suppose you want to find out whether a device file named `sbpcd` resides in your system's `/dev` directory because some documentation says you need that device file for a Sound Blaster Pro CD-ROM drive. You can use the `ls /dev` command to get a directory listing of the `/dev` directory and then browse through it to see whether that listing contains `sbpcd`.

Unfortunately, the `/dev` directory has a great many entries, so finding any item that has `sbpcd` in its name may be hard. You can, however, combine the `ls` command with `grep` and come up with a command line that does exactly what you want. Here's that command line:

```
ls /dev | grep sbpcd
```

The shell sends the output of the `ls` command (the directory listing) to the `grep` command, which searches for the string `sbpcd`. That vertical bar (|) is known as a *pipe* because it acts as a conduit (think of a water pipe) between the two programs — the output of the first command is fed into the input of the second one.

## Controlling command input and output

Most Linux commands have a common feature — they always read from the standard input (usually, the keyboard) and write to the standard output (usually, the screen). Error messages are sent to the standard error (usually to the screen as well). These three devices often are referred to as `stdin`, `stdout`, and `stderr`.

You can make a command get its input from a file and then send its output to another file. Just so you know, the highfalutin term for this feature is *input and output redirection* or *I/O redirection*.

### Getting command input from a file

If you want a command to read from a file, you can redirect the standard input to come from that file instead of the keyboard. For example, type the following command:

```
sort < /etc/passwd
```

This command displays a sorted list of the lines in the `/etc/passwd` file. In this case, the less-than sign (<) redirects `stdin` so that the `sort` command reads its input from the `/etc/passwd` file.

### Saving command output in a file

To save the output of a command in a file, redirect the standard output to a file. For example, type **cd** to change to your home directory and then type the following command:

```
grep typedef /usr/include/* > typedef.out
```

This command searches through all files in the /usr/include directory for the occurrence of the text typedef — and then saves the output in a file called typedef.out. The greater-than sign (>) redirects stdout to a file. This command also illustrates another feature of Bash. When you use an asterisk (*), Bash replaces the asterisk with a list of all filenames in the specified directory. Thus, /usr/include/* means *all the files in the* /usr/include *directory*.

 If you want to append a command's output to the end of an existing file instead of saving the output in a new file, use two greater-than signs (>>) like this:

```
command >> filename
```

### Saving error messages in a file

Sometimes you type a command and it generates a whole lot of error messages that scroll by so fast you can't tell what's going on. One way to see all the error messages is to save the error messages in a file so that you can see what the heck happened. You can do that by redirecting stderr to a file.

For example, type the following command:

```
find / -name COPYING -print 2> finderr
```

This command looks throughout the file system for files named COPYING, but saves all the error messages in the finderr file. The number 2 followed by the greater-than sign (2>) redirects stderr to a file.

 If you want to simply discard the error messages instead of saving them in a file, use /dev/null as the filename, like this:

```
find / -name COPYING -print 2> /dev/null
```

 That /dev/null is a special file — often called the *bit bucket* and sometimes glorified as the *Great Bit Bucket in the Sky* — that simply discards whatever it receives. So now you know what they mean when you hear phrases such as, "Your mail probably ended up in the bit bucket."

## Typing less with automatic command completion

Many commands take a filename as an argument. To view the contents of the /etc/modprobe.conf text file, for example, type the following command:

```
cat /etc/modprobe.conf
```

The cat command displays the /etc/modprobe.conf file. For any command that takes a filename as an argument, you can use a Bash feature to avoid having to type the whole filename. All you have to type is the bare minimum — just the first few characters — to uniquely identify the file in its directory.

To see an example, type **cat /etc/mod** but don't press Enter; press Tab instead. Bash automatically completes the filename, so the command becomes cat /etc/modprobe.conf. Now press Enter to run the command.

Whenever you type a filename, press Tab after the first few characters of the filename. Bash probably can complete the filename so that you don't have to type the entire name. If you don't enter enough characters to uniquely identify the file, Bash beeps. Just type a few more characters and press Tab again.

## Going wild with asterisks and question marks

You can avoid typing long filenames another way. (After all, making less work for users is the idea of computers, isn't it?)

This particular trick involves using the asterisk (*) and question mark (?) and a few more tricks. These special characters are called *wildcards* because they match zero or more characters in a line of text.

If you know MS-DOS, you may have used commands such as COPY *.* A: to copy all files from the current directory to the A drive. Bash accepts similar wildcards in filenames. As you'd expect, Bash provides many more wildcard options than the MS-DOS command interpreter does.

You can use three types of wildcards in Bash:

✦ The **asterisk (*)** character matches zero or more characters in a filename. That means * denotes all files in a directory.

✦ The **question mark (?)** matches any single character. If you type test?, that matches any five-character text that begins with test.

✦ A **set of characters in brackets** matches any single character from that set. The string [aB]*, for example, matches any filename that starts with a or B.

Wildcards are handy when you want to do something to a whole lot of files. For example, to copy all the files from the /mnt/cdrom directory to the current directory, type the following:

```
cp /mnt/cdrom/* .
```

Bash replaces the wildcard character * with the names of all the files in the /mnt/cdrom directory. The period at the end of the command represents the current directory.

You can use the asterisk with other parts of a filename to select a more specific group of files. Suppose you want to use the grep command to search for the text typedef struct in all files of the /usr/include directory that meet the following criteria:

✦ The filename starts with s.

✦ The filename ends with .h.

The wildcard specification s*.h denotes all filenames that meet these criteria. Thus you can perform the search with the following command:

```
grep "typedef struct" /usr/include/s*.h
```

The string contains a space that you want the grep command to find, so you have to enclose that string in quotation marks. That way, Bash does not try to interpret each word in that text as a separate command-line argument.

The question mark (?) matches a single character. Suppose that you have four files — image1.pcx, image2.pcx, image3.pcx, and image4.pcx — in the current directory. To copy these files to the /mnt/floppy directory, use the following command:

```
cp image?.pcx /mnt/floppy
```

Bash replaces the single question mark with any single character, and copies the four files to /mnt.

The third wildcard format — [...] — matches a single character from a specific set of characters enclosed in square brackets. You may want to combine this format with other wildcards to narrow down the matching filenames to a smaller set. To see a list of all filenames in the /etc/X11/xdm directory that start with x or X, type the following command:

```
ls /etc/X11/xdm/[xX]*
```

## *Repeating previously typed commands*

To make repeating long commands easy for you, Bash stores up to 500 old commands. Bash keeps a *command history* (a list of old commands). To see the command history, type **history**. Bash displays a numbered list of the old commands, including those that you entered during previous logins.

If the command list is too long, you can limit the number of old commands you want to see. To see only the most recent 10 commands, type this command:

```
history 10
```

To repeat a command from the list that the `history` command shows, simply type an exclamation point (!), followed by that command's number. To repeat command number 3, type **!3**.

You can repeat an old command without knowing its command number. Suppose you typed `more /usr/lib/X11/xdm/xdm-config` a few minutes ago, and now you want to look at that file again. To repeat the previous `more` command, type the following:

```
!more
```

Often, you may want to repeat the last command that you just typed, perhaps with a slight change. For example, you may have displayed the contents of the directory by using the `ls -l` command. To repeat that command, type two exclamation points as follows:

```
!!
```

Sometimes, you may want to repeat the previous command but add extra arguments to it. Suppose that `ls -l` shows too many files. Simply repeat that command, but pipe the output through the `more` command as follows:

```
!! | more
```

Bash replaces the two exclamation points with the previous command and then appends `| more` to that command.

Here's the easiest way to recall previous commands. Just press the up-arrow key and Bash keeps going backward through the history of commands you previously typed. To move forward in the command history, press the down-arrow key.

## *Learning Linux Commands*

You type Linux commands at the shell prompt. By *Linux commands,* I mean some of the commands that the Bash shell understands as well as the command-line utilities that come with Linux. In this section, I introduce you to a few major categories of Linux commands.

I can't possibly cover all the Linux commands in this chapter, but I want to give you a feel for the breadth of the commands by showing you a list of common Linux commands in Table 2-1. It lists common Linux commands by category. Before you start learning any Linux commands, browse this table.

| Table 2-1 | Overview of Common Linux Commands |
|---|---|
| *Command Name* | *Action* |
| ***Getting Online Help*** | |
| apropos | Finds online manual pages for a specified keyword. |
| info | Displays online help information about a specified command. |
| man | Displays online help information. |
| whatis | Similar to apropos, but searches for complete words only. |
| ***Making Commands Easier*** | |
| alias | Defines an abbreviation for a long command. |
| type | Shows the type and location of a command. |
| unalias | Deletes an abbreviation defined using alias. |
| ***Managing Files and Directories*** | |
| cd | Changes the current directory. |
| chmod | Changes file permissions. |
| chown | Changes file owner and group. |
| cp | Copies files. |
| ln | Creates symbolic links to files and directories. |
| ls | Displays the contents of a directory. |
| mkdir | Creates a directory. |
| mv | Renames a file as well as moves a file from one directory to another. |
| rm | Deletes files. |
| rmdir | Deletes directories. |
| pwd | Displays the current directory. |
| touch | Updates a file's time stamp. |
| ***Finding Files*** | |
| find | Finds files based on specified criteria such as name, size, and so on. |
| locate | Finds files using a periodically updated database. |

*(continued)*

**Table 2-1** *(continued)*

| Command Name | Action |
|---|---|
| whereis | Finds files based in the typical directories where executable (also known as *binary*) files are located. |
| which | Finds files in the directories listed in the PATH environment variable. |

***Processing Files***

| Command Name | Action |
|---|---|
| cat | Displays a file on standard output (can be used to concatenate several files into one big file). |
| cut | Extracts specified sections from each line of text in a file. |
| dd | Copies blocks of data from one file to another (used to copy data from devices). |
| diff | Compares two text files and finds any differences. |
| expand | Converts all tabs into spaces. |
| file | Displays the type of data in a file. |
| fold | Wraps each line of text to fit a specified width. |
| grep | Searches for regular expressions within a text file. |
| less | Displays a text file, one page at a time (can go backward also). |
| lpr | Prints files. |
| more | Displays a text file, one page at a time (goes forward only). |
| nl | Numbers all nonblank lines in a text file and prints the lines to standard output. |
| paste | Concatenates corresponding lines from several files. |
| patch | Updates a text file using the differences between the original and revised copy of the file. |
| sed | Copies a file to standard output while applying specified editing commands. |
| sort | Sorts lines in a text file. |
| split | Breaks up a file into several smaller files with specified size. |
| tac | Reverses a file (last line first and so on). |
| tail | Displays the last few lines of a file. |
| tr | Substitutes one group of characters for another throughout a file. |
| uniq | Eliminates duplicate lines from a text file. |
| wc | Counts the number of lines, words, and characters in a text file. |
| zcat | Displays a compressed file (after decompressing). |
| zless | Displays a compressed file one page at a time (can go backward also). |
| zmore | Displays a compressed file one page at a time. |

| Command Name | Action |
|---|---|
| *Archiving and Compressing Files* | |
| compress | Compresses files. |
| cpio | Copies files to and from an archive. |
| gunzip | Decompresses files compressed with GNU ZIP (gzip). |
| gzip | Compresses files using GNU ZIP. |
| tar | Creates an archive of files in one or more directories (originally meant for archiving on tape). |
| uncompress | Decompresses files compressed with compress. |
| *Managing Processes* | |
| bg | Runs an interrupted process in the background. |
| fg | Runs a process in the foreground. |
| free | Displays the amount of free and used memory in the system. |
| halt | Shuts down Linux and halts the computer. |
| kill | Sends a signal to a process (usually used to terminate a process). |
| ldd | Displays the shared libraries needed to run a program. |
| nice | Runs a process with lower priority (referred to as nice mode). |
| ps | Displays a list of currently running processes. |
| printenv | Displays the current environment variables. |
| pstree | Similar to ps, but shows parent-child relationships clearly. |
| reboot | Stops Linux and then restarts the computer. |
| shutdown | Shuts down Linux. |
| top | Displays a list of most processor- and memory-intensive processes. |
| uname | Displays information about the system and the Linux kernel. |
| *Managing Users* | |
| chsh | Changes the shell (command interpreter). |
| groups | Prints the list of groups that includes a specified user. |
| id | Displays the user and group ID for a specified username. |
| passwd | Changes the password. |
| su | Starts a new shell as another user or root (when invoked without any argument). |
| *Managing the File System* | |
| df | Summarizes free and available space in all mounted storage devices. |

**Book II
Chapter 2**

**Learning the Shell**

*(continued)*

**Table 2-1** *(continued)*

| Command Name | Action |
|---|---|
| du | Displays disk usage information. |
| fdformat | Formats a diskette. |
| fdisk | Partitions a hard disk. |
| fsck | Checks and repairs a file system. |
| mkfs | Creates a new file system. |
| mknod | Creates a device file. |
| mkswap | Creates a swap space for Linux in a file or a disk partition. |
| mount | Mounts a device (for example, the CD-ROM) on a directory in the file system. |
| swapoff | Deactivates a swap space. |
| swapon | Activates a swap space. |
| sync | Writes buffered (saved in memory) data to files. |
| tty | Displays the device name for the current terminal. |
| umount | Unmounts a device from the file system. |
| *Working with Date and Time* | |
| cal | Displays a calendar for a specified month or year. |
| date | Shows the current date and time or sets a new date and time. |

## Becoming root (superuser)

When you want to do anything that requires a high privilege level (for example, administering your system), you have to become root. Normally you log in as a regular user with your normal username. When you need the privileges of the superuser, though, use the following command to become root:

su -

That's su followed by the minus sign (or hyphen). The shell then prompts you for the root password. Type the password and press Enter.

After you're done with whatever you wanted to do as root (and you have the privilege to do anything as root), type **exit** to return to your normal self.

Instead of becoming root by using the su command, you can also type **sudo**, followed by the command that you want to run as root. If you are listed as an authorized user in the /etc/sudoers file, sudo executes the command as if you were logged in as root. Type **man sudoers** to read more about the /etc/sudoers file.

## Managing processes

Every time the shell executes a command that you type, it starts a process. The shell itself is a process. So are any scripts or programs that the shell runs.

Use the ps ax command to see a list of processes. When you type **ps ax**, Bash shows you the current set of processes. Here are a few lines of output from the ps ax command (I also included the --cols 132 option to ensure that you can see each command in its entirety):

```
ps ax --cols 132
  PID TTY       STAT   TIME COMMAND
    1 ?         S      0:06 init [5]
    2 ?         SWN    0:01 [ksoftirqd/0]
    3 ?         SW<    0:00 [events/0]
    4 ?         SW<    0:04 [kblockd/0]
    8 ?         SW<    0:00 [aio/0]
    5 ?         SW     0:00 [pdflush]
    6 ?         SW     0:01 [pdflush]
    7 ?         SW     0:20 [kswapd0]
    9 ?         SW     0:00 [kseriod]
   13 ?         SW     0:20 [kjournald]
... lines deleted ...
 8973 pts/2     R      0:00 ps ax --cols 132
```

In this listing, the first column has the heading PID and shows a number for each process. PID stands for *process ID* (identification), which is a sequential number assigned by the Linux kernel. If you look through the output of the ps ax command, you see that the init command is the first process and that it has a PID or process number of 1. That's why init is referred to as the "mother of all processes."

The COMMAND column shows the command that created each process.

The process ID or process number is useful when you have to forcibly stop an errant process. Look at the output of the ps ax command and note the PID of the offending process. Then, use the kill command with that process number. To stop process number 8550, for example, type the following command:

```
kill -9 8550
```

## Working with date and time

You can use the date command to display the current date and time or set a new date and time. Type the date command at the shell prompt and you get a result similar to the following:

```
date
Mon Apr 19 21:51:33 EST 2004
```

As you can see, the date command alone displays the current date and time.

To set the date, log in as root and then type **date** followed by the date and time in the MMDDhhmmYYYY format, where each character is a digit. For example, to set the date and time to December 31, 2004 and 9:30 p.m., you type

```
date 123121302004
```

The MMDDhhmmYYYY date and time format is similar to the 24-hour military clock, and has the following meaning:

+ MM is a two-digit number for the month (01 through 12).

+ DD is a two-digit number for the day of the month (01 through 31).

+ hh is a two-digit hour in 24-hour format (00 is midnight and 23 is 11:00 PM).

+ mm is a two-digit number for the minutes (00 through 59).

+ YYYY is the 4-digit year (such as 2004).

The other interesting date-related command is cal. If you type cal without any options, it prints a calendar for the current month. If you type cal followed by a number, cal treats the number as the year and prints the calendar for that year. To view the calendar for a specific month in a specific year, provide the month number (1 = January, 2 = February, and so on) followed by the year. Thus, to view the calendar for January 2005, type the following and you get the calendar for that month:

```
cal 1 2005
      January 2005
Su Mo Tu We Th Fr Sa
                   1
 2  3  4  5  6  7  8
 9 10 11 12 13 14 15
16 17 18 19 20 21 22
23 24 25 26 27 28 29
30 31
```

## Processing files

You can search through a text file with grep and view a text file, a screen at a time, with more. For example, to search for my username in the /etc/passwd file, I use

```
grep naba /etc/passwd
```

To view the /etc/inittab file a screenful at a time, I type

```
more /etc/inittab
```

As each screen pauses, I press the spacebar to go to the next page.

Many more Linux commands work on files — mostly on text files, but some commands also work on any file. I describe a few of the file-processing tools next.

### Counting words and lines in a text file

I am always curious about the size of files. For text files, the number of characters is basically the size of the file in bytes (because each character takes up a byte of storage space). What about words and the number of lines, though?

The Linux wc command comes to the rescue. The wc command displays the total number of characters, words, and lines in a text file. For example, try the following command:

Book II
Chapter 2

Learning the Shell

```
wc /etc/inittab
    53     229    1666 /etc/inittab
```

The second line shows the output. In this case, wc reports that 53 lines, 229 words, and 1666 characters are in the /etc/inittab file. If you simply want to see the number of lines in a file, use the -l option, such as this:

```
wc -l /etc/inittab
    53 /etc/inittab
```

As you can see, in this case, wc simply displays the line count.

If you don't specify a filename, the wc command expects input from the standard input. You can use the pipe feature of the shell to feed the output of another command to wc, which can be handy sometimes.

Suppose you want a rough count of the processes running on your system. You can get a list of all processes with the ps ax command, but instead of counting lines manually, just pipe the output of ps to wc and you get a rough count automatically:

```
ps ax | wc -l
    76
```

Here the ps command produced 76 lines of output. Because the first line simply shows the headings for the tabular columns, you can estimate that about 75 processes are running on your system. (Of course, this count probably includes the processes used to run the ps and wc commands as well, but who's *really* counting?)

### Sorting text files

You can sort the lines in a text file by using the sort command. To see how the sort command works, first type **more /etc/passwd** to see the current contents of the /etc/passwd file. Now type **sort /etc/passwd** to see the lines sorted alphabetically. If you want to sort a file and save the sorted version in another file, you have to use the Bash shell's output redirection feature like this:

```
sort /etc/passwd > ~/sorted.text
```

This command sorts the lines in the /etc/passwd file and saves the output in a file named sorted.text in your home directory.

### Substituting or deleting characters from a file

Another interesting command is tr — it substitutes one group of characters for another (or deletes a selected character) throughout a file. Suppose that you occasionally have to use MS-DOS text files on your Fedora Core system. Although you may expect to use a text file on any system without any problems, you find one catch: DOS uses a carriage return followed by a line feed to mark the end of each line, whereas Linux uses only a line feed.

On your Linux system, you can get rid of the extra carriage returns in the DOS text file by using the tr command with the -d option. Essentially, to convert the DOS text file filename.dos to a Linux text file named filename.linux, type the following:

```
tr -d '\015' < filename.dos > filename.linux
```

In this command, '\015' denotes the code for the carriage-return character in octal notation.

### Spilling a file into several smaller files

The split command is handy for those times when you want to copy a file to a floppy disk, but the file is too large to fit on a single floppy. You can then use the split command to break up the file into smaller files, each of which can fit on a floppy.

By default, split puts 1,000 lines into each file. The files are named by groups of letters such as aa, ab, ac, and so on. You can specify a prefix for the filenames. For example, to split a large file called hugefile.tar into smaller files that fit into several high-density 3.5-inch floppy disks, use split as follows:

```
split -b 1440k hugefile.tar part.
```

This command splits the hugefile.tar file into 1440K chunks so each one can fit onto a floppy disk. The command creates files named part.aa, part.ab, part.ac, and so on.

To combine the split files back into a single file, use the `cat` command as follows:

```
cat part.?? > hugefile.tar
```

# Writing Shell Scripts

If you have ever used MS-DOS, you may remember MS-DOS batch files. These are text files with MS-DOS commands. Similarly, shell scripts are also text files with a bunch of shell commands.

If you aren't a programmer, you may feel apprehensive about programming. But shell programming can be as simple as storing a few commands in a file. Right now you can't write complex shell scripts, but you can certainly try out a simple shell script.

To try your hand at a little shell programming, type the following text at the shell prompt exactly as shown and then press Ctrl+D when you're done:

```
cd
cat > simple
#!/bin/sh
echo "This script's name is: $0"
echo Argument 1: $1
echo Argument 2: $2
```

The `cd` command changes the current directory to your home directory. Then the `cat` command displays whatever you type; in this case, I'm sending the output to a file named `simple`. After you press Ctrl+D, the `cat` command ends and you see the shell prompt again. What you have done is created a file named `simple` that contains the following shell script:

```
#!/bin/sh
echo "This script's name is: $0"
echo Argument 1: $1
echo Argument 2: $2
```

The first line causes Linux to run the Bash shell program (its name is `/bin/bash`). The shell then reads the rest of the lines in the script.

Just as most Linux commands accept command-line options, a Bash script also accepts command-line options. Inside the script, you can refer to the options as $1, $2, and so on. The special name $0 refers to the name of the script itself.

To run this shell script, first you have to make the file executable (that is, turn it into a program) with the following command:

```
chmod +x simple
```

Now run the script with the following command:

```
./simple one two
This script's name is: ./simple
Argument 1: one
Argument 2: two
```

The ./ prefix to the script's name indicates that the simple file is in the current directory.

This script simply prints the script's name and the first two command-line options that the user types after the script's name.

Next, try running the script with a few arguments, as follows:

```
./simple "This is one argument" second-argument third
This script's name is: ./simple
Argument 1: This is one argument
Argument 2: second-argument
```

The shell treats the entire string within the double quotation marks as a single argument. Otherwise the shell uses spaces as separators between arguments on the command line.

Most useful shell scripts are more complicated than this simple script, but this simple exercise gives you a rough idea of how to write shell scripts.

Place Linux commands in a file and use the chmod command to make the file executable. Voilá! You have created a shell script!

# Chapter 3: Navigating the Linux File System

## In This Chapter

✔ Understanding the Linux file system

✔ Navigating the file system with Linux commands

✔ Understanding file permissions

✔ Manipulating files and directories with Linux commands

To use files and directories well, you need to understand the concept of a hierarchical file system. Even if you use the GUI file managers to access files and folders (folders are another name for directories), you can benefit from a lay of the land of the file system.

In this chapter, I introduce you to the Linux file system. Then you discover how to work with files and directories with several Linux commands.

## Understanding the Linux File System

Like any other operating system, Linux organizes information in files and directories. Directories, in turn, hold the files. A *directory* is a special file that can contain other files and directories. Because a directory can contain other directories, this method of organizing files gives rise to a hierarchical structure. This hierarchical organization of files is called the *file system*.

The Linux file system gives you a unified view of all storage in your PC. The file system has a single root directory, indicated by a forward slash (/). Within the root directory is a hierarchy of files and directories. Parts of the file system can reside in different physical media, such as hard disk, floppy disk, and CD-ROM. Figure 3-1 illustrates the concept of the Linux file system (which is the same in any Linux system) and how it spans multiple physical devices.

If you're familiar with MS-DOS or Windows, you may find something missing in the Linux file system: You don't find drive letters in Linux. All disk drives and CD-ROM drives are part of a single file system.

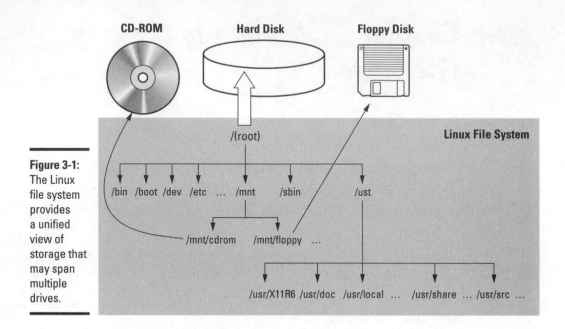

**Figure 3-1:** The Linux file system provides a unified view of storage that may span multiple drives.

In Linux, you can have long filenames (up to 256 characters), and filenames are case-sensitive. Often, these filenames have multiple extensions, such as `sample.tar.Z`. UNIX filenames can take many forms, such as the following: `index.html`, `Makefile`, `kernel-2.6.3-1.109.i386.rpm`, `.bash_profile`, and `httpd_src.tar.gz`.

To locate a file, you need more than just the file's name. You also need information about the directory hierarchy. The extended filename, showing the full hierarchy of directories leading to the file, is called the *pathname*. As the name implies, it's the path to the file through the maze of the file system. Figure 3-2 shows a typical pathname for a file in Linux.

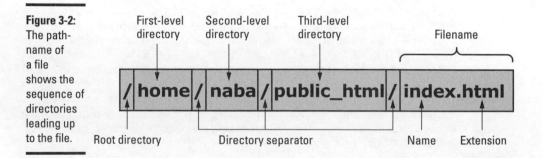

**Figure 3-2:** The pathname of a file shows the sequence of directories leading up to the file.

As Figure 3-2 shows, the pathname has the following parts:

✦ The `root` directory, indicated by a forward slash (/) character.

✦ The directory hierarchy, with each directory name separated from the previous one by a forward slash (/) character. A / appears after the last directory name.

✦ The filename, with a name and one or more optional extensions. (A period appears before each extension.)

The Linux file system has a well-defined set of top-level directories, and some of these directories have specific purposes. Finding your way around the file system is easier if you know the purpose of these directories. You'll also become adept at guessing where to look for specific types of files when you face a new situation. Table 3-1 briefly describes the top-level directories in the Linux file system.

**Book II
Chapter 3**

**Navigating the
Linux File System**

| Table 3-1 | Top-Level Directories in the Linux File System |
|---|---|
| *Directory* | *Description* |
| / | This `root` directory forms the base of the file system. All files and directories are contained logically in the `root` directory, regardless of their physical locations. |
| /bin | Contains the executable programs that are part of the Linux operating system. Many Linux commands, such as `cat`, `cp`, `ls`, `more`, and `tar`, are located in /bin. |
| /boot | Contains the Linux kernel and other files that the LILO and GRUB boot managers need (the kernel and other files can be anywhere, but placing them in the /boot directory is customary). |
| /dev | Contains special files that represent devices attached to the system. |
| /etc | Contains most system configuration files and the initialization scripts (in the /etc/rc.d subdirectory). |
| /home | Conventional location of the home directories of all users. User naba's home directory, for example, is /home/naba. |
| /lib | Contains library files for all programs stored in /sbin and /bin directories, including the loadable driver modules, needed to start Linux. |
| /lost+found | Directory for lost files. Every disk partition has a lost+found directory. |
| /mnt | A directory for temporarily mounted file systems, such as CD-ROM drives, floppy disks, and Zip drives. Contains the /mnt/floppy directory for mounting floppy disks and the /mnt/cdrom directory for mounting the CD-ROM drive. |
| /opt | Provides a storage area for large application software packages. |

*(continued)*

**Table 3-1** *(continued)*

| Directory | Description |
|---|---|
| /proc | A special directory that contains various information about the processes running in the Linux system. |
| /root | The home directory for the root user. |
| /sbin | Contains executable files representing commands typically used for system-administration tasks and used by the root user. Commands such as halt and shutdown reside in the /sbin directory. |
| /selinux | Contains information used by the Security Enhanced Linux (SELinux) kernel patch and utilities that provide a much secure access control system for Linux. |
| /sys | A special directory that contains information about the devices, as seen by the Linux kernel. |
| /tmp | Temporary directory that any user can use as a *scratch* directory, meaning that the contents of this directory are considered unimportant and usually are deleted every time the system boots. |
| /usr | Contains the subdirectories for many important programs, such as the X Window System (in the /usr/X11R6 directory), and the online manual. Table 3-2 shows some of the standard subdirectories in /usr. |
| /var | Contains various system files (such as logs), as well as directories for holding other information, such as files for the Web server and anonymous FTP server. |

The /usr and /var directories also contain a number of standard subdirectories. Table 3-2 lists the important subdirectories in /usr. Table 3-3 shows a similar breakdown for the /var directory.

**Table 3-2**  **Important /usr Subdirectories**

| Subdirectory | Description |
|---|---|
| /usr/X11R6 | Contains the X.org X11 (X Window System) software. |
| /usr/bin | Contains executable files for many more Linux commands, including utility programs commonly available in Linux, but is not part of the core Linux operating system. |
| /usr/games | Contains some old Linux games. |
| /usr/include | Contains the header files (files names ending in .h) for the C and C++ programming languages; also includes the X11 header files in the /usr/include/X11 directory and the Linux kernel header files in the /usr/include/linux directory. |
| /usr/lib | Contains the libraries for C and C++ programming languages; also contains many other libraries, such as database libraries, graphical toolkit libraries, and so on. |

| Subdirectory | Description |
|---|---|
| /usr/local | Contains local files. The /usr/local/bin directory, for example, is supposed to be the location for any executable program developed on your system. |
| /usr/sbin | Contains many administrative commands, such as commands for electronic mail and networking. |
| /usr/share | Contains shared data, such as default configuration files and images for many applications. For example, /usr/share/gnome contains various shared files for the GNOME desktop; and /usr/share/doc has the documentation files for many Linux applications (such as the Bash shell, the Sawfish window manager, and the GIMP image-processing program). |
| /usr/share/man | Contains the online manual (which you can read by using the man command). |
| /usr/src | Contains the source code for the Linux kernel (the core operating system). |

| Table 3-3 | Important /var Subdirectories |
|---|---|
| Subdirectory | Description |
| /var/cache | Storage area for cached data for applications. |
| /var/lib | Contains information relating to the current state of applications. |
| /var/lock | Contains locked files to ensure that a resource is used by one application only. |
| /var/log | Contains log files organized into subdirectories. The syslogd server stores its log files in /var/log, with the exact content of the files depending on the syslogd configuration file /etc/syslog.conf. For example, /var/log/messages is the main system log file, /var/log/secure contains log messages from secure services (such as sshd and xinetd), and /var/log/maillog contains the log of mail messages. |
| /var/mail | Contains user mailbox files. |
| /var/opt | Contains variable data for packages stored in /opt directory. |
| /var/run | Contains data describing the system since it was booted. |
| /var/spool | Contains data that's waiting for some kind of processing. |
| /var/tmp | Contains temporary files preserved between system reboots. |
| /var/yp | Contains Network Information Service (NIS) database files. |

# Navigating the File System with Linux Commands

Although GUI file managers such as Nautilus (in GNOME) or Konqueror (in KDE) are easy to use, you can use them only if you have a working GUI desktop. Sometimes, you may not have a graphical environment to run a graphical file manager. For example, you may be logged in through a text terminal, or X may not be working on your system. In those situations, you have to rely on Linux commands to work with files and directories. Of course, you can always use Linux commands, even in the graphical environment — all you have to do is open a terminal window and type the Linux commands.

In the sections that follow, I briefly show some Linux commands for moving around the Linux file system.

## Commands for directory navigation

In Linux, when you log in as `root`, your home directory is `/root`. For other users, the home directory is usually in the `/home` directory. My home directory (when I log in as `naba`) is `/home/naba`. This information is stored in the `/etc/passwd` file. By default, only you have permission to save files in your home directory, and only you can create subdirectories in your home directory to further organize your files.

Linux supports the concept of a current directory, which is the directory on which all file and directory commands operate. After you log in, for example, your current directory is the home directory. To see the current directory, type the `pwd` command.

To change the current directory, use the `cd` command. To change the current directory to `/usr/share/doc`, type the following:

```
cd /usr/share/doc
```

Then, to change the directory to the `bash-2.05b` subdirectory in `/usr/share/doc`, type this command:

```
cd bash-2.05b
```

Now, if you use the `pwd` command, that command shows `/usr/share/doc/bash-2.05b` as the current directory.

These two examples show that you can refer to a directory's name in two ways:

✦ An *absolute pathname* (such as `/usr/share/doc`) that specifies the exact directory in the directory tree

✦ A *relative directory name* (such as `bash-2.05b`, which represents the `bash-2.05b` subdirectory of the current directory, whatever that may be)

If you type `cd bash-2.05b` in `/usr/share/doc`, the current directory changes to `/usr/share/doc/bash-2.05b`. However, if I type the same command in `/home/naba`, the shell tries to change the current directory to `/home/naba/bash-2.05b`.

Use the `cd` command without any arguments to change the current directory back to your home directory. No matter where you are, typing **cd** at the shell prompt brings you back home!

By the way, the tilde character (~) refers to your home directory. Thus the command `cd ~` also changes the current directory to your home directory. You can also refer to another user's home directory by appending that user's name to the tilde. Thus, `cd ~superman` changes the current directory to the home directory of `superman`.

Wait, there's more. A single dot (.) and two dots (..) — often referred to as *dot-dot* — also have special meanings. A single dot (.) indicates the current directory, whereas two dots (..) indicate the parent directory. For example, if the current directory is `/usr/share`, you go one level up to `/usr` by typing

```
cd ..
```

## Commands for directory listings and permissions

You can get a directory listing by using the `ls` command. By default, the `ls` command — without any options — displays the contents of the current directory in a compact, multicolumn format. For example, type the next two commands to see the contents of the `/etc/X11` directory:

```
cd /etc/X11
ls
```

The output looks like this (on the console you see some items in different colors):

```
applnk   lbxproxy      starthere  xdm                      Xmodmap      xsm
dm       prefdm        sysconfig  XftConfig.README-OBSOLETE xorg.conf
fs       proxymngr     twm        xinit                    Xresources
gdm      serverconfig  X          xkb                      xserver
```

From this listing (without the colors), you cannot tell whether an entry is a file or a directory. To tell the directories and files apart, use the `-F` option with `ls` like this:

```
ls -F
```

This time the output gives you some more clues about the file types:

```
applnk/   lbxproxy/      starthere/   xdm/                    Xmodmap      xsm/
dm/       prefdm*        sysconfig/   XftConfig.README-OBSOLETE   xorg.conf
fs/       proxymngr/     twm/         xinit/                  Xresources
gdm/      serverconfig/  X@           xkb@                    xserver/
```

The output from `ls -F` shows the directory names with a slash (/) appended to them. Plain filenames appear as is. The *at sign* (@) appended to a file's name (for example, notice the file named X) indicates that this file is a link to another file (in other words, this filename simply refers to another file; it's a shortcut). An asterisk (*) is appended to executable files (see, for example, the `prefdm` file in the listing). The shell can run any executable file.

You can see even more detailed information about the files and directories with the `-l` option:

```
ls -l
```

For the `/etc/X11` directory, a typical output from `ls -l` looks like the following:

```
total 76
drwxr-xr-x  2 root root 4096 Mar 11 23:33 applnk
drwxr-xr-x  3 root root 4096 May 20 20:19 dm
drwxr-xr-x  2 root root 4096 May 20 19:58 fs
drwxr-xr-x  8 root root 4096 May 20 20:19 gdm
drwxr-xr-x  2 root root 4096 May 20 20:11 lbxproxy
-rwxr-xr-x  1 root root 1166 May  7 00:29 prefdm
drwxr-xr-x  2 root root 4096 May 20 20:11 proxymngr
drwxr-xr-x  2 root root 4096 Mar 11 23:33 serverconfig
drwxr-xr-x  2 root root 4096 May 20 19:59 starthere
drwxr-xr-x  2 root root 4096 Mar 11 23:33 sysconfig
drwxr-xr-x  2 root root 4096 May 20 20:12 twm
lrwxrwxrwx  1 root root   24 May 20 20:39 X -> ../../usr/X11R6/bin/Xorg
drwxr-xr-x  2 root root 4096 May 20 20:04 xdm
-rw-r--r--  1 root root  372 May  7 11:31 XftConfig.README-OBSOLETE
drwxr-xr-x  3 root root 4096 May  7 11:31 xinit
lrwxrwxrwx  1 root root   27 May 20 20:11 xkb -> ../../usr/X11R6/lib/X11/xkb
-rw-r--r--  1 root root  613 Mar 31 02:10 Xmodmap
-rw-r--r--  1 root root 2824 May 20 20:53 xorg.conf
-rw-r--r--  1 root root  492 Mar 31 02:10 Xresources
drwxr-xr-x  2 root root 4096 May 20 20:11 xserver
drwxr-xr-x  2 root root 4096 May 20 20:11 xsm
```

This listing shows considerable information about every directory entry — each of which can be a file or another directory. Looking at a line from the right column to the left, you see that the rightmost column shows the name of the directory entry. The date and time before the name show when the last modifications to that file were made. To the left of the date and time is the size of the file, in bytes.

The file's group and owner appear to the left of the column that shows the file size. The next number to the left indicates the number of links to the file.

(A *link* is like a shortcut in Windows.) Finally, the leftmost column shows the file's permission settings, which determine who can read, write, or execute the file.

The first letter of the leftmost column has a special meaning, as the following list shows:

✦ If the first letter is l, the file is a *symbolic link* (a shortcut) to another file.

✦ If the first letter is d, the file is a directory.

✦ If the first letter is a dash (-), the file is normal.

✦ If the first letter is b, the file represents a block device, such as a disk drive.

✦ If the first letter is c, the file represents a character device, such as a serial port or a terminal.

**Book II**
**Chapter 3**

**Navigating the**
**Linux File System**

After that first letter, the leftmost column shows a sequence of nine characters, which appear as rwxrwxrwx when each letter is present. Each letter indicates a specific permission. A hyphen (-) in place of a letter indicates no permission for a specific operation on the file. Think of these nine letters as three groups of three letters (rwx), interpreted as follows:

✦ The leftmost group of rwx controls the *read*, *write*, and *execute* permission of the file's owner. In other words, if you see rwx in this position, the file's owner can read (r), write (w), and execute (x) the file. A hyphen in the place of a letter indicates no permission. Thus the string rw- means the owner has read and write permission but no execute permission. Although executable programs (including shell programs) typically have execute permission, directories treat execute permission as equivalent to *use* permission — a user must have execute permission on a directory before he or she can open and read the contents of the directory.

✦ The middle three rwx letters control the read, write, and execute permission of any user belonging to that file's group.

✦ The rightmost group of rwx letters controls the read, write, and execute permission of all other users (collectively referred to as *the world*).

Thus, a file with the permission setting rwx------ is accessible only to the file's owner, whereas the permission setting rwxr--r-- makes the file readable by the world.

An interesting feature of the ls command is that it does not list any file whose name begins with a period. To see these files, you must use the ls command with the -a option, as follows:

```
ls -a
```

Try this command in your home directory (and then compare the result with what you see when you don't use the -a option):

1. **Type** cd **to change to your home directory.**

2. **Type** ls -F **to see the files and directories in your home directory.**

3. **Type** ls -aF **to see everything, including the hidden files.**

Most Linux commands take single-character options, each with a minus sign (think of this sign as a hyphen) as a prefix. When you want to use several options, type a hyphen and *concatenate* (string together) the option letters, one after another. Thus, ls -al is equivalent to ls -a -l as well as ls -l -a.

## Commands for changing permissions and ownerships

You may need to change a file's permission settings to protect it from others. Use the chmod command to change the permission settings of a file or a directory.

To use chmod effectively, you have to specify the permission settings. A good way is to concatenate letters from the columns of Table 3-4 in the order shown (Who/Action/Permission).

*Note:* You use only the single character from each column — the text in parentheses is for explanation only.

| Table 3-4 | Letter Codes for File Permissions | |
|-----------|-----------------|------------|
| *Who* | *Action* | *Permission* |
| u (user) | + (add) | r (read) |
| g (group) | - (remove) | w (write) |
| o (others) | = (assign) | x (execute) |
| a (all) | s (set user ID) | |

For example, to give everyone read access to all files in a directory, pick a (for *all*) from the first column, + (for *add*) from the second column, and r (for *read*) from the third column to come up with the permission setting a+r. Then use the whole set of options with chmod, like this:

chmod a+r *.

On the other hand, to permit everyone to execute one specific file, type

chmod a+x *filename*

Suppose you have a file named `mystuff` that you want to protect. You can make it accessible to no one but you if you type the following commands, in this order:

```
chmod a-rwx mystuff
chmod u+rw mystuff
```

The first command turns off all permissions for everyone, and the second command turns *on* the read and write permissions for the owner (you). Type `ls -l` to verify that the change took place (you see a permission setting of `-rw-------`). Here's a sample output from `ls -l`:

```
-rw-------   1 naba     naba     3 Jun 30 18:45 mystuff
```

*Note:* The third and fourth fields show `naba  naba`. These two fields show the file's user and group ownership. In this case, the name of the user is `naba` and the name of the group is `naba` as well (because Linux creates a group for each user).

Sometimes you have to change a file's user or group ownership for everything to work correctly. For example, suppose you are instructed (by a manual, what else?) to create a directory named `cups` and give it the ownership of user ID `lp` and group ID `sys`. How do you it?

Well, you can log in as `root` and create the directory with the command `mkdir`:

```
mkdir cups
```

If you check the file's details with the `ls -l` command, you see that the user and group ownership is `root root`.

To change the owner, use the `chown` command. For example, to change the ownership of the `cups` directory to user ID `lp` and group ID `sys`, type

```
chown lp.sys cups
```

## Commands for working with files

To copy files from one directory to another, use the `cp` command. For example, to copy the file `/usr/X11R6/lib/X11/xinit/Xclients` to the `Xclients.sample` file in the current directory (such as your home directory), type the following:

```
cp /usr/X11R6/lib/X11/xinit/Xclients Xclients.sample
```

If you want to copy a file to the current directory but retain the original name, use a period (`.`) as the second argument of the `cp` command. Thus,

**Book II**
**Chapter 3**

**Navigating the**
**Linux File System**

the following command copies the `xorg.conf` file from the `/etc/X11` directory to the current directory (denoted by a single period):

```
cp /etc/X11/xorg.conf .
```

The `cp` command makes a new copy of a file and leaves the original intact.

If you want to copy the entire contents of a directory — including all subdirectories and their contents — to another directory, use the command `cp -ar` *sourcedir destdir* (this command copies everything in *sourcedir* directory to *destdir*). For example, to copy all files from the `/etc/X11` directory to the current directory, type the following command:

```
cp -ar /etc/X11 .
```

To move a file to a new location, use the `mv` command. The original copy is gone, and a new copy appears at the destination. You can use `mv` to rename a file. If you want to change the name of `today.list` to `old.list`, use the `mv` command, as follows:

```
mv today.list old.list
```

On the other hand, if you want to move the `today.list` file to a subdirectory named `saved`, use this command:

```
mv today.list saved
```

An interesting feature of `mv` is that you can use it to move entire directories — with all their subdirectories and files — to a new location. If you have a directory named `data` that contains many files and subdirectories, you can move that entire directory structure to `old_data` by using the following command:

```
mv data old_data
```

To delete files, use the `rm` command. For example, to delete a file named `old.list`, type the following command:

```
rm old.list
```

Be careful with the `rm` command — especially when you log in as `root`. You can inadvertently delete important files with `rm` easily.

## Commands for working with directories

To organize files in your home directory, you have to create new directories. Use the `mkdir` command to create a directory. For example, to create a directory named `images` in the current directory, type the following:

```
mkdir images
```

After you create the directory, you can use the `cd images` command to change to that directory.

You can create an entire directory tree by using the `-p` option with the `mkdir` command. For example, suppose your system has a `/usr/src` directory and you want to create the directory tree `/usr/src/book/java/examples/applets`. To create this directory hierarchy, type the following command:

```
mkdir -p /usr/src/book/java/examples/applets
```

When you no longer need a directory, use the `rmdir` command to delete it.

You can delete a directory only when the directory is empty.

To remove an empty directory tree, you can use the `-p` option, like this:

```
rmdir -p /usr/src/book/java/examples/applets
```

This command removes the empty parent directories of `applets`. The command stops when it encounters a directory that's not empty.

## Commands for finding files

The `find` command is very useful for locating files (and directories) that meet your search criteria.

When I began using UNIX many years ago (Berkeley UNIX in the early 1980s), I was confounded by the `find` command. I stayed with one basic syntax of `find` for a long time before graduating to more complex forms. The basic syntax I learned first was for finding a file anywhere in the file system. Here's how it goes: Suppose you want to find any file or directory with a name that starts with `gnome`. Type the following `find` command to find these files:

```
find / -name "gnome*" -print
```

If you're not logged in as `root`, you may get a bunch of error messages. If these error messages annoy you, just modify the command as follows and the error messages are history (or, as UNIX aficionados say, *send 'em to the bit bucket*):

```
find / -name "gnome*" -print 2> /dev/null
```

This command tells `find` to start looking at the root directory (/), to look for filenames that match `gnome*`, and to display the full pathname of any

**Book II
Chapter 3**

**Navigating the
Linux File System**

matching file. The last part (`2> /dev/null`) simply sends the error messages to a special file that's the equivalent of simply ignoring them.

You can use variations of this simple form of `find` to locate a file in any directory (as well as any subdirectories contained in the directory). If you forget where in your home directory you have stored all files named `report*` (names that start with `report`), you can search for the files by using the following command:

```
find ~ -name "report*" -print
```

When you become comfortable with this syntax of `find`, you can use other options of `find`. For example, to find only specific types of files (such as directories), use the `type` option. The following command displays all top-level directory names in your Linux system:

```
find / -type d -maxdepth 1 -print
```

You probably don't have to use the complex forms of `find` in a typical Linux system — but if you ever need to, you can look up the rest of the `find` options by using the following command:

```
man find
```

An easy way to find all files that match a name is to use the `locate` command that searches a periodically updated database of files on your system. For example, here's what I get when I type **locate xorg.conf** on my system:

```
/usr/X11R6/man/man5/xorg.conf.5x.gz
/xorg.conf.new
/etc/X11/xorg.conf
```

## Commands for mounting and unmounting

Suppose you want to access the files on this book's companion DVD-ROM when you are logged in at a text console (with no GUI to help you). To do so, you have to first mount the DVD-ROM drive's file system on a specific directory in the Linux file system.

By the way, the procedure I am about to describe works for CDs as well as DVDs.

Log in as `root` (or type `su -` to become `root`), insert the DVD-ROM in the DVD drive, and then type the following command:

```
mount /dev/cdrom /mnt/cdrom
```

This command mounts the file system on the device named `/dev/cdrom` (the DVD/CD-ROM) on the `/mnt/cdrom` directory (which is also called the *mount point*) in the Linux file system.

After the `mount` command successfully completes its task, you can access the files on the DVD-ROM by referring to the `/mnt/cdrom` directory as the top-level directory of the disc. In other words, to see the contents of the DVD-ROM, type

```
ls -F /mnt/cdrom
```

When you're done using the DVD-ROM — and before you eject it from the drive — you have to "unmount" the disc drive with the following `umount` command:

```
umount /dev/cdrom
```

Mounting devices on directories in the `/mnt` directory is customary. Linux comes with the two predefined directories: `/mnt/cdrom` for mounting the DVD/CD-ROM and `/mnt/floppy` for mounting the floppy drive.

Book II
Chapter 3

Navigating the
Linux File System

## Commands for checking disk-space usage

I want to tell you about two commands — `df` and `du` — that you can use to check the disk-space usage on your system. These commands are simple to use. The `df` command shows you a summary of disk-space usage for all mounted devices, as shown in this example:

```
df
Filesystem          1K-blocks      Used Available Use% Mounted on
/dev/hda5            7392428    3855112   3161800  55% /
/dev/hda3             101105      15760     80124  17% /boot
none                  127880          0    127880   0% /dev/shm
/dev/cdrom            658144     658144         0 100% /mnt/cdrom
```

The output is a table that shows the device, the total kilobytes of storage, how much is in use, how much is available, the percentage being used, and the mount point.

To see the output of `df` in a more human-readable format, type `df -h`. Here is the output of the `df -h` command:

```
Filesystem          Size  Used Avail Use% Mounted on
/dev/hda5           7.1G  3.7G  3.1G  55% /
/dev/hda3            99M   16M   79M  17% /boot
none                125M     0  125M   0% /dev/shm
/dev/cdrom          643M  643M     0 100% /mnt/cdrom
```

If you compare this output with the output of plain df (see previous listing), you see that df -h prints the sizes with terms like M for megabytes and G for gigabytes. These are clearly easier to understand than 1K-blocks.

The other command — du — is useful for finding out how much space a directory takes up. For example, type the following command to view the contents of all the directories in the /etc/rc.d directory (this directory contains system startup files):

```
du /etc/rc.d
4       /etc/rc.d/rc1.d
4       /etc/rc.d/rc0.d
4       /etc/rc.d/rc5.d
4       /etc/rc.d/rc3.d
4       /etc/rc.d/rc4.d
4       /etc/rc.d/rc2.d
308     /etc/rc.d/init.d
4       /etc/rc.d/rc6.d
372     /etc/rc.d
```

Each directory name is preceded by a number — which tells you the number of kilobytes of disk space used by that directory. Thus the /etc/rc.d directory, as a whole, uses 372K disk space whereas the /etc/rc.d/init.d sub-directory uses 308K. If you simply want the total disk space used by a directory (including all the files and subdirectories contained in that directory), use the -s option, as follows:

```
du -s /etc/rc.d
372     /etc/rc.d
```

The -s option causes du to print just the summary information for the /etc/rc.d directory.

Just as df -h prints the disk-space information in megabytes and gigabytes, you can use the du -h command to view the output of du in more human-readable form. For example, here's how I combine it with the -s option to see the space I'm using in my home directory (/home/naba):

```
du -sh /home/naba
29M     /home/naba
```

# Chapter 4: Exploring Fedora Core Applications

## In This Chapter

✓ **Taking stock of Fedora Core applications**

✓ **Exploring office applications**

✓ **Setting up databases**

✓ **Playing with multimedia**

✓ **Working with images**

Fedora Core comes with a whole lot of applications. All you have to do is look at the menus in GNOME or KDE and you'll see what I mean. Often, there is more than one application of each type. Both GNOME and KDE come with the OpenOffice.org office application suite with a word processor, spreadsheet, presentation software, and more. You find many choices for CD players and multimedia players, not to mention the games, utility programs, and useful tools, such as a scanner and digital camera applications.

I give you an overview of some of these applications and briefly show you some interesting and useful applications. After you know about these applications, you can try them out when you need them.

## Taking Stock of the Fedora Core Applications

Table 4-1 shows a sampling of major Fedora Core applications, organized by category. For the major applications, I also show a relevant Web site where you can get more information about that application. This list is by no means comprehensive. Fedora Core distribution comes with many more applications and utilities than the ones I show in this table.

If your system has both GNOME and KDE installed, most of these applications are already available from either GUI desktop.

I briefly introduce some of the applications from Table 4-1, selecting one or two from each category. I describe the Internet applications in Book V.

| Table 4-1 | A Sampling of Fedora Core Applications |
| --- | --- |
| *Application* | *Description* |
| ***Office Applications*** | |
| OpenOffice.org Writer | A word-processing program similar to Microsoft Word (`www.openoffice.org`) |
| OpenOffice.org Calc | A spreadsheet program similar to Microsoft Excel (`www.openoffice.org`) |
| OpenOffice.org Impress | A presentation application similar to Microsoft PowerPoint (`www.openoffice.org`) |
| OpenOffice.org Draw | A drawing program (`www.openoffice.org`) |
| OpenOffice.org Math | An equation editor for writing mathematical equations, which you can then include in OpenOffice.org Writer documents (`www.openoffice.org`) |
| Dia | A drawing program, designed to be like the Windows application called Visio (`www.gnome.org/gnome-office/dia.shtml`) |
| ***Office Tools*** | |
| GNOME Calculator | A simple calculator |
| Kcalc | A calculator (part of KDE) |
| Aspell | A text-mode spell checker (`aspell.sourceforge.net`) |
| Dictionary | A graphical client for the dict.org dictionary server so you can look up words |
| ***Database*** | |
| PostgreSQL | A sophisticated object-relational database-management system that supports Structured Query Language (SQL) (`www.pgsql.com`) |
| MySQL | A popular relational database-management system that supports SQL (`www.mysql.com`) |
| ***Multimedia*** | |
| GNOME CD Player | An audio CD player (needs a working sound card) |
| KsCD | Audio CD player from KDE (needs a working sound card) |
| Rhythmbox | A multimedia audio player that can play several different sound formats (`rhythmbox.sourceforge.net`) — including MP3 files if you download a plugin for the purpose |
| XMMS | X Multimedia System — a multimedia audio player that can play many different sound formats (`www.xmms.org`) — including MP3 files if you download a plugin for the purpose (XMMS is not installed by default, but you can install it easily from the companion DVD) |

| Application | Description |
|---|---|
| *Multimedia* | |
| Cdrecord | A command-line application that can burn audio and data CD-R as well as DVD-R (`www.fokus.gmd.de/research/cc/glone/employees/joerg.schilling/private/cdrccord.html`) |
| X-CD-Roast | A GUI front end for `cdrecord` and `cdrdao` that makes burning data and audio CDs easy (`www.xcdroast.org`) |
| Gtkam | A digital camera application that works with over 150 digital cameras (`gphoto.sourceforge.net/proj/gtkam/`) |
| *Graphics and Imaging* | |
| The GIMP | The GNU Image Manipulation Program, an application suitable for tasks such as photo retouching, image composition, and image authoring (`www.gimp.org`) |
| GQView | A powerful image viewer (`gqview.sourceforge.net`) |
| Kview | A simple image viewer for KDE |
| GGV | Gnome Ghostview (GGV) is a PostScript document viewer (`www.gnu.org/directory/print/misc/ggv.html`) |
| Xsane | A graphical front end for accessing scanners with the SANE (Scanner Access Now Easy) library (`www.xsane.org`) |
| Ksnapshot | A screen-capture program |
| *Internet* | |
| Ximian Evolution | A personal information management application that integrates e-mail, calendar, contact management, and online task lists (`www.ximian.com/products/ximian_evolution`) |
| GFTP | An FTP client for downloading files from the Internet |
| Gaim | An AOL Instant Messenger client (`gaim.sourceforge.net`) |
| Mozilla | A well-known open-source Web browser that started with source code from Netscape (`www.mozilla.org`) |
| Kmail | An e-mail client for KDE (`kmail.kde.org`) |

# Office Applications and Tools

Word processor, spreadsheet, presentation software, calendar, calculator — these are some of the staples of the office. Both GNOME and KDE come with the OpenOffice.org (often shortened as *OO.o* or *Ooo*) suite of office applications and tools. You can try out all of them one by one and see which one takes your fancy. Each application is fairly intuitive to use. Even though some nuances of the user interface may be new to you, you can learn it after using it a few times. I briefly introduce a few of the following applications in this section:

✦ **OpenOffice.org Writer:** A Microsoft Word-like word processor

✦ **OpenOffice.org Calc:** A Microsoft Excel-like spreadsheet program

✦ **OpenOffice.org Impress:** A Microsoft PowerPoint-like presentation program

✦ **OpenOffice.org Draw:** A drawing and illustration application

✦ **OpenOffice.org Math:** A mathematical formula editor

✦ **Calculators:** GNOME calculator and KDE calculator

✦ **aspell:** Spelling checker

✦ **Commercially available office applications for Linux**

I cover the OpenOffice.org applications in separate chapters in Book III. Turn to that book to find out more about Writer, Calc, Impress, Draw, and Math.

## Calculators

You have a choice of the GNOME calculator or the KDE calculator. Both are scientific calculators, and you can do the typical scientific calculations, such as square root and inverse, as well as trigonometric functions, such as sine, cosine, and tangent.

To run the GNOME calculator, select Main Menu⇨Accessories⇨Calculator from the GNOME desktop. Figure 4-1 shows the GNOME calculator in its default view.

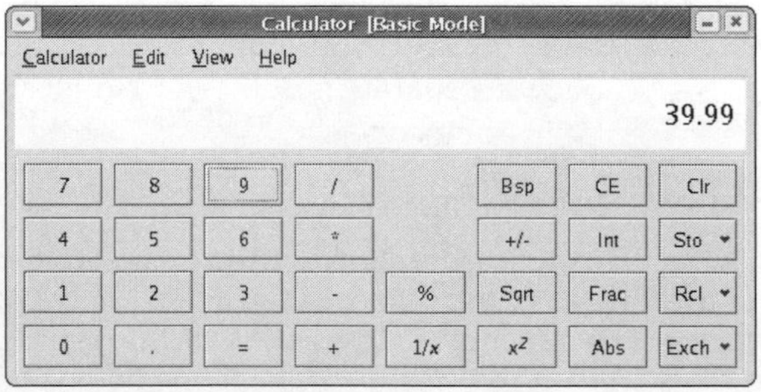

**Figure 4-1:**
Do your
calculations
in the
GNOME
calculator.

The GNOME calculator has three modes. By default, the calculator displays the Basic mode for typical calculations. The other two modes are Financial and Scientific. You can switch the mode from the View menu. For example, select View⇨Financial Mode to get a calculator capable of financial calculations, such as loan payment rates for a given principal, interest rate, and number of payments.

From the KDE desktop, you can start the KDE calculator by selecting Main Menu⇨Utilities⇨KCalc.

## Commercially available office applications for Linux

Because office applications are important to many businesses as well as individuals, I want to briefly mention some of the commercial office applications available for Fedora Core. These commercial offerings include Anyware Office (formerly Applixware Office) and StarOffice. These products do cost some money, but the cost is usually less than that for Microsoft Office — the leading office application suite for Windows. (In case you don't know, Microsoft Office is a collection of several applications: Microsoft Word for word processing; Microsoft Excel for spreadsheets; Microsoft PowerPoint for presentation graphics; and Microsoft Access for databases.)

Another recent commercial product for Linux is CrossOver Office from CodeWeavers. With CrossOver Office, you can run your existing Microsoft Office applications such as Word, Excel, and PowerPoint under Linux and X Window System.

This book's companion DVD-ROMs do not include any of these commercial office applications for Fedora Core, but I briefly describe them in the next few sections. You can visit each vendor's Web site for more about the products.

### Anyware Office

Anyware Office, formerly known as Applixware Office, is another prominent office application suite for all Linux distributions, including Fedora Core. In April 2000, Applix, Inc., formed a separate group — VistaSource, Inc. — that focuses solely on Linux applications.

Like other office suites, Anyware Office includes Words (for word processing), Spreadsheets (for spreadsheets), Graphics, and Presents (for presentation graphics). In addition, it also has Mail (an e-mail interface) and Data (an interactive relational database-browsing tool). Anyware Office can also read and write documents in Microsoft Office and Corel WordPerfect formats, as well as in several other file formats. Although trial versions are not offered, the entire Anyware Office suite is currently priced at less than $100 in the United States.

You can find out more about Applixware at the VistaSource Web site (www.vistasource.com/products).

### StarOffice

StarOffice is another commercial office applications suite; it was created by StarDivision of Hamburg, Germany, and recently purchased by Sun Microsystems. StarOffice is a cross-platform solution — it runs on Linux, Windows 95/98/Me/NT/2000/XP, Sun Solaris SPARC, and Sun Solaris x86. Also, StarOffice is available in several languages: English, French, German, Spanish, Italian, and Swedish.

StarOffice is unique in that it combines all its components into a common desktop from which you can open new documents, drag and drop documents from one application to another, and access the Internet. Here's what StarOffice 6.0 includes:

✦ StarOffice Writer for word processing (Microsoft Word-compatible)

✦ StarOffice Calc for spreadsheets (Microsoft Excel-compatible)

✦ StarOffice Impress for presentations (Microsoft PowerPoint-compatible)

✦ StarOffice Draw for vector graphics drawing

✦ StarOffice Base for data management

You can buy a copy of StarOffice or find the details of Sun's StarOffice licensing policy from www.sun.com/staroffice.

In October 2000, Sun released the source code of StarOffice under open-source licenses. OpenOffice.org, an open-source project that Sun supports, released the OpenOffice.org 1.0 office productivity suite in May 2002. Fedora Core comes with OpenOffice.org 1.1. To find out more about OpenOffice.org, consult Book III but also visit www.openoffice.org.

### CrossOver Office

Chances are better than good that you have Windows and Microsoft Office installed on your PC. When you decide to run Fedora Core on the PC, you can continue to run most Microsoft Office applications from the GNOME or KDE desktop. The convenience of running Microsoft Office in Linux comes from a commercial product called CrossOver Office.

CrossOver Office, from CodeWeavers, is a software package that enables you to install your Microsoft Office applications (only Office 97 or Office 2000, not Office XP) in Linux. You don't need Microsoft Windows to run the Office applications in CrossOver Office. You simply install CrossOver Office and then install Microsoft Office from the CD-ROM. After you install Microsoft Office, the Office applications are available directly from the GNOME or KDE desktop.

CrossOver Office uses Wine — an open-source implementation of the Windows Win32 and Win16 application programming interfaces (APIs) using the X Window System and designed to run in UNIX and Linux systems. Wine includes the Wine loader and WineLib. Wine loader can load and run Windows applications. WineLib is used for compiling and linking Windows applications in Linux. Wine is available free of charge from www.winehq.com.

CodeWeavers created CrossOver Office using a customized version of Wine so as to make sure that the Microsoft Office applications, especially Microsoft Word, Excel, and PowerPoint (from Office 97 or Office 2000) run properly on Wine. CodeWeavers charges a nominal amount for CrossOver Office — the list price is $54.95 for a single copy (with lower costs for multiple copies) — but all changes to Wine are returned to the Wine project. Thus, the Wine open-source project benefits from the sale of CrossOver Office.

You can find out more about CrossOver Office and purchase it at the CodeWeavers Web site (www.codeweavers.com/products/office/).

## aspell spelling checker

The aspell utility is an interactive spelling checker. You can use it to check the spelling of words in a text file. To do so, simply type the following command in a terminal window:

```
aspell check filename
```

If you want to try out aspell, type some notes and save them in a text file named notes.txt (the filename can be anything, but I use this filename in this section). To run the spelling checker on that file, type the following command in a terminal window:

```
aspell check notes.txt
This note describes the *concensus* reached during the August
    16 meeting.
1) consensus                        6) consensual
2) con census                       7) consciences
3) con-census                       8) incenses
4) condenses                        9) consensus's
5) concerns                         0) consensuses
i) Ignore                           I) Ignore all
r) Replace                          R) Replace all
a) Add                              x) Exit
?
```

Everything from the second line on is what aspell displays. When aspell finds a misspelled word (any word that does not appear in its dictionary), it displays the sentence with the misspelled word (concensus) and highlights that word by enclosing it in a pair of asterisks. Below that sentence, aspell lists possible corrections, numbering them sequentially from 1. In this case, aspell lists consensus — the right choice — as the first correction for concensus.

After the sentence, aspell displays a list of 16 options — 10 numbered 0 through 9 and 6 labeled with single letters i, r, a, I, R, and x — followed by a question mark prompt. You have to press one of the numbers or letters from the list shown in the output to indicate what you want aspell to do. The numbered options show 10 possible replacement words for the misspelled word. Here are the meanings of the letter options:

✦ Space means accept the word this time.

✦ i means ignore the misspelled word.

✦ I means ignore all occurrences of the word.

✦ r means replace this occurrence (you have to type a replacement word).

✦ R means replace all occurrences (you have to type a replacement word).

✦ a means accept the word and add it to the your private dictionary.

✦ x means save the rest of the file and exit, ignoring misspellings.

These options are case sensitive. Make sure you don't have Caps Lock engaged.

# Databases

Fedora Core comes with two relational databases — PostgreSQL and MySQL. I briefly show you how to use PostgreSQL.

PostgreSQL (pronounced *Post Gres Que Ell*), is a powerful and popular *relational database* (the type of database that works as a collection of connected tables). You can use the Structured Query Language (SQL) to work with the database.

PostgreSQL is developed by a team of developers and distributed under the BSD (Berkeley System Development) open-source license. The license has no restrictions on how the PostgreSQL source code may be used. To keep up with the latest PostgreSQL developments, visit www.PostgreSQL.org.

To check whether PostgreSQL is installed on your system, type **rpm -qa postgresql***. You see a list of at least three RPMs — postgresql, postgresql-libs, and postgresql-server. If a message informs you that the packages are not installed, you can install them from this book's companion DVD using these steps:

*1.* **Log in as** root **and insert the DVD into the DVD drive.**

   If you are using GNOME or KDE, the DVD mounts automatically. If not, type the following command in a terminal window to mount the DVD:

   ```
   mount /mnt/cdrom
   If you have a primary CD-ROM drive and you added a
       second DVD/CD drive, type mount /mnt/cdrom1 to mount
       the DVD.
   ```

*2.* **Type the following commands to install PostgreSQL:**

   ```
   cd /mnt/cdrom/Fedora/RPMS
   rpm -ivh postgresql*
   ```

   The packages you need to use PostgreSQL install on your system.

To use PostgreSQL, you have to first log in as root and start the database server with the following command:

```
service postgresql start
```

The PostgreSQL server process starts, called postmaster. The server is a daemon (a background process that runs continuously) that accepts database queries from client processes and performs database tasks (such as adding tables) on behalf of clients.

If you want the PostgreSQL database server to start whenever your system starts, type the following command to turn it on:

```
chkconfig postgresql on
```

Now you have to design a database, create that database in PostgreSQL, and load it with the data. To illustrate how to create and load a database, I set up a simple book catalog database.

## Adding a database user

PostgreSQL has its own concept of users, separate from the Linux user accounts. To enable a user to access PostgreSQL databases on your system, you have to add that username as a PostgreSQL user.

To add a PostgreSQL user, follow these steps:

1. **Log in as** `root`. **Then type the following command in a terminal window:**

   ```
   su - postgres
   ```

   You log in as `postgres` — the username under which the PostgreSQL database server runs. You have to perform PostgreSQL administrative tasks under this username.

2. **Type the following command in a terminal window:**

   ```
   createuser
   ```

   This utility program enables you to add PostgreSQL users. The program prompts for a username to add:

   ```
   Enter name of user to add:
   ```

3. **Type the Linux username of the user to whom you are giving database privileges.**

   For example, to add myself as a user, I type my Linux username `naba`.

4. **Answer the next two prompts:**

   ```
   Shall the new user be allowed to create databases?
     (y/n)
   Shall the new user be allowed to create more new users?
     (y/n)
   ```

   Typically, you don't want a user to create databases or add new users, so you press N to these prompts.

You can use this procedure to run `createuser` and add as many database users as you need.

## Reviewing the steps to build the database

Follow this basic sequence of steps to build a database:

1. **Design the database.**

   This step involves defining the tables and attributes that will be used to store the information.

2. **Create an empty database.**

   Before you can add tables, database systems require you to build an empty database.

3. **Create the tables in the database.**

   In this step, you define the tables using the CREATE TABLE statement of SQL.

4. **Load the tables with any fixed data.**

   For example, if you have a table of manufacturer names or publisher names (in the case of books), you want to load that table with information that's already known.

5. **Back up the initial database.**

   This step is necessary to ensure that you can create the database from scratch, if necessary.

6. **Load the data into tables.**

   You may either load data from an earlier dump of the database or interactively through forms.

7. **Use the database.**

   Make queries, update records, or insert new records using SQL commands.

## Designing the database

My simple example doesn't follow all the possible steps of database building. For the example, the database-design step is trivial because my book-catalog database includes only a single table. The attributes of that table are as follows:

+ Book title with up to 50 characters

+ Name of first author with up to 20 characters

+ Name of second author (if any) with up to 20 characters

+ Name of publisher with up to 30 characters

+ Page count as a number

+ Year published as a number (such as 2002)

+ International Standard Book Number (ISBN), as a 10-character text (such as 0764567934)

I store the ISBN without the dashes embedded in a typical book's ISBN. I also use the ISBN as the primary key of the table because the ISBN is a worldwide identification system for books. That means each book entry must have a unique ISBN, which is true for books.

## Creating an empty database

To create the empty database in PostgreSQL, use the `createdb` command. You have to log in as `root` and then become the postgres user to run the `createdb` program. Type the following commands in a terminal window to assume the `postgres` username:

```
su -
(Enter the root password at the prompt)
su - postgres
```

After becoming postgres, you can create the database. For example, to create an empty database named `books`, which the database user `naba` owns, I type the following commands:

```
createdb -O naba books
```

When you no longer need a database, run the `dropdb` command under the `postgres` username to remove the database. To learn more about the `createdb` and `dropdb` commands, type the following commands:

```
man createdb
man dropdb
```

## Using the PostgreSQL interactive terminal

After you create the empty database, all of your interactions with the database are through the `psql` program — the PostgreSQL interactive terminal that acts as a client to the database server. You have to run `psql` with the name of a database as an argument. The `psql` program then prompts you for input. Here is an example (the first line is what you type):

```
psql books
Welcome to psql 7.4, the PostgreSQL interactive terminal.

Type:  \copyright for distribution terms
       \h for help with SQL commands
       \? for help on internal slash commands
       \g or terminate with semicolon to execute query
       \q to quit

books=>
```

When creating tables or loading data into tables, a typical approach is to place the SQL statements (along with `psql` commands such as `\g`) in a file and then run `psql` with the standard input directed from that file. For example, suppose a file named `sample.sql` contains some SQL commands that you want to try out on a database named `books`. Then, you run `psql` with the following command:

```
psql books < sample.sql
```

I use `psql` in this manner to create a database table.

## Defining a table

To create a table named `books`, I edited a text file named `makedb.sql` and placed the following line in that file:

```
/*
 * Table structure for table 'books'
 */
CREATE TABLE books (
  isbn CHAR(10) NOT NULL PRIMARY KEY,
  title CHAR(80),
  author1 CHAR(20),
  author2 CHAR(20),
  pubname CHAR(30),
  pubyear INT,
  pagecount INT
) \g
```

`CREATE TABLE books` is an SQL statement to create the table named `books`. The `\g` at the end of the statement is a `psql` command. The attributes of the table appear in the lines enclosed in parentheses.

If a table contains fixed data, you can also include other SQL statements (such as `INSERT INTO`) to load the data into the table right after the table is created.

To execute the SQL statements in the `makedb.sql` file that creates the `books` table, I run `psql` as follows:

```
psql books < makedb.sql
```

Now the `books` database includes a table named `books`. (Okay, maybe I should have named them differently, but calling them by the same name seemed convenient.) I can now begin loading data into the table.

**Book II
Chapter 4**

Exploring Fedora
Core Applications

## *Inserting records into a table*

One way to load data into the table is to prepare SQL statements in another file and then run `psql` with that file as input. For example, suppose I want to add the following book information into the `books` table:

```
isbn = '0764541331'
title = 'Red Hat Linux 9 Professional Secrets'
author1 = 'Naba Barkakati'
author2 = NULL
pubname = 'Wiley Publishing, Inc.'
pubyear = 2003
pagecount = 1070
```

Then, the following SQL statement loads this information into the `books` table:

```
INSERT INTO books VALUES
('0764541331', 'Red Hat Linux 9 Professional Secrets',
'Naba Barkakati', NULL,
'Wiley Publishing, Inc.', 2003, 1070) \g
```

On the other hand, suppose you have the various fields available in a different order (than the order in which the table's attributes are defined by the `CREATE TABLE` statement). In that case, you can use a different form of the `INSERT INTO` command to add the row, as shown in the following example:

```
INSERT INTO books (pubyear, author1, author2, title,
    pagecount, pubname, isbn) values
(1996, 'Naba Barkakati', NULL, 'Linux SECRETS', 900, 'IDG
    Books Worldwide', '156884798X')\g
```

Essentially, you have to specify the list of attributes as well as the values and make sure that the order of the attributes matches that of the values.

If I save all `INSERT INTO` commands in a file named `additems.sql`, I can load the database from the `psql` command line by using the `\i` command like this (type **psql books** to start the PostgreSQL client):

```
books=> \i additems.sql
```

## *Querying the database*

You can query the database interactively through the `psql` interactive program. (Of course, you do have to know SQL to do this operation.) For example, to query the `books` database, I start the SQL client with the following command:

```
psql books
```

Then I type SQL commands at the `psql` prompt to look up items from the database. When done, I type **\q** to exit the `psql` program. Here's an example (the bold text is what I typed in a terminal window):

```
books=> select isbn, title from books where pubyear > 2002 \g
    isbn      |                          title
------------+--------------------------------------------------------
 0764542583 | Red Hat Linux Fedora All-in-One Desk Reference For Dummies
 0764541331 | Red Hat Linux 9 Professional Secrets
(2 rows)
books=> \q
```

To find out more about administering and using PostgreSQL, visit www. postgresql.org/docs/ and look for links to the latest version of online PostgreSQL documentation.

**Book II
Chapter 4**

**Exploring Fedora
Core Applications**

# Multimedia Applications

Fedora Core includes quite a few multimedia applications — mostly multimedia audio players and CD players, but also applications for using digital cameras and burning CD-ROMs. To play some other multimedia files (such as MPEG video), you have to download and install additional software in your Fedora Core system. Here's a quick sketch of a few typical multimedia tasks and the applications you can use to perform these tasks:

✦ **Using digital cameras:** Use the Digital Camera tool to download photos from your digital camera in Fedora Core.

✦ **Playing audio CDs:** Use one of many audio CD players that come with Fedora Core.

✦ **Playing sound files:** Use Rhythmbox or XMMS, multimedia audio players (you have to download some additional software to play MP3 files with Rhythmbox or XMMS). You can also download other players from the Internet.

✦ **Burning a CD:** Use X-CD-Roast to burn CDs.

## Using a digital camera

Fedora Core comes with gtkam — a digital-camera application you can use to download pictures from digital cameras. gtkam is a GUI front end to the gPhoto2 command-line application that works with many different makes and models of digital cameras. Depending on the model, the cameras can connect to the serial port or the Universal Serial Bus (USB) port. Visit the gPhoto Web site (`www.gphoto.org/proj/libgphoto2/support.php`) for the latest list of supported cameras.

To use gtkam with your digital camera, follow these steps:

*1.* **Connect your digital camera to the serial port or USB port (whichever interface the camera supports) and turn the camera on.**

*2.* **Choose Main Menu⇨Graphics⇨Digital Camera Tool to start gtkam.**

*3.* **From the gtkam menu, choose Camera⇨Add Camera.**

*4.* **In the dialog box that appears, click Detect.**

If your camera is supported, the camera is detected. If not, you can try an alternate method that I describe at the end of these steps.

gtkam displays a camera icon and the camera name on the left panel.

*5.* **Double-click the camera icon to download and view thumbnail pictures in the right panel.**

*6.* **Click the thumbnails to select the images you want to download; then choose File⇨Save or click the Save button on the toolbar.**

gtkam then downloads the images and places each image in a separate file in your home directory. You can now edit the photos in the GIMP or your favorite photo editor.

 Don't despair if gtkam does not recognize your digital camera. You can still access the digital camera's storage media (compact flash card, for example) as a USB mass storage device, provided your camera supports USB Mass Storage. To access the images on your USB digital camera, follow these steps:

*1.* **Read the camera manual and use the menu options of the camera to set the USB mode to Mass Storage.**

If the camera does not support USB Mass Storage, you cannot use this procedure to access the photos.

*2.* **Connect your digital camera to the USB port using the cable that came with the camera and turn the camera on.**

This causes Linux to detect the camera, create the `/mnt/camera` directory, and add a line to the `/etc/fstab` file so that you can easily mount the camera's storage media on the `/mnt/camera` directory.

*3.* **To see if the camera was detected, type the following command in a terminal window:**

```
cat /proc/bus/usb/devices
```

The output shows your camera as a mass storage device. For example, I get the following output when I connect my Nikon Coolpix 2500 as a USB mass storage device:

```
T:  Bus=01 Lev=00 Prnt=00 Port=00 Cnt=00 Dev#=  1 Spd=12  MxCh= 2
B:  Alloc=  0/900 us ( 0%), #Int=  0, #Iso=  0
D:  Ver= 1.00 Cls=09(hub ) Sub=00 Prot=00 MxPS= 8 #Cfgs=  1
P:  Vendor=0000 ProdID=0000 Rev- 0.00
S:  Product=USB UHCI Root Hub
S:  SerialNumber=fcc0
C:* #Ifs= 1 Cfg#= 1 Atr=40 MxPwr=  0mA
I:  If#= 0 Alt= 0 #EPs= 1 Cls=09(hub ) Sub=00 Prot=00 Driver=hub
E:  Ad=81(I) Atr=03(Int.) MxPS=   8 Ivl=255ms
T:  Bus=01 Lev=01 Prnt=01 Port=00 Cnt=01 Dev#=  2 Spd=12  MxCh= 0
D:  Ver= 1.10 Cls=00(>ifc ) Sub=00 Prot=00 MxPS= 8 #Cfgs=  1
P:  Vendor=04b0 ProdID=0108 Rev= 1.00
S:  Manufacturer=NIKON
S:  Product=Nikon Digital Camera E2500
S:  SerialNumber=000003365943
C:* #Ifs= 1 Cfg#= 1 Atr=c0 MxPwr=  0mA
I:  If#= 0 Alt= 0 #EPs= 2 Cls=08(stor.) Sub=06 Prot=50 Driver=usb-storage
E:  Ad=04(O) Atr=02(Bulk) MxPS=  64 Ivl=0ms
E:  Ad=83(I) Atr=02(Bulk) MxPS=  64 Ivl=0ms
```

All the lines starting with the second T: line pertain to the Nikon Coolpix 2500 camera. You can see some of the details in the output, such as manufacturer name and camera model.

4. **Mount the camera's storage media by typing the following command:**

```
mount /mnt/camera
```

A camera icon appears on the GNOME desktop.

5. **Double-click the camera icon on the GNOME desktop.**

The camera's contents appear in a Nautilus file manager window. You can double-click the folders and find the one that contains the photos. Typically, these digital photos are JPEG files with cryptic filenames that carry the .jpg extension. In the default view, Nautilus displays thumbnails of the photos, so you don't have to worry about the cryptic filenames.

6. **Click to select the photos and copy them to your hard disk.**

You can also type the cp command in a terminal window to copy all or some selected images to a directory on your hard disk. For example, to copy all JPEG photos from the camera to the current directory, type

```
cp /mnt/camera/*.jpg .
```

7. **When you're done downloading the photos, right-click the camera icon on the GNOME desktop and choose Unmount Volume from the pop-up menu.**

   Linux unmounts the camera from the /mnt/camera directory, removes the /mnt/camera directory, and removes the line that was added to the /etc/fstab file.

8. **Power off the camera and disconnect the USB cable from the PC.**

Who needs gtkam when you can access the camera just like any other storage device!

## Playing audio CDs

Both GNOME and KDE come with CD player applications. To play an audio CD, you need a sound card, and that sound card must be configured to work in Linux.

If you are using the GNOME desktop, you can play audio CDs by using the GNOME CD Player application. Launch the GNOME CD Player by selecting Main Menu⇨Sound & Video⇨CD Player. Figure 4-2 shows this CD player playing a track from an audio CD.

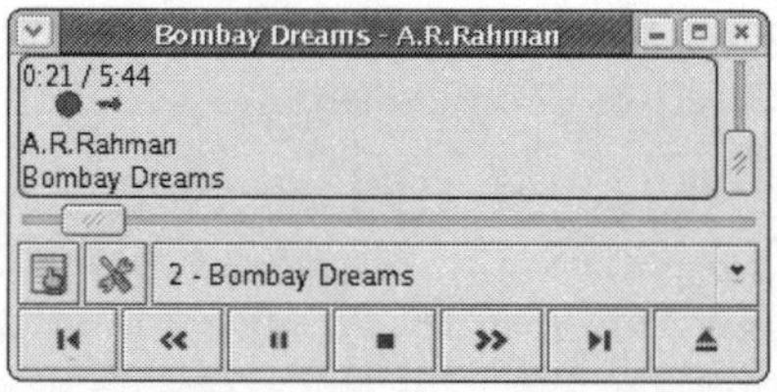

**Figure 4-2:** Play audio CDs with the GNOME CD Player.

The GNOME CD Player displays the title of the CD and the name of the current track. The GNOME CD Player gets the song titles from freedb.org — a free open-source CD database on the Internet (freedb.freedb.org at port 888). You need an active Internet connection for the CD Player to download song information from the CD database. After the CD Player downloads information about a particular CD, it caches that information in a local database for future use. The CD Player's user interface is intuitive, and you can learn it easily. One nice feature is that you can select a track by title, as shown in Figure 4-3.

If you use KDE as your desktop, you find a similar audio CD player in KDE. Start the KDE CD player by selecting Main Menu⇨Sound & Video⇨KsCD.

**Figure 4-3:**
In the
GNOME CD
Player, you
can select
a specific
audio track
to play.

## Playing sound files

You can use Rhythmbox or XMMS to open and play a sound file. Users with
large MP3 music libraries like Rhythmbox, but the version that comes with
Fedora Core does not include the MP3 capability. XMMS is not installed by
default, but you can install it from the companion DVD by following these
steps while logged in as `root`:

1. **Mount this book's companion DVD.**

   Insert the DVD into the DVD drive and type **mount /mnt/cdrom** in a terminal window (you may have to change `cdrom` to `cdrom1`, if the DVD
   drive is the second CD/DVD drive on your system).

2. **Install the XMMS RPM.**

   Type the following commands from a terminal window (these commands
   assume that the DVD drive is mounted on `/mnt/cdrom`):

   ```
   cd /mnt/cdrom/Fedora/RPMS
   rpm -ivh xmms*
   ```

XMMS can play many types of sound files, including Ogg Vorbis, FLAC
(Free Lossless Audio Codec, an audio file format that is similar to MP3), and
Windows WAV. You find many WAV sound files — which usually have names
that end with the `.wav` extension — in the `/usr/share/sounds` directory of
your Linux system.

You can also create WAV sound files from audio CD tracks by using the `cdda2wav` command-line application. For example, to convert the second track from an audio CD into a WAV file, type the following command:

```
cdda2wav -D /dev/cdrom -t2 -Owav
```

`cdda2wav` saves the track in a WAV file named `audio.wav`. You can then play the WAV file in XMMS. Watch out though — each track of an audio CD typically takes about 60MB of disk space in WAV format.

Because of legal reasons, the version of XMMS in Fedora Core does not include the code needed to play MP3 files, so you have to translate MP3s into a supported format such as WAV before you can play them. You can use the Ogg Vorbis format for compressed audio files because Ogg Vorbis is a patent- and royalty-free format.

To start XMMS from the GNOME or KDE desktop, choose Main Menu⇨Sound & Video⇨Audio Player. XMMS has a simple user interface. To open a sound file, choose Window Menu⇨Play File, or press L to select a `.wav` or `.ogg` file from the Load File dialog box. Select a file and click OK. XMMS starts playing the sound file. Figure 4-4 shows a typical XMMS window when it's playing a sound file.

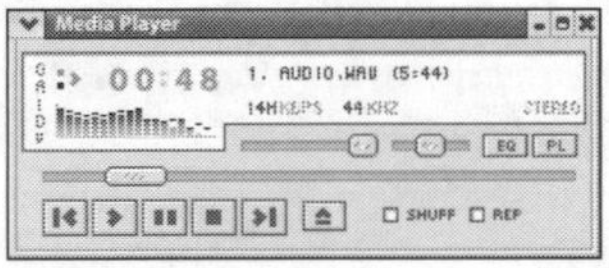

**Figure 4-4:**
You can play many different types of sound files in XMMS.

If you get an error message from XMMS, choose Window Menu⇨Options⇨ Preferences and then select ALSA as the Output Plugin.

Of course, many music files are in MP3 format. Wouldn't getting XMMS to play MP3 music be nice? Well, to play MP3 files in XMMS, you have to download the source code for XMMS and build it from scratch. I provide the instructions in Book VI, Chapter 4.

## Burning a CD

Fedora Core includes X-CD-Roast, a graphical CD burner application with a lot of features. It can create both data CDs and audio CDs. You can also *rip* (copy) music from audio CDs to files on the hard drive and then burn them onto a new audio CD. In the next few sections, I briefly explain how to use X-CD-Roast. If you want to find out more, visit `www.xcdroast.org`.

X-CD-Roast is on this book's companion DVD, but it is not installed by default. To install X-CD-Roast, follow these steps while you are logged in as `root`:

*1.* **Mount this book's companion DVD.**

Insert the DVD into the DVD drive and type **mount /mnt/cdrom** in a terminal window (you may have to change `cdrom` to `cdrom1`, if the DVD drive is the second CD/DVD drive on your system).

*2.* **Install the xcdroast RPM.**

Type the following commands from a terminal window (these commands assume that the DVD drive is mounted on `/mnt/cdrom`):

```
cd /mnt/cdrom/Fedora/RPMS
rpm -ivh xcdroast*
```

**Book II
Chapter 4**

**Exploring Fedora
Core Applications**

X-CD-Roast depends on many external programs to do its job. If these external programs do not exist, some X-CD-Roast features don't work. Although most programs used by X-CD-Roast come with Fedora Core, a few are not part of the Fedora Core distribution. For example, X-CD-Roast needs the `mpg123` program to convert MP3 audio files into a form suitable for recording on CD. Fedora Core does not come with the `mpg123` program, so you can't create audio CDs that include MP3 songs.

Before you can burn a CD, you need a CD-R or CD-RW drive (CD burner) connected to your PC. It can be an internal or an external CD burner. Internal CD burners are usually IDE (also known as ATAPI) devices connected to the same card that supports the PC's hard disk and any other CD-ROM drive.

If you have an external CD/DVD burner, it probably connects to your PC's USB port. When you connect such a burner to the USB port and power up the burner, Linux automatically recognizes the device and loads the appropriate USB driver. When you use X-CD-Roast to burn a CD on a USB CD-R/RW drive, you do not have to do anything special — X-CD-Roast automatically detects most CD/DVD-ROM and CD/DVD-R/RW drives on your system. You can, however, manually identify any CD/DVD drives that X-CD-Roast fails to detect.

To start X-CD-Roast, choose Main Menu⇨System Tools⇨CD Writer from the GNOME or KDE desktop (the CD Writer menu item appears only after you install the `xcdroast` RPM). If you aren't logged in as `root`, you're prompted for the `root` password. X-CD-Roast scans for all CD/DVD devices on your system and displays the results in a dialog box. Click OK to proceed. X-CD-Roast then gives you an opportunity to configure the software so that any user can activate it (this feature is called Non-Root Mode). If you want to get right on with burning CDs, click Launch X-CD-Roast and the main window appears, as shown in Figure 4-5. You can do everything — configure X-CD-Roast and burn audio and data CDs — from the main window.

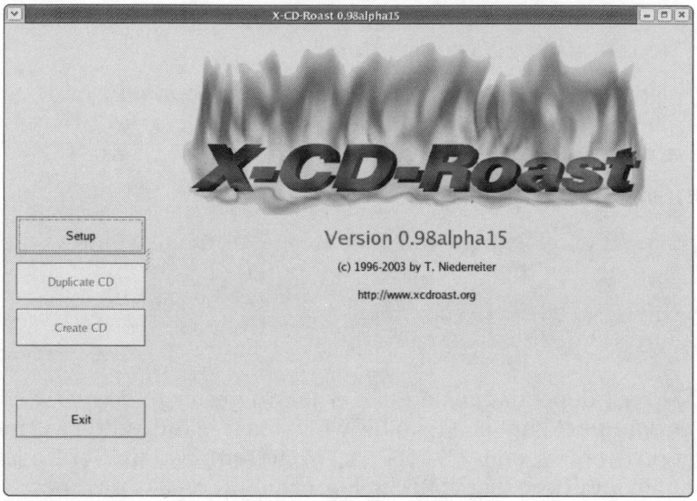

**Figure 4-5:**
You can
burn CDs
from the
X-CD-Roast
main
window.

### Exploring the Setup window

If this is your first time with X-CD-Roast, click Setup from the main menu (refer to Figure 4-5). X-CD-Roast displays the Setup window (shown in Figure 4-6) with six tabs.

Initially, X-CD-Roast displays the Device-Scan tab with a list of the CD/DVD devices it detects (shown in Figure 4-6). You also have to set up other parameters through the remaining tabs:

✦ **CD Settings:** Enables you to specify the CD reading and writing speeds, the default CD writer device, the primary and secondary CD read device (if you have multiple CD drives). You can also specify the CD writing mode. The default CD writing mode is Disk-At-Once (DAO). If this mode fails, try Track-At-Once (TAO) that puts a 2-second pause after each track, but that's supported by every CD writer.

✦ **HD Settings:** Specify the directory for temporary storage of CD images. Click the Browse button and select the directory you want to use. You could, for example, select the /tmp directory for temporary storage. After selecting the directory, click the Add button.

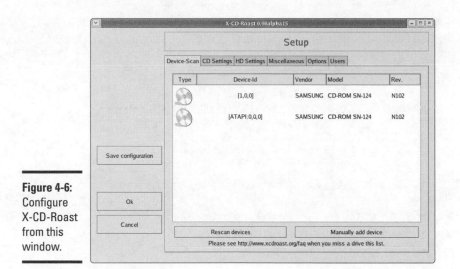

**Figure 4-6:**
Configure
X-CD-Roast
from this
window.

✦ **Miscellaneous:** Enables you to set up the way X-CD-Roast beeps to let you know about various events such as completion of CD burning, the server with a CD database where X-CD-Roast can look up information about a CD, and whether to turn on logging as X-CD-Roast burns a CD. The default CD database server is `freedb.freedb.org`.

✦ **Options:** Specifying some aspects of the X-CD-Roast application (for example, whether to display the tooltip help).

✦ **Users:** Specify which users are allowed to access the X-CD-Roast application to burn CDs.

After setting all the options, click the Save Configuration button on the left hand side of the window (refer to Figure 4-6). X-CD-Roast saves the configuration. Click OK to return from Setup to the main menu.

### Recording an audio CD

With X-CD-Roast, you can duplicate an audio CD or create a new audio CD by mixing and matching tracks you want. To make a new audio CD with all or some selected tracks from an existing audio CD, click the Create CD button in the main window (refer to Figure 4-5) and then follow these steps:

*1.* **Place the original CD in the CD reader device (the one you designated as the reader in the X-CD-Roast setup) and place a blank CD in the CD reader and click the Read Tracks button.**

X-CD-Roast displays the tracks in the Create CD window (shown in Figure 4-7) so that you can select the tracks to read.

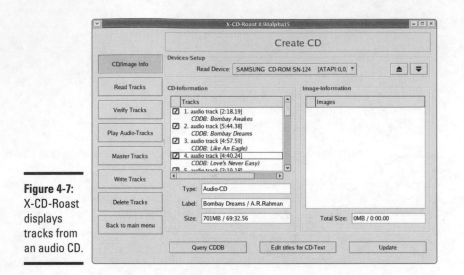

**Figure 4-7:**
X-CD-Roast
displays
tracks from
an audio CD.

2. **Select the tracks you want to copy to a new CD.**

   X-CD-Roast highlights the selected tracks.

3. **Click the Read Tracks button.**

   X-CD-Roast saves the tracks to the hard drive. It can take some time to read and save the tracks. X-CD-Roast displays the progress in an information window.

4. **Click the Write Tracks button.**

   X-CD-Roast displays the Create CD window.

5. **Click the Layout Tracks tab in the window. Select tracks from the list on the right hand side and click Add below that list to move the track to the list of tracks to write. You can select the tracks in the order in which you want them to appear on the CD.**

6. **Click the Write Tracks tab.**

   X-CD-Roast displays the options for writing the tracks to a CD.

7. **Click the Write Tracks button. X-CD-Roast prompts you to insert a blank CD-R into the CD writer. After inserting the blank CD-R, click OK.**

   X-CD-Roast then begins to burn the CD and shows the progress in a window. When the burn process is complete, X-CD-Roast ejects the CD.

8. **Click the Back to Main Menu button and then click Exit to quit X-CD-Roast.**

### Recording a data CD

Saving files from your hard drive onto a CD is easy. To create a data CD, follow these steps:

1. **Click the Create CD button in the main window (refer to Figure 4-5).**

   X-CD-Roast displays the Create CD window.

2. **Click the Master Tracks button.**

   X-CD-Roast displays a number of tabs with the Master Source tab on top. That tab shows two side by side panes — on the left you see the current layout of your data CD. The other tabs enable you to control other aspects of the data CD, such as making it bootable or specifying a label for the CD.

3. **Drag files and directories from the right pane onto the left pane.**

4. **Change to other directories as needed and continue until you have selected all the files and directories you want on the data CD.**

   In the left pane, X-CD-Roast displays the current set of files, including the directory hierarchies.

5. **Click the Create Session/Image tab.**

   X-CD-Roast displays options for either creating a CD image or burning a CD on the fly from the files that you have selected.

6. **Insert a blank CD-R or CD-RW into the CD burner and then click the Master button and write on the fly.**

   X-CD-Roast begins burning the data CD and ejects the disc when done.

# Graphics and Imaging

You can use graphics and imaging applications to work with images and graphics (line drawings and shapes). I discuss two applications:

- ✦ **The GIMP** *(GNU Image Manipulation Program)* is a program for viewing and performing image-manipulation tasks, such as photo retouching, image composition, and image creation.

- ✦ **Gnome Ghostview (GGV)** is a graphical application capable of displaying PostScript files.

## The GIMP

The GIMP (GNU Image Manipulation Program) is an image-manipulation program written by Peter Mattis and Spencer Kimball and released under the GNU General Public License (GPL). It is installed if you select the Graphics Manipulation package when you install Fedora Core from this book's companion DVD-ROM. The GIMP is comparable to other image-manipulation programs, such as Adobe Photoshop and Corel Photopaint.

To try out the GIMP, choose Main Menu⇔Graphics⇔The GIMP from the GNOME or KDE desktop. The GIMP starts and displays a window with copyright and license information. Click the Continue button to proceed with the installation. The next screen shows the directories that are created when you proceed with a personal installation of the GIMP.

GIMP installation involves creating a directory called .gimp-1.3 in your home directory and placing a number of files in that directory. This directory essentially holds information about any changes to user preferences you may make to the GIMP. Go ahead and click the Continue button at the bottom of the window. The GIMP creates the necessary directories, copies the necessary files to those directories, and guides you through a series of dialog boxes to complete the installation.

After the installation is done, click the Continue button. From now on, you don't see the installation window anymore; you have to deal with installation only when you run the GIMP for the first time.

The GIMP then loads any plugins — external modules that enhance its functionality. It displays a startup window that shows a message about each plugin as it loads. After finishing the startup, the GIMP displays a tip of the day in a window. You can browse the tips and click the Close button to close the tip window. At the same time, the GIMP displays a number of windows (see Figure 4-8).

These windows include a main toolbox window titled The GIMP, a Tool Options window, a Brush Selection window, and a Layers, Channels, Paths window. Of these, the main toolbox window is the most important — in fact, you can close the other windows and work by using the menus and buttons in the toolbox.

The toolbox has three menus on the menu bar:

✦ The **File menu** has options to create a new image, open an existing image, save and print an image, mail an image, and quit the GIMP.

✦ The **Xtns menu** gives you access to numerous extensions to the GIMP. The exact content of the Xtns menu depends on which extensions are installed on your system.

✦ The **Help menu** is where you can get help and view tips. For example, choose Help➪Help to bring up the GIMP Help Browser with online information about the GIMP.

To open an image file in the GIMP, select File➪Open. The Load Image dialog box comes up from which you can select an image file. You can change directories and select the image file you want to open. GIMP can read all common image-file formats, such as GIF, JPEG, TIFF, PCX, BMP, PNG, and PostScript. After you select the file and click the OK button, the GIMP loads the image into a new window. Figure 4-8 shows an image being touched up in the GIMP, along with all the other GIMP windows.

The toolbox also has many buttons that represent the tools you use to edit the image and apply special effects. You can get pop-up help on each tool button by placing the mouse pointer on the button. You can select a tool by clicking the tool button, and you can apply that tool's effects to the image.

For your convenience, the GIMP displays a pop-up menu when you right-click your mouse on the image window. The pop-up menu has most of the options from the File and Xtns menus in the toolbox. You can then select specific actions from these menus.

**Book II
Chapter 4**

Exploring Fedora
Core Applications

**Figure 4-8:**
Touch up
your photos
with the
GIMP.

You can do much more than just load and view images with the GIMP, but a complete discussion of all its features is beyond the scope of this book. If you want to try the other features of the GIMP, consult the GIMP User Manual (GUM), available online at `manual.gimp.org`. You can also choose Xtns⇨ Web Browser⇨GIMP.ORG⇨Documentation to access the online documentation for the GIMP (of course, you need an Internet connection for this command to work).

Some documentation about the GIMP is installed in the `/usr/share/doc` directory. To go to that directory, type **cd /usr/share/doc/gimp\*** (the actual directory name depends on the current version of the GIMP). The README file in that directory points you to other resources on the Web where you can discover more about the GIMP. In particular, visit the GIMP home page at `www.gimp.org` to find the latest news about the GIMP and links to other resources.

## Gnome Ghostview

Gnome Ghostview is a graphical application ideal for viewing and printing PostScript or PDF documents. For a long document, you can view and print selected pages. You can also view the document at various levels of magnification by zooming in or out.

To run Gnome Ghostview, select Main Menu⇨Graphics⇨PostScript Viewer from the GNOME or KDE desktop. The Gnome Ghostview application window appears. In addition to the menu bar and toolbar along the top edge, a vertical divide splits the main display area of the window into two parts.

To load and view a PostScript document in Gnome Ghostview, select File⇨Open, or click the Open icon on the toolbar. Gnome Ghostview displays a file-selection dialog box. Use this dialog box to navigate the file system and select a PostScript file. You can select one of the PostScript files that come with Ghostscript. For example, open the file `tiger.ps` in the `/usr/share/ghostscript/7.07/examples` directory. (If your system has a version of Ghostscript later than 7.07, you have to use the new version number in place of 7.07.)

To open the selected file, click the Open File button in the file-selection dialog box. Gnome Ghostview opens the selected file, processes its contents, and displays the output in its window, as shown in Figure 4-9.

Gnome Ghostview is useful for viewing various kinds of documentation that come in PostScript format (these files typically have the `.ps` extension in their names). You can also open PDF files (these files typically have `.pdf` extensions) in Gnome Ghostview.

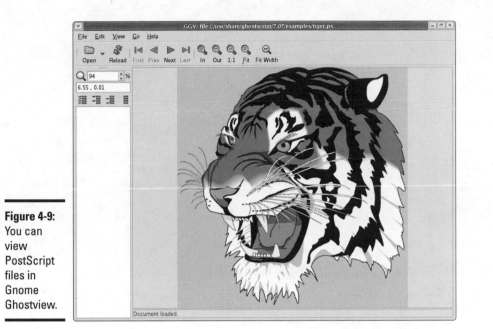

**Figure 4-9:**
You can view PostScript files in Gnome Ghostview.

**Book II
Chapter 4**

**Exploring Fedora
Core Applications**

# Chapter 5: Using Text Editors

## In This Chapter

✔ **Using GUI text editors**

✔ **Working with the** ed **text editor**

✔ **Learning the** vi **text editor**

*I*n Fedora Core, most system-configuration files are text files. If you write any shell scripts or other computer programs, they're text files too. Sometimes you have to edit these files using programs designed for that purpose: *text editors*. For example, you may need to edit files such as /etc/ hosts, /etc/modprobe.conf, /etc/X11/xorg.conf, /etc/xinetd.d/ telnet, and many more.

In this chapter, I introduce you to a few text editors — both the GUI editors and text-mode editors.

## Using GUI Text Editors

Each of the GUI desktops — GNOME and KDE — comes with GUI text editors (text editors that have graphical user interfaces).

To use the GNOME text editor, select Main Menu⇨Accessories⇨Text Editor from the GNOME desktop. You can open a file by clicking the Open button on the toolbar, which brings up the Open File dialog box. You can then change directories and select the file to edit by clicking the OK button.

The GNOME text editor then loads the file in its window. You can open more than one file and move among them as you edit the files. Figure 5-1 shows a typical editing session with the editor.

In this case, the editor has three files — fstab, hosts, and innittab (all from the /etc directory) — open for editing. The filenames appear as tabs below the toolbar of the editor's window. You can switch among the files by clicking the tabs.

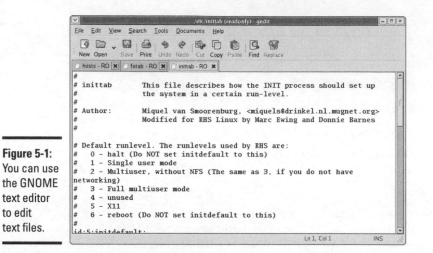

**Figure 5-1:**
You can use
the GNOME
text editor
to edit
text files.

If you open a file for which you have only read permission, the text RO- is appended to the filename to indicate that the file is "read-only." In Figure 5-1, all the files are opened read-only because here I'm logged in as a normal user and I'm opening system files that only root can modify.

The rest of the text-editing steps are intuitive. To enter new text, click to position the cursor and then begin typing. You can select text, copy, cut, and paste by using the buttons on the toolbar above the text-editing area.

From the KDE desktop, you can start the KDE text editor by selecting Main Menu⇨Accessories⇨Kate. To open a text file, choose File⇨Open from the menu. A dialog box appears. From this dialog box, you can go to the right directory, select the file to open, and click the OK button. The KDE text editor then opens the file and displays its contents in the window. You can then edit the file.

# Text Editing with ed and vi

Fedora Core comes with two text-mode text editors:

✦ ed, a line-oriented text editor

✦ vi, a full-screen text editor that supports the command set of an earlier editor named ex

The ed and vi editors are cryptic compared to the graphical text editors. However, you should still learn the basic editing commands of ed and vi because sometimes these two may be the only editors available.

For example, if Fedora Core refuses to boot from the hard drive, you may have to boot from a floppy disk. In that case, you have to edit system files with the ed editor because that editor is small enough to fit on the floppy. I walk you through the basic text-editing commands of ed and vi. You'll see — they're not that hard.

## Using ed

Typically, you have to use ed only when you boot a minimal version of Linux (for example, from a floppy you've set up as a boot disk), and the system doesn't support full-screen mode. In all other situations, you can use the vi editor that works in full-screen text mode.

When you use ed, you work in either command mode or text-input mode:

✦ **Command mode** is what you get by default. In this mode, anything that you type is interpreted as a command. The ed text editor has a simple command set where each command consists of one or more characters.

✦ **Text-input mode** is for typing text. You can enter input mode with the commands a (append), c (change), or i (insert). After entering lines of text, you can leave input mode by entering a period (.) on a line by itself.

To practice editing a file, copy the /etc/fstab file to your home directory by issuing the following commands:

```
cd
cp /etc/fstab .
```

Now you have a file named fstab in your home directory. Type the following command to begin editing a file in ed:

```
ed -p: fstab
783
:
```

This example uses the -p option to set the prompt to the colon character (:) and opens the fstab file (in the current directory, which is your home directory) for editing. The ed editor opens the file, reports the number of characters in the file (783), displays the prompt (:), and waits for a command.

When you're editing with ed, make sure you always turn on a prompt character (use the -p option). Without the prompt, distinguishing whether ed is in input mode or command mode is difficult.

After ed opens a file for editing, the current line is the last line of the file. To see the current line number (the current line is the line to which ed applies your command), use the . = command like this:

```
:.=
9
```

This output tells you that the fstab file has nine lines. (Your system's /etc/fstab file may have a different number of lines, in which case ed shows a different number.)

You can use the 1,$p command to see all lines in a file, as the following example shows:

```
:1,$p
LABEL=/                 /                   ext3    defaults        1 1
LABEL=/boot             /boot               ext3    defaults        1 2
none                    /dev/pts            devpts  gid=5,mode=620  0 0
none                    /dev/shm            tmpfs   defaults        0 0
none                    /proc               proc    defaults        0 0
none                    /sys                sysfs   defaults        0 0
/dev/hda6               swap                swap    defaults        0 0
/dev/cdrom              /mnt/cdrom          udf,iso9660 noauto,owner,kudzu,ro
    0 0
/dev/fd0                /mnt/floppy         auto    noauto,owner,kudzu 0 0
/dev/cdrom1             /mnt/cdrom1         udf,iso9660 noauto,owner,kudzu,ro
    0 0
:
```

To go to a specific line, type the line number:

```
:7
/dev/hda6               swap                swap    defaults        0 0
:
```

The editor responds by displaying that line.

Suppose you want to delete the line that contains cdrom. To search for a string, type a slash (/) followed by the string that you want to locate:

```
:/cdrom
/dev/cdrom              /mnt/cdrom          udf,iso9660 noauto,owner,kudzu,ro 0 0
:
```

The editor locates the line that contains the string and then displays it. That line becomes the current line.

To delete the current line, use the d command as follows:

```
:d
:
```

To replace a string with another, use the s command. To replace cdrom with the string cd, for example, use this command:

```
:s/cdrom/cd/
:
```

To insert a line in front of the current line, use the I command:

```
:i
    (type the line you want to insert)
.   (type a single period to indicate you're done)
:
```

You can enter as many lines as you want. After the last line, enter a period (.) on a line by itself. That period marks the end of text-input mode, and the editor switches to command mode. In this case, you can tell that ed switches to command mode because you see the prompt (:).

When you're happy with the changes, you can write them to the file with the w command. If you want to save the changes and exit, type **wq** to perform both steps at the same time:

```
:wq
785
```

The ed editor saves the changes in the file, displays the number of saved characters, and exits. If you want to quit the editor without saving any changes, use the Q command.

These examples give you an idea of how to use ed commands to perform the basic tasks of editing a text file. Table 5-1 lists some of the commonly used ed commands.

| Table 5-1 | Commonly Used ed Commands |
|---|---|
| *Command* | *Does the Following* |
| !command | Executes a shell command (for example, !pwd shows the current directory). |
| $ | Goes to last line in the buffer. |
| % | Applies a command that follows to all lines in the buffer (for example, %p prints all lines). |
| + | Goes to next line. |
| +n | Goes to *n*th next line (where *n* is a number you designate). |
| , | Applies a command that follows to all lines in the buffer (for example, ,p prints all lines); similar to %. |

*(continued)*

**Table 5-1** *(continued)*

| Command | Does the Following |
|---------|--------------------|
| - | Goes to preceding line. |
| -n | Goes to *n*th previous line (where *n* is a number you designate). |
| . | Refers to the current line in the buffer. |
| /text/ | Searches forward for the specified text. |
| ; | Refers to a range of lines; current through last line in the buffer. |
| = | Prints line number. |
| ?text? | Searches backward for the specified text. |
| ^ | Goes to the preceding line; also see the - command. |
| ^n | Goes to *n*th previous line (where *n* is a number you designate); also see the -n command. |
| a | Appends after current line. |
| c | Changes specified lines. |
| d | Deletes specified lines. |
| i | Inserts text before current line. |
| n | Goes to line number *n*. |
| Press Enter | Displays next line and makes that line current. |
| q | Quits editor. |
| Q | Quits editor without saving changes. |
| r file | Reads and inserts contents of file after the current line. |
| s/old/new/ | Replaces old string with new. |
| u | Undoes the last command. |
| W file | Appends contents of buffer to the end of the specified file. |
| w file | Saves buffer in the specified file (if no file is named, saves in the default file — the file whose contents ed is currently editing). |

## Using vi

The vi editor is a full-screen text editor, so you can view several lines at the same time. Most UNIX systems, including Fedora Core, come with vi. Therefore, if you know the basic features of vi, you can edit text files on almost any UNIX system.

When vi edits a file, it reads the file into a *buffer* — a block of memory — so you can change the text in the buffer. The vi editor also uses temporary files during editing, but the original file isn't altered until you save the changes.

To start the editor, type **vi** and follow it with the name of the file you want to edit, like this:

```
vi /etc/fstab
```

The vi editor then loads the file into memory and displays the first few lines in a text screen and positions the cursor on the first line (see Figure 5-2).

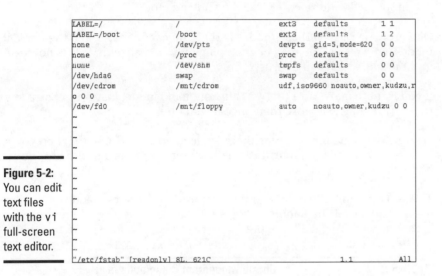

**Book II**
**Chapter 5**

**Using Text Editors**

**Figure 5-2:**
You can edit text files with the vi full-screen text editor.

The last line shows the pathname of the file as well as the number of lines (8) and the number of characters (621) in the file. In this case, the text [readonly] appears after the filename because I'm opening the /etc/fstab file while I am logged in as a normal user (which means I don't have permission to modify the file). Later, the last line in the vi display functions as a command-entry area. The rest of the lines display the file. If the file contains fewer lines than the screen, vi displays the empty lines with a tilde (~) in the first column.

The current line is marked by the cursor, which appears as a small black rectangle. The cursor appears on top of a character.

When using vi, you work in one of three modes:

✦ **Visual command mode** is what you get by default. In this mode, anything that you type is interpreted as a command that applies to the line containing the cursor. The vi commands are similar to the ed commands.

✦ **Colon command mode** is for reading or writing files, setting vi options, and quitting vi. All colon commands start with a colon (:). When you enter the colon, vi positions the cursor on the last line and waits for you to type a command. The command takes effect when you press Enter.

✦ **Text input mode** is for typing text. You can enter input mode with the command a (insert after cursor), A (append at end of line), or i (insert after cursor). After entering lines of text, you have to press Esc to leave input mode and re-enter visual command mode.

One problem with all these modes is that you cannot easily tell the current mode that vi is in. You may begin typing only to realize that vi is not in input mode, which can be frustrating.

If you want to make sure that vi is in command mode, just press Esc a few times. (Pressing Esc more than once doesn't hurt.)

To view online help in vi, type **:help** while in command mode. When you're done with help, type **:q** to exit the help screen and return to the file you're editing.

The vi editor initially positions the cursor on the first character of the first line — and one of the handiest things you can know is how to move the cursor around. To get a bit of practice, try the commands shown in Table 5-2.

| Table 5-2 | Cursor Movement Commands in vi |
|-----------|-------------------------------|
| *Key* | *Does the Following* |
| ↓ | Moves the cursor one line down. |
| ↑ | Moves the cursor one line up. |
| ← | Moves the cursor one character to the left. |
| → | Moves the cursor one character to the right. |
| W | Moves the cursor one word forward. |
| B | Moves the cursor one word backward. |
| Ctrl+D | Moves down half a screen. |
| Ctrl+U | Scrolls up half a screen. |

You can go to a specific line number at any time. Use the handy colon command: To go to line 6, for example, type the following and then press Enter:

```
:6
```

When you type the colon, vi displays the colon on the last line of the screen. From then on, vi uses any text you type as a command. You have to press Enter to submit the command to vi. In colon-command mode, vi accepts all commands that the ed editor accepts — and then some.

To search for a string, first type a slash (/). The vi editor displays the slash on the last line of the screen. Type the search string and then press Enter. The vi editor locates the string and positions the cursor at the beginning of that string. Thus, to locate the string cdrom in the file /etc/fstab, type

```
/cdrom
```

To delete the line that contains the cursor, type **dd** (two lowercase *ds*). The vi editor deletes that line of text and makes the next line the current one.

To begin entering text in front of the cursor, type **i** (a lowercase *i* all by itself). The vi editor switches to text input mode. Now you can enter text. When you finish entering text, press Esc to return to visual command mode.

After you finish editing the file, you can save the changes in the file with the :w command. To quit the editor without saving any changes, use the :q! command. If you want to save the changes and exit, you can type **:wq** to perform both steps at the same time. The vi editor saves the changes in the file and exits. You can also save the changes and exit the editor by pressing Shift+ZZ (hold the Shift key down and press the Z key twice).

In addition to these commands, vi accepts a large number of commands. Table 5-3 lists some commonly used vi commands, organized by task.

**Book II**
**Chapter 5**

**Using Text Editors**

| Table 5-3 | Commonly Used vi Commands |
|-----------|---------------------------|
| *Command* | *Does the Following* |
| **Insert Text** | |
| a | Inserts text after the cursor. |
| A | Inserts text at the end of the current line. |
| I | Inserts text at the beginning of the current line. |
| i | Inserts text before the cursor. |
| **Delete Text** | |
| D | Deletes up to the end of the current line. |
| dd | Deletes the current line. |
| dw | Deletes from the cursor to the end of the following word. |
| x | Deletes the character on which the cursor rests. |

*(continued)*

**Table 5-3** *(continued)*

| Command | Does the Following |
|---------|-------------------|
| *Change Text* | |
| C | Changes up to the end of the current line. |
| cc | Changes the current line. |
| J | Joins the current line with the next one. |
| rx | Replaces the character under the cursor with *x* (where *x* is any character). |
| *Move Cursor* | |
| h or ← | Moves one character to the left. |
| j or ↓ | Moves one line down. |
| k or ↑ | Moves one line up. |
| L | Moves cursor to the end of the screen. |
| l or → | Moves one character to the right. |
| w | Moves to the beginning of the following word. |
| *Scroll Text* | |
| Ctrl+D | Scrolls forward by half a screen. |
| Ctrl+U | Scrolls backward by half a screen. |
| *Refresh Screen* | |
| Ctrl+L | Redraws screen. |
| *Cut and Paste Text* | |
| P | Puts the yanked line above the current line. |
| p | Puts the yanked line below the current line. |
| yy | Yanks (copies) current line into an unnamed buffer. |
| *Colon Commands* | |
| :!*command* | Executes a shell command. |
| :q | Quits the editor. |
| :q! | Quits without saving changes. |
| :r *filename* | Reads the file and inserts it after current line. |
| :w *filename* | Writes a buffer to the file. |
| :wq | Saves changes and exits. |
| *Search Text* | |
| /*string* | Searches forward for a string. |
| ?*string* | Searches backward for a string. |

| Command | Does the Following |
|---|---|
| *Miscellaneous* | |
| u | Undoes the last command. |
| Esc | Ends input mode and enters visual command mode. |
| U | Undoes recent changes to the current line. |

# Book III

# OpenOffice.org

The 5th Wave          By Rich Tennant

"Get ready, Mona—here come the stats."

# Contents at a Glance

**Chapter 1: Writing with OpenOffice.org Writer** ...............................................................213

**Chapter 2: Preparing Spreadsheets with OpenOffice.org Calc** .......................................237

**Chapter 3: Making Presentations with OpenOffice.org Impress** ...................................249

**Chapter 4: Drawing with OpenOffice.org Draw** ...........................................................261

# Chapter 1: Writing with OpenOffice.org Writer

## In This Chapter

✔ Getting documents from others

✔ Taking stock of OpenOffice.org Writer

✔ Getting started with Writer

✔ Preparing documents in Writer

*L*et's face it! The whole world, or so it seems, uses Microsoft Office, especially Microsoft Word, to write stuff. You have to work with the world to get your job done. Until recently, the lack of a freely available and high-quality Microsoft Office-compatible office suite may have been holding you back from using Fedora Core as your primary desktop operating system. Well, your troubles are over. Fedora Core now comes with the OpenOffice.org office suite — a set of office productivity applications comparable to Microsoft Office and compatible with Microsoft Office as well. OpenOffice.org should already be installed on your system — all you have to do is select the *Office/Productivity* package group during Fedora Core installation. If you didn't install the *Office/Productivity* package group, follow the steps I describe in Book I, Chapter 3 to install that package group.

OpenOffice.org Writer, or *Writer* for short, is at the heart of the OpenOffice.org office suite. Writer is a word processor that makes preparing many different types of documents on your Fedora Core system easy and, best of all, you can share files with others who use Microsoft Word.

Typically you might work with Microsoft Word files that your coworkers and friends (and maybe even family) send you. This chapter starts by explaining the many different ways in which you may receive a Microsoft Word file — and what to do when you receive such a file. The chapter then gives you an overview of how to open the document, work on it, track changes, and save it to a folder. Along the way, I provide tables that summarize how to perform common word-processing tasks with Writer.

Before your expectations go sky-high, let me caution you that if you share files between Microsoft Word and Writer, you may run into some conversion problems; some Word features may not convert fully into equivalent Writer features. However, if you share only simple documents with Microsoft Word users (or if you simply want to prepare your own nicely formatted documents), Writer works well for you.

By the way, if you're already a proficient Microsoft Word user, you can start using Writer without much trouble because much of Writer works very much like Word.

# Getting Documents from Others

If you're like me, you often work on documents that you share with your coworkers. One of you prepares a draft and others then edit and add to that draft. You probably typically receive the documents as e-mail attachments or on some storage medium (such as a floppy disk, Zip disk, or CD-ROM).

Before you start working on the document, you have to save it in a folder (directory) on your hard disk. Here are the different ways you can get the documents onto your hard disk:

✦ **E-mail:** Your e-mail reader (such as Mozilla Mail or Ximian Evolution) has an option to save attachments to a directory.

✦ **Floppy disk:** (I assume it's a DOS/Windows-format floppy disk you're using.) Insert the floppy into the A drive, open a terminal window (by choosing Main Menu⇨System Tools⇨Terminal), and type **mdir** to look at the contents of the floppy. Then type the following command to copy a specified file to the current directory:

```
mcopy a:filename.doc .
```

Here `filename.doc` is the name of the Microsoft Word file you want to copy to the hard disk.

✦ **Zip disk:** Fedora Core creates an entry in the `/etc/fstab` file for the Zip drive so that you can mount it at the `/mnt/zip` directory. Insert the Zip disk into the drive and type **mount /mnt/zip** to mount it. You can now access the files on the Zip disk at the `/mnt/zip` directory. In other words, if a file is at the top-level directory on the Zip disk, you can copy that file to the current directory on your hard disk with the following command:

```
cp /mnt/zip/filename.doc .
```

✦ **DVD or CD-ROM:** If you're at the GNOME or KDE desktop, the contents of the DVD or CD-ROM appear in a file manager window soon after you insert the DVD/CD-ROM into the DVD/CD drive. You can then drag and drop the file into a directory on your hard disk. If you aren't using a GUI desktop, type **mount /mnt/cdrom** to mount the DVD/CD-ROM, and then you can access the DVD/CD-ROM's contents at the `/mnt/cdrom` directory.

Now that you have a Microsoft Word file in your hands, all you need to do is open it in Writer and start working on it!

# *Taking Stock of OpenOffice.org Writer*

Before you begin using Writer, I want to give you a quick overview of its major features. When you know what you can do with Writer, you can read the subsequent sections to find out how to perform specific tasks in Writer, such as formatting tables, printing documents, and tracking changes.

You can do the following with Writer:

✦ Open and edit Microsoft Word files or convert Microsoft Word files to Writer format. One advantage of converting to Writer format is that Writer files are much smaller in size than corresponding Microsoft Word files.

✦ Save documents in many different formats including Microsoft Word 97/2000/XP, Word 95, Word 6.0, Rich Text Format (RTF), StarWriter 5.0 (as well as 4.0 and 3.0), plain text, Adobe PDF, and Web page (HTML).

✦ Insert graphics files of many different formats, including JPEG, GIF, ZSoft Paintbrush (PCX), TIFF, Windows BMP, Macintosh PICT, Encapsulated PostScript (EPS), Adobe Photoshop (PSD), AutoCAD DXF, and many more.

✦ Create tables that can include calculations and add charts that update when the table contents change.

✦ Perform complex page layouts with desktop publishing features, such as text frames and floating frames.

✦ Easily create and organize multiple files that make up a large project, such as a book or a large report.

✦ Create a *mail merge* where you write a single document with generic fields and have Writer automatically create many different customized documents by filling in the specific fields (such as name, address, and phone number) from a database.

✦ Save versions of a document as you continue to change it, and revert to an older version if necessary.

✦ Compare changes and work collaboratively using the Versions system. Not only can you see what changed and who changed it, but you can also accept or reject those changes individually (or in groups) according to certain criteria.

A note of caution here: The versioning information doesn't export perfectly to some other formats — in particular, Microsoft Word.

✦ E-mail your documents directly from Writer.

✦ If you like, Writer can automatically complete the word you're typing by making a best guess — and you can accept the choice by pressing Enter. (If this feature drives you crazy, you can simply turn it off, just as you can configure many other features in Writer.)

**Book III
Chapter 1**

**Writing with
OpenOffice.org
Writer**

Writer enables you to export a Writer document directly to an Adobe Portable Document Format (PDF) file. To electronically share a document in its final form, you can print the document to a PDF file and distribute that file. Anyone can easily view and print PDF files by using the free Adobe Reader (available at `www.adobe.com/products/acrobat/readstep2.html`).

## Getting Started with Writer

The best way to find out how to use Writer is to simply start using it. To start Writer, click the Writer icon on the panel (the icon showing some pieces of paper with a pen) or choose Main Menu➪Office➪OpenOffice.org Writer.

Writer displays its main window (see Figure 1-1) with an empty document. In the following section, I describe this main window in some detail.

Using Writer is simple because it's so similar to other word processors that you've probably used, such as Microsoft Word. For example, you can type text into the blank document, format it, and save it when you're done. (I describe these tasks and more in a later section, "Preparing Documents in Writer.")

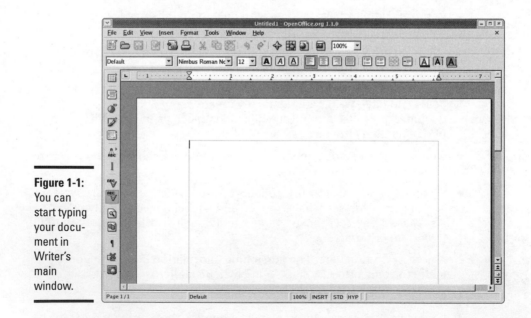

**Figure 1-1:**
You can start typing your document in Writer's main window.

If you want to work on an existing document (for example, a Microsoft Word file) that you saved on your hard disk, choose File➪Open and then pick the document from the Open dialog box. Then you can work on that document and save it in Word format, another word processing format, or in the default OpenOffice.org 1.0 Text Document format in a file with the .sxw extension.

## Examining the Writer main window

To familiarize yourself with Writer, start by examining the user interface components packed into its main window, shown in Figure 1-2.

As Figure 1-2 shows, you can view the Writer window in terms of the following major parts:

Object bar

Function bar

Menu bar

Ruler

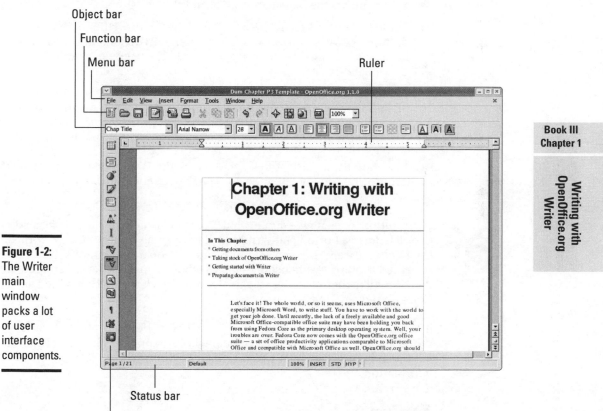

**Figure 1-2:** The Writer main window packs a lot of user interface components.

Status bar

Toolbar

**Book III Chapter 1**

**Writing with OpenOffice.org Writer**

✦ **Menu bar:** Provides the standard pull-down menus: File, Edit, Help, and so forth. Use these menus to perform all the tasks that Writer can do.

✦ **Function bar:** Shows the full pathname or the URL of the currently open file and also provides buttons for performing tasks, such as opening, saving, and printing a document. You can also click icons on the function bar to open the Stylist (a list of paragraph, character, and page styles), the Navigator (a list of document parts such as headings, tables, and bookmarks), and the Gallery (a collection of predefined graphic objects such as 3D shapes, backgrounds, and bullets).

✦ **Object bar:** Enables you to format the document by applying styles, selecting fonts, or changing text attributes such as bold, italic, and underline. This bar changes depending on the type of object (such as plain text or graphics) you click.

✦ **Ruler:** Shows the page dimensions and the tab stops.

✦ **Toolbar:** Located along the left side of the window, the toolbar provides buttons that you can use to perform common document-preparation tasks, such as insert tables, create forms, check spelling, and show the drawing functions.

✦ **Status bar:** Displays the usual information about the open document, including the current page number and the total page count. You can also click elements in the status bar to change certain settings, such as the text selection mode and the zoom factor for viewing the document.

In addition to these parts, the largest part of the Writer window is the work area where your document appears. That's where you focus most of your attention.

Use tooltips to get a clue about what a particular field or button does. Mouse over a field or a button and Writer displays a small tooltip window with a brief help message. If you want more information in the tooltips, turn on extended tooltips by choosing Help⇨Extended Tips. On the other hand, if you don't like these tooltips, toggle them off by choosing Help⇨Tips and Help⇨Extended Tips.

If you need it, help is available in Writer. Choose Help⇨Contents from the Writer menu. The OpenOffice.org Help window appears, shown in Figure 1-3, with help information about Writer. Click the links to view specific help information.

## Setting up Writer

You don't really have to do any special setup to start using Writer. Even tasks such as printing work right away provided you set up a printer using the steps I describe in Book I, Chapter 3. Some settings, however, you may want to tinker with so that Writer works to your liking. For example, you may want to turn off AutoCorrect so that it doesn't suggest word completion, or you may want to hide some toolbars to get more workspace. You can set up most of these options from the View and Tools menus, which are located on the menu bar (refer to Figure 1-2). In particular, you perform most of the setup tasks from the dialog box (see Figure 1-4) that appears when you choose Tools➪Options.

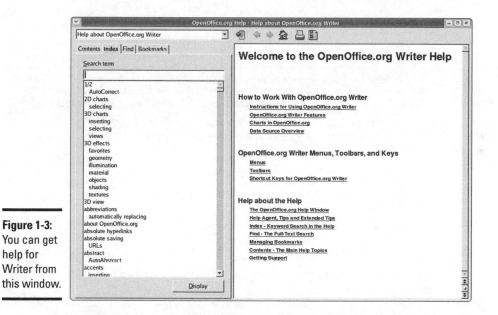

**Figure 1-3:** You can get help for Writer from this window.

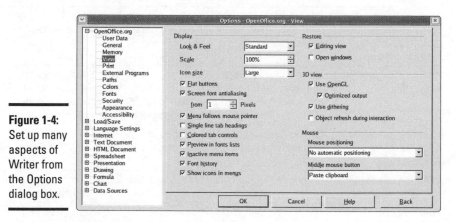

**Figure 1-4:** Set up many aspects of Writer from the Options dialog box.

Table 1-1 summarizes the common setup tasks and how you can perform them from Writer's menus.

| Table 1-1 | Common Setup Tasks in OpenOffice.org Writer |
|---|---|
| *To Do This* | *Use This Procedure* |
| Toggle various parts of Writer window on or off | Select the appropriate item such as Ruler, Status Bar, or Toolbars from the View menu and toggle that item on or off. |
| Customize toolbars | Choose View⇨Toolbars⇨Customize. You can also choose Tools⇨ Configure and then click the Status Bar and Toolbars tabs to config- ure the appropriate toolbar. You can also right-click a toolbar and choose Configure from the pop-up menu. |
| Customize menus | Choose Tools⇨Configure and then click the Menu tab. |
| Change default locations of various files | Choose Tools⇨Options. Then choose OpenOffice.org⇨Paths and click the path you want to change. For example, click My Documents and specify the pathname for the default location of your documents. |
| Display font names in their font in the drop- down font list on the object bar | Choose Tools⇨Options. Then choose OpenOffice.org⇨View and turn on the Preview in Fonts Lists check box. |
| Show full menus including items that are not applicable | Choose Tools⇨Options. Then choose OpenOffice.org⇨View and turn on the Inactive Menu Items check box. |
| Show or hide tooltips | Choose Help⇨Tips to toggle tooltips on or off and choose Help⇨ Extended Tips to toggle extended tooltips on or off. |
| Always create a backup copy of the file | Choose Tools⇨Options. Then choose Load/Save⇨General and select the Always Create Backup Copy check box. |
| Autosave every *XX* minutes | Choose Tools⇨Options. Then choose Load/Save⇨General and select the Autosave Every check box and select the number minutes speci- fying how often to save the file. |
| Show nonprintable characters, such as paragraph marks, tabs, and so on | Choose Tools⇨Options. Then choose Text Document⇨Formatting Aids and turn on the check box of characters you want Writer to display. |
| Choose language and currency | Choose Tools⇨Options. Then choose Language Settings⇨Languages and select the Locale setting, Default currency, and the language for documents. If you use any Asian language, turn on the Enabled check box in the text Asian Languages Support area. |
| Choose, create, or edit a custom dictionary. | Choose Tools⇨Options. Then choose Language Settings⇨Writing Aids and add a new dictionary or edit words in an existing dictionary. |
| Change options for tracking changes | Choose Tools⇨Options. Then choose Text Document⇨Changes and select the options for displaying changes to the document. |
| Change user information | Choose Tools⇨Options. Then choose OpenOffice.org⇨User Data and enter information about yourself. |

| To Do This | Use This Procedure |
|---|---|
| Turn off Help Agent that pops up when you perform certain tasks for the first time | Choose Tools⇨Options. Then choose OpenOffice.org⇨General and turn off the Activate check box for the Help Agent. |
| Set up AutoCorrect and AutoFormat options | Choose Tools⇨AutoCorrect/AutoFormat and click the Options tab in the resulting dialog box. Turn on (or turn off) the AutoCorrect options to suit your needs and click OK. For example, to turn off automatic word completion, click the Word Completion tab and select the Complete Words check box to remove the check mark. |

# Preparing Documents in Writer

You'll have no problem preparing documents using Writer. Typically, you can simply click to position a cursor and then type your text. To format text, select a style for the paragraph or select text and then apply formatting, such as boldface or italics. In the following sections, I provide some quick tips on how to perform specific document-preparation tasks in Writer. I organize the tips into the following categories of tasks:

+ Editing and reviewing documents
+ Using styles and templates
+ Performing page layout
+ Creating and inserting graphics
+ Using fields
+ Working with large documents

## Editing and reviewing documents

To edit a document, you have to open the file, move around within the document, insert and delete text, and save the file. You can perform most of these tasks intuitively because these steps are similar in most word processors. For that reason, I don't discuss in detail how to perform each of these tasks. Instead, in the following paragraphs, I highlight just a couple of features that you'll find particularly useful in your work. Then, in Table 1-2, I provide a list of commonly used tasks and how to perform them.

Typically, you review changes when you collaborate with others on a document and several of you make revisions to the document. To review changes, you need to track the changes. Writer has features to enable change tracking (or *redlining*, as it's commonly called). With Writer, you can examine the changes, accept or reject each change, and make more editing changes — even adding comments to explain why you made a change.

**Book III Chapter 1**

**Writing with OpenOffice.org Writer**

Writer has other features for easily editing a document. For example, you can search and replace text — even find all occurrences of text with a specific formatting style and change each occurrence.

Most of Writer's editing and change-tracking functions are on the Edit menu (shown in Figure 1-5). Some toolbar icons provide shortcuts to the menu.

**Figure 1-5:**
Perform most editing and reviewing tasks from the Edit menu and its submenus.

Table 1-2 summarizes some common editing and reviewing tasks and how to perform these tasks. The table does not mention the toolbar icons, but you can always mouse over each icon and read the tooltips to see which ones enable you to make specific editing and reviewing changes.

| Table 1-2 | Common Editing and Reviewing Tasks |
|---|---|
| *To Do This* | *Use These Steps* |
| Protect document for editing | Choose Edit⇨Changes⇨Protect Records and enter a password in the resulting dialog box. To enable changes, choose Edit⇨Changes⇨Protect Records again and enter the password you entered earlier. |
| Jump quickly to different parts of a document | Choose Edit⇨Navigator or press F5. Open the appropriate category, such as Headings, Tables, or Bookmarks, and then double-click an item to jump to that location. |

| To Do This | Use These Steps |
| --- | --- |
| Find and replace text with specific formatting and style | Choose Edit➪Find & Replace or press Ctrl+F. In the dialog box, enter the text to find, including any formatting, and enter the replacement text, if any. Then click Find or Replace depending on whether you simply want to find text or you want to find and replace with new text. |
| Select multiple blocks of text to copy, cut, or format as a group | Select the blocks of text while holding down the Ctrl key. Another way is to click STD on the status bar until it shows ADD and then select each block of text one by one. |
| Insert a special character | Position the cursor and choose Insert➪Special Character. Select the font and character to insert. |
| Set some text in initial uppercase | Select the text. Choose Format➪Character and click the Font Effects tab in the resulting dialog box. Choose Title from the Effects drop-down list. |
| Edit a hyperlink without activating the URL | Hold down the Alt key and click the hyperlink. Now you can edit the text in the hyperlink. |
| Move a paragraph up or down | Click in the paragraph and then press Ctrl+@@up or Ctrl+↓ to move the paragraph up or down. |
| Enable or disable change tracking | Choose Edit➪Changes➪Record to turn the check mark on or off. When the check mark is on, Writer tracks changes. |
| Show or hide changes in the document | Choose Edit➪Changes➪Show to turn the check mark on or off. When the check mark is on, Writer displays the changes with revision marks. |
| Insert comments to explain a change | Make the change, choose Edit➪Changes➪Comment, and then enter your comment in the dialog box that appears. |
| Insert notes — comments not associated with a change | Choose Insert➪Note and type the note in the dialog box that appears. |
| Print the document to a PDF file | Choose File➪Print. In the Print dialog box, click the list of printers and select PDF Converter from the drop-down list. Click OK. |
| Save a version of the document | Choose File➪Versions. From the resulting dialog box, select Save New Version. You can create new versions only after you save the document once. |
| Open an older version of a document | Choose File➪Versions and select the version to open from the dialog box. Click Open. |
| Merge documents | Choose Edit➪Changes➪Merge Document. From the resulting Insert dialog box, select the document with which you want to merge the current document. |
| Accept or reject changes | Choose Edit➪Changes➪Accept or Reject and then accept and reject changes from the list that appears in a dialog box. |
| Create an AutoText entry | Choose Edit➪AutoText or press Ctrl+F3. Then enter the text and the shortcut. |

*(continued)*

**Book III
Chapter 1**

**Writing with
OpenOffice.org
Writer**

**Table 1-2 *(continued)***

| To Do This | Use These Steps |
|---|---|
| Insert AutoText | Type the shortcut and press F3. For example, type BW and press F3 to enter the text "Best Wishes" (BW is a predefined shortcut for Best Wishes). |
| Count the number of words in the document | Choose File⇨Properties and click the Statistics tab in the resulting dialog box. |
| Edit document properties | Choose File⇨Properties. |
| Check spelling | Choose Tools⇨Spellcheck⇨Check or press F7. |
| Exclude a word from the spell check | Double-click to select the word. Right-click and select Character from the pop-up menu. Then click the Font tab and select [None] from the Language drop-down list. |

## Using styles and templates

In Writer, you can format pages, paragraphs, and blocks of text manually. For example, you can place the cursor in a paragraph, choose Format⇨Paragraph, and then format various characteristics of the paragraph (such as indentation, spacing, and borders). This paragraph-by-paragraph formatting is okay for a short document, but it can be tedious and time-consuming if you have to format hundreds of paragraphs one by one. A better approach is to define a *style* — a collection of formatting characteristics stored under a particular, usually descriptive, name. Then you can simply apply that style to all paragraphs. If you need to change any aspect of the paragraphs, simply edit the style and voilá — all paragraphs with that style get the new formatting.

You may be familiar with paragraph and character styles in Microsoft Word, but Writer relies more on styles than Microsoft Word. Writer supports five types of styles: page, paragraph, character, numbering, and frame. Table 1-3 summarizes what each of these styles control.

| Table 1-3 | Five Types of Styles in Writer |
|---|---|
| This Style | Controls This |
| Page style | The page layout, including the margins, number of columns, headers, and footers. |
| Paragraph style | The look of a paragraph, such as the font, paragraph spacing, borders, bullets, numbering, and the style of the following paragraph. |
| Character style | The font style of selected text in a paragraph. |
| Numbering style | The number or bullet character and spacing used for numbered or bulleted lists. |
| Frame style | The size and position of the frame and the text-wrapping options. |

In Writer, you can conveniently access and use all the document's styles in a floating window called the Stylist (see Figure 1-6). You can show and hide the Stylist by pressing F11 (or choosing Format⇨Stylist).

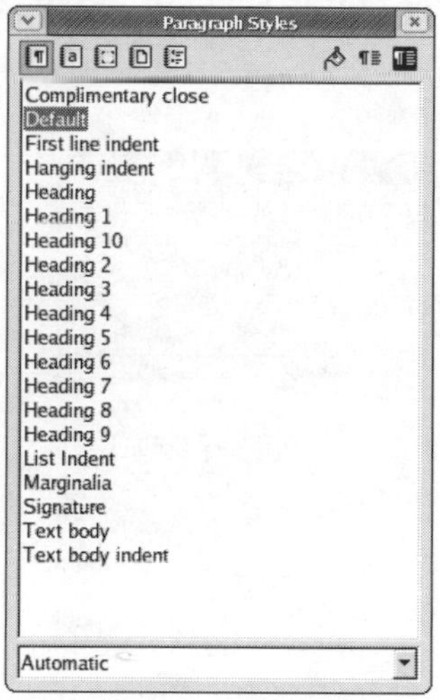

**Figure 1-6:**
Press F11
to toggle
the Stylist
on and off.

The Stylist makes organizing and using the styles easy. The five icons along the top part of the Stylist refer to the five types of styles — paragraph, character, frame, page, and numbering — from left to right. You can click an icon to see all styles of that type. To apply a style, position the cursor where you want to apply the style and double-click the appropriate icon from the Stylist. For character styles, select the text and then double-click the Character Style icon.

Writer also supports templates, just as Microsoft Word does. A *template* is a special document with a collection of styles for the kinds of layouts that the document needs. You can think of a template as a model for a specific type of document. For example, you may have templates for documents such as memos, letters, fax cover sheets, envelopes, and many more.

Writer does not come with any templates, but you can create or download templates from Web sites. A Writer template for writing manuscripts using the Modern Language Association (MLA) style (see owl.english.purdue. edu/handouts/research/r_mla.html for more information on the MLA style), for example, is available from www.cc.mie-u.ac.jp/~lq20100/ MLA-Template.stw. You have to install the template file — MLA-Template. stw — before you can create documents using that template. ***Note***: The .stw extension is used for OpenOffice.org template files.

To install a template file to use in Writer, follow these steps:

***1.*** **Choose File➪Templates➪Organize.**

The Template Management dialog box (shown in Figure 1-7) appears with the Default folder of templates on the left side and the current list of documents on the right.

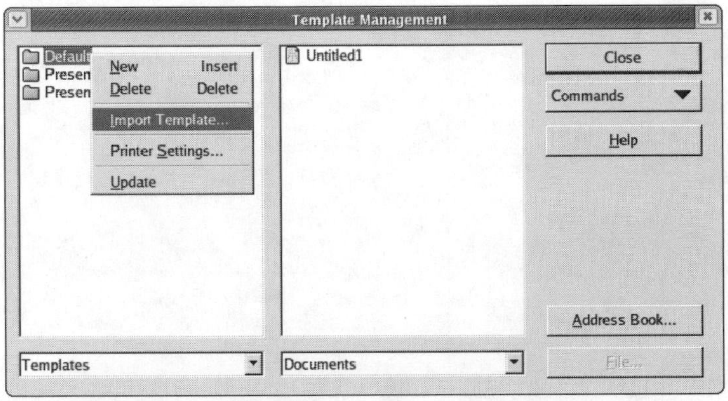

**Figure 1-7:**
Import the template file into the Default template folder.

***2.*** **Right-click the Default folder icon and select Import Template from the pop-up menu, as shown in Figure 1-7.**

The Open dialog box appears.

***3.*** **Navigate to the directory where you saved the template file, select the template file, and click Open.**

The Open dialog box closes; the template now appears in the Default folder in the Template Management dialog box.

***4.*** **Click Close to close the Template Management dialog box.**

To create a new document from a template you install, follow these steps:

***1.*** **Choose File➪New➪Templates and Documents.**

A dialog box appears with the templates. Double-click the Default folder to open it and view the templates.

***2.*** **Select the template you want to use and click Open.**

A new document appears, typically with some text illustrating the selected template's styles.

***3.*** **Erase the text in the new document and start typing what you want.**

To view the styles in that template, open the Stylist window by pressing F11 and apply styles by double-clicking them in the Stylist.

Writer also enables you to perform many other tasks related to styles and templates. For example, you can create a style, apply a style to text, copy styles from one template to another, and so on. Table 1-4 summarizes how you can perform some common tasks involving styles and templates in Writer.

| Table 1-4 | Common Tasks Involving Styles and Templates |
|---|---|
| *To Do This* | *Follow These Steps* |
| Determine what template is associated with a document | Choose File⇨Properties and click the General tab in the resulting dialog box. Look for the template name in the Template field in the lower part of that tab. |
| Install a template file | Choose File⇨Template⇨Organize. Right-click the Default folder icon and choose Import Template from the pop-up menu. Select the template from the Open dialog box and click Open. |
| Specify a default template | Choose File⇨Templates⇨Organize. Double-click the Default folder on the left-hand side of the dialog box to view the templates (you must have already installed templates). Select a template and click Commands on the right side of the dialog box. Then select Set As Default Template from the drop-down list. |
| Create a new template | Create a document layout with styles you want in the template. Choose File⇨Templates⇨Save and assign a name to save the current file as a template. |
| Edit a template | Choose File⇨Templates⇨Edit. From the resulting Open dialog box, select the template file to edit. |
| Copy styles between templates | Choose File⇨Templates⇨Organize. Open the two templates. Select styles from one template and drag and drop them onto another template. |
| Create a new document from a template | Choose File⇨New⇨Templates and Documents. In the resulting dialog box, open a template folder, select a template, and click Open. |
| Apply a different template to a document | Start a new document based on the template you want to use. Then copy the contents of the old document into the new document. |
| Apply a style to text | Position the cursor in the text and choose Format⇨Stylist or press F11. Click the first icon on the Stylist window's toolbar to view the paragraph styles. Then double-click a style to apply that style. After you apply a paragraph style once, the style appears in the drop-down list on the object bar. |
| Redefine a style | Choose the style in the Stylist, right-click, and choose Modify; or Format⇨Styles⇨Catalog, select the style, and click Modify. |
| Create a new style | Choose Format⇨Styles⇨Catalog, or press Ctrl+Y. Click New and define the style by filling in information in the resulting dialog box. |
| Use the AutoPilot to create a document | Choose File⇨AutoPilot and then the document type you want to create. Fill in the information requested by the AutoPilot and click Create. |

## Performing page layout

In Writer, page styles control the page layout, and each page can have its own style. The usual approach is to define three page styles: First Page, Left Page, and Right Page. Define the First Page with whatever applies to the first page, such as a special header and no page number. The Left Page is the style for the even numbered pages and the Right Page style is for odd numbered pages. For each page style, you can also define the page style that applies to the following page. The idea is to define Left Page as the next page style for First Page and Right Page as the style of the page that follows the Left Page style. That way, the page styles are correct for all the pages as long as you start with the First Page style. You may also want to define a Landscape page style so you can use it for pages that have to be in landscape orientation.

If you are familiar with Microsoft Word, you know that the page setup — paper size, orientation, margins, and so on — applies to all pages in the document. In Writer, a page style does not automatically apply to the entire document. Instead, each page has its own page style. Of course, you can choose to apply the same page style to all the pages. Essentially, you have more fine-grained control over page layouts in Writer.

A typical page layout task is to insert objects created in other OpenOffice.org applications, such as a Calc spreadsheet, an Impress slide, or a Draw drawing. You can insert such objects by choosing Insert⇨Object⇨OLE Object. Incidentally, OLE stands for *Object Linking and Embedding,* which is just a fancy term for the ability to create a document by adding components, such as charts and drawings, that are created in different applications.

When you add components, keep this caveat in mind: You can edit a component directly in the document only by using the application that originally created the component.

A component that you can insert into a Writer document is a mathematical formula, and I mean serious formulas with integral signs and Greek letters, such as alpha and sigma. If you're writing a scientific paper with complex equations, you'll really appreciate this feature of OpenOffice.org. Here's a typical sequence of steps to insert a formula into a Writer document (this process is similar for inserting other components):

*1.* **Position the cursor and select Insert⇨Object⇨Formula.**

The user interface changes to that of OpenOffice.org Math — an application for writing mathematical formulas and a small frame for the formula appears in the document. The formula is typeset in that frame.

*2.* **Select a formula type from the top two rows of the Selection window.**

The lower rows in the Selection window show available formulas of that type. For example, the summation category (denoted by an uppercase Greek letter sigma) includes integral signs.

3. **Click a specific formula, such as an integral.**

   The Math command for this formula appears in the Commands window and parts of the formula appear in the document.

4. **Fill in the arguments for the formula.**

   As you construct the formula with commands in the Commands window, the formatted formula appears in the document (see Figure 1-8).

5. **To change the font size of the formula, choose Format⇨Font Size and specify the font size.**

6. **Click anywhere else in the Writer document to return to the Writer user interface.**

7. **Double-click the formula to edit it again.**

Of course, Writer has many page layout features. You can use tables, numbered and bulleted lists, and columns. Writer also supports *frames* — rectangular boxes in which you can place text, graphics, and even other frames. Using frames, you can place just about anything anywhere on the document. Table 1-5 summarizes how you can perform some common page layout tasks in Writer.

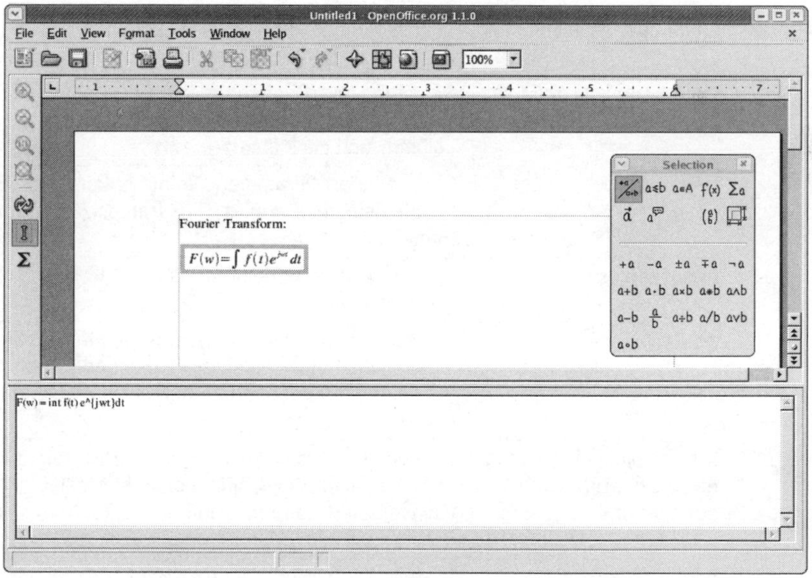

**Figure 1-8:**
Insert a math formula into a Writer document by using the Math application.

| Table 1-5 | Common Page Layout Tasks |
|---|---|
| *To Do This* | *Follow These Steps* |
| Insert a page break | Choose Insert⇨Manual Break and then select Page Break from the resulting dialog box. |
| Set page margins | Choose Format⇨Page. Then click the Page tab and specify the margins. |
| Insert headers and footers | Choose Insert⇨Header or Insert⇨Footer and select if you want the header or footer on all pages or just the first page. |
| Insert header on only the first page | Put the cursor in the first page and choose Format⇨Stylist (or press F11). Click the Page Style icon (fourth icon from left) and double-click the First Page style. Choose Insert⇨Header⇨ First Page, and then type the text you want in the first page header. |
| Change page numbers from the automatic numbering sequence | Choose Insert⇨Manual Break and then select Page Break and a style for the page. Then turn on the Change Page Number check box and enter the page number you want. |
| Insert a landscape page in a portrait document | Press F11 to open the Stylist. Click the Page Style icon (the fourth icon from left). Right-click Default style and select New. Name the new style Landscape and assign Default as next style, click the Page tab, select Landscape orientation, and click OK. Now choose Insert⇨Manual Break, select Page Break, and Landscape style. |
| Layout pages in columns | Choose Format⇨Page and click the Columns tab in the resulting dialog box. Then select the number of columns and click OK. |
| Layout the selected text in columns | Select the text. Choose Insert⇨Section and click the Columns tab in the resulting dialog box. Then select the number of columns and click Insert. |
| Use frames | Choose Insert⇨Frame and select options from the tabs in the Frame dialog box. You can link frames so that text flows from one frame to the next. |
| Insert tables | Choose Insert⇨Table or press Ctrl+F12. Format the table from the resulting dialog box. |
| Join two tables | Position the two tables one after the other, without any other text in between. Right-click either table and select the Join Tables option (that option appears only when the tables are next to each other). |
| Insert objects created in other OpenOffice.org applications | Position the cursor and choose Insert⇨Object⇨OLE Object. From the Insert OLE Object dialog box, select the type of object you want. If you are inserting an object from a file, click the Create from File radio button and click OK. |
| Insert a math formula | Position the cursor and choose Insert⇨Object⇨Formula. The user interface of the OpenOffice.org Math application appears. Use the formula Selection and Commands windows to create the formula and adjust the font size. As you construct the formula, it appears in the document. Click anywhere else in the document to return to Writer. Double-click the formula to edit it again. |

| To Do This | Follow These Steps |
|---|---|
| Insert a chart | Position the cursor and choose Insert⇨Chart to insert a chart with dummy data. Double-click the chart and the Impress user interface appears. To edit the chart's dummy data, choose Edit⇨ Chart Data. The dummy data appears in a mini-spreadsheet window. Edit the data and click the green check mark. To change the chart type, choose Format⇨Chart Type. Then pick the chart type from the resulting dialog box. Click elsewhere in the document to return to Writer. |
| Create an outline-style numbered list with items numbered 1, 1.1, 1.2, ... 2, 2.1, and so on | Type the list items, select them, and open the Stylist by pressing F11. Click the Numbering Style icon (fifth icon from left) and double-click the Numbering 5 style. Click in the list and note the right arrow on the object bar (the bar that shows the style name). Click the right arrow and the number list icons appear. Click each sub-numbered item and then click the right arrow icon. |
| Create a hanging indent | Press F11 to display the Stylist, if not already visible. Click the Paragraph Style icon (the first icon from left). Place the cursor in the text and then double-click the Hanging Indent style in the Stylist. |
| Preview page | Choose File⇨Page Preview. To return to editing, choose File⇨ Page Preview again. |
| Show a vertical ruler | Choose Tools⇨Options. Then choose Text Document⇨View from the resulting dialog box. Turn on the Vertical Ruler check box and click OK. |

## Creating and inserting graphics

Writer includes a drawing toolbar with tools that you can use to draw in the document. You can also insert into your document both line drawings and images from files in many different formats.

To create simple diagrams in your document, click the Show Draw Functions icon (on the toolbar along the left side of the Writer window). The Draw Functions toolbar appears, as shown in Figure 1-9.

**Figure 1-9:**
The Draw
Functions
toolbar.

Click in the document where you want to add a diagram. Select a tool from the Draw Functions toolbar (refer to Figure 1-9), and start drawing. To change the drawing tool, select another tool from the Draw Functions toolbar again.

Writer also comes with a gallery of predefined graphics. To view the Gallery (shown in Figure 1-10), choose Tools⇨Gallery or click the Gallery icon (the second- from right icon on the function bar). Select from the themes along the left side of the Gallery. If you see a graphic you want to use, drag and drop it from the Gallery to the location in the document where you want to insert it. Click the Gallery icon again to hide the Gallery.

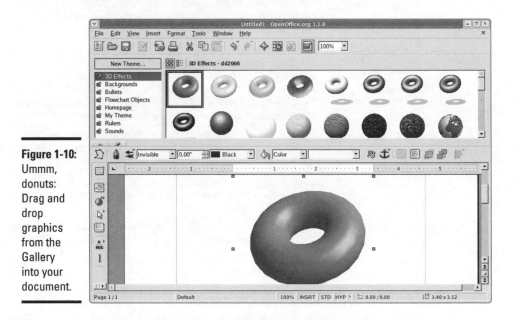

**Figure 1-10:** Ummm, donuts: Drag and drop graphics from the Gallery into your document.

Table 1-6 summarizes how you can work in Writer to perform some common tasks involving graphics.

| **Table 1-6** | **Common Tasks Involving Graphics** |
| --- | --- |
| *To Do This* | *Follow These Steps* |
| Create drawing objects | Click the Show Draw Functions icon on the left toolbar (mouse over and read the tooltips to locate the icon). Select a drawing tool, and then draw in the document. |
| Insert graphics files | Choose Insert⇨Graphics⇨From File. |
| Anchor graphics | Right-click the graphic, select Anchor from the pop-up menu, and then choose an option to anchor the graphic. |
| Wrap text around graphics | Right-click the graphic, select Wrap from the pop-up menu, and then choose one of several wrapping options. |
| Create captions for graphics | Right-click the graphic and select Caption from the pop-up menu. |

| To Do This | Follow These Steps |
|---|---|
| Insert a watermark | Choose Format⇨Page and click the Background tab in the resulting dialog box. Select Graphic from the As drop-down list, click the Browse button, and then select the graphic. Select other options, such as whether you want the graphic to tile the page or just have a single copy at a specified position. You can also prepare a graphic with the drawing tools, right-click the graphic and choose Arrange⇨To Background; right-click that graphic again and select Anchor⇨To Page. The graphic now appears as a watermark. |
| Insert a graphic (for example, a logo) on top of every page | Insert a header on each page by choosing Insert⇨Header⇨All. Click in the header, select Insert⇨Graphics⇨From File, and then select the graphics file to insert. |

## Using fields

Think of *fields* as bits of information that may change, but you want to call them by a name and use them in your document. For example, you may want to insert today's date and the page numbers into the header of a document. You can do so by inserting fields that refer to the date and page numbers. Some predefined fields (such as date and page numbers) are easy to use. Simply choose Insert⇨Fields and then select the field you want to insert (see Figure 1-11).

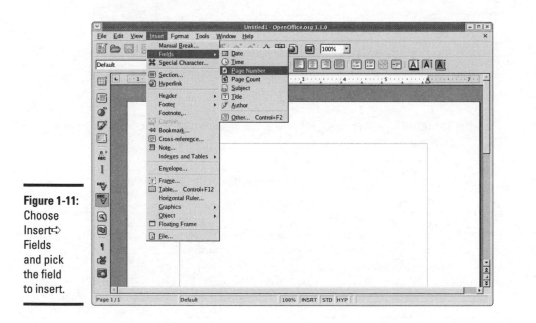

**Figure 1-11:**
Choose
Insert⇨
Fields
and pick
the field
to insert.

In addition to the fields you see in the Insert menu shown in Figure 1-11, you can pick from many more fields. Choose Insert⇨Fields⇨Other to open the Fields dialog box (see Figure 1-12) where you can browse and pick other fields to use in your document. From the Fields dialog box, you can also change the format for a field. For example, you can select how the date field is shown in the document.

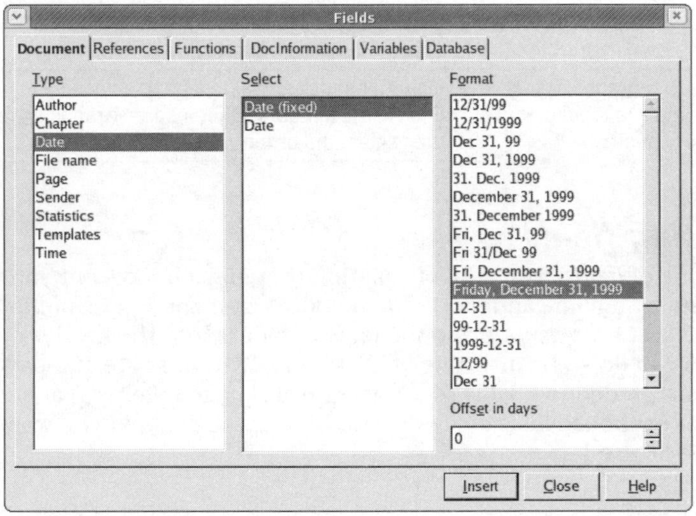

**Figure 1-12:** Use the Fields dialog box to pick other fields or select formats.

Another type of useful field is a *reference* or a *bookmark*. The idea is to mark a location in the document by a name and then refer to that location elsewhere by that assigned name. For example, you can insert a cross-reference to the page where that location occurs.

Table 1-7 summarizes a few common tasks involving fields and how you can perform them in Writer.

| Table 1-7 | Common Tasks Involving Fields |
|---|---|
| *To Do This* | *Follow These Steps* |
| Insert a field | Choose Insert⇨Fields and select a predefined field (such as Page Number, Page Count, Date, Time) you want or select Other to pick fields from a dialog box. |
| Insert the value of a formula in the text | Position the cursor and press F2. Enter the formula on the object bar and click the green check mark. The value of the formula appears in the text as a field. To edit the formula again, select the field and press F2. |
| Insert a bookmark | Click the location you want to bookmark and then choose Insert⇨Bookmark. Enter the name for the bookmark and click OK. |

| To Do This | Follow These Steps |
|---|---|
| Insert a cross-reference to a bookmark | Choose Insert⇨Cross-reference. Then select the bookmark you want to insert and the format in which the cross-reference appears in the text (for example, the page number or the name of the bookmark). |
| Set a reference | Click the text and then choose Insert⇨Cross-reference. Click Set Reference in the dialog box and assign a name to this reference. |
| Insert a cross-reference to a heading | Set a reference at the heading and position the cursor where you want to insert the cross-reference. Choose Insert⇨Cross-reference and click Insert Reference, select the reference, pick the format for the reference, and then click Insert. |

## Working with large documents

What's a large document? Well, I consider a large document any document over a hundred pages or so. Anything that has a couple of chapters and needs a table of contents and an index definitely qualifies as a large document — for example, a book. Writer includes features to do the "usual things" you want to do when working with these larger, more cumbersome documents, such as creating tables of content, inserting indexes, and adding entries to indexes.

Writer also enables you to tie together several Writer files into a single large document — what Writer refers to as a *master document*. Master documents are ideal for books, for example. You can keep the chapters in separate files and then organize these files into a book by using the master document feature. For a large project involving a master document, you have to plan a little and take care of the following key steps (see Table 1-8 for the specifics):

1. **Create a template with the styles you need as well as any fields you plan to use.**

   For more about styles and templates, see the appropriately named section "Using styles and templates," earlier in this chapter.

2. **Create the individual files and the master document by using the same template.**

3. **Insert the files into the master document — that's how you combine all the individual parts into the final product.**

4. **Add a table of contents, index, and a bibliography, if needed.**

5. **Work on the component files.**

6. **Update the table of contents and index.**

Table 1-8 summarizes some of the common tasks related to large documents and how you perform these tasks in Writer.

| Table 1-8 | Common Tasks Related to Large Documents |
|---|---|
| *To Do This* | *Follow These Steps* |
| Create a master document | Create a new file using a template you want. Then choose File⇨Send⇨Create Master Document. Assign a name, select a directory, and save the file. The Navigator window appears, from which you can select files to insert into the master document. |
| Insert a file into the master document | Use the Navigator to insert a file or choose Insert⇨File. |
| Insert index entries | Select the text you want to insert in the index. Then choose Insert⇨Indexes and Tables⇨Entry. |
| Create a table of contents, list of figures, or an index | Choose Insert⇨Indexes and Tables⇨Indexes and Tables. Click the Index/Table tab and select the type of table. For a table of contents, select Table of Contents as the type. To select the paragraph styles to include in the table, select the Additional Styles check box and then click the adjacent button to designate styles you want to include in the table. |
| Update a table of contents or index | Right-click the table and then select Update Index/Table. |
| Insert footnotes and endnotes | Choose Insert⇨Footnote, select your options, and then click OK. Then type the footnote text. |
| Create a bibliographic database | Choose Tools⇨Bibliography Database. Then fill in the bibliography information in the Bibliography Database window. |
| Insert bibliographic references into the text | Choose Insert⇨Indexes and Tables⇨Bibliographic Entry and pick the entry to insert. |

# Chapter 2: Preparing Spreadsheets with OpenOffice.org Calc

## In This Chapter

✔ Taking stock of OpenOffice.org Calc

✔ Getting started with Calc

✔ Using Calc

**D**oes the name VisiCalc mean anything to you? What about Lotus 1-2-3? I'm sure you have heard of Lotus 1-2-3, but maybe not VisiCalc — which was the first spreadsheet program that turned the IBM PC into a business tool. (Believe it or not, you can download and run VisiCalc even on today's PCs — for more information, visit Dan Bricklin's Web site at `www.bricklin.com/history/vcexecutable.htm`.)

Spreadsheet programs continue to be a staple of the office suite, and the OpenOffice.org suite is no exception. OpenOffice.org Calc, or just *Calc* for short, is the spreadsheet program in the OpenOffice.org suite.

All the spreadsheet programs that came after VisiCalc — from Lotus 1-2-3 to Microsoft Excel and Calc — still follow that visual model of a spreadsheet laid out in rows and columns. Of course, the newer spreadsheets (such as Excel and Calc) have many more bells and whistles, including fancy GUIs.

If you have used any other spreadsheet program, such as Microsoft Excel, you'll be right at home when you start using Calc. Therefore, in this chapter, I don't try to give you detailed instructions on how to use Calc; instead, I provide a quick overview and some tables that summarize how to perform some common tasks in Calc.

## Taking Stock of OpenOffice.org Calc

Before describing the types of tasks you can perform in Calc, I want to highlight the key features of Calc. Calc can do all the basic spreadsheet functions you expect in a spreadsheet program. Here are some things you can do with Calc:

✦ Open and edit Microsoft Excel files or convert Microsoft Excel files into the Calc format. Calc uses an XML format and saves files with the .sxc extension.

✦ Save documents in many different formats including Microsoft Excel 97/2000/XP, Excel 95, Excel 5.0, dBASE, StarCalc 5.0 (as well as 4.0 and 3.0), SYLK (an old Microsoft format), comma-separated values (CSV), and Web page (HTML).

✦ Visualize data in 2D or 3D plots with the charting tools.

✦ Insert graphics files of many different formats, including JPEG, GIF, ZSoft Paintbrush (PCX), TIFF, Windows BMP, Macintosh PICT, Encapsulated PostScript (EPS), Adobe Photoshop (PSD), AutoCAD DXF, and many more.

✦ Save versions of a spreadsheet as you continue to change it, allowing you to revert to an older version if necessary.

✦ Format your spreadsheet with styles and templates.

✦ Define cells to dynamically change the format depending on the value in the cell.

✦ Easily exchange — import and export — data with existing databases by using the DataPilot.

✦ Set up cells to accept values from a set of specific values or ranges of valid values.

✦ Lock cells so data cannot be changed inadvertently.

✦ Perform scenario analysis by storing multiple values in the same block of cells and define scenarios so you can select a set of values for a specific scenario.

✦ Determine the value of a cell that gives you the result you want from a formula with the Goal Seek feature.

## Getting Started with Calc

The best way to find out how to use Calc is to simply start using it. To start Calc, click the Calc icon — the icon showing a spreadsheet with a pie chart — on the panel or choose Main Menu⇨Office⇨OpenOffice.org Calc. The Calc window opens with a blank spreadsheet. You can then begin typing text and numbers into the cells and use formulas to calculate whatever you want.

## Examining the Calc main window

To familiarize yourself with Calc, take a moment to examine the tools and icons packed into Calc's main window (shown in Figure 2-1).

Notice the following major parts in the main Calc window (refer to Figure 2-1):

Formula bar

Object bar

Function bar

Menu bar

Function Autopilot

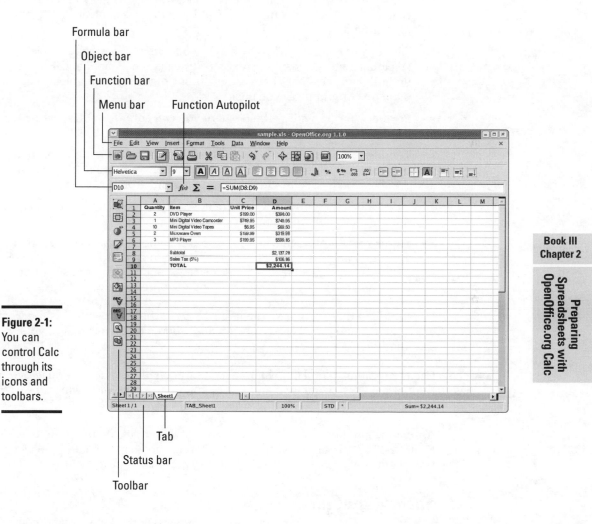

**Figure 2-1:**
You can control Calc through its icons and toolbars.

Tab

Status bar

Toolbar

✦ **Menu bar:** Provides the standard pull-down menus: File, Edit, Help, and so forth. Use these menus to perform all the tasks that Calc can do.

✦ **Function bar:** Shows the full pathname or the URL of the currently open file and also provides buttons for performing routine tasks: opening, saving, and printing a document. You can also click icons on the function bar to open the Stylist (a list of cell and page styles), the Navigator (a list of spreadsheet items such as sheets and graphics), and the Gallery (a collection of predefined graphic objects such as 3D shapes, backgrounds, and bullets).

✦ **Object bar:** Enables you to format the document by applying styles, selecting fonts, or changing text attributes (such as boldface, italics, and underlining). This bar changes depending on the type of object (such as plain text or graphics) you click.

✦ **Formula bar:** Provides a field where you can enter formulas, create sums, and launch the Function AutoPilot.

✦ **Toolbar:** Located along the left side of the window, the toolbar provides buttons that you can use to perform common tasks, such as inserting graphics, sorting cells, checking spelling, and grouping cells.

✦ **Tabs:** Along the bottom of the spreadsheet, tabs enable you to work with different sheets in the same file.

✦ **Status bar:** Displays information about the current sheet (the current sheet number, the page style, and so on). You can also click various elements in the status bar to change settings, such as the text selection mode and the zoom factor for viewing the spreadsheet.

In addition to these toolbars, the largest part of the Calc window is the work area where your spreadsheet appears and where you focus most of your attention.

Use the tooltips to find out what an icon or menu option does. Mouse over a toolbar icon or a menu item and Calc displays a small tooltip window with a brief help message.

*Note:* Curious about that Function AutoPilot icon that's pointed out in Figure 2-1? Check out the section "Calculating and charting data," later in this chapter, where I show you how to use that handy little feature.

## Setting up Calc

You can configure Calc through Tools➪Options. On the left side of the Options dialog box, click the plus sign (+) next to Spreadsheet. The plus sign turns to a minus sign (-) and a number of different categories of options appear (shown in Figure 2-2). You can then click each category to configure various aspects of Calc.

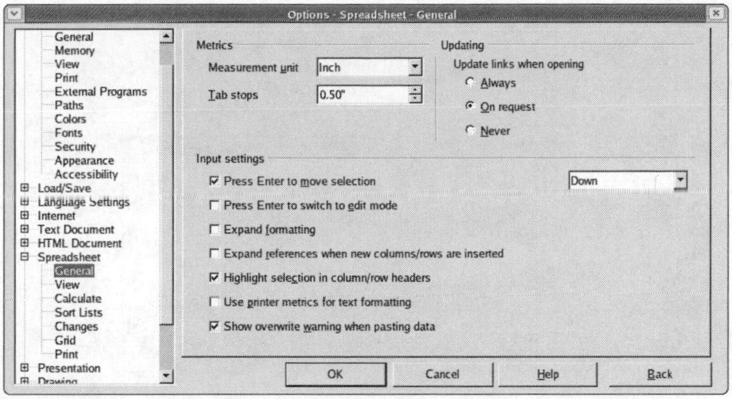

**Figure 2-2:**
Set up Calc
from the
Spread-
sheet
category in
the Options
dialog box.

# Using Calc

Preparing spreadsheets with Calc is a straightforward affair. Typically, you can enter text and numbers into the cells, resize the columns by dragging the vertical lines, and enter formulas to calculate the answers you need. To help you perform some common tasks in Calc, I provide some quick reference information organized into two broad categories of tasks:

✦ Entering and formatting data

✦ Calculating and charting data

## Entering and formatting data

When entering and formatting data, use Calc in the same way you use Microsoft Excel. You can type entries in cells, use formulas, and format the cells (such as specifying the type of value and the number of digits after the decimal point).

The Format menu (shown in Figure 2-3) contains many of the options for formatting the spreadsheet. Thanks to the tooltips, all you have to do is mouse over a menu item to get a hint about what that menu item does.

After you enter data into a spreadsheet, save it by choosing File➪Save As. A dialog box appears from which you can specify the file format, the directory location, and the name of the file. You've seen similar Save As dialog boxes a thousand times before. OpenOffice.org Calc can save the file in a number of formats, including Microsoft Excel 97/2000/XP, Microsoft Excel 95, Microsoft Excel 5.0, and a text file with comma-separated values (CSV).

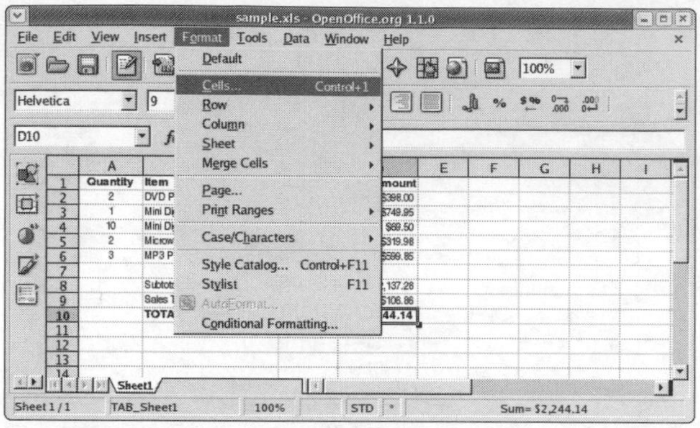

**Figure 2-3:**
Perform
many
formatting
tasks from
the Format
menu.

If you want to exchange files with Microsoft Excel, save the spreadsheet in
the Microsoft Excel format (choose an appropriate version of Excel). Then
you can transfer that file to a Windows system and open it in Microsoft
Excel.

After you save the spreadsheet once, you can also save intermediate versions of a spreadsheet. To save a new version, choose File⇨Versions and
then click Save New Version in the next dialog box.

Table 2-1 summarizes some of the common data entry and formatting tasks
in Calc. I also show the steps to print a spreadsheet to an Adobe Portable
Document Format (PDF) file. To share a spreadsheet with people who
don't use Calc or Excel, you can print the spreadsheet to a PDF file and then
send that to others because anyone can easily view and print PDF files by
using the free Adobe Reader (see `www.adobe.com/products/acrobat/
readstep2.html`).

| Table 2-1 | Common Data-Entry and Formatting Tasks |
|-----------|----------------------------------------|
| *To Do This* | *Follow These Steps* |
| Create a new spreadsheet | Choose File⇨New⇨Spreadsheet. |
| Create a spreadsheet from a template | Choose File⇨New⇨Templates and Documents. In the resulting dialog box, double-click a template folder, select a template, and click Open. *Note:* You don't see any templates if you haven't added any templates yet. |
| Open an existing spreadsheet | Choose File⇨Open and select the file from the resulting Open dialog box. |
| Add a sheet to the spreadsheet | Right-click the sheet tab where you want to add a new sheet. Select Insert from the pop-up menu, fill in the options in the resulting dialog box, and click OK. |
| Entering data or formula into a cell | Click the cell and type the data. To type a formula, click the green check mark in the formula bar. |

| To Do This | Follow These Steps |
|---|---|
| Wrap text | Right-click the cell and select Format Cells from the pop-up menu. Click the Alignment tab in the dialog box and turn on the Line Break check box at the bottom of the dialog box. |
| Edit contents directly in the cell | Double-click the cell and the cursor appears so you can edit the contents. |
| Automatically fill the cells | Fill the first cell with data (such as number, date, or cell reference) that you want to automatically increment as it fills in a range of cells. Select the cell and then drag the fill handle at the lower-right corner of the cell. As you move down (for instance), the cells automatically fill with numbers that get bigger as you go along. |
| Hide a row or a column | Right-click the row or column label and select Hide from the pop-up menu. |
| Show hidden row or column | Select the rows or columns on both side of the hidden row or column. Right-click the row or column label and select Show from the pop-up menu. |
| AutoFormat a range of cells | Drag and select the cells. Choose Format⇨AutoFormat. From the resulting dialog box, select the format and options you want. |
| Bring in data from a data source | Choose Data⇨DataPilot⇨Start. Use the subsequent dialog boxes to select a source of data, and to select the data you want to bring into the spreadsheet. |
| Move around the spreadsheet | Choose Edit⇨Navigator or press F5 to launch the Navigator window. Double-click an item, such as a sheet, to jump to that location. |
| Find and replace text in cells | Choose Edit⇨Find and Replace or press Ctrl+F. In the resulting dialog box, fill in the text to look for and the replacement text. Then click the appropriate buttons (such as Find All, Find, Replace All, or Replace) to find and replace the text. |
| Create a non-scrolling region of rows or columns | Select the last row or column in the range that you don't want to scroll. Choose Window⇨Freeze. |
| Apply style to cells | Press F11 or choose Format⇨Stylist to open the Stylist window. Click the cell to format and then double-click the style you want to apply. |
| Apply different styles depending on the cell value | Select the cell that you want to format conditionally. Choose Format⇨Conditional Formatting. In the resulting dialog box, specify the conditions (such as if the cell value is greater than something) and the style you want to apply for each condition. |
| Insert graphics from a file | Click the cell where you want to insert graphics and then choose Insert⇨Graphics⇨From File. Select the graphics file from the Insert Graphics dialog box and then click Open. |

Book III
Chapter 2

**Preparing
Spreadsheets with
OpenOffice.org Calc**

*(continued)*

**Table 2-1** *(continued)*

| To Do This | Follow These Steps |
|---|---|
| Protect a sheet against any changes | Choose Tools⇨Protect⇨Sheet. Enter a password in the next dialog box. |
| Create a PDF version of the spreadsheet | Choose File⇨Print. In the Print dialog box, click the list of printers and select PDF Converter from the drop-down list. Click OK. |
| Save a spreadsheet | Choose File⇨Save As. In the dialog box, enter a file-name and select the format in which you want to save the file. |
| Save a version of the spreadsheet | Choose File⇨Versions. From the resulting dialog box, choose Save New Version. (You can create new versions only after you save the spreadsheet once.) |
| Open an older version of a spreadsheet | Choose File⇨Versions and select the version to open from the dialog box. Click Open. |

## Calculating and charting data

To perform calculations, use formulas you normally use in Microsoft Excel. For example, use the formula SUM(D2:D6) to add the entries from cell D2 to D6. To set cell D2 as the product of the entries A2 and C2, type **=A2*C2** in cell D2.

To find out more about the functions available in OpenOffice.org Calc, choose Help⇨Contents from the menu. The OpenOffice.org Help window opens from which you can browse the functions by category and click a function to read more about it.

One interesting feature of Calc is the support for scenarios. A *scenario* is simply a collection of values for one or more cells. Scenarios are useful when you compare the effect of some cells on other calculations in the spread-sheet. For example, the monthly payment on a loan depends on the princi-pal, the interest rate, and the duration of the loan. You can use Calc's scenario feature to compare the monthly payments for a number of different scenarios where each scenario has a certain combination of interest rate and loan duration in months. To use a scenario for this comparison, follow these steps:

*1.* **Set up the spreadsheet cells with labels and values for the principal, annual interest rate in percentage, and loan duration in months. Calculate the monthly payment using this formula:**

```
-PMT(MONTHLY_RATE;MONTHS;PRINCIPAL)
```

For each of the fields, fill in the cell that contains that value. Remember to divide the annual percentage rate by 12 to get the monthly rate.

**2. Select the cells that you want to include in the scenario and choose Tools⇨Scenarios.**

The Create Scenario dialog box appears.

**3. Fill in the scenario name, and then click OK.**

**4. Enter values into the cells — principal, interest rate, and months to repay loan.**

The scenario name appears in a drop-down menu above the cells that constitute the scenario (as shown in Figure 2-4). The cell values define what that scenario means.

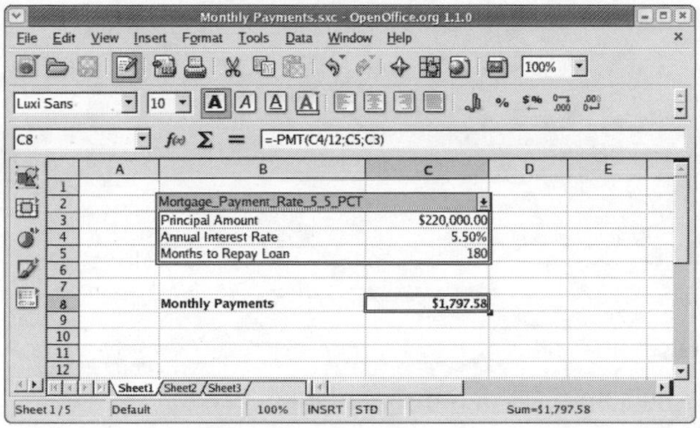

**Figure 2-4:**
Use scenarios to compare the effect of different sets of values on a calculation.

| | A | B | C | D | E |
|---|---|---|---|---|---|
| 1 | | | | | |
| 2 | | Mortgage_Payment_Rate_5_5_PCT | | | |
| 3 | | Principal Amount | $220,000.00 | | |
| 4 | | Annual Interest Rate | 5.50% | | |
| 5 | | Months to Repay Loan | 180 | | |
| 6 | | | | | |
| 7 | | | | | |
| 8 | | Monthly Payments | $1,797.58 | | |
| 9 | | | | | |
| 10 | | | | | |
| 11 | | | | | |
| 12 | | | | | |

*Monthly Payments.sxc - OpenOffice.org 1.1.0*
File Edit View Insert Format Tools Data Window Help
C8   =-PMT(C4/12;C5;C3)
Sheet1 / Sheet2 / Sheet3
Sheet 1 / 5    Default    100%    INSRT    STD    Sum=$1,797.58

**Book III
Chapter 2**

Preparing
Spreadsheets with
OpenOffice.org Calc

**5. Repeat Steps 2, 3, and 4 for other scenarios where each scenario has a combination of principal amount, rate, and loan duration in months.**

**6. Select a scenario from the drop-down list (refer to Figure 2-4) to see the monthly payment for that scenario.**

To figure out where a particular cell is being used in some calculation, click the cell and then choose Tools⇨Detective⇨Trace Dependents. Calc draws arrows to show where that cell is being used.

If you cannot remember a function, use the Function AutoPilot to build the formula in a cell. To use the Function AutoPilot, follow these steps:

**1. Click the Function AutoPilot icon (refer to Figure 2-1) on the formula bar.**

The AutoPilot dialog box appears.

**2. Scroll down the list of functions and double-click the function you want.**

Doing so causes the formula and its arguments to appear (see Figure 2-5), waiting for you to specify the values to be used as arguments.

3. **Click each argument and identify the cell that you want to use as that argument.**

When you specify all the arguments, the Result field (shown in Figure 2-5) shows the result of that formula.

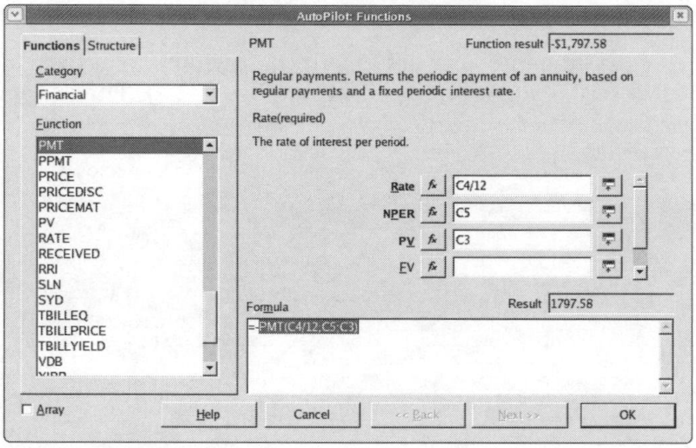

**Figure 2-5:**
Build
formulas
interactively
by using the
Function
AutoPilot.

4. **Click OK.**

The formula appears in the spreadsheet cell.

Table 2-2 summarizes some common computation and data-plotting tasks that you can perform in Calc.

| Table 2-2 | Common Calculation and Charting Tasks |
|---|---|
| *To Do This* | *Follow These Steps* |
| Add up rows or columns | Click the cell where you want the sum. Click the Sum icon (uppercase Greek letter sigma) on the formula bar. Calc inserts the sum of a logical range of cells. To change the range of cells, drag and highlight the cells you want to add. Then click the green check mark on the formula bar. |
| Build formulas with the Function AutoPilot | Click the cell where you want the function. Click the Function AutoPilot icon on the formula bar (refer to Figure 2-1). Click the Functions tab in the AutoPilot and select the function category and the specific function. Fill in the other necessary information such as the range of cells used as the argument to the function. |
| Insert a chart | Select the cells for the chart and choose Insert⇨Chart. Select the options and type of chart from the resulting AutoFormat Chart dialog box. Click Create to insert the chart. |

| *To Do This* | *Follow These Steps* |
|---|---|
| Edit a chart | Double-click the part of the chart you want to edit. Select the options from the resulting dialog box. Use icons on the toolbar (which change when you double-click a chart) to do other tasks (such as turning parts of the chart on or off and changing the chart type). |
| Perform a goal seek | Click in the cell with the formula. Choose Tools⇨Goal Seek. In the Goal Seek dialog box, enter the target value for the formula. In the Variable cell field, enter the cell whose value adjusts to reach the goal. Click OK to complete the goal seek. |
| Create scenarios | Select the cells whose values you plan to change for each scenario. Choose Tools⇨Scenarios. Assign a name to the scenario and click OK. Enter values in the cells. Repeat for each scenario you want to define. |
| Use scenarios | Define formulas that use the cells included in a scenario. You can then see the results for different scenarios by selecting each scenario from the drop-down list of scenarios. |

**Book III
Chapter 2**

**Preparing
Spreadsheets with
OpenOffice.org Calc**

# Chapter 3: Making Presentations with OpenOffice.org Impress

## In This Chapter

↙ Taking stock of OpenOffice.org Impress

↙ Getting started with Impress

↙ Using Impress to create presentations

**I**t seems the business world, or should I say the whole world, is full of PowerPoint rangers — those dedicated souls who live by their PowerPoint briefing packages (slide presentations). Imagining a meeting or a conference where someone isn't vigorously making points on-screen with PowerPoint is hard. Let's face it: Such programs are here to stay. Making presentations is a fact of life: Businesspeople have come to expect office-application suites to include some sort of presentation software.

Like Microsoft Office, the OpenOffice.org office-application suite comes with its own PowerPoint-like presentation software — OpenOffice.org Impress (or *Impress* for short). If you have used Microsoft PowerPoint and you're already familiar with its nuts and bolts — the concept of a slide, how to add text and graphics to a slide, how to organize the slides, and how to run a slide show — then you'll find getting started with Impress easy. Because some details of how you perform basic Impress tasks may differ from the way they're done in PowerPoint, I provide some quick reference tables to point you in the right direction. I start with an overview of Impress and then cover some categories of common tasks that you likely perform in Impress.

## Taking Stock of OpenOffice.org Impress

You'll find that Impress can do all the usual things that presentation software, such as Microsoft PowerPoint, can do. For example, you can create professional-looking slide shows in Impress, using capabilities such as these:

✦ Open and edit Microsoft PowerPoint files or convert Microsoft PowerPoint files to Impress format. One advantage of converting to Impress format is that Impress files are smaller in size than corresponding Microsoft PowerPoint files. Presentation files stored in Impress format are assigned the .sxi extension.

✦ Save documents in many different formats, including Microsoft PowerPoint 97/2000/XP, StarDraw 5.0 and 3.0, and StarImpress 5.0 and 4.0.

✦ Insert graphics and clip art from files of many different formats, including JPEG, GIF, ZSoft Paintbrush (PCX), TIFF, Windows BMP, Macintosh PICT, Encapsulated PostScript (EPS), Adobe Photoshop (PSD), AutoCAD DXF, and many more.

✦ Insert other OpenOffice.org documents (from programs such as Writer, Calc, and Draw) into a presentation.

✦ Quickly create a presentation with AutoPilot.

✦ Use all the drawing tools from OpenOffice.org Draw to add drawings to the slides.

✦ Export a presentation to a Web Page (HTML) with or without frames. You can also export the slides in any of the supported graphics file formats.

✦ Separate parts of the slide with layers so that you can edit or view each part separately.

✦ Use special effects such as animated text and graphics, sound, and slide transition effects.

✦ Create various text effects, such as aligning text along a curve, with FontWork (Format⇨Fontwork).

✦ Render text in 3D.

✦ Save versions of a presentation as you continue to change it and revert back to an older version, if necessary.

✦ Add speaker's notes to each slide and create handouts.

## Getting Started with Impress

The best way to get comfortable using Impress is simply to start using it. To start Impress, click the Impress icon — the icon showing a bar chart with a slide — on the panel or choose Main Menu⇨Office⇨OpenOffice.org Impress. The AutoPilot Presentation window appears and guides you through the steps of starting a new presentation. From the AutoPilot Presentation window, you can create an empty presentation, create a presentation from a template, or open an existing presentation. If you select an empty presentation and click Next, AutoPilot asks you to select the slide design and the slide-transition effect (that is, how Impress moves from one slide to the next). Then you can click Create to open the Impress window, where you can select the layout of your first slide. After you finish laying out a slide, you can proceed to insert new slides. For each slide, you can select the layout you want.

You can open and edit Microsoft PowerPoint files in Impress. To open an existing file, choose File➪Open and then select the file to open.

Before you start creating slides with Impress, take a moment to examine the Impress window (shown in Figure 3-1).

In Figure 3-1, note the major parts of the Impress window:

✦ **Menu bar:** Provides the standard pull-down menus such as File, Edit, and Help for performing all the tasks that Impress can do.

Object bar

Function bar

Menu bar

Ruler

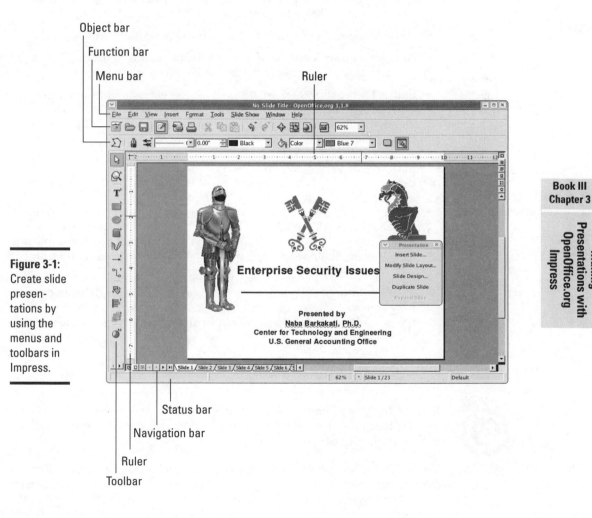

**Figure 3-1:**
Create slide presentations by using the menus and toolbars in Impress.

Status bar

Navigation bar

Ruler

Toolbar

**Book III
Chapter 3**

**Making
Presentations with
OpenOffice.org
Impress**

✦ **Function bar:** Shows the full pathname or the URL of the currently open file and also provides buttons for performing tasks such as opening, saving, and printing a document. You can also click icons on the function bar to open the Stylist, the Navigator, and the Gallery.

✦ **Object bar:** Enables you to format the document by applying styles, selecting fonts, or changing text attributes such as bold, italic, and underline. This bar changes according to the type of object you click (for example, plain text or graphic image).

✦ **Toolbar:** Along the left side of the window, the toolbar provides buttons that you can use to perform common tasks, such as inserting graphics, sorting cells, checking spelling, and grouping cells.

✦ **Rulers:** Shows the vertical and horizontal page dimensions.

✦ **Navigation bar:** Along the bottom of the slide, the navigation bar enables you to change the views and select a slide to work with.

✦ **Status bar:** Displays information about the current slide, such as the current slide number and the total count of slides. You can also click elements in the status bar and change settings, such as the zoom factor, for viewing the slide.

In addition to these toolbars, you can turn on two more toolbars (when visible, these toolbars appear at the bottom of the window, above the status bar):

✦ Choose View➪Toolbars➪Option Bar to turn on the option bar that appears below the navigation bar. The option bar displays icons through which you perform some drawing tasks such as edit curves, show grid lines, and indicate what happens when you click text and other objects.

✦ Choose View➪Toolbars➪Color Bar to turn on the color bar that appears at the bottom of the window, just above the status bar. The color bar displays colors that you can pick and use on objects. You can show or hide the color bar by clicking the downward-pointing arrow on the upper-left side of the color bar.

The largest part of the Impress window is the work area where you work on the current slide and where you focus most of your attention.

Use the tooltips to find out what an icon or menu option does. Mouse over a toolbar icon or a menu item and Impress displays a small tooltip window with a brief help message.

You don't have to set up anything to start using Impress. However, if you ever need to configure some aspects of Impress, you can do so through the Tools➪Options and Tools➪Configure menus. In particular, the Presentation category of the Options dialog box contains the options for Impress (shown in Figure 3-2). Go through each of the Presentation options to see what you can configure from this dialog box.

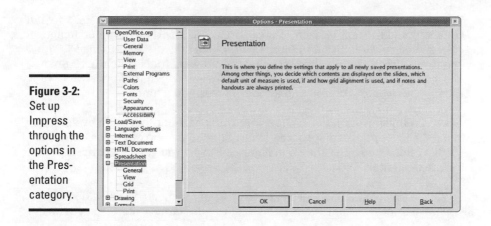

**Figure 3-2:**
Set up
Impress
through the
options in
the Pres-
entation
category.

# Using Impress

You get the AutoPilot when you choose File➪New➪Presentation. If you want
a blank presentation, simply click Create in the first step of the AutoPilot.
Impress displays the Modify Slide dialog box (shown in Figure 3-3) with a
gallery of slide layouts.

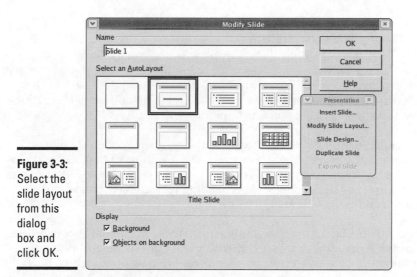

**Figure 3-3:**
Select the
slide layout
from this
dialog
box and
click OK.

**Book III
Chapter 3**

*Making
Presentations with
OpenOffice.org
Impress*

You can select a slide layout from the dialog box (refer to Figure 3-3) and
click OK. Impress then displays an empty slide with the selected layout.

Typically, a slide layout may have a title area and some text bullets. You can click and add the text to each of these areas. To insert any graphic image, choose Insert⇨Graphics and pick the graphics file you want to insert. You can draw directly in the slide by using the drawing tools from the toolbar along the left side of the Impress window. To see which tool does what, move the mouse over any button and a tooltip gives you a hint.

After you finish working on a slide, you can insert another slide by selecting Insert⇨Slide. Impress displays an Insert Slide dialog box (similar to the Modify Slide dialog box shown in Figure 3-3) and you can select the layout for the next slide.

To save a presentation, choose File⇨Save from the menu. For new documents, you have to provide a filename and select the directory where to save the file.

That, in a nutshell, is how you create presentations in PowerPoint. In the following sections, I provide some quick reference tips for performing the following types of tasks with Impress:

✦ Preparing presentations

✦ Adding graphics and special effects

✦ Delivering presentations

## *Preparing presentations*

Typically, you start with a blank slide with a specific layout. For example, the slide has a title area and a bulleted list for the points you want to make with the slide. You can click in the title area, type the title, and then click in the bulleted text area to start entering text. Then you add another slide and continue with the process until you finish the presentation.

If you're going to present information that's already in a Writer document (see Chapter 1 of this minibook), you can use the outline of that Writer document to start a presentation. The Writer document does have to follow one rule — it must use the heading styles (Heading 1, Heading 2, and so on) for the major sections in the document.

To create a presentation from the outline of a Writer document that uses the heading styles, open the document in Writer and choose Send⇨Outline to Presentation from the Writer menu. An Impress window opens with a new presentation with slides based on the headings in the Writer document. Each Heading 1 style becomes a new slide and the Heading 2 and Heading 3 styles appear as bulleted text in the slides.

After working on the set of slides, you may want to rearrange the slides. To rearrange slides in a different order, choose View⇨Workspace⇨Slides View. Impress displays an array of miniature-sized slides, arranged in a rectangular grid in the work area (shown in Figure 3-4). Think of this view as the slide sorter because you can move the slides around and sort them.

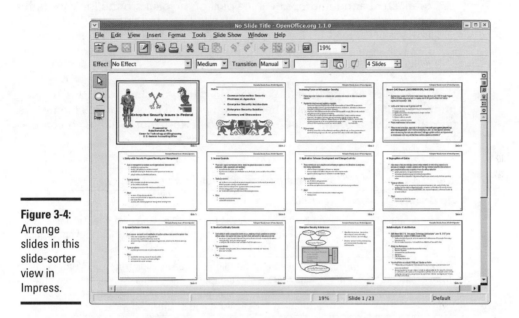

**Book III**
**Chapter 3**

Making
Presentations with
OpenOffice.org
Impress

In the slide-sorter view shown in Figure 3-4, you can drag and drop slides into different positions and rearrange them in the order you want. To delete a slide in this view, click the slide to select it and press Delete (or choose Edit⇨Delete). When prompted to confirm the deletion, you can click Yes if you really want to delete the slide. Double-click a slide to return to the usual single-slide view.

As you work on the presentation, keep in mind these concepts:

✦ **Master slide:** You can think of the *master slide* as the background of every slide. If you put text or other fields (such as date and page number) on the master slide, those elements appear on every slide in the presentation.

✦ **Layers:** You can have layers in both the master slide as well as each individual slide. Think of the layers as transparent sheets on which you place some related text and graphics. The slide is then made up of these layers superimposed on one another. You can use layers to group related information. For example, if you're drawing the plans for a house, you can put all the dimensions on a separate layer. The nice part is that you can hide or show layers easily. Just click the third icon from the left on the navigation bar (refer to Figure 3-1) or choose View➪Layer.

✦ **Master notes and master handouts:** The idea is the same as that for the master slide. You can define some fields and text on the master notes or master handout; these become part of the background for your notes and handouts. The *notes* refer to any explanatory text you add to the bottom of each slide. The *handouts* are printouts of the slides that you can hand out to an audience at a briefing. Typically, several slides fit on a page.

Well, I could go on and on, but you can learn best by simply starting to use Impress. But if you need some help as you prepare presentations in Impress, consult Table 3-1 for information on how to perform some of the common tasks.

| Table 3-1 | Common Presentation Preparation Tasks |
|---|---|
| *To Do This* | *Follow These Steps* |
| Create a blank presentation | Choose File➪New➪Presentation and click Create in the AutoPilot window that appears. Select the slide layout from the Modify Slide dialog box. |
| Create a presentation from a Writer document | Choose Send➪Outline to Presentation from the Writer menu A new presentation appears in an Impress window with the Writer document's outline, built out of the heading styles (Heading 1, Heading 2, and so on). |
| Open an existing presentation | Choose File➪Open and then pick the file to open. If you are in the AutoPilot window, click Open Existing Presentation, select <Other Position>, and click Create. Impress then displays the Open dialog box from which you can select a file to open. |
| Assign a title to the presentation | Choose File➪Properties. Click the Description tab in the resulting dialog box and type in the Title field. This title appears in the Impress window's title bar. |
| Insert a slide | Choose Insert➪Slide and select the slide layout from the Insert Slide dialog box. |
| Duplicate current slide | Choose Insert➪Duplicate Slide. |
| Delete a slide | Right-click the slide tab and select Delete Slide from the pop-up menu. Click Yes when asked to confirm. |
| Change layout of an existing slide | Choose Format➪Modify Layout. Select a layout from the Modify Slide dialog box and click OK. |
| Create a template | Prepare a presentation with slides representing all the styles you want. Choose File➪Save As and save the file as an OpenOffice.org Presentation template. |

| *To Do This* | *Follow These Steps* |
|---|---|
| Switch to slide view | Click the icon on the far left on the navigation bar along the bottom of the slide or choose View⇨Slide. |
| Edit master slide | Click the second icon from the left on the navigation bar along the bottom of the slide (or choose View⇨Master⇨Slide). Edit the master slide (used as a background for all slides). |
| Edit master notes | Choose View⇨Master⇨Notes. Edit the master notes page you want to use as the background for all the notes. You can insert fields, such as page numbers and dates. |
| Add notes to a slide | Choose View⇨Master⇨Notes View. Click in the notes area of slide and type the notes. |
| Work in outline view | Choose View⇨Master⇨Outline View. |
| View slides in miniature format | Choose View⇨Workspace⇨Slides View. You can rearrange the order of slides in this view. |
| Edit layers | Click the third icon from the left on the navigation bar along the bottom of the slide (or choose View⇨Layer). Click a layer tab to edit that layer. |
| Insert layer | While editing a layer, right click a layer tab and select Insert Layer from the pop-up menu. |
| Hide or show a layer | While editing a layer, right-click the layer tab and select Modify Layer from the pop-up menu. Deselect the Visible property and click OK. Turning on the Visible property makes the layer visible again. |
| Change zoom level | Right-click the zoom level on the status bar and select the new zoom level from the pop-up menu. |
| View slides in color, gray-scale, or black and white | Choose View⇨Display Quality and then pick whether you want color, grayscale, or black and white. |

## Adding graphics and special effects

To jazz up your presentation, you may want to add graphics, charts, and other special effects to the slides. With Impress, you can do nearly everything you can think of — all you have to decide is how many bells and whistles your presentation needs. It's your call, but I recommend using these features judiciously lest they detract from your presentation's main message.

If you want to add some simple drawings to the slide, you can pick from the drawing tools on the toolbar on the left side of the Impress window (refer to Figure 3-1) and start drawing on the slide. To insert an image into the slide, choose Insert⇨Graphics and then select the image file you want to insert.

You can also insert charts to graphically depict data. You start by inserting a chart with dummy data, and then you edit the data as well as other features of the chart. To add a chart and edit the data, follow these steps:

**Book III**
**Chapter 3**

**Making Presentations with OpenOffice.org Impress**

*1.* **Choose Insert⇨Chart.**

A chart with a default chart type and dummy data appears.

*2.* **Resize the chart by dragging the handles around the border of the chart; then right-click the chart and select Chart Data from the pop-up menu that appears (see Figure 3-5).**

A mini-spreadsheet appears with the dummy chart data.

*3.* **Edit the row and column labels and enter the data you want the chart to display.**

*4.* **When you're done editing the chart, click the green check mark (located to the right of the data entry area) to apply the changes and close the Chart Data window.**

*5.* **To change the chart type, right-click the chart and choose Chart Type from the pop-up menu that appears; choose a new type and click OK.**

You can do a lot more than just add graphics and charts to your slide presentations. You can insert spreadsheets and Writer documents into a slide, add text that runs along a curve, and add special effects to various elements in a slide. Table 3-2 summarizes some common graphics and special-effects tasks, including information on how to perform each task.

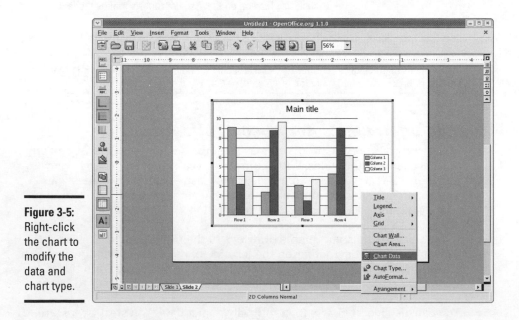

**Figure 3-5:**
Right-click
the chart to
modify the
data and
chart type.

| Table 3-2 | Common Graphics and Special Effects Tasks |
|---|---|
| *To Do This* | *Follow These Steps* |
| Draw in a slide | Select the drawing tools from the toolbar on the left side of the Impress window and draw in the slide using the mouse. You can also add text and text callouts (a text box with a line pointing to something you are trying to explain) |
| Apply text effects | Choose Format➪FontWork. Select the text and use the FontWork tools to apply special effects to the text, such as placing text along a curve and showing a shadow. |
| Convert text or graphics to 3D | Right-click the text or graphic and choose Convert➪To 3D. For text, make sure that you click the text frame, and not the text itself. |
| Insert graphics from a file | Choose Insert➪Graphics and then select the graphics file you want to insert. |
| Add a chart | Choose Insert➪Chart to insert a dummy chart. Right-click the chart and select Chart Data from the pop-up menu. The dummy data appears in a mini-spreadsheet window. Edit the data. To change the chart type, right-click the chart and select Chart Type. Then pick a chart type from the resulting dialog box. |
| Adding graphics to a slide | Choose Insert➪Graphics to select a graphics file to insert. |
| Insert a drawing prepared in Draw | Choose Insert➪OLE Object. In the resulting dialog box, choose Create from File➪Search. Select the drawing file from the Open dialog box and click Open. Click OK to insert the drawing from the file. Double-click the drawing to edit it later on. |
| Insert a formula | Choose Insert➪Object➪Formula. The OpenOffice.org Math application appears. Use the formula Selection and Commands windows to create the formula and adjust the font size. As you construct the formula, it appears in the slide. Click anywhere else in the slide to return to Impress. Double-click the formula to edit it again. |
| Apply effects on objects in a slide | Choose Slide Show➪Effects to open the Effects window. Choose View➪Preview so you can see the effects in a small preview window as you try them. Select the object to which you want to apply an effect, select the effect from the Effects window, and then click the green check mark. Observe the effect in the preview window. Stop when you like the effects. Apply effects to more objects if you want. |
| Control how slides transition | Choose Slide Show➪Slide Transition to open the Slide Transition window. Choose View➪Preview so you can see the effect of a transition in a small preview window as you apply each transition. Select a transition effect from the Slide Transition window, and click the green check mark. Observe the effect in the preview window. Stop when you like the effects. Apply transition effects to other slides as needed. |

**Book III
Chapter 3**

**Making
Presentations with
OpenOffice.org
Impress**

## Delivering presentations

After you prepare a spectacular set of slides, you have to deliver it to your audience. Delivering presentations typically involves tasks such as preparing speaker's notes, running a slide show, converting the presentation into HTML for delivery via the Web, and printing handouts. Table 3-3 summarizes some common presentation delivery tasks.

You can also export an Impress presentation directly to an Adobe Portable Document Format (PDF) file. PDFs make electronically sharing a presentation with everyone easy because anyone can view and print PDF files by using the free Adobe Reader (available at www.adobe.com/products/acrobat/readstep2.html).

| Table 3-3 | Common Presentation Delivery Tasks |
|---|---|
| *To Do This* | *Follow These Steps* |
| Edit the master handout | Choose View⇨Master⇨Handout. Edit the master handout that gets used as the background for all the handouts. |
| Prepare handouts | Choose View⇨Master View⇨Handout View. The view shows the handout page with a number of slides per page. To change the layout, right-click the handout and choose Slide⇨Modify Slide from the pop-up menu. Select the layout (how many slides per page of handout) you want. |
| Print handouts | Choose View⇨Master View⇨Handout View. Choose File⇨Print. |
| Run a slide show | Choose Slide Show⇨Slide Show, or press Ctrl+F2. Click to advance through slides. Press Esc to stop the slide show or at the last slide click to end show. |
| Create a custom slide show | Choose Slide Show⇨Custom Slide Show. Click New in the Custom Slide Show window. Assign a name and then select the slides you want in the slide show, in the order you want them to appear. Drag the slides up or down to change that order. Click OK and then click Close. |
| Run a custom slide show | Choose Slide Show⇨Custom Slide Show. Select the custom slide show (you see the name you used when creating the slide show). Turn on the Use Custom Slide Show check box and then click Start. |
| Print the slides to a PDF file | Choose File⇨Export as PDF. In the Export dialog box, enter the filename. Click OK. |
| Create an HTML version of the presentation | Choose File⇨Export. In the Export dialog box, enter a filename and select Web Page as the format. Click Save. Go through the HTML Export steps, select the file type you want (for example, HTML with or without frames) as well as the format for the images (JPEG or GIF) used to represent each slide. |

# Chapter 4: Drawing with OpenOffice.org Draw

## In This Chapter

↙ **Taking stock of OpenOffice.org Draw**

↙ **Getting started with Draw**

↙ **Using Draw**

Sometimes you need images, diagrams, and illustrations to make a point. Whether you need a quick sketch or a complex diagram, OpenOffice.org Draw, or *Draw* for short, provides you with the tools you need to prepare your drawing.

Draw is a separate drawing program in the OpenOffice.org office application suite, but you can also access many of Draw's drawing tools from other OpenOffice.org applications, such as Writer and Impress. When you use Draw to prepare drawings, you save the drawing in a file. You can later insert the drawing as a Draw object into other OpenOffice.org documents, such as a Writer document or an Impress presentation. The nice part about inserting a Draw object into a Writer or Impress document is that you can always double-click and edit the drawing directly, even while it's in the Writer or Impress document.

In this chapter, I introduce you to the Draw application. I provide an overview and then provide quick references to help you perform some common drawing tasks in Draw.

## Taking Stock of OpenOffice.org Draw

You'll find that Draw can do all the usual things that a typical drawing program can do. To give you a feel for Draw's features, here are some things you can do with Draw:

✦ Use an array of standard drawing tools, such as polygons, circles, and Bézier curves.

✦ Draw flow charts, organization charts, and network diagrams with smart connector lines.

✦ Mix *vector graphics* (lines, geometric shapes, text) with *raster* images (JPEG, GIF, and other bitmapped formats).

✦ Access Draw tools from other OpenOffice.org applications, such as Writer and Impress.

✦ Apply special effects to text (such as laying out text along a curve and adding shadows) with FontWork.

✦ Insert other OpenOffice.org objects (such as spreadsheets and slides) into your drawing.

✦ Draw 3D shapes and intersect 3D objects.

✦ Convert text and curves to 3D objects.

✦ Crop images.

✦ Control many aspects of image colors, such as brightness, contrast, and transparency.

✦ Separate various parts of the drawing with layers so that you can edit and view each part separately.

✦ Export a drawing to a Web Page (HTML) or other image-file formats, such as EPS, JPEG, and GIF.

## Getting Started with Draw

The best way to find out how to use Draw is to simply start using it. To start Draw, select Main Menu⇨Office⇨OpenOffice.org Draw. The Draw window appears with an empty drawing area. You can then select tools from the toolbar that appears on the left side of the Draw window and begin drawing. Figure 4-1 shows the Draw window with a not-so-typical drawing that includes text, 3D shapes, and an image.

Before you start using Draw, take some time to study the Draw window and the various toolbars (as shown in Figure 4-1). Notice that the Draw window has the following major parts:

✦ **Menu bar:** Provides the standard pull-down menus (such as File, Edit, and Help) for performing all the tasks that Draw can do.

✦ **Function bar:** Shows the full pathname or the URL of the currently open file and also provides buttons for performing tasks such as opening, saving, and printing a document. You can also click icons on the function bar to open the Stylist (a list of graphics styles), the Navigator (a list of drawing items), and the Gallery (a collection of predefined graphic objects such as 3D shapes, backgrounds, and bullets).

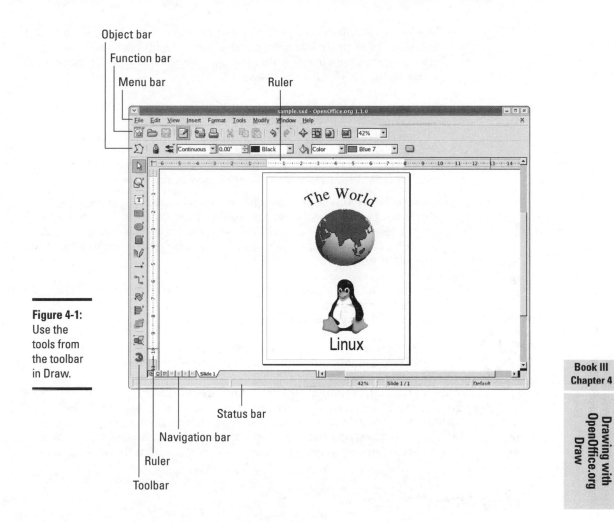

Object bar

Function bar

Menu bar

Ruler

**Figure 4-1:**
Use the
tools from
the toolbar
in Draw.

Status bar

Navigation bar

Ruler

Toolbar

Book III
Chapter 4

Drawing with
OpenOffice.org
Draw

✦ **Object bar:** Shows the common formatting and style attributes, including colors, that apply to the currently selected type of object such as
text, image, or vector graphics.

✦ **Toolbar:** Located along the left side of the window, the toolbar provides
icons that you can click to select tools for drawing or editing objects in
the drawing.

✦ **Rulers:** Shows the vertical and horizontal page dimensions.

✦ **Navigation bar:** Located along the bottom of the window, the navigation
bar enables you to change views and select a drawing to work with.

✦ **Status bar:** Displays information about the current drawing, such as the location of the pointer and which object is currently selected. You can also click elements in the status bar and change settings, including the zoom factor for viewing the drawing.

In addition to these toolbars, you can turn on two more toolbars:

✦ Choose View⇨Toolbars⇨Option Bar to turn on the option bar that appears below the navigation bar. The option bar displays icons through which you perform tasks, such as edit curves, show grid lines, and indicate what happens when you click text and other objects.

✦ Choose View⇨Toolbars⇨Color Bar to turn on the color bar that appears at the bottom of the window, just above the status bar. The color bar displays colors that you can pick and use on objects. You can show or hide the color bar by clicking the downward-pointing arrow on the upper-left side of the color bar.

As with other OpenOffice.org applications, the largest part of the Draw window is the work area where you work on the current drawing and where you spend most of your time in the application.

If you don't know what an icon or a menu does, mouse over that item and Draw displays a small tooltip window with a brief help message.

You don't have to set up anything to start using Draw. However, if you ever need to configure anything in Draw, you can do so through the Tools⇨ Options and Tools⇨Configure menus. In particular, the Drawing category of the Options dialog box contains the options for Draw. Go through each of the Presentation options to see what you can configure from this dialog box.

## Using Draw

For the most part, you use the drawing tools located on the toolbar along the left side of the Draw window (refer to Figure 4-1). For some tasks, you use the menus and the color toolbar that you make visible by choosing View⇨Toolbars⇨Color Bar.

When using tools from the vertical toolbar, you have to *long-click*. Don't worry, it's nothing complicated. You simply click an icon and hold down the mouse button until a small window appears. That's a long click. After you try it and see it in action, you'll immediately get the hang of it. If you click normally, you simply get to use the currently selected icon instead of being shown a selection of icons to pick from.

Long-clicking works with any icon that has a small, right-pointing arrow. The icon shows the currently selected tool, but a long click brings out all the icons on a *tearoff menu* — a small window that floats in the Draw window and shows all the choices you can make. To use the tools from the tearoff menu, follow these steps:

*1.* **Long-click (click and hold down the mouse) any icon with a right-pointing arrow until a tearoff menu appears (see Figure 4-2).**

The tearoff menu shows icons representing the available tools (if a tool does not apply to the currently selected object, it's grayed out). The tools remain available in the tearoff menu (see Figure 4-2), labeled for the name of the tool you've clicked on the toolbar. You can click and use any tool you want. When you don't need the tearoff menu anymore, click the X to close the menu.

**Figure 4-2:**
A tearoff
menu.

*2.* **To reuse the same tool again, click the icon as you normally do on the vertical toolbar.**

The cursor changes shape, and you can use the tool to draw.

You may wonder how to remember what each icon on the toolbar does. My advice: Don't try. Simply mouse over and read the tooltip. That's what the tooltips are for!

Try using the tools to prepare drawings. Consult Table 4-1 for hints on how to perform some common drawing tasks in Draw.

| Table 4-1 | Common Drawing Tasks |
|---|---|
| *To Do This* | *Follow These Steps* |
| Create a new drawing | Choose File⇨New⇨Drawing. |
| Open an existing drawing file | Choose File⇨Open and then select the file to open from the Open dialog box. |
| Insert an image | Choose Insert⇨Graphics and then select the file to insert from the Open dialog box. |
| Apply styles | Press F11 to open the Stylist window, if it isn't already open. Select the object to which you want to apply a style. Double-click the style in the Stylist. |

*(continued)*

**Table 4-1** *(continued)*

| To Do This | Follow These Steps |
|---|---|
| Adding text and graphics objects to a drawing | Click the icon for a drawing tool from the vertical toolbar. Use the mouse to draw, using the selected tool. Mouse over and use the tooltip to figure out what the different tools do. |
| Change an object's attributes | Right-click the object and select the attribute such as the line, area, position, and size that you want to change. |
| Duplicate an object | Select the object and choose Edit⇨Duplicate. In the Duplicate dialog box, make selections for the placement and the number of copies and click OK. |
| Select multiple objects | Click objects while holding down the Shift key. |
| Group objects | Select the objects you want to group. Right-click the selection and select Group from the pop-up menu. |
| Ungroup objects | Right-click the group and select Ungroup from the pop-up menu. |
| Rotate objects | Select one or more objects. Click the Effects icon on the toolbar (use the tooltip to find this icon) and click the Rotate icon. Grab one of the handles that appear on the object and use it to rotate the object. |
| Align objects | Select the objects. Right-click the selection and select Alignment and the alignment type such as Left, Top, Center, and so on. |
| Distribute objects evenly | Select three or more objects. Right-click the selection and select Distribution. Use the Distribution dialog box to choose how you want the objects distributed on-screen. |
| Arrange the order of objects | Select the objects. Right-click the selection and select Arrange and the placement order, such as Bring to Front, Send Backward, and so on. |
| Add 3D objects to a drawing | Click the 3D Object icon on the toolbar (the last icon from the top). |
| Convert text to 3D | Click to select the text frame. Then right-click the frame and select Convert⇨To 3D. Click and rotate the 3D text to your liking. |
| Apply special effects to text | Choose Format⇨FontWork. Select the text frame to which you want to apply special effects. Select the effects you want from the FontWork window. (For example, you can place the text along a curve and show a shadow for the text.) |
| Add a background to text | Right-click the text frame and select Area. Select options for the text background from the resulting Area dialog box. |
| Apply font effects to text | Right-click the text frame and select Character from the pop-up menu. Click the Font Effects tab in the resulting Character dialog box. Select the effects (such as embossed or engraved characters) from the Font Effects tab. |
| Crop an image | Select the image and click the Crop icon — the icon on the right on the object bar. Select the options you want from the Crop dialog box and click OK. |

| *To Do This* | *Follow These Steps* |
|---|---|
| Change an image's characteristics | Click an image and use the icons on the object bar to adjust the color, contrast, brightness, and transparency. You can change the red, green, and blue components in the image colors, and adjust an on-screen object's transparency from 0% (opaque) to 100% (fully transparent). |
| Merge two 3D objects into a single 3D object | Bring the two 3D objects near each other. Select the 3D object you want to appear in the front and press Ctrl+X to cut it. Click the second object and press F3. Now press Ctrl+V to paste the front object onto the second object. The objects now appear merged. Click and adjust the objects individually. Press Ctrl+F3 to end the process of merging the objects. |
| Export drawings to an image file | Choose File⇨Export. In the resulting Export dialog box, enter a filename and select the format you want. Supported formats include BMP (Windows Bitmap), EPS (Encapsulated PostScript), GIF, JPEG, PNG (Portable Network Graphics), PPM (Portable Pixmap), TIFF, and many more. |

# Book IV

# Networking

The 5th Wave          By Rich Tennant

"It's okay. One of the routers must have gone down and we had a brief broadcast storm."

# Contents at a Glance

Chapter 1: Connecting to the Internet .............................................................................271

Chapter 2: Setting Up a Local Area Network .................................................................295

Chapter 3: Adding a Wireless Ethernet LAN .................................................................307

Chapter 4: Managing the Network ...................................................................................319

Chapter 5: Cool Networking Projects ..............................................................................329

# Chapter 1: Connecting to the Internet

## In This Chapter

✔ **Understanding the Internet**

✔ **Deciding how to connect to the Internet**

✔ **Connecting to the Internet with DSL**

✔ **Connecting to the Internet with cable modem**

✔ **Setting up a dial-up PPP link**

The Internet is fast becoming a lifeline for most of us. Seems we can't get through a day without it (and I know I could not write this book without it). Sometimes I wonder how we ever managed without the Internet — and that you want to connect your Fedora Core system to the Internet is a pretty safe bet. In this chapter, I show you how to connect to the Internet in several different ways — depending on whether you have DSL, cable modem, or dial-up network connection.

Two of the options for connecting to the Internet — DSL and cable modem — involve connecting a special modem to an Ethernet card on your Fedora Core system. In these cases, you have to set up Ethernet networking on your Fedora Core system. (I explain networking in Chapter 2 of this minibook.) In this chapter, I show you in detail how to set up a DSL or a cable modem connection.

I also show you the other option — dial-up networking — that involves dialing up an Internet Service Provider (ISP) from your Fedora Core system.

## Understanding the Internet

How you view the Internet depends on your perspective. Common folks like us see the Internet in terms of the services we use. For example, as users we think of the Internet as an information-exchange medium — with features such as

✦ **E-mail:** Send e-mail to any other user on the Internet, using addresses such as `mom@home.net`.

✦ **Web:** Download and view documents from millions of servers throughout the Internet.

✦ **Newsgroups:** Read newsgroups and post news items to newsgroups with names such as `comp.os.linux.networking` or `comp.os.linux.setup`.

✦ **Information sharing:** Download software, music files, videos, and so on. Reciprocally, you may provide files that users on other systems can download.

✦ **Remote access:** Log on to another computer on the Internet, assuming that you have access to that remote computer.

The techies among us say the Internet is a worldwide *network of networks*. The term *internet* (without capitalization) is a short form of *internetworking* — the interconnection of networks. The Internet Protocol (IP) was designed with the idea of connecting many separate networks.

In terms of physical connections, the Internet is similar to a network of highways and roads. This similarity is what has prompted the popular press to dub the Internet "the Information Superhighway." Just as the network of highways and roads includes some interstate highways, many state roads, and many more residential streets, the Internet has some very high-capacity networks (for example, a 10-Gbps backbone can handle 10 billion bits per second) and a large number of lower-capacity networks ranging from 56 Kbps dial-up connections to 45 Mbps T3 links (*Kbps* is thousand-bits-per-second and *Mbps* is million-bits-per-second). The high-capacity network is the backbone of the Internet.

In terms of management, the Internet is not run by a single organization, nor is it managed by any central computer. You can view the physical Internet as a "network of networks" managed collectively by thousands of cooperating organizations. Yes, a collection of networks managed by *thousands* of organizations — sounds amazing, but it works!

## Deciding How to Connect to the Internet

So you want to connect to the Internet, but don't know how? Let me count the ways. Nowadays you have three popular options for connecting homes and small offices to the Internet (of course, huge corporations and governments have many other ways to connect):

✦ **Digital Subscriber Line (DSL):** Your local telephone company, as well as other telecommunications companies, may offer DSL. DSL provides a way to send high-speed digital data over a regular phone line. Typically, DSL offers data-transfer rates of between 128 Kbps and 1.5 Mbps. You can download from the Internet at much higher rates than when you send data from your PC to the Internet (upload). One caveat with DSL is that your home must be between 12,000 and 15,000 feet from your local central office (the phone-company facility where your phone lines end up). The distance limitation varies from provider to provider. In the United States, you can check out the distance limits for many providers at www.dslreports.com/distance.

✦ **Cable modem:** If the cable television company in your area offers Internet access over cable, you can use that service to hook up your Fedora Core system to the Internet. Typically, cable modems offer higher data-transfer rates than DSL — for the same cost. Downloading data from the Internet via cable modem is much faster than sending data from your PC to the Internet. You can expect routine download speeds of 1.5 Mbps and upload speeds of around 128 Kbps, but sometimes you may get even higher speeds than these.

✦ **Dial-up networking:** A dial-up connection is what most of us were using before DSL and cable modems came along. You hook up your PC to a modem that's connected to the phone lines. Then dial up an ISP to connect to the Internet. That's why it's called dial-up networking — establishing a network connection between your Fedora Core PC and another network (the Internet) through a dial-up modem. In this case, the maximum data-transfer rate is 56 Kbps.

DSL and cable-modem service connect you to the Internet and also act as your Internet Service Provider (ISP); in addition to improved speed, what you're paying for is an IP address and your e-mail accounts. If you use a dial-up modem to connect to the Internet, first you have to connect to the phone line (for which you pay the phone company) and then select and pay a separate ISP — which gives you a phone number to dial and all the other necessary goodies (such as an IP address and e-mail accounts).

Table 1-1 summarizes all these options. You can consult that table and select the type of connection that's available to you and that best suits your needs.

| Table 1-1 | Comparison of Dial-up, DSL, and Cable | | |
|---|---|---|---|
| *Feature* | *Dial-up* | *DSL* | *Cable* |
| Equipment | Modem | DSL modem, Ethernet card | Cable modem, Ethernet card |
| Also requires | Phone service and an Internet Service Provider (ISP) | Phone service and location within 12,000 to 15,000 feet of central office | Cable TV connection |
| Connection type | Dial to connect | Always on, dedicated | Always on, shared |

*(continued)*

**Table 1-1** *(continued)*

| Feature | Dial-up | DSL | Cable |
|---|---|---|---|
| Typical speed | 56 Kbps maximum | 640 Kbps download, 128 Kbps upload (higher speeds cost more) | 1.5 Mbps download, 128 Kbps upload |
| One-time costs (estimate) | None | Install = $100-200; Equipment = $200-300 (may be leased and may require activation cost) | Install = $100-200; Equipment = $60-100 (may be leased) |
| Typical monthly cost (2004) | Phone charges = $20/month; ISP charges = $15-30/month | $50/month; may require monthly modem lease | $50/month; may require monthly modem lease |

*Note:* Costs vary by region and provider. Costs shown are typical ones for U.S. metropolitan areas.

# Connecting with DSL

DSL stands for *Digital Subscriber Line*. DSL uses your existing phone line to send digital data in addition to the normal analog voice signals (*analog* means continuously varying, whereas digital data is represented by 1s and 0s). The phone line goes from your home to a central office, where the line connects to the phone company's network — by the way, the connection from your home to the central office is called the *local loop*. When you sign up for DSL service, the phone company hooks up your phone line to some special equipment at the central office. That equipment can separate the digital data from voice. From then on, your phone line can carry digital data that is then directly sent to an Internet connection at the central office.

## How DSL works

A special box called a *DSL modem* takes care of sending digital data from your PC to the phone company's central office over your phone line. Your PC can connect to the Internet with the same phone line that you use for your normal telephone calls — you can make voice calls even as the line is being used for DSL. Figure 1-1 shows a typical DSL connection to the Internet.

Your PC talks to the DSL modem through an Ethernet connection, which means that you need an Ethernet card in your Fedora Core system.

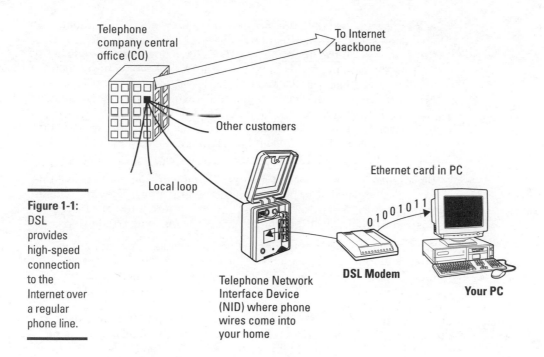

Telephone
company central
office (CO)

To Internet
backbone

Other customers

Ethernet card in PC

Local loop

01001011

**DSL Modem**

Telephone Network
Interface Device
(NID) where phone
wires come into
your home

**Your PC**

**Figure 1-1:**
DSL
provides
high-speed
connection
to the
Internet over
a regular
phone line.

Your PC sends digital data over the Ethernet connection to the DSL modem.
The DSL modem sends the digital data at different frequencies than those
used by the analog voice signals. The voice signals occupy a small portion of
all the frequencies that the phone line can carry. DSL uses the higher frequencies to transfer digital data, so both voice and data can travel on the
same phone line.

The distance between your home and the central office — the *loop length* —
is a factor in DSL's performance. Unfortunately, the phone line can reliably
carry the DSL signals over only a limited distance — typically three miles or
less, which means that you can get DSL service only if your home (or office)
is located within about three miles of your phone company's central office.
Your phone company can tell you whether your location can get DSL or not.
Often it has a Web site where you can type in your phone number and get a
response about DSL availability. For example, try www.dslavailability.com
for U.S. locations.

## DSL alphabet soup: ADSL, IDSL, SDSL

I have been using the term *DSL* as if there were only one kind of DSL. As you
may imagine, nothing is ever that simple. There are in fact three variants of
DSL, each with different features. Take a look:

✦ **ADSL:** Asymmetric DSL, the most common form of DSL, has much higher download speeds (from the Internet to your PC) than upload speeds (from your PC to the Internet). ADSL can have download speeds of up to 8 Mpbs and upload speeds of up to 1 Mbps. ADSL works best when your location is within about 2½ miles (12,000 feet) of your central office. ADSL service is priced according to the download and upload speeds you want. A popular form of ADSL, called G.lite, is specifically designed to work on the same line you use for voice calls. G.lite has a maximum download speed of 1.5 Mbps and maximum upload speed of 512 Kbps.

✦ **IDSL:** ISDN DSL (ISDN is an older technology called *Integrated Services Digital Network*) is a special type of DSL that works at distances of up to five miles between your phone and the central office. The downside is that IDSL only offers downstream (from the Internet to your PC) and upstream (from your PC to the Internet) speeds of up to 144 Kbps.

✦ **SDSL:** Symmetric DSL provides the equal download and upload speed of up to 1.5 Mbps. SDSL is priced according to the speed you want, with the higher speeds costing more. The closer your location is to the phone company central office, the faster the connection you can get.

DSL speeds are typically specified by two numbers separated by a slash, such as this: 1500/384. The numbers refer to data-transfer speeds in kilobits per second (that is, thousands-of-bits per second, abbreviated Kbps). The first number is the download speed, the second the upload. Thus 1500/384 means you can expect to download from the Internet at a maximum rate of 1,500 Kbps (or 1.5 Mbps) and upload to the Internet at 384 Kbps. If your phone line's condition is not perfect, you may not get these maximum rates — both ADSL and SDSL adjust the speeds to suit existing line conditions.

The price of DSL service depends on which variant — ADSL, IDSL, or SDSL — you select. For most home users, the primary choice is ADSL (or, more accurately, the G.lite form of ADSL) with transfer speed ratings of 1500/128.

## Typical DSL setup

To get DSL for your home or business, you have to contact a DSL provider. In addition to your phone company, you can find many other DSL providers. No matter who provides the DSL service, some work has to be done at your central office — the place where your phone lines connect to the rest of the phone network. The work involves connecting your phone line to equipment that can work with the DSL modem at your home or office. The central office equipment and the DSL modem at your location can then do whatever magic is needed to send and receive digital data over your phone line.

Because of the need to set up your line at the central office, it takes some time after you place an order to get your line ready for DSL.

The first step for you is to check out the DSL providers that provide service and see if you can actually get the service. Because DSL can work only over certain distances — typically less than 2.5 miles — between your location and the central office, you have to check to see if you are within that distance limit. Contact your phone company to verify. You may be able to check this availability on the Web. Try typing into Google (`www.google.com`) the words **DSL**, **availability**, and your local phone company's name. You probably get a Web site where you can type in your phone number to find out if DSL is available for your number.

If DSL is available, you can look for the types of service — ADSL versus SDSL — and the pricing. The price depends on the download and upload speeds you want. Sometimes phone companies offer a simple residential DSL (basically the G.lite form of ADSL) with a 1500/128 speed rating — meaning you can download at up to 1,500 Kbps and upload at 128 Kbps. Of course, these are the *maximums*, and your mileage may vary.

After selecting the type of DSL service and provider, you can place an order and have the provider install the necessary equipment at your home or office. Figure 1-2 shows a sample connection diagram for typical residential DSL service.

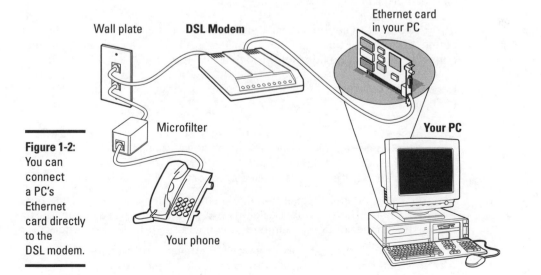

**Figure 1-2:** You can connect a PC's Ethernet card directly to the DSL modem.

Book IV
Chapter 1

Connecting to
the Internet

Here are some key points to note in Figure 1-2:

✦ Connect your DSL modem's data connection to the phone jack on a wall plate.

✦ Connect the DSL modem's Ethernet connection to the Ethernet card on your PC.

✦ When you connect other telephones or fax machines on the same phone line, install a *microfilter* between the wall plate and each of these devices.

Because the same phone line carries both voice signals and DSL data, you need the microfilters to protect the DSL data from possible interference. You can buy them at electronic stores or from the DSL provider.

When you connect your Fedora Core PC to the Internet using DSL, the connection is always on — and with more potential for outsiders to break into the PC. You need to make sure that the Fedora Core firewall setting is set at High Security. To configure the firewall settings, choose Main Menu⇨System Settings⇨Security Level from the GNOME desktop.

You can protect your Fedora Core system from intruders and, as an added bonus, share the high-speed connection with other PCs in a local-area network (LAN). You need a router that can perform Network Address Translation (NAT). Such a *NAT router* translates multiple private Internet Protocol (IP) addresses from an internal LAN into a single public IP address, which allows all the internal PCs to access the Internet.

If you also want to set up a local-area network, you need an Ethernet hub to connect the other PCs to the network. Figure 1-3 shows a typical setup that connects a LAN to the Internet through a NAT router and a DSL modem.

Here are the points to note when setting up a connection like the one shown in Figure 1-3:

✦ You need a NAT router with two 10BaseT Ethernet ports (the 10BaseT port looks like a large phone jack, also known as an *RJ-45 jack*). Typically one Ethernet port is labeled *Internet* (or *External* or *WAN* for *wide-area network*) and the other one is labeled *Local* or *LAN* (for *local-area network*).

✦ You also need an Ethernet hub. For a small home network, you can buy a 4- or 8-port Ethernet hub. Basically, you want a hub with as many ports as the number of PCs you intend to connect to your local-area network.

✦ Connect the Ethernet port of the DSL modem to the Internet port of the NAT router, using a 10BaseT Ethernet cable (these look like phone wires with bigger RJ-45 jacks and are often labeled *Category 5* or *Cat 5* wire).

✦ Connect the Local Ethernet port of the NAT router to one of the ports on the Ethernet hub, using a 10BaseT Ethernet cable.

✦ Now connect each of the PCs to the Ethernet hub. (Of course, to do so you must first have an Ethernet card installed and configured in each PC.)

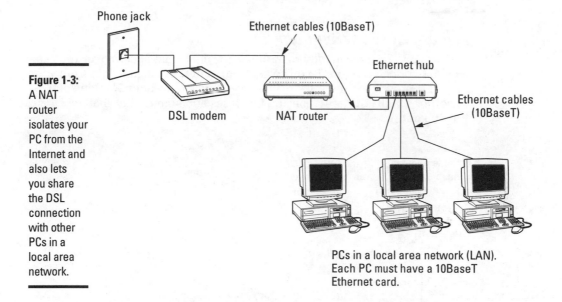

**Figure 1-3:**
A NAT router isolates your PC from the Internet and also lets you share the DSL connection with other PCs in a local area network.

You can also buy a NAT router with a built-in 4- or 8-port Ethernet hub. With such a combined router-hub, you need only one box to set up a LAN and connect it to the Internet via a DSL modem. These boxes are typically sold under the name Cable/DSL router because they work with both DSL and a cable modem.

Consult Chapter 2 of this minibook for information on how to configure networking on the Fedora Core system so your system can access the Internet.

DSL providers typically use a protocol known as PPP over Ethernet (PPPoE) to establish a connection between your PC and the equipment at the provider's central office. PPPoE requires you to provide a username and password to establish the network connection over Ethernet. To set up your system for a PPPoE DSL connection, all you have to do is select Main Menu⇨System Tools⇨Internet Configuration Wizard and click *xDSL connection* from the list. Then go through the successive screens and provide the requested information such as login name and password.

## Connecting with a Cable Modem

Cable TV companies also offer high-speed Internet access over the same coaxial cable that carries television signals to your home. After the cable company installs the necessary equipment at its facility to send and receive digital data over the coaxial cables, customers can sign up for cable Internet service. You can then get high-speed Internet access over the same cable that delivers cable TV signals to your home.

## How cable modem works

A box called a *cable modem* is at the heart of Internet access over the cable TV network (see Figure 1-4). The cable modem takes digital data from your PC's Ethernet card and puts in an unused block of frequency (think of it as another TV channel, but instead of pictures and sound, this channel carries digital data).

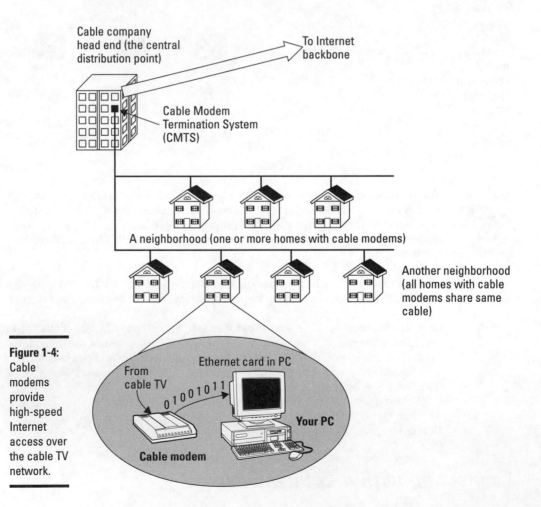

**Figure 1-4:** Cable modems provide high-speed Internet access over the cable TV network.

The cable modem places *upstream data* — data that's being sent from your PC to the Internet — in a different channel than the *downstream* data that's coming from the Internet to your PC. By design, the speed of downstream data transfers is much higher than that of upstream transfers. The assumption is that people download far more stuff from the Internet than they upload. (Probably true for most of us.)

The coaxial cable that carries all those hundreds of cable TV channels to your home is a very capable signal carrier. In particular, the coaxial cable can carry signals covering a huge range of frequencies — hundreds of megahertz (MHz). Each TV channel requires 6 MHz — and the coaxial cable can carry hundreds of such channels. The cable modem places the upstream data in a small frequency band and expects to receive the downstream data in a whole other frequency band.

At the other end of your cable connection to the Internet is the *Cable Modem Termination System* (CMTS) — also known as the *head end* — that your cable company installs at its central facility (refer to Figure 1-4). The CMTS connects the cable TV network to the Internet. It also extracts the upstream digital data sent by your cable modem (and by those of your neighbors as well), and sends all of it to the Internet. The CMTS also puts digital data into the upstream channels so your cable modem can extract that data and provide it to your PC via the Ethernet card.

Cable modems can receive downstream data at the rate of about 30 Mbps and send data upstream at around 3 Mbps. However, all the cable modems in a neighborhood share the same downstream capacity. Each cable modem filters out — separates — the data it needs from the stream of data that the CMTS sends out. Cable modems follow a modem standard called DOCSIS, which stands for Data Over Cable Service Interface. You can buy any DOCSIS-compliant modem and use it with your cable Internet service; all you have to do is call the cable company and give them the modem's identifying information so that the CMTS can recognize and initialize the modem.

In practice, with a cable modem you can get downstream transfer rates of around 1.5 Mbps and upstream rates of 128 Kbps. These are maximum rates and your transfer rate is typically lower, depending on how many users in your neighborhood are using cable modems at the same time.

If you want to check your downstream transfer speed, go to `bandwidth place.com/speedtest` and click the link to start the test. For my cable modem connection (for example), the tests reported a downstream transfer rate of about 1.4 Mbps.

**Book IV Chapter 1**

Connecting to the Internet

## Typical cable modem setup

To set up cable modem access, your cable TV provider must offer high-speed Internet access. If the service is available, you can call to sign up. The cable companies often have promotional offers such as no installation fee or a reduced rate for three months. Look for these offers. If you are lucky, it may have a promotion going on just when you want to sign up.

The installation is typically done by a technician, who splits your incoming cable into two — one side goes to the TV and the other to the cable modem. The technician provides information about the cable modem to the cable company's head end for set up at its end. When all that is done, you can plug in your PC's Ethernet card to the cable modem and you're all set to enjoy high-speed Internet access. Figure 1-5 shows a typical cable-modem hookup.

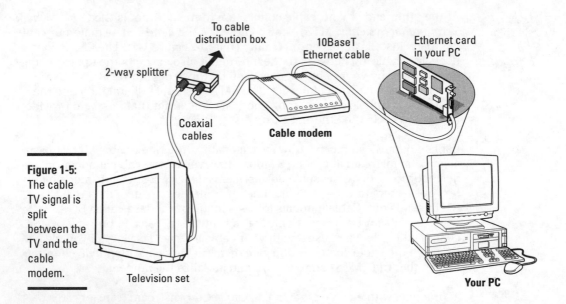

**Figure 1-5:** The cable TV signal is split between the TV and the cable modem.

The cable modem connects to an Ethernet card in your PC. If you don't have an Ethernet card in your PC, the cable company technician often provides one.

Here are some key points to note about the cable modem setup in Figure 1-5:

✦ Split the incoming cable TV signal into two parts by using a two-way splitter (the cable company technician installs the splitter). By the way, the two-way splitter needs to be rated for 1 GHz; otherwise, it may not pass through the frequencies that contain the downstream data from the Internet.

✦ Connect one of the video outputs from the splitter to your cable modem's F-type video connector using a coaxial cable.

✦ Connect the cable modem's 10BaseT Ethernet connection to the Ethernet card on your PC.

✦ Connect your TV to the other video output from the two-way splitter.

When you use cable modem to connect your Fedora Core PC to the Internet, the connection is always on, so you have more of a chance that someone may try to break into the PC. Set the firewall setting to High Security. To configure the firewall settings, choose Main Menu⇨System Settings⇨Security Level from the GNOME desktop.

You may want to add a NAT (Network Address Translation) router between your PC and the cable modem. As an added bonus, you can even share a cable modem connection with all the PCs in your own local-area network (LAN) by adding an Ethernet hub. Better yet, buy a combination NAT-router-and-hub so you have only one box do the whole job. By the way, the NAT router/hubs are typically sold under the name *Cable/DSL router* because they work with both DSL and cable modem.

The NAT router translates private Internet Protocol (IP) addresses into a public IP address. When connected through a NAT router, any PC in the internal LAN can access the Internet as if it had its own unique IP address. Result: You can share a single Internet connection among many PCs. (An ideal solution for an entire family of Net surfers!)

Figure 1-6 shows a typical setup with a cable modem connection being shared by a number of PCs in a LAN.

Here are the points to note when setting up a connection like the one shown in Figure 1-6:

✦ You need a Cable/DSL NAT router with two 10BaseT Ethernet ports (the 10BaseT port — also known as an RJ-45 jack — looks like a large phone jack). Typically, one Ethernet port is labeled *Internet* (or *External* or *WAN* for *wide area network*) and the other one is labeled *Local*.

✦ If you plan to set up a LAN, you also need an Ethernet hub. For a small home network, you can buy a 4- or 8-port Ethernet hub. Basically, you want a hub with as many ports as the number of PCs you intend to connect to your local area network.

✦ Consider buying a single box that acts as a NAT router and also a hub with a number of Ethernet ports.

**Book IV
Chapter 1**

**Connecting to
the Internet**

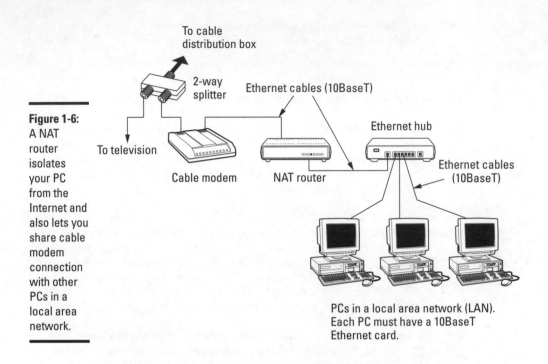

**Figure 1-6:**
A NAT router isolates your PC from the Internet and also lets you share cable modem connection with other PCs in a local area network.

To cable distribution box

2-way splitter

Ethernet cables (10BaseT)

Ethernet hub

To television

Cable modem

NAT router

Ethernet cables (10BaseT)

PCs in a local area network (LAN). Each PC must have a 10BaseT Ethernet card.

✦ Connect the video cable to the video input port of the cable modem.

✦ Connect the Ethernet port of the cable modem to the Internet port of the NAT router using a 10BaseT Ethernet cable (these look like phone wires, except that the Ethernet cables have bigger RJ-45 jacks and are often labeled Category 5 or Cat 5 wire).

✦ Connect the Local Ethernet port of the NAT router to one of the ports on the Ethernet hub using a 10BaseT Ethernet cable.

✦ Now connect each of the PCs to the Ethernet hub. Of course, each PC must have an Ethernet card.

In Chapter 2 of this minibook, I explain how to configure the PCs in such a LAN so that they can all access the Internet.

## Setting Up Dial-Up Networking

*Dial-up networking* refers to connecting a PC to a remote network through a dial-up modem. If you are ancient enough to remember the days of dialing up with Procomm or some serial communications software, realize that there is a significant difference between dial-up networking and the old days of serial communication. Both approaches use a modem to dial up a remote computer and to establish a communication path, but the serial-communication software makes your computer behave like a dumb terminal connected to the remote computer. The serial-communication software exclusively uses dial-up connection. You cannot run another copy of the communication software and use the same modem connection, for example.

In dial-up networking, both your PC and the remote system run network-protocol (called TCP/IP) software. When your PC dials up and sets up a communication path, the network protocols exchange data packets over that dial-up connection. The neat part is that any number of applications can use the same dial-up connection to send and receive data packets. So your PC becomes a part of the network to which the remote computer belongs. (If the remote computer is not on a network, dial-up networking creates a network that consists of the remote computer and your PC.)

In Chapter 2 of this minibook, I describe TCP/IP protocol some more, but I have to use the term as well as a few concepts such as *Internet Protocol* (IP) address and *Domain Name Service* (DNS) when describing how to set up dial-up networking.

Setting up a TCP/IP network over a dial-up link involves specifying the protocol — the convention — for packaging a data packet over the communication link. *Point-to-Point Protocol* (PPP) is such a protocol for establishing a TCP/IP connection over any point-to-point link, including dial-up phone lines. Fedora Core supports PPP, and it comes with the configuration tools you can use to set up PPP so that your system can establish a PPP connection with your ISP.

Here's what you have to do to set up dial-up networking in Fedora Core:

1. Install an internal or external modem in your PC. If your PC did not already come with an internal modem, you can buy an external modem and connect it to the PC's serial or USB port.

2. Connect the modem to the phone line.

3. Get an account with an ISP. Every ISP provides you a phone number to dial, a username, and a password. Additionally, the ISP gives you the full names of servers for e-mail and news. Typically, your system automatically gets an IP address.

4. Test your modem and make sure it's working. You can do this testing with the Minicom serial communication package that comes with Fedora Core.

5. Run the Internet Configuration Wizard to set up a PPP connection.

6. Activate the PPP connection to connect to the Internet.

I briefly go over these steps in the following sections.

**Book IV
Chapter 1**

**Connecting to
the Internet**

# Winmodems: They *only* do Windows

A quick word of caution about the *winmodems* that come with many new PCs and laptops. Winmodems are software-based internal modems — totally different from the traditional hardware modems. Also known as *Windows modems* or *software modems* (*softmodem* for short), they work only with special driver software (which in turn works only with Microsoft Windows). With winmodems and Linux, you're pretty much on your own — but you can find some useful guidance online at the Linux Winmodem Support home page at `www.lin modems.org`. For example, I found out that the winmodem in my laptop uses a Conexant chipset and that a Linux driver is available from `www.linuxant.com/drivers/hsf/full /downloads.php`. Then I downloaded the zipped RPM file for Fedora core that matches my kernel version (as reported by the `uname -r` command). Then I unzipped the RPM file with the `unzip` command and installed it on the laptop, using the `rpm` command. Now I can use my laptop's winmodem from Fedora Core applications. By the way, the free version of the driver is limited to 14.4 Kbps only. To go up to 56 Kbps, you have to get the full version for a modest price of around $15 U.S. The free version, however, is good for testing to make sure that the driver works with your softmodem.

## Connecting the modem

*Modem* is a contraction of modulator/demodulator — a device that converts digital signals (string of 1s and 0s) into continuously varying analog signals that transmit over telephone lines and radio waves. Thus, the modem is the intermediary between the digital world of the PC and the analog world of telephones. Figure 1-7 illustrates the concept of a modem.

**Figure 1-7:** A modem bridges the digital world of PCs and the analog world of telephones.

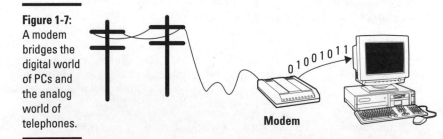

Modem

Inside the PC, 1s and 0s are represented with voltage levels, but signals carried over telephone lines are usually tones of different frequencies. The modem sits between the PC and the telephone lines and makes data communication possible over the phone lines. The modem converts information back and forth between the voltage/no voltage representation of digital circuits and different frequency tones that are appropriate for transmission over phone lines.

Before you can dial out using an external modem, you have to make sure that the modem is properly connected to one of the serial or USB ports of your PC.

If you have an external modem, make sure that your modem is properly connected to the power supply and that the modem is connected to the telephone line. Buy the right type of cable to connect the modem to the PC. You need a straight through serial cable to connect the modem to the PC. The connectors at the ends of the cable depend on the type of serial connector on your PC. The modem end of the cable needs a male 25-pin connector. The PC end of the cable often is a female 9-pin connector. You can buy modem cables at most computer stores. Often you can find 9-pin-female-to-25-pin-male modem cables sold under the label *AT Modem Cable*. Connect USB modems by using a USB cable.

If your PC has an internal modem, all you have to do is connect the phone line to the phone jack at the back of the internal-modem card. If it's a winmodem, you still connect the phone line, but you also have to do a bit of research on the Internet and download a driver that makes the winmodem work in Fedora Core. After you install a working Linux driver for a winmodem, it works just like the older serial-port modems. See the sidebar "Winmodems: They *only* do Windows" for more information.

### Learning the serial-device names

The PC typically has two serial ports, called COM1 and COM2 in MS-DOS parlance. Many new PCs with *Universal Serial Bus* (USB) have only one serial port. The PC also can support two more serial ports: COM3 and COM4. Because of these port names, serial ports are often referred to as *COM ports*.

Like other devices, the serial-port devices are represented by device files in the /dev directory. The serial ports also need *interrupt-request* (IRQ) numbers and I/O port addresses. Two IRQs — 3 and 4 — are shared among the four COM ports. Table 1-2 lists the serial-device names corresponding to the PC's COM ports, as well as the IRQs and I/O port addresses assigned to the four serial ports.

| Table 1-2 | Device Names for Serial Ports | | |
|-----------|-------------------------------|-----|-------------|
| *COM port* | *Device name* | *IRQ* | *I/O address* |
| COM1 | /dev/ttyS0 | 4 | 0x3f8 |
| COM2 | /dev/ttyS1 | 3 | 0x2f8 |
| COM3 | /dev/ttyS2 | 4 | 0x3e8 |
| COM4 | /dev/ttyS3 | 3 | 0x2e8 |

**Book IV
Chapter 1**

**Connecting to
the Internet**

All these devices are already in your Fedora Core system. In a terminal window, type **ls -l /dev/ttyS\*** | **more** to see a listing of these device files.

The device name is different if your modem connects to a USB port or if you have a winmodem. For winmodems, you have to first download and install a driver. You can locate Linux drivers for many winmodems by checking the www.linmodems.org Web site. In many cases, Linux winmodem drivers set up the modem device /dev/modem as a symbolic link to the actual device file. For example, the Conexant HSF driver sets up /dev/modem as a symbolic link to /dev/ttySHSF0, which is the actual device name for that softmodem. Because of the symbolic link, I can refer to the modem device by the generic name /dev/modem instead of the somewhat complicated device names.

### Checking if the Linux kernel detected the serial port

To verify that the Linux kernel detects the serial port correctly, check the boot messages with the following command:

```
dmesg | grep ttyS
```

If you see a message such as the following, Linux detects a serial port in your PC:

```
ttyS0 at 0x03f8 (irq = 4) is a 16550A
```

In this case, the message indicates that the Linux kernel has detected the first serial port (COM1). It shows the I/O address (in hexadecimal), 0x3f8 and IRQ 4. The last part of the message — 16550A — refers to the identifying number of the *universal asynchronous receiver/transmitter* (UART) chip, which is at the heart of all serial communications hardware (the UART converts each byte to a stream of 1s and 0s, and vice versa when it receives such a stream).

Of course, if you have a softmodem installed, you may see something similar to the following in response to the **dmesg** | **grep ttyS** command:

```
ttySHSF0 at I/O 0x2400 (irq = 10) is a Conexant HSF softmodem
```

You can also check for the serial ports with the setserial command. Type the following command to see detailed information about the serial ports:

```
setserial -g /dev/ttyS?
```

Any serial device listed in the output of this command with an unknown UART is either not installed or not detected by the Linux kernel. For softmodems, you don't see a UART listed because for softmodems the UART functionality is performed in software.

## Testing the modem

After you complete the physical installation of the modem and verify that the Linux kernel detects the serial port, you can try to dial out through the modem. The best approach is to use the Minicom serial communications program that comes with Fedora Core.

Minicom is similar to other communications software, such as Procomm or Crosstalk, that you may have used under MS-DOS or Windows.

To run Minicom, log in as root and type **minicom** at the shell prompt in the terminal window (or in a virtual console). Minicom runs and resets the modem. Figure 1-8 shows the result of running Minicom in a terminal window.

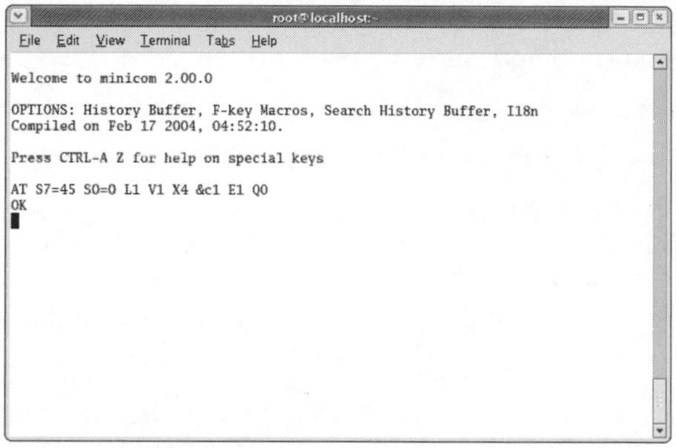

**Figure 1-8:**
You can test your modem manually with Minicom.

If you don't see the words OK, it probably means that this particular serial-device name is not set correctly. To set the serial device, follow these steps:

*1.* **Press Ctrl+A and then Z.**

   Minicom displays its help screen.

*2.* **Press O.**

   Minicom displays its configuration menu.

*3.* **Use the arrow key to select Serial port setup and press Enter.**

   Minicom displays the serial port settings.

*4.* **Press A.**

   Minicom puts the cursor in the line that shows the serial-device name. Edit the device name to match where your modem is connected. For example, if the modem device is set up with the /dev/modem symbolic link, make sure that the device name is set to /dev/modem.

5. **Press Enter twice.**

   Minicom returns to the configuration menu.

6. **Select Save setup as dfl and press Enter.**

   Minicom saves the settings.

7. **Select Exit and press Enter.**

   Minicom returns to online mode.

8. **Press Ctrl+A and X.**

   Minicom prompts you to ask whether you really want to exit.

9. **Press Enter to exit.**

   After setting the correct device name for the serial port where the modem is connected, make sure that your modem is powered on and connected to the phone line.

10. **Start Minicom again (type** minicom **in the terminal window).**

11. **Press Ctrl+A to get the attention of the Minicom program.**

    After you press Ctrl+A, if you press Z, a help screen appears in the form of a text window. In the help screen, you can get information about other Minicom commands.

12. **From the help screen, press Enter to go back to online mode.**

    In online mode, you can use the modem's AT commands to dial out. In particular, you can use the ATDT command to dial the phone number of another modem (for example, dial your ISP's number). When you get the login prompt, you know that the modem is working. Figure 1-9 shows the results of a typical dial-up using Minicom: The line that says Connect 38400 indicates that it's a 38.4 Kbps connection. Only 38.4 Kbps with a 56 Kbps modem. (No wonder I needed DSL or a cable modem!)

**Figure 1-9:**
Use the
ATDT
command to
manually
dial out
using
Minicom.

*13.* **To exit Minicom, press Ctrl+A and then type X.**

*14.* **Press Enter again to close Minicom.**

## Setting up and activating a PPP connection

Most ISPs provide PPP dial-up access to the Internet through one or more systems that the ISP maintains. If you sign up for such a service, the ISP provides you the information that you need to make a PPP connection to the ISP's system. Typically, this information includes the following:

✦ The phone number to dial to connect to the remote system

✦ The username and password that you must use to log in to the remote system

✦ The names of the ISP's mail and news servers

✦ The IP address for your PPP connection. Your ISP does not provide this address if the IP address is assigned dynamically (which means the IP address may change every time your system establishes a connection).

✦ IP addresses of the ISP's *Domain Name Servers* (DNS). The ISP does not provide these addresses if it assigns the IP address dynamically.

Of this information, the first two items are what you need to set up a PPP connection.

Follow these steps to set up a PPP connection using the Internet Configuration Wizard:

*1.* **Log in as** root **and choose Main Menu⇨System Tools⇨Internet Configuration Wizard from the GNOME desktop.**

If you are not logged in as root, type the root password when you're prompted for it.

The Select Device Type dialog box appears (as shown in Figure 1-10).

*2.* **Select Modem Connection from the Device Type list, and then click Forward.**

The Select Modem dialog box shows information about your modem.

*3.* **Click Forward to continue.**

The Select Provider dialog box appears.

*4.* **Fill in the connection information — the ISP's phone number, your login name, and password — in the text boxes (shown in Figure 1-11); click Forward to continue.**

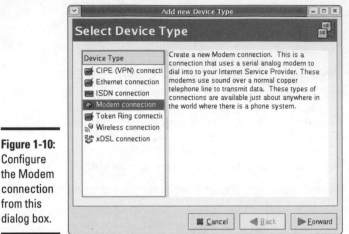

**Figure 1-10:**
Configure
the Modem
connection
from this
dialog box.

5. **Enter the IP settings — whether you want to automatically get an IP address or provide a static IP address, and then click Forward to continue.**

   Typically, you select the option to automatically obtain an IP address and name server settings from the ISP.

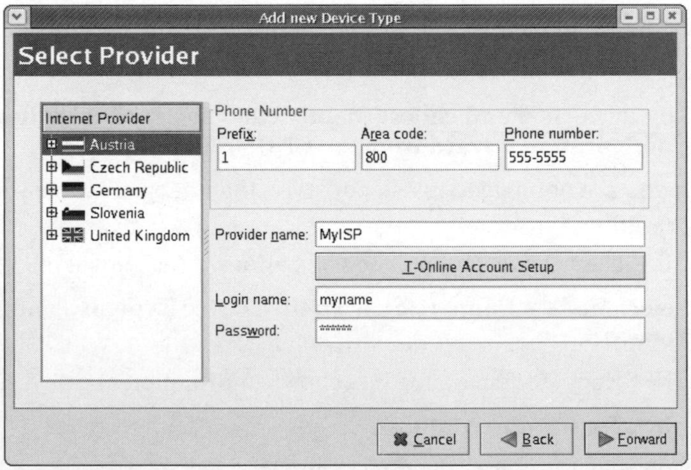

**Figure 1-11:**
Fill in the
connection
information
in this
dialog box.

6. **Click Apply to save the dial-up configuration information, and then close the Internet Configuration Wizard.**

   The Network Configuration dialog box appears with the name of the new dial-up connection in a list (see Figure 1-12).

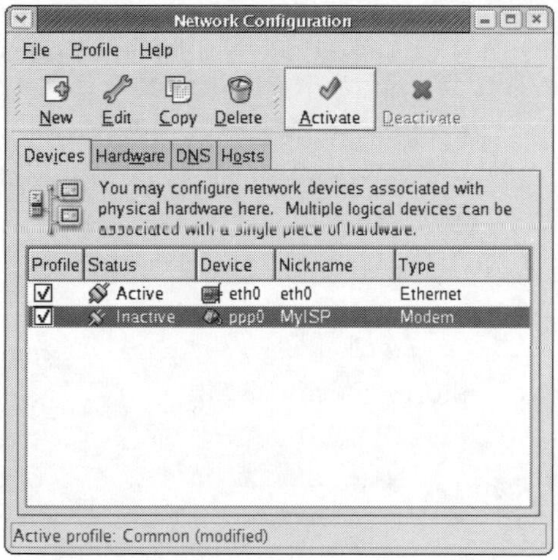

**Figure 1-12:**
Click
Activate in
the Network
Configura-
tion dialog
box to
establish
the PPP
connection.

7. **Select the connection name, and then click Activate.**

8. **When you're done, click Deactivate to turn the PPP connection off.**

## Configuring CHAP and PAP authentication

The PPP server on your system has to authenticate itself to the ISP's
PPP server before the PPP connection can get fully up and running.
*Authentication* requires proving that you have a valid account with the ISP;
essentially providing a username and a *secret* (that is, a password). PPP
specifies two ways of exchanging the authentication information between
the two ends of the connection:

✦ **Challenge Handshake Authentication Protocol (CHAP)** requires the
remote end to send a randomly generated challenge string along with
the remote server's name. The local system looks up the secret, using
the server's name; then it sends back a response that includes its name
and a value that combines the secret and the challenge, using a one-way
hash function. The remote system then checks that value against its own
calculation of the expected hash value. If the values match, the authentication succeeds; otherwise, the remote system terminates the connection. In this case, the name and secret are stored in the /etc/ppp/
chap-secrets file. Note that the remote system can repeat the CHAP
authentication any time while the PPP link is up.

✦ **Password Authentication Protocol (PAP)** is like the normal login process.
When using PAP, the local system repeatedly sends a username (name)
and password (secret) until the remote system acknowledges the authentication or ends the connection. The name and secret are stored in the
/etc/ppp/pap-secrets file. Note that the username and password are
sent in the clear (that is, unencrypted).

The Linux PPP server supports both types of authentication. For both PAP and CHAP, the information that the PPP server needs is a name and a secret — a username-password pair. This authentication information is stored in the following configuration files:

◆ `/etc/ppp/chap-secrets` stores the information for CHAP. Here's what a typical `chap-secrets` file looks like:

```
# Secrets for authentication using CHAP
# client        server        secret        IP addresses
"naba"          *             "mypassword"
```

◆ `/etc/ppp/pap-secrets` stores the information for PAP. Here's a typical `pap-secrets` file:

```
# Secrets for authentication using PAP
# client        server        secret        IP addresses
"naba"          *             "mypassword"
```

As you can see, the formats of the entries are the same for both `chap-secrets` and `pap-secrets`. Four fields are in each line, in the following order:

◆ `client`: This field contains the name that is used during authentication. You get this username from the ISP.

◆ `server`: This field contains the name of the remote system to which you are authenticating the local system. If you don't know the server's name, put an asterisk to indicate any server.

◆ `secret`: This field is the secret that your system's PPP server has to send to the remote system to authenticate itself. You receive this password from the ISP.

◆ `IP addresses`: This optional field can contain a list of the IP addresses that the local system may use when connecting to the specified server. Typically, this field is left blank because the local system usually gets a dynamic IP address from the server and (therefore) doesn't know what IP address it uses.

# Chapter 2: Setting Up a Local Area Network

## In This Chapter

✔ Understanding TCP/IP networks

✔ Setting up an Ethernet LAN

✔ Configuring TCP/IP networking

✔ Connecting your LAN to the Internet

*L*inux comes with built-in support for TCP/IP (*Transmission Control Protocol/Internet Protocol*) networking, as do most modern operating systems from Windows to Mac OS. You can have TCP/IP networking over many different physical interfaces, such as Ethernet cards, serial ports, and parallel ports.

Typically, you use an Ethernet network for your local area network (LAN) — at your office or even your home (if you happen to have several systems at home). To connect to remote systems over a modem, you use TCP/IP networking over *Point-to-Point Protocol* (PPP).

This chapter describes how to set up an Ethernet network. Even if you have a single PC, you may need to set up an Ethernet network interface so you can connect your PC to high-speed Internet access that uses DSL or cable modem. (I cover DSL and cable modems in Chapter 1 of this minibook.)

## Understanding TCP/IP

You can understand TCP/IP networking best if you think in terms of a layered model with four layers. Think of each layer as responsible for performing a particular task. The layered model describes the flow of data between the physical connection to the network and the end-user application. Figure 2-1 shows the four-layer network model for TCP/IP.

In this four-layer model, information always moves from one layer to the next. For example, when an application sends data to another application, the data goes through the layers in this order: Application⇨Transport⇨ Network⇨Physical. At the receiving end, the data goes up from Physical⇨ Network⇨Transport⇨Application.

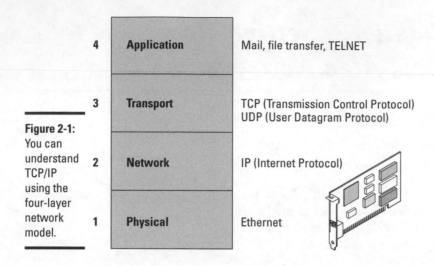

**Figure 2-1:**
You can understand TCP/IP using the four-layer network model.

| 4 | Application | Mail, file transfer, TELNET |
| 3 | Transport | TCP (Transmission Control Protocol) UDP (User Datagram Protocol) |
| 2 | Network | IP (Internet Protocol) |
| 1 | Physical | Ethernet |

Each layer has its own set of *protocols* — conventions — for handling and formatting the data. If you think of sending data as something akin to sending letters through the postal service, a typical protocol is a preferred sequence of actions for a task such as addressing an envelope (first the name, then the street address, and then city, state, and Zip or other postal code).

Here's what each of the four layers does, top to bottom:

✦ **Application:** Runs the applications that users use, such as e-mail readers, file transfers, and Web browsers. Application-level protocols are Simple Mail Transfer Protocol (SMTP) and Post Office Protocol (POP) for e-mail; HyperText Transfer Protocol (HTTP) for the Web; and File Transfer Protocol (FTP) for file transfers. Application-level protocols also have a port number that you can think of as an identifier for a specific application. For example, port 80 is associated with HTTP or the Web server.

✦ **Transport:** Sends data from one application to another. The two most important protocols in this layer are Transmission Control Protocol (TCP) and User Datagram Protocol (UDP). TCP guarantees delivery of data; UDP just sends the data without ensuring that it actually reaches the destination.

✦ **Network:** This layer is responsible for getting data packets from one network to another. If the networks are far apart, the data packets are routed from one network to the next until they reach their destination. The primary protocol in this layer is the Internet Protocol (IP).

✦ **Physical:** Refers to the physical networking hardware (such as an Ethernet card or Token Ring card) that carries the data packets in a network.

The beauty of the layered model is that each layer only takes care of its specific task, leaving the rest to the other layers. The layers can mix and match — you can have TCP/IP network over any type of physical network medium, from Ethernet to radio waves (in a wireless network). The software is modular as well because each layer can be implemented in different modules. For example, typically the Transport and Network layers already exist as part of the operating system and any application can make use of these layers.

## TCP/IP and the Internet

TCP/IP has become the protocol of choice on the Internet — *the* "network of networks" that evolved from ARPAnet. The U.S. Government's Advanced Research Projects Agency (ARPA) initiated research in the 1970s on a new way of sending information, using packets of data sent over a network. The result was ARPAnet: a national network of linked computers. Subsequently, ARPA acquired a Defense prefix and became DARPA. Under the auspices of DARPA, the TCP/IP protocols emerged as a popular collection of protocols for *internetworking* — communication among networks.

TCP/IP has flourished because the protocol is open. That means the technical descriptions of the protocol appear in public documents, so anyone can implement TCP/IP on specific hardware and software.

TCP/IP also made great inroads because stable, working software was available. Instead of a paper description of network architecture and protocols, the TCP/IP protocols *started out* as working software — and who can argue with what's already working? These days (as a result), TCP/IP rules the Internet.

## IP addresses

When you have many computers on a network, you need a way to identify each one uniquely. In TCP/IP networking, the address of a computer is the IP address. Because TCP/IP deals with internetworking, the address is based on the concepts of a network address and a host address. You may think of the idea of a network address and a host address as having to provide two addresses to identify a computer uniquely:

✦ Network address indicates the network on which the computer is located.

✦ Host address indicates a specific computer on that network.

The network and host addresses together constitute an *IP address* and it's a 4-byte (32-bit) value. The convention is to write each byte as a decimal value and to put a dot (.) after each number. Thus you see network addresses such as 132.250.112.52. This way of writing IP addresses is known as *dotted-decimal* or *dotted-quad* notation.

Book IV
Chapter 2

Setting Up a Local
Area Network

---

# Next-generation IP (IPv6)

When the 4-byte IP address was created, the number of available addresses seemed adequate. Now, however, the 4-byte addresses are running out. The Internet Engineering Task Force (IETF) recognized the potential for running out of IP addresses in 1991, and began work on the next-generation IP addressing scheme. They called it IPng (for Internet Protocol Next Generation) and intended that it will eventually replace the old 4-byte addressing scheme (called IPv4, for IP Version 4).

Several alternative addressing schemes for IPng were proposed and debated. The final contender, with a 128-bit (16-byte) address, was dubbed IPv6 (for IP Version 6). On September 18, 1995, the IETF declared the core set of IPv6 addressing protocols to be an IETF Proposed Standard.

IPv6 is designed to be an evolutionary step from IPv4. The proposed standard provides direct interoperability between hosts using the older IPv4 addresses and any new IPv6 hosts. The idea is that users can upgrade their systems to use IPv6 when they want and that network operators are free to upgrade their network hardware to use IPv6 without affecting current users of IPv4. Sample implementations of IPv6 are being developed for many operating systems, including Linux. For more information about IPv6 in Linux, consult the Linux IPv6 FAQ/HOWTO at www.linuxhq.com/IPv6/.

The IPv6 128-bit addressing scheme allows for 340,282,366,920,938,463,463,374,607,431,768,211,456 unique hosts! That should last us for a while!

---

In decimal notation, a byte (which has 8 bits) can have a value between 0 and 255. Thus a valid IP addresses can use only the numbers between 0 and 255 in the dotted-decimal notation.

## *Internet services and port numbers*

The TCP/IP protocol suite has become the *lingua franca* of the Internet because many standard services are available on any system that supports TCP/IP. These services make the Internet tick by facilitating the transfer of mail, news, and Web pages. These services go by well-known names such as the following:

✦ **DHCP** (Dynamic Host Configuration Protocol) is for dynamically configuring TCP/IP network parameters on a computer. DHCP is primarily used to assign dynamic IP addresses and other networking information (such as name server, default gateway, and domain names) needed to configure TCP/IP networks. The DHCP server listens on port 67.

✦ **FTP** (File Transfer Protocol) is used to transfer files between computers on the Internet. FTP uses two ports — data is transferred on port 20, while control information is exchanged on port 21.

✦ **HTTP** (HyperText Transfer Protocol) is a protocol for sending documents from one system to another. HTTP is the underlying protocol of the Web. By default, the Web server and client communicate on port 80.

✦ **SMTP** (Simple Mail Transfer Protocol) is for exchanging e-mail messages between systems. SMTP uses port 25 for information exchange.

✦ **NNTP** (Network News Transfer Protocol) is for distribution of news articles in a store-and-forward fashion across the Internet. NNTP uses port 119.

✦ **SSH** (Secure Shell) is a protocol for secure remote login and other secure network services over an insecure network. SSH uses port 22.

✦ **TELNET** is used when a user on one system logs in to another system on the Internet (the user must provide a valid user ID and password to log in to the remote system). TELNET uses port 23 by default, but the TELNET client can connect to any port.

✦ **SNMP** (Simple Network Management Protocol) is for managing all types of network devices on the Internet. Like FTP, SNMP uses two ports: 161 and 162.

✦ **TFTP** (Trivial File Transfer Protocol) is for transferring files from one system to another (typically used by X terminals and diskless workstations to download boot files from another host on the network). TFTP data transfer takes place on port 69.

✦ **NFS** (Network File System) is for sharing files among computers. NFS uses Sun's Remote Procedure Call (RPC) facility, which exchanges information through port 111.

A well-known port is associated with each of these services. The TCP protocol uses each such port to locate a service on any system. (A *server process* — a special computer program running on a system — provides each service.)

# Setting Up an Ethernet LAN

*Ethernet* is a standard way to move packets of data between two or more computers connected to a single cable. (You can create larger networks by connecting multiple Ethernet segments with gateways.) To set up an Ethernet local area network (LAN), you need an Ethernet card for each PC. Linux supports a wide variety of Ethernet cards for the PC.

Ethernet is a good choice for the physical data-transport mechanism for the following reasons:

✦ Ethernet is a proven technology that has been in use since the early 1980s.

✦ Ethernet provides good data-transfer rates: typically 10 million bits per second (10 Mbps), although 100-Mbps Ethernet and Gigabit Ethernet (1,000 Mbps) are now available.

✦ Ethernet hardware is relatively low-cost. (PC Ethernet cards cost about $20 U.S.)

✦ With wireless Ethernet, you can easily connect laptop PCs to your Ethernet LAN — without having to run wires all over the place. (Go to Chapter 3 of this minibook for more information on wireless Ethernet.)

## How Ethernet works

So what makes Ethernet tick? In essence, it's the same thing that makes playground recess work: taking turns.

In an Ethernet network, all systems in a segment are connected to the same wire. Because a single wire is used, a protocol is used for sending and receiving data because only one data packet can exist on the cable at any time. An Ethernet LAN uses a data-transmission protocol known as *Carrier-Sense Multiple Access/Collision Detection* (CSMA/CD) to share the single transmission cable among all the computers. Ethernet cards in the computers follow the CSMA/CD protocol to transmit and receive Ethernet packets.

The idea behind the CSMA/CD protocol is similar to the way in which you have a conversation at a party. You listen for a pause (that's sensing the carrier) and talk when no one else is speaking. If you and another person begin talking at the same time, both of you realize the problem (that's collision detection) and pause for a moment; then one of you starts speaking again. As you know from experience, everything works out.

In an Ethernet LAN, each Ethernet card checks the cable for signals — that's the carrier-sense part. If the signal level is low, the Ethernet card sends its packets on the cable; the packet contains information about the sender and the intended recipient. All Ethernet cards on the LAN listen to the signal, and the recipient receives the packet. If two cards send out a packet simultaneously, the signal level in the cable rises above a threshold, and the cards know a collision has occurred (two packets have been sent out at the same time). Both cards wait for a random amount of time before sending their packets again.

Ethernet was invented in the early 1970s at the Xerox Palo Alto Research Center (PARC) by Robert M. Metcalfe. In the 1980s, Ethernet was standardized by the cooperative effort of three companies: Digital Equipment Corporation (DEC), Intel, and Xerox. Using the first initials of the company names, that Ethernet standard became known as the DIX standard. Later, the

DIX standard was included in the 802-series standards developed by the Institute of Electrical and Electronics Engineers (IEEE). The final Ethernet specification is formally known as IEEE 802.3 CSMA/CD, but people continue to call it *Ethernet*.

Ethernet sends data in *packets* (discrete chunks also known as *frames*). You don't have to hassle much with the innards of Ethernet packets, except to note the 6-byte source and destination addresses. Each Ethernet controller has a unique 6-byte (48-bit) address — at the Physical level, every packet must have one.

## Ethernet cables

Any time you hear experts talking about Ethernet, you're also going to hear some bewildering terms used for the cables that carry the data. Here's a quick rundown.

The original Ethernet standard used a thick coaxial cable, nearly half an inch in diameter. This wiring is called *thickwire* or *thick Ethernet*, although the IEEE 802.3 standard calls it 10Base5. That designation means several things: The data-transmission rate is 10 megabits per second (10 Mbps); the transmission is baseband (which simply means that the cable's signal-carrying capacity is devoted to transmitting Ethernet packets only); and the total length of the cable can be no more than 500 meters. Thickwire was expensive, and the cable was rather unwieldy. Unless you're a technology history buff, you don't have to care one whit about 10Base5 cables.

Nowadays, two other forms of Ethernet cabling are more popular. The first alternative to thick Ethernet cable is *thinwire*, or 10Base2, which uses a thin, flexible coaxial cable. A thinwire Ethernet segment can be, at most, 185 meters long. The other, more recent, alternative is Ethernet over unshielded twisted-pair cable (UTP), known as 10BaseT.

To set up a 10BaseT Ethernet network, you need an Ethernet hub — a hardware box with RJ-45 jacks (these look like big telephone jacks). You build the network by running twisted-pair wires (usually, Category 5, or Cat5, cables) from each PC's Ethernet card to this hub. You can get a 4-port 10BaseT hub for about $50 U.S. Figure 2-2 shows a typical small 10BaseT Ethernet LAN that you may set up at a small office or your home.

When you install Fedora Core from this book's companion DVD-ROMs on a PC connected with an Ethernet card, the Fedora Core installer automatically detects the Ethernet card and installs the appropriate drivers. The installer also lets you set up TCP/IP networking.

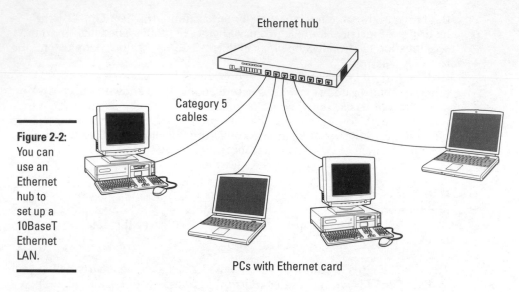

**Figure 2-2:**
You can use an Ethernet hub to set up a 10BaseT Ethernet LAN.

Ethernet hub

Category 5 cables

PCs with Ethernet card

TIP

When properly installed, the Linux kernel loads the driver for the Ethernet card every time it boots. To verify that the Ethernet driver is loaded, type the following command in a terminal window:

```
dmesg | grep -A 2 'grep eth0 /etc/modprobe.conf | cut -d ' ' -f 3`
```

This command searches the boot messages for any line that contains the name of the first Ethernet card (the command in backquotes — `grep eth0 /etc/modprobe.conf | cut -d ' ' -f 3` — picks out the alias for the eth0 device from the /etc/modprobe.conf file). The -A 2 option for grep causes it to print two lines after the line that matches the search criteria.

On my PC, I have a 3Com PCI 3c905C Ethernet card installed, so I get the following output when I type that command on my system:

```
3c59x: Donald Becker and others. www.scyld.com/network/vortex.html
0000:02:01.0: 3Com PCI 3c905C Tornado at 0x3000. Vers LK1.1.19
divert: allocating divert_blk for eth0
```

You see something similar, showing the name of your Ethernet card and other related information.

## Configuring TCP/IP Networking

When you set up TCP/IP networking during Fedora Core installation, the installation program prepares all appropriate configuration files using the information you provide. However, Fedora Core does come with the graphical network configuration tool that you can use to add a new network interface or alter information such as name servers and host names.

Use the Fedora Core network-configuration tool to set up networking if you're adding a new Ethernet card (or if your Ethernet card was not configured during installation).

To start the network-configuration tool, log in as `root` and from the GNOME desktop, choose Main Menu⇨System Settings⇨Network. If you are not logged in as `root`, you're prompted for the `root` password.

The network-configuration tool displays a tabbed dialog box, as shown in Figure 2-3.

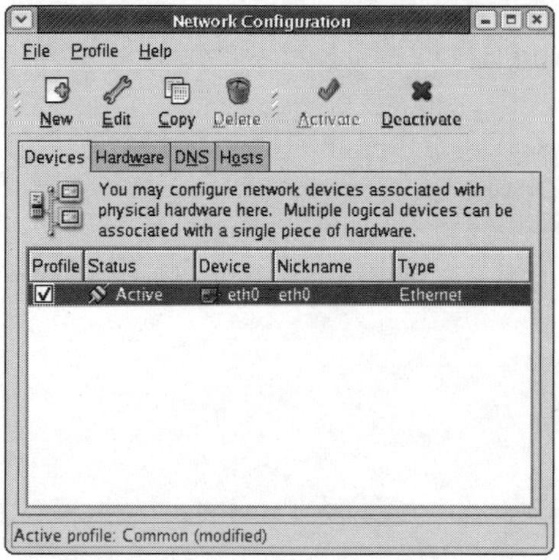

**Figure 2-3:**
Configure the Ethernet network with the network-configuration tool.

You can configure your network through the four tabs that appear along the top of the dialog box. Here's what each of the tabs does:

✦ **Devices:** Here's where you find options for a new network interface (for example, an Ethernet card). You can set the IP address of the interface and then activate it. Information that you enter about a device is stored in various files in the `/etc/sysconfig` directory.

✦ **Hardware:** Here you add a new hardware device, such as an Ethernet card, modem, or an ISDN device. You can then provide information such as interrupt request (IRQ), I/O port numbers, and DMA channels for the device.

✦ **DNS:** Here you enter the host name for your system and enter the IP addresses of name servers. The name server addresses are stored in the /etc/resolv.conf file. The host name is stored in the HOSTNAME variable in the /etc/sysconfig/network file.

✦ **Hosts:** This tab shows you the local table of hosts and IP addresses from the /etc/hosts file and lets you add, remove, or edit entries.

To add and activate a new Ethernet network interface, do the following:

*1.* **On the Devices tab, click the New button.**

The Select Device Type dialog box appears.

*2.* **Select Ethernet connection and click Forward.**

The Select Ethernet Device dialog box appears.

*3.* **Select your Ethernet Card and click Forward.**

The Configure Network Settings dialog box appears (shown in Figure 2-4).

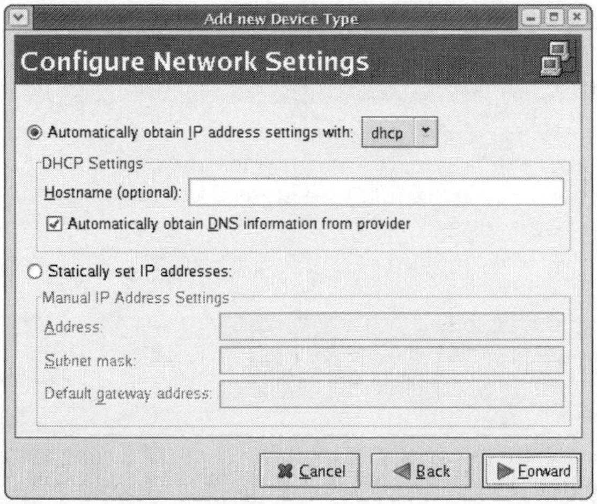

**Figure 2-4:**
Configure
the network
settings
in this
dialog box.

*4.* **Select the way in which the Ethernet card gets its IP address:**

If it can automatically obtain an IP address (which is the case when the Ethernet card is connected to DSL or cable modem), select the Automatically Obtain IP Address Settings with DHCP radio button. When you do so, also select the Automatically Obtain DNS Information from Provider check box.

Otherwise, select the Statically Set IP Addresses radio button, and then enter an IP address in the provided text box. For a home network, use a private IP address such as 192.168.0.2. (Anything that begins with *192.168.* works.)

5.  **Click Forward, and then Apply to complete the Ethernet setup.**

    You're back in the Network Configuration dialog box (refer to Figure 2-3).

6.  **Select the** eth0 **device and then click Activate to turn the Ethernet network on.**

If you are running a private network, you may use IP addresses in the 192.168.0.0 to 192.168.255.255 range. (Other ranges of addresses are reserved for private networks, but this range suffices for most needs.)

## Connecting Your LAN to the Internet

If you have a LAN with several PCs, you can connect the entire LAN to the Internet by using DSL or cable modem. Basically, you can share the high-speed DSL or cable modem connection with all the PCs in the LAN.

In Chapter 1 of this minibook, I explain how to set up DSL or cable modem. In this section, I briefly explain how to connect a LAN to the Internet so that all the PCs can access the Internet.

The most convenient way to connect a LAN to the Internet via DSL or cable modem is to buy a hardware device called DSL/Cable Modem NAT Router with a 4- or 8-port Ethernet hub. NAT stands for *Network Address Translation* and the NAT router can translate many private IP addresses into a single externally known IP address. The Ethernet hub part appears to you as a number of RJ-45 Ethernet ports where you can connect the PCs to set up a LAN. In other words, you need only one extra box besides the DSL or cable modem.

Figure 2-5 shows how you might connect your LAN to the Internet through a NAT router with a built-in Ethernet hub. Of course, you need a DSL or cable modem hookup for this scenario to work (and you have to sign up with the phone company for DSL service or with the cable provider for cable Internet service).

When you connect a LAN to the Internet, the NAT router acts as a gateway for your LAN. The NAT router also dynamically provides IP addresses to the PCs in your LAN. Therefore, on each PC, you have to set up the networking options to obtain the IP address dynamically.

**Book IV
Chapter 2**

**Setting Up a Local
Area Network**

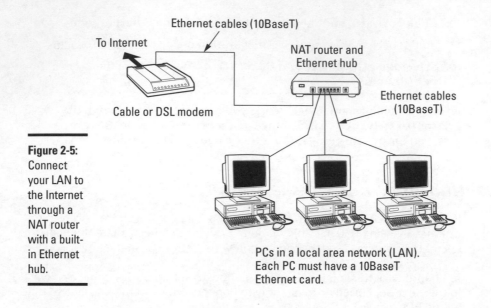

Ethernet cables (10BaseT)

To Internet

NAT router and
Ethernet hub

Cable or DSL modem

Ethernet cables
(10BaseT)

**Figure 2-5:**
Connect
your LAN to
the Internet
through a
NAT router
with a built-
in Ethernet
hub.

PCs in a local area network (LAN).
Each PC must have a 10BaseT
Ethernet card.

Your LAN can mix and match all kinds of computers — some may be running
Fedora Core and some may be running Microsoft Windows or any other
operating system that supports TCP/IP. On the Fedora Core PCs, you can
set up Ethernet networking using the network configuration tool (choose
Main Menu⇨System Settings⇨Network from GNOME desktop). When configuring the network settings (refer to Figure 2-4), remember to select the
Automatically Obtain IP Address Settings with DHCP radio button. Also
select the Automatically Obtain DNS Information from Provider check box.

# Chapter 3: Adding a Wireless Ethernet LAN

## In This Chapter

- ✓ Understanding wireless Ethernet networks
- ✓ Setting up the wireless hardware
- ✓ Configuring the wireless network

*I*f you have laptop computers on your LAN — or if you don't want to run a rat's nest of wires to connect a PC to the LAN — you have the option of using a wireless Ethernet network. In a typical scenario, you have a cable modem or DSL connection to the Internet, and you want to connect one or more laptops with wireless network cards to access the Internet through the cable or DSL modem. This chapter shows you how to set up wireless networking for connecting to an Ethernet LAN and accessing the Internet.

## Understanding Wireless Ethernet Networks

You've probably heard about Wi-Fi network. Wi-Fi stands for *Wireless Fidelity* network — a short-range wireless network similar to the wired Ethernet networks. A number of standards from an organization known as IEEE (the Institute of Electrical and Electronics Engineers) defines the technical details of how Wi-Fi networks work. Manufacturers use these standards to build the components that you can buy to set up a wireless network, also known as WLAN for short.

Until mid-2003, two popular IEEE standards — 802.11a and 802.11b — were for wireless Ethernet networks. These two standards were finalized in 1999. A third standard — 802.11g — was finalized by the IEEE in the summer of 2003. All these standards specify how the wireless Ethernet network works at the physical level. You don't have to fret all the details of all those standards to set up a wireless network, but knowing some pertinent details is good so you can buy the right kind of equipment for your wireless network.

The three wireless Ethernet standards have the following key characteristics:

✦ **802.11b:** Operates in the 2.4GHz radio band (2.4GHz to 2.4835GHz) in up to three non-overlapping frequency bands or channels. Supports a maximum bit rate of 11 Mbps per channel. One disadvantage of 802.11b is that the 2.4GHz frequency band is crowded — many devices (such as microwave ovens, cordless phones, medical and scientific equipment, as well as Bluetooth devices), all work within the 2.4GHz frequency band. Nevertheless, 802.11b is very popular in corporate and home networks.

✦ **802.11a:** Operates in the 5GHz radio band (5.725GHz to 5.850GHz) in up to eight non-overlapping channels. Supports a maximum bit rate of 54 Mbps per channel. The 5GHz band is not as crowded as the 2.4GHz band, but the 5GHz band is not approved for use in Europe. Products conforming to 802.11a standard are available on the market, and wireless access points are designed to handle both 802.11a and 802.11b connections.

✦ **802.11g:** Supports up to 54 Mbps data rate in the 2.4GHz band (the same band that 802.11b uses). 802.11g achieves the higher bit rate by using a technology called *OFDM* (orthogonal frequency-division multiplexing), which is also used by 802.11a. Although 802.11g was only recently finalized, equipment that complies with it is already on the market. That's probably because 802.11.g has generated excitement by working in the same band as 802.11b but promising much higher data rates. Vendors are currently offering access points that can support both the 802.11b and 802.11g connection standards.

The maximum data throughput that a user sees is much less because all users of that radio channel share the capacity of the channel. Also, the data transfer rate decreases as the distance between the user's PC and the wireless access point increases.

To find out more about wireless Ethernet, visit www.wi-fi.org, the home page of the Wi-Fi Alliance — a nonprofit international association formed in 1999 to certify interoperability of wireless LAN products based on IEEE 802.11 standards.

## Understanding infrastructure and ad hoc modes

The 802.11 standard defines two modes of operation for wireless Ethernet networks: infrastructure and ad hoc. *Ad-hoc mode* is simply two or more wireless Ethernet cards communicating with each other without an access point.

*Infrastructure mode* refers to the approach in which all the wireless Ethernet cards communicate with each other and to the wired LAN through an access point. For the example in this book, set your wireless Ethernet card to infrastructure mode. In the configuration files, this mode is referred to as *Managed mode*.

# Is the WEP stream cipher good enough?

WEP uses the RC4 encryption algorithm, which is known as a *stream cipher*. Such an algorithm works by taking a short secret key and generating an infinite stream of *pseudorandom bits.* Before sending the data, the sending station performs an *exclusive-OR operation* between the pseudorandom bits and the bits representing the data packet, which results in a 1 when two bits are different and 0 if they are the same. The receiver has a copy of the same secret key, and generates an identical stream of pseudorandom bits — and performs an identical exclusive-OR operation between this pseudorandom stream and the received bits. Doing so regenerates the original, unencrypted data packet.

Such a method of stream cipher has a few problems. If a bit is flipped (from a 0 to 1 or vice versa) in the encrypted data stream, the corresponding bit is flipped in the decrypted output — which can help an attacker derive the encryption key. Also, an eavesdropper who intercepts two encoded messages *that were encoded with the same stream* can generate the exclusive-OR of the original messages. That knowledge is enough to mount attacks that can eventually break the encryption.

To counter these weaknesses, WEP uses some defenses:

✦ **Integrity Check (IC) Field:** To make sure that data packets are not modified in transit, WEP uses an Integrity Check field in each packet.

✦ **Initialization Vector (IV):** To avoid encrypting two messages with the same key stream, WEP uses a 24-bit initialization vector (IV) that augments the shared secret key to produce a different RC4 key for each packet. The IV itself is also included in the packet.

Experts say that both these defenses are poorly implemented, making WEP ineffective. IC and IV have two main problems:

✦ The Integrity Check field is implemented by using a checksum algorithm called 32-bit cyclic redundancy code (CRC-32); that checksum *is then included as part of the data packet.* Unfortunately, an attacker can flip arbitrary bits in an encrypted message and correctly adjust the checksum so the resulting message appears valid.

✦ The 24-bit IV is sent in the clear (unencrypted). There are only $2^{24}$ possible initialization vectors (no big challenge for a fast machine), and they have to be reused after running through all of them. In other words, after sending $2^{24}$, or 16,777,216 packets, the IV is repeated. The number may sound like a lot, but consider the case of a busy access point that sends 1,500-byte packets at a rate of 11 Mbps. Each packet has 8 × 1,500 = 12,000 bits. That means each second the access point sends 11,000,000/12,000 = 916 packets. At that rate, the access point sends 16,777,216 packets in 16,777,216/916 = 18,315 seconds or 5 hours. That means the IV is reused after 5 hours, and the time may be less than that because many messages are smaller than 1,500 bytes. Thus an attacker has ample opportunities to collect two encrypted messages encrypted with the same key stream — and perform *statistical attacks* (which amount to trying the possible "combinations" really fast) to decrypt the message.

### *Understanding wired equivalent privacy (WEP)*

The 802.11 standard includes the Wired Equivalent Privacy (WEP) for protecting wireless communications from eavesdropping. WEP relies on a 40-bit or 104-bit secret key that is shared between a *mobile station* (such as a laptop with a wireless Ethernet card) and an *access point* (also called a *base station*). The secret key is used to encrypt data packets before they transmit and an integrity check performs to ensure that packets are not modified in transit. The 802.11 standard does not explain how the shared key is established. In practice, most wireless LANs use a single key that is shared between all mobile stations and access points. Such an approach, however, does not scale up very well to an environment such as a college campus because the keys are shared with all users — and you know how it is if you share a "secret" with hundreds of people. That's why WEP is typically not used on large wireless networks such as the ones at universities. In such wireless networks, you have to use other security approaches such as SSH (Secure Shell) to log in to remote systems. WEP, however, is good to use on your home wireless network.

WEP has its weaknesses, but it's better than nothing. You can use it in smaller wireless LANs where sharing the same key among all wireless stations is not an onerous task.

Work is underway to provide better security than WEP for wireless networks. The soon-to-be-finalized 802.11i standard uses public-key encryption with digital certificates — along with an authentication, authorization, and accounting done on a RADIUS (Remote Authentication Dial-In User Service) server — to provide better security for wireless Ethernet networks.

While the 802.11i standard is in progress, the Wi-Fi Alliance — a multivendor consortium that supports Wi-Fi — has developed an interim specification called Wi-Fi Protected Access (WPA) that's a precursor to 802.11i. WPA replaces the existing WEP standard and improves security by making some changes. For example, unlike WEP (which uses fixed keys), the WPA standard uses Temporal Key-Integrity Protocol (TKIP), which generates new keys for every 10K of data transmitted over the network. TKIP makes WPA more difficult to break. You may want to consider wireless products that support WPA while waiting for products that implement 802.11i.

## *Setting Up the Wireless Hardware*

To set up the wireless connection, you need a wireless access point and a wireless network card in each PC. You can also set up an ad hoc wireless network among two or more PCs with wireless network cards, but that is a standalone wireless LAN among those PCs only. In this section, I focus on the scenario where you want to set up a wireless connection to an established LAN that has a wired Internet connection through a cable modem or DSL.

In addition to the wireless access point, you also need a cable modem or DSL connection to the Internet, along with a NAT router/hub, as described in the previous sections. Figure 3-1 shows a typical setup for wireless Internet access through an existing cable modem or DSL connection.

As Figure 3-1 shows, the LAN has both wired and wireless PCs. In this example, a cable or DSL modem connect the LAN to the Internet through a NAT router/hub. Laptops with wireless network cards connect the LAN through a wireless access point attached to one of the RJ-45 ports on the hub. To connect desktop PCs to this wireless network, you can use a USB wireless network card (which connects to a USB port).

If you have not yet purchased a NAT router/hub for your cable or DSL connection, consider buying a router/hub that has a built-in wireless access point.

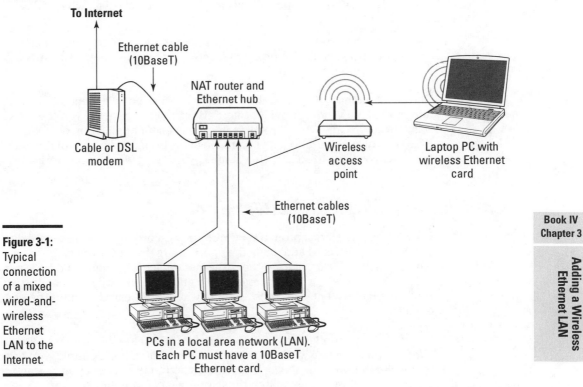

**Figure 3-1:**
Typical connection of a mixed wired-and-wireless Ethernet LAN to the Internet.

## Configuring the wireless access point

Configuring the wireless access point involves the following tasks:

◆ Setting a name for the wireless network (the technical term is ESSID).

◆ Setting the frequency or channel on which the wireless access point communicates with the wireless network cards. The access point and the cards must use the same channel.

◆ Deciding whether to use encryption.

◆ If encryption is to be used, setting the number of bits in the encryption key and the value of the encryption key. Twenty-four bits of the encryption key are internal to the access point; you specify only the remaining bits. Thus, for 64-bit encryption, you have to specify a 40-bit key, which comes to 10 hexadecimal digits (a *hexadecimal digit* is an integer from 0 through 9 or a letter from A through F). For a 124-bit encryption key, you specify 104 bits, or 26 hexadecimal digits.

◆ Setting the access method that wireless network cards must use when connecting to the access point. You can opt for either open access or shared key. The open-access method is typical (even when using encryption).

◆ Setting the wireless access point to operate in infrastructure (managed) mode (because that's the way you connect wireless network cards to an existing Ethernet LAN).

The exact method of configuring a wireless access point depends on make and model; the vendor provides instructions to configure the wireless access point. You typically work through a graphical client application on a Windows PC to do the configuration. If you enable encryption, make note of the encryption key; you have to specify that same key for each wireless network card.

# Configuring Wireless Networking

On your Fedora Core laptop, the PCMCIA or PC Card manager recognizes the wireless network card and loads the appropriate driver for the card. Treat the wireless network card like another Ethernet device — assign it a device name such as eth0 or eth1. If you already have an Ethernet card in the laptop, that card gets the eth0 device name, and the wireless PC card becomes the eth1 device.

You do have to configure certain parameters to enable the wireless network card to communicate with the wireless access point. For example, you have to specify the wireless network name assigned to the access point — and the encryption settings must match those on the access point. You can do everything from the graphical Network Configuration tool.

Follow these steps to configure and activate the wireless network connection on your Fedora Core system:

1. **Log in as** root **at the graphical login screen, and then choose Main Menu⇨System Settings⇨Network.**

   The Network Configuration tool runs and its main window appears.

2. **Click New in the Network Configuration window's toolbar.**

   The Add New Device Type window (shown in Figure 3-2) appears.

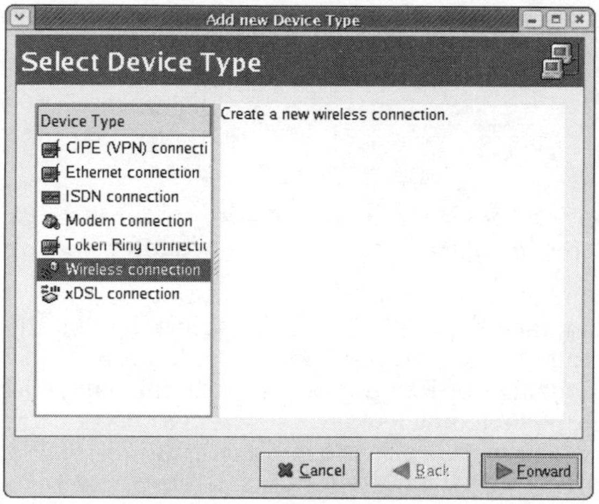

**Figure 3-2:**
Select Wireless Connection from this window to configure a wireless Ethernet connection.

3. **Select Wireless Connection from the window (refer to Figure 3-2), and then click Forward.**

   The Select Wireless Device window (shown in Figure 3-3) appears.

4. **Select your wireless card from the list in the window (refer to Figure 3-3), and then click Forward.**

   The Configure Wireless Connection window (shown in Figure 3-4) appears.

5. **Set the Mode to Managed, specify the name of the wireless network (the one you want to connect to), and set the encryption key, if any. Then click Forward.**

   The Configure Network Settings window (shown in Figure 3-5) appears.

**Book IV
Chapter 3**

**Adding a Wireless
Ethernet LAN**

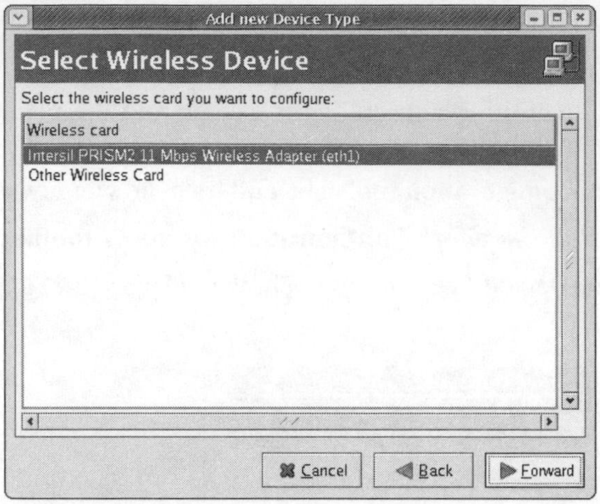

**Figure 3-3:**
Select your
wireless
card from
the listed
devices.

*6.* **Select the option for obtaining the IP address for the wireless network interface (refer to Figure 3-5); click Forward after making your selections.**

You can either specify a static IP address (meaning that the IP address does not change every time you boot) or let Linux automatically get an IP address by using DHCP (a protocol for obtaining network configuration parameters, including IP addresses from a server on the network). Typically, you select the option to automatically get an IP address.

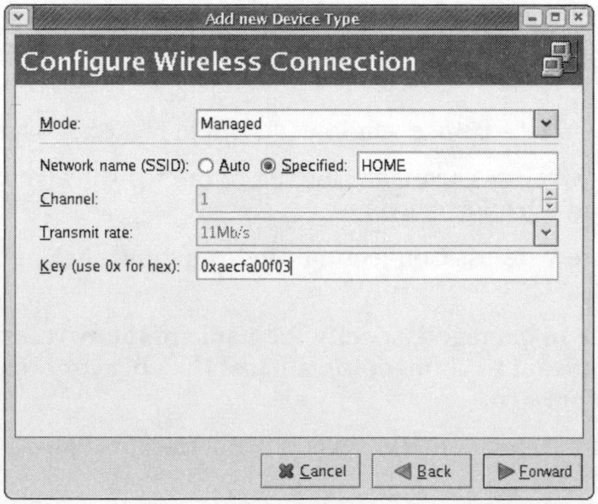

**Figure 3-4:**
Set the
parameters
for the
wireless
connection
from this
window.

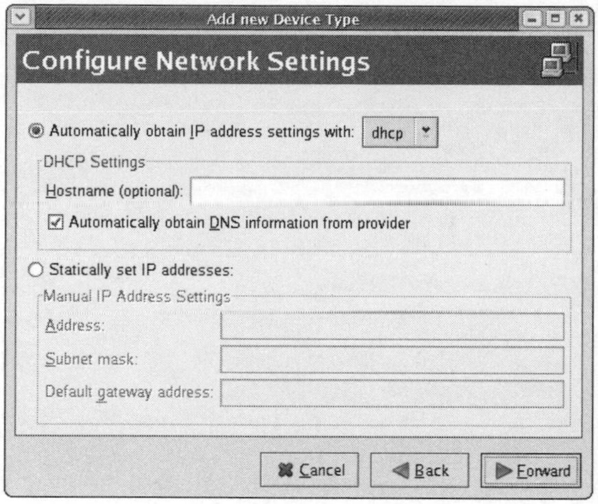

**Add new Device Type**

## Configure Network Settings

● Automatically obtain IP address settings with: [ dhcp ▾ ]

DHCP Settings

Hostname (optional): [                          ]

☑ Automatically obtain DNS information from provider

○ Statically set IP addresses:

Manual IP Address Settings

Address: [                          ]

Subnet mask: [                          ]

Default gateway address: [                          ]

[ ✖ Cancel ]  [ ◀ Back ]  [ ▶ Forward ]

**Figure 3-5.**
Configure
the network
settings of
the wireless
network
interface
from this
window.

The Create Wireless Device window (see Figure 3-6) appears with a summary of the wireless network connection you're about to create.

7. **Verify that the information shown in the Create Wireless Device window is correct, and then click Apply to create the wireless device.**

The information shows the device name (in this case, eth1) that you're creating.

The new device appears in the Network Configuration tool (as shown in Figure 3-7).

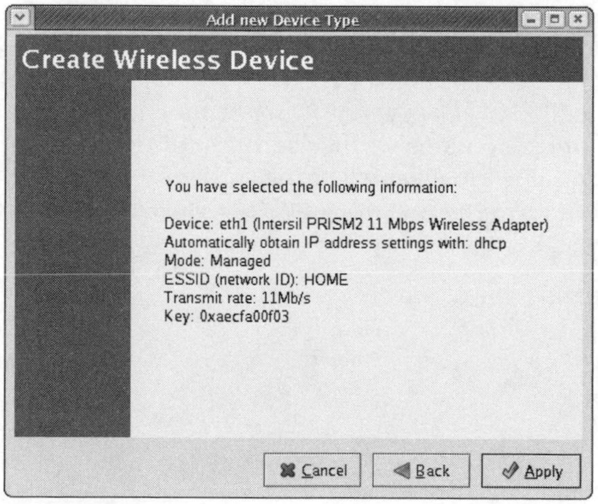

**Add new Device Type**

## Create Wireless Device

You have selected the following information:

Device: eth1 (Intersil PRISM2 11 Mbps Wireless Adapter)
Automatically obtain IP address settings with: dhcp
Mode: Managed
ESSID (network ID): HOME
Transmit rate: 11Mb/s
Key: 0xaecfa00f03

[ ✖ Cancel ]  [ ◀ Back ]  [ ✓ Apply ]

**Figure 3-6:**
Check the
information
about the
wireless
connection
and click
Apply if the
information
is correct.

**Book IV
Chapter 3**

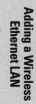

Adding a Wireless
Ethernet LAN

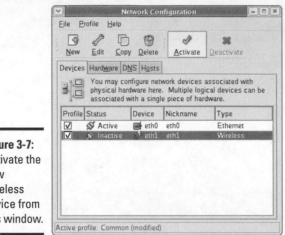

**Figure 3-7:**
Activate the new wireless device from this window.

8. **Select the new wireless device, and then click the Activate button on the toolbar (refer to Figure 3-7).**

   A dialog box informs you that the changes have to be saved before activating the wireless device and asks if you want to continue.

9. **Click Yes and then OK when another dialog box prompts you to activate the network device.**

   If all goes well, the wireless network is up and running after a few moments.

The Network Configuration tool saves your wireless network settings in a text file whose name depends on the wireless network device name. If the wireless network device name is eth0, the configuration is stored in the text file /etc/sysconfig/network-scripts/ifcfg-eth0. If the wireless device name is eth1, the file is /etc/sysconfig/network-scripts/ifcfg-eth1. This configuration file contains various settings for the wireless network card. Table 3-1 explains the meaning of the settings. Here is a slightly edited version of the /etc/sysconfig/network-scripts/ifcfg-eth1 file from my laptop PC:

```
IPV6INIT=no
USERCTL=no
PEERDNS=yes
TYPE=Wireless
DEVICE=eth1
HWADDR=00:02:2d:8c:f9:c4
BOOTPROTO=dhcp
ONBOOT=no
```

```
DHCP_HOSTNAME=
NAME=
ESSID='HOME'
CHANNEL=6
MODE=Managed
RATE=auto
```

The encryption key is stored separately. For an wireless Ethernet card whose device name is eth1, the encryption key is stored in the /etc/sysconfig/network-scripts/keys-eth1 file. For example, here is the what this file contains for my example:

```
KEY=AECFA00F03
```

Note that the key has 10 hexadecimal digits for a 40-bit key (for example, 1fdf-3fde-fe) or 26 hexadecimal digits for a 104-bit key. The keys are, in fact, 64-bit and 128-bit, but the encryption algorithm automatically generates 24 bits of the key, so you need to specify only the remaining bits. Needless to say, the longer the key, the more secure the encryption.

If you ever manually edit the parameters in the wireless Ethernet configuration file, type the following command to reactivate the wireless network interface after editing the configuration file:

```
service pcmcia restart
```

| Table 3-1 | Settings in Configuration File for a Wireless Ethernet Network Interface |
|---|---|
| *This Parameter* | *Means the Following* |
| BOOTPROTO | The name of the protocol to use to get the IP address for the interface. Is either dhcp or bootp for Ethernet interface. |
| CHANNEL | Channel number (between 1 and 14 in United States and Canada). Must be the same as that set for the wireless access point. In Managed mode, you don't need to specify the channel. |
| DEVICE | The device name for the wireless Ethernet network interface (eth0 for the first interface, eth1 for second, and so on). |
| ESSID | Extended Service Set (ESS) Identifier, also known as the wireless network name. It is case sensitive and must be the same as the name specified for the wireless access point. Provide the name within single quotes (for example, 'HOME'). |
| HWADDR | The hardware address (also called the MAC address) of the wireless network card (six pairs of colon-separated hexadecimal numbers; for example, 00:02:2d:8c:f9:c4). The wireless card's device driver automatically detects this address. |

*(continued)*

Book IV
Chapter 3

Adding a Wireless
Ethernet LAN

**Table 3-1** *(continued)*

| | |
|---|---|
| IPV6INIT | When set to yes, initializes IPv6 configuration for the wireless interface. Set it to no if you are not using IPv6. |
| MODE | The mode of operation of the wireless network card. Set to Managed for a typical network that connects through a wireless access point. |
| NAME | A nickname for your wireless network. If you don't specify it, the host name is used as the nickname. |
| ONBOOT | Set to yes to activate the wireless interface at boot time; otherwise set to no. |
| PEERDNS | Set to yes to enable the interface to modify your system's /etc/resolv.conf file to use the DNS servers obtained from the DHCP server (the same server that provides the IP address for the interface). If you set this parameter to no, the /etc/resolv.conf file is left unchanged. |
| RATE | Bit rate for the wireless connection (set to one of 1M, 2M, 5.5M, 11M, or auto). The M means Mbps or a million bits per second. Set to auto to use the maximum possible transmission rate. |
| TYPE | Set to Wireless for wireless network interface. |
| USERCTL | When set to yes, a non-root user can control the device. Set it to no so that only root can control the device. |

To check the status of the wireless network interface, type the following command:

```
iwconfig
```

Here's a typical output from a Fedora Core laptop with a wireless Ethernet PC card:

```
lo        no wireless extensions.

eth0      no wireless extensions.

eth1      IEEE 802.11-DS  ESSID:"HOME"  Nickname:"localhost.localdomain"
          Mode:Managed  Frequency:2.437GHz  Access Point: 00:30:AB:06:2E:5D
          Bit Rate=11Mb/s   Tx-Power=15 dBm   Sensitivity:1/0
          Retry limit:4   RTS thr:off   Fragment thr:off
          Encryption key:AECF-A00F-03
          Power Management:off
          Link Quality:66/0  Signal level:-27 dBm  Noise level:-93 dBm
          Rx invalid nwid:0  Rx invalid crypt:0  Rx invalid frag:0
          Tx excessive retries:0  Invalid misc:0   Missed beacon:0
```

Here the eth1 interface refers to the wireless network card. I edited the encryption key and some other parameters here, but the sample output shows what you typically see when the wireless link is working.

# Chapter 4: Managing the Network

## In This Chapter

✓ Learning the TCP/IP configuration files

✓ Checking TCP/IP networks

✓ Configuring networks at boot time

*L*ike almost everything else in Fedora Core, TCP/IP setup is a matter of preparing numerous configuration files (text files you can edit with any text editor). Most of these configuration files are in the /etc directory. The Fedora Core installer helps by hiding the details of the TCP/IP configuration files. Nevertheless, if you know the names of the files and their purposes, editing the files manually, if necessary, is easier.

## Learning the TCP/IP Configuration Files

Running the Network Configuration tool is enough to get TCP/IP configured on your system. However, if you want to effectively manage the network, you need to become familiar with the TCP/IP configuration files so you can edit the files, if necessary. (For example, if you want to check whether the name servers are specified correctly, you have to know about the /etc/resolv.conf file, which stores the IP addresses of name servers.)

Table 4-1 summarizes the basic TCP/IP configuration files. I describe these configuration files in the next few sections.

| Table 4-1 | Basic TCP/IP Network Configuration Files |
|---|---|
| *This File* | *Contains the Following* |
| /etc/hosts | IP addresses and host names for your local network as well as any other systems you access often |
| /etc/networks | Names and IP addresses of networks |
| /etc/host.conf | Instructions on how to translate host names into IP addresses |
| /etc/resolv.conf | IP addresses of name servers |
| /etc/hosts.allow | Instructions on which systems can access Internet services on your system |
| /etc/hosts.deny | Instructions on which systems must be denied access to Internet services on your system |
| /etc/nsswitch.conf | Instructions on how to translate host names into IP addresses |

## /etc/hosts

The /etc/hosts text file contains a list of IP addresses and host names for your local network. In the absence of a name server, any network program on your system consults this file to determine the IP address that corresponds to a host name. Think of /etc/hosts as the local phone directory where you can look up the IP address (instead of a phone number) for a local host.

Here is the /etc/hosts file from a system, showing the IP addresses and names of other hosts on a typical LAN:

```
127.0.0.1        localhost          localhost.localdomain
# Other hosts on the LAN
192.168.0.100    lnbp933
192.168.0.50     lnbp600
192.168.0.200    lnbp200
192.168.0.233    lnbp233
192.168.0.40     lnbp400
```

As the example shows, each line in the file starts with an IP address, followed by the host name for that IP address. (You can have more than one host name for any given IP address.)

## /etc/networks

/etc/networks is another text file that contains the names and IP addresses of networks. These network names are commonly used in the routing command (/sbin/route) to specify a network by name instead of by its IP address.

Don't be alarmed if your Linux PC does not have the /etc/networks file. Your TCP/IP network works fine without this file. In fact, the Fedora Core installer does not create a /etc/networks file.

## /etc/host.conf

Linux uses a special *library* (that is, a collection of computer code) called the *resolver library* to obtain the IP address that corresponds to a host name. The /etc/host.conf file specifies how names are resolved (that is, how the name gets converted to a numeric IP address). A typical /etc/host.conf file might contain the following lines:

```
order hosts, bind
multi on
```

The entries in the /etc/host.conf file tell the resolver library what services to use (and in which order) to resolve names.

The `order` option indicates the order of services. The sample entry tells the resolver library to first consult the `/etc/hosts` file, and then check the name server to resolve a name.

Use the `multi` option to indicate whether or not a host in the `/etc/hosts` file can have multiple IP addresses. Hosts that have more than one IP address are called *multihomed* because the presence of multiple IP addresses implies that the host has several network interfaces. (In effect, the host "lives" in several networks simultaneously.)

## /etc/resolv.conf

The `/etc/resolv.conf` file is another text file used by the resolver — the library that determines the IP address for a host name. Here is a sample `/etc/resolv.conf` file:

```
search nrockv01.md.comcast.net
nameserver 68.48.0.12
nameserver 68.48.0.13
```

The first line tells the resolver how to search for a host name. For example, when trying to locate a host name `myhost`, the `search` directive in the example causes the resolver to try `myhost.nrockv01.md.comcast.net` first, then `myhost.md.comcast.net`, and finally `myhost.comcast.net`.

The `nameserver` line provides the IP addresses of name servers for your domain. If you have multiple name servers, list them on separate lines. They are queried in the order in which they appear in the file.

If you do not have a name server for your network, you can safely ignore this file. TCP/IP still works, even though you may not be able to refer to hosts by name (other than those listed in the `/etc/hosts` file).

## /etc/hosts.allow

The `/etc/hosts.allow` file specifies which hosts are allowed to use the Internet services (such as TELNET and FTP) running on your system. This file is consulted before certain Internet services start. The services start only if the entries in the `hosts.allow` file imply that the requesting host is allowed to use the services.

The entries in `/etc/hosts.allow` are in the form of a *servername:IP address* format, where *server* refers to the name of the program providing a specific Internet service, and *IP address* identifies the host allowed to use that service. For example, if you want all hosts in your local network

Book IV
Chapter 4

Managing the
Network

(which has the network address 192.168.0.0) to access the Telnet service (provided by the `in.telnetd` program), add the following line in the `/etc/hosts.allow` file:

`in.telnetd:192.168.0.`

If you want to let all local hosts have access to all Internet services, you can use the `ALL` keyword and rewrite the line as follows:

`ALL:192.168.0.`

Finally, to open all Internet services to all hosts, you can replace the IP address with `ALL`, as follows:

`ALL:ALL`

You can also use host names in place of IP addresses.

To find out the detailed syntax of the entries in the `/etc/hosts.allow` file, type **man hosts.allow** at the shell prompt in a terminal window.

## /etc/hosts.deny

This file is just the opposite of `/etc/hosts.allow` — whereas `hosts.allow` specifies which hosts may access Internet services (such as TELNET and TFTP) on your system, the `hosts.deny` file identifies the hosts that must be denied services. The `/etc/hosts.deny` file is consulted if no rules are in the `/etc/hosts.allow` file that apply to the requesting host. Service is denied if the `hosts.deny` file has a rule that applies to the host.

The entries in `/etc/hosts.deny` file have the same format as those in the `/etc/hosts.allow` file — they are in the form of a *server:IP address* format, where *server* refers to the name of the program providing a specific Internet service and *IP address* identifies the host that must not be allowed to use that service.

If you already set up entries in the `/etc/hosts.allow` file to allow access to specific hosts, you can place the following line in `/etc/hosts.deny` to deny all other hosts access to any service on your system:

`ALL:ALL`

To find out the detailed syntax of the entries in the `/etc/hosts.deny` file, type **man hosts.deny** at the shell prompt in a terminal window.

## /etc/nsswitch.conf

This file, known as the *name service switch* (NSS) file, specifies how services such as the name resolver library, NIS, NIS+, and local configuration files (such as /etc/hosts and /etc/shadow) interact.

NIS and NIS+ are *network information services* — another type of name-lookup service. Newer versions of the Linux kernel use the /etc/nsswitch.conf file to determine what takes precedence: a local configuration file, a service such as DNS (Domain Name Service), or NIS.

As an example, the following hosts entry in the /etc/nsswitch.conf file says that the resolver library first tries the /etc/hosts file, and then tries NIS+, and finally tries DNS:

```
hosts:        files nisplus dns
```

You can find out more about the /etc/nsswitch.conf file by typing **info libc "Name Service Switch"** (including the quotes) in a terminal window.

# Checking Out TCP/IP Networks

After you configure Ethernet and TCP/IP (whether during Fedora Core installation or by running the Network Configuration tool later on), you can use various networking applications without any problem. If you do run into trouble, Fedora Core includes several tools to help you monitor and diagnose problems.

## Checking the network interfaces

Use the /sbin/ifconfig command to view the currently configured network interfaces. The ifconfig command is used to configure a network interface (that is, to associate an IP address with a network device). If you run ifconfig without any command-line arguments, the command displays information about current network interfaces. The following is a typical invocation of ifconfig and the resulting output:

```
/sbin/ifconfig
eth0      Link encap:Ethernet  HWaddr 00:08:74:E5:C1:60
          inet addr:192.168.0.6  Bcast:192.168.0.255  Mask:255.255.255.0
          inet6 addr: fe80::208:74ff:fee5:c160/64 Scope:Link
          UP BROADCAST RUNNING MULTICAST  MTU:1500  Metric:1
          RX packets:93700 errors:0 dropped:0 overruns:1 frame:0
          TX packets:74097 errors:0 dropped:0 overruns:0 carrier:0
          collisions:0 txqueuelen:1000
          RX bytes:33574333 (32.0 Mb)  TX bytes:8832457 (8.4 Mb)
```

```
            Interrupt:10 Base address:0x3000

eth1        Link encap:Ethernet  HWaddr 00:02:2D:8C:F8:C5
            inet addr:192.168.0.8  Bcast:192.168.0.255  Mask:255.255.255.0
            inet6 addr: fe80::202:2dff:fe8c:f8c5/64 Scope:Link
            UP BROADCAST RUNNING MULTICAST  MTU:1500  Metric:1
            RX packets:3403 errors:0 dropped:0 overruns:0 frame:0
            TX packets:22 errors:1 dropped:0 overruns:0 carrier:0
            collisions:0 txqueuelen:1000
            RX bytes:254990 (249.0 Kb)  TX bytes:3120 (3.0 Kb)
            Interrupt:3 Base address:0x100

lo          Link encap:Local Loopback
            inet addr:127.0.0.1  Mask:255.0.0.0
            inet6 addr: ::1/128 Scope:Host
            UP LOOPBACK RUNNING  MTU:16436  Metric:1
            RX packets:3255 errors:0 dropped:0 overruns:0 frame:0
            TX packets:3255 errors:0 dropped:0 overruns:0 carrier:0
            collisions:0 txqueuelen:0
            RX bytes:2686647 (2.5 Mb)  TX bytes:2686647 (2.5 Mb)
```

This output shows that three network interfaces — the loopback interface (`lo`) and two Ethernet cards (`eth0` and `eth1`) — are currently active on this system. For each interface, you can see the IP address, as well as statistics on packets delivered and sent. If the Fedora Core system has a dial-up PPP link up and running, you also see an item for the `ppp0` interface in the output.

## Checking the IP routing table

The other network configuration command, `/sbin/route`, also provides status information when it is run without any command-line argument. If you're having trouble checking a connection to another host (that you specify with an IP address), check the IP routing table to see whether a default gateway is specified. Then check the gateway's routing table to ensure that paths to an outside network appear in that routing table.

A typical output from the `/sbin/route` command looks like the following:

```
/sbin/route
Kernel IP routing table
Destination     Gateway         Genmask         Flags Metric Ref    Use Iface
192.168.0.0     *               255.255.255.0   U     0      0        0 eth0
192.168.0.0     *               255.255.255.0   U     0      0        0 eth1
169.254.0.0     *               255.255.0.0     U     0      0        0 eth1
127.0.0.0       *               255.0.0.0       U     0      0        0 lo
default         192.168.0.1     0.0.0.0         UG    0      0        0 eth0
```

As this routing table shows, the local network uses the `eth0` and `eth1` Ethernet interfaces, and the default gateway is the `eth0` Ethernet interface. The default gateway is a routing device that handles packets addressed to any network other than the one in which the Fedora Core system resides. In this example, packets addressed to any network address other than those beginning with 192.168.0 are sent to the gateway — 192.168.0.1. The gateway forwards those packets to other networks (assuming, of course, that the gateway is connected to another network, preferably the Internet).

## Checking connectivity to a host

To check for a network connection to a specific host, use the `ping` command. `ping` is a widely used TCP/IP tool that uses a series of Internet Control Message Protocol (ICMP, pronounced *eye-comp*) messages. ICMP provides for an Echo message to which every host responds. Using the ICMP messages and replies, `ping` can determine whether or not the other system is alive and can compute the round-trip delay in communicating with that system.

The following example shows how I run `ping` to see whether a system on my network is alive:

```
ping 192.168.0.1
```

Here is what this command displays on my home network:

```
PING 192.168.0.1 (192.168.0.1) from 192.168.0.7 : 56(84) bytes of data.
64 bytes from 192.168.0.1: icmp_seq=1 ttl=254 time=1.36 ms
64 bytes from 192.168.0.1: icmp_seq=2 ttl=254 time=1.33 ms
64 bytes from 192.168.0.1: icmp_seq=3 ttl=254 time=1.36 ms
64 bytes from 192.168.0.1: icmp_seq=4 ttl=254 time=1.34 ms

--- 192.168.0.1 ping statistics ---
4 packets transmitted, 4 received, 0% loss, time 3026ms
rtt min/avg/max/mdev = 1.338/1.352/1.366/0.038 ms
```

In Fedora Core, `ping` continues to run until you press Ctrl+C to stop it; then it displays summary statistics showing the typical time it takes to send a packet between the two systems. On some systems, `ping` simply reports that a remote host is alive. However, you can still get the timing information by using appropriate command-line arguments.

## Checking network status

To check the status of the network, use the `netstat` command. This command displays the status of network connections of various types (such as TCP and UDP connections). You can view the status of the interfaces quickly with `netstat -i`, as follows:

```
netstat -i
Kernel Interface table
Iface  MTU Met   RX-OK RX-ERR RX-DRP RX-OVR   TX-OK TX-ERR TX-DRP TX-OVR Flg
eth0  1500   0   94237      0      0      1   74889      0      0      0 BMRU
eth1  1500   0    3942      0      0      0      24      1      0      0 BMRU
lo   16436   0    3255      0      0      0    3255      0      0      0 LRU
```

In this case, the output shows the current status of the loopback and Ethernet interfaces. Table 4-2 describes the meanings of the columns.

| Table 4-2 | Meaning of Columns in the Kernel Interface Table |
|---|---|
| *Column* | *Meaning* |
| Iface | Name of the interface |
| MTU | Maximum Transfer Unit — the maximum number of bytes that a packet can contain |
| RX-OK, TX-OK | Number of error-free packets received (RX) or transmitted (TX) |
| RX-ERR, TX-ERR | Number of packets with errors |
| RX-DRP, TX-DRP | Number of dropped packets |
| RX-OVR, TX-OVR | Number of packets lost due to overflow |
| Flg | A = receive multicast; B = broadcast allowed; D = debugging turned on; L = loopback interface (notice the flag on lo), M = all packets received, N = trailers avoided; O = no ARP on this interface; P = point-to-point interface; R = interface is running; and U = interface is up. |

Another useful form of netstat option is -t, which shows all active TCP connections. Following is a typical result of netstat -t on one Fedora Core PC:

```
netstat -t
Active Internet connections (w/o servers)
Proto Recv-Q Send-Q Local Address          Foreign Address       State
tcp    0      0 dhcppc4:1031       www.redhat.com:http   ESTABLISHED
tcp    0    126 dhcppc4:telnet     192.168.0.6:1238      ESTABLISHED
tcp    0      0 dhcppc4:1032       www.redhat.com:https  ESTABLISHED
tcp    0      0 dhcppc4:1033       www.redhat.com:https  ESTABLISHED
tcp    0    138 dhcppc4:telnet     192.168.0.6:1238      ESTABLISHED
tcp    0      0 dhcppc4:ftp        192.168.0.6:1548      TIME_WAIT
```

In this case, the output columns show the protocol (Proto); the number of bytes in the receive and transmit queues (Recv-Q, Send-Q); the local TCP port in hostname:service format (Local Address); the remote port (Foreign Address); and the state of the connection.

Type **netstat -ta** to see all TCP connections — both active and the ones your Fedora Core system is listening to (with no connection established yet). For example, here's a typical output from the netstat -ta command:

```
Active Internet connections (servers and established)
Proto Recv-Q Send-Q Local Address          Foreign Address       State
tcp    0      0 *:1024             *:*                   LISTEN
tcp    0      0 localhost.localdom:1025 *:*              LISTEN
tcp    0      0 *:sunrpc           *:*                   LISTEN
tcp    0      0 *:x11              *:*                   LISTEN
tcp    0      0 *:ftp              *:*                   LISTEN
tcp    0      0 *:ssh              *:*                   LISTEN
tcp    0      0 *:telnet           *:*                   LISTEN
tcp    0      0 localhost.localdom:smtp *:*              LISTEN
tcp    0    138 dhcppc3:telnet     dhcppc4:1037          ESTABLISHED
tcp    0      0 dhcppc3:ftp        dhcppc4:1060          ESTABLISHED
```

## Sniffing network packets

Sniffing network packets — sounds like something illegal, doesn't it? Nothing like that. *Sniffing* simply refers to viewing the TCP/IP network data packets. The concept is to capture all the network packets so you can examine them later.

If you feel like sniffing TCP/IP packets, you can use `tcpdump`, a command-line utility that comes with Fedora Core. As its name implies, it "dumps" (prints) the headers of TCP/IP network packets.

To use `tcpdump`, log in as `root` and type the `tcpdump` command in a terminal window. Typically, you want to save the output in a file and examine that file later. Otherwise, `tcpdump` starts spewing out results that just flash by on the window. For example, to capture 1,000 packets in a file named `tdout` and attempt to convert the IP addresses to names, type the following command:

```
tcpdump -a -c 1000 > tdout
```

After capturing 1,000 packets, `tcpdump` quits. Then you can examine the output file, `tdout`. It's a text file, so you can simply open it in a text editor or type **more tdout** to view the captured packets.

Just to whet your curiosity, here are some lines from a typical output from `tcpdump`:

```
20:39:56.929241 dhcppc6.telnet > 192.168.0.6.4272: P 3225722544:3225722572(28)
    ack 1449612018 win 5840 (DF) [tos 0x10]
20:39:57.120308 192.168.0.6.4272 > dhcppc6.telnet: . ack 28 win 16199 (DF)
20:39:57.155930 arp who-has 192.168.0.1 tell dhcppc6
20:39:57.156915 arp reply 192.168.0.1 is-at 0:a0:c5:e1:ae:ae
20:39:57.156956 dhcppc6.1025 > 192.168.0.1.domain: 33598+ PTR? 6.0.168.192.in-
    addr.arpa. (42) (DF)
20:39:57.838984 192.168.0.1.domain > dhcppc6.1025: 33598 NXDomain* 0/1/0 (119)
    (DF)
20:39:57.840892 dhcppc6.1025 > 192.168.0.1.domain: 33599+ PTR? 1.0.168.192.in-
    addr.arpa. (42) (DF)
20:39:57.855757 192.168.0.1.domain > dhcppc6.1025: 33599 NXDomain 0/1/0 (119)
    (DF)
20:40:05.513863 192.168.0.1.router > 192.168.0.255.router: RIPv1-resp [items 2]:
    {0.0.0.0}(1) {68.49.48.0}(1) [ttl 1]
... lines deleted...
```

The output does offer some clues to what's going on — each line shows information about one network packet. Each line starts with a timestamp, followed by details of the packet, information such as where it originates and where it is going. I don't try to explain the details here, but you can type **man tcpdump** to find out more about some of the details (and, more importantly, see what other ways you can use `tcpdump`).

**Book IV
Chapter 4**

**Managing the
Network**

Fedora Core comes with another packet sniffer called Ethereal. To find out more about Ethereal, visit www.ethereal.com and consult the documentation located in the /usr/share/doc/ethereal* directory (type **ls /usr/ share/doc/ethereal\*** to see the contents of that directory).

## Configuring Networks at Boot Time

You want to start your network automatically every time you boot the system. For that to happen, various startup scripts must contain appropriate commands. You don't have to do anything special other than configure your network (either during installation or by using the Network Configuration tool at a later time). If the network balks at startup, however, you can troubleshoot by checking the files I mention in this section.

To initialize your network, the network-activation script uses a set of text files in the /etc/sysconfig directory. For example, the script checks the variables defined in the /etc/sysconfig/network file to decide whether to activate the network. In /etc/sysconfig/network, you see a line with the NETWORKING variable as follows:

NETWORKING=yes

The network activates only if the NETWORKING variable is set to yes.

A number of scripts in the /etc/sysconfig/network-scripts directory activate specific network interfaces. For example, the configuration file for activating the Ethernet interface eth0, is the file /etc/sysconfig/ network-scripts/ifcfg-eth0. Here is what a typical /etc/sysconfig/ network-scripts/ifcfg-eth0 file contains:

DEVICE=eth0
BOOTPROTO=dhcp
ONBOOT=yes

The DEVICE line provides the network device name. The BOOTPROTO variable is set to dhcp, indicating that the IP address is obtained dynamically by using the Dynamic Host Configuration Protocol (DHCP), a standard method. The ONBOOT variable states whether this network interface activates when Fedora Core boots. If your PC has an Ethernet card and you want to activate the eth0 interface at boot time, ONBOOT must be set to yes.

Of course, the configuration file ifcfg-eth0 in the /etc/sysconfig/ network-scripts directory works only if your PC has an Ethernet card and the Linux kernel has detected and loaded the specific driver for that card.

# Chapter 5: Cool Networking Projects

## In This Chapter

✔ Building your own home network

✔ Adding wireless to your current network

✔ Turning your Fedora Core system into a NAT router

*I*n other chapters of this minibook, I describe how to connect your PC or your home network to the Internet. The first project in this chapter guides you through the steps of building a home network. After you have a home network, you probably want to add wireless so you can connect to the network from anywhere in your home. The second project goes over the steps to add wireless networking to an existing network. The third project gives you a taste of Linux's networking abilities — you find out how to use a Linux PC as a network address translator (NAT) and router.

## Building Your Own Home Network

Face it: Many people have multi-PC households nowadays — at least in the United States. With all those PCs for your spouse and children, you need a home network. With a home network, you can share a single Internet connection so everyone can surf the Web and have e-mail. You can also share a printer and easily swap files with each other. As you are about to discover, setting up a home network is simple.

### Things you need

Here's what you need to set up your own home network:

✦ **Two or more PCs.** They don't have to run Fedora Core: Windows PCs or Mac OS X computers do just fine. The operating systems on these computers must, however, support TCP/IP networking.

✦ **Ethernet network interface cards on all the computers you want to network.** Some computers come with Ethernet built into the motherboard, whereas others need a plug-in interface card.

✦ **An Ethernet hub with enough ports for all the systems being connected to the network.** If you plan to connect the home network to the Internet through a DSL or cable modem, you can buy a combined hub and NAT router. A hub enables you to use private IP addresses in the LAN and connect the LAN to the Internet with a unique public IP addresses assigned by your ISP. If you start with a hub, you can still add a NAT router later on. By the way, you can use an Ethernet switch in place of the hub (the switch provides better performance than a hub).

✦ **10BaseT cables (also called CAT 5 UTP) with RJ-45 plugs at both ends.** You need as many of these cables as the number of computers you plan to connect to the Ethernet hub. You can buy cables of different lengths from the local computer store. Make sure to buy the correct lengths, depending on the distance between each computer and the hub. By the way, the length of each Cat 5 UTP cable cannot exceed 100 meters (about 328 feet).

## Steps to follow

Follow these steps to set up your home network:

*1.* **Connect one end of a Cat 5 UTP cable to the RJ-45 Ethernet plug on a computer's network interface and connect the other end to an RJ-45 plug on the hub (or hub/router or switch).**

How you want to snake the wire from the computer to the hub or switch is up to you. For quick-and-dirty networking, simply stringing the wire along the wall may be okay, but for a more permanent setup, you may want to pull the wire through walls and/or ceilings.

*2.* **Repeat Step 1 for each computer on the network.**

*3.* **Connect the hub to the power supply.**

Physically, the network is ready now. You still have to, however, configure the networking in the operating system to use the network.

*4.* **Configure TCP/IP networking on each PC.**

If you are connecting the home network to the Internet through a NAT router (see Chapter 1 of this minibook for more information), you configure each PC to dynamically obtain an IP addresses because the NAT router usually serves as a DHCP server (a DHCP server can dynamically configure networking on a host). Otherwise, you can assign IP addresses with the 192.168 prefix. Make sure all PCs have IP addresses that begin with 192.168.$X$ where $X$ is a number from 0 to 254. For example, you could use addresses such as 192.168.0.1, 192.168.0.2, 192.168.0.3, and so on. (You get the idea.) See Chapter 2 of this minibook for more information on configuring TCP/IP networking.

5. **Test the connectivity among the PCs.**

   One way to test that a PC can reach another one is by using the `ping` command. For example, to see if a PC can reach another one whose IP address is 192.168.0.5, type **ping 192.168.0.5** in a terminal window.

# Adding Wireless to Your Current Network

If you already have a home network, consider adding wireless to the network so that you can cut the umbilical cord of wires and work from anywhere in your home. Of course, you need a wireless-capable laptop or desktop. Typically, laptops are the ones with wireless cards because it makes sense — a wireless-capable laptop enables you to work from anywhere there's a wireless access to a network.

## Things you need

Here's what you need to add wireless to your home network:

✦ **A wireless access point.** This hardware device comes with a power connection and a RJ45 jack where you can plug in a Cat 5 UTP cable and connect the access point to the Ethernet hub on the home network. Make sure you buy an access point compatible with the wireless standard available in the PCs and laptops that connect to the access point. Typically, you might buy a 802.11b or 802.11g access point. You can also buy access points that support both 802.11b and 802.11g (see Chapter 3 of this minibook to find more about these wireless standards).

✦ **A laptop with wireless capability (either built-in or through a plug-in PC card).** You use this laptop to access your home network through the wireless access point.

✦ **One Cat 5 UTP cable with RJ-45 plugs at both ends.** You need this cable to connect the wireless access point to the Ethernet hub in your home network. Buy a cable that's long enough to reach from the access point to the hub.

## Steps to follow

Follow these steps to set up the wireless access point:

1. **Mount the wireless access point on the wall high enough so that it's not obstructed. You can also place it on the top of a bookshelf or file cabinet.**

2. **Connect one end of a Cat 5 UTP cable to the RJ-45 Ethernet plug on the wireless access point and connect the other end to an RJ-45 plug on the hub (or hub/router or switch).**

3. **Connect the wireless access point to the power supply.**

4. **Configure the wireless access point from any PC on the home network.**

    The exact steps depend on the wireless access point. You can read the access point's manual for more information. Often the access point comes with Windows software that you have to use to configure the access point. The configuration steps involve setting the name of the access point, setting the IP address (either dynamic or static), enabling encryption, and setting the encryption key (if you are using encryption).

5. **Test the connectivity from a wireless-capable laptop.**

    If the laptop is already configured for wireless, you can simply power it on and it detects the wireless access point. You can recognize the access point by the name you assigned to it when you configured it. If you turned on encryption, you have to enter the encryption key — the same key that you enter into the wireless access point. After that, the laptop can access the other PCs in the home network via the wireless access point.

# Turning Your Fedora Core System into a NAT Router

In Chapter 1 of this minibook, I mention that you can use a network address translation (NAT) router to connect your home network to the Internet. If you have a spare PC lying around, you can turn that PC into a NAT router. You do have to install two Ethernet cards, install Fedora Core, and do a bit of configuring. This section shows you how.

## Things you need

Here's what you need to turn a PC into NAT router:

✦ A PC running Red Hat Linux or Fedora Core — the system that you plan to turn into a NAT router.

✦ Install two Ethernet network cards in the PC and make sure that Fedora Core can recognize both Ethernet cards.

✦ Configure TCP/IP networking for both Ethernet interfaces — these are named eth0 and eth1. You have to know which of these interfaces you are connecting to the Internet.

✦ Cat 5 UTP cables to connect the two Ethernet cards to their networks —
one goes to the Ethernet hub on the home network and the other to the
Internet connection (a DSL or cable modem).

✦ A connection to the Internet, the higher the bandwidth the better.

## Steps to follow

Log in as `root` and follow these steps to set up the Fedora Core system as a
NAT router:

*1.* **Enable IP forwarding in the kernel by typing the following command
in a terminal window:**

```
echo "1" > /proc/sys/net/ipv4/ip_forward
```

This step is necessary because IP forwarding is disabled by default. To
ensure that IP forwarding is enabled when you reboot your system, add
this line to the `/etc/rc.d/rc.local` text file.

*2.* **Type** iptables **to run the IP packet filter administration program and
set up the rules that enable the Fedora Core PC to perform network
address translation (NAT) for your home network.**

The exact `iptables` command depends on the network interface
through which the Fedora Core system connects to the Internet. For
example, if the Internet connection is through the `eth0` network interface, use the following command:

```
iptables -t nat -A POSTROUTING -o eth0 -j MASQUERADE
```

You can also add packet filtering to ensure that no new connections can
come in through the `eth0` interface. The following two commands turn
on this packet filtering:

```
iptables -A INPUT -i ppp0 -m state --state NEW,INVALID
   -j DROP
iptables -A FORWARD -i ppp0 -m state --state
   NEW,INVALID -j DROP
```

*3.* **Save the** iptables **settings with the following command:**

```
service iptables save
```

This command saves the `iptables` rules in the `/etc/sysconfig/ipta-
bles` file. From then on, whenever you start the Fedora Core system,
`iptables` automatically loads these rules and sets up the system as a
NAT router.

4. **Configure networking on other PCs on the home network so that each system uses the Fedora Core system as the gateway.**

   Run the network configuration tool for the operating system running each PC. For the gateway address, specify the IP address of the Fedora Core system (the address of the network interface that connects to the home network, not the one that connects to the Internet). Use the same ISP-provided name server addresses on all systems. After you perform these steps, you can access the Internet from any PC on the home network. Consult Chapter 2 of this minibook for more information on how to configure networking in Fedora Core.

# Book V

# Internet

The 5th Wave    By Rich Tennant

"I think you're just jealous that I found a community of people on MSN.com that worship the yam as I do, and you haven't."

# Contents at a Glance

**Chapter 1: Exchanging E-mail and Instant Messages** ......................................................337

**Chapter 2: Using the Web** ...............................................................................351

**Chapter 3: Reading Newsgroups**..........................................................................371

**Chapter 4: Transferring Files with FTP** ...................................................................383

# Chapter 1: Exchanging E-Mail and Instant Messages

## In This Chapter

✔ Understanding electronic mail

✔ Taking stock of mail readers and IM (Instant Messaging) clients

✔ Using Ximian Evolution

✔ Using Mozilla Mail

✔ Instant messaging with Gaim

*E*lectronic mail (e-mail) is a mainstay of the Internet. E-mail is great because you can exchange messages and documents with anyone on the Internet. One of the most common ways people use the Internet is to keep in touch with friends, acquaintances, loved ones, and strangers through e-mail. You can send a message to a friend thousands of miles away and get a reply within a couple of minutes. Essentially, you can send messages anywhere in the world from an Internet host, and that message typically makes its way to its destination within minutes — something you cannot do with paper mail (also known as *snail mail*, and appropriately so).

I love e-mail because I can communicate without having to play the game of "phone tag," in which two people can seemingly infinitely leave telephone messages for each other without ever successfully making contact. When I send an e-mail message, it waits in the recipient's mailbox to be read at the recipient's convenience. I guess I like the converse even better — when people send me e-mail, I can read and reply at *my* convenience.

Fedora Core comes with several mail clients that can download mail from your Internet Service Provider (ISP). You can also read and send e-mail using these mail clients. In this chapter, I mention most of the mail clients available in Fedora Core and describe a few of them. And when you know one, you can easily use any of the mail readers.

There is yet another type of "keeping in touch" that's more in line with today's teenagers. I'm talking about *IM* — instant messaging. IM is basically one-to-one chat, and Fedora Core includes IM clients for AOL Instant Messenger (or AIM). I briefly describe the AIM client in this chapter.

# Understanding Electronic Mail

E-mail messages are addressed to a username at a host (*host* is just a fancy name for an online computer). That means if John Doe logs in with the *username* `jdoe`, e-mail to him is addressed to `jdoe`. The only other piece of information needed to identify the recipient uniquely is the fully qualified *domain name* of the recipient's system. Thus, if John Doe's system is named `someplace.com`, his complete e-mail address becomes `jdoe@someplace.com`. Given that address, anyone on the Internet can send e-mail to John Doe.

## How MUA and MTA work

There are two types of mail software.

✦ **Mail-user agent (MUA)** is the fancy name for a mail reader — a client that you use to read your mail messages, write replies, and compose new messages. Typically, the mail-user agent retrieves messages from the mail server by using the POP3 or IMAP4 protocol. POP3 is the Post Office Protocol Version 3, and IMAP4 is the Internet Message Access Protocol Version 4. Fedora Core comes with mail-user agents such as Balsa, Mozilla Mail, KMail, and Ximian Evolution.

✦ **Mail-transport agent (MTA)** is the fancy name for a mail server that actually sends and receives mail-message text. The exact method used for mail transport depends on the underlying network. In TCP/IP networks, the mail-transport agent delivers mail using the *Simple Mail-Transfer Protocol* (SMTP). Fedora Core includes sendmail, a powerful and popular mail-transport agent for TCP/IP networks.

Figure 1-1 shows how the MUAs and MTAs work with one another when Alice sends an e-mail message to Bob. (In case you didn't know, using *Alice* and *Bob* to explain e-mail and cryptography is customary — just pick up any book on cryptography and you'll see what I mean). And you may already know this, but the Internet is always diagrammed as a cloud — the boundaries of the Internet are so fuzzy that a cloud seems just right to represent it (or is it because no one knows where it starts and where it ends?).

The scenario in Figure 1-1 is typical of most people. Alice and Bob both connect to the Internet through an ISP and get and send their e-mail through their ISPs. When Alice types a message and sends it, her mail-user agent (MUA) sends the message to her ISP's mail-transfer agent (MTA) using the Simple Mail-Transfer Protocol (SMTP). The sending MTA then sends that message to the receiving MTA — Bob's ISP's MTA — using SMTP. When Bob connects to the Internet, his MUA downloads the message from his ISP's MTA using the POP3 (or IMAP4) protocol. That's the way mail moves around the Internet — from sending MUA to sending MTA to receiving MTA to receiving MUA.

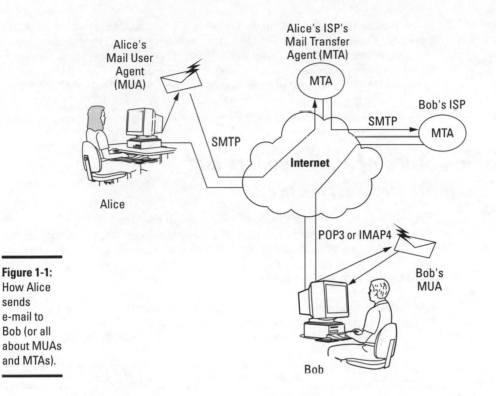

**Figure 1-1:**
How Alice
sends
e-mail to
Bob (or all
about MUAs
and MTAs).

## Mail message enhancements

Mail messages used to be plain text (and most still are), but many messages today have much more than text. Two typical new features of today's mail are

✦ **Attachments:** Many messages today include attached files, which can be anything from documents to images. The recipient can save the attachment on disk or open it directly from the mail reader. Unfortunately, attachments are one way hackers try to get viruses and worms into your PC. (If it's any consolation, most Windows-based viruses and worms do not work in Linux.)

✦ **HTML messages:** Mail messages can be in *HTML* (HyperText Markup Language), the language used to lay out Web pages. When you read an HTML message on a capable mail reader, the message appears in its full glory with nice fonts and embedded graphics.

While HTML messages are nice, they don't appear right when you use a text-based mail reader. In a text mail reader, HTML messages appear as a bunch of gobbledygook (which is just the HTML code).

If you have an ISP account, all you need is a *mail client* (excuse me, a mail-user agent) to access your e-mail. In this case, your e-mail resides on your ISP's server and the mail reader downloads mail when you run it. You have to do some setup before you can start reading mail from your ISP's mail server. The setup essentially requires you to enter information that you get from your ISP — the mail server's name, server type (POP3, for example), your username, and your password.

## Taking Stock of Mail Readers and 1M Clients in Fedora Core

Time was when most mail readers were text programs, but times have changed. Now mail readers are graphical applications capable of displaying HTML messages and handling attachments with ease. They are easy to use. If you can work with one, you can use any of the graphical mail readers. Fedora Core comes with several mail readers.

IM (instant messaging) is a more recent phenomenon, but Fedora Core tries to stay on top of things, so it comes with two AOL IM clients. Table 1-1 gives you an overview of the mail readers and IM clients in Fedora Core.

| Table 1-1 | Fedora Core Mail Readers and AIM Clients |
|---|---|
| *Software* | *Description* |
| KMail | The KDE e-mail client that supports both POP3 and IMAP |
| Mozilla Mail | A mail client as well as a newsreader, part of the Mozilla open-source Web browser (open source incarnation of Netscape Communicator) |
| Ximian Evolution | A *personal information manager* (PIM) that includes e-mail, calendar, contact management, and an online task list |
| Gaim | An IM client for GNOME that supports a number of instant-messaging protocols such as AOL IM, ICQ, Yahoo!, MSN, Gadu-Gadu, and Jabber |
| Kit | An AOL IM client for KDE |

## Using Ximian Evolution

I have heard so much about Ximian Evolution that I want to start with it. What better way than to jump right in!

Choose Main Menu⇨Internet⇨Evolution Email from the GNOME or KDE desktop. If you're working with Evolution for the first time, the Evolution Setup Assistant starts up (as in Figure 1-2).

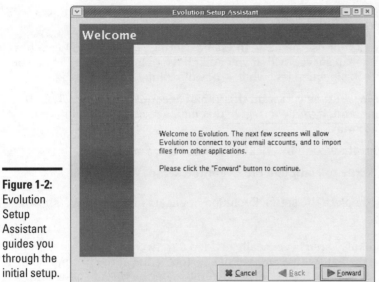

**Figure 1-2:**
Evolution
Setup
Assistant
guides you
through the
initial setup.

Click Forward in the Welcome screen and the Setup Assistant guides you
through the following steps:

1. **Enter your name and e-mail address in the Identity screen and click
   Forward.**

   For example, if your e-mail address is joe@someplace.com, that's what
   you enter.

2. **Set up the options for receiving e-mail and click Forward.**

   Select the type of mail download protocol — POP or IMAP. Then provide
   the name of the mail server (for example, mail.comcast.net). You are
   prompted for the password when Evolution connects to the mail server
   for the first time.

3. **Provide further information about receiving e-mail — how often to
   check for mail and whether to leave messages on the server — and
   then click Forward.**

   Typically, you want to download the messages and delete them from the
   server (otherwise the ISP complains when your mail piles up).

4. **Set up the following options for sending e-mail and click Forward
   when you're done:**

   • Select the server type as SMTP.

   • Enter the name of the server such as smtp.comcast.net.

- If the server requires you to log in, select the Server Requires Authentication check box.

- Enter your username — the same username you use to log in to your ISP's mail server. (Often you don't have to log in to send mail; you only log in when receiving — downloading — mail messages.)

5. **Indicate whether you want this e-mail account to be your default account, and, if you want, give this mail account a descriptive name; click Forward.**

6. **Set your time zone by clicking a map; click Forward.**

7. **Click Apply to complete the Evolution setup.**

After you complete the setup, Evolution opens its main window (shown in Figure 1-3).

The main display area is vertically divided into two windows: a narrow window on the left (with a number of shortcut icons at the bottom), and a bigger window that's further divided into two. In the right hand window, Evolution displays information relevant to the currently selected shortcut icon. Initially, the Mail icon is selected by default.

You can click the icons in the lower left hand area to switch to different views. Table 1-2 describes what happens when you click each of the four shortcut icons in Evolution's Shortcuts window.

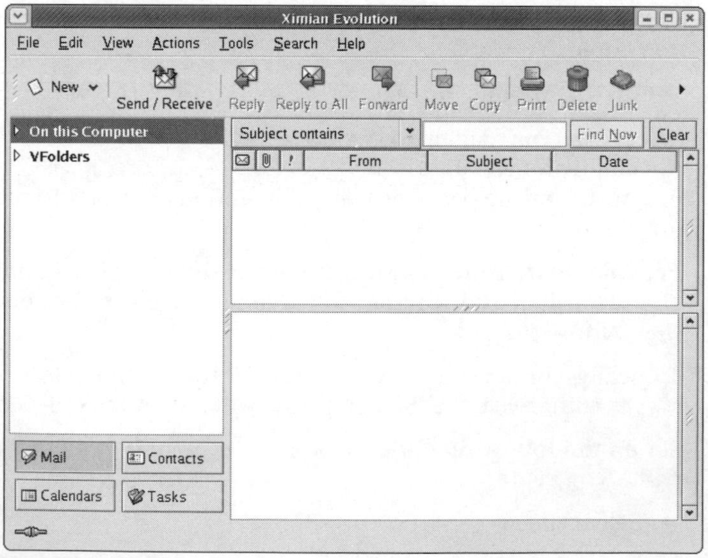

**Figure 1-3:** Evolution takes care of mail, calendar, contact management, and to-do lists.

| Table 1-2 | Shortcut Icons in Ximian Evolution |
|---|---|
| *Name of Icon* | *What It Does* |
| Mail | Switches to mail display where you can read mail and send mail. |
| Calendars | Opens your calendar where you can look up and add appointments. |
| Tasks | Shows your task ("to do") list where you can add new tasks and check what's due when. |
| Contacts | Opens your contact list where you can add new contacts or look up someone from your current list. |

As the icons listed in Table 1-2 show, Ximian Evolution has all the necessary components of a PIM — e-mail, calendar, task list, and contacts.

Above the shortcut icons, Evolution displays folders that you can open by clicking. For example, to read mail, click the Mail icon and then click the arrow next to On This Computer. You see a number of folders containing mail messages.

To access your e-mail, click the Inbox icon. Evolution opens your Inbox (as shown in Figure 1-4). If you turn on the feature to automatically check for mail every so often, Evolution already prompted you for your mail password and downloaded your mail. The e-mail Inbox looks very much like any other mail reader's inbox, such as the Outlook Express Inbox.

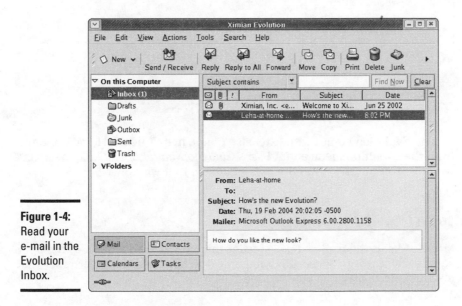

**Figure 1-4:**
Read your
e-mail in the
Evolution
Inbox.

To read a message, click the message in the upper window of the Inbox and the message text appears in the lower window.

To reply to the current message, click the Reply button on the toolbar. A message composition window pops up (as shown in Figure 1-5). You can write your reply and then click the Send button on the toolbar to send the reply. Simple, isn't it?

To send a new e-mail, click the New Message button on the Evolution toolbar. A new message composition window appears and you can type your message in that window; then click Send.

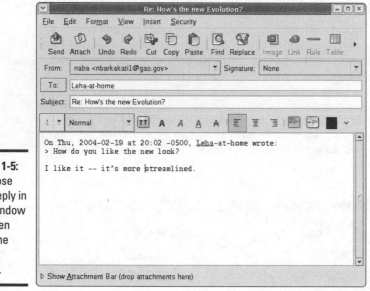

**Figure 1-5:**
Compose
your reply in
this window
and then
click the
Send
button.

Ximian Evolution comes with extensive online help. Choose Help⇨Contents from the Evolution menu and *A User's Guide to Ximian Evolution* appears in a window. You can then read the user's guide in that window.

# Using Mozilla Mail

Mozilla Mail is the mail and newsreader that comes with Mozilla — the open source successor to Netscape Communicator. Mozilla is a Web browser that also includes a mail and newsreader.

To use Mozilla Mail, start by running the Mozilla Web browser. Click the Mozilla icon (the earth lassoed by the mouse cord) on the panel, and the Mozilla Web browser window appears. To access the Mozilla Mail mail and newsreader, choose Window⇨Mail and Newsgroups from the menu. Mozilla Mail runs, starts the Account Wizard (shown in Figure 1-6), and prompts you for information about your e-mail account.

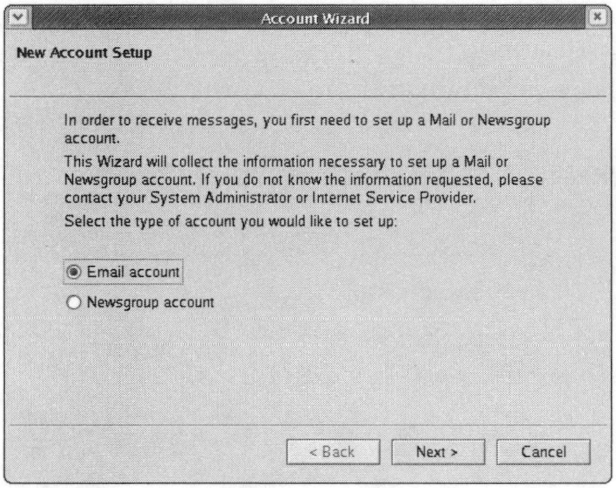

**Figure 1-6:**
Provide your
e-mail
account
information
to Mozilla
Mail's
Account
Wizard.

**Account Wizard**

**New Account Setup**

In order to receive messages, you first need to set up a Mail or Newsgroup account.

This Wizard will collect the information necessary to set up a Mail or Newsgroup account. If you do not know the information requested, please contact your System Administrator or Internet Service Provider.

Select the type of account you would like to set up:

● Email account
○ Newsgroup account

< Back    Next >    Cancel

Select the Email Account radio button and click Next. The Account Wizard then takes you through the following steps:

1. **Enter your identity information — your name and your full e-mail address such as** joe@someplace.com **— and then click Next.**

2. **Provide information about your ISP's mail server — the protocol type (POP or IMAP) as well as the incoming and outgoing server names — and click Next.**

   The incoming server is the POP or IMAP server, whereas the outgoing server is the one through which you send mail out (it's the SMTP server).

3. **Enter the username that your ISP has given you; click Next.**

4. **Enter a name that you want to use to identify this account and click Next.**

   This name is just for Mozilla Mail, so you can pick anything you want such as "My home account."

   The Account Wizard then displays a summary of the information you entered.

5.  **Verify the information; if it's correct, click Finish. Otherwise click Back and fix the errors.**

After you set up the e-mail account, Mozilla Mail's main window appears and shows you the contents of your Inbox. Soon a dialog box pops up and asks you for your e-mail password. Mozilla Mail needs your password to download your e-mail messages from your ISP. Enter your password and click OK.

Mozilla Mail downloads your messages and displays them in a familiar format. To read a message, click that message, and the full text appears in the lower window (as shown in Figure 1-7).

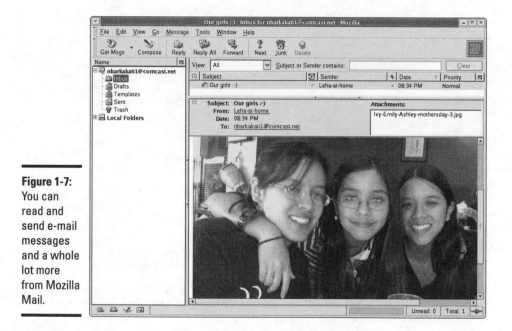

**Figure 1-7:**
You can read and send e-mail messages and a whole lot more from Mozilla Mail.

Mozilla Mail is intuitive to use. Most of the time you can click the toolbar buttons to do most anything you want to do with the e-mail messages. Here's what each toolbar button does:

✦ **Get Msgs:** Downloads messages from your e-mail accounts (you can set up as many as you want).

✦ **Compose:** Opens a window where you can compose and send a message.

✦ **Reply:** Opens a window where you can send back a reply to the person who sent you the message you are reading now.

✦ **Reply All:** Opens a window for sending a reply to everyone who was on the addressee list of the message you are reading now.

✦ **Forward:** Brings up the current message in a window so that you can forward it to someone else.

✦ **Next:** Shows the next unread message.

✦ **Junk:** Marks the selected messages as junk.

✦ **Delete:** Deletes the selected message.

If you use any GUI mail reader — from Microsoft Outlook Express to Novell GroupWise — you find a similar set of toolbar buttons. In the following sections, I describe how to perform a few common e-mail-related tasks.

## Managing your Inbox

Mozilla Mail downloads your incoming mail and stores it in the Inbox folder. You can see the folders organized along the narrow window on the left-hand side (refer to Figure 1-7). Each e-mail account you have set up has a set of folders. You have the following folders by default:

✦ **Inbox:** Holds all your incoming messages for this e-mail account.

✦ **Drafts:** Contains the messages that you save as a draft (click the Save button on the message composition window).

✦ **Templates:** Contains the messages you save as templates.

✦ **Sent:** Holds all the messages you send.

✦ **Trash:** Contains the messages you delete (to empty the Trash folder, choose File⇨Empty Trash from the Mozilla Mail menu).

You can create other folders to better organize your mail. To create a folder, do the following:

*1.* **Choose File⇨New⇨Folder.**

The New Folder dialog box appears.

*2.* **Fill in the folder name and select where you want to put the folder (see Figure 1-8); then click OK.**

The new folder appears in the left window of Mozilla Mail.

When you select a folder from the left window, Mozilla Mail displays the contents of that folder in the upper window on the right-hand side. The list is normally sorted by date, with the latest messages shown at the end of the list. If you want to sort the list any other way — say, by sender or by subject — simply click that column heading and Mozilla Mail sorts the list according to that column.

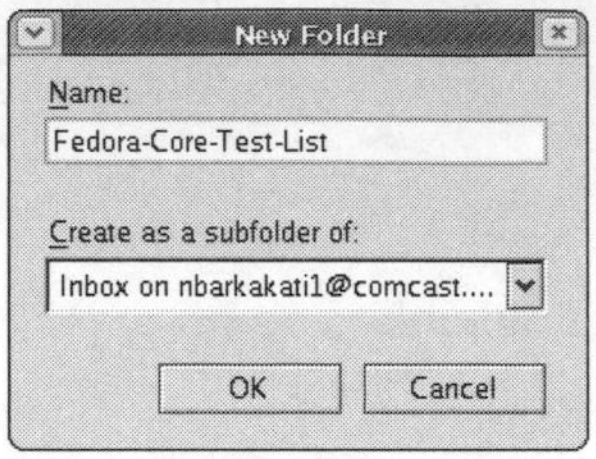

**Figure 1-8:**
You can
create new
folders to
organize
your mail
messages
in Mozilla
Mail.

## Composing and sending messages

To send an e-mail message, you either write a new message or reply to a
message you are reading. The general steps for sending an e-mail message
are as follows:

1. **To reply to a message, click the Reply or Reply All button on the tool-
   bar as you are reading the message. To write a new message, click the
   Compose button on the toolbar. To forward a message, click the
   Forward button.**

   A message composition window appears (as shown in Figure 1-9).

2. **In the message composition window, fill in the subject line and type
   your message.**

   The message can include links to Web sites and images. To insert any of
   these items, choose Insert⇨Link or Insert⇨Image from the menu.

3. **If you're creating a new message or forwarding a message, type the
   e-mail addresses of the recipients.**

   To select addressees from the Address Book, click the Address button
   on the toolbar. Your Address Book opens, from which you can select the
   addressees.

4. **When you're done composing the message, click the Send button.**

   Mozilla Mail asks whether you want to send the message in HTML
   format or plain text or both.

5. **Select a format and then click Send to send the message.**

   If you inserted images and Web links and you know the recipient can
   read HTML mail, be sure to select HTML format; otherwise, choose plain
   text.

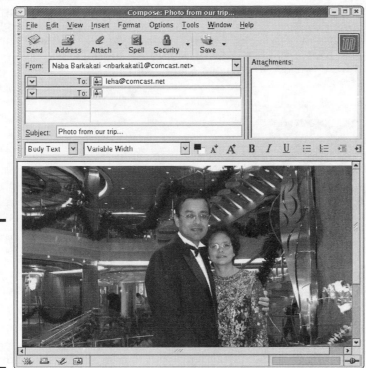

**Figure 1-9:**
Compose
your
message
and then
enter the
addresses
of the
recipients.

If you want to complete a message later, click Save in the message composition window and then close the window. Mozilla Mail saves the message in the Drafts folder. When you're ready to work on that message again, go to the Drafts folder and then double-click the saved message to open it.

## Instant Messaging with Gaim

You can use Gaim to keep in touch with all of your buddies on AOL Instant Messenger (or *AIM*, as it's commonly known). If you use AOL's AIM, you'll be right at home with Gaim, a client for the AOL AIM service. You need an AOL AIM screen name to use Gaim.

Start Gaim by choosing Main Menu⇨Internet⇨Messaging Client from the GNOME desktop. The initial Gaim window appears (see Figure 1-10).

If you've used AIM before, you already have a screen name. Just type it in, enter the password, and then click the Sign On button. Gaim logs you in and opens the standard Buddy List window. The Buddy List is initially empty. To add buddies, select Buddies⇨Add a Buddy. In the Add Buddy window that appears, enter the screen name of the buddy and click Add. To create a new group, choose Buddies⇨Add a Group. Type the name of the new group in the Add Group window that appears and then click Add.

**Figure 1-10:**
Sign on to AIM with Gaim.

If any of your buddies are online, their names show up in the Buddy List window. To send a message to a buddy, double-click the name and a message window pops up. If someone sends you a message, a message window pops up with the message and you can begin conversing in that window.

Well, if you know AIM, you know what to do: Have fun IMing with Gaim!

# Chapter 2: Using the Web

## In This Chapter

↳ Discovering the World Wide Web

↳ Understanding a URL

↳ Checking out Web servers and Web browsers

↳ Web browsing with Mozilla

↳ Creating Web pages with Mozilla Composer

*I* suspect you already know about the Web, but did you know that the Web, or more formally the World Wide Web, made the Internet what it is today? The Internet was around for quite a while, but it did not reach the masses until the Web came along in 1993.

Before the Web came along, you had to use arcane UNIX commands to download and use files, which was simply too complicated for most of us. With the Web, however, anyone can enjoy the benefits of the Internet by using a *Web browser* — a graphical application that downloads and displays Web documents. A click of the mouse is all you need to go from reading a document from your company Web site to downloading a video clip from across the country.

In this chapter, I briefly describe the Web and introduce Mozilla — the primary Web browser (and, for that matter, mail and newsreader, too) in Fedora Core. I also briefly discuss how you can create your own Web pages.

## Discovering the World Wide Web

If you have used a file server at work, you know the convenience of sharing files. You can use the word processor on your desktop to get to any document on the shared server.

Now imagine a word processor that enables you to open and view a document that resides on any computer on the Internet. You can view the document in its full glory, with formatted text and graphics. If the document makes a reference to another document (possibly residing on yet another computer), you can open that linked document by clicking the reference. That kind of easy access to distributed documents is essentially what the World Wide Web provides.

Of course, the documents have to be in a standard format, so that any computer (with the appropriate Web browser software) can access and interpret the document. And a standard protocol is necessary for transferring Web documents from one system to another.

The standard Web document format is *HyperText Markup Language* (HTML), and the standard protocol for exchanging Web documents is *HyperText Transfer Protocol* (HTTP). HTML documents are text files and don't depend on any specific operating system, so they work on any system from Windows and Mac to any type of UNIX and Linux.

A *Web server* is software that provides HTML documents to any client that makes the appropriate HTTP requests. A *Web browser* is the client software that actually downloads an HTML document from a Web server and displays the contents graphically.

## Like a giant spider's web

The World Wide Web is the combination of the Web servers and the HTML documents that the servers offer. When you look at the Web in this way, the Web is like a giant book whose pages are scattered throughout the Internet. You use a Web browser running on your computer to view the pages — the pages are connected like a giant spider's web, with the documents everywhere (shown in Figure 2-1).

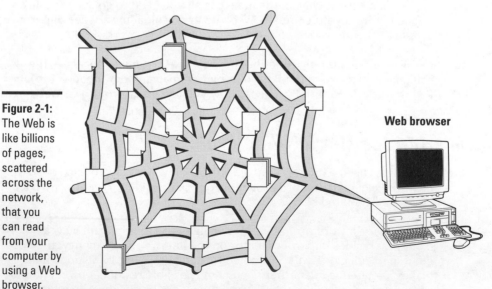

**Figure 2-1:** The Web is like billions of pages, scattered across the network, that you can read from your computer by using a Web browser.

**Web browser**

**Web pages**

Imagine that the Web pages — HTML documents — are linked by network connections that resemble a giant spider's web, so you can see why the Web is called "the Web." The "World Wide" part comes from the fact that the Web pages are scattered around the world.

## Links and URLs

Like the pages of real books, Web pages contain text and graphics. Unlike real books, however, Web pages can include multimedia, such as video clips, sound, and links to other Web pages that can actually take you to those Web pages.

The *links* in a Web page are references to other Web pages that you can follow to go from one page to another. The Web browser typically displays these links as underlined text (in a different color) or as images. Each link is like an instruction to you — something like, "For more information, please consult Chapter 4," that you might find in a real book. In a Web page, all you have to do is click the link; the Web browser brings up the referenced page, even though that document may actually reside on a far-away computer somewhere on the Internet.

The links in a Web page are referred to as *hypertext links* because when you click a link, the Web browser jumps to the Web page referenced by that link.

This arrangement brings up a question. In a real book, you might ask the reader to go to a specific chapter or page in the book. How does a hypertext link indicate the location of the referenced Web page? In the World Wide Web, each Web page has a special name, called a *Uniform Resource Locator* (URL). A URL uniquely specifies the location of a file on a computer. Figure 2-2 shows the parts of a URL.

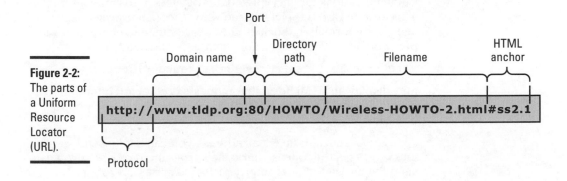

**Figure 2-2:**
The parts of a Uniform Resource Locator (URL).

Port

Domain name    Directory path    Filename    HTML anchor

`http://www.tldp.org:80/HOWTO/Wireless-HOWTO-2.html#ss2.1`

Protocol

As Figure 2-2 shows, a URL has the following parts:

✦ **Protocol:** Name of the protocol that the Web browser uses to access the data from the file the URL specifies. In Figure 2-2, the protocol is `http://`, which means that the URL specifies the location of a Web page. Here are some of the common protocol types and their meanings:

- `file://` means the URL is pointing to a local file. You can use this URL to view HTML files without having to connect to the Internet. For example, `file:///var/www/html/index.html` opens the file `/var/www/html/index.html` from your Fedora Core system.

- `ftp://` means you can download a file using the File Transfer Protocol (FTP). For example, `ftp://ftp.purdue.edu/pub/uns/NASA/nasa.jpg` refers to the image file `nasa.jpg` from the `/pub/uns/NASA` directory of the FTP server `ftp.purdue.edu`. If you want to access a specific user account via FTP, use a URL in the following form:

  `ftp://username:password@ftp.somesite.com/`

  with the username and password embedded in the URL (note that the password is in plain text and not secure).

- `http://` means the file is downloaded using the HyperText Transfer Protocol (HTTP). This protocol is the well-known format of URLs for all Web sites, such as `http://fedora.redhat.com` for the Fedora Project's home page. If the URL does not have a filename, the Web server sends a default HTML file named `index.html` (that's the default filename for the popular UNIX-based Apache Web servers; Microsoft Windows Web servers use a different default filename).

- `https://` specifies that the file is accessed through a Secure Sockets Layer (SSL) connection — a protocol designed by Netscape Communications for encrypted data transfers across the Internet. This form of URL is typically used when the Web browser sends sensitive information (such as credit card number, username, and password) to a Web server. For example, a URL such as

  `https://some.site.com/secure/takeorder.html`

  may display an HTML form that requests credit card information and other personal information (such as name, address, and phone number).

- `mailto://` specifies an e-mail address you can use to send an e-mail message. This URL opens your e-mail program from where you can send the message. For example, `mailto:webmaster@someplace.com` refers to the Webmaster at the host `someplace.com`.

- `news://` specifies a newsgroup you can read by means of the Network News Transfer Protocol (NNTP). For example,

  `news://news.md.comcast.giganews.com/comp.os.linux.setup`

  accesses the `comp.os.linux.setup` newsgroup at the news server `news.md.comcast.giganews.com`. If you have a default news server configured for the Web browser, you can omit the news server's name and use the URL `news: comp.os.linux.setup` to access the newsgroup.

✦ **Domain name:** Contains the fully qualified domain name of the computer that has the file this URL specifies. You can also provide an IP address in this field. The domain name is not case sensitive.

✦ **Port:** Port number that is being used by the protocol listed in the first part of the URL. This part of the URL is optional; all protocols have default ports. The default port for HTTP, for example, is 80. If a site configures the Web server to listen to a different port, the URL has to include the port number.

✦ **Directory path:** Directory path of the file being referred to in the URL. For Web pages, this field is the directory path of the HTML file. The directory path is case sensitive.

✦ **Filename:** Name of the file. For Web pages, the filename typically ends with `.htm` or `.html`. If you omit the filename, the Web server returns a default file (often named `index.html`). The filename is case sensitive.

✦ **HTML anchor:** Optional part of the URL that makes the Web browser jump to a specific location in the file. If this part starts with a question mark (?) instead of a hash mark (#), the browser takes the text following the question mark to be a query. The Web server returns information based on such queries.

## Web servers and Web browsers

The Web server serves up the Web pages, and the Web browser downloads them and displays them to the user. That's pretty much the story with these two cooperating software packages that make the Web work.

In a typical scenario, the user sits in front of a computer that's connected to the Internet and runs a Web browser. When the user clicks a link or types a URL into the Web browser, the browser connects to the Web server and requests a document from the server. The Web server sends the document (usually in HTML format) and ends the connection. The Web browser interprets and displays the HTML document with text and graphics. Figure 2-3 illustrates this typical scenario of a user browsing the Web.

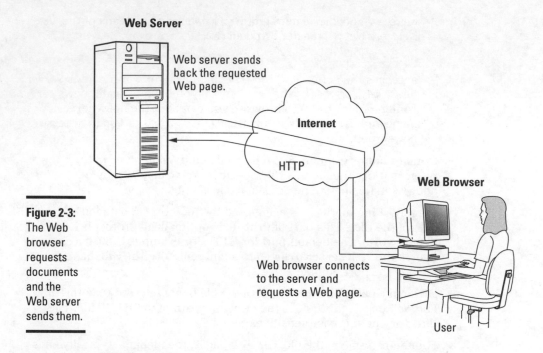

**Web Server**

Web server sends
back the requested
Web page.

**Internet**

HTTP

**Web Browser**

**Figure 2-3:**
The Web
browser
requests
documents
and the
Web server
sends them.

Web browser connects
to the server and
requests a Web page.

User

The Web browser's connection to the Web server ends after the server
sends the document. When the user browses through the downloaded document and clicks another hypertext link, the Web browser again connects to
the Web server named in the hypertext link, downloads the document, ends
the connection, and displays the new document. That's how the user can
move from one document to another with ease.

A Web browser can do more than simply "talk" HTTP with the Web server —
in fact, Web browsers can also download documents using FTP and many
have integrated mail and newsreaders as well.

## Web Browsing in Fedora Core

Web browsing is fun because many of today's Web pages are so full of graphics and multimedia. Then there's the element of surprise — you can click a
link and end up at unexpected Web pages. Links are the most curious (and
useful) aspect of the Web. You can start at a page that shows today's
weather and a click later, you can be reading this week's issue of *Time*
magazine.

To browse the Web, all you need is a Web browser and an Internet connection. I assume that you've already taken care of the Internet connection, so all you need to know are the Web browsers in Fedora Core.

## Checking out the Web browsers in Fedora Core

Fedora Core comes with the Mozilla Web browser. Mozilla is an open source version of Netscape Communicator, and it is the primary Web browser in Fedora Core.

Fedora Core includes several other Web browsers. I briefly mention the other browsers, but I focus on Mozilla in the rest of the discussions. Here are the major Web browsers that come with Fedora Core:

✦ **Mozilla:** The reincarnation of that old workhorse — Netscape Communicator — only better. Includes mail and a newsreader. The Web browser is called the Mozilla Navigator, or simply Navigator (just as it was in Netscape Communicator).

✦ **Epiphany:** The GNOME Web browser that uses parts of the Mozilla code to draw the Web pages, but has a simpler user interface than Mozilla. Epiphany is not installed by default, but it's on the DVD included with this book. If you can't find Epiphany on the DVD, you can download it from `www.gnome.org/projects/epiphany/`.

✦ **Konqueror:** The KDE Web browser that also doubles as a file manager and a universal viewer.

In addition to these three, many other applications are capable of downloading and displaying Web pages.

## Starting Mozilla

From the GNOME desktop, you can start Mozilla in one of two ways:

✦ Click the Web Browser icon (the earth and mouse) on the GNOME or KDE panel.

✦ Choose Main Menu⇨Internet⇨Mozilla Web Browser from GNOME.

When Mozilla starts, it displays a browser window with a default home page (the main Web page on a Web server is known as the *home page*). You can configure Mozilla to use a different Web page as the default home page.

## Learning Mozilla's user interface

Figure 2-4 shows a Web page from a U.S. government Web site (`www.gao.gov`), as well as the main elements of the Mozilla browser window.

Personal toolbar

Navigation toolbar

Menu bar

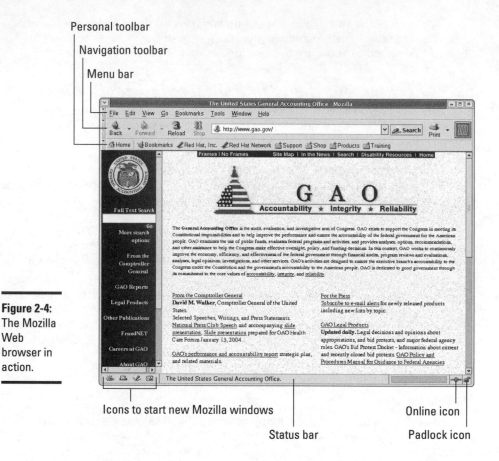

**Figure 2-4:**
The Mozilla
Web
browser in
action.

Icons to start new Mozilla windows

Online icon

Status bar

Padlock icon

The Mozilla Web browser includes lots of features in its user interface, but you can master it easily. You can turn off some of the items that make it look busy. You can also start with just the basics to get going with Mozilla and then gradually expand to areas that you haven't yet explored.

### Mozilla toolbars

Starting from the top of the window, you see a menu bar with the standard menus (File, Edit, and so forth), followed by the two toolbars — Navigation toolbar and Personal toolbar. The area underneath the Personal toolbar is where the current Web page appears.

Here's what you can do with the buttons on the Navigation toolbar that appear just below the menu bar:

+ **Back:** Move to the previous Web page.

+ **Forward:** Move to the page from which you may have gone backward.

+ **Reload:** Reload the current Web page.

+ **Stop:** Stop loading the current page.

+ **Location text box:** Show the URL of the current Web page. (Type a URL in this box to view that Web page.)

+ **Search:** Takes you to the Google Web Search page (www.google.com).

+ **Print:** Print the current Web page (you can also preview how the page will appear when printed).

+ **Mozilla icon:** Go to the Mozilla.org Web site (www.mozilla.org).

Immediately below the Navigation toolbar comes the Personal toolbar with the Home and Bookmarks buttons. These two buttons serve the following purposes:

+ **Home:** Takes you to the home page.

+ **Bookmarks:** Displays a menu from which you can bookmark the current page as well as manage your bookmarks.

More links are on the Personal toolbar. Clicking the Red Hat, Inc. button takes you to the Red Hat home page (www.redhat.com). The rest of the links are organized into folders. Click a folder to view the drop-down list of links, and click the link you want to visit.

### Status bar

You can think of the bar along the bottom edge of the Mozilla window as the status bar because the middle part of that area displays status information as Mozilla loads a Web page.

The left side of the status bar includes a number of icons. If you want a hint about what any of these icons do, simply mouse over the button, and Mozilla displays a small balloon help message. You can click these icons to open other Mozilla windows to perform various tasks. Table 2-1 explains what you can do with these icons.

| Table 2-1 | Icons on Mozilla's Status Bar |
|---|---|
| *When You Click This Icon* | *It Does the Following* |
| | Opens another Navigator (Web browser) window. |
| | Opens a Mozilla Mail window for reading mail and newsgroups. |
| | Opens an HTML composer window where you can prepare an HTML document. |
| | Opens the Address Book window for looking up addresses. |

In the right corner of Mozilla's status bar, to the right of the status message, you see two icons. The icon on the left indicates that you're online; if you click it, Mozilla goes offline. The rightmost icon is a security padlock. Mozilla supports a secure version of HTTP that uses a protocol called *Secure Sockets Layer* (SSL) to transfer encrypted data between the browser and the Web server. When Mozilla connects to a Web server that supports secure HTTP, the security padlock appears locked. Otherwise the security padlock is open, signifying an insecure connection. The URL for secure HTTP transfers begins with `https://` instead of the usual `http://` (note the extra `s` in `https`).

Mozilla displays status messages in the middle portion of the status bar. You can watch the messages in this area to see what's going on. When Mozilla is done downloading a Web page, it displays a message showing the number of seconds it took to download that page.

### Mozilla menus

I haven't mentioned the Mozilla menus much. That's because you can usually get by without having to go to them. Nevertheless, taking a quick look through the Mozilla menus is worthwhile so you know what each one offers. Table 2-2 gives you an overview of the Mozilla menus.

| Table 2-2 | Mozilla Menus |
|---|---|
| *This Menu* | *Enables You to Do the Following* |
| File | Open a file or Web location, close the browser, send a Web page or link by mail, edit a Web page, print the current page, and quit Mozilla. |
| Edit | Copy and paste selections, find text in the current page, and edit your preferences. |
| View | Show or hide various toolbars, reload the current page, make the text larger or smaller, view the HTML code for the page, and view information about the page. |

| This Menu | Enables You to Do the Following |
| --- | --- |
| Go | Go backward and forward in the list of pages you have visited, or jump to other recently visited Web pages. |
| Bookmarks | Bookmark a page, manage the bookmarks, and add links to the Personal toolbar folder (these then appear in the Personal toolbar). |
| Tools | Search the Web and manage various aspects of the Web page such as image loading, cookies, and stored passwords. |
| Window | Open other Mozilla windows (such as Mozilla Mail, Navigator, Address Book, and Composer). |
| Help | Get online help on Mozilla. |

## Changing your home page

Your *home page* is the page that Mozilla loads when you start it. By default, Mozilla loads the Fedora Core Release Notes from your system's hard drive. Changing the home page is easy.

First locate the page that you want to be the home page. You can get to that page any way you want. You can search with a search engine to find the page you want, you can type in the URL in the Location text box, or you may even accidentally end up on a page that you want to make your home page. It does not matter.

When you're viewing the Web page that you feel is good as your home page, choose Edit⇨Preferences from the Mozilla menu. The Preferences window appears (shown in Figure 2-5).

On the right side of Figure 2-5, notice that the Home Page radio button is selected. This option means Mozilla Navigator displays the home page when you start it up. Then you see the URL for the home page, and underneath the address is a Use Current Page button. Click that button to make the current page your home page.

You can set a lot of other options using the Preferences window. Although I am not explaining all the options, you can click around to explore everything that you can do from this window. For example, you can click the Choose File button to select a file on your local system as the home page.

## Changing Mozilla's appearance

Mozilla supports themes. A *theme* is basically the look and feel of Mozilla's user interface (which includes how the background and the buttons look). The default theme is called the Classic theme, which gives you a look and feel that's similar to what Netscape used to have.

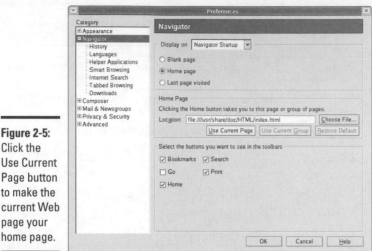

**Figure 2-5:**
Click the
Use Current
Page button
to make the
current Web
page your
home page.

Mozilla comes with another theme called Modern, and you can download
many other themes from the Net. Visit `themes.mozdev.org` to browse some
of the available themes and download the ones you want to try. You can also
get new themes by choosing View⇨Apply Theme⇨Get New Themes from the
Mozilla menu.

Changing the theme is easy. If you want to see the theme that you're selecting before you select it, follow these steps:

*1.* **Choose Edit⇨Preferences from the Mozilla menu.**

The Preferences window appears.

*2.* **Click the plus sign next to Appearance on the left side of the window.**

The Appearance item opens up.

*3.* **Click the Themes item.**

The right side now shows the available themes.

*4.* **Choose the theme you want.**

You see a preview of the buttons and the color in the area underneath
the list of themes (see Figure 2-6).

*5.* **After you select a theme, click OK to close the Preferences window.**

A dialog box tells you that the new theme takes effect the next time you
start Mozilla.

To see the full effect of a theme, choose the theme from View⇨Apply Theme
or close Mozilla and then start it again.

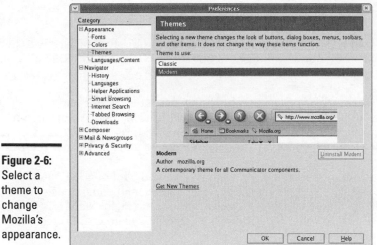

**Figure 2-6:**
Select a
theme to
change
Mozilla's
appearance.

## Surfing the Net with Mozilla

Where you go from the Mozilla home page depends on you. All you have to
do is click and see where you end up. Move your mouse around. You know
when you are on a link because the mouse pointer changes to a hand with an
extended index finger. Click the link, and Mozilla downloads the Web page
referenced by that link.

How you use the Web depends on what you want to do. When you first get
started, you may explore a lot — browsing through Web sites and following
links without any specific goal in mind; what you may call Web window-
shopping.

The other, more purposeful, use of the Web is to find specific information
from the Net. For example, you might want to locate all the Web sites that
contain documents with a specified keyword. For such searches, you can use
one of many Web search tools available on the Net. Mozilla's Search button
takes you to the Google Web Search page (www.google.com).

A third type of use is a visit to a specific site with a known URL. For example,
when reading about a specific topic in this book, you may come across a
specific URL. In that case, you want to go directly to that Web page.

If you want to surf the Net with Mozilla, all you need is a starting Web page —
then you can click whatever catches your fancy. For example, select the text
in the Location text box in Mozilla's Navigation toolbar, type **www.yahoo.
com**, and then press Enter. You get to the Yahoo home page that shows
Yahoo's Web directory — organized by subject. There's your starting point.
All you have to do is click and you're on your way!

# Creating Web Pages

If you get your Internet access from an ISP, you probably get a free Web page as well. The only catch is you have to upload an HTML file for your Web page, which means you have to somehow prepare a Web page.

One way to prepare a Web page is to simply use a text editor and type HTML code. After all, a Web page is just a text file with HTML tags. Even though I won't put anyone through the agony of typing all those HTML tags, I want to show you a very basic HTML document, just so you know the structure.

Before I get into the HTML code, I want to give you a bit of good news. Mozilla comes with something called Composer, which you can use to prepare HTML documents — Web pages — without having to learn HTML tags. Now that you know relief is on the way, I can quickly show you the innards of an HTML document.

## Introducing HTML

Typically, when a client (a Web browser) connects to a Web server, the server sends back an HTML file named `index.html`. When you have your Web site, the `index.html` file is your home page. I introduce HTML by creating an `index.html` file and improving it through iterations. In the process, you see most of the important HTML features.

To begin, open any text editor and type the following lines of text:

```
<html>

<head>
<TITLE>
My Home Page
</TITLE>
</head>

<body>

<center>
<h1>
My Home Page
</h1>
</center>

<hr>
This page is under construction.
<hr>
```

```
Copyright &copy; 2004 Someone
<a href="mailto:webmaster@myplace.com">
<address>
webmaster@myplace.com
</address>
</a>

</body>
</html>
```

This example is a bare-bones HTML file. Go ahead and save it with the file-name `index.html`.

To see how this page looks, choose File⇨Open File from the Mozilla menu. Browse through the directories and pick the `index.html` file from wherever you stored it. Click Open to open the file in Mozilla. Figure 2-7 shows how the Web page looks in Mozilla.

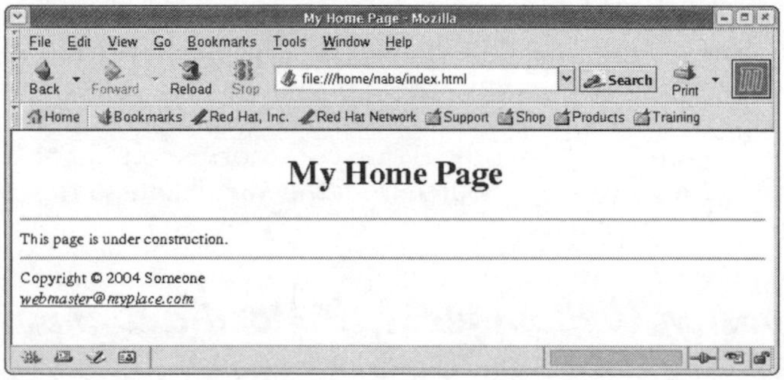

**Figure 2-7:**
View your
HTML file
in Mozilla
to see how
it looks.

Getting back to the Web page itself, it looks quite nice, doesn't it? No wonder we love Web pages.

At this point, correlate the Web page in Figure 2-7 with the HTML codes so that you can see the effect of each HTML tag. In particular, notice the following things:

✦ HTML tags are enclosed in angle brackets ⟨...⟩, and a pair of tags — a beginning tag and an ending tag — goes like this ⟨/...⟩.

✦ HTML tags are not case sensitive. Thus, you can type the title tag as ⟨title⟩ or ⟨TITLE⟩; both mean the same.

✦ The ⟨html⟩ ... ⟨/html⟩ tag pair simply indicates that the document is an HTML document; that tag does not have any visual effect.

✦ The `<head>` ... `</head>` tags enclose the header information. In this case, the header defines the title of the page. That title appears in the title bar of the Mozilla window.

✦ The `<body>` ... `</body>` tag pair encloses the entire HTML document.

✦ The body of the Web page shows the text `My Home Page` in header level 1 (`<h1>` ... `</h1>`) and centered (`<center>` ... `</center>`).

✦ The `<hr>` tag causes the browser to display a horizontal rule.

✦ The HTML keyword `&copy;` displays a copyright symbol.

✦ The `<a href= ...>` ... `</a>` tag adds a hyperlink. All the lines between the start tag `<a href="mailto:webmaster@myplace.com">` and the end tag `</a>` are called the *anchor* (or `<a>`) *element*. The `href` keyword that appears in the start tag of the anchor element is called an *attribute*.

✦ The `<address>` ... `</address>` tags display the enclosed text as an address (in italics).

I won't go any further with the HTML tags; this section gives you a feel for the overall structure of a typical Web page.

If you're ever curious about the HTML code corresponding to any Web page, simply choose View⇨Page Source from the Mozilla menu to see the HTML code for the current page.

## Composing Web pages with Mozilla Composer

Mozilla Composer is a graphical tool for creating Web pages without having to know much HTML. If you know HTML, you can certainly make use of that knowledge in Composer. One nice part is that you can create an attractive Web page even if you don't know any HTML.

### A sample editing session in Composer

If you are creating a new Web page from scratch, choose Window⇨Composer from the Mozilla menu.

If you want to edit an existing Web page and you open it in Mozilla, choose File⇨Edit Page. Mozilla opens a Composer window with the same HTML file.

You can start with the page shown in Figure 2-7 and begin editing it. In the Composer window, the Web page looks similar to that in Figure 2-7, but now it behaves like a word processor. You can start editing the text and changing the layout, just as you do in a word processor. To add text, simply click and type. To apply text-formatting effects, such as boldface, italics, and underlining, use the text-formatting toolbar (which looks very much like similar toolbars in any word processor).

You can also insert images. Here's how:

1.  **Gather the image files you want to use (in formats such as JPEG or GIF), and then save them somewhere on your Fedora Core PC.**

    You can either prepare the images in a drawing and paint program or get the images from some other source (for example, from a Web site such as thefreesite.com/Free_Graphics/Free_clipart/index.html).

2.  **Position the cursor where you want an image; then choose Insert⇨Image from the Composer menu.**

    The Image Properties dialog box, shown in Figure 2-8, appears.

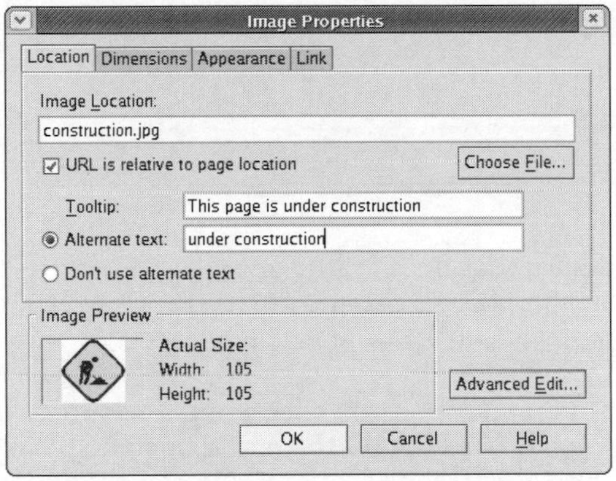

**Figure 2-8:**
You can add an image to a Web page from this dialog box.

3.  **Click the Choose File button and select the image file from the Select Image File dialog box.**

4.  **Enter alternate text for the image — this text appears in text-only browsers.**

    You can also enter a tooltip (the text that appears as a user places the mouse over the image).

5.  **After filling in all the information, click OK.**

    The image appears where you positioned the cursor in Step 2 (see Figure 2-9).

6.  **Repeat Steps 2 through 5 for other images. After inserting all the images, choose File⇨Save to save the HTML file.**

    If you're creating a new Web page, Composer prompts you for a filename.

Figure 2-9 shows the Web page of Figure 2-7 after I inserted an image.

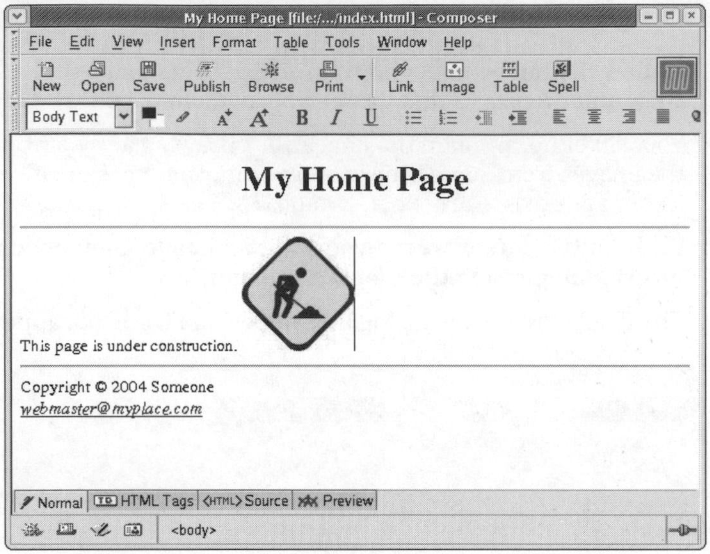

**Figure 2-9:**
You can
create
or edit
your Web
pages in
Composer.

With this brief example, I have barely scratched the surface as far as what Composer can do. If you begin to try these features on sample Web pages, you'll figure out Composer's features in no time.

As you are working in Composer, if you ever wonder what any of the toolbar buttons do, simply mouse over the button and a small help balloon pops up with a helpful hint. Figure 2-10 shows an example of what happens when you mouse over the Link button.

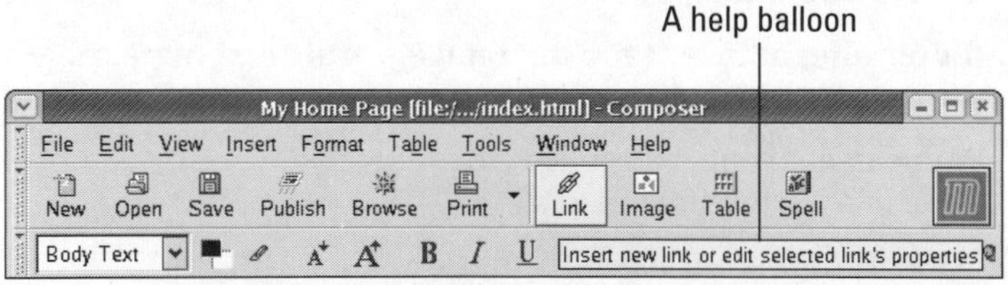

**Figure 2-10:**
Mouse over
a button and
Composer
displays
a balloon
help.

A help balloon

### Views in Composer

Notice that the Composer window has four tabs along the bottom. These tabs enable you to view the Web page in different forms. You typically edit the file in Normal view, but you can switch to the other views; for example, you can edit HTML directly if you so desire. To change to a different view, click the tab.

The four tabs are as follows:

✦ **Normal:** This view shows the Web page in nearly complete layout, but also lets you edit the page. You typically do most of your editing and formatting in this view.

✦ **HTML Tags:** This view shows the Web page with the HTML tags as small icons. You can quickly check what HTML tags are affecting which parts of the document and, perhaps, fix any formatting problems.

✦ **<HTML> Source:** This view shows you the HTML text in its full glory. If you use WordPerfect, this view is like WordPerfect's Reveal Codes option. If something weird happens to the Web page layout, you can switch to this view, find the offending code, and fix it. Of course, you have to know some HTML, but don't worry — you'll pick it up if you start working with Web pages. You can also use this view to write the Web page directly in HTML and go to Normal or Preview views to check up on the layout.

✦ **Preview:** This view essentially shows you what the Web page looks like in Mozilla Navigator. Preview is a quick way to check the final layout without having to open the file in a Navigator window. You cannot edit the page in this view.

The HTML Tags view can be handy when you want to quickly spot extraneous HTML tags. Figure 2-11 shows the HTML Tags view of the Web page shown in Figure 2-9.

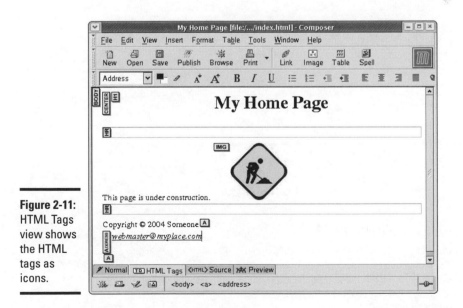

**Figure 2-11:**
HTML Tags view shows the HTML tags as icons.

Each tag appears in yellow, with a tag name such as CENTER (for centered text), H1 (for header level 1), IMG (for image), HR for a horizontal rule, and so on. You can see whether any extraneous tags appear in the Web page — and remove them if you want (although the extras often don't do any harm — such as those that are inserted, for example, when a blank line is centered).

# Chapter 3: Reading Newsgroups

## In This Chapter

✔ **Understanding newsgroups**

✔ **Reading newsgroups from your ISP**

✔ **Reading and searching newsgroups at some Web sites**

Internet newsgroups are like the bulletin-board systems (BBSs) of the pre-Web age or the forums offered on online systems such as AOL and MSN. Essentially, newsgroups provide a distributed conferencing system that spans the globe. You can post articles — essentially e-mail messages to a whole group of people — and respond to articles others have posted.

Think of an Internet newsgroup as a gathering place — a virtual meeting place where you can ask questions and discuss various issues (and best of all, everything you discuss gets archived for posterity).

To participate in newsgroups, you need access to a news server — your Internet Service Provider (ISP) can give you this access. You also need a newsreader. Luckily, Fedora Core comes with software that you can use to read newsgroups: Pan and Mozilla Mail. In this chapter, I introduce you to newsgroups and show you how to read newsgroups with a few of the newsreaders. I also briefly explain how you can read and search newsgroups for free from a few Web sites.

## Understanding Newsgroups

Newsgroups originated in Usenet — a store-and-forward messaging network that was widely used for exchanging e-mail and news items. Usenet works like a telegraph in that news and mail are relayed from one system to another. In Usenet, the systems are not on any network; they simply dial up and use the UNIX-to-UNIX Copy Protocol (UUCP) to transfer text messages.

Although it's a very loosely connected collection of computers, Usenet works well and continues to be used because very little expense is involved in connecting to it. All you need is a modem and a site willing to store and forward your mail and news. You have to set up UUCP on your system, but you don't need a sustained network connection; just a few phone calls are all you need to keep the e-mail and news flowing. The downside is that you cannot use TCP/IP services such as the Web, TELNET, or FTP.

From their Usenet origins, the newsgroups have now migrated to the Internet (even though the newsgroups are still called *Usenet newsgroups*). Instead of UUCP, the Network News Transfer Protocol (NNTP) now transports the news.

Although (for most of the online world) the news-transport protocol has changed from UUCP to NNTP, the store-and-forward concept of news transfer remains. Thus, if you want to get news on your Fedora Core system, you have to find a news server from which your system can download news. Typically, you can use your ISP's news server.

## Newsgroup hierarchy

The Internet newsgroups are organized in a hierarchy for ease of maintenance as well as ease of use. The newsgroup names show the hierarchy — written in Internet-speak — but easy to understand with a little bit of explanation.

A typical newsgroup name looks like this:

```
comp.os.linux.announce
```

This name says that `comp.os.linux.announce` is a newsgroup for announcements (`announce`) about the Linux operating system (`os.linux`) and that these subjects fall under the broad category of computers (`comp`).

As you can see, the format of a newsgroup name is a sequence of words separated by periods. These words denote the hierarchy of the newsgroup. Figure 3-1 illustrates the concept of hierarchical organization of newsgroups.

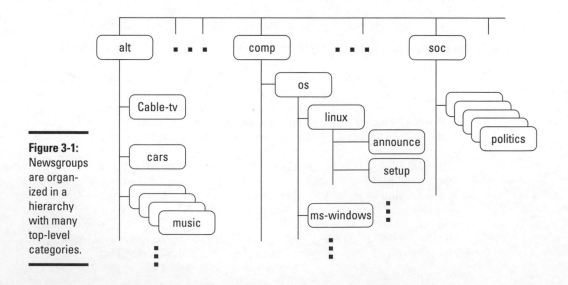

**Figure 3-1:** Newsgroups are organized in a hierarchy with many top-level categories.

To understand the newsgroup hierarchy, compare the newsgroup name with the path name of a file (for example, `/usr/lib/X11/xinit/Xclients`) in Linux. Just as a file's path name shows the directory hierarchy of the file, the newsgroup name shows the newsgroup hierarchy. In filenames, a slash (/) separates the names of directories; in a newsgroup's name, a period (.) separates the different levels in the newsgroup hierarchy.

In a newsgroup name, the first word represents the newsgroup *category*. The `comp.os.linux.announce` newsgroup, for example, is in the `comp` category, whereas `alt.books.technical` is in the alt category.

## Top-level newsgroup categories

Table 3-1 lists some of the major newsgroup categories. You'll find a wide variety of newsgroups covering subjects ranging from politics to computers. The Linux-related newsgroups are in the `comp.os.linux` hierarchy.

| Table 3-1 | Some Major Newsgroup Categories |
|---|---|
| *Category* | *Subject* |
| alt | "Alternative" newsgroups (not subject to any rules), which run the gamut from the mundane to the bizarre |
| bionet | Biology newsgroups |
| bit | Bitnet newsgroups |
| biz | Business newsgroups |
| clari | Clarinet news service (daily news) |
| comp | Computer hardware and software newsgroups (includes operating systems such as Linux and Microsoft Windows) |
| ieee | Newsgroups for the Institute of Electrical and Electronics Engineers (IEEE) |
| k12 | Newsgroups devoted to elementary and secondary education |
| linux | Newsgroups devoted to Linux (includes a `linux.redhat` hierarchy) |
| misc | Miscellaneous newsgroups |
| news | Newsgroups about Internet news administration |
| rec | Recreational and art newsgroups |
| sci | Science and engineering newsgroups |
| soc | Newsgroups for discussing social issues and various cultures |
| talk | Discussions of current issues (think "talk radio") |

This short list of categories is deceptive because it doesn't really tell you about the wide-ranging variety of newsgroups available in each category. The top-level categories alone number close to a thousand, but many top-level categories are distributed only in specific regions of the world. Because each newsgroup category contains several levels of subcategories, the overall count of newsgroups can be close to 60,000 or 70,000! The `comp` category alone has more than 500 newsgroups.

To browse newsgroup categories and get a feel for the breadth of topics covered by the newsgroups, visit the Free Usenet Newsgroup News Web site at `newsone.net`.

## Linux-related newsgroups

Typically, you have to narrow your choice of newsgroups according to your interests. If you're interested in Linux, for example, you can pick one or more of these newsgroups:

✦ `comp.os.linux.admin`: Information about Linux system administration.

✦ `comp.os.linux.advocacy`: Discussions about promoting Linux.

✦ `comp.os.linux.announce`: Important announcements about Linux. This newsgroup is moderated, which means you must mail the article to a moderator, who then posts it to the newsgroup if the article is appropriate for the newsgroup (this method keeps the riff-raff from clogging up the newsgroup with marketing pitches).

✦ `comp.os.linux.answers`: Questions and answers about Linux. All the Linux HOWTOs are posted in this moderated newsgroup.

✦ `comp.os.linux.development`: Current Linux development work.

✦ `comp.os.linux.development.apps`: Linux application development.

✦ `comp.os.linux.development.system`: Linux operating-system development.

✦ `comp.os.linux.hardware`: Discussions about Linux and various types of hardware.

✦ `comp.os.linux.help`: Help with various aspects of Linux.

✦ `comp.os.linux.misc`: Miscellaneous Linux-related topics.

✦ `comp.os.linux.networking`: Networking under Linux.

✦ `comp.os.linux.redhat`: Red Hat Linux-related topics.

✦ `comp.os.linux.setup`: Linux setup and installation.

✦ `comp.os.linux.x`: Discussions about setting up and running the X Window System under Linux.

✦ `linux.redhat`: Discussions about Red Hat Linux.

You have to be selective about what newsgroups you read because keeping up with all the news is impossible, even in a specific area such as Linux. When you first install and set up Red Hat Linux, you might read newsgroups such as `comp.os.linux.redhat`, `comp.os.linux.setup`, `comp.os.linux.hardware`, and `comp.os.linux.x` (especially if you run X). After you have Linux up and running, you may want to find out about only new things happening in Linux. For such information, read the `comp.os.linux.announce` newsgroup.

## Reading Newsgroups from Your ISP

If you sign up with an ISP for Internet access, it can provide you with access to a news server. Such Internet news servers communicate by using the Network News Transfer Protocol (NNTP). You can use an NNTP-capable newsreader, such as Pan, to access the news server and read selected newsgroups. You can also read news by using the newsreader that comes with Mozilla (included with Fedora Core). Using a newsreader is the easiest way to access news from your Fedora Core Internet system.

My discussion of reading newsgroups assumes that you obtained access to a news server from your ISP. The ISP provides you the name of the news server and any username and password needed to set up your news account on the newsreader you use.

To read news, you need a *newsreader* — a program that enables you to select a newsgroup and view the items in that newsgroup. You also have to understand the newsgroup hierarchy and naming conventions (which I describe in the "Newsgroup hierarchy" section of this chapter). Now I show you how to read news from a news server.

If you don't have access to newsgroups through your ISP, you can try using one of the many public news servers that are out there. For a list of public news servers, visit NewzBot at `www.newzbot.com`. At this Web site, you can search for news servers that carry specific newsgroups.

## Reading newsgroups with Mozilla Mail

You can browse newsgroups and post articles from Mozilla Mail, one of the components of Mozilla. When you're starting to read newsgroups for the first time, follow these steps to set up the news account:

*1.* **Click the Mozilla icon (the earth and mouse icon) or choose Main Menu➪Internet➪Mozilla Web Browser from the GNOME panel.**

Mozilla starts.

*2.* **Choose Windows➪Mail & Newsgroups from the Mozilla menu.**

If you have not yet defined any mail or newsgroup account, the Account Wizard appears. Otherwise the Mozilla Mail and News (Mozilla Mail for short) window appears.

*3.* **Choose Edit➪Mail & Newsgroups Account Settings from the Mozilla Mail menu.**

A dialog box appears.

*4.* **Click Add Account.**

The Account Wizard appears (shown in Figure 3-2).

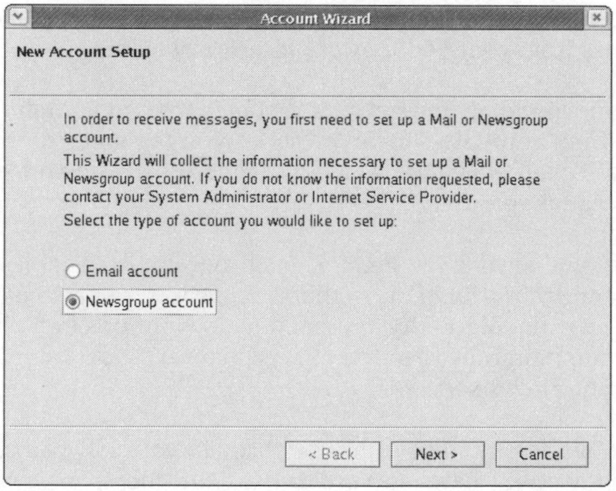

**Figure 3-2:**
Mozilla's
Account
Wizard
guides you
through the
newsgroup
account
setup.

*5.* **Select the Newsgroup Account radio button and click Next.**

*6.* **Fill in your identity information — name and e-mail address — and click Next.**

7. **Enter your news server name and click Next.**

8. **Enter a descriptive name of the newsgroup account and click Next.**

9. **Click Finish to complete the newsgroup account setup.**

The new newsgroup account now appears in the list of accounts on the left side of the Mozilla Mail window. Click the newsgroup account name, and the right side of the window shows the options for the newsgroup account.

Click the <u>Subscribe to Newsgroups</u> link. Mozilla Mail starts to download the list of newsgroups from the news server.

If your ISP's news server requires a username and password, you're prompted for that information. After that, Mozilla Mail downloads the list of newsgroups and displays them in the Subscribe dialog box. (You can enter a search string in a text box to narrow the list.) When you find the newsgroups you want, click the check box to subscribe to these newsgroups (shown in Figure 3-3). Then click OK to close the dialog box.

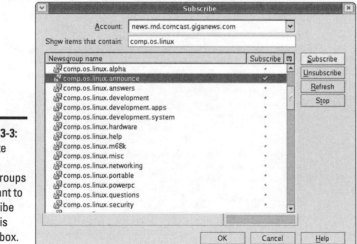

**Figure 3-3:** Indicate which newsgroups you want to subscribe to in this dialog box.

After you subscribe to newsgroups, these newsgroups appear under the newsgroup account name in the left side of the Mozilla Mail window. You can then read a newsgroup using these steps:

1. **Click a newsgroup name (for example,** comp.os.linux.announce**).**

   If your news server requires a username and password, a dialog box prompts you for this information. Then another dialog box asks you how many message headers you want to download.

2. **Specify the number of headers (for example, 500) you want and then click Download to proceed.**

   Mozilla Mail downloads the headers from the newsgroup and displays a list in the upper-right area of the window.

3. **From the list of headers, click an item to read that article (shown in Figure 3-4).**

To select other subscribed newsgroups, simply click the newsgroup's name in the left side of the window.

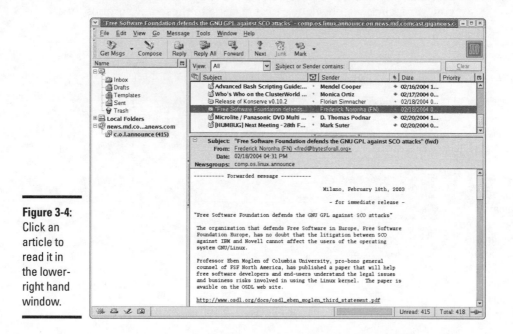

**Figure 3-4:**
Click an article to read it in the lower-right hand window.

## Newsgroup subscriptions

Unlike magazines or newspapers, newsgroups don't require that you subscribe to them; you can read any available newsgroup on the news server. The news server's administrator may decide to exclude certain newsgroups, however; if they aren't included, you cannot read them.

The only thing that can be called "subscribing" is when you indicate the newsgroups you routinely want to read. The news server does not receive any of this subscription information — the information is used only by the newsreader to determine what to download from the news server.

## Posting news

You can use any newsreader to post a news article (a new item or a reply to an old posting) to one or more newsgroups. The exact command for posting a news item depends on the newsreader. For example, in the Mozilla Mail newsreader, you follow these steps to post an article:

1. **Click Reply on the toolbar to post a follow-up to a news item you're reading. To post a new news article, click Compose.**

   A window appears where you can compose the message.

2. **Type the names of the newsgroups, just as you type the addresses of recipients when sending e-mail; then enter the subject and your message.**

   For this test posting, type `ignore` as the subject line and enter `misc.test` as the name of the newsgroup.

   Otherwise, any site that receives your article replies by mail to tell you the article has reached the site; that's in keeping with the purpose of the `misc.test` newsgroup. Figure 3-5 shows the message being composed in Netscape Communicator.

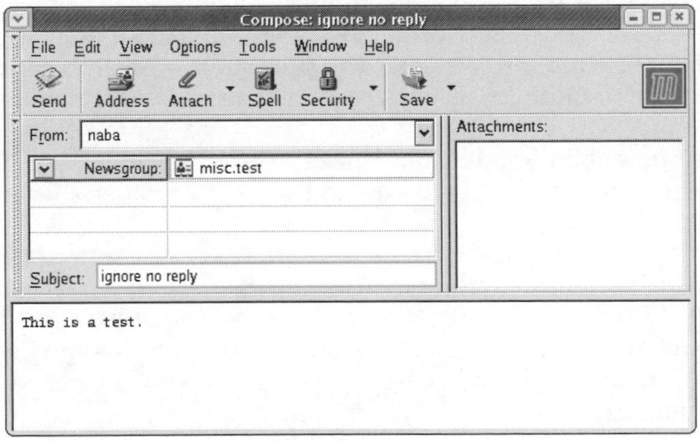

**Figure 3-5:**
You can post follow-ups or new news articles from the Mozilla Mail newsreader.

3. **After you finish composing the message, click Send on the toolbar (see Figure 3-5).**

   Mozilla Mail sends the message to the news server, which in turn sends it to other news servers, and soon it's all over the world!

4. **To verify that the test message reaches the newsgroup, choose File⇨Subscribe; then subscribe to the** `misc.test` **newsgroup (that's where you recently posted the new article). Look at the latest article (or one of the most recent ones) in** `misc.test`, **which is the article you recently posted.**

If you post an article and read the newsgroup immediately, you see the new article, but that does not mean the article has reached other sites on the Internet. After all, your posting shows up on your news server immediately because that's where you posted the article. Because of the store-and-forward model of news distribution, the news article gradually propagates from your news server to others around the world.

The `misc.test` newsgroup provides a way to see whether or not your news posting is really getting around. If you post to that newsgroup and don't include the word *ignore* in the subject, news servers acknowledge receipt of the article by sending an e-mail message to the address listed in the Reply To field of the article's header.

## Reading and Searching Newsgroups at Web Sites

If you don't have access to newsgroups through your ISP, you can still read newsgroups and post articles to newsgroups at a number of Web sites. Some of them archive old news articles and provide good search capabilities, so you can search these for articles related to some question you may have.

The best part about reading newsgroups through a Web site is that you don't even need access to a news server and you can read news from your Web browser.

Table 3-2 lists Web sites that offer free access to Usenet newsgroups. Some sites offer Usenet newsgroup service for a fee. I don't list them here, but you can search for them with Google (`www.google.com`) — type the search words **usenet newsgroup access** and you get a list of all Web sites that offer newsgroup access (including the ones that charge a fee).

| Table 3-2 | Web Sites with Free Access to Usenet Newsgroups |
|-----------|-------------------------------------------------|
| *Web Site* | *URL* |
| Google Groups | `groups.google.com` |
| NewsOne.Net | `newsone.net` |
| Mailgate | `www.mailgate.org` |

One of the best places to read newsgroups, post articles, and search old newsgroup archives is Google Groups — Google's Usenet discussion forums — on the Web at `groups.google.com`. At that Web site, you can select a newsgroup to browse and you can post replies to articles posted on various newsgroups.

The best part of Google Groups is the search capability. You already know how good Google's Web search is; you get that same comprehensive search capability to locate newsgroup postings that relate to your search words. To search newsgroups, fill in the search form at `groups.google.com` and press Enter.

To browse newsgroups in Google Groups, ignore the search box and look at the list of high-level newsgroup categories such as `alt`, `comp`, and `soc`. Click the category, and you can gradually drill down to specific newsgroups. When viewing an article in Google Groups, you can click a link that enables you to post a follow-up to that article.

# Chapter 4: Transferring Files with FTP

## In This Chapter

✔ Using the GNOME FTP client

✔ Using the Mozilla Web browser as FTP client

✔ Learning to use the FTP command

*J*ust as the name implies, *File Transfer Protocol* (FTP) is used to transfer files between computers. For example, if your Internet Service Provider (ISP) gives you space for a personal Web page, you may have already used FTP to upload the Web page. Using an FTP client on your computer, you log in to your ISP account, provide your password, and then copy the files from your home system to the ISP's server.

You can also use FTP to download other files anonymously, such as open-source software from other computers on the Internet — in which case, you don't need an account on the remote system to download files. You can simply log in using the word anonymous as the username and provide your e-mail address as the password (in fact, your Web browser can do this on your behalf, so you may not even know this process is happening). This type of anonymous FTP is great for distributing files to anyone who wants them. For example, a hardware vendor might use anonymous FTP to provide updated device drivers to anyone who needs them.

Fedora Core comes with several FTP clients, both command-line ones and GUI ones. In this chapter, I introduce you to a few GUI FTP clients and, for the command-line FTP client, describe the commands you use to work with remote directories.

## Using Graphical FTP Clients

You can use one of the following GUI FTP clients in Fedora Core:

✦ gFTP (a graphical FTP client)

✦ Mozilla Web browser for anonymous FTP downloads

For uploading files, you want to use gFTP because you typically have to provide a username and password for such transfers. Web browsers work fine for anonymous downloads, which is how you typically download software from the Internet.

I briefly describe both GUI FTP clients in the next two sections.

## Using gFTP

GNOME comes with gFTP, a graphical FTP client. gFTP is not installed by default, but you can easily install it from the companion DVD by following these steps while you are logged in as `root`:

*1.* **Mount this book's companion DVD.**

Insert the DVD into the DVD drive and type **mount /mnt/cdrom** in a terminal window (you may have to change `cdrom` to `cdrom1`, if the DVD drive is the second CD/DVD drive on your system).

*2.* **Install the gftp RPM.**

Type the following commands from a terminal window (these commands assume that the DVD drive is mounted on `/mnt/cdrom`):

```
cd /mnt/cdrom/Fedora/RPMS
rpm -ivh gftp*
```

To start gFTP, choose from the GNOME or KDE desktop Main Menu⇨ Internet⇨gFTP. The gFTP window appears (as shown in Figure 4-1).

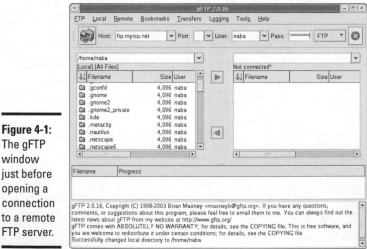

**Figure 4-1:**
The gFTP window just before opening a connection to a remote FTP server.

The gFTP window has a menu bar with menus for performing various tasks. Just below the menu bar is a toolbar with a number of buttons and text fields. Here you can type the name or IP address of the remote host, the username, and the password needed to log in to the remote host. Figure 4-1 shows the gFTP window after you fill in this information.

To upload or download files using gFTP, follow these steps.

1. **Fill in the host name or the IP address of the remote system in the Host field.**

   If you have used that host before, you can select it from the drop-down list that appears when you click the downward-pointing arrow next to the Host field.

2. **Provide the username in the User field and the password in the Pass field, and then click the button with the icon showing two computers (to the left of the Host field).**

   This operation causes gFTP to connect to your chosen host and to log in with the username and password you provided. The lower part of the gFTP window shows the FTP protocol messages exchanged between the two systems.

3. **Observe this area for any indication of error messages.**

   The directory listing of the remote system appears in the right half of the gFTP window. The left half shows the current local directory.

4. **To upload one or more files from the current system to the remote system, select the files in the list on the left, and then click the right arrow button.**

5. **To download files from the remote system, select the filenames in the list on the right, and then click the left arrow button.**

6. **When you're done transferring files, choose FTP⇨Quit from the menu.**

As these steps show, transferring files with a GUI FTP client, such as gFTP, is a simple task.

Believe it or not, gFTP isn't for FTP transfers alone. It can also transfer files using the HTTP protocol and secure file transfers using the Secure Shell (SSH) protocol.

## Using a Web browser as an FTP client

Any Web browser can act as an FTP client, but such programs are best for anonymous FTP downloads, where the Web browser can log in using the anonymous username and any password.

In Fedora Core, you can use the Mozilla Web browser as an FTP client. All you have to know is how to write the URL so the Web browser can tell that you want to download a file using FTP. The syntax of the FTP URL is like this:

```
ftp://hostname/pathname
```

The first part (`ftp://`) indicates that you want an FTP transfer. The `hostname` part is the name of the FTP server (the name often starts with an `ftp` — for example, `ftp.netscape.com`). The `pathname` is the full directory path and filename of the file you want to download.

If you simply provide the hostname for the FTP server, the Web browser displays the contents of the anonymous FTP directory. If you want to find an anonymous FTP on your Fedora Core system, start Mozilla (click the Mozilla icon on the GNOME panel) and then type the following line in the Location text box:

```
ftp://localhost
```

Then press Enter. Mozilla shows the contents of the anonymous FTP directory on your Fedora Core system. Figure 4-2 shows a typical appearance of an anonymous FTP directory in Mozilla. You can click folders to see their contents and download any files.

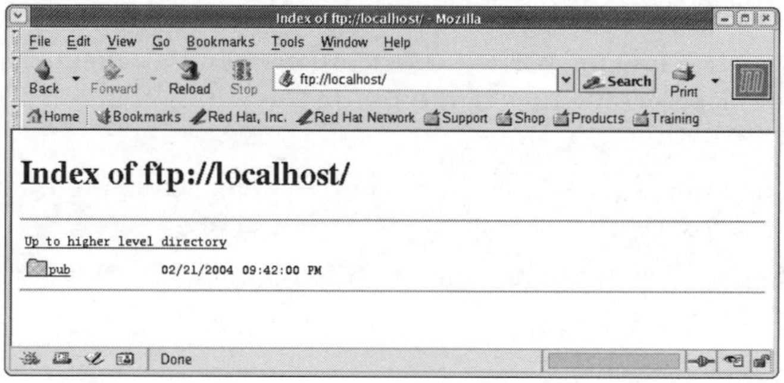

**Figure 4-2:** You can use Mozilla to download files from anonymous FTP servers.

> Index of ftp://localhost/ - Mozilla
>
> File  Edit  View  Go  Bookmarks  Tools  Window  Help
>
> Back  Forward  Reload  Stop   ftp://localhost/   Search  Print
>
> Home  Bookmarks  Red Hat, Inc.  Red Hat Network  Support  Shop  Products  Training
>
> ## Index of ftp://localhost/
>
> Up to higher level directory
>
> 📁 pub          02/21/2004 09:42:00 PM
>
> Done

When you use the `ftp://localhost` URL, you won't get a response from your system if you're not running an FTP server or if you have set up your firewall so that no FTP connections are allowed. On your system, log in as `root` and type **service vsftpd start** (in a terminal window) to start the FTP server.

The same approach of accessing anonymous FTP sites works if you type the hostname of some other anonymous FTP server. For example, try typing the following URL:

```
ftp://ftp.netscape.com
```

You get the directory of the ftp.netscape.com server.

# Using the Command-Line FTP Client

Knowing how to use FTP from the command line is a good idea — just in case. For example, your GUI desktop may not be working and to fix the problem, you may have to download some files. If you know how to use the command-line FTP client, you can download the files and take care of the problem. It's not that hard.

The best way to learn the command-line FTP client is to try it out. The command is called ftp, and you can try out the ftp commands from your Fedora Core system. You don't even need any Internet connection because you can use the ftp command to connect to your own system — I show you how.

In the following sample FTP session, I use the command-line FTP client to log in using my username (naba) and browse the directories on my system. When you try a similar operation, replace the name with your username and provide your password. Here's the listing showing the commands (my comments appear in italics):

```
ftp localhost
Connected to localhost (127.0.0.1).
220 (vsFTPd 1.2.1)
Name (localhost:naba):     (I press Enter.)
331 Please specify the password.
Password:          (I type my password.)
230 Login successful.
Remote system type is UNIX.
Using binary mode to transfer files.
ftp> help        (I type help to see a list of FTP commands.)
Commands may be abbreviated.  Commands are:

!             debug       mdir      sendport    site
$             dir         mget      put         size
account       disconnect  mkdir     pwd         status
append        exit        mls       quit        struct
ascii         form        mode      quote       system
bell          get         modtime   recv        sunique
```

```
binary       glob        mput        reget       tenex
bye          hash        newer       rstatus     tick
case         help        nmap        rhelp       trace
cd           idle        nlist       rename      type
cdup         image       ntrans      reset       user
chmod        lcd         open        restart     umask
close        ls          prompt      rmdir       verbose
cr           macdef      passive     runique     ?
delete       mdelete     proxy       send
ftp> help mget    (I can get help on a specific command.)
mget       get multiple files
ftp> cd /var/ftp (This changes directory to /var/ftp.)
250 Directory successfully changed.
ftp> ls   (This command lists the contents of the directory.)
227 Entering Passive Mode (127,0,0,1,38,142)
150 Here comes the directory listing.
drwxr-xr-x    2 0         0            4096 Feb 21 21:42 pub
226 Directory send OK.
ftp> bye          (This command ends the session.)
221 Goodbye.
```

As the listing shows, you can start the command-line FTP client by typing the command `ftp` *hostname*, where *hostname* is the name of the system you want to access. When the FTP client establishes a connection with the FTP server at the remote system, the FTP server prompts you for a username and password. After you supply the information, the FTP client displays the `ftp>` prompt, and you can begin typing commands to perform specific tasks. If you can't remember a specific FTP command, type **help** to view a list of them. You can get additional help for a specific command by typing **help *command***, where *command* is what you want help on.

Many FTP commands are similar to the Linux commands for navigating the file system. For example, `cd` changes directory, `pwd` prints the name of the current working directory, and `ls` lists the contents of the current directory. Two other common commands are `get` and `put` — `get` is what downloads a file from the remote system to your system, and `put` uploads (sends) a file from your system to the remote host.

Table 4-1 describes some commonly used FTP commands. You don't have to type the entire FTP command. For a long command, you have to type the first few characters only — enough to identify the command uniquely. For example, to delete a file, you can type **dele** and to change the file transfer mode to binary, you can type **bin**.

When downloading files from the Internet, you almost always want to transfer the files in binary mode because the software is usually archived and compressed in a binary form (its files aren't plain text files). So always use the `binary` command to set the mode to binary. Then use the `get` command to download the files.

| Table 4-1 | Commonly Used FTP Commands |
|-----------|----------------------------|
| **Command** | **Description** |
| ! | Executes a shell command on the local system. For example, `!ls` lists the contents of the current directory on the remote system. |
| ? | Displays a list of commands (same as `help`). |
| append | Appends a local file to a remote file. |
| ascii | Sets the file-transfer type to ASCII (or plain text). This command is the default file-transfer type. |
| binary | Sets the file-transfer type to binary. |
| bye | Ends the FTP session with the remote FTP server and quits the FTP client. |
| cd | Changes the directory on the remote system. For example, `cd /pub/Linux` changes the remote directory to `/pub/Linux`. |
| chmod | Changes the permission settings of a remote file. For example, `chmod 644 index.html` changes the permission settings of the `index.html` file on the remote system. |
| close | Ends the FTP session with the FTP server and returns to the FTP client's prompt. |
| delete | Deletes a remote file. For example, `delete bigimage.jpg` deletes that file on the remote system. |
| dir | Lists the contents of the current directory on the remote system. |
| disconnect | Ends the FTP session and returns to the FTP client's prompt. (This command is the same as `close`.) |
| get | Downloads a remote file. For example, `get junk.tar.gz junk.tgz` downloads the file `junk.tar.gz` from the remote system and saves it as the file `junk.tgz` on the local system. |
| hash | Turns on or off the hash-mark (#) printing that shows the progress of file transfer. When this feature is turned on, a hash mark prints on-screen for every 1,024 bytes transferred from the remote system. (It's the command-line version of a progress bar.) |
| help | Displays a list of commands. |
| image | Same as `binary`. |
| lcd | Changes the current directory on the local system. For example, `lcd /var/ftp/pub` changes the current local directory to `/var/ftp/pub`. |
| ls | Lists the contents of the current remote directory. |
| mdelete | Deletes multiple files on a remote system. For example, `mdelete *.jpg` deletes all remote files with names ending in `.jpg` in the current directory. |
| mdir | Lists multiple remote files and saves the listing in a specified local file. For example, `mdir /usr/share/doc/w* wlist` saves the listing in the local file named `wlist`. |

*(continued)*

**Table 4-1** *(continued)*

| Command | Description |
|---------|-------------|
| mget | Downloads multiple files. For example, mget *.jpg downloads all files with names ending in .jpg. If the prompt is turned on, the FTP client asks for confirmation before downloading each file. |
| mkdir | Creates a directory on the remote system. mkdir images creates a directory named images in the current directory on the remote system. |
| mls | Same as mdir. |
| mput | Uploads multiple files. For example, mput *.jpg sends all files with names ending in .jpg to the remote system. If the prompt is turned on, the FTP client asks for confirmation before sending each file. |
| open | Opens a connection to the FTP server on the specified host. For example, an open ftp.netscape.com connects to the FTP server on the host ftp.netscape.com. |
| prompt | Turns the prompt on or off. When the prompt is on, the FTP client prompts you for confirmation before downloading or uploading each file during a multifile transfer. |
| put | Sends a file to the remote system. For example, put index.html sends the index.html file from the local system to the remote system. |
| pwd | Displays the full path name of the current directory on the remote system. When you log in as a user, the initial current working directory is your home directory. |
| quit | Same as bye. |
| recv | Same as get. |
| rename | Renames a file on the remote system. For example, rename old.html new.html renames the file old.html to new.html on the remote system. |
| rmdir | Deletes a directory on the remote system. For example, rmdir images deletes the images directory in the current directory of the remote system. |
| send | Same as put. |
| size | Shows the size of a remote file. For example, size bigfile.tar.gz shows the size of that remote file. |
| status | Shows the current status of the FTP client. |
| user | Sends new user information to the FTP server. For example, user naba sends the username naba; the FTP server then prompts for the password for that username. |

# Book VI

# Administration

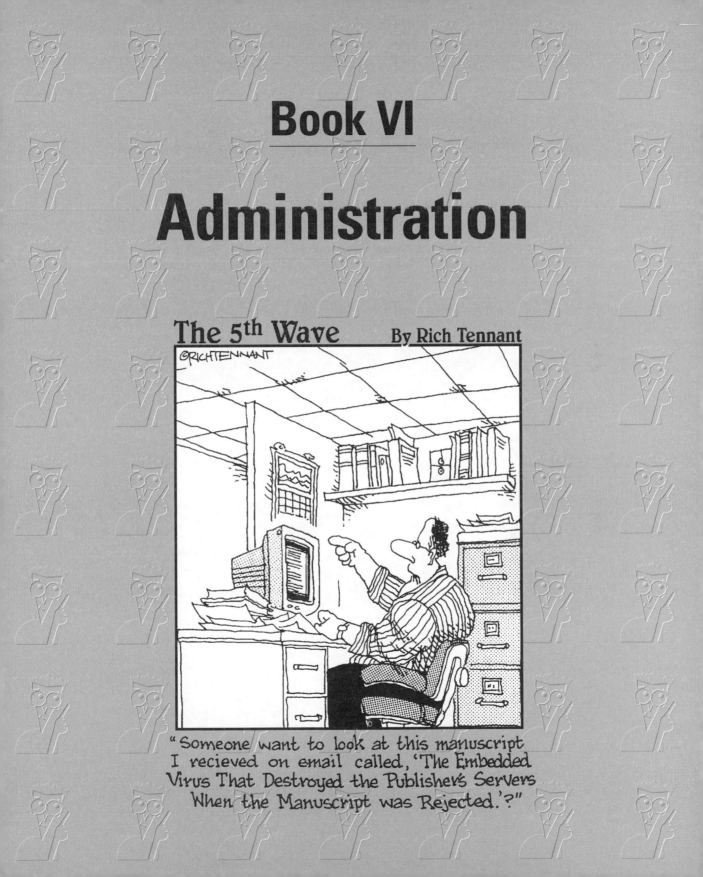

The 5th Wave By Rich Tennant

@RICHTENNANT

"Someone want to look at this manuscript I recieved on email called, 'The Embedded Virus That Destroyed the Publisher's Servers When the Manuscript was Rejected.'?"

# Contents at a Glance

**Chapter 1: Performing Basic System Administration** ......................................................393

**Chapter 2: Managing Users** ................................................................................425

**Chapter 3: Managing the File System** ....................................................................437

**Chapter 4: Managing Applications** .......................................................................461

**Chapter 5: Managing Devices and Printers** ...............................................................479

**Chapter 6: Upgrading and Customizing the Kernel** ........................................................493

# Chapter 1: Performing Basic System Administration

## In This Chapter

✔ **Becoming** root

✔ **Understanding the system startup process**

✔ **Taking stock of the system configuration files**

✔ **Viewing system information through the** /proc **file system**

✔ **Monitoring system performance**

✔ **Scheduling jobs**

*S*ystem administration refers to whatever has to be done to keep a computer system up and running; the *system administrator* is whoever is in charge of taking care of these tasks.

If you're running Fedora Core at home or in a small office, you're most likely the system administrator. Or maybe you're the system administrator for a whole LAN full of Fedora Core systems. No matter. In this chapter, I introduce you to basic system-administration procedures and show you how to perform some common tasks.

Fedora Core comes with quite a few graphical tools for performing specific system administration tasks. I describe some of these tools in this chapter, and the other chapters of this minibook.

## Taking Stock of System-Administration Tasks

So what *are* system-administration tasks? My off-the-cuff reply is *anything you have to do to keep the system running well.* More accurately, though, a system administrator's duties include the following:

✦ **Adding and removing user accounts.** You have to add new user accounts and remove unnecessary user accounts. If a user forgets the password, you have to change the password.

✦ **Managing the printing system.** You have to turn the print queue on or off, check print-queue status, and delete print jobs if necessary.

✦ **Installing, configuring, and upgrading the operating system and various utilities.** You have to install or upgrade parts of the Linux operating system and other software packages.

✦ **Installing new software.** You have to install software that comes in Red Hat Package Manager (RPM) files. You also have to download and unpack software that comes in source-code form — and then build executable programs from the source code.

✦ **Managing hardware.** Sometimes you have to add new hardware and install drivers so the devices work properly.

✦ **Making backups.** You have to back up files, either in a Zip drive or on tape (if you have a tape drive).

✦ **Mounting and unmounting file systems.** When you want to access the files on a CD-ROM (for example), you have to mount that CD-ROM's file system on one of the directories in your Linux file system. You also have to mount floppy disks, in both Linux format and DOS format.

✦ **Automating tasks.** You have to schedule Linux tasks to take place automatically (at specific times) or jobs for people to perform periodically.

✦ **Monitoring the system's performance.** You may want to keep an eye on system performance to see where the processor is spending most of its time, and to see the amount of free and used memory in the system.

✦ **Starting and shutting down the system.** Although starting the system typically involves nothing more than powering up the PC, you do have to take some care when you want to shut down your Linux system. If your system is set up for a graphical login screen, you can perform the shutdown operation by selecting a menu item from the login screen. Otherwise, use the `shutdown` command to stop all programs before turning off your PC's power switch.

✦ **Monitoring network status.** If you have a network presence (whether a LAN, a DSL line, or cable-modem connection), you may want to check the status of various network interfaces and make sure your network connection is up and running.

✦ **Setting up host and network security.** You have to make sure that system files are protected and protect your system against attacks over the network.

✦ **Monitoring security.** You have to keep an eye on any intrusions, usually by checking the log files.

That's a long list of tasks! I don't cover all of them in this chapter, but the rest of the minibook describes most of these tasks. Here I focus on some of the basics, such as how to become root (the superuser), setting system-configuration files, monitoring system performance, and setting up periodic jobs.

# How to Become root

You have to log in as root to perform the system administration tasks. The root user is the superuser and the only account with all the privileges needed to do anything in the system.

Common wisdom says you should *not* normally log in as root. When you're root, one misstep and you can easily delete all the files — especially when typing commands. Take, for example, the command rm *.html that you may type to delete all files that have the .html extension. What if you accidentally press the spacebar after the asterisk (*)? The shell takes the command to be rm * .html and — because * matches any filename — deletes everything in the current directory. Seems implausible until it happens to you!

## Using the su - command

If you're logged in as a normal user, how do you do any system administration chores? Well, you become root for the time being. If you're working at a terminal window or console, type

```
su -
```

Then enter the root password in response to the prompt. From this point on, you're root. Do whatever you have to do. To return to your usual self, type

```
exit
```

That's it! It's that easy.

# Becoming root for the GUI Utilities

If you use any of Fedora Core's GUI utilities to perform a system administration chore, it's even easier. Typically, the utility pops up a dialog box that prompts you for the root password (as in Figure 1-1). Just type the password and press Enter. If you don't want to use the utility, click Close.

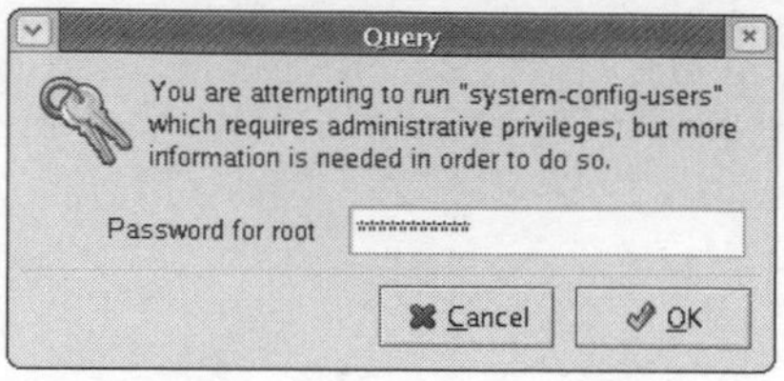

**Figure 1-1:**
Type the
root
password
and press
Enter to gain
root
privileges.

## Recovering from a forgotten root password

To perform system-administration tasks, you have to know the root password. What happens if you forget the root password? Not to worry: Just reboot the PC and you can reset the root password by following these steps:

1. **Reboot the PC (select Reboot as you log out of the GUI screen) or power up as usual.**

   Soon you see the graphical GRUB boot loader screen that shows the names of the operating systems you can boot.

2. **If you have more than one operating system installed, use the arrow key to select Fedora Core as your operating system. Then press the A key.**

   GRUB prompts you for commands to add to its default boot command.

3. **If you see the word** rhgb, **press Backspace to delete it and then press the spacebar, type the following, and then press Enter:**

   ```
   single
   ```

   Linux starts up as usual but runs in a single-user mode that does not require you to log in. After Linux starts, you see the following command-line prompt:

   ```
   sh-2.05b#
   ```

4. **Type the** passwd **command to change the** root **password as follows:**

   ```
   sh-2.05b# passwd
   Changing password for user root.
   New password:
   ```

5. **Type the new** root **password that you want to use (it doesn't appear on-screen) and then press Enter.**

   Linux asks for the password again, like this:

   ```
   Retype new password:
   ```

6. **Type the password again, and press Enter.**

   If you enter the same password both times, the passwd command changes the password and displays the following message:

   ```
   passwd: all authentication tokens updated successfully.
   ```

7. **Now type** reboot **to reboot the PC.**

   After Linux starts, it displays the familiar login screen. Now you can log in as root with the new password.

Make sure your Fedora Core PC is *physically* secure. As these steps show, anyone who can physically access your Fedora Core PC can simply reboot, set a new root password, and do whatever they want with the system. Another way to protect against resetting the password is to set a GRUB password, which causes GRUB to require a valid password before it boots Fedora Core. Of course, you must then remember to enter the GRUB password every time you boot your system!

# Understanding How Fedora Core Boots

Knowing the sequence in which Fedora Core starts processes as it boots is important. You can use this knowledge to start and stop services, such as the Web server and Network File System (NFS). The next few sections provide you with an overview of how Fedora Core boots and starts the initial set of processes. These sections also familiarize you with the shell scripts that start various services on a Fedora Core system.

## Understanding the init process

When Fedora Core boots, it loads and runs the core operating-system program from the hard drive. The core operating system is designed to run other programs. A process named init starts the initial set of processes on your Linux system.

To see the processes currently running on the system, type

```
ps ax | more
```

You get an output listing that starts off like this:

```
PID TTY      STAT    TIME COMMAND
  1 ?        S       0:05 init [5]
```

The first column, with the heading `PID`, shows a number for each process. PID stands for *process ID* (identification) — a sequential number assigned by the Linux kernel. The first entry in the process list, with a *process ID* (PID) of 1, is the `init` process. It's the first process, and it starts all other processes in your Fedora Core system. That's why `init` is sometimes referred to as the "mother of all processes."

What the `init` process starts depends on the following:

✦ The *run level,* an identifier that identifies a system configuration in which only a selected group of processes can exist

✦ The contents of the `/etc/inittab` file, a text file that specifies which processes to start at different run levels

✦ A number of shell scripts (located in the `/etc/rc.d` directory and its subdirectories) that are executed at specific run levels

Fedora Core has seven run levels — 0 through 6 — and Table 1-1 shows their meanings.

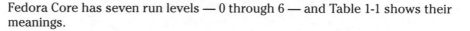

| Table 1-1 | Run Levels in Fedora Core |
|-----------|---------------------------|
| **Run Level** | **Meaning** |
| 0 | Shuts down the system |
| 1 | Runs in single-user stand-alone mode (no one else can log in; you work at the text console) |
| 2 | Runs in multiuser mode without the network services (in multiuser mode, other users can log in) |
| 3 | Runs in full multiuser mode, but with a text-mode login |
| 4 | Unused in Fedora Core |
| 5 | All services running and enables graphical login |
| 6 | Reboots the system |

The current run level, together with the contents of the `/etc/inittab` file, controls which processes `init` starts. The initial default run level is 3 for text-mode login screens and 5 for the graphical login screen. You can change the default run level by editing a line in the `/etc/inittab` file.

To check the current run level, type the following command in a terminal window:

```
/sbin/runlevel
```

The `runlevel` command prints an output like this:

```
N 5
```

The first character of the output shows the previous run level (`N` means no previous run level), and the second character shows the current run level (5). In this case, the system started at run level 5.

## Examining the /etc/inittab file

The `/etc/inittab` file is the key to understanding the processes that `init` starts at various run levels. You can look at the contents of the file by using the `more` command, as follows:

```
more /etc/inittab
```

To see the contents of the `/etc/inittab` file with the `more` command, you don't have to log in as `root`.

To interpret the contents of the `/etc/inittab` file, follow these steps:

*1.* **Look for the line that looks like this:**

```
id:5:initdefault:
```

That line shows the default run level. In this case, it's 5.

*2.* **Find all the lines that specify what `init` runs at run level 5. Look for a line that has a 5 between the first two colons (:). Here are the two relevant lines:**

```
l5:5:wait:/etc/rc.d/rc 5
x:5:respawn:/etc/X11/prefdm -nodaemon
```

The first line specifies that `init` executes the file `/etc/rc.d/rc` with 5 as an argument. The second line causes `init` to run `/etc/X11/prefdm`, a shell script that starts the graphical display manager. The display manager, in turn, displays the graphical login dialog box that enables you to log in to the system.

If you look at the file `/etc/rc.d/rc`, you find it's a shell script. You can study this file to see how it starts various processes for run levels 1 through 5.

Each entry in the /etc/inittab file tells init what to do at one or more run levels — you simply list all run levels at which the process runs. Each inittab entry has four fields — separated by colons — in the following format:

*id:runlevels:action:process*

Table 1-2 shows what each of these fields means.

| Table 1-2 | Meaning of the Fields in Each inittab Entry |
|-----------|---------------------------------------------|
| *Field* | *Meaning* |
| id | A unique one- or two-character identifier. The init process uses this field internally. You can use any identifier you want, as long as you don't use the same identifier on more than one line. |
| runlevels | A sequence of zero or more characters, each denoting a run level. For example, if the runlevels field is 12345, that entry applies to each of the run levels 1 through 5. This field is ignored if the action field is set to sysinit, boot, or bootwait. |
| action | Tells the init process what to do with that entry. If this field is initdefault, for example, init interprets the runlevels field as the default run level. If this field is set to wait, init starts the program or script specified in the process field and waits until that process exits. |
| process | Name of the script or program that init starts. Of course, some settings of the action field require no process field. For example, when the action field is initdefault, there is no need for a process field. |

## Trying a new run level with the init command

To try a new run level, you don't have to change the default run level in the /etc/inittab file. If you log in as root, you can change the run level (and, consequently, the processes that run in Fedora Core) by typing **init** followed by the run level (usually 1, 3, or 5).

For example, to put the system in single-user mode, type the following:

init 1

Thus, if you want to try run level 5 (assuming your system isn't set up for a graphical login screen yet) without changing the /etc/inittab file, enter the following command at the shell prompt:

init 5

The system ends all current processes and enters run level 5. By default, the init command waits 20 seconds before stopping all current processes and starting the new processes for run level 5.

To switch to run level 5 immediately, type the command **init -t0 5**. The number after the `-t` option indicates the number of seconds `init` waits before changing the run level.

You can also use the `telinit` command, which is simply a symbolic link (a shortcut) to `init`. If you make changes to the `/etc/inittab` file and want `init` to reload its configuration file, use the command `telinit q`.

## Understanding the Fedora Core startup scripts

The `init` process runs a number of scripts at system startup. If you look at the `/etc/inittab` file, you find the following line near the beginning of the file:

```
# System initialization.
si::sysinit:/etc/rc.d/rc.sysinit
```

The first one is a comment line. The second line causes `init` to run the `/etc/rc.d/rc.sysinit` script — the first Fedora Core startup script that `init` runs. The `rc.sysinit` script performs many initialization tasks, such as mounting the file systems, setting the clock, configuring the keyboard layout, starting the network, and loading many other driver modules. The `rc.sysinit` script performs these initialization tasks by calling many other scripts and reading configuration files located in the `/etc/sysconfig` directory.

After executing the `/etc/rc.d/rc.sysinit` script, the `init` process runs the `/etc/rc.d/rc` script with the run level as argument. For example, for run level 5, the following line in `/etc/inittab` specifies what `init` executes:

```
l5:5:wait:/etc/rc.d/rc 5
```

This example says `init` executes the command `/etc/rc.d/rc 5` and waits until that command completes.

The `/etc/rc.d/rc` script is somewhat complicated. Here's how it works:

✦ It changes to the directory corresponding to the run level. For example, to change to run level 5, the script changes to the `/etc/rc.d/rc5.d` directory.

✦ In the directory that corresponds with the run level, `/etc/rc.d/rc` looks for all files that begin with a `K` and executes each of them with the `stop` argument. This argument kills any currently running processes. Then it locates all files that begin with an `S` and executes each file with a `start` argument. This argument starts the processes needed for the specified run level.

To see what gets executed at run level 5, type the following command:

```
ls -l /etc/rc.d/rc5.d
```

In the resulting listing, the K scripts — the files whose names begin with K — stop (or "kill") servers, whereas the S scripts start servers. The /etc/rc.d/rc script executes these files in exactly the order in which they appear in the directory listing.

A script with the name /etc/rc.d/rc.local executes after all other scripts. So you can place in that script any command you want to execute whenever your Fedora Core system boots.

## Manually starting and stopping servers

Most server startup scripts reside in the /etc/init.d directory (the scripts are actually in /etc/rc.d/init.d, but /etc/init.d is a shortcut to /etc/rc.d/init.d). You can manually invoke scripts in this directory to start, stop, or restart specific processes — usually servers. For example, to stop the Web server (the server program is called httpd), type the following command:

```
/etc/rc.d/init.d/httpd stop
```

If httpd is already running and you want to restart it, type the following command:

```
/etc/init.d/httpd restart
```

You can enhance your system-administration skills by familiarizing yourself with the scripts in the /etc/init.d directory. To see its listing, type the following command:

```
ls /etc/init.d
```

For example, here is a typical list of scripts in my system:

| | | | | | |
|---|---|---|---|---|---|
| acpid | dovecot | killall | nfslock | rpcgssd | syslog |
| aep1000 | firstboot | kudzu | nscd | rpcidmapd | tux |
| anacron | functions | mdmonitor | ntpd | rpcsvcgssd | vncserver |
| apmd | gpm | mdmpd | pcmcia | saslauthd | vsftpd |
| atd | halt | messagebus | portmap | sendmail | winbind |
| autofs | httpd | microcode_ctl | postgresql | single | xfs |
| bcm5820 | innd | named | psacct | smartd | xinetd |
| cpuspeed | iptables | netdump | random | smb | ypbind |
| crond | irda | netfs | rawdevices | snmpd | yppasswdd |
| cups | irqbalance | netplugd | readahead | snmptrapd | ypserv |
| dc_client | isdn | network | readahead_early | squid | ypxfrd |
| dc_server | kdcrotate | nfs | rhnsd | sshd | yum |

The script names give you some clue about which server the script can start and stop. For example, the nfs script starts and stops the processes required for NFS (Network File System) services. At your leisure, you may want to study some of these scripts to see what each one does. You don't have to understand all the shell programming; the comments help you learn the purpose of each script.

Use the service command as a shortcut to run the scripts in /etc/init.d that you use to start, stop, or restart servers. For example, to start the Web server, you type this command:

```
service httpd stop
```

To restart that server, type the following command:

```
service httpd restart
```

## Automatically starting servers at system startup

You want some servers to start automatically every time you boot the system. For example, if you run a Web server, you want the httpd server to start whenever the system starts. You can make that happen by using the chkconfig command. For example, to set httpd to start whenever the system boots into run level 3, 4, or 5, you type the following command (while logged in as root):

```
chkconfig --level 345 httpd on
```

You can also use the chkconfig command to check which servers are turned on or off. For example, to see the complete list of all servers for all run levels, type the following command:

```
chkconfig --list
```

If you want to view the status of a single server, such as httpd, add that server's name to the chkconfig command, like this:

```
chkconfig --list httpd
```

You see an output similar to the following:

```
httpd     0:off  1:off  2:off  3:on  4:on  5:on  6:off
```

## Understanding the GUI startup

The graphical login screen starts at run level 5. When the `init` process starts up the system at run level 5, the last line of the `/etc/inittab` file causes `init` to start the graphical login process. Here's what the last line in the `/etc/inittab` file looks like (the number 5 denotes run level 5):

```
x:5:respawn:/etc/X11/prefdm -nodaemon
```

This line causes `init` to run `/etc/X11/prefdm`, a shell script that starts a specific display manager — `gdm`, `kdm`, or `xdm` — depending on the setting of a variable named `DISPLAYMANAGER`, which is defined in the `/etc/sysconfig/desktop` file. The display manager is a program responsible for displaying the graphical login window, authenticating users who log in, running initialization scripts at the start of a session, and cleaning up after the session. The display manager process manages the display, making it available to the users and cleaning up after the user finishes a session.

If the `DISPLAYMANAGER` variable is not defined, the `/etc/X11/prefdm` script checks for `gdm`, `kdm`, and `xdm` — in that order — and runs whichever display manager it finds first. The end result is that you get `gdm` if you installed GNOME and `kdm` if you installed KDE as your sole desktop. If you install both GNOME and KDE, you get `gdm` by default because the `prefdm` script looks for `gdm` first. If you do have both GNOME and KDE installed on your system and you want `kdm` as the display manager, define the `DISPLAYMANAGER` variable in the `/etc/sysconfig/desktop` file like this:

```
DISPLAYMANAGER="KDE"
```

The next time you reboot the system, the `kdm` display manager runs.

### GNOME display manager (gdm)

The `gdm` program is a display manager similar to `xdm`, the X display manager. Like `xdm`, `gdm` starts an X server for each local display, displays a login dialog box, and enables the user to log in to the system.

When `gdm` runs, it reads various configuration parameters from the configuration file `/etc/X11/gdm/gdm.conf`, which has a structure similar to a Windows INI file. For example, here are a few lines from a typical `gdm.conf` file:

```
[daemon]
AutomaticLoginEnable=false
AutomaticLogin=
TimedLoginEnable=false
TimedLogin=
TimedLoginDelay=30
Greeter=/usr/bin/gdmgreeter
... lines deleted ...
```

The /etc/X11/gdm/gdm.conf file has many comment lines — these lines begin with a hash mark (#). Labels within square brackets ([...]) identify various sections of the file. The different sections in the configuration file control different aspects of the graphical login screen as well as the tasks the user can perform from that screen.

You see the term *greeter* used often in the display manager configuration file. Greeter refers to the login screen — the user interface through which the display manager prompts the user to log in to the system.

Edit the Welcome= line in /etc/X11/gdm/gdm.conf to change the welcome message on the graphical login screen. The default message says welcome to the hostname, which can be somewhat cryptic. You can edit that line and change the message to something more meaningful with the syntax Welcome=Welcome to ABC Corp.

### GNOME session startup under gdm

For the default configuration after a typical Fedora Core installation with the GNOME desktop, gdm manages the login session as follows:

1. The gdm program starts the X server and looks for a script named after the local display's name (for the first display, the filename is :0) in the /etc/X11/gdm/Init directory. If it does not find that file, gdm executes the file named Default from that directory. Typically, the /etc/X11/gdm/Init/:0 script sets the background to a solid color and displays a logo. The gdm program runs this script as root and waits until the commands finish.

2. The gdm program runs the /usr/bin/gdmgreeter program, which displays a dialog box that contains fields in which the user can enter a name and a password.

3. After a user enters a name and password and presses Enter, gdm verifies the password and tries to execute the startup script /etc/X11/gdm/PreSession/*DisplayName*, where *DisplayName* is :0 for the first display. If that file is not found, gdm executes the /etc/X11/gdm/PreSession/Default script, if it exists.

4. The gdm program runs the session script from the /etc/X11/gdm/Sessions directory. The exact script that gdm runs depends on the session the user selects in the Sessions menu in the login dialog box gdmgreeter displays. For a GNOME session, gdm runs the /etc/X11/xdm/Xsession script with gnome as the argument. For a KDE session, gdm runs the /etc/X11/xdm/Xsession script with kde as the argument. The /etc/X11/xdm/Xsession script looks for another script file, named .xsession, in the user's home directory and executes that script, if it

exists. Next, it looks for the `.Xclients` script file in the user's home directory and executes that file, if it exists. Otherwise, `Xsession` executes the `/etc/X11/xinit/Xclients` script. When you follow through these scripts, you find that the `Xclients` script executes the `/usr/bin/gnome-session` program if the `/etc/sysconfig/desktop` file contains the line `DESKTOP="GNOME"`. The `gnome-session` program then starts the GNOME session (which includes a set of applications and a window manager). Initially, `gnome-session` uses the session file `/usr/share/gnome/default.session` (a text file) to start the applications and the window manager. Later, the GNOME session is re-stored to the values saved in a file in the `~/.metacity/sessions` directory (this path refers to a subdirectory in your home directory). The default session file runs a script named `/usr/bin/gnome-wm`, which, in turn, starts an appropriate window manager. The default window manager is `metacity`, but you can specify a different window manager by defining the `WINDOW_MANAGER` environment value to the name of a window manager you want.

**5.** From this point on, the user can interact with the system through the X display and through the window manager (started by the `gnome-session` program).

**6.** When the user ends the GNOME session (by selecting Log Out from the Main Menu), `gdm` attempts to run the script `/etc/X11/gdm/PostSession/`*DisplayName*, where *DisplayName* is `:0` for the first display. If that file does not exist, `gdm` executes the `/etc/X11/gdm/PostSession/Default` script, if it exists.

Although this brief description of `gdm` does not show you all the details, `gdm` is what provides the GUI login and takes care of starting a GNOME session. Like many other X programs, `gdm` is highly configurable. For example, the names of the script files in the preceding list are the typical ones, but you can specify other names through the file named `gdm.conf`, which, by default, also resides in the `/etc/X11/gdm` directory.

# Taking Stock of Fedora Core System Configuration Files

Fedora Core includes a host of configuration files. All these files share text files that you can edit with any text editor. To edit these configuration files, you must log in as `root`. I don't discuss the files individually, but I show a selection of the configuration files in Table 1-3, along with a brief description of each. This listing gives you an idea of what types of configuration files a system administrator has to work with. In many cases, Fedora Core includes GUI utility programs to set up many of these configuration files.

| Table 1-3 | Some Fedora Core Configuration Files |
|---|---|
| *Configuration File* | *Description* |
| /boot/System.map | Map of the Linux kernel (maps kernel addresses into names of functions and variables) |
| /boot/vmlinuz | The Linux kernel (the operating system's core) |
| /etc/at.allow | Usernames of users allowed to use the at command to schedule jobs for later execution |
| /etc/at.deny | Usernames of users forbidden to use the at command |
| /etc/bashrc | Systemwide functions and aliases for the BASH shell |
| /etc/cups/cupsd.conf | Printer configuration file for the Common UNIX Printing System (CUPS) scheduler |
| /etc/fonts | Directory with font configuration files |
| /etc/fstab | Information about file systems available for mounting |
| /etc/group | Information about groups |
| /etc/grub.conf | The configuration for the Grand Unified Bootloader (GRUB) — the default boot loader in Fedora Core (this file is a symbolic link to /boot/grub/grub.conf) |
| /etc/hosts | List of IP numbers and their corresponding hostnames |
| /etc/hosts.allow | Hosts allowed to access Internet services on this system |
| /etc/hosts.deny | Hosts forbidden to access Internet services on this system |
| /etc/httpd/conf/httpd.conf | Configuration file for the Apache Web server conf |
| /etc/init.d | Directory with scripts to start and stop many servers |
| /etc/inittab | Configuration file used by the init process that starts all the other processes |
| /etc/issue | File containing a message to be printed before displaying the text-mode login prompt (usually the Fedora Core version number) |
| /etc/lilo.conf | The configuration for the Linux Loader (LILO) — one of the boot loaders that can load the operating system from disk (present only if you use the LILO boot loader) |
| /etc/login.defs | Default information for creating user accounts, used by the useradd command |
| /etc/modprobe.conf | Configuration file with directives for loading kernel modules (for example, Ethernet and sound drivers) |
| /etc/mtab | Information about currently mounted file systems |

*(continued)*

**Table 1-3** *(continued)*

| | |
|---|---|
| `/etc/passwd` | Information about all user accounts (actual passwords are stored in `/etc/shadow`) |
| `/etc/profile` | Systemwide environment and startup file for the BASH shell |
| `/etc/rc.d` | Directory that holds startup and shutdown scripts for the Fedora Core system |
| `/etc/rc.d/rc.sysinit` | Fedora Core initialization script |
| `/etc/shadow` | Secure file with encrypted passwords for all user accounts (can be read only by `root`) |
| `/etc/shells` | List of all the shells on the system that the user can use |
| `/etc/skel` | Directory that holds initial versions of files such as `.bash_profile` that copy to a new user's home directory |
| `/etc/sysconfig` | Fedora Core configuration files |
| `/etc/sysctl.conf` | Configuration file with kernel parameters that are read in and set by `sysctl` at system startup |
| `/etc/termcap` | Database of terminal capabilities and options |
| `/etc/udev` | Directory containing configuration files for `udev` — the program that provides the ability to dynamically name hot-pluggable devices and create device files in the `/dev` directory |
| `/etc/X11/xorg.xonf` | Configuration file for X.org X11 — the X Window System |
| `/etc/X11/gdm` | Directory with configuration files for the GNOME display manager (`gdm`) |
| `/etc/xinetd.conf` | Configuration for the `xinetd` daemon that starts a number of Internet services on demand |
| `/etc/yum.conf` | Configuration for the `yum` package updater and installer |
| `/var/log/cron` | Log file with messages from the `cron` process that runs scheduled jobs |
| `/var/log/httpd/access_log` | Web-server access log |
| `/var/log/httpd/error_log` | Web-server error log |
| `/var/log/messages` | System log |

# Monitoring System Performance

When you're the system administrator, you must keep an eye on how well your Fedora Core system is performing. You can monitor the overall performance of your system by looking at information such as

✦ Central Processing Unit (CPU) usage

✦ Physical memory usage

✦ Virtual memory (swap-space) usage

✦ Hard-drive usage

Fedora Core comes with a number of utilities you can use to monitor one or more of these performance parameters. Here I introduce a few of these utilities and show you how to understand the information presented by these utilities.

## Using the top utility

To view the top CPU processes — the ones that are using most of the CPU time — you can use the text mode `top` utility. To start that utility, type **top** in a terminal window (or text console). The `top` utility then displays a text screen listing the current processes, arranged in the order of CPU usage, along with various other information, such as memory and swap-space usage. Figure 1-2 shows a typical output from the `top` utility.

**Book VI
Chapter 1**

Performing Basic
System
Administration

```
                          naba@localhost:~                        _ □ x
File   Edit   View   Terminal   Tabs   Help
top - 21:56:56 up 3 days, 10:49,  4 users,  load average: 0.48, 0.32, 0.32
Tasks:  84 total,   1 running,  83 sleeping,   0 stopped,   0 zombie
Cpu(s):  3.6% us,  1.3% sy,  0.0% ni, 95.0% id,  0.0% wa,  0.0% hi,  0.0% si
Mem:   255828k total,   253404k used,     2424k free,     8632k buffers
Swap:  522072k total,    76144k used,   445928k free,   108368k cached

 PID USER      PR  NI  VIRT  RES  SHR S %CPU %MEM    TIME+  COMMAND
 2901 root      15   0 68232  25m  40m S  2.7 10.3  1384:35 X
 4756 naba      15   0 36360  12m  18m S  1.3  5.1 88:02.45 gnome-panel
10197 naba      16   0  2804  948 1904 R  0.7  0.4  0:00.21 top
10169 naba      15   0 25412  11m  20m S  0.3  4.7  0:00.71 gnome-terminal
    1 root      16   0  3312  120 1428 S  0.0  0.0  0:05.92 init
    2 root      34  19     0    0    0 S  0.0  0.0  0:00.15 ksoftirqd/0
    3 root       5 -10     0    0    0 S  0.0  0.0  0:00.09 events/0
    4 root       5 -10     0    0    0 S  0.0  0.0  0:02.13 kblockd/0
    8 root      15 -10     0    0    0 S  0.0  0.0  0:00.00 aio/0
    5 root      25   0     0    0    0 S  0.0  0.0  0:00.00 pdflush
    6 root      15   0     0    0    0 S  0.0  0.0  0:01.00 pdflush
    7 root      15   0     0    0    0 S  0.0  0.0  0:10.22 kswapd0
    9 root      19   0     0    0    0 S  0.0  0.0  0:00.00 kseriod
   13 root      15   0     0    0    0 S  0.0  0.0  0:10.92 kjournald
   92 root      15   0     0    0    0 S  0.0  0.0  0:00.06 khubd
  222 root      15   0     0    0    0 S  0.0  0.0  0:00.46 usb-storage
  223 root      20   0     0    0    0 S  0.0  0.0  0:00.00 scsi_eh_0
```

**Figure 1-2:**
You can see the top CPU processes by using the `top` utility.

The `top` utility updates the display every 5 seconds. If you keep `top` running in a window, you can continually monitor the status of your Fedora Core system. To quit `top`, press Q or Ctrl+C or close the terminal window.

The first five lines of the output screen (refer to Figure 1-2) provide summary information about the system. Here is what these five lines show:

✦ The first line shows the current time, how long the system has been up, how many users are logged in, and three *load averages* — the average number of processes ready to run during the last 1, 5, and 15 minutes.

✦ The second line lists the total number of processes and the status of these processes.

✦ The third line shows CPU usage — what percentage of CPU time is used by user processes, what percentage by system (kernel) processes, and during what percentage of time the CPU is idle.

✦ The fourth line shows how the physical memory is being used — the total amount, how much is used, how much is free, and how much is allocated to buffers (for reading from disk, for example).

✦ The fifth line shows how the virtual memory (or swap space) is being used — the total amount of swap space, how much is used, how much is free, and how much is being cached.

The table that appears below the summary information (refer to Figure 1-2) lists information about the current processes, arranged in decreasing order by amount of CPU time used. Table 1-4 summarizes the meanings of the column headings in the table that top displays.

If the RSS field is drastically smaller than the SIZE field for a process, the process is using too little physical memory compared to what it needs. The result is a lot of swapping as the process runs. You can use the vmstat utility (which I discuss later in this section) to find out how much your system is swapping.

| Table 1-4 | Meanings of Column Headings in top Utility's Output |
|---|---|
| *Heading* | *Meaning* |
| PID | The process ID of the process |
| USER | Username under which the process is running |
| PR | Priority of the process |
| NI | *Nice value* of the process — the value ranges from –20 (highest priority) to 19 (lowest priority) and the default is 0 |
| VIRT | The total amount of virtual memory used by the process, in kilobytes |
| RES | Total physical memory used by a task (typically shown in kilobytes, but an m suffix indicates megabytes) |
| SHR | Amount of shared memory used by the process |
| S | State of the process (S for sleeping, D for uninterruptible sleep, R for running, Z for zombies — processes that should be dead, but are still running — or T for stopped) |
| %CPU | Percentage of CPU time used since last screen update |

| Heading | Meaning |
|---------|---------|
| %MEM | Percentage of physical memory used by the process |
| TIME+ | Total CPU time the process has used since it started |
| COMMAND | Shortened form of the command that started the process |

## Using the GNOME system monitor

Like the text mode `top` utility, the GNOME System Monitor tool also enables you to view the system load in terms of the number of currently running processes, their memory usage, and the free disk space on your system. To run the tool, select Main Menu⇨System Tools⇨System Monitor. The tool starts and displays its output in a window, as shown in Figure 1-3.

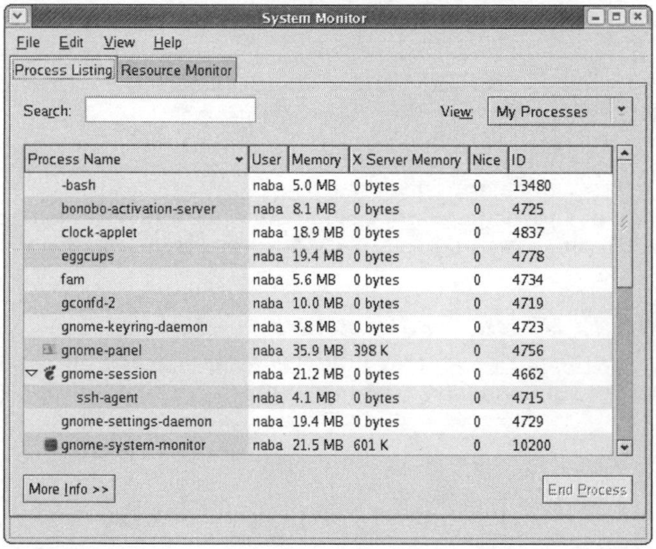

**Figure 1-3:**
Use the
GNOME
System
Monitor
to view
information
about the
current
processes.

The output is similar to the output you see when you type **top** in a text-mode console or a terminal window, except that with the System Monitor, you can decide which columns you want to see. Figure 1-3 shows the default view (the Process Listing tab) with the process name, the user who is running the process, the memory used, and the process ID. The GNOME System Monitor keeps updating the display to reflect the current state of the system.

The GNOME System Monitor window has another tab labeled Resource Monitor. Click that tab to view a summary of CPU, memory, and disk usage. Figure 1-4 shows a typical view of the Resource Monitor tab.

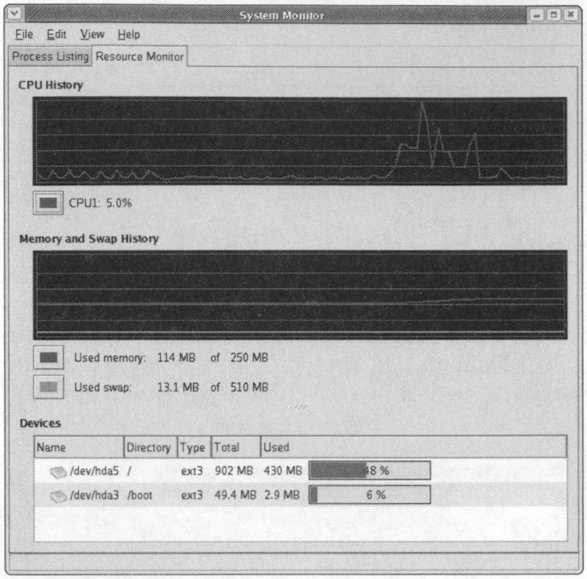

**Figure 1-4:**
GNOME
System
Monitor
displays
summary
CPU,
memory,
and disk
usage
information.

The upper plot in Figure 1-4 shows the percentage of CPU usage with time. The next plot shows the history of memory use and swap-space use. Disk-space use is summarized in a table at the bottom.

## Using the uptime command

You can use the uptime command to get a summary of the system's state. Just type the command like this:

```
uptime
```

It displays output similar to the following:

```
15:03:21 up 32 days, 57 min, 3 users, load average: 0.13,
    0.23, 0.27
```

This output shows the current time, how long the system has been up, the number of users, and (finally) the three load averages — the average number of processes that were ready to run in the past 1, 5, and 15 minutes. Load averages greater than 1 imply that many processes are competing for CPU time simultaneously.

The load averages give you an indication of how busy the system is.

## Using the vmstat utility

You can get summary information about the overall system usage with the
vmstat utility. To view system usage information averaged over 5-second
intervals, type the following command (the second argument indicates the
total number of lines of output vmstat displays):

```
vmstat 5 8
```

You see output similar to the following listing:

```
procs -----------memory---------- ---swap-- -----io---- --system-- ----cpu----
 r  b   swpd   free   buff  cache   si   so    bi    bo   in    cs us sy id wa
 0  0  31324   4016  18568 136004    1    1    17    16    8   110 33  4 61  1
 0  1  31324   2520  15348 139692    0    0  7798   199 1157   377  8  8  6 78
 1  0  31324   1584  12936 141480    0   19  5784   105 1099   437 12  5  0 82
 2  0  31324   1928  13004 137136    7    0  1586   138 1104   561 43  6  0 51
 3  1  31324   1484  13148 132064    0    0  1260    51 1080   427 50  5  0 46
 0  0  31324   1804  13240 127976    0    0  1126    46 1082   782 19  5 47 30
 0  0  31324   1900  13240 127976    0    0     0     0 1010   211  3  1 96  0
 0  0  31324   1916  13248 127976    0    0     0    10 1015   224  3  2 95  0
```

The first line of output shows the averages since the last reboot. After that,
vmstat displays the 5-second average data seven more times, covering the
next 35 seconds. The tabular output is grouped as six categories of information, indicated by the fields in the first line of output. The second line shows
further details for each of the six major fields. You can interpret these fields
using Table 1-5.

**Book VI
Chapter 1**

**Performing Basic
System
Administration**

| Table 1-5 | Meaning of Fields in the vmstat Utility's Output |
|---|---|
| *Field Name* | *Description* |
| procs | Number of processes and their types: r = processes waiting to run; b = processes in uninterruptible sleep; w = processes swapped out, but ready to run |
| memory | Information about physical memory and swap-space usage (all numbers in kilobytes): swpd = virtual memory used; free = free physical memory; buff = memory used as buffers; cache = virtual memory that's cached |
| swap | Amount of swapping (the numbers are in kilobytes per second): si = amount of memory swapped in from disk; so = amount of memory swapped to disk |
| io | Information about input and output (the numbers are in blocks per second where the block size depends on the disk device): bi = rate of blocks sent to disk; bo = rate of blocks received from disk |
| system | Information about the system: in = number of interrupts per second (includ-ing clock interrupts); cs = number of context switches per second — how many times the kernel changed which process was running |
| cpu | Percentages of CPU time used: us = percentage of CPU time used by user processes; sy = percentage of CPU time used by system processes; id = percentage of time CPU is idle; wa = time spent waiting for input or output (I/O) |

In the `vmstat` utility's output, high values in the `si` and `so` fields indicate too much swapping (*swapping* refers to the copying of information between physical memory and the virtual memory on the hard drive). High numbers in the `bi` and `bo` fields indicate too much disk activity.

## Checking disk performance and disk usage

Fedora Core comes with the `/sbin/hdparm` program that you can use to control IDE or ATAPI hard drives that are common on most PCs. One feature of the `hdparm` program is that you can use the `-t` option to determine the rate at which data is read from the disk into a buffer in memory. For example, here's the result of the command on my system:

```
/sbin/hdparm -t /dev/hda

/dev/hda:
 Timing buffered disk reads:  64 MB in  3.04 seconds = 21.05
    MB/sec
```

The command requires the IDE drive's device name (`/dev/hda`) as an argument. If you have an IDE hard drive, you can try this command to see how fast data is read from your system's disk drive.

To display the space available in the currently mounted file systems, use the `df` command. If you want a more human-readable output from `df`, type the following command:

```
df -h
```

Here's a typical output from this command:

```
Filesystem            Size  Used Avail Use% Mounted on
/dev/hda5             7.1G  3.9G  2.9G  59% /
/dev/hda3              99M   18M   77M  19% /boot
none                 125M     0  125M   0% /dev/shm
/dev/scd0            3.8G  3.8G     0 100% /mnt/cdrom1
```

As this example shows, the `-h` option causes the `df` command to show the sizes in gigabytes (G) and megabytes (M).

To check the disk space being used by a specific directory, use the `du` command — you can specify the `-h` option to view the output in kilobytes (k) and megabytes (M), as shown in the following example:

```
du -h /var/log
```

Here's a typical output of that command:

```
152K    /var/log/cups
4.0K    /var/log/vbox
4.0K    /var/log/httpd
508K    /var/log/gdm
4.0K    /var/log/samba
8.0K    /var/log/mail
4.0K    /var/log/news/OLD
8.0K    /var/log/news
4.0K    /var/log/squid
2.2M    /var/log
```

The du command displays the disk space used by each directory and the last line shows the total disk space used by that directory. If you want to see only the total space used by a directory, use the -s option, like this:

```
du -sh /home
89M     /home
```

# Viewing System Information via the /proc File System

Your Fedora Core system has a special file system called the /proc file system. You can find out many things about your system from this file system. In fact, you can even change kernel parameters through the /proc file system (just by writing to a file in that file system), thereby modifying the system's behavior.

The /proc file system isn't a real directory on the disk but a collection of data structures in memory, managed by the Linux kernel, that appears to you as a set of directories and files. The purpose of /proc (also called the *process file system*) is to give you access to information about the Linux kernel as well as to help you find out about all processes currently running on your system.

You can access the /proc file system just as you access any other directory, but you have to know the meaning of various files to interpret the information. Typically, you can use the cat or more commands to view the contents of a file in /proc; the file's contents provide information about some aspect of the system.

As with any directory, start by looking at a detailed directory listing of /proc. To do so, log in as root and type ls -l /proc in a terminal window. In the output, the first set of directories (indicated by the letter d at the beginning of the line) represents the processes currently running on your system. Each directory that corresponds to a process has the process ID (a number) as its name.

Notice also a very large file named /proc/kcore; that file represents the *entire* physical memory of your system. Although /proc/kcore appears in the listing as a huge file, no single physical file is occupying that much space on your hard drive — so don't try to remove the file to reclaim disk space.

Several files and directories in /proc contain interesting information about your Fedora Core PC. The /proc/cpuinfo file, for example, lists the key characteristics of your system, such as processor type and floating-point processor information. You can view the processor information by typing **cat /proc/cpuinfo**. For example, here's what I get when I type **cat /proc/cpuinfo** on my system:

```
processor        : 0
vendor_id        : GenuineIntel
cpu family       : 15
model            : 2
model name       : Mobile Intel(R) Celeron(R) CPU 1.50GHz
stepping         : 7
cpu MHz          : 1496.271
cache size       : 256 KB
fdiv_bug         : no
hlt_bug          : no
f00f_bug         : no
coma_bug         : no
fpu              : yes
fpu_exception    : yes
cpuid level      : 2
wp               : yes
flags            : fpu vme de pse tsc msr pae mce cx8 sep mtrr
                   pge mca cmov pat pse36 clflush dts acpi mmx
                   fxsr sse sse2 ss ht tm pbe cid
bogomips         : 2957.31
```

This output is from a 1.5 GHZ Celeron system. The listing shows many interesting characteristics of the processor. Notice the line that starts with fdiv_bug. Remember the infamous Pentium floating-point-division bug? The bug is in an instruction called fdiv (for *floating-point division*). Thus, the fdiv_bug line indicates whether this particular Pentium has the bug (fortunately, my PC's processor does not).

The last line in the /proc/cpuinfo file shows the BogoMips for the processor, as computed by the Linux kernel when it boots. BogoMips is something that Linux uses internally to time-delay loops.

Table 1-6 summarizes some of the files in the /proc file system that provide information about your Fedora Core system. You can view some of these files on your system to see what they contain, but note that not all files shown in Table 1-6 are present on your system. The specific contents of the /proc file system depends on the kernel configuration and the driver modules that are loaded (which, in turn, depend on your PC's hardware configuration).

You can navigate the /proc file system just as you work with any other directories and files in Fedora Core. Use the more or cat commands to view the contents of a file.

Book VI
Chapter 1

Performing Basic
System
Administration

| Table 1-6 | Some Files and Directories in /proc |
|---|---|
| *Filename* | *Content* |
| /proc/acpi | Information about Advanced Configuration & Power Interface (ACPI) — an industry-standard interface for configuration and power management on laptops, desktops, and servers |
| /proc/bus | Directory with bus-specific information for each bus type, such as PCI |
| /proc/cmdline | The command line used to start the Linux kernel (for example, ro root=LABEL=/ rhgb) |
| /proc/cpuinfo | Information about the CPU (the microprocessor) |
| /proc/devices | Available block and character devices in your system |
| /proc/dma | Information about DMA (direct memory access) channels that are being used |
| /proc/driver/rtc | Information about the PC's real-time clock (RTC) |
| /proc/filesystems | List of supported file systems |
| /proc/ide | Directory containing information about IDE devices |
| /proc/interrupts | Information about interrupt request (IRQ) numbers and how they are being used |
| /proc/ioports | Information about input/output (I/O) port addresses and how they are being used |
| /proc/kcore | Image of the physical memory |
| /proc/kmsg | Kernel messages |
| /proc/loadavg | Load average (average number of processes waiting to run in the last 1, 5, and 15 minutes) |
| /proc/locks | Current kernel locks (used to ensure that multiple processes don't write to a file at the same time) |
| /proc/meminfo | Information about physical memory and swap space usage |
| /proc/misc | Miscellaneous information |
| /proc/modules | List of loaded driver modules |

*(continued)*

**Table 1-6** *(continued)*

| Filename | Content |
|---|---|
| /proc/mounts | List of mounted file systems |
| /proc/net | Directory with many subdirectories that contain information about networking |
| /proc/partitions | List of partitions known to the Linux kernel |
| /proc/pci | Information about PCI devices found on the system |
| /proc/scsi | Directory with information about SCSI devices found on the system (present only if you have a SCSI device) |
| /proc/stat | Overall statistics about the system |
| /proc/swaps | Information about the swap space and how much is used |
| /proc/sys | Directory with information about the system; you can change kernel parameters by writing to files in this directory (using this method to tune system performance requires expertise to do properly) |
| /proc/uptime | Information about how long the system has been up |
| /proc/version | Kernel version number |

# Scheduling Jobs in Fedora Core

As a system administrator, you may have to run some programs automatically at regular intervals or execute one or more commands at a specified time in the future. Your Fedora Core system includes the facilities to schedule jobs to run at any future date or time you want. You can also set up the system to perform a task periodically or just once. Here are some typical tasks you can perform by scheduling jobs on your Linux system:

✦ Back up the files in the middle of the night.

✦ Download large files in the early morning when the system isn't busy.

✦ Send yourself messages as reminders of meetings.

✦ Analyze system logs periodically and look for any abnormal activities.

You can set up these jobs by using the at command or the crontab facility of Fedora Core. In the next few sections, I introduce these job-scheduling features of Fedora Core.

## Scheduling one-time jobs

If you want to run one or more commands at a later time, you can use the at command. The atd *daemon* — a program designed to process jobs submitted using at — runs your commands at the specified time and mails the output to you.

Before you try the at command, you need to know that the following configuration files control which users can schedule tasks using the at command:

✦ /etc/at.allow contains the names of the users who may submit jobs using the at command.

✦ /etc/at.deny contains the names of users not allowed to submit jobs using the at command.

If these files aren't present, or if you find an empty /etc/at.deny file, any user can submit jobs by using the at command. The default in Fedora Core is an empty /etc/at.deny file; with this default in place, anyone can use the at command. If you don't want some users to use at, simply list their usernames in the /etc/at.deny file.

To use at to schedule a one-time job for execution at a later time, follow these steps:

*1.* **Run the at command with the date or time when you want your commands executed.**

When you press Enter, the at> prompt appears, as follows:

```
at 21:30
at>
```

This method is the simplest way to indicate the time when you want to execute one or more commands — simply specify the time in a 24-hour format. In this case, you want to execute the commands at 9:30 p.m. tonight (or tomorrow, if it's already past 9:30 p.m.). You can, however, specify the execution time in many different ways (see Table 1-7 for examples).

*2.* **At the at> prompt, type the commands you want to execute as if typing at the shell prompt; after each command, press Enter and continue with the next command. When you finish entering the commands you want to execute, press Ctrl+D to indicate the end.**

Here is an example showing how to execute the `ps` command at a future time:

```
at> ps
at> <EOT>
job 1 at 2004-02-29 21:30
```

After you press Ctrl+D, the `at` command responds with a job number and the date and time when the job will execute.

| Table 1-7 | Formats for the Time of Execution with the at Command |
|-----------|-------------------------------------------------------|
| *Command* | *When the Job Will Run* |
| `at now` | Immediately |
| `at now + 15 minutes` | 15 minutes from the current time |
| `at now + 4 hours` | 4 hours from the current time |
| `at now + 7 days` | 7 days from the current time |
| `at noon` | At noontime today (or tomorrow, if already past noon) |
| `at now next hour` | Exactly 60 minutes from now |
| `at now next day` | At the same time tomorrow |
| `at 17:00 tomorrow` | At 5:00 p.m. tomorrow |
| `at 4:45pm` | At 4:45 p.m. today (or tomorrow, if it's already past 4:45 p.m.) |
| `at 3:00 Aug 16, 2004` | At 3:00 a.m. on August 16, 2004 |

After you enter one or more jobs, you can view the current list of scheduled jobs with the `atq` command:

```
atq
```

The output looks similar to the following:

```
4        2004-08-16 03:00 a root
5        2004-10-26 21:57 a root
6        2004-10-26 16:45 a root
```

The first field on each line shows the job number — the same number that the `at` command displays when you submit the job. The next field shows the year, month, day, and time of execution. The last field shows the jobs pending in the queue named `a`.

If you want to cancel a job, use the `atrm` command to remove that job from the queue. When removing a job with the `atrm` command, refer to the job by its number, as follows:

```
atrm 4
```

This command deletes job 4 scheduled for 3:00 a.m. August 16, 2004.

When a job executes, the output is mailed to you. Type **mail** at a terminal window to read your mail and to view the output from your jobs.

## Scheduling recurring jobs

Although at is good for running commands at a specific time, it's not useful for running a program automatically at repeated intervals. You have to use crontab to schedule such recurring jobs — for example, if you want to back up your files to tape at midnight every day.

You schedule recurring jobs by placing job information in a file with a specific format and submitting this file with the crontab command. The cron daemon — crond — checks the job information every minute and executes the recurring jobs at the specified times. Because the cron daemon processes recurring jobs, such jobs are also referred to as *cron jobs*.

**Book VI
Chapter 1**

**Performing Basic
System
Administration**

Any output from a cron job is mailed to the user who submits the job. (In the submitted job-information file, you can specify a different recipient for the mailed output.)

Two configuration files control who can schedule cron jobs using crontab:

✦ /etc/cron.allow contains the names of the users who may submit jobs using the crontab command.

✦ /etc/cron.deny contains the names of users not allowed to submit jobs using the crontab command.

If the /etc/cron.allow file exists, only users listed in this file can schedule cron jobs. If only the /etc/cron.deny file exists, users listed in this file cannot schedule cron jobs. If neither file exists, the default Fedora Core setup enables any user to submit cron jobs.

To submit a cron job, follow these steps:

*1.* **Prepare a shell script (or an executable program in any programming language) that can perform the recurring task you want to perform.**

You can skip this step if you want to execute an existing program periodically.

*2.* **Prepare a text file with information about the times when you want the shell script or program (from Step 1) to execute, and then submit this file by using** crontab.

You can submit several recurring jobs with a single file. Each line with timing information about a job has a standard format with six fields — the first five specify when the job runs, and the sixth field constitutes the actual command that runs. For example, here is a line that executes the `myjob` shell script in a user's home directory at five minutes past midnight each day:

```
5 0 * * * $HOME/myjob
```

Table 1-8 shows the meaning of the first five fields. *Note:* An asterisk (*) means all possible values for that field. Also, an entry in any of the first five fields can be a single number, a comma-separated list of numbers, a pair of numbers separated by a dash (indicating a range of numbers), or an asterisk.

3. **Suppose the text file `jobinfo` (in the current directory) contains the job information. Submit this information to `crontab` with the following command:**

```
crontab jobinfo
```

That's it! You are set with the `cron` job. From now on, the `cron` job runs at regular intervals (as specified in the job information file), and you receive mail messages with the output from the job.

To verify that the job is indeed scheduled, type the following command:

```
crontab -l
```

The output of the `crontab -l` command shows the `cron` jobs currently installed in your name. To remove your `cron` jobs, type **crontab -r**.

| Table 1-8 | Format for the Time of Execution in crontab Files | |
|-----------|--------------------------|--------------------------|
| *Field Number* | *Meaning of Field* | *Acceptable Range of Values** |
| 1 | Minute | 0–59 |
| 2 | Hour of the day | 0–23 |
| 3 | Day of the month | 0–31 |
| 4 | Month | 1–12 (1 means January, 2 means February, and so on) or the names of months using the first three letters (Jan, Feb, Mar, Apr, May, Jun, Jul, Aug, Sep, Oct, Nov, Dec) |
| 5 | Day of the week | 0–6 (0 means Sunday, 1 means Monday, and so on) or the three-letter abbreviations of weekdays (Sun, Mon, Tue, Wed, Thu, Fri, Sat) |

*\* An asterisk in a field means all possible values for that field. For example, if an asterisk is in the third field, the job is executed every day.*

If you log in as `root`, you can also set up, examine, and remove `cron` jobs for any user. To set up `cron` jobs for a user, use this command:

```
crontab -u username filename
```

Here, *username* is the user for whom you install the `cron` jobs, and *filename* is the file that contains information about the jobs.

Use the following form of the `crontab` command to view the `cron` jobs for a user:

```
crontab -u username -l
```

To remove a user's `cron` jobs, use the following command:

```
crontab -u username -r
```

***Note:*** The `cron` daemon also executes the `cron` jobs listed in the system-wide `cron`-job file `/etc/crontab`. Here's the default `/etc/crontab` file in Fedora Core (type **cat /etc/crontab** to view the file):

```
SHELL=/bin/bash
PATH=/sbin:/bin:/usr/sbin:/usr/bin
MAILTO=root
HOME=/

# run-parts
01 * * * * root run-parts /etc/cron.hourly
02 4 * * * root run-parts /etc/cron.daily
22 4 * * 0 root run-parts /etc/cron.weekly
42 4 1 * * root run-parts /etc/cron.monthly
```

The first four lines set up several environment variables for the jobs listed in this file. The `MAILTO` environment variable specifies the user who receives the mail message with the output from the `cron` jobs in this file.

The line that begins with a # is a comment line. The four lines following the `run-parts` comment execute the `run-parts` shell script (located in the `/usr/bin` directory) at various times with the name of a specific directory as argument. Each of the arguments to `run-parts` — `/etc/cron.hourly`, `/etc/cron.daily`, `/etc/cron.weekly`, and `/etc/cron.monthly` — are directories. Essentially, `run-parts` executes all scripts located in the directory that you provide as an argument.

Table 1-9 lists the directories where to locate these scripts and when they execute. You have to look at the scripts in these directories to know what executes at these periodic intervals.

| Table 1-9 | Script Directories for cron Jobs |
|---|---|
| *Directory Name* | *Contents* |
| /etc/cron.hourly | Scripts execute every hour |
| /etc/cron.daily | Scripts execute each day at 4:02 a.m. |
| /etc/cron.weekly | Scripts execute weekly on Sunday at 4:22 a.m. |
| /etc/cron.monthly | Scripts execute at 4:42 a.m. on the first day of each month |

# Chapter 2: Managing Users

## In This Chapter

✔ Adding user accounts

✔ Understanding the password file

✔ Managing groups

✔ Exploring the user environment

✔ Changing user and group ownerships of files and directories

Fedora Core is a multiuser system, so it has many user accounts. Even if you are the only user on your system, many servers require a unique username and group name. Take, for example, the Apache Web server. It runs under the username apache. A whole host of system users are not for people, but just for running specific programs.

Also, users can belong to one or more groups. Typically, each username has a corresponding private group name. By default, each user belongs to that corresponding private group. However, you can define other groups for the purpose of providing access to specific files and directories based on group membership.

User and group ownerships of files are a way to make sure that only the right people (or the right process) can access the right files and directories. Managing the user and group accounts is a typical system administration job. It's not that hard to do this part of the job, given the tools that come with Fedora Core. I show you how.

## Adding User Accounts

You get the chance to add user accounts when you boot your system for the first time after installing Fedora Core. The root account is the only one that you must set up during installation. If you didn't add other user accounts during the initial boot, you can do so later on, using the User Manager or the useradd command to add new users on your system.

Creating other user accounts besides root is a good idea. Even if you're the only user of the system, logging in as a less-privileged user is good practice because that way you can't damage any important system files inadvertently. If necessary, you can type the su - command to log in as root and then perform any system administration tasks.

## Using the User Manager to add user accounts

You can use the User Manager to add user accounts. To start the User Manager, log in as root at the graphical login screen and then choose Main Menu⇨ System Settings⇨Users and Groups from the GNOME panel. If you're not logged in as root, the User Manager prompts you for the root password. If prompted, enter the password and click OK. Then the User Manager window appears.

The window has two tabs: Users and Groups (as shown in Figure 2-1). The Users tab displays the current list of users from the /etc/passwd file. The Groups tab lists the names of groups from the /etc/group. Initially, the User Manager filters out any system users and groups. However, you can turn off the filter by choosing Preferences⇨Filter System Users and Groups, so that the check mark next to that menu item disappears. Figure 2-1 shows the User Manager window with a listing of all user accounts, including the system ones.

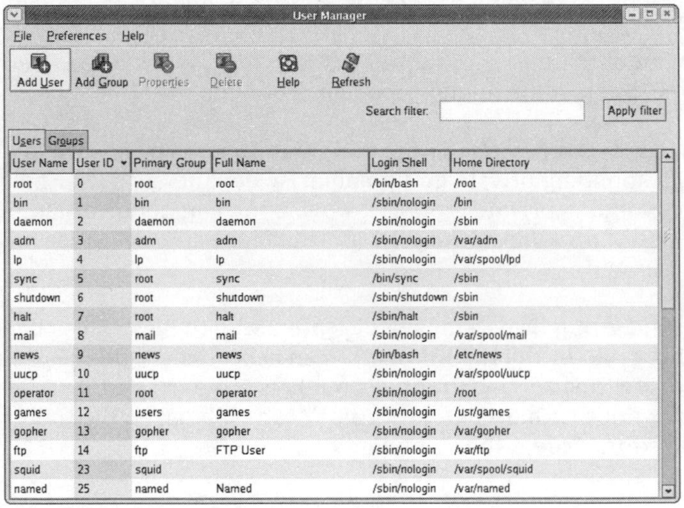

**Figure 2-1:** You can manage user accounts and groups from the User Manager window.

You can add new users and groups or edit existing users and groups from the User Manager window.

To edit the information for an existing user, follow these steps:

1. **Click the username in the list on the Users tab and then click the Properties button on the toolbar.**

   That user's information appears in a User Properties dialog box (see Figure 2-2).

2. **Edit the information and click OK to make the changes.**

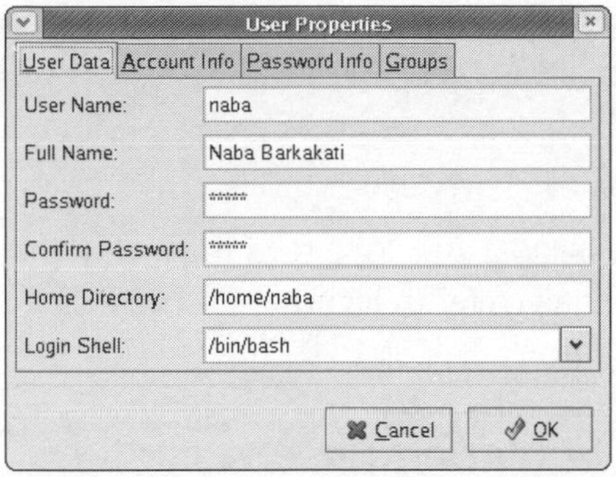

**User Properties**

User Data | Account Info | Password Info | Groups

| User Name: | naba |
| Full Name: | Naba Barkakati |
| Password: | ***** |
| Confirm Password: | ***** |
| Home Directory: | /home/naba |
| Login Shell: | /bin/bash |

**✖ Cancel**    **✓ OK**

**Figure 2-2:**
Edit an existing user's information in this dialog box.

**Book VI
Chapter 2**

**Managing Users**

To add a new user, follow these steps:

*1.* **Click the Add User button on the toolbar (refer to Figure 2-1).**

This action opens the Create New User dialog box (shown in Figure 2-3).

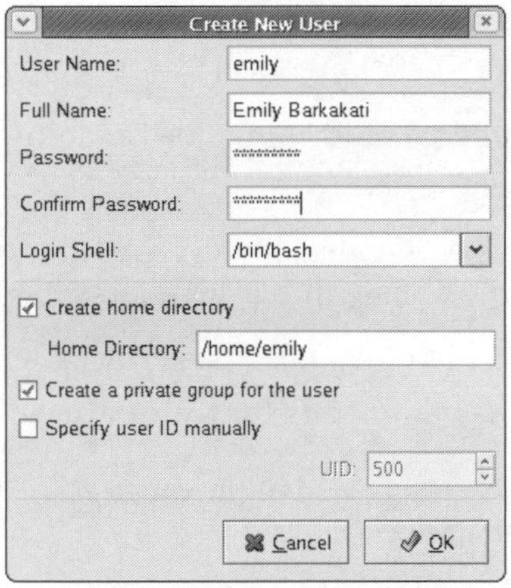

**Create New User**

| User Name: | emily |
| Full Name: | Emily Barkakati |
| Password: | ********* |
| Confirm Password: | ********* |
| Login Shell: | /bin/bash |

☑ Create home directory

Home Directory: /home/emily

☑ Create a private group for the user

☐ Specify user ID manually

UID: 500

**✖ Cancel**    **✓ OK**

**Figure 2-3:**
Create a new user account by filling in the information in this dialog box.

*2.* **Fill in the requested information.**

In particular, you must enter the username and the password. After filling in all the fields, click the OK button. The new user now appears in the list on the Users tab in the User Manager window.

Notice the Create a Private Group for the User check box. It's checked by default, and that means each new user is in a separate private user group. Sometimes you want a user to be in a specific group, however, so that the user can access the files owned by that group. Adding a user to another group is easy. For example, suppose I want to add the username naba to the group called wheel. I simply type the following command in a terminal window:

```
usermod -G wheel naba
```

To remove a user account, click the username in the list on the Users tab that displays all user accounts (refer to Figure 2-1). Then click the Delete button on the toolbar.

## Using commands to manage user accounts

If you're working from a text console, you can create a new user account by using the useradd command. Follow these steps to add an account for a new user:

*1.* **Log in as** root.

If you're not already logged in as root, type su - to become root.

*2.* **Type the following** useradd **command with the** -c **option to create the account:**

```
/usr/sbin/useradd -c "Ashley Barkakati" ashley
```

*3.* **Set the password by using the** passwd **command, as follows:**

```
passwd ashley
```

You're prompted for the password twice. If you type a password that someone can easily guess, the passwd program rejects it.

The useradd command consults the following configuration files to obtain default information about various parameters for the new user account:

✦ /etc/default/useradd: Specifies the default shell (/bin/bash) and the default home directory location (/home).

✦ /etc/login.defs: Provides system-wide defaults for automatic group and user IDs, as well as password-expiration parameters.

Examine these files with the cat or more commands to see what they contain.

You can delete a user account by using the userdel command. Simply type **/usr/sbin/userdel *username*** at the command prompt to delete a user's account. To wipe out that user's home directory as well, type **/usr/sbin/ userdel -r *username***.

To modify any information in a user account, use the usermod command. For example, if I want my username, naba, to have root as the primary group, I type the following:

```
usermod -g root naba
```

To find out more about the useradd, userdel, and usermod commands, type **man useradd**, **man userdel**, or **man usermod** in a terminal window.

# Understanding the /etc/passwd File

The /etc/passwd file is a list of all user accounts. It's a text file and any user can read it — no special privileges needed. Each line in /etc/passwd has seven fields, separated by colons (:).

Here is a typical entry from the /etc/passwd file:

```
naba:x:500:10:Naba Barkakati:/home/naba:/bin/bash
```

Figure 2-4 explains the meaning of the seven fields in this entry.

**Figure 2-4:**
This typical /etc/ passwd entry illustrates the meaning of the various fields.

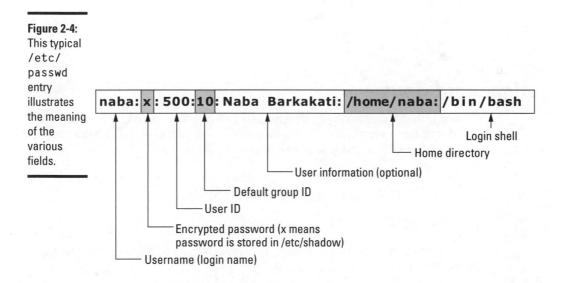

As the example shows, the format of each line in /etc/passwd looks like this:

```
username:password:UID:GID:GECOS:homedir:shell
```

Table 2-1 explains the meaning of the seven fields in each /etc/passwd entry.

| Table 2-1 | Meaning of the Fields in /etc/passwd File |
| --- | --- |
| *This Field* | *Contains* |
| username | An alphanumeric username, usually eight characters long and unique (Linux allows usernames to be longer than eight characters, but some other operating systems do not) |
| password | When present, a 13-character encrypted password (an empty field means that no password is required to access the account, an x means the password is stored in the /etc/shadow file, which is more secure) |
| UID | A unique number that serves as the user identifier (root has a UID of 0 and usually the UIDs between 1 to 100 are reserved for non-human users such as servers; keeping the UID less than 32,767 is best) |
| GID | The default group ID of the group to which the user belongs (GID 0 is for group root, other groups are defined in /etc/group and users can be and usually are in more than one group at a time) |
| GECOS | Optional personal information about the user (the finger command uses this field and GECOS stands for General Electric Comprehensive Operating System, a long-forgotten operating system that's immortalized by the name of this field in /etc/passwd) |
| homedir | The name of the user's home directory |
| shell | The command interpreter (shell), such as Bash (/bin/bash), that executes when this user logs in |

# Managing Groups

A group is a something to which users belong. A group has a name and an identification number (ID). After a group is defined, users can belong to one or more of these groups.

You can find all the existing groups listed in /etc/group. For example, here is the line that defines the group named wheel:

```
wheel:x:10:root,naba
```

As this example shows, each line in /etc/group has the following format, with four fields separated by colons:

*groupname:password:GID:membership*

Table 2-2 explains the meaning of the four fields in a group definition.

| Table 2-2 | Meaning of Fields in /etc/group File |
|-----------|--------------------------------------|
| *Field Name* | *Meaning* |
| groupname | The name of the group (for example, wheel) |
| password | The group password (an x means the password is stored in the /etc/shadow file) |
| GID | The numerical group ID (for example, 10) |
| membership | A comma-separated list of usernames that belong to this group (for example, root,naba) |

If you want to create a new group, you can simply click the Add Group button in the User Manager (refer to Figure 2-1). An even quicker way is to use the groupadd command. For example, to add a new group called class with an automatically selected group ID, just type the following command in a terminal window (you have to be logged in as root):

```
groupadd class
```

Then you can add users to this group with the usermod command. For example, to add the users naba and ashley to the group named class, I type the following commands:

```
usermod -G class naba
usermod -G class ashley
```

That's it. Now I check /etc/group to find that it contains the following definition of class:

```
class:x:502:naba,ashley
```

It's that simple!

If you want to remove a group, use the groupdel command. For example, to remove a group named class, type

```
groupdel class
```

# Exploring the User Environment

When you log in as a user, you get a set of environment variables that control many aspects of what you see and do on your Fedora Core system. If you want to see your current environment, go ahead and type the following command in a terminal window:

```
env
```

(By the way, the `printenv` command also displays the environment, but `env` is shorter.)

The `env` command prints a long list of lines. That whole collection of lines is the current environment, and each line defines an environment variable. For example, the `env` command displays this typical line:

```
HOSTNAME=localhost.localdomain
```

This line defines the environment variable `HOSTNAME`, and it's defined as `localhost.localdomain`.

An *environment variable* is nothing more than a name associated with a string. For example, the environment variable named `PATH` is typically defined as follows:

```
PATH=/usr/local/bin:/bin:/usr/bin:/usr/X11R6/bin
```

The string to the right of the equal sign is the value of the `PATH` environment variable. By convention, the `PATH` environment variable is a sequence of directory names, each name separated from the preceding one by a colon (`:`).

Each environment variable has a specific purpose. For example, when the shell has to search for a file, it simply searches the directories listed in the `PATH` environment variable. The shell searches the directories in `PATH` in the order of their appearance. Therefore, if two programs have the same name, the shell executes the one it finds first.

In a fashion similar to the shell's use of the `PATH` environment variable, an editor such as `vi` uses the value of the `TERM` environment variable to figure out how to display the file you are editing with `vi`. To see the current setting of `TERM`, type the following command at the shell prompt:

```
echo $TERM
```

If you type this command in a terminal window, the output is as follows:

```
xterm
```

To define an environment variable in Bash, use the following syntax:

```
export NAME=Value
```

Here, *NAME* denotes the name of the environment variable, and *Value* is the string representing its value. Therefore, you set `TERM` to the value `xterm` by using the following command:

```
export TERM=xterm
```

After you define an environment variable, you can change its value by simply specifying the new value with the syntax NAME=new-value. For example, to change the definition of TERM to vt100, type **TERM=vt100** at the shell prompt.

With an environment variable such as PATH, you typically want to append a new directory name to the existing definition, rather than define the PATH from scratch. For example, if you download and install the Java 2 Software Development Kit (available from java.sun.com/j2se/downloads/index.html), you have to add the location of the Java binaries to PATH. Here's how you accomplish that task:

```
export PATH=$PATH:/usr/java/j2sdk1.4.2_02/bin
```

This command appends the string :/usr/java/j2sdk1.4.2_02/bin to the current definition of the PATH environment variable. The net effect is to add /usr/java/j2sdk1.4.2_02/bin to the list of directories in PATH.

*Note:* You also can write this export command as follows:

```
export PATH=${PATH}:/usr/java/j2sdk1.4.2_02/bin
```

After you type that command, you can access programs in the /usr/java/j2sdk1.4.2_02/bin directory such as javac, the Java compiler that converts Java source code into a form that the Java interpreter can execute.

PATH and TERM are only two of a handful of common environment variables. Table 2-3 lists some of the environment variables for a typical Fedora Core user.

**Book VI
Chapter 2**

**Managing Users**

| Table 2-3 | Typical Environment Variables in Fedora Core |
|---|---|
| *Environment Variable* | *Contents* |
| DISPLAY | The name of the display on which the X Window System displays output (typically set to :0.0) |
| HOME | Your home directory |
| HOSTNAME | The host name of your system |
| LOGNAME | Your login name |
| MAIL | The location of your mail directory |
| PATH | The list of directories in which the shell looks for programs |
| SHELL | Your shell (SHELL=/bin/bash for Bash) |
| TERM | The type of terminal |

# Changing User and Group Ownership of Files

In Linux, each file or directory has two types of owners — a user and a group. In other words, a user and group own each file and directory. The user and group ownerships can control who can access a file or directory.

To view the owner of a file or directory, use the `ls -l` command to see the detailed listing of a directory. For example, here's a typical file's information:

```
-rw-rw-r-- 1 naba   naba    40909 07-14 20:37 composer.txt
```

In this example, the first set of characters shows the file's permission setting — who can read, write, or execute the file. The third and fourth fields (in this example, `naba naba`) indicate the user and group owner of the file. Each user has a private group that has the same name as the username. So most files' user and group ownership appear to show the username twice.

As a system administrator, you may decide to change the group ownership of a file to a common group. For example, suppose you want to change the group ownership of the `composer.txt` file to the `class` group. To do that, log in as `root` and type the following command:

```
chgrp class composer.txt
```

This `chgrp` command changes the group ownership of `composer.txt` to `class`. After I tried this, I typed **ls -l** again to verify the ownership, and here's what I got:

```
-rw-rw-r-- 1 naba   class   40909 07-14 20:37 composer.txt
```

You can use the `chown` command to change the user owner. The command has the following format:

```
chown username filename
```

For example, to change the user ownership of a file named `sample.jpg` to `naba`, I type

```
chown naba sample.jpg
```

In fact, `chown` can change both the user and group owner at the same time. For example, to change the user owner to `naba` and the group owner to `class`, I type

```
chown naba.class composer.txt
```

In other words, you simply append the group name to the username with a period in between, and use that as the name of the owner.

# Chapter 3: Managing the File System

## In This Chapter

✔ Navigating the Linux file system

✔ Sharing files with NFS

✔ Backing up and restoring files

✔ Mounting the NTFS file system

✔ Accessing MS-DOS files

*T*he *file system* refers to the organization of files and directories. As a system administrator, you have to perform certain operations to manage the file system. For example, you have to know how to *mount* — add a file system on a storage medium by attaching it to the overall Linux file system. You also have to back up important data and restore files from a backup. Other file system operations include sharing files with the *Network File System* (NFS) and accessing MS-DOS files. In this chapter, I show you how to perform all the file-system-management tasks.

## Learning the Linux File System

The files and directories in your PC store information in an organized manner just like paper filing systems. When you store information on paper, you typically put several pages in a folder and then save the folder in a file cabinet. If you have many folders, you probably have some sort of filing system. For example, you may label each folder's tab and then arrange them alphabetically in the file cabinet. You probably have several file cabinets, each with lots of drawers, which, in turn, contain folders full of pages.

Operating systems such as Linux organize information in your computer in a manner similar to your paper filing system. Linux uses a file system to organize all information in your computer. Of course, unlike a filing cabinet, the storage medium isn't a metal cabinet and paper. Instead, Linux stores information on devices such as hard drives, floppy-disk drives, and CD-ROM drives.

To draw an analogy between your computer's file system and a paper filing system, think of a disk drive as the file cabinet. The drawers in the file cabinet correspond to the directories in the file system. The folders in each drawer are also directories — because a directory in a computer file system can contain other directories. You can think of files as the pages inside the folder — and that's where the actual information is stored. Figure 3-1 illustrates the analogy between a file cabinet and the Linux file system.

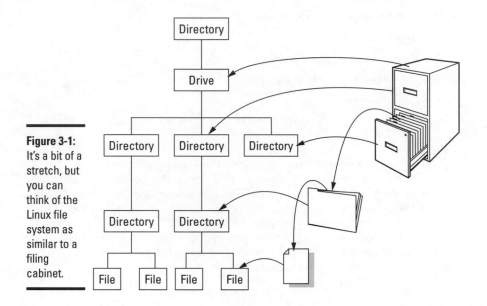

**Figure 3-1:** It's a bit of a stretch, but you can think of the Linux file system as similar to a filing cabinet.

The Linux file system has a *hierarchical* structure — directories can contain other directories, which in turn contain individual files.

Everything in your Fedora Core system is organized in files and directories in the file system. To access and use documents and programs on your system, you have to be familiar with the file system.

## Understanding the file-system hierarchy

The Linux file system is organized like a tree, with a *root directory* from which all other directories branch out. When you write a complete pathname, the root directory is represented by a single slash (/). Then there is a hierarchy of files and directories. Parts of the file system can be in different physical drives or different hard-drive partitions.

Linux uses a standard directory hierarchy. Figure 3-2 shows the standard parts of the Linux file system. Of course, you can create new directories anywhere in this structure.

**Figure 3-2:**
The Linux
file system
uses this
standard
directory
hierarchy.

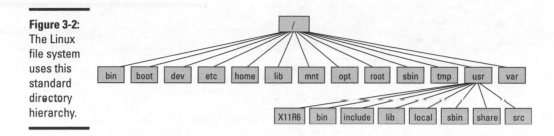

Write the name of any file or directory by concatenating the names of directories that identify where that file or directory is and using the forward slash (/) as a separator. For example, in Figure 3-2, the usr directory at the top level is written as /usr because the root directory (/) contains usr. On the other hand, the X11R6 directory is inside the usr directory, which is inside the root directory (/). Therefore, the X11R6 directory is uniquely identified by the name /usr/X11R6. This type of full name is called a *pathname* because the name identifies the path you take from the root directory to reach a file. Thus /usr/X11R6 is a pathname.

Book VI
Chapter 3

Managing the
File System

Each of the standard directories in the Linux file system has a specific purpose. Table 3-1 summarizes these directories.

| Table 3-1 | Standard Directories in Linux File System |
|---|---|
| *Directory* | *Used to Store* |
| /bin | Executable files for user commands (for use by all users) |
| /boot | Files needed by the boot loader to load the Linux kernel |
| /dev | Device files |
| /etc | Host-specific system configuration files |
| /home | User home directories |
| /lib | Shared libraries and kernel modules |
| /mnt | Mount point for a temporarily mounted file system |
| /opt | Add-on application software packages |
| /root | Home directory for the root user |
| /sbin | Utilities for system administration |
| /selinux | Files for Security Enhanced Linux (SELinux) kernel extensions |
| /tmp | Temporary files |

*(continued)*

**Table 3-1** *(continued)*

| Directory | Used to Store |
|---|---|
| **The /usr Hierarchy** | |
| /usr/X11R6 | X Window System, Version 11 Release 6 |
| /usr/bin | Most user commands |
| /usr/include | Directory for standard included files used in developing Linux applications |
| /usr/lib | Libraries used by software packages and for programming |
| /usr/libexec | Libraries for applications |
| /usr/local | Any local software |
| /usr/sbin | Nonessential system administrator utilities |
| /usr/share | Shared data that does not depend on the system architecture (whether the system is an Intel PC or a Sun SPARC workstation) |
| /usr/src | Source code |
| **The /var Hierarchy** | |
| /var/cache | Cached data for applications |
| /var/lib | Information relating to the current state of applications |
| /var/lock | Lock files to ensure that a resource is used by one application only |
| /var/log | Log files organized into subdirectories |
| /var/mail | User mailbox files |
| /var/opt | Variable data for packages stored in the /opt directory |
| /var/run | Data describing the system since it was booted |
| /var/spool | Data that's waiting for some kind of processing |
| /var/tmp | Temporary files preserved between system reboots |
| /var/yp | Network Information Service (NIS) database files |

## Mounting a device on the file system

The storage devices that you use in Fedora Core contain Linux file systems. Each device has its own local file system consisting of a hierarchy of directories. Before you can access the files on a device, you have to attach the device's directory hierarchy to the tree that represents the overall Linux file system.

*Mounting* is the operation you perform to cause the file system on a physical storage device (a hard-drive partition or a CD-ROM) to appear as part of the Linux file system. Figure 3-3 illustrates the concept of mounting.

Figure 3-3 shows each device with a name that begins with /dev. For example, /dev/cdrom is the first DVD/CD-ROM drive and /dev/fd0 is the floppy drive. These physical devices are mounted at specific mount points on the Linux file system. For example, the DVD/CD-ROM drive, `/dev/cdrom`, is mounted on `/mnt/cdrom` in the file system. After mounting the CD-ROM in this way, the `Fedora` directory on a CD-ROM or DVD-ROM appears as `/mnt/cdrom/Fedora` in the Linux file system.

Book VI
Chapter 3

Managing the
File System

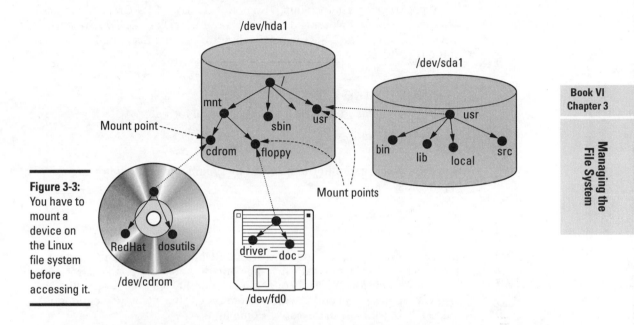

**Figure 3-3:** You have to mount a device on the Linux file system before accessing it.

You can use the `mount` command to manually mount a device on the Linux file system at a specified directory. That directory is the *mount point*. For example, to mount the DVD/CD-ROM drive at `/mnt/cdrom` directory, you type the following command (after logging in as `root`):

```
mount /dev/cdrom /mnt/cdrom
```

The `mount` command reports an error if the DVD/CD-ROM device is mounted already or if no CD or DVD media is in the drive. Otherwise, the `mount` operation succeeds, and you can access the DVD or CD's contents through the `/mnt/cdrom` directory.

You can use any directory as the mount point. If you mount a device on a nonempty directory, however, you cannot access the files in that directory until you unmount the device by using the `umount` command. Therefore, always use an empty directory as the mount point.

Fedora Core comes with the `/mnt/cdrom` directory for mounting DVDs or CDs and `/mnt/floppy` for mounting floppy drives.

To unmount a device when you no longer need it, use the `umount` command. For example, to unmount the DVD/CD-ROM device, type

```
umount /dev/cdrom
```

The `umount` command succeeds as long as no one is using the DVD/CD-ROM. If you get an error when trying to unmount the DVD/CD-ROM, check to see whether the current working directory is on the DVD or CD. If you're currently working in one of the DVD/CD-ROM's directories, that also qualifies as a use of the DVD/CD-ROM.

## Examining the /etc/fstab file

The `mount` command has the following general format:

```
mount device-name mount-point
```

However, you can mount the CD-ROM by typing one of the following commands:

```
mount /dev/cdrom
mount /mnt/cdrom
```

You can mount by specifying only the CD-ROM device name or the mount-point name because of what's in a file named `/etc/fstab`. A line is in the `/etc/fstab` file for the `/mnt/cdrom` mount point. That entry specifies the CD-ROM device name and the file-system type. That's why you can mount the CD-ROM with a shorter `mount` command.

The `/etc/fstab` file is a *configuration file* — a text file containing information that the `mount` and `umount` commands use. Each line in the `/etc/fstab` file provides information about a device and its mount point in the Linux file system. Essentially, the `/etc/fstab` file associates various mount points within the file system with specific devices, which enables the `mount` command to work from the command line with only the mount point or the device as argument.

Here is a `/etc/fstab` file from a Fedora Core system:

```
LABEL=/            /              ext3      defaults                    1 1
LABEL=/boot        /boot          ext3      defaults                    1 2
none               /dev/pts       devpts    gid=5,mode=620              0 0
none               /dev/shm       tmpfs     defaults                    0 0
none               /proc          proc      defaults                    0 0
none               /sys           sysfs     defaults                    0 0
/dev/hda6          swap           swap      defaults                    0 0
/dev/cdrom         /mnt/cdrom     udf,iso9660 noauto,owner,kudzu,ro 0 0
/dev/fd0           /mnt/floppy    auto      noauto,owner,kudzu          0 0
/dev/cdrom1        /mnt/cdrom1    udf,iso9660 noauto,owner,kudzu,ro 0 0
```

The first field on each line shows a device name, such as a hard-drive partition (or it identifies a partition by a LABEL keyword). The second field is the mount point, and the third field indicates the type of file system on the device. You can ignore the last three fields for now.

This /etc/fstab file shows that the /dev/hda6 device (the second logical partition on the first IDE hard drive) functions as a swap device for virtual memory, which is why both the mount point and the file-system type are set to swap.

The Linux operating system uses the contents of the /etc/fstab file to mount various file systems automatically. During Fedora Core startup, the init process executes a shell script that runs the mount -a command. That command reads the /etc/fstab file and mounts all listed file systems (except those with the noauto option). The third field on each line of /etc/fstab specifies the type of file system on that device and the fourth field shows a comma-separated list of options that the mount command uses when mounting that device on the file system. Typically, you find the defaults option in this field. The defaults option implies — among other things — that the device mounts at boot time; that only the root user can mount the device; and that the device mounts for both reading and writing. If the options include noauto, the device doesn't mount automatically as the system boots.

The kudzu option in the fourth field of /etc/fstab entries indicates that these lines were added to the fstab file by the kudzu hardware-detection utility — kudzu runs the updfstab command to add an entry in the /etc/fstab file for each removable drive it detects. You typically find that the entries for DVD/CD-ROM drives (/dev/cdrom and /dev/cdrom1) and the floppy drive (dev/fd0) have the kudzu option in the fourth field. On a PC with an IDE Zip drive, for instance, the /etc/fstab file has another entry set up by kudzu that associates the /mnt/zip mount point with the Zip drive device (/dev/hdd4), as follows:

```
/dev/hdd4  /mnt/zip    auto  noauto,owner,kudzu   0 0
```

## Sharing Files with NFS

Sharing files through the Network File System (NFS) is simple and involves two basic steps:

✦ On the NFS server, export one or more directories by listing them in the /etc/exports file and by running the /usr/sbin/exportfs command. In addition, you must run the NFS server (you can do so by logging in as root and typing **service nfs start**).

✦ On each client system, use the mount command to mount the directories the server has exported.

The only problem in using NFS is that each client system must support it. Most PCs don't come with NFS — that means you have to buy NFS software separately if you want to share files by using NFS. If, however, all systems on your LAN run Linux (or other variants of UNIX with built-in NFS support), using NFS makes sense.

*Note:* NFS has security vulnerabilities. Therefore do not set up NFS on systems directly connected to the Internet.

In the upcoming section, I walk you through an NFS setup, using an example of two Linux PCs on a LAN.

## Exporting a file system with NFS

Start with the server system that *exports* — makes available to the client systems — the contents of a directory. On the server, you must run the NFS service and also designate one or more file systems to be exported, or made available to the client systems.

To export a file system, you have to add an appropriate entry to the /etc/ exports file. For example, suppose you want to export the /home directory and you want to enable the host named LNBP75 to mount this file system for read-and-write operations (you can use a host's IP address in place of the host name). You can do so by adding the following entry to the /etc/ exports file:

```
/home LNBP75(rw)
```

After adding the entry in the /etc/exports file, manually export the file system by typing **/usr/sbin/exportfs -a** in a terminal window. This command exports all file systems defined in the /etc/exports file.

Now start the NFS server — log in as root and type the following command in a terminal window:

```
service nfs start
```

To restart the NFS service, type **service nfs restart**.

When the NFS service is up, the server side of NFS is ready. Now you can try to mount the exported file system from a client system and access the exported file system.

If you ever make any changes to the exported file systems listed in the /etc/exports file, remember to restart the NFS service. To do so, type **service nfs restart** in a terminal window.

## Mounting an NFS file system

To access an exported NFS file system on a client system, you have to mount that file system on a mount point — which is, in practical terms, nothing more than a local directory. For example, suppose you want to access the /home directory exported from the server named LNBP200 at the local directory /mnt/lnbp200 on the client system. To do so, follow these steps:

1. **Log in as** root, **and create the directory with the following command:**

   mkdir /mnt/lnbp200

2. **Type the following command to perform the** mount **operation:**

   mount lnbp200:/home/public /mnt/lnbp200

3. **Change the directory to** /mnt/lnbp200 **with the command** cd /mnt/lnbp200.

   Now you can view and access exported files from this directory.

To confirm that the NFS file system is indeed mounted, log in as root on the client system and type **mount** in a terminal window. You see a line similar to the following one about the NFS file system:

lnbp200:/home/public on /mnt/lnbp200 type nfs (rw,addr=192.168.1.200)

# Backing Up and Restoring Files

Backing up and restoring files is a crucial system-administration task. If something happens to your system's hard drive, you have to rely on the backups to recover important files. Here I present some backup strategies, describe several backup media, and explain how to back up and restore files by using the *tape archiver* (tar) program that comes with Fedora Core. Also, you find out how to perform incremental and automatic backups on tapes.

If you have a CD burner, you can also back up files by recording them on a CD-R. Consult Book II, Chapter 4 for information on how to burn a data CD.

## Selecting a backup strategy and media

Your Fedora Core system's hard drive contains everything you need to keep the system running — as well as other files (such as documents and databases) that keep your business running. You have to back up these files so you can recover quickly and bring the system back to normal in case the hard drive crashes. Typically, you have to follow a strict regimen of regular backups because you can never tell when the hard drive may fail or the file system may corrupt. To implement such a regimen, first decide which files you want to back up, how often, and what backup storage media to use. This process is what I mean by selecting a backup strategy and backup media.

Your choice of backup strategy and backup media depends on your assessment of the risk of business disruption due to hard-drive failure. Depending on how you use your Fedora Core system, a disk failure may or may not have much impact on you.

For example, if you use your Fedora Core system as a learning tool (to learn about Linux or programming), all you may need are backup copies of some system files required to configure Linux. In this case, your backup strategy can be to save important system-configuration files on one or more floppies every time you change any system configuration.

On the other hand, if you use your Fedora Core system as an office server that provides shared file storage for many users, the risk of business disruption due to disk failure is much higher. In this case, you have to back up all the files every week and back up any new or changed files every day. You can perform these backups in an automated manner (where you can use the job-scheduling features that I describe in Chapter 1 of this minibook). Also, you probably need a backup storage medium that can store large amounts (multiple gigabytes) of data on a single tape. In other words, for high-risk situations, your backup strategy is more elaborate and requires additional equipment (such as a tape drive).

Your choice of backup media depends on the amount of data you have to back up. For a small amount of data (such as system-configuration files), you can use floppy disks or USB flash disks as the backup media. If your PC has a Zip drive, you can use Zip disks as backup media; these are good for backing up a single-user directory. To back up entire servers, use a tape drive, typically a 4mm or 8mm tape drive that connects to a SCSI controller. Such tape drives can store several gigabytes of data per tape, and you can use them to back up an entire file system on a single tape.

When backing up files to these media, you have to refer to the backup device by name. Table 3-2 lists device names for some common backup devices.

| Table 3-2 | Device Names for Common Backup Devices |
|---|---|
| *Backup Device* | *Linux Device Name* |
| Floppy disk | `/dev/fd0` |
| IDE Zip drive | `/dev/hdc4` or `/dev/hdd4` |
| SCSI Zip drive | `/dev/sda` (assuming it's the first SCSI drive; otherwise, the device name depends on the SCSI ID) |
| SCSI tape drive | `/dev/st0` or `/dev/nst0` (the n prefix means that the tape isn't rewound after files copy to the tape) |

## Commercial backup utilities for Linux

In the next section, I explain how to back up and restore files using the tape archiver (`tar`) program that comes with Fedora Core. Although you can manage backups with `tar`, a number of commercial backup utilities come with graphical user interfaces and other features to simplify backups. Here are some well-known commercial backup utilities for Fedora Core:

✦ **BRU:** A backup and restore utility from The TOLIS Group, Inc. (`www.tolisgroup.com`)

✦ **LONE-TAR:** Tape-backup software package from Lone Star Software Corporation (`www.cactus.com`)

✦ **Arkeia:** Backup and recovery software for heterogeneous networks from Arkeia (`www.knox-software.com`)

✦ **CTAR:** Backup and recovery software for UNIX systems from UniTrends Software Corporation (`www.unitrends.com`)

✦ **BrightStor ARCserve Backup for Linux:** Data-protection technology for Linux systems from Computer Associates (`www3.ca.com/Solutions/Product.asp?ID=3370`)

## Using the tape archiver — tar

You can use the `tar` command to archive files to a device, such as a floppy disk or tape. The `tar` program creates an archive file that can contain other directories and files and (optionally) compress the archive for efficient storage. The archive is then written to a specified device or another file. In fact, many software packages are distributed in the form of a compressed `tar` file.

The command syntax of the `tar` program is as follows:

```
tar options destination source
```

Here, *options* are usually specified by a sequence of single letters, with each letter specifying what `tar` will do. The *destination* is the device name of the backup device. And *source* is a list of file or directory names denoting the files to back up.

### Backing up and restoring a single-volume archive

For example, suppose you want to back up the contents of the /etc/X11 directory on a floppy disk. Log in as `root`, place a disk in the floppy drive, and type the following command:

```
tar zcvf /dev/fd0 /etc/X11
```

The `tar` program displays a list of filenames as each file copies to the compressed `tar` archive on the floppy disk. In this case, the options are `zcvf`, the destination is `/dev/fd0` (the floppy disk), and the source is the `/etc/X11` directory (which implies all its subdirectories and their contents). You can use a similar `tar` command to back up files to a tape — simply replace `/dev/fd0` with the tape device — such as `/dev/st0` for a SCSI tape drive.

Table 3-3 defines a few common `tar` options.

| Table 3-3 | Common tar Options |
|---|---|
| **Option** | **Does the Following** |
| c | Creates a new archive |
| f | Specifies the name of the archive file or device on the next field in the command line |
| M | Specifies a multivolume archive (the next section describes multivolume archives) |
| t | Lists the contents of the archive |
| v | Displays verbose messages |
| x | Extracts files from the archive |
| z | Compresses the `tar` archive using `gzip` |

To view the contents of the `tar` archive you create on the floppy disk, type the following command:

```
tar ztf /dev/fd0
```

You see a list of the filenames (each begins with `/etc/X11`) indicating what's in the backup. In this `tar` command, the `t` option lists the contents of the `tar` archive.

To extract the files from a `tar` backup, follow these steps while logged in as `root`:

*1.* **Change the directory to `/tmp` by typing this command:**

```
cd /tmp
```

This step is where you can practice extracting the files from the `tar` backup. For a real backup, change the directory to an appropriate location (typically, you type `cd /`).

*2.* **Type the following command:**

```
tar zxvf /dev/fd0
```

This `tar` command uses the `x` option to extract the files from the archive stored on `/dev/fd0` (the floppy disk).

Now if you check the contents of the /tmp directory, you notice that the tar command creates an etc/X11 directory tree in /tmp and restores all the files from the tar archive into that directory. The tar command strips off the leading / from the filenames in the archive and restores the files in the current directory. If you want to restore the /etc/X11 directory from the archive on the floppy, use this command:

```
tar zxvf /dev/fd0 -C /
```

The / at the end of the command denotes the directory where you want to restore the backup files.

You can use the tar command to create, view, and restore an archive. You can store the archive in a file or in any device you specify with a device name.

### Backing up and restoring a multivolume archive

Sometimes the capacity of a single storage medium is less than the total storage space needed to store the archive. In this case, you can use the M option for a multivolume archive — meaning the archive can span multiple tapes or floppies. Note, however, that you cannot create a compressed, multivolume archive. That means you have to drop the z option. To see how multivolume archives work, log in as root, place one disk in the floppy drive, and type the following tar command:

```
tar cvfM /dev/fd0 /usr/share/doc/ghostscript*
```

*Note:* The M option is in the option letters; it tells tar to create a multivolume archive. The tar command prompts you for a second floppy when the first one is filled. Take out the first floppy, and insert another floppy when you see the following prompt:

```
Prepare volume #2 for `/dev/fd0' and hit return:
```

When you press Enter, the tar program continues with the second floppy. In this example, you need only two floppies to store the archive; for larger archives, the tar program continues to prompt for floppies in case more floppies are needed.

To restore from this multivolume archive, type **cd /tmp** to change the directory to /tmp. Then type

```
tar xvfM /dev/fd0
```

The tar program prompts you to feed the floppies as necessary.

Use the `du -s` command to determine the amount of storage you need for archiving a directory. For example, here's how you can get the total size of the `/etc` directory in kilobytes:

```
du -s /etc
35724   /etc
```

The resulting output shows that the `/etc` directory requires at least 35,724K of storage space to back up.

### Backing up on tapes

Although backing up on tapes is as simple as using the right device name in the `tar` command, you do have to know some nuances of the tape device to use it well. When you use `tar` to back up to the device named `/dev/st0` (the first SCSI tape drive), the tape device automatically rewinds the tape after the `tar` program finishes copying the archive to the tape. The `/dev/st0` device is called a rewinding tape device because it rewinds tapes by default.

If your tape can hold several gigabytes of data, you may want to write several `tar` archives — one after another — to the same tape (otherwise much of the tape may be left empty). If you plan to do so, your tape device can't rewind the tape after the `tar` program finishes. To help you with scenarios like this one, several Linux tape devices are nonrewinding. The nonrewinding SCSI tape device is called `/dev/nst0`. Use this device name if you want to write one archive after another on a tape.

After each archive, the nonrewinding tape device writes an *end-of-file* (EOF) marker to separate one archive from the next. Use the `mt` command to control the tape — you can move from one marker to the next or rewind the tape. For example, after you finish writing several archives to a tape using the `/dev/nst0` device name, you can force the tape to rewind with the following command:

```
mt -f /dev/nst0 rewind
```

After rewinding the tape, you can use the following command to extract files from the first archive to the current disk directory:

```
tar xvf /dev/nst0
```

After that, you must move past the EOF marker to the next archive. To do so, use the following `mt` command:

```
mt -f /dev/nst0 fsf 1
```

This positions the tape at the beginning of the next archive. Now use the `tar` `xvf` command again to read this archive.

If you save multiple archives on a tape, you have to keep track of the archives yourself. The order of the archives can be hard to remember, so you may be better off simply saving one archive per tape.

### Performing incremental backups

Suppose you use `tar` to back up your system's hard drive on a tape. Because such a full backup can take quite some time, you don't want to repeat this task every night. (Besides, only a small number of files may have changed during the day.) To locate the files that need backing up, you can use the `find` command to list all files that have changed in the past 24 hours:

```
find / -mtime -1 -type f -print
```

Book VI
Chapter 3

Managing the
File System

This command prints a list of files that have changed within the last day. The `-mtime -1` option means you want the files that were last modified less than one day ago. You can now combine this `find` command with the `tar` command to back up only those files that have changed within the last day:

```
tar cvf /dev/st0 'find / -mtime -1 -type f -print'
```

When you place a command between single back quotes, the shell executes that command and places the output at that point in the command line. The net result is that the `tar` program saves only the changed files in the archive. What this process gives you is an *incremental backup* of only the files that have changed since the previous day.

### Performing automated backups

In Chapter 1 of this minibook, I show you how to use `crontab` to set up recurring jobs (called *cron jobs*). The Linux system performs these tasks at regular intervals. Backing up your system is a good use of the `crontab` facility. Suppose your backup strategy is as follows:

✦ Every Sunday at 1:15 a.m., your system backs up the entire disk on the tape.

✦ Monday through Saturday, your system performs an incremental backup at 3:10 a.m. by saving only those files that have changed during the past 24 hours.

To set up this automated backup schedule, log in as `root` and type the following lines in a file named `backups` (this example assumes that you use a SCSI tape drive):

```
15 1 * * 0 tar zcvf /dev/st0 /
10 3 * * 1-6 tar zcvf /dev/st0 `find / -mtime -1 -type f -print`
```

Next, submit this job schedule by using the following `crontab` command:

```
crontab backups
```

Now you are set for an automated backup. All you need to do is to place a new tape in the tape drive everyday. Remember to also give each tape an appropriate label.

# Accessing DOS/Windows File Systems

If you have Microsoft Windows 95/98/Me installed on your hard drive, you've probably already mounted the DOS partition under Fedora Core. If not, you can easily mount DOS partitions in Fedora Core. Mounting makes the DOS directory hierarchy appear as part of the Linux file system. To identify the DOS partitions easily, you may want to mount the first DOS partition as `/dosc`, the second one as `/dosd`, and so on.

To determine whether your DOS hard drive partitions are set up to mount automatically, type the following `grep` command to look for the string `vfat` in the file `/etc/fstab`:

```
grep vfat /etc/fstab
```

If the output shows one or more lines that contain `vfat`, your Fedora Core system mounts DOS/Windows hard-drive partitions automatically.

If the `grep` command doesn't show any lines that contain the string `vfat` in `/etc/fstab`, your system doesn't mount any DOS/Windows hard-drive partitions automatically. Of course, a very good reason for this situation may be that your hard drive doesn't *have* any DOS partitions.

Even if you don't have any DOS partitions on your hard drive, you should learn how to access a DOS file system from Fedora Core because you may have to access a DOS floppy disk on your Fedora Core system.

## Mounting a DOS disk partition

To mount a DOS hard drive partition or floppy, use the `mount` command but include the option `-t vfat` to indicate the file system type as DOS. For example, if your DOS partition happens to be the first partition on your *IDE* (Integrated Drive Electronics) drive and you want to mount it on `/dosc`, use the following `mount` command:

```
mount -t vfat /dev/hda1 /dosc
```

The `-t vfat` part of the `mount` command specifies that the device you mount — `/dev/hda1` — has an MS-DOS file system. Figure 3-4 illustrates the effect of this `mount` command.

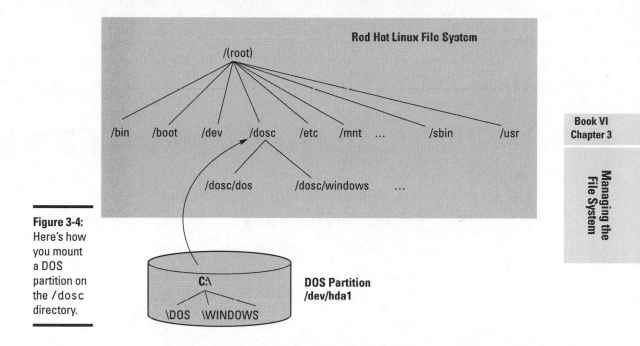

**Figure 3-4:** Here's how you mount a DOS partition on the `/dosc` directory.

Figure 3-4 shows how directories in your DOS partition map to the Linux file system. What was the `C:\DOS` directory under DOS becomes `/dosc/dos` under Fedora Core. Similarly, `C:\WINDOWS` now is `/dosc/windows`. You probably can see the pattern. To convert a DOS filename to Linux (when you `mount` the DOS partition on `/dosc`), perform the following steps:

*1.* **Change the DOS names to lowercase.**

*2.* **Change `C:\` to `/dosc/`.**

*3.* **Change all backslashes (\\) to forward slashes (/).**

## Mounting DOS floppy disks

Just as you mount a DOS hard-drive partition on the Linux file system, you can also mount a DOS floppy disk. You must log in as `root` to mount a floppy, but you can follow the steps I show in the latter part of this section to set up your system so that any user can mount a DOS floppy disk. You also have to know the device name for the floppy drive. By default, Linux defines the following two generic floppy-device names:

✦ /dev/fd0 is the A drive (the first floppy drive)

✦ /dev/fd1 is the B drive (the second floppy drive, if you have one)

As for the mount point, you can use any empty directory in the file system as the mount point, but the Fedora Core system comes with a directory, /mnt/floppy, to specifically mount a floppy disk.

To mount a DOS floppy disk on the /mnt/floppy directory, put the floppy in the drive and type the following command:

```
mount -t vfat /dev/fd0 /mnt/floppy
```

After you mount the floppy, you can copy files to and from the floppy by using the Linux copy command (cp). To copy the file gnome1.pcx from the current directory to the floppy, type the following:

```
cp gnome1.pcx /mnt/floppy
```

Similarly, to see the contents of the floppy disk, type the following:

```
ls /mnt/floppy
```

If you want to remove the floppy disk from the drive, first *unmount* the floppy drive. Unmounting removes the association between the floppy disk's file system and the mount point on the Linux file system. Use the umount command to unmount the floppy disk like this:

```
umount /dev/fd0
```

You can set up your Fedora Core system so that any user can mount a DOS floppy. To enable any user to mount a DOS floppy in the A drive on the /a directory, for example, perform the following steps:

*1.* **Log in as** root.

*2.* **Create the** /a **directory (the mount point) by typing the following command in a terminal window:**

```
mkdir /a
```

*3.* **Edit the** /etc/fstab **file in a text editor (such as** vi **or emacs), insert the following line and then save the file and quit the editor:**

```
/dev/fd0    /a    vfat    noauto,user    0 0
```

The first field in that line is the device name of the floppy drive (/dev/fd0); the second field is the mount directory (/a); and the third field shows the type of file system (vfat). The user option (which appears next to noauto) is what enables all users to mount DOS floppy disks.

4. **Log out and log in as a normal user.**

5. **To confirm that you can mount a DOS floppy as a normal user and not just as** root, **insert a DOS floppy in the A drive and type the following command:**

   ```
   mount /a
   ```

   The mount operation succeeds, and you see a listing of the DOS floppy when you type the command **ls /a**.

6. **To unmount the DOS floppy, type** umount /a.

## Mounting an NTFS Partition

Nowadays, most PCs come with Windows XP or Windows 2000 preinstalled on the hard drive. Both Windows XP and 2000, as well as Windows NT, typically use the NT File System (NTFS). Linux supports read-only access to NTFS partitions, but Fedora Core does not come with the ntfs.ko kernel module that's needed to access an NTFS partition.

If you have installed Fedora Core on a Windows XP system and want to access files on the NTFS partition, you can build the kernel after selecting an NTFS module during the kernel configuration step (see Chapter 6 of this minibook for detailed instructions on configuring, building, and installing the kernel).

After rebuilding and booting from the new kernel, log in as root, and type the following command to create a mount point for the NTFS partition (in this case I am creating a mount point in the /mnt directory):

```
mkdir /mnt/xp
```

Now, you can mount the NTFS partition with the following command:

```
mount /dev/hda2 /mnt/xp -t ntfs -r -o umask=0222
```

Replace /dev/hda2 with the device name for the NTFS partition on your system. On most PCs that come with Windows XP preinstalled, the NTFS partition is the second one (/dev/hda2) — the first partition (/dev/hda1) is usually a hidden partition used to hold files used for Windows XP installation.

# Using mtools

One way to access the MS-DOS file systems is to mount the DOS hard drive or floppy disk by using the mount command and then use regular Linux commands, such as ls and cp, to work with the mounted DOS file system. This approach of mounting a DOS file system is fine for hard drives. Linux can mount the DOS partition automatically at startup, and you can access the DOS directories on the hard drive at any time.

If you want a quick directory listing of a DOS floppy disk, however, mounting can soon become quite tedious. First, you have to mount the floppy drive. Then you must use the `ls` command. Finally, you must use the `umount` command before ejecting the floppy out of the drive.

This situation is where the `mtools` package comes to the rescue. The `mtools` package implements most common DOS commands; the commands use the same names as in DOS except that you add an `m` prefix to each command. Thus the command for getting a directory listing is `mdir`, and `mcopy` copies files. The best part of `mtools` is the fact that you don't have to mount the floppy disk to use the `mtools` commands.

Because the `mtools` commands write to and read from the physical device (floppy disk), you must log in as `root` to perform these commands. If you want any user to access the `mtools` commands, you must alter the permission settings for the floppy drive devices. Use the following command to permit anyone to read from and write to the first floppy drive:

```
chmod o+rw /dev/fd0
```

## Trying mtools

To try out `mtools`, follow these steps:

1. **Place an MS-DOS floppy disk in your system's A drive.**
2. **Type** `mdir`.

   You see the directory of the floppy disk (in the standard DOS directory-listing format).

Typically, you use the `mtools` utilities to access the floppy disks. The default configuration file, `/etc/mtools.conf`, is set up to access the floppy drive as the A drive. Although you can edit that file to define C and D drives for your DOS hard-drive partitions, you can as well access the hard drive partitions by using the Linux `mount` command to mount them. Because you can mount the hard-drive partitions automatically at startup, accessing them through the Linux commands is normally just as easy.

## Understanding the /etc/mtools.conf file

The `mtools` package works with the default setup, but if you get any errors, check the `/etc/mtools.conf` file. That file contains the definitions of the drives (such as A, B, and C) that the `mtools` utilities see. Following are a few lines from a typical `/etc/mtools.conf` file:

```
drive a: file="/dev/fd0" exclusive mformat_only
drive b: file="/dev/fd1" exclusive mformat_only

# First SCSI hard disk partition
#drive c: file="/dev/sda1"

# First IDE hard disk partition on a Windows 98 PC
drive c: file="/dev/hda1"

# Internal IDE Zip drive
drive e: file="/dev/hdd4" exclusive
```

The pound sign (#) indicates the start of a comment. Each line defines a drive letter, the associated Linux device name, and some keywords that indicate how to access the device. In this example, the first two lines define drives A and B. The third noncomment line defines drive C as the first partition on the first IDE drive (/dev/hda1). If you have other DOS drives (D, for example), you can add another line that defines drive D as the appropriate disk partition.

If your system's A drive is a high-density, 3.5-inch drive, you don't need to change anything in the default /etc/mtools.conf file to access the floppy drive. If you also want to access any DOS partition in the hard drive, uncomment and edit an appropriate line for the C drive.

You also can access Iomega Zip drives through mtools. Simply specify a drive letter and the appropriate device's filename. For built-in IDE (ATAPI) Zip drives, try /dev/hdd4 as the device file and add the following line in the /etc/mtools.conf file:

```
drive e: file="/dev/hdd4"
```

After that, you can use mtools commands to access the Zip drive (refer to it as the E drive). For example, to see the directory listing, place a Zip disk in the Zip drive and type:

```
mdir e:
```

## Learning the mtools commands

The mtools package is a collection of utilities. So far, I have been using mdir — the mtools counterpart of the DIR command in DOS. The other mtools commands are fairly easy to use.

If you know MS-DOS commands, using the mtools commands is easy. Type the DOS command in lowercase letters, and remember to add m in front of each command. Because the Linux commands and filenames are case-sensitive, you must use all lowercase letters as you type mtools commands.

Table 3-4 summarizes the commands available in mtools.

| Table 3-4 | | The mtools Commands |
|---|---|---|
| *mtools Utility* | *MS-DOS Command (If Any)* | *The mtools Utility Does the Following* |
| mattrib | ATTRIB | Changes MS-DOS file-attribute flags |
| mbadblocks | | Tests a floppy disk and marks the bad blocks in the file allocation table (FAT) |
| mcd | CD | Changes an MS-DOS directory |
| mcopy | COPY | Copies files between MS-DOS and Linux |
| mdel | DEL or ERASE | Deletes an MS-DOS file |
| mdeltree | DELTREE | Recursively deletes an MS-DOS directory |
| mdir | DIR | Displays an MS-DOS directory listing |
| mdu | | Lists the space that a directory and its contents occupy |
| mformat | FORMAT | Places an MS-DOS file system on a low-level-formatted floppy disk (use fdformat to low-level-format a floppy disk in Fedora Core) |
| minfo | | Gets information about an MS-DOS file system |
| mkmanifest | | Makes a list of short name equivalents |
| mlabel | LABEL | Initializes an MS-DOS volume label |
| mmd | MD or MKDIR | Creates an MS-DOS directory |
| mmove | | Moves or renames an MS-DOS file or subdirectory |
| mmount | | Mounts an MS-DOS disk |
| mpartition | | Creates an MS-DOS file system as a partition |
| mrd | RD or RMDIR | Deletes an MS-DOS directory |
| mren | REN or RENAME | Renames an existing MS-DOS file |
| mshowfat | | Shows FAT entries for an MS-DOS file |
| mtoolstest | | Tests and displays the current mtools configuration |
| mtype | TYPE | Displays the contents of an MS-DOS file |
| mwrite | COPY | Copies a Linux file to MS-DOS |
| mzip | | Performs certain operations on SCSI Zip disks |

You can use the `mtools` commands just as you use the corresponding DOS commands. The `mdir` command, for example, works the same as the `DIR` command in DOS. The same goes for all the other `mtools` commands shown in Table 3-4.

You can use wildcard characters (such as *) with `mtools` commands, but you must remember that the Linux shell is the first program to see your command. If you don't want the shell to expand the wildcard character all over the place, use quotation marks around filenames that contain any wildcard characters. For example, to copy all *.txt files from the A drive to your current directory, use the following command:

```
mcopy "a:*.txt".
```

If you omit the quotation marks, the shell tries to expand the string a:*.txt with filenames from the current Linux directory. It also tries to copy those files (if any) from the DOS floppy disk.

On the other hand, if you want to copy files from the Linux directory to the DOS floppy disk, you do want the shell to expand any wildcard characters. To copy all *.jpg files from the current Linux directory to the DOS floppy disk, for example, use `mcopy` like this:

```
mcopy *.jpg a:
```

With the `mtools` utilities you can use the backslash character (\) as the directory separator, just as you do in DOS. However, when you type a filename that contains the backslash character, you must enclose the name in double quotation marks (" "). For example, here's a command that copies a file from a subdirectory on the A drive to the current Linux directory:

```
mcopy "a:\test\sample.dat".
```

## Formatting a DOS floppy

Suppose you run Fedora Core on your home PC and MS-DOS is no longer on your system, but you want to copy some files onto an MS-DOS floppy disk and take the disk to your office. If you already have a formatted MS-DOS floppy, you can simply mount that floppy and copy the file to the floppy by using the Linux `cp` command. But what if you don't have a formatted DOS floppy? The `mtools` package again comes to the rescue.

The `mtools` package provides the `mformat` utility, which can format a floppy disk for use in MS-DOS. Unlike the DOS format command that formats a floppy in a single step, the `mformat` command requires you to follow a two-step process:

*1.* **Use the** `fdformat` **command to low-level-format a floppy disk.**

The `fdformat` command uses the floppy device name as the argument; the device name includes all parameters necessary for formatting the floppy disk.

Figure 3-5 illustrates the device-naming convention for the floppy-drive device. As shown in Figure 3-5, you use the following command to format a 3.5-inch, high-density floppy disk in your system's A drive:

```
fdformat /dev/fd0H1440
```

**Figure 3-5:** Here's how you can construct the name of a floppy disk drive in Fedora Core.

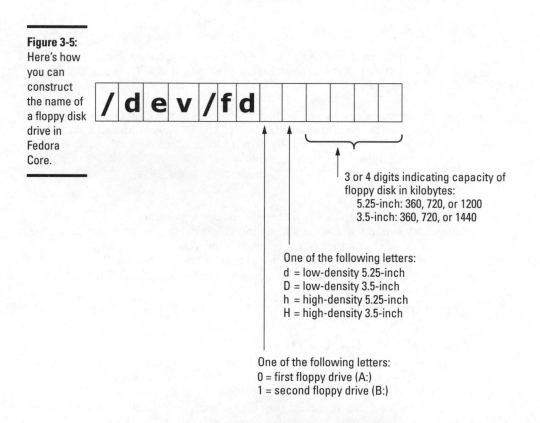

/dev/fd

3 or 4 digits indicating capacity of floppy disk in kilobytes:
5.25-inch: 360, 720, or 1200
3.5-inch: 360, 720, or 1440

One of the following letters:
d = low-density 5.25-inch
D = low-density 3.5-inch
h = high-density 5.25-inch
H = high-density 3.5-inch

One of the following letters:
0 = first floppy drive (A:)
1 = second floppy drive (B:)

*2.* **Use the** `mformat` **command to put an MS-DOS file system on the low-level-formatted floppy disk.**

If the floppy is in drive A, type the following command to create a formatted DOS floppy:

```
mformat a:
```

# Chapter 4: Managing Applications

## In This Chapter

✔ Finding out about RPMs

✔ Installing and removing software RPMs

✔ Building applications from source files

✔ Updating Fedora Core applications with Up2date and Yum

Most software packages for Fedora Core are distributed in special files called *Red Hat Package Manager* (RPM) files, which is why you have to know how to install or remove software packages that come in the form of RPM files. In this chapter, I show you how to work with RPM files.

Many other open-source software packages come in source-code form, usually in compressed archives. You have to build and install the software to use it. I describe the steps you typically follow when downloading, building, and installing source-based software packages.

Finally, I briefly describe how you can use Up2date (Red Hat's Update Agent) and Yum to update Fedora Core applications.

## Working with Red Hat Package Manager

Red Hat Package Manager (RPM) is a system for packaging all the necessary files for a software product in a single file — called an *RPM file* or simply an *RPM*. In fact, the entire Fedora Core distribution is a whole lot of RPMs. The best way to work with RPMs is through the RPM commands. You have to type these commands at the shell prompt in a terminal window or a text console.

### Using the RPM commands

When you install Fedora Core from the companion DVD-ROMs, the Fedora Core installer uses the rpm command to unpack the packages (RPM files) and to copy the contents to your hard drive.

You don't have to understand the internal structure of an RPM file, but you need to know how to use the `rpm` command to work with RPM files. Here are some of the things you can do with the `rpm` command:

✦ Find out the version numbers and other information about the RPMs installed on your system.

✦ Install a new software package from an RPM. For example, you may install a package you skipped during the initial installation. You can do that with the `rpm` command.

✦ Remove (uninstall) unneeded software you previously installed from an RPM. You may uninstall a package to reclaim the disk space, if you find that you rarely (or never) use the package.

✦ Upgrade an older version of an RPM with a new one. You may upgrade after you download a new version of a package from Fedora Core download sites (listed online at `fedora.redhat.com/download/mirrors.html`). Often you must upgrade an RPM to benefit from the fixes in the new version.

✦ Verify that an RPM is in working order. You can verify a package to check that all necessary files are in the correct locations.

As you can see, the `rpm` command is versatile — it can do a lot of different things depending on the options you use.

If you ever forget the `rpm` options, type the following command to see a list:

```
rpm --help | more
```

The number of `rpm` options will amaze you!

## Understanding RPM filenames

An RPM contains a number of files, but it appears as a single file on your Fedora Core system. By convention, the RPM filenames have a specific format. To see the names of some of the RPM files on the companion DVD-ROMs, follow these steps:

1. **Place the DVD-ROM in the DVD drive. The DVD-ROM automatically mounts if you're using the GNOME or KDE graphical desktops. Otherwise, mount it with the following command (you must be logged in as** `root`**):**

   ```
   mount /dev/cdrom
   ```

   If you are inserting the DVD-ROM into your system's second CD/DVD drive, type **mount /dev/cdrom1** to mount the DVD-ROM.

2. **Type the following command to go to the directory in which the RPMs are located:**

```
cd /mnt/cdrom/Fedora/RPMS
```

3. **View the listing using the** ls **command. For example, to see RPMs with names that start with** cups, **type**

```
ls cups*
```

You see a listing that looks like this:

```
cups-1.1.20-6.i386.rpm
cups-libs-1.1.20-6.i386.rpm
```

As you may guess from the listing, the names of RPM files end with an .rpm extension. To understand the various parts of the filename, consider the following RPM:

```
cups-1.1.20-6.i386.rpm
```

This filename has the following parts, separated by dashes (-):

Book VI
Chapter 4

Managing
Applications

✦ **Package name:** cups

✦ **Version number:** 1.1.20

✦ **Release number:** 6 (a Red-Hat-assigned release number)

✦ **Architecture:** i386 (this package is for Intel 80386-compatible processors)

Usually, the package name is descriptive enough for you to guess what the RPM may contain. The version number is the same as that of the software package's current version number (even when it's distributed in some other form, such as a tar file). Developers assign the release number to keep track of changes. The architecture is i386 or noarch for the RPMs you want to install on a PC with an Intel x86-compatible processor.

## Finding out about RPMs

As it installs packages, the rpm command builds a database of installed RPMs. You can use the rpm -q command to query this database to find out information about packages installed on your system.

For example, to find out the version number of the Linux kernel installed on your system, type the following rpm -q command:

```
rpm -q kernel
```

You see a response similar to the following:

```
kernel-2.6.5-1.358
```

The response is the name of the RPM for the kernel (this version is the executable version of the kernel, not the source files). The name is the same as the RPM filename, except that the last part — `.i386.rpm` — isn't shown. In this case, the version part of the RPM tells you that the kernel is 2.6.5.

You can see a list of all installed RPMs by using the following command:

```
rpm -qa
```

You see a long list of RPMs scroll by your screen. To view the list one screen at a time, type

```
rpm -qa | more
```

If you want to search for a specific package, feed the output of `rpm -qa` to the `grep` command. For example, to see all packages with `kernel` in their names, type

```
rpm -qa | grep kernel
```

The result depends on what parts of the kernel RPMs are installed on a system. For example, on my system this command shows the following:

```
kernel-2.6.5-1.358
kernel-source-2.6.5-1.358
```

You can query much more than a package's version number with the `rpm -q` command. By adding single-letter options, you can find out other useful information. For example, try the following command to see the files in the kernel package:

```
rpm -ql kernel
```

Here are a few lines from the output of this command:

```
/boot/System.map-2.6.5-1.358
/boot/config-2.6.5-1.358
/boot/vmlinuz-2.6.5-1.358
/lib/modules/2.6.5-1.358
/lib/modules/2.6.5-1.358/build
/lib/modules/2.6.5-1.358/build/.config
/lib/modules/2.6.5-1.358/build/Makefile
/lib/modules/2.6.5-1.358/build/arch
/lib/modules/2.6.5-1.358/build/arch/alpha
/lib/modules/2.6.5-1.358/build/arch/alpha/Kconfig
/lib/modules/2.6.5-1.358/build/arch/alpha/Makefile
```

```
/lib/modules/2.6.5-1.358/build/arch/alpha/boot
/lib/modules/2.6.5-1.358/build/arch/alpha/boot/Makefile
/lib/modules/2.6.5-1.358/build/arch/alpha/kernel
/lib/modules/2.6.5-1.358/build/arch/alpha/kernel/Makefile
(rest of the listing deleted)
```

Here are a few more useful forms of the `rpm -q` commands to query information about a package (to use any of these `rpm -q` commands, type the command, followed by the package name):

+ `rpm -qc`: Lists all configuration files in a package.

+ `rpm -qd`: Lists all documentation files in a package. These are usually the online manual pages (also known as *man pages*).

+ `rpm -qf`: Displays the name of the package (if any) to which a specified file belongs.

+ `rpm -qi`: Displays detailed information about a package, including version number, size, installation date, and a brief description.

+ `rpm -ql`: Lists all the files in a package. For some packages, you see a very long list.

+ `rpm -qs`: Lists the state of all files in a package.

Book VI
Chapter 4

Managing
Applications

These `rpm` commands provide information about installed packages only. If you want to find information about an uninstalled RPM file, add the letter *p* to the command-line option of each command. For example, to view the list of files in the RPM file named `rdist-6.1.5-32.i386.rpm`, go to the directory where that file is located and then type the following command:

```
rpm -qpl rdist-*.rpm
```

Of course, this command works only if the current directory *contains* that RPM file.

Two handy `rpm -q` commands enable you to find out which RPM file provides a specific file and which RPMs need a specified package. To find out the name of the RPM that provides a file, use the following command:

```
rpm -q --whatprovides filename
```

For example, to see which RPM provides the file `/etc/yum.conf`, type

```
rpm -q --whatprovides /etc/yum.conf
```

RPM then prints the name of the package that provides the file, like this:

```
yum-2.0.7-1.1
```

If you provide the name of a package instead of a filename, RPM displays the name of the RPM package that contains the specified package.

On the other hand, to find the names of RPMs that need a specific package, use the following command:

```
rpm -q --whatrequires packagename
```

For example, to see which packages need the `openssl` package, type

```
rpm -q --whatrequires openssl
```

Here is a typical output from this command showing all the RPM packages that need `openssl`:

```
libpcap-0.8.3-3
sendmail-8.12.11-4.6
curl-7.11.1-1
mod_ssl-2.0.49-4
openssl-devel-0.9.7a-35
dovecot-0.99.10.4-4
```

## Installing an RPM

To install an RPM, use the `rpm -i` command. You have to provide the name of the RPM file as the argument. A typical example is installing an RPM from this book's companion DVD-ROM containing the Fedora Core RPMs. As usual, you have to mount the DVD-ROM and change to the directory in which the RPMs are located. Then use the `rpm -i` command to install the RPM. If you want to view the progress of the RPM installation, use `rpm -ivh`. A series of hash marks (#)displays as the package is unpacked.

For example, to install the `kernel-source` RPM (which contains the source files for the Linux operating system) from the companion DVD-ROM, I insert the DVD and after it's mounted, type the following commands:

```
cd /mnt/cdrom/Fedora/RPMS
rpm -ivh kernel-source*
```

You don't have to type the full RPM filename — you can use a few characters from the beginning of the name followed by an asterisk (*). Make sure you type enough of the name to identify the RPM file uniquely.

If you try to install an RPM that's already installed, the `rpm -i` command displays an error message. For example, here is what happens when I type the following command to install the `man` package on my system:

```
rpm -i man-1*
```

I get the following error message from the `rpm -i` command:

```
package man-1.5m2-6 is already installed
```

To force the `rpm` command to install a package even if errors are present, just add `--force` to the `rpm -i` command, like this:

```
rpm -i --force man-1*
```

## Removing an RPM

You may want to remove — uninstall — a package if you realize you don't really need the software. For example, if you have installed the X Window System development package but discover you're not interested in writing X applications, you can easily remove the package by using the `rpm -e` command.

You have to know the name of the package before you can remove it. One good way to find the name is to use `rpm -qa` in conjunction with `grep` to search for the appropriate RPM file. For example, to locate the X Window System development RPM, try the following command:

```
rpm -qa | grep xorg
```

`xorg-x11-devel` happens to be the package name of the X Window System development RPM. To remove that package, type

```
rpm -e xorg-x11-devel
```

To remove an RPM, you don't need the full RPM filename; all you need is the package name — the first part of the filename up to the dash (-) before the version number.

The `rpm -e` command does not remove a package other packages need. For example, to remove the `vim-common` package, I type the following command:

```
rpm -e vim-common
```

Then I get the following error message:

```
error: Failed dependencies:
        vim-common is needed by (installed) vim-enhanced-6.2.457-1
```

## Upgrading an RPM

Use the `rpm -U` command to upgrade an RPM. You must provide the name of the RPM file that contains the new software. For example, if I have version 2.0.48 of Apache `httpd` (Web server) installed on my system but I want to upgrade to version 2.0.49, I download the RPM file `httpd-2.0.49-4.i386.rpm` from one of Red Hat update sites (listed at `fedora.redhat.com/download/mirrors.html`) and use the following command:

```
rpm -U httpd-2.0.49-4.i386.rpm
```

The `rpm` command performs the upgrade by removing the old version of the `httpd` package and installing the new RPM.

Whenever possible, upgrade rather than remove the old package and install a new one. Upgrading automatically saves your old configuration files, which saves you the hassle of reconfiguring the software after a fresh installation.

When you're upgrading the `kernel` packages that contain a ready-to-run Linux kernel, install it by using the `rpm -i` command (instead of the `rpm -U` command). That way you won't overwrite the current kernel.

## Verifying an RPM

You may not do so often, but if you suspect that a software package isn't properly installed, use the `rpm -V` command to verify it. For example, to verify the kernel package, type the following:

```
rpm -V kernel
```

This command causes `rpm` to compare the size and other attributes of each file in the package against those of the original files. If everything verifies correctly, the `rpm -V` command does not print anything. If it finds any discrepancies, you see a report of them. For example, I have modified the configuration files for the Apache `httpd` Web server. Here is what I type to verify the `httpd` package:

```
rpm -V httpd
```

Here's the result I get:

```
S.5....T c /etc/httpd/conf/httpd.conf
```

In this case, the output from `rpm -V` tells me that a configuration file has changed. Each line of this command's output has three parts:

✦ The line starts with eight characters: each character indicates the type of discrepancy found. For example, `S` means the size is different, and `T` means the time of last modification is different. Table 4-1 shows each character and its meaning. A period means that that specific attribute matches the original.

✦ For configuration files, a c appears next; otherwise, this field is blank. That's how you can tell whether or not a file is a configuration file. Typically, you don't worry if a configuration file has changed; you probably made the changes yourself.

✦ The last part of the line is the full pathname of the file. From this part, you can tell exactly where the file is located.

| Table 4-1 | Characters Used in RPM Verification Reports |
|-----------|---------------------------------------------|
| *Character* | *Meaning* |
| S | Size has changed |
| M | Permissions and file type are different |
| 5 | Checksum computed with the MD5 algorithm is different |
| D | Device type is different |
| L | Symbolic link is different |
| U | File's user is different |
| G | File's group is different |
| T | File's modification time is different |

# Building Software Packages from Source Files

Many open-source software packages are distributed in source-code form, without executable binaries. Before you can use such software, you have to build the executable binary files by compiling, and you have to follow some instructions to install the package. In this section, I show you how to build software packages from source files.

## Downloading and unpacking the software

Open-source software source files are typically distributed in compressed tar archives. These archives are created by the tar program and compressed with the gzip program. The distribution is in the form of a single large file with the .tar.gz or .tar.Z extension — often referred to as a *compressed tarball*. If you want the software, you have to download the compressed tarball and unpack it.

Download the compressed tar file by using anonymous FTP or through your Web browser. Typically, this process involves no effort on your part beyond clicking a link and saving the file in an appropriate directory on your system.

To try your hand at downloading and building a software package, you can practice on the X Multimedia System (XMMS) — a graphical X application for playing MP3 and other multimedia files. XMMS is bundled with Fedora

Core and already installed on your system. However, you do no harm in downloading and rebuilding the XMMS package again.

Download the source files for XMMS from www.xmms.org/download.php. The files are packed in the form of a compressed tar archive. Click the ftp link for the source files and then save them in the /usr/local/src directory in your Fedora Core system (be sure to log in as root; otherwise you cannot save in the /usr/local/src directory).

After downloading the compressed tar file, examine the contents with the following tar command:

```
tar ztf xmms*.gz | more
```

You see a listing similar to the following:

```
xmms-1.2.10/
xmms-1.2.10/intl/
xmms-1.2.10/intl/ChangeLog
xmms-1.2.10/intl/Makefile.in
xmms-1.2.10/intl/config.charset
xmms-1.2.10/intl/locale.alias
xmms-1.2.10/intl/ref-add.sin
xmms-1.2.10/intl/ref-del.sin
xmms-1.2.10/intl/gmo.h
xmms-1.2.10/intl/gettextP.h
xmms-1.2.10/intl/hash-string.h
xmms-1.2.10/intl/loadinfo.h
... rest of the output not shown ...
```

The output of this tar command shows you what's in the archive and gives you an idea of the directories that are created after you unpack the archive. In this case, a directory named xmms-1.2.10 is created in the current directory, which, in my case, is /usr/local/src. From the listing, you also learn the programming language used to write the package. If you see .c and .h files, the source files are in the C programming language used to write many open-source software packages.

To extract the contents of the compressed tar archive, type the following tar command:

```
tar zxvf xmms*.gz
```

You again see the long list of files as they extract from the archive and copy to the appropriate directories on your hard drive.

Now you're ready to build the software.

## Building the software from source files

After you unpack the compressed `tar` archive, all source files are in a directory whose name is usually that of the software package with a version-number suffix. For example, the XMMS version 1.2.10 source files extract to the `xmms-1.2.10` directory. To start building the software, change directories with the following command:

```
cd xmms*
```

You don't have to type the entire name — the shell can expand the directory name and change to the `xmms-1.2.10` directory.

Nearly all software packages come with some sort of `README` or `INSTALL` file — a text file that tells you how to build and install the package. XMMS is no exception; it comes with a `README` file you can peruse by typing **more README**. An `INSTALL` file contains instructions for building and installing XMMS.

Most open-source software packages, including XMMS, also come with a file named `COPYING`. This file contains the full text of the *GNU General Public License* (GPL), which spells out the conditions under which you can use and redistribute the software. If you're not familiar with the GNU GPL, read this file and show the license to your legal counsel for a full interpretation and an assessment of applicability to your business.

To build the software package, follow the instructions in the `README` or `INSTALL` file. For the XMMS package, the `README` file lists some of the prerequisites (such as libraries) and tells you what commands to type to build and install the package. In the case of XMMS, the instructions tell you to use the following steps:

1.  **Type** ./configure **to run a shell script that checks your system configuration and creates a file named** Makefile **— a file the** make **command uses to build and install the package. (You can type** ./configure -help **to see a list of options that** configure **accepts.)**

2.  **Type** make **to build the software.**

    This step compiles the source files in all the subdirectories (compiling source code converts each source file into an object file — a file containing binary instructions that your PC's processor can understand).

3.  **Type** make install **to install the software.**

    This step copies libraries and executable binary files to appropriate directories on your system.

Although these steps are specific to XMMS, most other packages follow these steps — `configure`, `make`, and `install`. The `configure` shell script guesses system-dependent variables and creates a `Makefile` with commands needed to build and install the software.

Usually, you don't have to do anything but type the commands to build the software, but you must install the software-development tools on your system. You must install the Software Development package when you install Fedora Core. To build and run XMMS, you must also install the X Software Development package because it's an X application.

To begin building XMMS, type the following command to run the `configure` script (you must be in the `xmms-1.2.10` directory when you type this command):

```
./configure
```

The `configure` script starts running and prints lots of messages as it checks various features of your system — from the existence of the C compiler to various libraries needed to build XMMS. Finally, the `configure` script creates a `Makefile` you can use to build the software.

If the `configure` script displays error messages and fails, review the `INSTALL` and `README` files to find any clues to solving the problem. You may be able to circumvent it by providing some information to the `configure` script through command-line arguments.

After the `configure` script finishes, build the software by typing **make**. This command runs the GNU `make` utility, which reads the `Makefile` and starts compiling the source files according to information specified in the `Makefile`. The `make` command goes through all the source directories, compiles the source files, and creates the executable files and libraries needed to run XMMS. You see a lot of messages scroll by as each file is compiled. These messages show the commands used to compile and link the files.

The `make` command can take 10 to 15 minutes to complete. After `make` is done, you can install the XMMS software with the following command:

```
make install
```

This command also runs GNU `make`, but the `install` argument instructs GNU `make` to perform a specific set of commands from the `Makefile`. These instructions essentially go through all the subdirectories and copy various files to their final locations. For example, the binary executable files `xmms`, `gnomexmms`, `wmxmms`, and `xmms-config` copy to the `/usr/bin directory`.

Now that you have installed XMMS, try running it from the GNOME or KDE desktop by typing **xmms** in a terminal window or by choosing Main Menu➪ Sound & Video➪Audio Player. XMMS already comes with Fedora Core, but now you get the new version of XMMS (the difference is that the newly-built version can play MP3 files without any add-ons). From the XMMS window, press the L key to get the Load File dialog box and select an MP3 file to play. Your PC must have a sound card, and the sound card must be configured correctly for XMMS to work. Figure 4-1 shows a typical view of XMMS playing an MP3 music clip.

**Figure 4-1:** You can play MP3 music with the version of XMMS you built from source files.

Here's an overview of the steps you follow to download, unpack, build, and install a typical software package:

*1.* Use a Web browser to download the source code, usually in the form of a `.tar.gz` file, from the anonymous FTP site or Web site.

*2.* Unpack the file with a `tar zxvf filename` command.

*3.* Change the directory to the new subdirectory where the software is unpacked, with a command such as `cd software_dir`.

*4.* Read any `README` or `INSTALL` files to get a handle on any specific instructions you must follow to build and install the software.

*5.* The details of building the software may differ slightly from one software package to another, but typically you type the following commands to build and install the software:

```
./configure
make
make install
```

*6.* Read any other documentation that comes with the software to learn how to use the software and whether you must configure the software further before using it.

## Installing SRPMS

If you have the source CDs for Fedora Core (you can download the source CD images from one of the sites listed at fedora.redhat.com/download/mirrors.html), you can install the source files and build various applications directly from the source files. Red Hat provides the source-code files in RPMs, just as with the executable binary files, and these source RPM files are generally known as SRPMS (for *source RPMs*).

To install a specific source RPM and build the application, follow these steps:

1. **Mount the DVD-ROM by typing** mount /mnt/cdrom **or waiting for the GNOME desktop to mount the DVD.**

2. **Typically source RPMs are in the SRPMS directory. Change to that directory by typing the following command:**

   ```
   cd /mnt/cdrom/SRPMS
   ```

3. **Install the source RPM file by using the** rpm -i **command. For example, to install the Web server (**httpd**) source, type**

   ```
   rpm -ivh httpd*.src.rpm
   ```

   The files install in the /usr/src/redhat/SOURCES directory. A spec file with a .spec extension is placed in the /usr/src/redhat/SPECS directory. The *spec file* describes the software and also contains information used to build and install the software.

4. **Use the** rpmbuild **command with the spec file to build the software. You perform different tasks from unpacking the source files to building and installing the binaries by using different options with the** rpmbuild **command. For example, to process the entire spec file, type:**

   ```
   rpmbuild -ba packagename.spec
   ```

   Here *packagename* is the name of the SRPM. This command typically builds the software and installs the binary files.

# Updating Fedora Core Applications with Up2date

Fedora Core comes with Up2date — a graphical Update Agent that can download any new RPM files your system requires and install those files for you. I briefly provide an overview of how to update your system by using the Up2date. Up2date is also known as the Red Hat Update Agent because Red Hat developed it for its Red Hat Network through which Red Hat provides services to its commercial customers.

To update software packages using Up2date, follow these steps:

1. **Log in as** `root`**, and choose Main Menu⇨System Tools⇨ Red Hat Network. You can also type** up2date **in a terminal window.**

   The Red Hat Update Agent starts, and, if you're using Up2date for the first time, a dialog box prompts you to install a public key in your GPG key ring. *(GPG refers to GNU Privacy Guard or GnuPG, a program for encrypting, decrypting, and signing e-mail and other data using the OpenPGP Internet standard.)* That public GPG key verifies that the package developer has securely signed the package that Up2date has downloaded. If prompted to do so, click Yes to install the public key.

2. **Up2date displays a window with a welcome message. Click the Forward button to proceed.**

3. **Up2date displays a list of what it calls channels — repositories from where the agent downloads package headers. Click Forward to continue.**

   By default, the Update Agent uses a channel that works with Yum — a command-line package updater/installer that I describe in the next section. The channels are identified in the text configuration file `/etc/ sysconfig/rhn/sources`. Besides Yum, the Up2date can also access repositories meant for Apt — another package updater.

   After you click Forward, Up2date figures out what needs to be updated and retrieves a list of all headers from the specified channel.

4. **After Up2date downloads the headers, it displays a list of packages. You can then scroll through the list and pick the packages you want to update; click the box to the left of a package's name to select it. Click Forward to continue.**

   Up2date then checks for any package dependencies and begins down-loading the packages. Progress bars show the status of the download.

5. **After the download finishes, click the Forward button to proceed with the installation.**

6. **Up2date displays progress bars as it installs each package update. Click the Forward button when the installation is complete.**

   Up2date displays a message about the package(s) it installs successfully.

7. **Click the Finish button to exit Up2date.**

## Using Yellow dog Updater, Modified (Yum)

Yellow dog Updater, Modified (Yum) is a command-line utility for updating as well as installing and removing RPM packages. Yum downloads RPM package headers from a specified Web site and then uses the `rpm` utility to figure out any interdependencies among packages and what needs to be installed on your system. Then it downloads and uses `rpm` to install the necessary packages. Yum downloads just the headers to do its job and the headers are much smaller in size than the complete RPM packages. Yum is much faster than the alternative where you manually download the complete RPM packages using the `rpm` command.

Typically, you keep your system up to date with the graphical Update Agent because it's easy to use. However, knowing how to run Yum from a command-line is good, just in case you have problems with the Update Agent.

You can read more about Yum and keep up with Yum news by visiting the Yum Web page at `linux.duke.edu/projects/yum/`.

The command-line for Yum has the following syntax:

```
yum [options] command [packagenames]
```

where *options* is a list of Yum options, *command* specifies what you want Yum to do, and *packagenames* are the names of a packages on which Yum performs that action. You must provide the *command*, but the *options* and *packagenames* are optional. That's why I show them in square brackets in the syntax. Table 4-2 summarizes the Yum commands and Table 4-3 lists some common Yum options.

| Table 4-2 | Yum Commands |
|---|---|
| *Command* | *What Yum Does for This Command* |
| `check-update` | Checks for available updates for your system. |
| `clean` | Cleans up the cache directory. |
| `info` | Displays summary information about the specified packages. |
| `install` | Installs latest versions of specified packages, making sure that all dependencies are satisfied. |
| `list` | Lists information about available packages. |
| `provides` | Provides information on which package provides a file. |
| `remove` | Removes specified packages as well as any packages that depend on the packages being removed. |
| `search` | Finds packages whose header contains what you specify as the package name. |
| `update` | Updates specified packages, making sure that all dependencies are satisfied. |

| Table 4-3 | Some Common Yum Options |
| --- | --- |
| *Option* | *Causes Yum to Do the Following* |
| `--download-only` | Downloads the packages, but does not install them. |
| `--exclude=`*pkgname* | Excludes the specified package. (You can use this option more than once on the command line.) |
| `--help` | Displays a help message and quits. |
| `--installroot=`*path* | Uses the specified path name as the directory under which all packages are installed. |
| `-y` | Assumes that your answer to any question is yes. |

If you simply want Yum to update your system, just type the following (you have to be logged in as `root`):

```
yum update
```

Yum consults its configuration file, `/etc/yum.conf`, and does everything needed to update the packages installed on your system.

You can specify package names to update only some packages. For example, to update the kernel and xorg-x11 packages, use the following Yum command:

```
yum update kernel* xorg-x11*
```

This command updates all packages whose names begin with `kernel` and `xorg-x11`.

You may use the options to further instruct Yum what to do. For example, if you want to download the updated packages, but not install them, type

```
yum --download-only update
```

Another typical option is `--exclude`, which enables you to exclude one or more packages from the update process. Suppose you want to update everything except the GNOME packages (whose names begin with `gnome`) and the `rhythmbox` package. Then you type the following Yum command:

```
yum --exclude=gnome* --exclude=rhythmbox update
```

# Chapter 5: Managing Devices and Printers

## In This Chapter

✔ **Understanding Linux devices**

✔ **Managing loadable driver modules**

✔ **Managing USB devices**

✔ **Managing print queues**

*E*verything you use to work with your computer is a device. The keyboard and mouse you use to type and click with, the hard drive where you store everything, and the printer where you get your hard copies — these are all devices. And guess what? You have to manage them, but don't worry: It's not as hard as it sounds. All you have to do is load the device driver and (perhaps) configure the device a bit. This managing is easier to do if you understand device drivers a bit and get some practice using the tools Fedora Core includes to help you manage devices. In this chapter, I provide a brief overview of device drivers and explain how to manage driver modules. Because printers are a common type of device you have to manage, I also show you how to manage print queues.

## Understanding Linux Devices

Linux treats all devices as files and uses a device just as it uses a file — opens it, writes data to it, reads data from it, and closes it when done. This ability to treat every device as a file comes through the use of device drivers. A *device driver* is a special program that controls a particular type of hardware. When the kernel writes data to the device, the device driver does whatever is appropriate for that device. For example, when the kernel writes data to the floppy drive, the floppy device driver puts that data onto the physical medium of the floppy disk. On the other hand, if the kernel writes data to the parallel port device, the parallel-port driver sends the data to the printer connected to the parallel port.

Thus the device driver isolates the device-specific code from the rest of the kernel and makes a device look like a file. Any application can access a device by opening the file specific to that device. Figure 5-1 illustrates this concept of a Linux device driver.

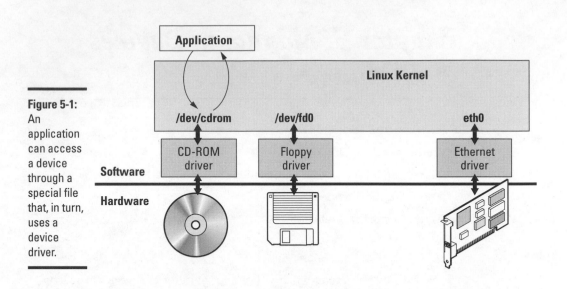

## Device files

As Figure 5-1 shows, applications can access a device as if it were a file. These files are special files called *device files*, and they appear in the /dev directory in the Linux file system.

If you use the ls command to look at the list of files in the /dev directory, you see several thousand files. These files do not mean that your system has several thousand devices. The /dev directory has files for all possible types of devices — that's why the number of device files is so large.

So how does the kernel know which device driver to use when an application opens a specific device file? The answer is in two numbers called the *major* and *minor device numbers*. Each device file is mapped to a specific device driver through these numbers.

To see an example of the major and minor device numbers, type the following command in a terminal window:

```
ls -l /dev/hda
```

You see a line of output similar to the following:

```
brw-rw----  1 root   disk   3,  0 Jul 23 14:50 /dev/hda
```

In this line, the major and minor device numbers appear just before the date. In this case, the major device number is 3 and the minor device number is 0. The kernel selects the device driver for this device file by using the major device number.

You don't really have to know much about the device files and the device numbers, except to be aware of their existence.

In case you are curious, all the major and minor numbers for devices are assigned according to device type. The Linux Assigned Names And Numbers Authority (LANANA) assigns these numbers. You can see the current device list at `www.lanana.org/docs/device-list/devices.txt`.

**Book VI**
**Chapter 5**

**Managing Devices and Printers**

### Block devices

The first letter in the listing of a device file also provides an important clue. For the `/dev/hda` device, the first letter is a `b`, which indicates that `/dev/hda` is a *block device* — one that can accept or provide data in chunks (typically 512 bytes or 1KB). By the way, `/dev/hda` refers to the first IDE hard drive on your system (the C drive in Windows). Hard drives, floppy drives, and CD-ROM drives are all examples of block devices.

### Character devices

If the first letter in the listing of a device file is a `c`, the device is a *character device* — one that can receive and send data one character (one byte) at a time. For example, the serial port and parallel ports are character devices. To see the specific listing of a character device, type the following command in a terminal window:

```
ls -l /dev/ttyS0
```

The listing of this device is similar to the following:

```
crw-rw----   1 root    uucp    4, 64 Jul 23 14:50 /dev/ttyS0
```

Notice that the very first letter is a `c` because `/dev/ttyS0` — the first serial port — is a character device.

### Network devices

*Network devices* that enable your system to interact with a network — for example, Ethernet and dial-up *point-to-point protocol* (PPP) connections — are somewhat special because they need no file to correspond to the device. Instead, the kernel uses a special name for the device. For example, the Ethernet devices are named `eth0` for the first Ethernet card, `eth1` for the second one, and so on. PPP connections are named `ppp0`, `ppp1`, and so on.

Because network devices aren't mapped to device files, no files corresponding to these devices are in the `/dev` directory.

### Persistent device naming with udev

Linux kernel 2.6 introduces a new approach for handling devices, based on the following features:

✦ **sysfs:** Kernel 2.6 provides the sysfs file system that is mounted on the /sys directory of the file system. The sysfs file system shows all the devices in the system as well as lots of information about each device. The information includes the location of the device on the bus, attributes such as name and serial number, and the major and minor numbers of the device.

✦ /sbin/hotplug: This program is called whenever a device is added or removed. It can then do whatever is necessary to handle the device.

✦ /sbin/udev: This program takes care of dynamically named devices based on device characteristics such as serial number, device number on a bus, or a user-assigned name based on a set of rules that are set through the text file /etc/udev/udev.rules.

Currently, the 2.6 kernel includes both udev as well as the older static /dev device directory. The udev program's configuration file is /etc/udev/udev.conf. Based on settings in that configuration file, udev creates device nodes automatically in the /udev directory. If you edit the udev_root="/udev/" line in /etc/udev/udev.conf, only then udev can start to manage the device nodes in the /dev directory. For now, just be aware of udev, but in some future kernel release, it could become the only way to dynamically manage devices in Linux.

## Managing Loadable Driver Modules

To use any device, the Linux kernel must contain the driver. If the driver code is linked into the kernel as a *monolithic* program (a program that's in the form of a single large file), adding a new driver means rebuilding the kernel with the new driver code. Rebuilding the kernel means you have to reboot the PC with the new kernel before you can use the new device driver. Luckily, the Linux kernel uses a modular design that does away with rebooting hassles. Linux device drivers can be created in the form of modules that the kernel can load and unload without having to restart the PC.

Driver modules are one type of a broader category of software modules called Loadable Kernel Modules. Other types of kernel modules include code that can support new types of file systems, modules for network protocols, and modules that interpret different formats of executable files.

## Loading and unloading modules

You can manage the loadable device driver modules by using a set of commands. You have to log in as `root` to use some of these commands. In Table 5-1, I summarize a few of the commonly used module commands.

| Table 5-1 | Commands to Manage Kernel Modules |
|-----------|-----------------------------------|
| *This Command* | *Does the Following* |
| insmod | Inserts a module into the kernel |
| rmmod | Removes a module from the kernel |
| depmod | Determines interdependencies between modules |
| ksyms | Displays a list of symbols along with the name of the module that defined the symbol |
| lsmod | Lists all currently loaded modules |
| modinfo | Displays information about a kernel module |
| modprobe | Inserts or removes a module or a set of modules intelligently (for example, if module A requires B, then modprobe automatically loads B when asked to load A) |

**Book VI
Chapter 5**

**Managing Devices
and Printers**

If you have to use any of these commands, log in as `root` or type **su** - in a terminal window to become `root`.

To see what modules are currently loaded, type

```
lsmod
```

You see a list of modules. For example, here is a list on one of my laptops running Fedora Core:

```
Module              Size   Used by
hid                 50580  0
ntfs                78924  1
ide_cd              32644  0
snd_mixer_oss       14336  1
snd_intel8x0        30120  1
snd_ac97_codec      53768  1 snd_intel8x0
snd_pcm             84744  1 snd_intel8x0
snd_timer           25604  1 snd_pcm
gameport             4352  1 snd_intel8x0
snd_page_alloc       9092  2 snd_intel8x0,snd_pcm
snd_mpu401_uart      7680  1 snd_intel8x0
snd_rawmidi         21792  1 snd_mpu401_uart
snd_seq_device       6792  1 snd_rawmidi
snd                 44516  8
    snd_mixer_oss,snd_intel8x0,snd_ac97_codec,snd_pcm,snd_time
    r,snd_mpu401_uart,snd_rawmidi,snd_seq_device
```

```
soundcore              8032   2 snd
nls_utf8               2048   1
cifs                 145280   2
ipv6                 211200  10
lp                     9452   0
autofs                17536   0
orinoco_cs             7816   1
orinoco               45196   1 orinoco_cs
hermes                 7040   2 orinoco_cs,orinoco
ds                    10628   3 orinoco_cs
yenta_socket          12928   1
pcmcia_core           52964   3 orinoco_cs,ds,yenta_socket
ipt_REJECT             5248   1
ipt_state              1920   6
ip_conntrack          25008   1 ipt_state
iptable_filter         2560   1
ip_tables             13952   3
       ipt_REJECT,ipt_state,iptable_filter
3c59x                 33192   0
ohci1394              31896   0
ieee1394             286776   1 ohci1394
sd_mod                13216   0
parport_pc            20928   1
parport               36808   2 lp,parport_pc
microcode              5792   0
floppy                54192   0
sg                    28448   0
sr_mod                13988   0
cdrom                 29852   2 ide_cd,sr_mod
usb_storage           59360   0
scsi_mod             102332   4 sd_mod,sg,sr_mod,usb_storage
uhci_hcd              35740   0
usbcore               92724   5 hid,usb_storage,uhci_hcd
button                 5016   0
battery                7436   0
asus_acpi              8984   0
ac                     3980   0
ext3                  94760   2
jbd                   65432   1 ext3
```

As you may expect, the list of modules depends on the types of devices installed on your system.

The first column lists the names of the modules in the last-to-first order. Thus, the first module in the list is the last one to be loaded. The Size column shows the number of bytes that the module occupies in your PC's memory. The remaining columns show other information about each module, such as how many applications are currently using the module and the names of the modules that require the module.

The list displayed by lsmod includes all types of Linux kernel modules, not just device drivers. For example, the last two modules — jbd and ext3 — are all part of the EXT3 file system (the latest file system for Linux).

Besides lsmod, one commonly used module command is modprobe. Use modprobe whenever you need to manually load or remove one or more modules. The best thing about modprobe is that you don't need to worry if a module requires other modules to work. The modprobe command automatically loads any other module needed by a module. On my system, for example, I can manually load the sound driver with the command

```
modprobe sound-slot-0
```

This command causes modprobe to load everything needed to make sound work.

You can use modprobe with the -r option to remove modules. For example, to remove the sound modules, I use the following command:

```
modprobe -r sound-slot-0
```

This command gets rid of all the modules that the modprobe sound-slot-0 command had loaded.

## Using the /etc/modprobe.conf file

How does the modprobe command know that it needs to load the snd-intel8x0 driver module when I use a module name sound-slot-0? The answer is in the /etc/modprobe.conf configuration file. That file contains a line that tells modprobe what it loads when it sees the module name sound-slot-0.

To view the contents of /etc/modprobe.conf, type

```
cat /etc/modprobe.conf
```

On one of my Fedora Core PCs, the file contains the following lines:

```
alias eth0 3c59x
alias usb-controller uhci-hcd
alias sound-slot-0 snd-intel8x0
```

Each line that begins with the keyword alias defines a standard name for an actual driver module. For example, the first line defines 3c59x as the actual driver name for the alias eth0, which stands for the first Ethernet card. Similarly, the third line defines snd-intel8x0 as the module to load when I use the name sound-slot-0.

The `modprobe` command consults the `/etc/modprobe.conf` file to convert an alias to the real name of a driver module as well as for other tasks, such as obtaining parameters for driver modules. For example, you can insert lines that begin with the `options` keyword to provide values of parameters that a driver may need.

For example, to set the debug level parameter for the Ethernet driver to 5 (this parameter generates lots of information in `/var/log/messages`), I add the following line to the `/etc/modprobe.conf` file:

```
options 3c59x debug=5
```

This line specifies 5 as the value of the parameter named `debug` in the `3c59x` module.

If you want to know the names of the parameters that a module accepts, use the `modinfo` command. For example, to view information about the `3c59x` driver module, I type

```
modinfo 3c59x | more
```

From the resulting output, I can tell that `debug` is the name of the parameter for setting the debug level.

Unfortunately, the information shown by the `modinfo` command can be somewhat cryptic. The only saving grace is that you may not have to do much more than use a graphical utility to configure the device, and the utility takes care of adding whatever is needed to configuration files, such as `/etc/modprobe.conf`.

# Managing USB Devices

Fedora Core comes with built-in support for the Universal Serial Bus (USB) — a serial bus that's gradually replacing the functionality of the PC's serial and parallel ports, as well as that of the keyboard and mouse ports. Nowadays, many PC peripherals — such as mouse, keyboard, printer, CD burner, scanner, modem, digital camera, memory card, and so on — are designed to connect to the PC through a USB port.

USB version 1.1 supports data-transfer rates as high as 12 Mbps — 12 million bits per second or 1.5MB per second — compared with 115 Kbps or the 0.115 Mbps transfer rate of a standard serial port. You can daisy chain up to 127 devices on a single USB bus. The bus also provides power to the devices, and you can attach or remove devices while the PC is running — a capability commonly referred to as *hotplug* or *hot swap*. USB version 2.0 (or USB 2.0 or

USB2, for short) ups the ante by raising the data transfer rates to a whopping 480 Mbps, slightly faster than the competing IEEE 1394 (FireWire) bus. Nowadays many devices, such as CD burners and scanners, come with the high-speed USB2 interface. If your PC has older USB 1.1 ports, the USB2 devices can still work, albeit at lower data-transfer rates. Fedora Core supports both USB 1.1 and USB2 interfaces.

Using USB devices in Fedora Core is easy. You can hotplug a device into a USB port, and the Linux kernel can detect and load the appropriate device drivers so applications can make use of the device. To be more precise, the `kudzu` hardware detection utility takes care of the chores necessary to make the USB device accessible to applications. For USB mass storage devices, such as CD drives or hard drivers, `kudzu` can also mount the device on the Linux file system. For examples of using USB mass-storage devices, see Book II, Chapter 4 where I discuss how Linux detects a USB CD burner and how to access the photos in a digital camera through the USB interface.

**Book VI
Chapter 5**

To use a USB printer in Fedora Core, simply connect the printer to the USB port, power it up, and then follow the steps in Book I, Chapter 3 to configure a locally connected queue for the printer. The printer shows up with a device name such as `/dev/usb/lp0` (for the USB printer detected by `kudzu`), `/dev/usb/lp1` (for the second USB printer), and so on.

Using USB scanners in Fedora Core is as simple as using USB printers. Just plug the scanner into the USB port, power it up, and you can access it by using `xsane` — a graphical front end for scanners that you can start by choosing Main Menu➪Graphics➪Scanning. Of course, `xsane` must support the USB scanner make and model. To quickly check whether `kudzu` has detected your USB scanner, log in as `root` and type **sane-find-scanner** in a terminal window.

The kernel can also automatically mount a USB mass storage device for easy access. Consider, for example, the USB keychain storage device. Just as the name says, these are small memory cards, capable of storing anywhere from 32MB to 1GB. You can carry them around on a keychain — in effect, taking all your data with you wherever you go. Here's how you can use a USB keychain storage device that's already formatted for use in Microsoft Windows:

**1. Plug the keychain storage device to the PC's USB port.**

Sometimes the device plugs directly into the port, but for some devices you have to attach the keychain device to a USB cable and then plug the cable into the USB port.

Some USB keychain devices have a small switch on the side that controls whether the keychain is write-protected. If you plan to write to the device, first make sure it's not write-protected or locked.

2. **Kudzu detects the USB storage device and adds an entry in** `/etc/fstab` **that associates the USB device with the mount point** `/mnt/flash`. **Mount the device with the command:**

```
mount /mnt/flash
```

3. **To check that the USB device is mounted, type the following command and look for a line in the output that shows** `/mnt/flash`:

```
df
```

For example, the following line of output is for a 32MB USB keychain device:

```
/dev/sda1  31520    64    31456   1% /mnt/flash
```

If you don't have any other USB device plugged in, the device name is `/dev/sda1` (USB storage devices appear as SCSI devices). The next USB storage devices gets the `/dev/sda2` device name and so on.

Now you can access the files on the keychain at the `/mnt/flash` directory. To save a file to the USB keychain storage device, use a command of the following form:

```
cp filename /mnt/flash
```

where `filename` is the name of the file you want to save.

When you're done using the device, unmount the USB keychain with this command:

```
umount /dev/sda1
```

That's it!

# Managing Print Queues in Fedora Core

PCs typically come with one parallel port, typically used to connect the printer to the PC. You can set up a printer fairly easily by using Fedora Core's graphical printer-configuration utility, but you also have to know how to manage the print queue.

## Spooling and print jobs

*Spooling* refers to the capability to print in the background. When you print from a word processor in Windows, for example, the output first goes to a file on the disk. Then, while you continue working with the word processor, a background process sends that output to the printer. The Fedora Core printing environment also supports spooling.

*Print job* refers to what you print with a single print command. The printing environment queues print jobs by storing them in the spool directory. A background process periodically sends the print jobs from the spool directory to the printer.

Fedora Core uses the Common UNIX Printing System (CUPS) for its printing environment. CUPS is a printing system based on the Internet Printing Protocol (IPP) — a protocol for distributed printing using Internet technologies. IPP assumes a client/server model with the client being an application and the server a "Printer" — an abstraction of an output device or a printing service provider. IPP supports a distributed printing environment with the clients and Printer servers communicating over the Internet. You could use an IPP client to print on a printer anywhere on the Internet. The client and Printer exchange data using the HTTP 1.1 protocol — the same protocol that Web servers use. The client application uses IPP to inquire about capabilities of a printer, submit print jobs, and inquire about — or cancel — print jobs.

If you have set up a CUPS print queue for a printer connected to your Fedora Core system (following the directions in Book I, Chapter 3), you can print on that printer from Windows XP and 2000 systems on your local-area network. Windows 2000 and XP have built-in support for IPP — the protocol used by CUPS. To print on a CUPS print queue from a Windows XP system, add a network printer on the XP. In the Add Printer Wizard, select Connect to a Printer on the Internet or on a Home or Office Network and then enter the URL for the CUPS print queue. For example, for a CUPS print queue named `HPLaserjetRoom210` on a Fedora Core host whose IP address is 192.168.0.8, I enter the following URL for the print queue:

```
http://192.168.0.8:631/printers/HPLaserjetRoom210
```

As a Fedora Core user, you use a client program — `lp` or `lpr` — to send the files to print to a print scheduler called `cupsd` over a TCP/IP network connection. The `cupsd` scheduler then queues the files, processes them according to their file extensions (such as `.txt` or `.ps`), and sends them to the printer one by one. Thanks to various configuration files, the `cupsd` scheduler knows what to do to make sure that the file — be it a text file or an image file — gets printed properly.

Although you typically have only one printer connected to your PC, one advantage of the CUPS printing system is the capability to print on a printer connected to another system on a network. Printing to a remote printer is handled in the same fashion as printing to a local printer; the local `lp` or `lpr` program simply sends the files to the remote system's `cupsd` scheduler.

## Printing with the lp command

You can print a file by using the `lp` or `lpr` command. For example, to print the file `/etc/inittab`, type the following in a terminal window:

```
lp /etc/inittab
```

The `lp` command queues a print job by sending the file and appropriate control information to the `cupsd` print scheduler. By default, the `cupsd` print scheduler accepts files to be printed, holds them in the print queue, and forwards them to the default printer (or to another system if the default printer is attached to a remote system on the network). The default printer is identified by the `<DefaultPrinter queuename>` entry in the CUPS configuration file `/etc/cups/cupsd.conf` (where *queuename* is the name of the print queue).

You can embellish the simple `lp` command with some options. If you have many different print queues defined, you can specify the destination of the print job with the `-d` option. For example, to send a print job to the Hewlett-Packard LaserJet print queue named `HPLaserjetRoom210`, you type the following command (the print queue name appears in the `/etc/cups/printers.conf` file):

```
lp -d HPLaserjetRoom210 testprint.ps
```

## Checking the print queue using lpq

If you mistakenly print a large file and want to stop the print job before you waste too much paper, you can use the `lpq` command to look at the current print jobs and then cancel the large print job. Following is a typical listing of print jobs I get when I type **lpq** after submitting a file to the `HPLaserjetRoom210` print queue:

```
HPLaserjetRoom210 is ready and printing
Rank    Owner   Job    File(s)                    Total Size
active  root    2      testprint.ps               15360 bytes
```

The `lpq` command shows the job number (2) and the name of the file that I am printing (`testprint.ps`).

## Canceling the print job using cancel

To remove a job from the print queue, use the `cancel` command. For example, to remove print job 2, I type the following command:

```
cancel 2
```

You can get the same result with the following `lprm` command:

```
lprm 2
```

If you're in a hurry and want to cancel all print jobs you have submitted so far, use `cancel` with `-a` as the argument, as follows:

```
cancel -a
```

## Checking the printer status using lpstat

To see the status of print jobs, use the `lpstat` command. Here is a typical output from the `lpstat` command:

```
lpstat
HPLaserjetRoom210-2      root      15360   Wed 25 Feb 2004 04:25:48 PM EST
```

The first field of the output shows the name of the queue with a job number appended to it (that number identifies the print job). You need that job number to cancel the print job.

## Controlling the print queue

To see the names of printers connected to your system, use the `lpc status` command. On my system, the `lpc status` command shows the following:

```
lpc status
HPLaserjetRoom210:
        printer is on device 'parallel' speed -1
        queuing is enabled
        printing is enabled
        no entries
        daemon present
```

Notice that queuing and printing are both enabled for this printer. The last line tells you that the `cupsd` *daemon* (a server that runs all the time) is running and available to handle print jobs.

You can use the `accept` and `reject` commands to enable or disable queuing for a print queue. For example, to stop queuing further print jobs for the `HPLaserjetRoom210` printer, I type:

```
reject HPLaserjetRoom210
```

This command disables queuing jobs for this printer. If anyone tries to send a print job using the `lp` command, the user receives an error message like this:

```
lp: unable to print file: server-error-not-accepting-jobs
```

If you want to allow queuing of print jobs, but want to start or stop the printing, use the `enable` and `disable` commands. When you disable printing, users can submit print jobs, but nothing gets printed until you enable printing again. For example, here is the command I use to disable printing on the `HPLaserjetRoom210` printer:

```
disable HPLaserjetRoom210
```

If you're trying to print, but nothing seems to be coming out of the printer, check the printer status with the `lpc status` command and make sure that the `cupsd` scheduler is present and that both queuing and printing are enabled. To allow the queuing of print jobs, use the `accept` command. To start printing, use the `enable` command.

# Chapter 6: Upgrading and Customizing the Kernel

## In This Chapter

✔ Upgrading with a kernel RPM

✔ Configuring the kernel

✔ Building a new kernel and any modules

✔ Installing the modules

✔ Building and installing a new initial RAM disk file

✔ Installing the kernel and setting up GRUB

One reason Linux is so exciting is that many programmers are constantly improving it. Some programmers, for example, write drivers that add support for new hardware, such as a new sound card or a new networking card. All these innovations come to you in the form of new versions of the Linux kernel.

Although you don't have to upgrade or modify the Linux operating system — the kernel — every time a new version is available, sometimes you have to upgrade simply because the new version corrects some problems or supports your hardware better. On the other hand, if an earlier kernel version has everything you need, you don't have to rush out and upgrade.

Sometimes you may want to rebuild the kernel even when it has no fixes or enhancements. The Linux kernel on the companion DVD-ROM is generic and uses modules to support all types of hardware. You may want to build a new kernel that links in the drivers for only the devices installed on your system. In particular, if you have a SCSI hard drive, you may want to create a kernel that supports your SCSI adapter. Depending on your needs, you may also want to change some of the kernel-configuration options, such as creating a kernel that's specific for your processor (instead of a generic Intel 386 processor).

In this chapter, I explain how to upgrade a kernel using a kernel RPM as well as how to rebuild and install a new Linux kernel.

# Upgrading with a Kernel RPM

Fedora Core software updates, including new versions of kernels, come in the form of RPM files. To download and install the kernel RPMs, follow these steps:

1. **Use a Web server to download the kernel RPM files from a Fedora Core download site (I explain the details in the next section).**

   If you want to rebuild the kernel, you have to download the `kernel-source` RPM corresponding to the new version of the kernel.

2. **Install the RPMs by using the `rpm -i` command.**

3. **Create a new, initial RAM disk by running the `/sbin/mkinitrd` command.**

4. **Reconfigure GRUB to boot the new kernel.**

5. **Try out the new kernel by rebooting the system.**

I further describe these steps in the next few sections.

## Downloading new kernel RPMs

Fedora Core software updates are distributed in the form of RPMs — packages — from one of the mirror sites listed at `fedora.redhat.com/download/mirrors.html`. The updates are organized in directories according to Fedora Core version numbers. For example, any updates for Fedora Core 1 for 32-bit Intel x86 systems reside in the `fedora/linux/core/updates/1/i386/` directory (for Fedora Core 2 updates, just replace the 1 with a 2 in that pathname). Use a Web browser such as Mozilla to visit a mirror site and download any kernel RPMs available at that site. Another way to get the new kernel RPM is through the normal update process using Up2date or Yum (see Chapter 4 of this minibook for more on how to use Up2date and Yum).

## Installing the kernel RPMs

To install the kernel and the modules, follow these steps:

1. **Log in as `root`.**

2. **Use the `cd` command to change the directory to where the RPM files (the ones you download from a Fedora Core download server) are located.**

3. **Type the following command to install the kernel RPM:**

   ```
   rpm -ivh kernel*.rpm
   ```

You have to install the `kernel-source` RPM only if you want to build a new kernel.

When you install a new kernel RPM, the installation process creates a new initial RAM disk image — a file that the kernel can copy into a block of memory and use as a memory-resident disk to load modules needed to access the hard disk. That file's name begins with `initrd` (`initrd` is shorthand for *initial RAM disk*) and has the kernel version number in the filename. The kernel RPM install also adds a description of the kernel to the GRUB configuration file — `/etc/grub.conf`. For example, here is a typical GRUB configuration file after I install a new kernel RPM:

```
title Fedora Core (2.6.3-2.1.240)
        root (hd0,2)
        kernel /vmlinuz-2.6.3-2.1.240 ro root=LABEL=/ rhgb
        initrd /initrd-2.6.3-2.1.240.img
title Fedora Core (2.6.3-2.1.238)
        root (hd0,2)
        kernel /vmlinuz-2.6.3-2.1.238 ro root=LABEL=/ rhgb
        initrd /initrd-2.6.3-2.1.238.img
```

Next time you reboot the system, these two kernels appear as choices in the GRUB boot screen. From that screen, you can select which kernel you want to boot.

## Trying out the new kernel

After installing the new kernel RPM, creating the initial RAM disk file, and reconfiguring GRUB, it's time to try the new kernel. To restart the system, log in as `root` and type the following command from the Linux prompt:

```
reboot
```

You may also reboot the system from the graphical login screen. Select Reboot from the Options menu in the login dialog box.

When the system reboots and you see the GRUB screen, press the arrow key to select the new kernel's name.

After Fedora Core starts, you see the usual graphical login screen. Log in as a user, open a terminal window, and type **uname -sr** to see the version number. The response shows that your system is running the new version of the kernel.

# Rebuilding the Kernel

*Rebuilding the kernel* refers to creating a new binary file for the core Linux operating system. This binary file is the one that runs when Fedora Core boots. You may wonder why you ever want to rebuild the kernel. Well, here are a few reasons:

✦ After you initially install Linux, you may want to create a new kernel that includes support for only the hardware installed on your system. In particular, if you have a SCSI adapter, you may want to create a kernel that links in the SCSI driver. The kernel on the companion DVD-ROM includes the SCSI driver as an external module that the kernel loads at startup.

✦ If you have a system with hardware for which only experimental support is available, you have to rebuild the kernel to include that support into the operating system.

✦ You may want to recompile the kernel and generate code that works well on your specific Pentium processor (instead of the generic 386 processor code that comes in the standard Fedora Core distribution).

To rebuild the Linux kernel, you need the kernel source files. The kernel source files are not normally installed. Use the following steps to install the kernel source files on your system:

1. **Log in as** `root` **and insert the Fedora Core DVD-ROM into the DVD drive.**

2. **If the DVD-ROM does not mount automatically, type the following command to mount the DVD-ROM:**

   ```
   mount /mnt/cdrom
   ```

   If you're using GNOME or KDE, the DVD-ROM automatically mounts, and you do not have to perform this step manually.

3. **Change the directory to the** `Fedora/RPMS` **directory on the DVD-ROM, and use the** `rpm` **command to install the kernel source files. Type the following commands:**

   ```
   cd /mnt/cdrom/Fedora/RPMS
   rpm -ivh kernel-source*
   ```

   After the `rpm` command finishes installing the kernel source package, the source files appear in the `/usr/src/linux-VERSION` directory, where VERSION is the version number of the kernel. Thus, for kernel version 2.6.3-2.1.240, the source files are in the `/usr/src/linux-2.6.3-2.1.240` directory.

Building the kernel involves the following phases:

✦ Configuring the kernel

✦ Building the kernel

✦ Building and installing the modules

✦ Building a new file for the initial RAM disk

✦ Installing the kernel and setting up GRUB

I explain these phases in the next few sections, but first you need to know the difference between linking in a driver versus building a driver as a loadable module.

## Creating a monolithic versus a modular kernel

You have two options for the device drivers needed to support various hardware devices in Linux:

✦ **Link in support:** You can link the drivers for all hardware on your system into the kernel. The size of the kernel grows as device-driver code incorporates into the kernel. A kernel that links in all necessary code is called a *monolithic kernel* because it's one big file.

✦ **Use modules:** You can create the device drivers in the form of loadable kernel modules. A *module* is a block of code the kernel can load after it starts running. A typical use of modules is to add support for a device without having to rebuild the kernel for each new device. Modules don't have to be device drivers; they can also add new functionality to the kernel. A kernel that uses modules is called a *modular kernel*.

You don't have to create a fully monolithic or fully modular kernel. In fact, linking some support directly into the kernel but building infrequently used device drivers in the form of modules is common practice. For a Fedora Core distribution, including a mostly modular kernel makes sense, along with a large number of modules that can support many different types of hardware. Then the Fedora Core installer configures the system to load only modules needed to support the hardware installed in a user's system.

When you create a custom kernel for your hardware configuration, you may want to link all required device drivers into the kernel. You can still keep the size of such a monolithic kernel under control because you link in device drivers only for the exact set of hardware installed on your system.

## Configuring the kernel

The first phase in rebuilding a kernel is to configure it. To configure the kernel, log in as `root`. Then change the kernel source directory by using the `cd` command as follows:

```
cd /usr/src/linux*
```

To configure the kernel, you have to indicate which features and device drivers you want to include in your Linux kernel. In essence, you build your very own version of the Linux kernel with just the features you want.

Fedora Core provides several ways for you to configure the kernel:

✦ Type **make menuconfig** to enter the kernel-configuration parameters through a text-based interface similar to the one the Fedora Core installation program uses.

✦ Type **make xconfig** to use an X Window System-based configuration program to configure the kernel. You have to run X to use this configuration program with a graphical interface.

✦ Type **make config** to use a shell script that prompts you for each configuration option one by one. You can use this configuration program from the Linux command prompt. When you use this option, you undergo a long question-and-answer process to specify the configuration parameters. For each question, respond with a *y* to link support into the kernel, *m* to build a module, and *n* to skip the support for that specific device.

The `make menuconfig`, `make xconfig`, and `make config` commands achieve the same end result — each stores your choices in a text file named `.config` located in the `/usr/src/linux*` directory. Because the filename starts with a period, you don't see it when you use the `ls` command alone to list the directory. Instead, type **ls -a** to see the `.config` file in the directory listing.

The kernel-configuration step merely captures your choices in the `.config` file. (In fact, the `.config` file does not exist until you configure the kernel once.) The kernel file does not change until you compile the kernel with the `make` command. That means you can go through the kernel-configuration option as many times as you want. If you want to start over with default settings, type the following command before you start configuring the kernel:

```
make mrproper
```

For an overview of the kernel configuration build steps that you can perform with the `make` command, type the following in a terminal window (after you type **cd /usr/src/linux*** to change the current directory to the correct location):

```
make help | more
```

## *Running the kernel configuration tool*

You can use any of the configuration tools — make xconfig, make menu-config, or make config — to configure the kernel, but the easiest way is to log in as root and type the following command in a terminal window:

make xconfig

This command builds an X Window System-based configuration tool and runs it. The initial graphical kernel configuration window displays a window split vertically into two panels. The left hand panel displays a tree organization of configuration options organized by category, as shown in Figure 6-1. The right panel is further divided horizontally, with the upper part showing the detailed options for the item selected on the left panel. The lower right panel shows a help message for the currently selected option (see Figure 6-1).

**Book VI
Chapter 6**

**Upgrading and
Customizing
the Kernel**

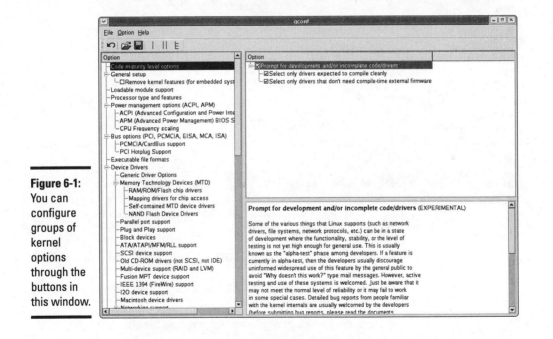

**Figure 6-1:**
You can
configure
groups of
kernel
options
through the
buttons in
this window.

Through the six buttons on the toolbar, you can perform tasks such as save the configurations and change the layout of the panes through which you specify the options.

To pick a category of configuration options, click the relevant category in the left hand pane. For example, if you click the Processor Type and Features option in the left pane, the configuration program displays in the upper-right pane all the options for that category. You can then set specific options by clicking each item in the upper-right pane. For example, Figure 6-2 shows the options for the processor type (in this case, the selection shows a Pentium Pro with PC-compatible subarchitecture).

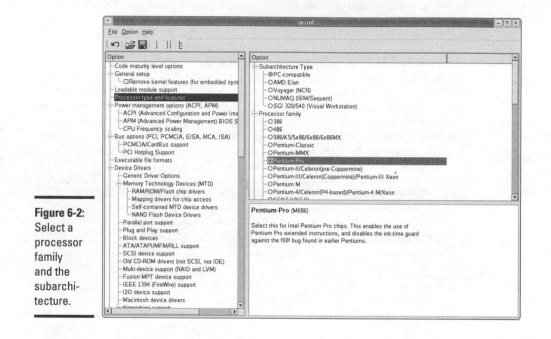

**Figure 6-2:** Select a processor family and the subarchitecture.

Notice the Help message in the lower-right pane. Whenever you have a question about a configuration option, click the item in the upper-right pane. The lower-right pane displays help information for that option. Figure 6-2 shows the result of clicking the Pentium-Pro option.

You can follow these steps to specify options for each category of options:

*1.* **In the left pane of the main window (refer to Figure 6-1), click the option category.**

The configuration program displays the options for that category in the upper-right pane (refer to Figure 6-2).

*2.* **Set the options you want.**

Click the box to the left of each option to toggle between three choices — unchecked means the option is not enabled, a check mark means the option is built into the kernel, and a dot means that the option is built as a loadable module. Clicking an option that asks for a yes-no answer toggles the box between a check mark and unchecked. If you need help on an option, click the option label (not the box) and a relevant help message appears in the lower-right pane (see Figure 6-2).

3. **After completing all the options, click the floppy disk icon on the toolbar or choose File⇨Save to save the configurations.**

Next I describe some of the important and interesting categories of options. The section headings match the text for the options, as shown in the left pane of the configuration window (refer to Figure 6-2), so you can easily locate a section that interests you.

A final word of caution before you start configuring the kernel options: Many kernel options depend on one another. For example, if the parallel port option isn't enabled, the configuration program hides all options related to parallel port devices. The best way to logically proceed through the configuration steps is to start with the topmost option category in the left pane — Code Maturity Level Options — and then continue down the list of option categories. That way, you always set the options in the correct order.

### Code maturity level options

The very first group of options enables you to indicate if you want to use experimental device drivers or code. If you enable these options, you can try some experimental features, such as support for a PCI hotplug (available on machines that allow you to add or remove a PCI card while the machine is powered up and running).

### Loadable module support

This group of options asks you about support for loadable modules. You definitely want to include support for modules, so enable the Enable Loadable Module Support option. The rest of the options are about the following features: unloading modules, including version information in each module, and automatically loading required kernel modules. Enable module unloading and automatic loading of kernel modules. That way, parts of the kernel are built in the form of modules and the kernel automatically loads these modules when needed.

### Processor type and features

This set of options (refer to Figure 6-2) is for setting the subarchitecture type, the processor family, and support for specific processor-related features. The Subarchitecture Type options enable you to select from different types of fundamental system designs that make use of the Intel x86 processor family but that may differ fundamentally from the well-known

PC-compatible machines. Prior to version 2.6, the Linux kernel made an implicit assumption that the system's architecture was based on the old IBM PC-AT family. Starting with kernel version 2.6, you can build the kernel for other types of Intel x86-based architectures such as SGI Visual Workstation and multiprocessor systems with non-uniform memory access (NUMA). You probably can select the default PC-compatible subarchitecture, but the other options are available if you have to build the kernel for a different type of x86-based system.

The Processor Family options are for specifying your system's processor type. If you select 386, the compiled kernel can run on any other processor (such as a 486 or any type of Pentium). However, if you're creating a kernel specifically for your system's processor, select your processor type from the list that appears in the Processor Family options. You can also enable symmetric multiprocessing (SMP) support, but do so only if your system's motherboard has two or more processors. There are a host of other options, which you can leave in their default settings.

### Power management options

This set of options deals with managing the system's power and includes advanced configuration and power interface (ACPI), advanced power management (APM) BIOS support, and CPU frequency scaling. You can simply accept the default settings for these options. If you don't understand what an option means, click the option text to get help on that option.

### Bus options

These options ask you about supporting specific buses: PCI, ISA, EISA, MCA, and PCMCIA. The Industry Standard Architecture (ISA) bus was once the most widely used bus (until the PCI bus came along); this bus was used in the original IBM PC-AT. The Micro Channel Architecture (MCA) bus is IBM's proprietary bus, which first appeared in the PS/2 PCs. IBM designed this bus as a high-speed bus, but its proprietary nature kept it from being widely used in PCs. The Extended Industry Standard Architecture (EISA) bus came about as an alternative to the MCA bus, with performance comparable to that of the MCA. The EISA bus is not widely used because the EISA bus peripheral cards are more expensive than their ISA bus counterparts. The Peripheral Component Interconnect (PCI) bus is the latest high-performance bus; the current crop of PCs use the PCI bus, but also offer ISA bus slots so that you can continue to use ISA cards.

PCMCIA stands for Personal Computer Memory Card International Association, a nonprofit organization that standardized the interface for adding memory cards to laptop computers. Although originally conceived for memory cards, PCMCIA devices became popular for a wide variety of add-ons for laptops. The PCMCIA devices are called PC cards and the term CardBus refers to the electrical specification of PC cards.

Typically, you want to build in support for PCI and ISA and build modules for PCMCIA support. You can also add support for the PCI hotplug if your system supports adding or removing PCI cards while the system is powered up and running.

### Executable file formats

Turn on the support for Executable and Linkable Format (ELF), which is the standard format for executables and libraries in Linux. Prior to ELF, the format for executables was called a.out (based on the default name of the executable generated by the C compiler). In kernel version 2.6, you can build a module to support the old a.out format.

### Device drivers

This category of options provides support for file systems resident on memory technology devices, such as flash memory and random-access memory. These file systems are often used in embedded devices. This category includes a number of options for building kernel modules to support various memory devices. There is no harm in building the modules because they are not loaded if you don't have the appropriate memory device.

### Parallel port support

These options are important if you use any devices such as printers or parallel-port Zip drives connected to the parallel port of your PC. Select the Parallel Port Support and PC-Style Hardware options to show dots so the drivers are built as modules.

### Plug-and-Play support

These options ask if you want to enable Plug-and-Play (PnP) support in the kernel. If you enable PnP support, the kernel automatically configures PnP devices (just as Windows does). Enable these two options.

### Block devices

Block devices (such as disk drives) transfer data in chunks (as opposed to keyboards, which transfer data one character at a time). This set of options (shown in Figure 6-3) involves the floppy and IDE (Integrated Drive Electronics) devices connected to the PC's parallel port as well as other block devices.

The first option asks whether you want floppy-drive support. Because most PCs do have a floppy drive, select this option to show a check mark in the box. Click the Parallel Port IDE Device Support option to show a dot if you have an external CD-ROM or disk devices that connect through your PC's parallel port. That way, a module is built to support these devices.

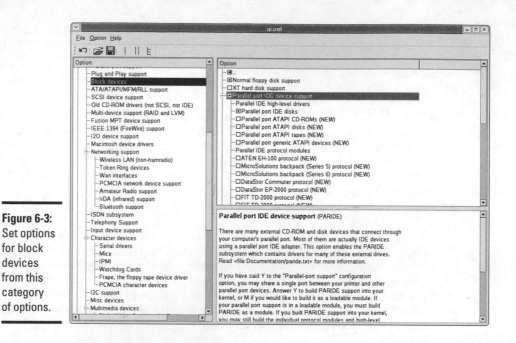

**Figure 6-3:**
Set options
for block
devices
from this
category
of options.

If you scroll down the list of options in the upper-right pane in Figure 6-3, you find more options for block devices. Turning on the Loopback Device Support option lets the Linux kernel manipulate an entire file system image stored in a single large file. This option is useful if you want to mount a CD image (for example, a Fedora Core ISO file) and check it out before actually burning the CD.

The RAM Disk Support option allows the kernel to use a portion of your system's memory as a disk capable of storing a file system. The Initial RAM Disk Support option creates a RAM disk that is used by the boot loader before the system boots. The Initial RAM disk functions only during system startup when the hard drive may not be available yet. The Initial RAM disk is essential for loading the driver modules needed to access the hard disk before the kernel can boot from a hard drive partition.

### ATA/ATAPI/MFM/RLL support

When you're configuring an operating system, you have to expect a fair share of acronyms — this one has four acronyms: ATA, ATAPI, MFM, and RLL. All these relate to hard drives or the interface that links disk drives to the PC. Here's what they mean:

✦ **ATA** stands for *AT Attachment* and refers to the PC-AT style interface that connects hard drives and CD-ROM drives to the PC's motherboard.

✦ **ATAPI** stands for *AT Attachment Packet Interface* and refers to the original PC hard drives that integrate the disk controller onto the hard drive itself. This interface used to be called *Integrated Drive Electronics* or IDE. You typically see the terms IDE, ATA, and ATAPI used interchangeably.

✦ **MFM** stands for *Modified Frequency Modulation,* the way data was encoded on older hard drives. These hard drives can work over an IDE interface.

✦ **RLL** stands for *Run Length Limited,* an old technique for storing data on a hard drive from the early days of the PC. RLL disks can work over an IDE interface.

Enable the ATA/ATAPI/MFM/RLL Support option by clicking it until a check mark appears. When you enable this support, you get many more configuration options (see Figure 6-4) involving IDE devices, such as hard drives and ATAPI CD-ROM drives.

The first option is for enhanced IDE support, which refers to full-featured IDE controllers that can control up to 10 IDE interfaces. Because each IDE interface can have a master and a slave device, Linux can access a total of up to 20 IDE devices (such as disks or CD-ROM drives). Make sure this option has a check mark.

**Book VI
Chapter 6**

Upgrading and
Customizing
the Kernel

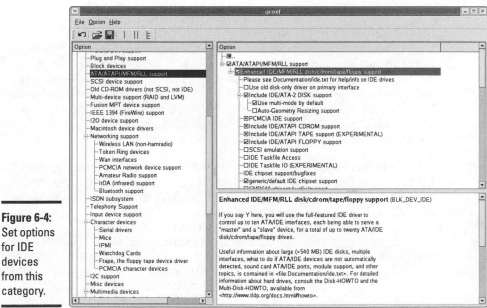

**Figure 6-4:**
Set options
for IDE
devices
from this
category.

The second item the in upper-right pane of Figure 6-4 is a comment that refers you to the file Documentation/ide.txt for help with IDE devices. To read these help files (these are all text files), type the following command to change the directory:

```
cd /usr/src/linux*/Documentation
```

Now you can browse the directory for text files relating to specific devices. You can also use the GNOME or KDE file managers to browse the documentation.

*Note:* The IDE/ATAPI FLOPPY Support option refers to IDE floppy drives, such as the Iomega Zip drive or Imation Superdisk LS-120 drive. If you have an IDE ZIP drive, enable this option to show a check mark or a dot.

### SCSI device support

SCSI stands for *Small Computer Systems Interface* — a type of interface through which you can connect multiple devices (such as hard drives and scanners) to the PC. This set of options has to do with SCSI devices. If your system has a SCSI adapter, start by clicking the SCSI Support option to show a dot (which means a module is built). After that, you can set the options relating to the types of devices (disk, tape, CD-ROM) connected to the SCSI adapter. Finally, you must look in the SCSI low-level drivers category and enable support for the specific SCSI adapter model on your system.

### IEEE 1394 (FireWire) support

IEEE 1394 is a high-speed serial bus for connecting peripherals to PCs. Apple calls this bus FireWire; Sony calls it i.Link. IEEE 1394 is similar to USB, but it can transfer data at rates up to 400Mbps, which is more than 30 times the data rate of the older USB version 1.1 (note that USB 2.0 is even faster; it can transfer data at rates of up to 480Mbps). Because of its high data-transfer rates, IEEE 1394 is ideal for connecting high-speed peripherals such as digital audio and video devices and external hard drives to the PC.

You can build a module for the IEEE 1394 bus. Currently, Linux supports IEEE 1394 chipsets that are compatible with Texas Instruments PCILynx/PCILynx2 and OHCI chipsets. If your PC has an IEEE 1394 adapter, you can build the necessary drivers through these options.

To find out more about using IEEE 1394 peripherals in Linux, visit the Web site of the IEEE 1394 for Linux project at www.linux1394.org.

### I2O device support

Pronounced *eye-two-oh*, I2O refers to Intelligent Input/Output — a new device driver architecture independent of the operating system and the controlled device. The basic concept of I2O is to separate the part responsible for managing the device from the part that contains operating system-specific details (it's called the I2O Split Driver model). The two parts of an I2O driver are the OS Services Module (OSM), which works with the operating system, and the Hardware Device Module (HDM) that interfaces with the particular device the driver manages. The OSM and HDM communicate by passing messages to each other. Linux comes with some I2O drivers for SCSI and PCI devices. You can configure these drivers from this category of options.

### Networking support

This set of options (shown in Figure 6-5) deals with networking. How you set these options depends on how you want to use your Fedora Core system in a network. Always enable the TCP/IP Networking option because the X Window System uses TCP/IP networking (even if your PC isn't on any network).

**Book VI
Chapter 6**

**Upgrading and Customizing the Kernel**

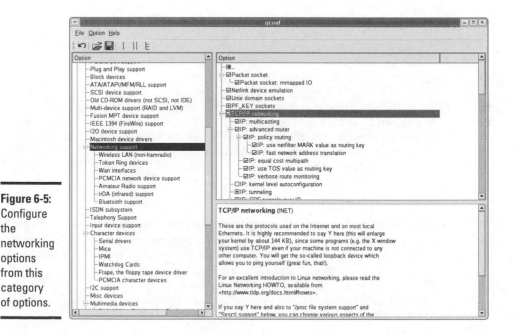

**Figure 6-5:**
Configure the networking options from this category of options.

Set the Network Packet Filtering option to a check mark if you want to use your Fedora Core system as a firewall — an intermediary system that controls information flowing between a local area network (LAN) and the Internet.

Other categories in the Networking Support options include wireless LAN, Token Ring, wide area network (WAN), PCMCIA network devices, amateur radio, infrared, and Bluetooth.

The infrared support is for infrared communication using the protocols specified by the Infrared Data Association (IrDA). IrDA communication is used by many laptops and personal digital assistants (PDAs), such as Palm and Handspring.

Bluetooth is a low-power, short-range wireless technology for connecting devices on the 2.4 GHz frequency band. Devices that use Bluetooth can usually connect when they are within 10 meters of one another. To find out more about Bluetooth, visit `www.bluetooth.com`. Linux supports Bluetooth through a core driver and several other modules. You can click the option to enable Bluetooth support and then select other options specific to your Bluetooth devices.

### ISDN subsystem

This set of options enables you to include support for *ISDN* (Integrated Services Digital Network) — a digital telephone line you can use to connect the Linux system to the Internet. These ISDN-related options include the configuration of specific ISDN adapters.

Build the ISDN driver only if your PC has an ISDN card. If you anticipate adding an ISDN card and purchase ISDN service from the phone company, you can build the driver as a module. Read the file `/usr/src/linux*/Documentation/isdn/README` for more information on how to set up and use the ISDN driver in Linux.

### Telephony support

With the right hardware and software, the Telephony Support options enable you to use the Fedora Core system for making phone calls over the Internet (also known as *voiceover IP* or *VoIP*). You can choose to build driver modules for telephony support if you have a telephony card, such as the Internet PhoneJACK or Internet LineJACK manufactured by Quicknet Technologies, Inc. If you have no Quicknet telephony cards, you can safely leave these options turned off.

### Character devices

These options deal with configuring character devices, which include devices connected to the serial and parallel ports. These options also include configuration of multiport serial interface cards that enable you to connect multiple terminals or other devices to your Fedora Core system.

Other subcategories of character devices include

+ **Mice:** You can include support for bus mice in this option category.

+ **Watchdog cards:** You can enable support for special watchdog cards that can monitor the PC's status (including the temperature, for instance) and reboots the PC when necessary. This option can be helpful if you want to have a networked PC automatically reboot after it hangs up for whatever reason.

+ `Ftape` **or the floppy-tape device driver:** If you have a tape drive connected to your floppy controller, you can configure it through this category of options.

+ **PCMCIA character devices:** These options are for configuring PC card serial adapters that are meant for laptop PCs.

## I2C Support

I2C — pronounced *eye-squared-see* — is a protocol Philips has developed for communication over a pair of wires at rates between 10 and 100kHz. System Management Bus (SMBus) is a subset of the I2C protocol. Many modern motherboards have an SMBus meant for connecting devices such as EEPROM (electrically erasable programmable read-only memory) and chips for hardware monitoring. Linux supports the I2C and SMBus protocols. You need this support for video for Linux. If you have any hardware sensors or video equipment that needs I2C support, set the I2C Support option to a dot (for module) and click to show a dot for the specific driver for your hardware. To find out more about the I2C, read the documentation in the `/usr/src/linux*/Documentation/i2c` directory. In particular, the `summary` file briefly describes the I2C and SMBus protocols.

## Multimedia devices

This category of options configures support for multimedia devices such as video cameras, television tuners, and FM radio cards. For more information on these devices, consult the documentation in the `/usr/src/linux*/Documentation/video4linux` directory.

## Sound

Use this set of options to configure sound-card support. If you have a sound card installed, start by enabling the Sound Card Support option. After that, click Advanced Linux Sound Architecture (ALSA) and select the options to build modules for the sound devices. You can always build the sound modules for all types of sound cards. That way, the modules needed for your system's sound card are available when needed.

## USB support

Use this category of options (see Figure 6-6) to configure support for the Universal Serial Bus (USB) — a serial bus that comes built into most new PCs. USB version 1.1 supports data-transfer rates as high as 12Mbps — 12 million bits per second or 1.5MB per second — compared with 115Kbps or the 0.115Mbps transfer rate of a standard serial port (such as COM1). You can daisy chain up to 127 devices on a USB bus. The bus also provides power to the devices, and you can attach or remove devices while the PC is running — a capability commonly referred to as *hot swapping* or *hotplug*. USB version 2.0 (or USB 2.0 or USB2, for short) ups the data-transfer ante to 480Mbps, slightly faster than the competing IEEE 1394 (FireWire) bus.

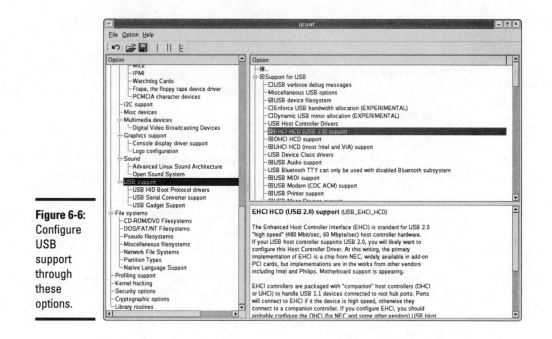

**Figure 6-6:**
Configure
USB
support
through
these
options.

USB can replace the functionality of the PC's serial and parallel ports, as well as the keyboard and mouse ports. Nowadays, many PC peripherals — such as mouse, keyboard, printer, scanner, modem, digital camera, and so on — are designed to connect to the PC through a USB port.

If your PC has a USB Port, set the Support for USB option to a dot (so that a module is built). Then you have to select the UHCI or OHCI option, depending on the type of USB interface — UHCI (Intel) or OHCI (Compaq and others) — your PC has. To determine the type of USB interface, type **lspci** in a terminal window and look for the USB controller's make and model in the output. If the controller is by Intel, use the UHCI driver.

For USB 2.0 support, you can set the EHCI HCD (that's host controller device) option to a dot (module).

After you select the UHCI or OHCI interface support, you have to build the driver modules for specific USB devices on your system. For more information on USB devices, consult the documentation in the `/usr/src/linux*/Documentation/usb` directory — especially the links in the `usb-help.txt` file.

## File systems

Through this category of options (shown in Figure 6-7), you can turn on support for specific types of file systems. You'd be amazed by the many different file systems that the Linux kernel can support. Table 6-1 lists some of the file systems that Linux can support. You typically build a kernel with support for the core Linux file systems (ext2 and ext3), CD-ROM file system (ISO 9660 and Joliet), and DOS/Windows file systems (MSDOS, FAT, and VFAT). For sharing files with Windows 2000/XP systems, you also build the module for CIFS.

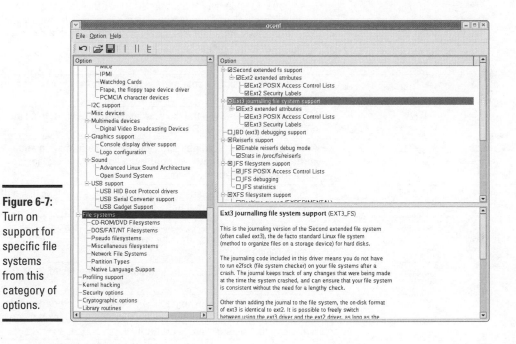

**Figure 6-7:** Turn on support for specific file systems from this category of options.

| Table 6-1 | Some File Systems Supported by the Linux Kernel |
|---|---|
| *File System* | *Description* |
| Apple Macintosh | The Macintosh HFS file system (Linux can read and write Macintosh-formatted floppy disks and hard drives). |
| CIFS | The Common Internet File System (CIFS) — a successor to the Server Message Block (SMB) protocol — is the new file system for Windows servers such as Windows 2000, Windows XP, and Samba. |
| Coda | An advanced network file system that is similar to NFS but that better supports disconnected operation (for example, laptops) and is a better security model. |
| Ext2 | The second extended file system — the current standard file system for Linux. |
| Ext3 | Ext2 file system with support for journaling — a facility that allows quick recovery of the disk after a crash. |
| FAT | Refers to any File Allocation Table (FAT)-based file system (including MS-DOS and Windows 95 VFAT file systems). |
| HPFS | The OS/2 HPFS file system (Linux can only read HPFS files). |
| ISO 9660 | The standard ISO 9660 file system used on CD-ROMs (this system is also known as the High Sierra File System and is referred to as `hsfs` on some UNIX workstations). |
| Joliet | Microsoft's Joliet extension for the ISO 9660 CD-ROM file system, which allows for long filenames in Unicode format. (Unicode is the new 16-bit character code that can encode the characters of almost all languages of the world.) |
| MSDOS | The MS-DOS file system. |
| NFS | Network File System for sharing files and directories from other systems on a network. |
| NTFS | NT file system (NTFS) — the file system used by Microsoft Windows NT (Linux can only read NTFS disks). |
| `/proc` | A virtual file system through which you can get information about the kernel. The `/proc` file system does not exist on the disk; files are created when you access them. |
| ReiserFS | An efficient file system that stores both filenames and files in a balanced tree and uses journaling. |
| SMB | File system that uses Server Message Block (SMB) protocol to access shared directories from networked PCs running Windows 95/98/NT/2000. |
| System V | File system used by SCO, Xenix, and Coherent variants of UNIX for Intel PCs. |
| UDF | A new file system used on some CD-ROMs and DVDs (for example, UDF file system is used on rewritable CDs written in packet mode or written by UDF utilities such as DirectCD). |

| File System | Description |
| --- | --- |
| UFS | File system used by the BSD (Berkeley Software Distribution) variants of UNIX (such as SunOS, FreeBSD, NetBSD, and NeXTstep). |
| VFAT | Windows 95/98/NT/2000 file systems with long filenames. |

### Kernel hacking

This set of options enables you to debug the kernel and use the SysRq key (usually the PrintScrn key on your keyboard) to get important status information right after a system crash. This information is useful if you're a Linux developer who expects to debug the kernel. Most users disable these options (because most users run a stable version of the kernel and don't expect to fix kernel errors).

### Security options

Through these options, you can include support for the Security Enhanced Linux (SELinux), which was developed by the National Security Agency (NSA) — a U.S. government agency. SELinux comes with Fedora Core, but you can turn it off during booting by providing `selinux=0` as a boot option. For more information on SELinux, visit `www.nsa.gov/selinux/`.

## Building the Kernel and the Modules

After configuring the kernel options, click the Save and Exit button in the main configuration window (refer to Figure 6-7). Now you have to build the kernel. This part can take a while. Depending on your system, making a new kernel can take anywhere from a few minutes to over an hour.

Type the following on a single line to initiate the process:

```
make
```

The `make` command creates the new kernel as well as any modules that you have specified through the configuration step.

As the kernel is built, you see a lot of messages on-screen. When it's all over, a new kernel in the form of a compressed file named `bzImage` is in the `/usr/src/linux*/arch/i386/boot` directory.

To use the new kernel, you have to copy the kernel to the `/boot` directory under a specific name and edit the `/etc/grub.conf` file to set up GRUB — the boot loader. Before you proceed with the kernel installation, however, you have to install the modules and build a new initial RAM disk.

# Installing the Modules

If you select any modules during the kernel configuration, the kernel building step also builds the modules. All you have to do is install them. Perform this task with the following commands:

```
cd /usr/src/linux*
make modules_install
```

The `make modules_install` command copies all the modules to a new subdirectory named `2.6.3-2.1.240custom` in the `/lib/modules` directory. Appending the word `custom` to the kernel version number creates the directory name.

Now you can install the kernel and make it available for GRUB to boot.

# Creating the Initial RAM Disk File

The new kernel needs a new initial RAM disk file that you can create by using the `mkinitrd` command. Usually, the initial RAM disk image is stored in a file whose name begins with `initrd`. As you might have guessed, `initrd` is shorthand for initial RAM disk, and the `mkinitrd` command is so named because it makes an `initrd` file.

The `mkinitrd` program is in the `/sbin` directory, and you have to log in as `root` and use a command line of the following form to create the `initrd` file:

```
/sbin/mkinitrd /boot/initrd-filename.img   module-directory
```

The `initrd` file has to be in the `/boot` directory where the kernel is also located. You can use any filename for *initrd- filename*. The *module-directory* is the name of the directory in `/lib/modules` where the module files for the new kernel are located. The `make modules_install` step places the modules in a directory whose name is the kernel version number with the word *custom* appended to it. For example, if your kernel version (as reported by the `uname -r` command) is 2.6.3-2.1.240, the *module-directory*, after the make `modules_install` step, is `2.6.3-2.1.240custom`.

Another common practice is to use an `initrd` filename created by appending the module directory name to the `initrd-` prefix. Thus, for module directory `2.6.3-2.1.240custom`, the `initrd` file is `initrd-2.6.3-2.1.240custom.img`.

To create the initial RAM disk image for the newly built kernel, type the following command:

```
/sbin/mkinitrd /boot/initrd-2.6.3-2.1.240custom.img 2.6.3-2.1.240custom
```

This command creates the file `initrd-2.6.3-2.1.240custom.img` in the `/boot` directory. You have to refer to this `initrd` file in the GRUB configuration file (`/etc/grub.conf`).

# *Installing the New Kernel and Setting Up GRUB*

Fedora Core uses GRUB to load the Linux kernel from the disk. The configuration file `/etc/grub.conf` lists the kernel binary file that GRUB runs. You can examine the contents of the GRUB configuration file by typing the following command:

```
cat /etc/grub.conf
```

**Book VI
Chapter 6**

**Upgrading and
Customizing
the Kernel**

Here is what I see when I try this command on one of my systems:

```
# grub.conf generated by anaconda
#
# Note that you do not have to rerun grub after making changes to this file
# NOTICE:  You have a /boot partition.  This means that
#          all kernel and initrd paths are relative to /boot/, eg.
#          root (hd0,2)
#          kernel /vmlinuz-version ro root=/dev/hda5
#          initrd /initrd-version.img
#boot=/dev/hda
default=0
timeout=10
splashimage=(hd0,2)/grub/splash.xpm.gz
title Fedora Core (2.6.3-2.1.240)
        root (hd0,2)
        kernel /vmlinuz-2.6.3-2.1.240 ro root=LABEL=/ rhgb
        initrd /initrd-2.6.3-2.1.240.img
title Windows XP
        rootnoverify (hd0,1)
        chainloader +1
```

Here's what the lines in `/etc/grub.conf` file mean (the lines that begin with # are comments):

✦ `default=0`: Specifies the first boot entry as the default one that GRUB boots. If this line is set to 1, GRUB boots the second boot.

✦ `timeout=10`: Causes GRUB to boot the default entry automatically after waiting for 10 seconds. If other boot entries are in the file, the user may select another one from a boot menu GRUB displays.

✦ The four lines starting with `title Fedora Core (2.6.3-2.1.240)` constitute the first boot entry — and this entry defines a specific kernel file GRUB can boot. You can make GRUB boot another kernel by adding a similar section to the configuration file. Here's the meaning of the lines in this boot entry:

- root (hd0,2): Sets the root device to the third partition of the first hard drive. This partition is where the Linux kernel is installed on this particular system.

- kernel /vmlinuz-2.6.3-2.1.240 ro root=LABEL=/ rhgb: Identifies the kernel GRUB loads if the user selects this boot entry. In this case, the kernel file is vmlinuz-2.6.3-2.1.240, which is located in the root device. In my system, that partition is mounted on the /boot directory. In other words, GRUB loads the kernel file /boot/vmlinuz-2.6.3-2.1.240. The items following the kernel name are options provided to the kernel. For example, the rhgb option enables a graphical boot that shows a nice graphical screen instead of scrolling text messages.

- initrd /initrd-2.6.3-2.1.240.img: Specifies a file that contains an initial RAM disk (initrd stands for initial RAM disk) image that serves as a file system before the disks are available. The Linux kernel uses the RAM disk — a block of memory used as a disk — to get started; then it loads other driver modules and begins using the hard drive.

✦ The three lines starting with title Windows XP are the second boot entry and refer to the Windows XP operating system that happens to be on this system. The text next to the title line appears in the GRUB menu from which the user selects which operating system to boot.

To configure GRUB to boot the new Linux kernel (the one you just built), follow these steps:

*1.* **Copy the new kernel binary to the /boot directory.**

The new, compressed kernel file is in the /usr/src/linux*/arch/ i386/boot directory. The kernel filename is bzImage. I simply copy that file to the /boot directory with the same name:

```
cp /usr/src/linux*/arch/i386/boot/bzImage /boot
```

If the kernel filename is vmlinux, make sure you use vmlinux instead of bzImage. You can change the kernel filename in /boot to anything you want, as long as you use the same filename when referring to the kernel in the /etc/grub.conf file in Step 3.

*2.* **Save the old System.map file in the /boot directory, and copy the new map file.**

(I assume you have rebuilt kernel version 2.6.3-2.1.240 after changing some configuration options):

```
mv /boot/System.map-2.6.3-2.1.240 /boot/System.map-2.6.3-2.1.240-old
cp /usr/src/linux*/System.map /boot/System.map-2.6.3-2.1.240
cd /boot
ln -s System.map-2.6.3-2.1.240 System.map
```

3. **Use your favorite text editor to edit the** `/etc/grub.conf` **file to add the following lines just after the** `splashimage` **line in the file:**

```
title Fedora Core (2.6.3-2.1.240 NEW)
        root (hd0,2)
        kernel /bzImage ro root=LABEL=/ rhgb
        initrd /initrd-2.6.3-2.1.240custom.img
```

On your system, make sure the `root` line is correct — instead of (`hd0,2`), list the correct disk partition where the Linux `root` directory (`/`) is located. Also, use the correct filename for the kernel image file (for example, `/vmlinux` If the kernel file is so named).

*Note:* The `initrd` line refers to the `initrd` file that you created in an earlier step.

4. **Save the** `/etc/grub.conf` **file and exit the editor.**

Now you're ready to reboot the system and try out the new kernel.

Book VI
Chapter 6

Upgrading and
Customizing
the Kernel

# Rebooting the System

After you finish configuring GRUB, you can restart the system. While you're still logged in as `root`, type the following command to reboot the system:

```
reboot
```

When you see the GRUB screen, select the name you assigned to the new kernel in the `/etc/grub.conf` file.

After the system reboots, you see the familiar graphical login screen. To see proof that you're indeed running the new kernel, log in as a user, open a terminal window, and type **uname -srv**. This command shows you the kernel version, as well as the date and time when this kernel was built. If you upgraded the kernel source, you see the version number for the new kernel. If you have simply rebuilt the kernel for the same old kernel version, the date and time matches the time when you rebuilt the kernel. That's your proof that the system is running the new kernel.

If the system hangs (nothing seems to happen — you don't see any output on-screen or disk activity), you may have skipped a step during the kernel rebuild. You can power the PC off and on to reboot. This time, select the name of the old working kernel at the GRUB screen.

# Book VII

# Security

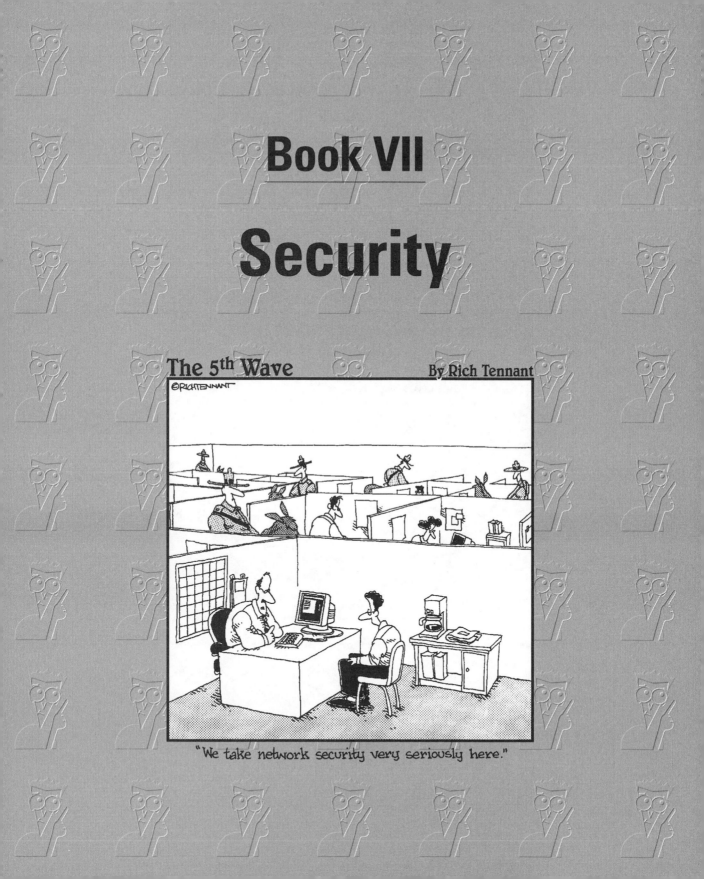

The 5th Wave                    By Rich Tennant

"We take network security very seriously here."

# Contents at a Glance

Chapter 1: Understanding Network and Host Security ..................................................521

Chapter 2: Securing the Host ....................................................................................535

Chapter 3: Securing the Network ...............................................................................557

Chapter 4: Performing Security Audits ........................................................................577

# Chapter 1: Understanding Network and Host Security

## In This Chapter

✔ Establishing a security policy and framework

✔ Understanding host-security issues

✔ Understanding network-security issues

✔ Translating computer-security terminology

✔ Keeping up with security news and updates

*I*n this chapter, I explain why you need to worry about security and then give you a high-level view of how to get a handle on security. I explain the idea of an overall security framework and explain the two key aspects of security — host security and network security. I end this chapter by introducing you to the terminology used in discussing computer security.

## Why Worry About Security?

In today's networked world, you have to worry about your Fedora Core system's security. For a standalone system, or a system used in an isolated local-area network (LAN), you have to focus on protecting the system from the users and the users from one another. In other words, you don't want a user to modify or delete system files, whether intentionally or unintentionally. Also, you don't want a user destroying another user's files.

If your Fedora Core system is connected to the Internet, you have to secure the system from unwanted accesses over the Internet. These intruders — or *crackers,* as they are commonly known — typically impersonate a user, steal or destroy information, and even deny you access to your own system (known as a *Denial of Service* or *DoS* attack).

By its very nature, an Internet connection makes your system accessible to any other system on the Internet. After all, the Internet connects a huge number of networks across the globe. In fact, the client/server architecture of Internet services, such as HTTP (Web) and FTP, rely on the wide-open network access the Internet provides. Unfortunately, the easy accessibility to Internet services running on your system also means anyone on the Net can easily access your system.

If you operate an Internet host that provides information to others, you certainly want everyone to access your system's Internet services, such as FTP and Web servers. However, these servers often have vulnerabilities that crackers may exploit in order to cause harm to your system. You need to know about the potential security risks of Internet services — and the precautions you can take to minimize the risk of someone exploiting the weaknesses of your FTP or Web server.

You also want to protect your company's internal network from outsiders, even though your goal is to provide information to the outside world through a Web or FTP server. You can protect your internal network by setting up an Internet *firewall* — a controlled access point to the internal network — and placing the Web and FTP servers on a host outside the firewall.

## Establishing a Security Framework

The first step in securing your Fedora Core system is to set up a *security policy* — a set of guidelines that state what you enable users (as well as visitors over the Internet) to do on your Fedora Core system. The level of security you establish depends on how you use the Fedora Core system — and on how much is at risk if someone gains unauthorized access to your system.

If you're a system administrator for one or more Fedora Core systems at an organization, you probably want to involve company management, as well as the users, in setting up the security policy. Obviously, you cannot create a draconian policy that blocks all access (that would prevent anyone from effectively working on the system). On the other hand, if the users are creating or using data valuable to the organization, you have to set up a policy that protects the data from disclosure to outsiders. In other words, the security policy should strike a balance between the users' needs and your need to protect the system.

For a stand-alone Fedora Core system, or a home system that you occasionally connect to the Internet, the security policy can be just a listing of the Internet services you want to run on the system and the user accounts you plan to set up on the system. For any larger organization, you probably have one or more Fedora Core systems on a LAN connected to the Internet — preferably through a firewall (to reiterate, a *firewall* is a device that controls the flow of Internet Protocol — IP — packets between the LAN and the Internet). In such cases, thinking of computer security across the entire organization systematically is best. Figure 1-1 shows the key elements of an organization-wide framework for computer security.

The security framework outlined in Figure 1-1 starts with the development of a security policy based on business requirements and risk analysis.

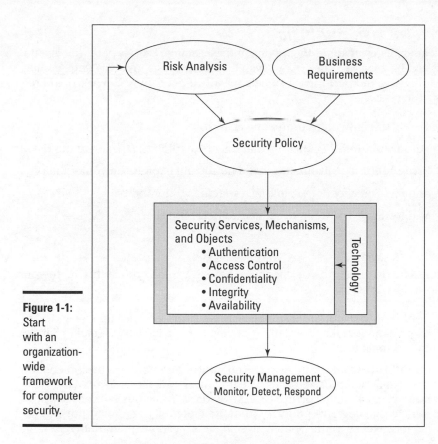

**Figure 1-1:**
Start
with an
organization-
wide
framework
for computer
security.

## Determine business requirements for security

The business requirements identify the security needs of the business — the computer resources and information you have to protect (including any requirements imposed by applicable laws, such as the requirement to protect the privacy of some types of data). Typical security requirements may include items such as the following:

✦ Enable access to information by authorized users

✦ Implement business rules that specify who has access to what information

✦ Employ a strong user-authentication system

✦ Deny malicious or destructive actions on data

✦ Protect data from end to end as it moves across networks

✦ Implement all security and privacy requirements that applicable laws impose

## Perform risk analysis

Risk analysis is all about identifying and assessing risks — potential events that can harm your Fedora Core system. The analysis involves determining the following and performing some analysis to determine the priority of handling the risks:

+ **Threats:** What you're protecting against

+ **Vulnerabilities:** Weaknesses that may be exploited (these are the risks)

+ **Probability:** The likelihood that a threat will exploit the vulnerability

+ **Impact:** The effect of exploiting a specific vulnerability

+ **Mitigation:** What to do to reduce vulnerabilities

### Typical threats

Before I further describe risk analysis, here are some typical threats to your Fedora Core system:

+ **Denial of Service:** The computer and network are tied up so legitimate users cannot make use of the systems. For businesses, Denial of Service can mean loss of revenue.

+ **Unauthorized access:** Use of the computer and network by someone who isn't an authorized user. The unauthorized user can steal information or maliciously corrupt or destroy data. Some businesses may be hurt by the negative publicity from the mere act of an unauthorized user gaining access to the system, even if data has no explicit damage.

+ **Disclosure of information to the public:** The unauthorized release of information to the public. For example, the disclosure of a password file enables potential attackers to figure out username and password combinations for accessing a system. Exposure of other sensitive information, such as financial and medical data, may be a potential liability for a business.

### Typical vulnerabilities

The threats to your system and network come from exploitation of vulnerabilities in your organization's resources — both computer and people. Some common vulnerabilities are the following:

+ People's foibles (divulging passwords, losing security cards, and so on)

+ Internal network connections (routers, switches)

+ Interconnection points (gateways — routers and firewalls — between the Internet and the internal network)

✦ Third-party network providers (ISPs, long-distance carriers) with looser security

✦ Operating-system security holes (potential holes in Internet servers, such as those associated with `sendmail`, `named`, `bind`, and so on)

✦ Application security holes (known security holes in specific applications)

### *The 1-2-3 of risk analysis (probability and impact)*

To perform risk analysis, assign a numeric value to the probability and impact of each potential vulnerability. To develop a workable risk analysis, do the following for each vulnerability or risk:

*1.* Assign subjective ratings of Low, Medium, and High for the probability. As the ratings suggest, Low probability means a lesser chance that the vulnerability will be exploited; High probability means a greater chance.

*2.* Assign similar ratings to impact. What you consider impact is up to you. If the exploitation of a vulnerability will affect your business greatly, assign it a High impact.

*3.* Assign a numeric value to the three levels — Low = 1, Medium = 2, and High = 3 — for both probability and impact.

*4.* Multiply the probability by the impact — you can think of this product as the *risk level*. Then make a decision to develop protections for vulnerabilities that exceed a specific threshold for the product of probability and impact. For example, you may choose to handle all vulnerabilities with a probability-times-impact greater than 6.

If you want to characterize the probability and impact with finer gradations, pick a scale of 1 through 5 (for example) instead of 1 through 3, and follow the same steps as before.

## *Establish security policy*

Using risk analysis and any business requirements you may have to address (regardless of risk level) as a foundation, you can craft a security policy for the organization. The security policy typically addresses the following areas:

✦ **Authentication:** What method is used to ensure that a user is the real user? Who gets access to the system? What is the minimum length and complexity of passwords? How often do users change passwords? How long can a user be idle before that user is logged out automatically?

✦ **Authorization:** What can different classes of users do on the system? Who can have the `root` password?

✦ **Data protection:** What data must be protected? Who has access to the data? Is encryption necessary for some data?

✦ **Internet access:** What are the restrictions on users (from the LAN) accessing the Internet? What Internet services (such as Web, Internet Relay Chat, and so on) can users access? Are incoming e-mails and attachments scanned for viruses? Is there a network firewall? Are virtual private networks (VPNs) used to connect private networks across the Internet?

✦ **Internet services:** What Internet services are allowed on each Linux system? Are there any file servers? Mail servers? Web servers? What services run on each type of server? What services, if any, run on Linux systems used as desktop workstations?

✦ **Security audits:** Who tests whether the security is adequate? How often is the security tested? How are problems found during security testing handled?

✦ **Incident handling:** What are the procedures for handling any computer security incidents? Who must be informed? What information must be gathered to help with the investigation of incidents?

✦ **Responsibilities:** Who is responsible for maintaining security? Who monitors log files and audit trails for signs of unauthorized access? Who maintains the database of security policy?

## Implement security solutions (mitigation)

After you analyze the risks — vulnerabilities — and develop a security policy, you have to select the mitigation approach: how to protect against specific vulnerabilities. This is where you develop an overall security solution based on security policy, business requirements, and available technology — a solution that includes the following:

✦ Services (authentication, access control, encryption)

✦ Mechanisms (username/password, firewalls)

✦ Objects (hardware, software)

## Manage security

In addition to implementing security solutions, you have to install security management that continually monitors, detects, and responds to any security incidents.

The combination of the risk analysis, security policy, security solutions, and security management provides the overall security framework. Such a framework helps establish a common level of understanding of security concerns — and a common basis for the design and implementation of security solutions.

# Securing Linux

After you define a security policy, you can proceed to secure the system according to the policy. The exact steps depend on what you want to do with the system — whether it's a server or a workstation and how many users must access the system.

To secure the Fedora Core system, you have to handle two broad categories of security issues:

✦ Host security issues that relate to securing the operating system and the files and directories on the system

✦ Network security issues that refer to the threat of attacks over the network connection

## Understanding the host security issues

Here are some high-level guidelines to address host security (I cover some of these topics in detail in Chapter 2 of this minibook):

✦ When installing Fedora Core, select only the package groups you need for your system. Don't install unnecessary software. For example, if your system is used as a workstation, you don't have to install most of the servers (Web server, news server, and so on).

✦ Create initial user accounts and make sure all passwords are strong enough that password-cracking programs can't "guess" them. Linux includes tools to enforce strong passwords.

✦ Set file ownerships and permissions to protect important files and directories.

✦ Enable mandatory access control capabilities provided by the Security Enhanced Linux (SELinux). Fedora Core enables SELinux access control by default.

✦ Use the GNU Privacy Guard (GnuPG) to encrypt or decrypt files with sensitive information and to authenticate files that you download from Red Hat. GnuPG comes with Fedora Core and you can use the `gpg` command to perform tasks, such as encrypt or decrypt a file and digitally sign a file.

✦ Use file-integrity checking tools, such as Tripwire, to monitor any changes to crucial system files and directories.

✦ Periodically check various log files for signs of any break-ins or attempted break-ins. These log files are in the `/var/log` directory of your system.

✦ Install security updates, as soon as they become available. These security updates fix known vulnerabilities in Linux.

**Book VII
Chapter 1**

Understanding
Network and
Host Security

## *Understanding network security issues*

The issue of security comes up as soon as you connect your organization's internal network to the Internet. You need to think of security even if you connect a single computer to the Internet, but security concerns are more pressing when an entire internal network is opened to the world.

If you're an experienced system administrator, you already know that the cost of managing an Internet presence doesn't worry corporate management; their main concern is security. To get your management's backing for the Web site, you have to lay out a plan to keep the corporate network secure from intruders.

You may think that you can avoid jeopardizing the internal network by connecting only the external servers, such as Web and FTP servers, to the Internet. However, employing this simplistic approach isn't wise. It's like deciding not to drive because you may have an accident. Not having a network connection between your Web server and your internal network also has the following drawbacks:

✦ You cannot use network file transfers, such as FTP, to copy documents and data from your internal network to the Web server.

✦ Users on the internal network cannot access the corporate Web server.

✦ Users on the internal network don't have access to Web servers on the Internet. Such a restriction makes a valuable resource — the Web — inaccessible to the users in your organization.

A practical solution to this problem is to set up an Internet firewall and to put the Web server on a highly secured host outside the firewall.

In addition to using a firewall, here are some of the other steps to take to address network security (I explain these further in Chapter 3 of this minibook):

✦ Enable only those Internet services you need on a system. In particular, don't enable services that are not properly configured.

✦ Use Secure Shell (`ssh`) for remote logins. Don't use the `r` commands, such as `rlogin` and `rsh`.

✦ Secure any Internet services such as FTP or TELNET that you want to run on your system. You can use the TCP wrapper access control files — `/etc/hosts.allow` and `/etc/hosts.deny` — to secure some of these services.

✦ Promptly fix any known vulnerabilities of Internet services that you choose to run. Typically you can download and install the latest server RPM file from Red Hat.

# Learning Computer Security Terminology

Computer books, magazine articles, and experts on computer security use a number of terms with unique meanings. You need to know these terms to understand discussions about computer security (and to communicate effectively with security vendors). Table 1-1 describes some of the commonly used computer security terms.

| Table 1-1 | Commonly Used Computer-Security Terminology |
|---|---|
| *Term* | *Description* |
| Application gateway | A proxy service that acts as a gateway for application-level protocols, such as FTP, TELNET, and HTTP. |
| Authentication | The process of confirming that a user is indeed who he or she claims to be. The typical authentication method is a challenge-response method wherein the user enters a username and secret password to confirm his or her identity. |
| Backdoor | A security weakness a cracker places on a host in order to bypass security features. |
| Bastion host | A highly secured computer that serves as an organization's main point of presence on the Internet. A bastion host typically resides on the perimeter network, but a dual-homed host (with one network interface connected to the Internet and the other to the internal network) is also a bastion host. |
| Buffer overflow | A security flaw in a program that enables a cracker to send an excessive amount of data to that program and to overwrite parts of the running program with code in the data being sent. The result is that the cracker can execute arbitrary code on the system and possibly gain access to the system as a privileged user. The new `exec-shield` feature of the Linux kernel protects against buffer overflows. |
| Certificate | An electronic document that identifies an entity (such as an individual, an organization, or a computer) and associates a public key with that identity. A certificate contains the certificate holder's name, a serial number, expiration date, a copy of the certificate holder's public key, and the digital signature of the Certificate Authority so a recipient can verify that the certificate is real. |
| Certificate Authority (CA) | An organization that validates identities and issues certificates. |

*(continued)*

**Table 1-1** *(continued)*

| Term | Description |
|------|-------------|
| Cracker | A person who breaks into (or attempts to break into) a host, often with malicious intent. |
| Confidentiality | Of data, a state of being accessible to no one but you (usually achieved by encryption). |
| Decryption | The process of transforming encrypted information into its original, intelligible form. |
| Denial of Service (DoS) | An attack that uses so many of the resources on your computer and network that legitimate users cannot access and use the system. |
| Digital signature | A one-way MD5 or SHA-1 hash of a message encrypted with the private key of the message originator, used to verify the integrity of a message and ensure nonrepudiation. |
| DMZ | Another name for the perimeter network. (DMZ originally stood for *demilitarized zone*, the buffer zone separating the warring North and South in Korea and Vietnam.) |
| Dual-homed host | A computer with two network interfaces (think of each network as a home) |
| Encryption | The process of transforming information so it's unintelligible to anyone but the intended recipient. The transformation is done by a mathematical operation between a key and the information. |
| Firewall | A controlled-access gateway between an organization's internal network and the Internet. A dual-homed host can be configured as a firewall. |
| Hash | The result when a mathematical function converts a message into a fixed-size numeric value known as a *message digest* (or *hash*). The MD5 algorithm, for example, produces a 128-bit message digest; the Secure Hash Algorithm-1 (SHA-1) generates a 160-bit message digest. The hash of a message is encrypted with the private key of the sender to produce the digital signature. |
| Host | A computer on a network that is configured to offer services to other computers on the network. |
| Integrity | Of received data, a state of being the same as originally sent (that is, unaltered in transit). |
| IPSec (IP Security) Protocol | A security protocol for the Network layer of the OSI Networking Model, designed to provide cryptographic security services for IP packets. IPSec provides encryption-based authentication, integrity, access control, and confidentiality (visit `www.ietf.org/html.charters/ipsec-charter.html` for the list of RFCs related to IPSec). |

| Term | Description |
| --- | --- |
| IP spoofing | An attack in which a cracker figures out the IP address of a trusted host and then sends packets that appear to come from the trusted host. The attacker can send packets but cannot see responses. However, the attacker can predict the sequence of packets and essentially send commands that set up a backdoor for future break-ins. |
| Nonrepudiation | A security feature that prevents the sender of data from being able to deny ever having sent the data. |
| Packet | A collection of bytes, assembled according to a specific protocol, that serves as the basic unit of communication on a network. On TCP/IP networks, for example, the packet may be referred to as an *IP packet* or a *TCP/IP packet*. |
| Packet filtering | Selective blocking of packets according to type of packet (as specified by the source and destination IP address or port). |
| Perimeter network | A network between the Internet and the protected internal network. The perimeter network (also known as DMZ) is where the bastion host resides. |
| Port scanning | A method of discovering which ports are open (in other words, which Internet services are enabled) on a system. Performed by sending connection requests to the ports, one by one. This procedure is usually a precursor to further attacks. |
| Proxy server | A server on the bastion host that enables internal clients to access external servers (and enables external clients to access servers inside the protected network). There are proxy servers for various Internet services, such as FTP and HTTP. |
| Public-key cryptography | An encryption method that uses a pair of keys — a private key and a public key — to encrypt and decrypt the information. Anything encrypted with the public key is decrypted only with the corresponding private key, and vice versa. |
| Public-Key Infrastructure (PKI) | A set of standards and services that enables the use of public-key cryptography and certificates in a networked environment. PKI facilitates tasks, such as issuing, renewing, and revoking certificates, and generating and distributing public-and-private key pairs. |
| Screening router | An Internet router that filters packets. |

*(continued)*

**Book VII
Chapter 1**

**Understanding
Network and
Host Security**

**Table 1-1** *(continued)*

| Term | Description |
|------|-------------|
| `setuid` program | A program that runs with the permissions of the owner regardless of who runs the program. For example, if `root` owns a `setuid` program, that program has `root` privileges regardless of who started the program. Crackers often exploit vulnerabilities in `setuid` programs to gain privileged access to a system. |
| Symmetric-key encryption | An encryption method wherein the same key is used to encrypt and decrypt the information. |
| Threat | An event or activity, deliberate or unintentional, with the potential for causing harm to a system or network. |
| Trojan Horse | A program that masquerades as a benign program, but in fact is a backdoor used for attacking a system. Attackers often install a collection of Trojan Horse programs that enable the attacker to freely access the system with `root` privileges, yet hide that fact from the system administrator. Such collections of Trojan Horse programs are called *rootkits*. |
| Virus | A self-replicating program that spreads from one computer to another by attaching itself to other programs. |
| Vulnerability | A flaw or weakness that may cause harm to a system or network. |
| Worm | A self-replicating program that copies itself from one computer to another over a network. |

# Keeping Up with Security News and Updates

To keep up with the latest security alerts, you may want to visit one or more of the following sites on a daily basis:

✦ CERT Coordination Center at `www.cert.org`

✦ Computer Incident Advisory Capability (CIAC) at `www.ciac.org/ciac/`

✦ National Infrastructure Protection Center at `www.nipc.gov`

If you have access to Internet newsgroups, you can periodically browse the following:

✦ `comp.security.announce`: A moderated newsgroup that includes announcements from CERT about security.

✦ `comp.security.unix`: A newsgroup that includes discussions of UNIX security issues, including items related to Linux, which also apply to Fedora Core.

If you prefer to receive regular security updates through e-mail, you can also sign up for (subscribe to) various mailing lists:

✦ **FOCUS-LINUX:** Fill out the form at `www.securityfocus.com/cgi-bin/subscribe.pl` to subscribe to this mailing list focused on Linux security issues.

✦ **US-CERT National Cyber Alert System:** Follow the directions at `www.us-cert.gov` to subscribe to this mailing list. The Cyber Alert System features four categories of security information through its mailing lists:

   • Technical Cyber Security Alerts provides technical information about vulnerabilities in various common software products.

   • Cyber Security Alerts are sent when vulnerabilities affect the general public. They outline the steps and actions that non-technical home and corporate computer users can take to protect themselves from attacks.

   • Cyber Security Bulletins are bi-weekly summaries of security issues and new vulnerabilities along with patches, workarounds, and other actions that users can take to help reduce the risk.

   • Cyber Security Tips offers advice on common security issues for non-technical computer users.

Finally, check the Fedora Core Web site at `fedora.redhat.com/download/updates.html` for updates that may fix any known security problems with Fedora Core.

# Chapter 2: Securing the Host

## In This Chapter

✔ **Securing passwords**

✔ **Protecting files and directories**

✔ **Encrypting and signing files with GnuPG**

✔ **Monitoring system security**

*H*ost is the techie term for your Fedora Core system — especially when you use it to provide services on a network. But the term makes sense even when you think of the computer by itself; it's the host for everything that runs on it — the operating system and all the applications. A key aspect of computer security is to secure the host.

In this chapter, I take you through a few key steps to follow in securing your Fedora Core host. These steps include installing operating system updates, protecting passwords, protecting the files and directories, using encryption if necessary, and monitoring the security of the system. You can monitor host security by examining log files for any suspicious activities and by using the Tripwire tool to see whether anyone has messed with important files on your system.

## Installing Operating System Updates

Fedora Core and related application updates come in RPM files. To manually download and install the updates, follow these steps:

*1.* **Log in as** root **and create a directory for the updates:**

```
mkdir /usr/local/updates
cd /usr/local/updates
```

*2.* **Use the** wget **command to download the updates from the Red Hat FTP site.**

For example, to download the updates for the i386 version of Fedora Core 2, type

```
wget ftp://download.fedora.redhat.com/pub/fedora/
    linux/core/updates/2/i386/\*.rpm
```

3. **Install all updates with the following command:**

```
rpm -F *
```

4. **Delete the update files with the command:**

```
rm -fr /usr/local/updates
```

# Securing Passwords

Historically, UNIX passwords are stored in the `/etc/passwd` file, which any user can read. For example, a typical old-style `/etc/passwd` file entry for the `root` user looks like this:

```
root:t6Z7NWDK1K8sU:0:0:root:/root:/bin/bash
```

The fields are separated by colons (`:`), and the second field contains the password in encrypted form. To check whether a password is valid, the login program encrypts the plain-text password the user enters and compares the password with the contents of the `/etc/passwd` file. If there is a match, the user is allowed to log in.

Password-cracking programs work just like the login program, except that these programs pick one word at a time from a dictionary, encrypt the word, and compare the encrypted word with the encrypted passwords in the `/etc/passwd` file for a match. To crack the passwords, the intruder needs the `/etc/passwd` file. Often, crackers use weaknesses of various Internet servers (such as mail and FTP) to get a copy of the `/etc/passwd` file.

Recently, several improvements have made passwords more secure in Fedora Core. These include shadow passwords and pluggable authentication modules, and you can install these easily as you install Fedora Core. During Fedora Core installation, one step involves making selections in an Authentication Configuration screen. If you accept the default selections — Enable MD5 Passwords and Enable Shadow Passwords — you automatically enable more secure passwords in Fedora Core.

## Shadow passwords

Obviously, leaving passwords lying around where anyone can get at them — even if they're encrypted — is bad security. So instead of storing passwords in the `/etc/passwd` file (which any user can read), Fedora Core now stores them in a shadow password file, `/etc/shadow`. Only the superuser (`root`) can read this file. For example, here is the entry for `root` in the new-style `/etc/passwd` file:

```
root:x:0:0:root:/root:/bin/bash
```

In this case, note that the second field contains an x instead of an encrypted password. The x is the *shadow password*; the actual encrypted password is now stored in the /etc/shadow file where the entry for root is like this:

```
root:$1$AAAn1/yN$uESHbzUpy9CyfoolBfOtSO.11077:0:99999:7: 1:-1:134540356
```

The format of the /etc/shadow entries with colon-separated fields resembles the entries in the /etc/passwd file, but the meanings of most of the fields differ. The first field is still the username, and the second one is the encrypted password.

The remaining fields in each /etc/shadow entry control when the password expires. You don't have to interpret or change these entries in the /etc/shadow file. Instead, use the chage command to change the password-expiration information. For starters, you can check a user's password-expiration information by using the chage command with the -l option, as follows (in this case, you have to be logged in as root):

```
chage -l root
```

This command displays expiration information, including how long the password lasts and how often you can change the password.

If you want to ensure that the user is forced to change a password every 90 days, you can use the -M option to set the maximum number of days that a password stays valid. For example, to make sure that user naba is prompted to change the password in 90 days, I log in as root and type the following command:

```
chage -M 90 naba
```

You can use the command for each user account to ensure that all passwords expire when appropriate, and that all users must pick new passwords.

**Book VII
Chapter 2**

**Securing the Host**

## *Pluggable authentication modules (PAMs)*

In addition to improving the password file's security by using shadow passwords, Fedora Core also improves the actual encryption of the passwords stored in the /etc/shadow file, using the MD5 message-digest algorithm described in RFC 1321 (www.ietf.org/rfc/rfc1321.txt or www.cis.ohio-state.edu/cgi-bin/rfc/rfc1321.html). MD5 reduces a message of any length to a 128-bit message digest (or *fingerprint*) of a document so you can digitally sign it by encrypting it with your private key. MD5 works quite well for password encryption, too.

Another advantage of MD5 over older-style password encryption is that the older passwords were limited to a maximum of eight characters; new passwords (encrypted with MD5) can be much longer. Longer passwords are harder to guess, even if the /etc/shadow file falls into the wrong hands.

You can tell that MD5 encryption is in effect in the /etc/shadow file. The encrypted passwords are longer and they all sport the $1$ prefix, as in the second field of the following sample entry:

```
root:$1$AAAni/yN$uESHbzUpy9Cgfoo1Bf0tSO:11077:0:99999:7:-1:-1:134540356
```

An add-in program module called a *pluggable authentication module* (PAM) performs the actual MD5 encryption. Fedora Core PAMs provide a flexible method for authenticating users. By setting the PAMs' configuration files, you can change your authentication method on the fly, without having to actually modify vital programs (such as login and passwd) that verify a user's identity.

Fedora Core uses PAM capabilities extensively. The PAMs reside in many different modules (more about that momentarily); their configuration files are in the /etc/pam.d directory of your system. Check out the contents of this directory on your system by typing the following command:

```
ls /etc/pam.d
```

Each configuration file in this directory specifies how users are authenticated for a specific utility. For example, you find a file for login, passwd, and su. Here's what I see when I type cat /etc/pam.d/passwd file on my system:

```
#%PAM-1.0
auth        required        pam_stack.so service=system-auth
account     required        pam_stack.so service=system-auth
password    required        pam_stack.so service=system-auth
```

These lines indicate that authentication, account management, and password checking are all done by using the pam_stack module (/lib/security/ pam_stack.so) with the argument service=system-auth. Essentially, the pam_stack module refers to another configuration file in the /etc/pam.d directory. In this case, the configuration file is /etc/pam.d/system-auth. Here's the content of the /etc/pam.d/system-auth file on my Fedora Core PC:

```
#%PAM-1.0
# This file is auto-generated.
# User changes will be destroyed the next time authconfig is run.
auth    required /lib/security/$ISA/pam_env.so
```

```
auth     sufficient /lib/security/$ISA/pam_unix.so likeauth nullok
auth     required   /lib/security/$ISA/pam_deny.so
account  required   /lib/security/$ISA/pam_unix.so
password required   /lib/security/$ISA/pam_cracklib.so retry=3 type=
password sufficient /lib/security/$ISA/pam_unix.so nullok use_authtok md5 shadow
password required   /lib/security/$ISA/pam_deny.so
session  required   /lib/security/$ISA/pam_limits.so
session  required   /lib/security/$ISA/pam_unix.so
```

Here's a brief explanation of what some of these lines in the configuration file do:

✦ The first `auth` line loads the PAM module `/lib/security/pam_env.so`. This module can set or unset environment variables (the `$ISA` in `/lib/security/$ISA/pam_env.so` refers to an environment variable that's typically not defined, so the effective pathname for the PAM module is `/lib/security/pam_env.so`).

✦ The second `auth` line specifies an authentication module that checks the user's identity by using the PAM module `/lib/security/pam_unix.so` with the argument string `likeauth nullok`. The options in the argument string have the following meanings:

  • `likeauth`: Returns the same value whether the module is used to set new credentials or authenticate an existing username.

  • `nullok`: Allows a blank password.

✦ The third `auth` line in the `/etc/pam.d/system-auth` file denies access to the system if the `pam_unix.so` module's authentication is unsuccessful.

✦ The `account` line in the `/etc/pam.d/system-auth` file checks to make sure that the user account has not expired, that the user is allowed to log in at a given time of day, and so on.

✦ The next two `password` lines in the `/etc/pam.d/system-auth` file specify how passwords are set:

  • The first password line uses the `/lib/security/pam_cracklib.so` module to try to crack the new password (that's what the `cracklib` in the module's name indicates).

  • The `retry=3` part indicates that the user can try to enter a new password three times at most. The second `password` line indicates that the MD5 encryption is used to store the password in the `/etc/shadow` file.

When you're done setting the `/etc/pam.d/passwd` configuration file, your choices apply when you use the `passwd` command to change passwords. Here's an example where I am trying to change my password (*my comments are shown in italics*):

```
passwd
Changing password for user naba.
Changing password for naba
(current) UNIX password:   I type my current password
New password: I type "xyzz"
BAD PASSWORD: it is too short
New password:   I type "transport" as password
BAD PASSWORD: it is based on a dictionary word
New password:   I type "naba12" as the new password
BAD PASSWORD: it is based on your username
passwd: Authentication token manipulation error
```

In this case, the passwd program is using the PAM module to check my identity (when I first type my current password) and make sure that each of the new passwords I try are strong. Finally, the PAM module aborts the passwd program after I fail to select a good password in three tries.

# Protecting Files and Directories

One important aspect of securing the host is to protect important system files — and the directories that contain these files. You can protect the files through the file ownership and through the permission settings that control who can read, write, or (in case of executable programs) execute the file.

The default Fedora Core file security is controlled through the following settings for each file or directory:

- ✦ User ownership
- ✦ Group ownership
- ✦ Read, write, execute permissions for owner
- ✦ Read, write, execute permissions for group
- ✦ Read, write, execute permissions for others (everyone else)

## Viewing ownerships and permissions

You can see these settings for a file when you look at the detailed listing with the ls -l command. For example, type the following command to see the detailed listing of the /etc/inittab file:

```
ls -l /etc/inittab
```

The resulting listing looks something like this:

```
-rw-r--r--  1 root root 1666 Feb 16 07:57 /etc/inittab
```

The first set of characters describes the file permissions for user, group, and others. The third and fourth fields show the user and group that own this file. In this case, both user and group names are the same: root.

## Changing file ownerships

You can set the user and group ownerships with the chown command. For example if the file /dev/hda is owned by the user root and the group disk, then you type the following command as root to set up this ownership:

```
chown root.disk /dev/hda
```

To change the group ownership alone, use the chgrp command. For example, here's how you can change the group ownership of a file to the group named accounting:

```
chgrp accounting ledger.out
```

## Changing file permissions

Use the chmod command to set the file permissions. To use chmod effectively, you have to specify the permission settings. One way is to *concatenate* one or more letters from each of the following tables, in the order shown (Who/Action/Permission) in Table 2-1.

| Table 2-1 | File Permission Codes | |
|---|---|---|
| *Who* | *Action* | *Permission* |
| u user | + add | r read |
| g group | - remove | w write |
| o others | = assign | x execute |
| a all | s set user ID | |

To give everyone read and write access to all files in a directory, type **chmod a+rw \***. On the other hand, to permit everyone to execute a specific file, type **chmod a+x *filename***.

Another way to specify a permission setting is to use a three-digit sequence of numbers. In a detailed listing, the read, write, and execute permission settings for the user, group, and others appear as the sequence

```
rwxrwxrwx
```

with dashes in place of letters for disallowed operations. Think of `rwxrwxrwx` as three occurrences of the string `rwx`. Now assign the values r=4, w=2, and x=1. To get the value of the sequence `rwx`, simply add the values of r, w, and x. Thus, `rwx = 7`. Using this formula, you can assign a three-digit value to any permission setting. For example, if the user can read and write the file but everyone else can only read the file, the permission setting is `rw-r--r--` (that's how it appears in the listing), and the value is 644. Thus, if you want all files in a directory to be readable by everyone but writable only by the user, use the following command:

```
chmod 644 *
```

## Setting default permission

What permission setting does a file get when you (or a program) create a new file? The answer is in what is known as the user file-creation mask that you can see and set using the `umask` command.

Type **umask**, and it prints out a number showing the current file-creation mask. The default setting is different for the `root` user and other normal users. For the `root` user the mask is set to 022, whereas the mask for normal users is 002. To see the effect of this file-creation mask and to interpret the meaning of the mask, follow these steps:

*1.* **Log in as** `root` **and type the following command:**

```
touch junkfile
```

This command creates a file named `junkfile` with nothing in it.

*2.* **Type** ls -l junkfile **to see that file's permissions.**

You see a line similar to the following:

```
-rw-r--r--  1 root    root       0 Aug 24 10:56 junkfile
```

Interpret the numerical value of the permission setting by converting each three-letter permission in the first field (excluding the very first letter) into a number between 0 and 7. For each letter that's present, the first letter gets a value of 4, the second letter is 2, and the third is 1. For example, `rw-` translates to 4+2+0 (because the third letter is missing) or 6. Similarly, `r--` is 4+0+0 = 4. Thus the permission string `-rw-r--r--` becomes 644.

*3.* **Subtract the numerical permission setting from 666 and what you get is the** umask **setting.**

In this case, 666 - 644 results in an `umask` of 022.

Thus an `umask` of 022 results in a default permission setting of 666-022 = 644. When you rewrite 644 in terms of a permission string, it becomes `rw-r--r--`.

To set a new `umask`, type **umask** followed by the numerical value of the mask. Here is how you go about it:

1.  **Figure out what permission settings you want for new files.**

    For example, if you want new files that can be read and written only by the owner and by nobody else, the permission setting looks like this:

    ```
    rw-------
    ```

2.  **Convert the permissions into a numerical value by using the conversion method that assigns 4 to the first field, 2 to the second, and 1 to the third.**

    Thus, for files that are readable and writable only by their owner, the permission setting is 600.

3.  **Subtract the desired permission setting from 666 to get the value of the mask.**

    For a permission setting of 600, the mask becomes 666 - 600 = 066.

4.  **Use the `umask` command to set the file-creation mask:**

    ```
    umask 066
    ```

A default `umask` of 022 is good for system security because it translates to files that have read and write permission for the owner and read permissions for everyone else. The bottom line is that you don't want a default `umask` that results in files that are writable by the whole wide world.

## Checking for set user ID permission

Another permission setting can be a security hazard. This permission setting, called the set user ID (or `setuid` for short), applies to executable files. When the `setuid` permission is enabled, the file executes under the user ID of the file's owner. In other words, if an executable program is owned by `root` and the `setuid` permission is set, no matter who executes that program, it runs as if `root` is executing it. This permission means that the program can do a lot more (for example, read all files, create new files, and delete files) than what a normal user program can do. Another risk is that if a `setuid` program file has some security hole, crackers can do a lot more damage through such programs than through other vulnerabilities.

You can find all `setuid` programs with a simple `find` command:

```
find / -type f -perm +4000 -print
```

You see a list of files such as the following:

```
/usr/bin/chage
/usr/bin/gpasswd
/usr/bin/chfn
/usr/bin/chsh
/usr/bin/newgrp
/usr/bin/passwd
/usr/bin/at
/usr/bin/rcp
/usr/bin/rlogin
/usr/bin/rsh
/usr/bin/sudo
/usr/bin/crontab
... lines deleted ...
```

Many of the programs have the `setuid` permission because they need it, but check the complete list and make sure that there are no strange `setuid` programs (for example, `setuid` programs in a user's home directory).

If you want to see how these permissions are listed by the `ls` command, type **ls -l /usr/bin/passwd** and you see the permission settings:

```
-r-s--x--x   1 root     root        16128 Jun  5 23:03 /usr/bin/passwd
```

The `s` in the owner's permission setting (`r-s`) tells you that the `setuid` permission is set.

## Using exec-shield

Buffer overflow is (if you'll pardon the expression) the root cause of many Linux security holes. When buffer overflow occurs, a cracker can overwrite data-storage areas of memory with instructions designed to execute nasty commands. But what if the Linux kernel refuses to execute instructions from any data area? Poof! — no more buffer overflows! That's exactly what the latest Linux kernel does: It protects against the common buffer overflow type of vulnerabilities by making many parts of a program's memory (including the stack where temporary variables are stored) not executable. This feature of the Linux kernel is called `exec-shield`.

The best part about `exec-shield` is that you don't have to fix the applications that have the buffer-overflow problem. All you have to do is turn on the feature. To make the process even easier, Fedora Core enables `exec-shield` by default.

Some programs may have trouble working correctly when `exec-shield` is enabled. If you have to turn off `exec-shield`, log in as `root` and type the following command from a terminal window:

```
echo 0 > /proc/sys/kernel/exec-shield
```

That command sets the `exec-shield` kernel option to 0. The `exec-shield` option can take one of three values — 0, 1, and 2. Think of these values as three different levels of security. Table 2-2 summarizes the meaning of the three values of `exec-shield`. Fedora Core sets `exec-shield` to 1 by default.

| Table 2-2 | Four Levels of Security Using Exec Shield |
|---|---|
| *This Value of exec-shield* | *Has This Meaning* |
| 0 | exec-shield is always disabled. |
| 1 | exec-shield is enabled for programs compiled with the newest version of gcc compiler. |
| 2 | exec-shield is always enabled. |

To set `exec-shield` to its default value, type:

```
echo 1 > /proc/sys/kernel/exec-shield
```

# Using SELinux

Fedora Core comes with Security Enhanced Linux (SELinux), which provides mandatory access control with a much finer-grained control than just user and group ownership of files and processes. The access control is determined by the SELinux policy that specifies the access permissions for everything — files, devices, programs, and users — in the system. Fedora Core comes with a default security policy that works right out of the box. If you install Fedora Core with SELinux enabled (by typing **selinux** at the `boot:` prompt), you don't have to do anything to use SELinux — it works behind the scenes controlling which users or processes can access various system resources, such as files and devices.

To provide the fine-grained access control, SELinux requires that each file include a security context — think of it as the security attributes of the file or directory. Adding contexts to the files is referred to as labeling the filesystem. The filesystem is already labeled when you install Fedora Core and enable SELinux. However, if you need to re-label a filesystem, you can do so with the `setfiles` or `fixfiles` command.

You can easily check the context of a file, a user, or a process by using a new -Z option with the usual Linux commands such as ls, id, and ps. For example, to see the details of the /etc/passwd file including its security context, type **ls -lZ /etc/passwd**. Here is a typical output of this command (if SELinux is not enabled, you get an error message):

```
-rw-r--r--+ root   root    system_u:object_r:etc_t    /etc/passwd
```

*Note:* The context is in the form of three colon-separated fields that precede the filename — the first field is the identity, the second field is the role, and the third field is the type.

If you want to know the context of whatever user ID you are currently logged in as, type **id -Z**. For example, here is the output of the id -Z command when you are logged in as a root:

```
root:sysadm_r:sysadm_t
```

To see the processes with their security contexts, type **ps axZ**. Here is a partial listing of output from the ps axZ command (the context appears in the second column):

```
PID CONTEXT                               COMMAND
  1 system_u:system_r:init_t              init [5]
  2 system_u:system_r:kernel_t            [ksoftirqd/0]
  3 system_u:system_r:kernel_t            [events/0]
  4 system_u:system_r:kernel_t            [kblockd/0]
  5 system_u:system_r:kernel_t            [pdflush]
  6 system_u:system_r:kernel_t            [pdflush]
  8 system_u:system_r:kernel_t            [aio/0]
  7 system_u:system_r:kernel_t            [kswapd0]
  9 system_u:system_r:kernel_t            [kseriod]
 13 system_u:system_r:kernel_t            [kjournald]
102 system_u:system_r:kernel_t            [khubd]
240 system_u:system_r:kernel_t            [usb-storage]
241 system_u:system_r:kernel_t            [scsi_eh_0]
770 system_u:system_r:kernel_t            [kjournald]
... lines deleted ...
```

To perform some tasks such as system administration with SELinux enabled, you have to assume a specific role. You can assume a new role (provided you have access to that new role) by using the newrole command. For example, to change to the sysadm_r role (the system administrator role), type the following command:

```
newrole -r sysadm_r
```

When SELinux is installed and enabled, you must also take care to start various servers such as the Web server and the mail server with the correct context. Use the `run_init` command to execute the scripts in the `/etc/init.d` directory to start (or stop) the servers. For example, to start the secure shell server (`sshd`) in the correct context, type the following command:

```
run_init /etc/init.d/sshd start
```

The `run_init` command prompts you for your password before performing the function, which prevents unauthorized users from starting or stopping servers.

In this section, I only touch briefly on how to use SELinux. To find more about SELinux in Fedora Core, see the online documentation at `people. redhat.com/kwade/fedora-docs/selinux-faq-en/`.

# Encrypting and Signing Files with GnuPG

Fedora Core comes with the *GNU Privacy Guard* (GnuPG or, simply GPG) encryption and authentication utility. With GPG, you can create your public and private key pair, encrypt files using your key, and also digitally sign a message to authenticate that it's really from you. If you send a digitally signed message to someone who has your public key, the recipient can verify that it was you who signed the message.

## Understanding public-key encryption

The basic idea behind public-key encryption is to use a pair of keys — one private and the other public — that are related but can't be used to guess one from the other. Anything encrypted with the private key can be decrypted only with the corresponding public key, and vice versa. The public key is for distribution to other people while you keep the private key in a safe place.

You can use public-key encryption to communicate securely with others; Figure 2-1 illustrates the basic idea. Suppose Alice wants to send secure messages to Bob. Each of them generates public-and-private-key pairs, after which they exchange their public keys. Then, when Alice wants to send a message to Bob, she simply encrypts the message using Bob's public key and sends the encrypted message to him. Now the message is secure from any eavesdropping because only Bob's private key can decrypt the message — and only Bob has that key. When Bob receives the message, he uses his private key to decrypt the message and read it.

At this point, you need to stop and think and say "Wait a minute!" How does Bob know the message really came from Alice? What if someone else uses Bob's public key and sends a message as if it came from Alice? This situation is where digital signature comes in.

**Figure 2-1:**
Bob and
Alice
can com-
municate
securely
with
public-key
encryption.

Alice encrypts the message
using Bob's public key.

Bob decypts the message
using his private key.

Bob's public key

Bob's private key

Alice

Bob

## Understanding digital signatures

The purpose of digital or electronic signatures is the same as pen-and-ink
signatures, but how you sign digitally is completely different. Unlike pen-and-
ink signatures, your digital signature depends on the message you're signing.
The first step in creating a digital signature is to apply a mathematical function on the message and reduce it to a fixed-size message digest (also called
*hash* or a *fingerprint*). No matter how big your message is, the message
digest is always around 128 or 160 bits, depending on the hashing function.

The next step is to apply public-key encryption. Simply encrypt the message
digest with your private key, and you get the digital signature for the message. Typically, the digital signature is appended to the end of the message,
and voilà — you get an electronically signed message.

What good does the digital signature do? Well, anyone who wants to verify
that the message is indeed signed by you takes your public key and decrypts
the digital signature. What they get is the message digest (the encrypted hash)
of the message. Then they apply the same hash function to the message and
compare the computed hash with the decrypted value. If the two match, then
no one has tampered with the message. Because your public key was used to
verify the signature, the message must have been signed with the private key
known only to you. So the message must be from you!

In the theoretical scenario of Alice sending private messages to Bob, Alice
can digitally sign her message to make sure that Bob can tell that the message is really from her. Figure 2-2 illustrates the use of digital signature along
with normal public-key encryption.

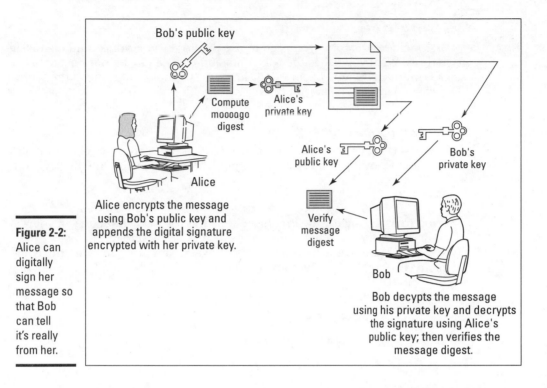

**Figure 2-2:**
Alice can digitally sign her message so that Bob can tell it's really from her.

Here's how Alice sends her private message to Bob with the assurance that Bob can really tell it's from her:

1. Alice uses software to compute the message digest of the message and then encrypts the digest, using her private key. This is her digital signature for the message.

2. Alice encrypts the message (again, using some convenient software *and* Bob's public key).

3. She sends both the encrypted message and the digital signature to Bob.

4. Bob decrypts the message using his private key.

5. Bob decrypts the digital signature using Alice's public key. This gives him the message digest.

6. Bob computes the message digest of the message and compares it with what he got by decrypting the digital signature.

7. If the two message digests match, Bob can be sure that the message really came from Alice.

## Using GPG

GPG includes the tools you need to use public key encryption and digital signatures. What you use is the `gpg` command. You can figure out how to use GPG gradually as you begin using encryption. I show you some of the typical tasks you may perform with GPG.

### Generating the key pair

The first thing you have to do is generate your own private-public key pair. Type the following command in a terminal window to generate the key pair:

```
gpg --gen-key
```

If you're using `gpg` for the first time, it creates a `.gnupg` directory in your home directory and a file named `options` in that directory. Then `gpg` exits with a message that asks you to run `gpg` again. Now you can rerun the command. The steps for generating the key pairs go like this:

1. **Type the** `gpg --gen-key` **command again.**

    You see a message like this:

    ```
    Please select what kind of key you want:
       (1) DSA and ElGamal (default)
       (2) DSA (sign only)
       (5) RSA (sign only)
    Your selection?
    ```

2. **Press Enter for the default choice because it's good enough.**

    GPG then prompts you for the key size (the number of bits).

3. **Press Enter again to accept the default value of 1024 bits.**

    GPG asks you when the keys expire. The default is to never expire.

4. **If the default is what you want (and why not?), press Enter.**

5. **When GPG asks if you really want the keys to never expire, press the Y key to confirm.**

    GPG prompts you for your name, your e-mail address, and finally a comment so that the key pair is associated with your name.

6. **Type each piece of requested information and press Enter.**

7. **When GPG gives you a chance to change the information or confirm it as is, confirm by typing** o **and then pressing Enter.**

    GPG next prompts you for a passphrase that protects your private key.

8. **Type a long phrase that includes lower- and uppercase letters, numbers, and punctuation marks — the longer the better — and then press Enter.**

   Careful though; pick a passphrase that you can easily remember.

   GPG generates the keys. It may ask you to perform some work on the PC so that the random number generator can generate enough random numbers for the key-generation process.

## Exchanging keys

To communicate with others, you have to give them your public key. You also have to get public keys from those who may send you a message (or someone who might sign a file and you want to verify the signature). GPG keeps the public keys in your key ring. To list the keys in your key ring, type

```
gpg --list-keys
```

To send your public key to someone or place it on a Web site, you have to export the key to a file. The best way is to put the key in what GPG documentation calls an *ASCII-armored* format with a command like this:

```
gpg --armor --export naba@comcast.net > nabakey.asc
```

This command saves my public key in an ASCII-armored format (it basically looks like garbled text) in the file named `nabakey.asc`. Of course, you replace the e-mail address with your e-mail address (the one you used when you created the key) and the output filename to something different.

After you export the public key to a file, you can mail that file to others or place it on a Web site for use by others.

When you import a key from someone else, you typically get it in an ASCII-armored format as well. For example, if I have a `fedora@redhat.com` GPG public key in a file named `fedorakey.asc`, I import it into my key ring with the following command:

```
gpg --import fedorakey.asc
```

Use the `gpg --list-keys` command to verify that the key is in your key ring. For example, here's what I see when I type **gpg –list-keys** on my system:

```
gpg: please see http://www.gnupg.org/faq.html for more information
/home/naba/.gnupg/pubring.gpg
----------------------------
pub   1024D/D1929123 2004-04-15 Naba Barkakati <naba@comcast.net>
sub   1024g/6D1AE9B8 2004-04-15
```

```
pub  1024D/4F2A6FD2 2003-10-27 Fedora Project <fedora@redhat.com>
sub  1024g/FB939E34 2003-10-27
```

The next step is to check the fingerprint of the new key. I type the following command to get the fingerprint of the Fedora key:

```
gpg --fingerprint fedora@redhat.com
```

GPG prints the fingerprint:

```
pub  1024D/4F2A6FD2 2003-10-27 Fedora Project <fedora@redhat.com>
     Key fingerprint = CAB4 4B99 6F27 744E 8612  7CDF B442 69D0 4F2A 6FD2
sub  1024g/FB939E34 2003-10-27
```

At this point, you need to verify the key fingerprint with someone at Red Hat. For a large project such as Fedora, you can verify the fingerprint from the Fedora Web page (`fedora.redhat.com/about/security/`). If you think the key fingerprint is good, you can sign the key and validate it. Here's the command you use to sign the key:

```
gpg --sign-key fedora@redhat.com
```

GPG displays a message and prompts you on the level of key verification you have performed:

```
gpg: checking the trustdb
gpg: checking at depth 0 signed=0 ot(-/q/n/m/f/u)=0/0/0/0/0/1
pub 1024D/4F2A6FD2  created: 2003-10-27 expires: never      trust: -/-
sub 1024g/FB939E34  created: 2003-10-27 expires: never
(1). Fedora Project <fedora@redhat.com>

pub 1024D/4F2A6FD2  created: 2003-10-27 expires: never      trust: -/-
 Primary key fingerprint: CAB4 4B99 6F27 744E 8612  7CDF B442 69D0 4F2A 6FD2

     Fedora Project <fedora@redhat.com>

How carefully have you verified the key you are about to sign actually belongs
to the person named above?  If you don't know what to answer, enter "0".

   (0) I will not answer. (default)
   (1) I have not checked at all.
   (2) I have done casual checking.
   (3) I have done very careful checking.

Your selection?
```

After you answer and press Enter, GPG asks for confirmation and then prompts you for your passphrase. After that GPG signs the key.

Because the key verification and signing is a potential weak link in GPG, be careful about what keys you sign. By signing a key, you basically say that you trust the key to be from that person or organization.

### Signing a file

You may find signing files useful if you send out a file to someone and want to assure the recipient no one tampered with the file and you sent the file. GPG makes signing a file very easy. You can compress and sign a file named `message` with the following command:

```
gpg -o message.sig -s message
```

To verify the signature, type

```
gpg --verify message.sig
```

To get back the original document, simply type

```
gpg -o message --decrypt message.sig
```

Sometimes you don't care about keeping a message secret, but simply want to sign it to indicate that the message is from you. In such a case, you can generate and append a clear-text signature with the following command:

```
gpg -o message.asc --clearsign message
```

This command basically appends a clear-text signature to the text message. Here's a typical clear-text signature block:

```
-----BEGIN PGP SIGNATURE-----
Version: GnuPG v1.2.4 (GNU/Linux)

iD8DBQFAfdhOH/butdGSkSMRAo5VAJsFGSlwA3z6PQJwXZVSDCVMjphZFACeIYfB
YSZSM86EedATw/Hexeqa6TM=
=vyUl
-----END PGP SIGNATURE-----
```

When a message has a clear-text signature appended, you can use GPG to verify the signature with the following command:

```
gpg --verify message.asc
```

The last line of the output says that it's a good signature.

### Encrypting and decrypting documents

To encrypt a message meant for a recipient, you can use the `--encrypt` (or `-e`) GPG command. Here's how you might encrypt a message for me if you had my public GPG key:

```
gpg -o message.gpg -e -r naba@comcast.net message
```

The message is encrypted using my public key (without any signature, but you can add the signature with an `-s` command).

When I receive the `message.gpg` file, I have to decrypt it using my private key. Here's the command I use:

```
gpg -o message --decrypt message.gpg
```

GPG then prompts me for the passphrase to unlock my private key and then decrypts the message and saves the output in the file named `message`.

If you simply want to encrypt a file and no one else has to decrypt the file, you can use GPG to perform what is called *symmetric encryption*. In this case, you provide a passphrase to encrypt the file with the following GPG command:

```
gpg -o secret.gpg -c somefile
```

GPG prompts you for the passphrase and asks you to repeat the passphrase (to make sure that you didn't mistype anything). Then GPG encrypts the file using a key generated from the passphrase.

To decrypt a file encrypted with a symmetric key, type

```
gpg -o myfile --decrypt secret.gpg
```

GPG prompts you for the passphrase. If you enter the correct passphrase, GPG decrypts the file and saves the output (in this example) in the file named `myfile`.

# Monitoring System Security

Even if you secure your system, you have to monitor the log files periodically for signs of intrusion. You may want to install the Tripwire software to monitor the integrity of critical system files and directories. Fedora Core does not come with the Tripwire package. To use Tripwire, you have to download it from `www.tripwire.org/downloads/index.php`. You have to download the source tarball (a compressed archive of source files) and then build Tripwire. (Book VI, Chapter 4 provides more information on how to build software packages from source files.) After you build and install Tripwire, you can configure it to monitor any changes to specified system files and directories on your system.

Periodically examine the log files. Many Fedora Core applications, including some servers, write log information using the logging capabilities of `syslogd`.

On Fedora Core systems, the log files written by syslogd reside in the /var/log directory. Make sure that only the root user can read and write these files.

The syslogd configuration file is /etc/syslog.conf. The default configuration of syslogd generates the necessary log files; however, if you want to examine and understand the configuration file, type **man syslog.conf** for more information.

Routinely monitor the following log files:

✦ /var/log/messages contains a wide variety of logging messages, from user logins to messages from services started by the TCP wrapper.

✦ /var/log/secure contains reports from services, such as in.telnetd and in.ftpd, which xinetd starts through the TCP wrapper.

✦ /var/log/maillog contains reports from sendmail.

✦ /var/log/xferlog contains a log of all FTP file transfers.

Fedora Core comes with a graphical log-file viewer utility. To use this tool, select Main Menu⇨System Tools⇨System Logs from the GNOME panel. Figure 2-3 shows the System Logs utility.

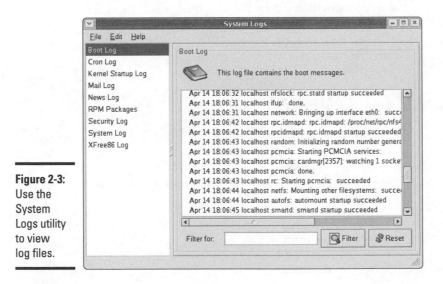

**Figure 2-3:**
Use the System Logs utility to view log files.

The System Logs utility is simple to use. Click the log filename in the left window and view the contents in the scrolling text window to the right.

Because many potential intruders use port-scanning tools in an attempt to establish TCP/IP connections to well-known ports on your system, you need to look for messages that indicate attempted connections from unknown hosts (as indicated by names or IP addresses). To do this type of checking, click Security Log in the left window and then browse the log messages that appear in the right window. You see lines such as the following:

```
Apr 13 19:30:37 localhost xinetd[1691]: START: telnet pid=15174 from=192.168.0.4
Apr 13 20:50:54 localhost userhelper[4722]: running '/usr/sbin/printconf-gui'
    with root privileges on behalf of 'root'
```

Where applicable, these lines show you the type of connection (telnet, sshd, and so on) and the IP addresses from where the connections originated. If you want to browse through these messages using a text editor, you can find them in the /var/log/secure file.

In Fedora Core, the LogWatch log-monitoring system is installed by default. LogWatch goes through your system's log files and sends an e-mail message to root with a report of anything worth noting such as a summary of FTP transfers, invalid login attempts, mail messages transferred by sendmail, and current disk space information. You can read these messages by logging in as root and typing **mail** in a terminal window.

# Chapter 3: Securing the Network

## In This Chapter

✔ **Securing Internet services**

✔ **Using Secure Shell (SSH) for secure remote logins**

✔ **Setting up simple firewalls**

✔ **Enabling packet filtering on your Fedora Core system**

To secure your Fedora Core system, you have to pay attention to both host security and network security. The distinction between the two types of security is somewhat arbitrary because securing the network involves fixing up things on the host that relate to what Internet services your system offers. In this chapter, I explain how you can secure the Internet services (mostly by not offering unnecessary services), how you can use a firewall to stop unwanted network packets from reaching your network, and how to use Secure Shell for secure remote logins.

## Securing Internet Services

For an Internet-connected Fedora Core system (or even one on a TCP/IP LAN that's not connected to the Internet), a significant threat is the possibility that someone could use one of many Internet services to gain access to your system. Each service — such as mail, Web, or FTP — requires running a server program that responds to client requests arriving over the TCP/IP network. Some of these server programs have weaknesses that can allow an outsider to log in to your system — maybe with `root` privileges. Luckily, Fedora Core comes with some facilities you can use to make the Internet services more secure.

Potential intruders can employ a port-scanning tool — a program that attempts to establish a TCP/IP connection at a port and to look for a response — to check which Internet servers are running on your system. Then, to gain access to your system, the intruders can potentially exploit any known weaknesses of one or more services.

## Using chkconfig to disable standalone services

To provide Internet services such as Web, mail, and FTP, your Fedora Core system has to run server programs that listen to incoming TCP/IP network requests. Some of these servers are started when your system boots, and they run all the time. Such servers are called *standalone servers*. The Web server and mail server are examples of standalone servers. Another server, called `xinetd`, starts on demand the other servers.

You can turn the standalone servers on or off by using the `chkconfig` command. Here's how you use `chkconfig` to stop unneeded services:

✦ Log in as `root` and type **chkconfig –list** to view all the services set to start automatically at run levels 0 through 6 (see Book VI, Chapter 1 for more on run levels).

✦ The services for run levels 3 and 5 matter most because your Fedora Core system is usually at run level 3 (text mode) or 5 (graphical login). Type **runlevel** to see the current run level.

✦ Decide which services you don't need. What you need or don't need depends on how you use your Fedora Core system. For example, if it's just a personal workstation, you don't have to run most services.

✦ To stop a service, use the following form of the `chkconfig` command:

```
chkconfig --level 345 service_name off
```

where `service_name` is the name of the service you want to turn off. For example, to prevent the `ypserv` service from automatically starting at run levels 3, 4, and 5, type the following command:

```
chkconfig --level 345 ypserv off
```

Using this approach, you can use `chkconfig` to stop all unneeded services from starting at boot time.

To stop a service immediately, use the `service` command like this:

```
service service_name stop
```

where `service_name` is the name of the service to stop. For example, if the mail server (`sendmail`) is already running, you can stop it with the following command:

```
service sendmail stop
```

## Configuring the xinetd server to disable services

In addition to standalone servers such as a Web server (`httpd`), mail (`sendmail`), and domain name server (`named`), you have to configure another server separately. That other server, xinetd (the Internet super server), starts a host of other Internet services, such as FTP, TELNET, and so on whenever a client makes a request over the network. The xinetd server includes some security features that you can use to disable the services that it can start on demand.

The xinetd server reads a configuration file named /etc/xinetd.conf at startup. This file, in turn, refers to configuration files stored in the /etc/xinetd.d directory. The configuration files in /etc/xinetd.d tell xinetd which ports to listen to and which server to start for each port. Type **ls /etc/xinetd.d** to see a list of the files in the /etc/xinetd.d directory on your system. On my system, here's what the ls /etc/xinetd.d command lists:

```
chargen      cups-lpd  daytime-udp  echo-udp  rsync     sgi_fam  time
chargen-udp  daytime   echo         ktalk     services  telnet   time-udp
```

This list shows all the services xinetd can start. However, the configuration file for a service can also turn off a service simply by having a disable = yes line in the file. For example, here's the telnet file's content:

```
# default: on
# description: The telnet server serves telnet sessions;
#      it uses unencrypted username/password pairs for
#      authentication.
service telnet
{
        flags            = REUSE
        socket_type      = stream
        wait             = no
        user             = root
        server           = /usr/sbin/in.telnetd
        log_on_failure  += USERID
        disable          = yes
}
```

Notice the last line in the configuration file — that line disables the TELNET service.

I don't explain the format of the xinetd configuration files, except to reiterate that you can turn off a service simply by adding the following line in the configuration file somewhere between the two curly braces {...}:

```
        disable          = yes
```

You can also use the chkconfig command to turn on or off the services controlled by xinetd. For example, to allow the TELNET service, type the following command:

```
chkconfig telnet on
```

**Book VII
Chapter 3**

**Securing the
Network**

Depending on how you use your system, you may be able to disable many of the services. If you don't want anyone to log in remotely or download files from your system, simply disable the TELNET and FTP services.

After you make any changes to the `xinetd` configuration files, you must restart the `xinetd` server; otherwise the changes don't take effect. To restart the `xinetd` server, type the following command:

```
service xinetd restart
```

This command stops the `xinetd` server and then starts it again. When it restarts, it reads the configuration files, and the changes take effect.

Another security feature of `xinetd` is its use of the TCP wrapper to start various services. The *TCP wrapper* is a block of code that provides an access-control facility for Internet services, acting like a protective package for your message. The TCP wrapper can start other services, such as FTP and TELNET; but before starting a service, it consults the `/etc/hosts.allow` file to see whether the host requesting service is allowed that service. If nothing appears in `/etc/hosts.allow` about that host, TCP wrapper checks the `/etc/hosts.deny` file to see if it denies the service. If both files are empty, TCP wrapper provides access to the requested service.

Here are the steps to follow to tighten the access to the services that `xinetd` is configured to start:

1. **Use a text editor to edit the** `/etc/hosts.deny` **file, adding the following line into that file:**

   ```
   ALL:ALL
   ```

   This setting denies all hosts access to any Internet services on your system.

2. **Edit the** `/etc/hosts.allow` **file and add to it the names of hosts that can access services on your system.**

   For example, to enable only hosts from the 192.168.1.0 network and the `localhost` (IP address 127.0.0.1) to access the services on your system, place the following line in the `/etc/hosts.allow` file:

   ```
   ALL: 192.168.1.0/255.255.255.0 127.0.0.1
   ```

3. **If you want to permit access to a specific Internet service to a specific remote host, you can do so by using the following syntax for a line in** `/etc/hosts.allow`**:**

   ```
   server_program_name: hosts
   ```

Here *server_program_name* is the name of the server program (for example, `in.telnetd` for TELNET), and *hosts* is a comma-separated list of hosts that can access the service. You may also write *hosts* as a network address or an entire domain name, such as .mycompany.com. For example, here's how you can give TELNET access to all systems in the mycompany.com domain:

```
in.telnetd: .mycompany.com
```

 Edit the configuration files in the /etc/xinetd.d directory to turn off unneeded services; use the /etc/hosts.deny and /etc/hosts.allow files to control access to the services that are allowed to run on your system. After you edit the files in the /etc/xinetd.d directory, remember to type **service xinetd restart** to restart the xinetd server.

# Using Secure Shell (SSH) for Remote Logins

Fedora Core comes with the *Open Secure Shell* (OpenSSH) software, a suite of programs that provides a secure replacement for the Berkeley r commands: `rlogin` (remote login), `rsh` (remote shell), and `rcp` (remote copy). OpenSSH uses public-key cryptography to authenticate users and to encrypt the communication between two hosts, so users can securely log in from remote systems and copy files securely.

In this section, I briefly describe how to use the OpenSSH software in Fedora Core. To find out more about OpenSSH and read the latest news about it, visit www.openssh.com or www.openssh.org.

The OpenSSH software is installed during Fedora Core installation. Table 3-1 lists the main components of the OpenSSH software.

**Book VII**
**Chapter 3**

**Securing the Network**

| Table 3-1 | Components of the OpenSSH Software |
|---|---|
| *Component* | *Description* |
| /usr/sbin/sshd | This Secure Shell daemon must run on a host if you want users on remote systems to use the ssh client to log in securely. When a connection from a ssh client arrives, sshd performs authentication using public-key cryptography and establishes an encrypted communication link with the ssh client. |
| /usr/bin/ssh | Users can run this Secure Shell client to log in to a host that is running sshd. Users can also use ssh to execute a command on another host. |
| /usr/bin/slogin | A symbolic link to /usr/bin/ssh. |

*(continued)*

**Table 3-1** *(continued)*

| Component | Description |
|---|---|
| /usr/bin/scp | The secure-copy program that works like rcp, but securely. The scp program uses ssh for data transfer and provides the same authentication and security as ssh. |
| /usr/bin/ssh-keygen | You use this program to generate the public-and-private key pairs you need for the public-key cryptography used in OpenSSH. The ssh-keygen program can generate key pairs for both RSA and DSA (Digital Signature Algorithm) authentication. |
| /etc/ssh/sshd_config | This configuration file for the sshd server specifies many parameters for sshd — including the port to listen to, the protocol to use (there are two versions of SSH protocols, SSH1 and SSH2, both supported by OpenSSH), and the location of other files. |
| /etc/ssh/ssh_config | This configuration file is for the ssh client. Each user can also have a ssh configuration file named config in the .ssh subdirectory of the user's home directory. |

OpenSSH uses public-key encryption where the sender and receiver both have a pair of keys — a public key and a private key. The public keys are freely distributed, and each party knows the other's public key. The sender encrypts data by using the recipient's public key. Only the recipient's private key can then decrypt the data.

To use OpenSSH, do both of the following:

✦ If you want to support SSH-based remote logins on a host, start the sshd server on your system. Type **ps ax | grep sshd** to see if the server is already running. If not, log in as root, and type the following command at the shell prompt to ensure that the sshd server starts at a system reboot:

```
chkconfig --level 35 sshd on
```

To start the sshd server immediately, type the following command:

```
service sshd start
```

✦ Generate the host keys with the following command:

```
ssh-keygen -d -f /etc/ssh/ssh_host_key -N ''
```

The -d flag causes the ssh-keygen program to generate DSA keys, which the SSH2 protocol uses. If you see a message saying that the file /etc/ssh/ssh_host_key already exists, that means that the key pairs were generated during Fedora Core installation. You can then use the existing file without having to regenerate the keys.

A user who wants to log in using ssh must also generate the public-and-private key pair. For example, here is what I do so I can log in from another system on my Fedora Core system using SSH:

*1.* I type the following command to generate the DSA keys for use with SSH2:

```
ssh-keygen -d
```

I am prompted for a passphrase and the last message informs me that my public key is saved in /home/naba/.ssh/id_dsa.pub.

*2.* I copy my public key — the /home/naba/.ssh/id_dsa.pub file — to the remote system and save it as the ~/.ssh/authorized_keys2 file (this name refers to the authorized_keys2 file in the .ssh subdirectory of the other system, assuming that the remote system is also another Fedora Core system). Note that the 2 in the name of the authorized_keys2 file refers to the SSH2 protocol.

*3.* To log in to my account on my Fedora Core system (with host name lnbp200), I type the following command on the remote system:

```
ssh lnbp200 -l naba
```

*4.* When prompted for my password on the lnbp200 host, I enter the password. I can also log in to this account with the following equivalent command:

```
ssh naba@lnbp200
```

If I simply want to copy a file securely from the lnbp200 system, I can use scp like this:

```
scp lnbp200:/etc/ssh/ssh_config .
```

This command securely copies the /etc/ssh/ssh_config file from the lnbp200 host to the system from which I type the command.

# Setting Up Simple Firewalls

An Internet *firewall* is an intermediary between your internal network and the Internet. The firewall controls access to and from the protected internal network.

If you connect an internal network directly to the Internet, you have to make sure that every system on the internal network is properly secured — which can be nearly impossible because only one careless user can render the entire internal network vulnerable. A firewall is a single point of connection to the Internet: You can direct all your efforts toward making that firewall system a daunting barrier to unauthorized external users.

To be useful, a firewall has the following general characteristics:

✦ It must control the flow of packets between the Internet and the internal network.

✦ It must *not* provide dynamic routing because dynamic routing tables are subject to route *spoofing* — use of fake routes by intruders. Instead, the firewall uses static routing tables (which you can set up with the `route` command on Fedora Core systems).

✦ It must not allow any external user to log in as `root`. That way, even if the firewall system is compromised, the intruder is blocked from using `root` privileges from a remote login.

✦ It must be kept in a physically secure location.

✦ It must distinguish between packets that come from the Internet and packets that come from the internal protected network. This feature allows the firewall to reject packets that come from the Internet, but have the IP address of a trusted system on the internal network.

✦ It acts as the SMTP mail gateway for the internal network. Set up the sendmail software so that all outgoing mail appears to come from the firewall system.

✦ It cannot have any user accounts. However, the firewall system may have to have a few user accounts for those internal users who need access to external systems. External users who need access to the internal network should use SSH for remote login (see discussion of SSH earlier in this chapter).

✦ It keeps a log of all system activities, such as successful and unsuccessful login attempts.

✦ It provides DNS name-lookup service to the outside world to resolve any host names that are known to the outside world.

✦ It provides good performance so it doesn't hinder the internal users' access to specific Internet services (such as HTTP and FTP).

A firewall can take many different forms. Here are three common forms of a firewall:

✦ **Screening router with packet filtering:** This simple firewall uses a router capable of filtering (blocking) packets according to their IP addresses.

✦ **Dual-homed host with proxy services:** In this case, a host with two network interfaces — one on the Internet and the other on the internal network — runs proxy services that act as a gateway for services, such as FTP and HTTP.

✦ **Perimeter network with bastion host:** This firewall configuration includes a perimeter network between the Internet and the protected internal network. A secure bastion host resides on the perimeter network and provides various services.

In a large organization, you may also have to isolate smaller internal networks from the corporate network. You can set up such internal firewalls the same way you set up Internet firewalls.

In the next few sections, I describe the common forms of a firewall: screening router with packet filtering, dual-homed host, perimeter network with bastion host, and application gateway.

## Screening the router with packet filtering

If you directly connect your organization's internal network to the Internet, you have to use a router to ensure proper exchange of packets between the internal network and the Internet. Most routers can block a packet according to its source or its destination IP address (as well as the port number it seeks to use). The router's packet-filtering capability can serve as a simple firewall. Figure 3-1 illustrates the basic concept of packet filtering.

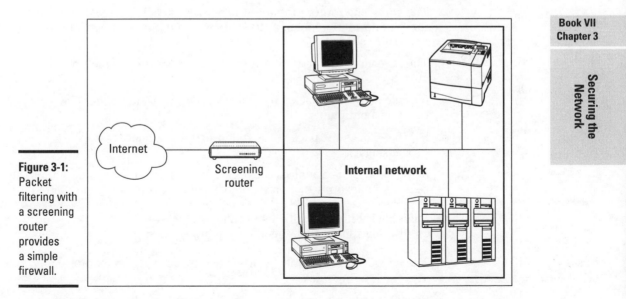

**Figure 3-1:** Packet filtering with a screening router provides a simple firewall.

Many router vendors, such as Cisco and 3Com, offer routers that can be programmed to perform packet filtering. The exact details of filtering depend on the router vendor, but all routers operate according to rules that refer to the basic attributes of an Internet packet:

✦ Source IP address

✦ Destination IP address

✦ Protocol (TCP, UDP, or ICMP)

✦ Source port number (if protocol is TCP or UDP)

✦ Destination port number (if protocol is TCP or UDP)

✦ ICMP message type

In addition, the router knows the physical interface on which the packet arrived and the interface on which the packet goes out (if it's not blocked by the filtering rules).

Most packet filters operate in the following sequence:

*1.* You define the rules for allowing or blocking specific types of packets based on IP addresses and port numbers. These packet-filtering rules are stored in the router.

*2.* The screening router examines the header of each packet that arrives for the information (such as IP addresses and port numbers) to which your rules apply.

*3.* The screening router applies the rules in the order in which they are stored.

*4.* If a rule allows the packet to be forwarded, the router sends the packet to its destination.

*5.* If a rule blocks the packet, the router drops the packet (stops processing it).

*6.* If none of the rules applies, the packet is blocked. This rule epitomizes the security philosophy that one should "deny unless expressly permitted."

Although packet filtering with a screening router is better than no security, packet filtering suffers from the following drawbacks:

✦ The network administrator can easily introduce errors inadvertently into the filtering rules.

✦ Packets are filtered on the basis of IP addresses, which represent specific hosts. Essentially, packet filtering either blocks or routes all packets from a specific host. That means that anyone who breaks into a trusted host can immediately gain access to your protected network.

✦ Because it's based on IP addresses, packet filtering can be defeated by a technique known as *IP spoofing,* whereby a cracker sends packets with the IP address of a trusted host (by appropriating the IP address of a trusted host and setting up an appropriate route); packets with these fake IP addresses can then gain access to your system.

✦ Packet filtering is susceptible to routing-attack programs that can create a bogus route, allowing an intruder to receive all packets meant for the protected internal network.

✦ Screening routers that implement packet filtering don't keep logs of activities. That makes determining if anyone is attempting to break into the protected network hard for you. As you see in the next section, a dual-homed host can provide logging.

✦ A screening router does not hide the host names and IP addresses of the internal network. Outsiders can access and use this exposed information to mount attacks against the protected network.

A more sophisticated approach is to use an application gateway that controls network traffic, based on specific applications instead of on a per-packet basis. You can implement an application gateway with a dual-homed host, known also as a *bastion host*.

## Dual-homed host

A *dual-homed host* is a system with two network interfaces — one connected to the Internet and the other on an internal network that needs protection. The term "dual-homed" refers to the fact that the host "lives" in two networks.

In fact, if your operating system supports IP routing — the ability to forward network packets from one interface to another — the dual-homed host can serve as a router. However, you must turn off the IP forwarding feature to use the dual-homed host as a firewall system.

The Linux kernel supports the IP forwarding feature. If you plan to use a dual-homed host as a firewall, you have to use the `sysctl` command to disable IP forwarding.

With IP forwarding turned off, systems on both networks — the internal network as well as the Internet — can reach the dual-homed host, but no one from the Internet can access the internal network (nor can anyone from the internal network access the Internet). In this configuration, the dual-homed host completely isolates the two networks. Figure 3-2 shows the basic architecture of a dual-homed host.

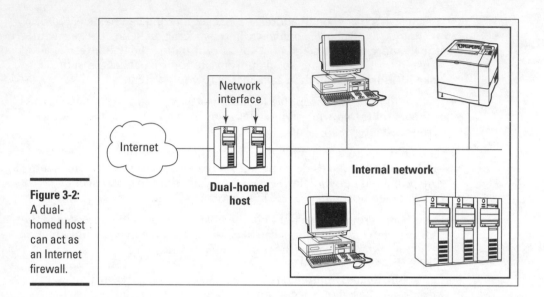

**Figure 3-2:**
A dual-
homed host
can act as
an Internet
firewall.

The dual-homed host is turned into a firewall by running application gateways — proxy services — on the dual-homed host. These proxy services allow specific applications, such as FTP and HTTP, to work across the dual-homed host. That means that you can configure the firewall so that internal clients (on the internal network) are able to access Web and FTP servers on the Internet.

Your public Web site can also run on the dual-homed host and be accessible to everyone on the Internet.

Don't allow user logins on the dual-homed host. Anyone logged in to the host can have access to both the internal network *and* the Internet. Because the dual-homed host is your only barrier between the Internet and the internal network, not increasing the chances of a break-in is best by allowing users to log in to the firewall system. Putting user accounts there increases the chance of an intruder gaining access to the firewall by cracking a user's password.

## *Perimeter network with bastion host*

An Internet firewall is often more complicated than a single dual-homed host that connects to both the Internet and the protected internal network. In particular, if you provide a number of Internet services, you may need more than one system to host them. Imagine that you have two systems: one to run the Web and FTP servers and the other to provide mail (SMTP) and domain name system (DNS) lookups. In this case, you place these two systems on a network that sits between the Internet and the internal network. Figure 3-3 illustrates this concept of an Internet firewall.

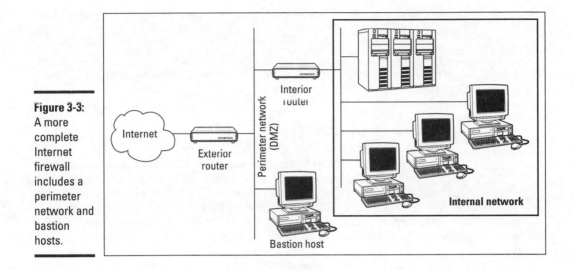

**Figure 3-3:**
A more
complete
Internet
firewall
includes a
perimeter
network and
bastion
hosts.

In this case, the firewall includes a perimeter network that connects to the Internet through an exterior router. The perimeter network, in turn, connects to the internal network through an interior router. The perimeter network has one or more hosts that run Internet services, including proxy servers (about which more in a moment) that allow internal hosts to access Web servers on the Internet.

The term *bastion host* refers to any system on the perimeter network, because such a system is on the Internet and has to be well fortified. The dual-homed host is also a bastion host because the dual-homed host is also accessible from the Internet and has to be protected.

In the firewall configuration shown in Figure 3-3, the perimeter network is known as a DMZ (demilitarized zone) network because that network acts as a buffer between the Internet and the internal network (just as a real-life DMZ is a buffer between North and South Korea).

Usually, you combine a packet-filtering router with a bastion host. Your Internet Service Provider typically provides the external router, which means you don't have much control over that router's configuration. But you provide the internal router, which means you can choose a screening router and employ some packet-filtering rules. For example, you might employ the following packet-filtering rules:

✦ From the internal network, allow only packets addressed to the bastion host.

✦ From the DMZ, allow only packets originating from the bastion host.

✦ Block all other packets.

These rules ensure that the internal network communicates only with the bastion host (or hosts).

Like the dual-homed host, the bastion host also runs an application gateway that provides proxy services for various Internet services, such as TELNET, FTP, SMTP, and HTTP.

## Application gateway

The bastion host or the dual-homed host is the system that acts as the intermediary between the Internet and the protected internal network. As such, that system serves as the internal network's gateway to the Internet. Toward this end, the system runs software to forward and filter TCP/IP packets for various services, such as TELNET, FTP, and HTTP. The software for forwarding and filtering TCP/IP packets for specific applications are known as *proxy servers*. Figure 3-4 illustrates a proxy server's role in a firewall.

A *proxy server* accepts a connection for a specific protocol, such as FTP, and forwards the request to another server. In other words, the proxy server acts as a proxy for an actual server. Because it acts as a gateway for a specific application (such as HTTP or FTP), a proxy server is also known as an *application gateway*.

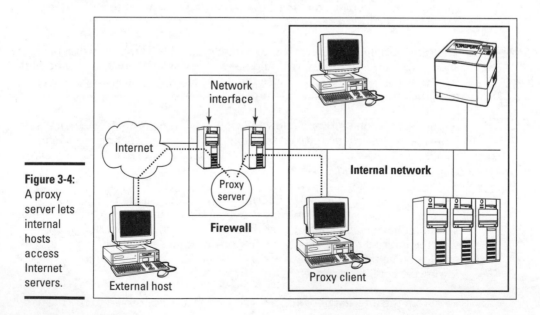

**Figure 3-4:**
A proxy server lets internal hosts access Internet servers.

Unlike a screening router, which blocks packets only on the basis of information in the packet header (such as source and destination IP addresses), a proxy server uses the packet's data to decide what to do. For example, a proxy server does not blindly forward packets to an Internet service. The proxy server can enforce a site's security policy and disallow certain operations, depending on the specific application. For example, an FTP proxy server may prevent users from internal networks from using the FTP put command to send files to the Internet.

Accessing an Internet service through a proxy server can be a bit more involved than accessing that service directly. For example, a user on the internal network establishes a TELNET session with an Internet host with the following steps:

*1.* The user establishes a TELNET session with the firewall host — the system that runs the TELNET proxy. To establish a session, the user has to enter a username and password so that the firewall host can verify that the user has permission to connect to the Internet.

*2.* The user enters a command (which the TELNET proxy accepts) to connect to the Internet host. The TELNET proxy, in turn, establishes a TELNET connection between itself and the Internet host.

*3.* The TELNET proxy on the firewall begins passing packets back and forth between the Internet host and the user's system (until the user ends the TELNET session with the Internet host).

Besides acting as a gateway, the TELNET proxy also logs the user's session with the Internet host. The logging is part of an application gateway's security feature because the log file keeps track of all firewall accesses (as well as attempted accesses that may fail because of a wrong username or password).

Although the TELNET session involves two steps — first TELNET to the firewall host and then connect to the Internet host — the process of accessing services through a proxy need not be too cumbersome. The exact steps you take to access services through a firewall depend on the proxy software and the client program you use to access a service. With the right client program, proxies can be transparent to the user. For example, many Web browsers make accessing a Web site through an HTTP proxy easy. All you have to do is indicate through a menu choice the HTTP proxy you want to use.

## Enabling Packet Filtering on Your Fedora Core System

Your Fedora Core system comes with built-in packet-filtering software in the form of something called netfilter that's in the Linux kernel. All you have to do is use the iptables command to set up the rules for what happens to the packets based on the IP addresses in their header and the network connection type.

The built-in packet-filtering capability is handy when you don't have a dedicated firewall between your Fedora Core system and the Internet. This is the case, for example, when you connect your Fedora Core system to the Internet through a DSL or cable modem. You can essentially have a packet-filtering firewall inside your Fedora Core system, sitting between the kernel and the applications.

## Using the security level configuration tool

You can turn on different levels of packet filtering through the graphical Security Level Configuration tool. To run the tool, log in as `root` and select Main Menu⇨System Settings⇨Security Level. The Security Level Configuration window appears (see Figure 3-5).

**Figure 3-5:**
You can set up packet filtering with this tool.

From the Security Level drop-down menu (refer to Figure 3-5), you can select two predefined levels of simple firewalling (more precisely, packet filtering) with the Security Level Configuration tool:

✦ **Disable Firewall:** Does not perform any filtering, and all connections are allowed (you can still turn off Internet services by not running the servers or disabling them in the `xinetd` configuration files). This security level is fine if your Fedora Core system is inside a protected local area network or if you have a separate firewall device.

✦ **Enable Firewall:** Turns on packet filtering. You can then select the services that you want to allow and the network devices that you trust.

You can allow incoming packets meant for specific Internet services such as SSH, TELNET, and FTP. If you select a network interface such as `eth0` (the first Ethernet card) as trusted, all network traffic over that interface is allowed without any filtering.

## Using the iptables command

Using the `iptables` command is somewhat complex. `iptables` uses the concept of a chain, which is a sequence of rules. Each rule says what to do with a packet if the header contains certain information (such as the source or destination IP address). If a rule does not apply, `iptables` consults the next rule in the chain. By default, there are three chains:

✦ **INPUT:** The first set of rules against which packets are tested. The packets continue to the next chain only if the input chain does not specify `DROP` or `REJECT`.

✦ **FORWARD:** Contains the rules that apply to packets attempting to pass through this system to another system (for example, when you use the Fedora Core system as a router between your LAN and the Internet).

✦ **OUTPUT:** Includes the rules applied to packets before they are sent out (either to another network or to an application).

You can add rules to these chains or create new chains of rules by using the `iptables` command. You can also view the current chains and save them to a file. For example, if you do nothing else, the `iptables -L` command shows the following:

```
Chain INPUT (policy ACCEPT)
target      prot opt source                destination

Chain FORWARD (policy ACCEPT)
target      prot opt source                destination

Chain OUTPUT (policy ACCEPT)
target      prot opt source                destination
```

In this case, all three chains — `INPUT`, `FORWARD`, and `OUTPUT` — show the same `ACCEPT` policy, which means everything is wide open.

If you're setting up a packet filter, the first thing you do is specify the packets that you want to accept. For example, to accept packets from the 192.168.0.0 network, add the following rule to the input chain:

```
iptables -A INPUT -s 192.168.0.0/24 -j ACCEPT
```

Now add a rule to drop everything except local loopback (the `lo` network interface) traffic and stop all forwarding with the following commands:

```
iptables -A INPUT -i ! lo -j REJECT
iptables -A FORWARD -j REJECT
```

**Book VII
Chapter 3**

**Securing the
Network**

The first `iptables` command, for example, appends to the input chain (`-A INPUT`) the rule that if the packet does not come from the `lo` interface (`-i ! lo`), `iptables` rejects the packet (`-j REJECT`).

Before rejecting all other packets, you may also add more rules to each INPUT chain to allow specific packets in. You can select packets to accept or reject based on many different parameters such as IP addresses, protocol types (TCP, UDP), network interface, and port numbers.

Don't type `iptables` commands from a remote login session. A rule that begins denying packets from all addresses can also stop what you type from reaching the system; once that happens, you may have no way of accessing the system over the network. To avoid unpleasant surprises, always type `iptables` rules at the console — the keyboard and monitor connected directly to your Fedora Core PC that is running the packet filter. If you want to delete all filtering rules in a hurry, you can flush them by typing the following command:

```
iptables -F
```

I don't provide all the details of the `iptables` commands in this section. Suffice to say that you type **man iptables** to read a summary of the commands. You can also read about netfilter and `iptables` at `www.iptables.org`.

After you define the rules by using the `iptables` command, they are in the memory and are gone when you reboot the system. To save them, use the `iptables-save` command to store the rules in a file. For example, you can save the rules in a file named `iptables.rules` by using the following command:

```
iptables-save > iptables.rules
```

Here's a listing of the `iptables.rules` file, generated on a Fedora Core system:

```
# Generated by iptables-save v1.2.9 on Wed Apr 14 20:56:40 2004
*filter
:INPUT ACCEPT [44:2024]
:FORWARD ACCEPT [0:0]
:OUTPUT ACCEPT [2572:1426880]
-A INPUT -s 192.168.0.0/255.255.255.0 -j ACCEPT
-A INPUT -i ! lo -j REJECT --reject-with icmp-port-unreachable
-A FORWARD -j REJECT --reject-with icmp-port-unreachable
COMMIT
# Completed on Wed Apr 14 20:56:40 2004
```

In case you're curious, these rules correspond to the following iptables commands I use to configure the filter:

```
iptables -A INPUT -s 192.168.0.0/24 -j ACCEPT
iptables -A INPUT -i ! lo -j REJECT
iptables -A FORWARD -j REJECT
```

If you want to load these saved rules into iptables, use the following command:

```
iptables-restore < iptables.rules
```

On a Fedora Core system, the process of saving and restoring firewall rules is automated by saving the iptables rules in the file /etc/sysconfig/ iptables and by enabling iptables with the following command:

```
chkconfig iptables on
```

That ensures the /etc/init.d/iptables start command executes at the system startup. The /etc/init.d/iptables script then runs the /sbin/ iptables-restore command to restore the iptables rules from the /etc/ sysconfig/iptables file.

# Chapter 4: Performing Security Audits

## In This Chapter

✔ Understanding computer security audits

✔ Learning a security test methodology

✔ Reviewing host and network security

✔ Exploring security testing tools

*Y*ou see the term "audit" and you think tax audit, right? Well, there are many different types of audits, and one of them is a *computer security audit*. The purpose of a computer security audit is to basically test your system and network security. For larger organizations, an independent auditor (much like the auditing of financial statements) can do the security audit. If you have only a few Fedora Core systems or a small network, you can do the security audit as a self-assessment, just to figure out if you're doing everything okay or not.

In this chapter, I explain how to perform computer security audits and show you a number of free tools and resources to help you test your system's security.

## Understanding Security Audits

An *audit* is simply an independent assessment of whatever it is you're auditing. So a computer security audit is an independent assessment of computer security. If someone is conducting a computer security audit of your organization, he or she focuses typically on two areas:

✦ Independent verification of whether your organization is complying with its existing policies and procedures for computer security. This part is the nontechnical aspect of the security audit.

✦ Independent testing of how effective your security controls (any hardware and software mechanisms you use to secure the system) are. This part is the technical aspect of the security audit.

Why do you need security audits? For the same reason you need financial audits — mainly to verify that everything is being done the way it's supposed to be done. For public as well as private organizations, management may want independent security audits to assure themselves that their security is A-okay. Irrespective of your organization's size, you can always perform security audits on your own, either to prepare for independent security audits or simply to know that you're doing everything right.

No matter whether you have independent security audits or a self-assessment, here are some of the benefits you get from security audits:

✦ Periodic risk assessments that consider internal and external threats to systems and data.

✦ Periodic testing of the effectiveness of security policies, security controls, and techniques.

✦ Identification of any significant deficiencies in your system's security (so you know what to fix).

✦ In case of self-assessments, preparation for any annual independent security testing that your organization might have to face.

## Nontechnical aspects of security audits

The nontechnical side of computer security audits focuses on your organization-wide security framework. The audit examines how well the organization is set up and implemented the policies, plans, and procedures for computer security. Some of the items to be verified include

✦ Risks are periodically assessed.

✦ There is an entitywide security program plan.

✦ A security program-management structure is put in place.

✦ Computer security responsibilities are clearly assigned.

✦ Effective security-related personnel policies are in place.

✦ The security program's effectiveness is monitored and changes are made when needed.

As you may expect, the nontechnical aspects of the security audit involve reviewing documents and interviewing appropriate individuals to find out how the organization manages computer security. Of course, for a small organization or a home PC, expecting plans and procedures in documents is ridiculous. In those cases, all you have to make sure is that you have some technical controls in place to secure your system and your network connection.

## Technical aspects of security audits

The technical side of computer security audits focuses on testing the technical controls that secure your hosts and network. The testing involves determining

✦ **How well the host is secured.** Are all operating system patches applied? Are the file permissions set correctly? Are user accounts protected? Are file changes monitored? Are log files monitored? And so on.

✦ **How well the network is secured.** Are unnecessary Internet services turned off? Is a firewall installed? Are remote logins secured with tools such as SSH? Are TCP wrapper access controls used? And so on.

Typically, security experts use automated tools to perform these two security reviews — host and network.

# Learning a Security Test Methodology

A key element of a computer security audit is the security test that checks the technical mechanisms used to secure a host and the network. The security test methodology follows these high-level steps:

*1.* Take stock of the organization's networks, hosts, network devices (routers, switches, firewalls, and so on), and how the network connects to the Internet.

*2.* If there are many hosts and network connections, determine what are the important hosts and network devices that need to be tested. The importance of a host depends on the kind of applications it runs.

*3.* Test the hosts individually. Typically, this step involves logging in as a system administrator and then checking various aspects of host security, from passwords to system log files.

*4.* Test the network. This step is usually done by attempting to break through the network defenses from another system on the Internet. If there is a firewall, the testing checks that the firewall is indeed configured correctly.

*5.* Analyze the test results of both host and network tests to determine the vulnerabilities and risks.

Each of the two types of testing — host and network — focuses on three areas that comprise overall computer security:

✦ **Prevention:** Includes the mechanisms (nontechnical and technical) that help prevent attacks on the system and the network.

✦ **Detection:** Refers to techniques such as monitoring log files, checking file integrity, and intrusion detection systems that can detect when someone is about to or has already broken into your system.

✦ **Response:** Includes the steps such as reporting an incident to authorities and restoring important files from backup that you perform when a computer security incident occurs.

For host and network security, each of these areas has some overlaps. For example, prevention mechanisms for host security such as good passwords or file permissions can also provide network security. Nevertheless, thinking in terms of the three areas helps — prevention, detection, and response.

Before you can think of prevention, however, you have to know the types of problems you're trying to prevent. In other words, what are the common security vulnerabilities? The prevention and detection steps typically depend on what these vulnerabilities are.

## Some common computer vulnerabilities

The specific tests of the host and network security depend on the common vulnerabilities. Basically, the idea is to check if a host or a network has the vulnerabilities that crackers are most likely to exploit.

### Online resources on computer vulnerabilities

Several online resources identify and categorize computer security vulnerabilities:

✦ **SANS Institute** publishes a list of the Top 20 most critical Internet security vulnerabilities at `www.sans.org/top20/`.

✦ **CVE** (Common Vulnerabilities and Exposures) is a list of standardized names of vulnerabilities. For more information on CVE, see `cve.mitre.org` (the list has over 2,500 names of vulnerabilities). Using the CVE name to describe vulnerabilities is common practice.

✦ **ICAT Metabase** is a searchable index of information on computer vulnerabilities, published by the National Institute of Standards and Technology (NIST), a United States government agency. The ICAT vulnerability index is online at `icat.nist.gov`. ICAT lists over 6,500 vulnerabilities, and it provides links to vulnerability advisory and patch information for each vulnerability. ICAT also has a Top 10 List that lists the vulnerabilities that were most queried during the past year.

### Typical Top 20 computer vulnerabilities

The SANS/FBI Top 20 vulnerabilities list includes two types of vulnerabilities — Windows and UNIX. Of these, the UNIX vulnerabilities are relevant to Fedora

Core. Table 4-1 summarizes some common UNIX vulnerabilities that apply to Fedora Core. You can read the complete details about these vulnerabilities at www.sans.org/top20/.

| Table 4-1 | Some Common Vulnerabilities to UNIX Systems |
|---|---|
| **Vulnerability Type** | **Description** |
| Remote Procedure Calls (RPC) | Services such as Network File System (NFS) and Network Information System (NIS) use remote procedure calls (RPC) and some known vulnerabilities are in RPC. |
| Apache Web server | Some Apache Web server modules (such as mod_ssl) have known vulnerabilities. Any vulnerability in common gateway interface (CGI) programs used with Web servers to process interactive Web pages can provide attackers a way to gain access to a system. |
| Secure Shell (SSH) | SSH is used for securely logging in, executing commands, and transferring files across a network. Some SSH implementations have vulnerabilities. |
| Simple Network Management Protocol (SNMP) | SNMP is used to remotely monitor and administer various network-connected systems ranging from routers to computers. SNMP lacks good access control, so, if SNMP is running on a system, an attacker may be able to use SNMP to reconfigure or shut down the system. |
| File Transfer Protocol (FTP) | FTP transmits a username and password in the clear, so attackers may be able to pick these up by eavesdropping. Some FTP servers have flaws that enable attackers to gain superuser (administrator) access to a system. |
| R-services — Trust | The so-called r commands allow an attacker to easily access Relationships any system that has an implicit trust relationship with others (the r commands assume a trust relationship). |
| Line Printer Daemon (LPD) | LPD is the print server process and it listens on port 515 for remote printing requests. Unfortunately, the remote printing capability has a buffer overflow vulnerability. |
| Sendmail | Sendmail is a complex program used to send, receive, and forward most electronic mail messages on UNIX and Linux systems. Older versions of sendmail have vulnerabilities such as buffer overflow and bad configurations that allow anyone to relay mail through the system. |
| BIND/DNS | Berkeley Internet Name Domain (BIND) is a package that implements Domain Name System (DNS), the Internet's name service that translates a name to an IP address. Some versions of BIND have vulnerabilities. |
| General UNIX Authentication — Accounts with No Passwords or Weak Passwords | User accounts often have weak passwords that are easily cracked by password-cracking programs. |

**Book VII Chapter 4**

**Performing Security Audits**

## Host security review

When reviewing host security, focus on assessing the security mechanisms in each of the following areas:

✦ **Prevention:** Install operating system updates, secure passwords, improve file permissions, set up a password for a boot loader, and use encryption.

✦ **Detection:** Capture log messages and check file integrity with Tripwire.

✦ **Response:** Make routine backups and develop incident response procedures.

I review a few of these host-security mechanisms in the upcoming sections.

### Operating-system updates

Fedora Core updates are released as soon the Fedora team learns of any security vulnerabilities, but you or a system administrator has to download and install the updates. One way to keep up with the Fedora Core security patches is to use Up2date to update your system routinely.

You can install any updates by using the `rpm` command. If you place all current updates in a single directory, you can use the following command to install them:

```
rpm -F *.rpm
```

For larger organizations, an authorized system administrator can install the operating-system updates.

To assess whether the operating system updates are current, an auditor gets a current list of updates for key Fedora Core components and then uses the `rpm` command to check if they are installed. For example, if a list shows that `glibc` version 2.3.3 is what the system should have, the auditor types the following command to view the current `glibc` version number:

```
rpm -q glibc
```

If the version number is less than 2.3.3, the conclusion is that operating system updates are not being installed.

### File permissions

Key system files need to be protected with appropriate file ownerships and file permissions. The key procedures in assigning file-system ownerships and permissions are as follows:

✦ Figure out which files contain sensitive information and why. Some files may contain sensitive data related to your work or business, whereas many other files are sensitive because they control the Fedora Core system configuration.

✦ Maintain a current list of authorized users and what they are authorized to do on the system.

✦ Set up passwords, groups, file ownerships, and file permissions to allow only authorized users to access the files.

Table 4-2 lists some important system files in Fedora Core, showing the numeric permission setting for each file.

| Table 4-2 | Important System Files and Their Permissions | |
|---|---|---|
| **File Pathname** | **Permission** | **Description** |
| `/boot/grub/grub.conf` | 600 | GRUB bootloader configuration file |
| `/etc/cron.allow` | 400 | List of users permitted to use `cron` to submit periodic jobs |
| `/etc/cron.deny` | 400 | List of users who cannot use `cron` to submit periodic jobs |
| `/etc/crontab` | 644 | Systemwide periodic jobs |
| `/etc/hosts.allow` | 644 | List of hosts allowed to use Internet services that are started using TCP wrappers |
| `/etc/hosts.deny` | 644 | List of hosts denied access to Internet services that are started using TCP wrappers |
| `/etc/logrotate.conf` | 644 | File that controls how log files are rotated |
| `/etc/pam.d` | 755 | Directory with configuration files for pluggable authentication modules (PAMs) |
| `/etc/passwd` | 644 | Old-style password file with user-account information but not the passwords |
| `/etc/rc.d` | 755 | Directory with system-startup scripts |
| `/etc/securetty` | 600 | TTY interfaces (terminals) from which `root` can log in |
| `/etc/security` | 755 | Policy files that control system access |
| `/etc/shadow` | 400 | File with encrypted passwords and password-expiration information |
| `/etc/shutdown.allow` | 400 | Users who can shut down or reboot by pressing Ctrl+Alt+Delete |
| `/etc/ssh` | 755 | Directory with configuration files for the Secure Shell (SSH) |

**Book VII Chapter 4**

**Performing Security Audits**

*(continued)*

**Table 4-2** *(continued)*

| File Pathname | Permission | Description |
|---|---|---|
| /etc/sysconfig | 755 | System-configuration files |
| /etc/sysctl.conf | 644 | Kernel-configuration parameters |
| /etc/syslog.conf | 644 | Configuration file for the syslogd server that logs messages |
| /etc/vsftpd | 600 | Configuration file for the very secure FTP server |
| /etc/vsftpd.ftpusers | 600 | List of users who cannot use FTP to transfer files |
| /etc/xinetd.conf | 644 | Configuration file for the xinetd server |
| /etc/xinetd.d | 755 | Directory containing configuration files for specific services that the xinetd server can start |
| /var/log | 755 | Directory with all log files |
| /var/log/lastlog | 644 | Information about all previous logins |
| /var/log/messages | 644 | Main system message log file |
| /var/log/secure | 400 | Security-related log file |
| /var/log/wtmp | 664 | Information about current logins |

Another important check is to look for executable program files that have the setuid permission. If a program has setuid permission and it's owned by root, then the program runs with root privileges, no matter who is actually running the program. You can find all setuid programs with the following find command:

```
find / -perm +4000 -print
```

You may want to save the output in a file (just append > *filename* to the command) and then examine the file for any unusual setuid programs. For example, a setuid program in a user's home directory is unusual.

### Password security

Verify that the password, group, and shadow password files are protected. In particular, the shadow password file has to be write-protected and readable only by root. The filenames and their recommended permissions are shown in Table 4-3.

| Table 4-3 | Ownership and Permission of Password Files | |
| --- | --- | --- |
| *File Pathname* | *Ownership* | *Permission* |
| /etc/group | root.root | 644 |
| /etc/passwd | root.root | 644 |
| /etc/shadow | root.root | 400 |

## Incident response

*Incident response* is the policy that answers the question of what to do if something unusual does happen to the system — it tells you how to proceed if someone has broken into your system.

Your response to an incident depends on how you use your system and how important it is to you or your business. For a comprehensive incident response, here are some key points to remember:

✦ Figure out how critical and important your computer and network are and identify who or what resources can help you protect your system.

✦ Take steps to prevent and minimize potential damage and interruption.

✦ Develop and document a comprehensive contingency plan.

✦ Periodically test the contingency plan and revise the procedures as appropriate.

## Network-security review

*Network-security review* focuses on assessing the security mechanisms in each of the following areas:

✦ **Prevention:** Set up a firewall, enable packet filtering, disable unnecessary xinetd services, turn off unneeded Internet services, use TCP wrappers for access control, and use SSH for secure remote logins.

✦ **Detection:** Use network intrusion detection and capture system logs.

✦ **Response:** Develop incident-response procedures.

I briefly describe some key steps in assessing the network security.

### Services started by xinetd

The xinetd server starts many Internet services such as TELNET and sgi_fam (sgi_fam monitors changes to files). The decision to turn on some of these services depends on factors such as how the system connects to the Internet and how the system is being used. You can usually turn off most xinetd services.

Check which xinetd services are turned on by using one of the following ways:

✦ Check the configuration files in the /etc/xinetd.d directory for all the services that xinetd can start. If a service is turned off, the configuration file has a line like this:

```
disable = yes
```

**Remember:** The disable = yes line doesn't count if it's commented out by placing a # at the beginning of the line.

✦ Type the following command to disable a service that xinetd can start:

```
chkconfig servicename off
```

where *servicename* is the name of the service (such as telnet or sgi_fam). To check the names of the services that xinetd can start, type the following command:

```
chkconfig --list | more
```

In the output, look for the lines that follow:

```
xinetd based services:
```

These lines list all the services that xinetd can start and whether they are on or off. For example, here are a few lines showing the status of xinetd services on a system:

```
telnet:        on
sgi_fam:       on
echo-udp:      off
chargen:       off
cups-lpd:      off
services:      off
finger: off
... lines deleted ...
```

In this case, telnet (a server that enables users to remotely log in to the system) and sgi_fam (a server that reports changes to any file) services are on, but everything else is off.

Also check the following files for any access controls used with the xinetd services:

✦ /etc/hosts.allow lists hosts allowed to access specific services.

✦ /etc/hosts.deny lists hosts denied access to services.

### Standalone services

Many services such as the httpd (Web server) and sendmail (mail server) start automatically at boot time, assuming they are configured to start that way. You can use the chkconfig command to check which of these stand-alone servers is set to start at various run levels (see Book VI, Chapter 1 for more about run levels). Typically, your Fedora Core system starts up at run level 3 (for text login) or 5 (for graphical login). Therefore, what matters is the setting for the servers in levels 3 and 5. To view the list of servers, type the following command:

```
chkconfig --list | more
```

Here's a partial listing of what you might see:

```
xinetd          0:off   1:off   2:off   3:on    4:on    5:on    6:off
syslog          0:off   1:off   2:on    3:on    4:on    5:on    6:off
rpcsvcgssd      0:on    1:off   2:off   3:on    4:off   5:on    6:on
bcm5820         0:off   1:off   2:off   3:off   4:off   5:off   6:off
rhnsd           0:off   1:off   2:off   3:on    4:on    5:on    6:off
iptables        0:off   1:off   2:on    3:on    4:on    5:on    6:off
smartd          0:off   1:off   2:on    3:on    4:on    5:on    6:off
ypxfrd          0:off   1:off   2:off   3:off   4:off   5:off   6:off
dc_server       0:off   1:off   2:off   3:off   4:off   5:off   6:off
saslauthd       0:off   1:off   2:off   3:off   4:off   5:off   6:off
mdmonitor       0:off   1:off   2:on    3:on    4:on    5:on    6:off
nfslock         0:off   1:off   2:off   3:on    4:on    5:on    6:off
sendmail        0:off   1:off   2:on    3:on    4:on    5:on    6:off
apmd            0:off   1:off   2:on    3:on    4:on    5:on    6:off
readahead       0:off   1:off   2:off   3:off   4:off   5:on    6:off
psacct          0:off   1:off   2:off   3:off   4:off   5:off   6:off
netfs           0:off   1:off   2:off   3:on    4:on    5:on    6:off
microcode_ctl   0:off   1:off   2:off   3:on    4:on    5:on    6:off
...lines deleted...
```

The first column shows the names of the servers. Look at the column of entries that begin with 3: and the ones that begin with 5:. These columns show the status of the server for run levels 3 and 5. The ones that appear as on automatically start when your Fedora Core system starts.

If you're doing a self-assessment of your network security and you find that some servers should not be running, you can turn them off for run levels 3 and 5 with the chkconfig command like this:

```
chkconfig --level 35 servicename off
```

Replace servicename with the name of the server you want to turn off.

If you're auditing network security, make a note of all the servers that are turned on — and then try to determine whether they should really *be* on, according to what you know about the system. The decision to turn a particular service on depends on how your system is used (for example, as a Web server or as a desktop system) and how it's connected to the Internet (say, through a firewall or directly).

### Penetration test

A penetration test is the best way to tell what services are really running on a Fedora Core system. *Penetration testing* involves trying to get access to your system from an attacker's perspective. Typically, you perform this test from a system on the Internet and try to see if you can break in or, at a minimum, get access to services running on your Fedora Core system.

One aspect of penetration testing is to see what ports are open on your Fedora Core system. The port number is simply a number that identifies specific TCP/IP network connections to the system. The attempt to connect to a port succeeds only if a server is running on that port (or put another way, if a server is "listening on that port"). A port is considered to be open if a server responds when a connection request for that port arrives.

The first step in penetration testing is to perform a port scan. The term *port scan* is used to describe the automated process of trying to connect to each port number to see if a valid response comes back. Many available automated tools can perform port scanning — Fedora Core comes with a popular port-scanning tool called nmap (which I describe later in this chapter).

After performing a port scan, you know the potential vulnerabilities that could be exploited. Not all servers have security problems, but many servers have well-known vulnerabilities, and an open port provides a cracker a way to attack your system through one of the servers. In fact, you can use automated tools called *vulnerability scanners* to identify vulnerabilities that exist in your system. (I describe some vulnerability scanners next.) Whether your Fedora Core system is connected to the Internet directly (through DSL or cable modem) or through a firewall, use the port-scanning and vulnerability- scanning tools to figure out if you have any holes in your defenses. Better you than them!

## Exploring Security Testing Tools

Many automated tools are available to perform security testing. Some of these tools are meant for finding the open ports on every system in a range of IP addresses. Others look for the vulnerabilities associated with open ports. Yet other tools can capture (or *sniff*) those weaknesses and help you analyze them so you can glean useful information about what's going on in your network.

You can browse a list of the top 75 security tools (based on an informal poll of nmap users) at www.insecure.org/tools.html. Table 4-4 lists a number of these tools by category. I describe a few of the freely available vulnerability scanners in the next few sections.

| Table 4-4 | Some Popular Computer Security Testing Tools |
|---|---|
| *Type* | *Names of Tools* |
| Port scanners | nmap, Strobe |
| Vulnerability scanners | Nessus Security Scanner, SAINT, SARA, Whisker (CGI scanner), ISS Internet Scanner, CyberCop Scanner, Vetescan, Retina Network Security Scanner |
| Network utilities | Netcat, hping2, Firewalk, Cheops, ntop, ping, ngrep, AirSnort (802.11 WEP encryption cracking tool) |
| Host-security tools | Tripwire, lsof |
| Packet sniffers | tcpdump, Ethereal, dsniff, sniffit |
| Intrusion-detection systems (IDSs) | Snort, Abacus portsentry, scanlogd, NFR, LIDS |
| Password-checking tools | John the Ripper, LC4 |
| Log-analysis and monitoring tools | logcolorise, tcpdstats, nlog, logcheck, LogWatch, Swatch |

## *Nmap*

Nmap (short for *network mapper*) is a port-scanning tool. It can rapidly scan large networks and determine what hosts are available on the network, what services they are offering, what operating system (and the operating system version) they are running, what type of packet filters or firewalls are in use, and dozens of other characteristics. Fedora Core comes with nmap. You can read more about nmap at www.insecure.org/nmap.

If you want to try out nmap to scan your local area network, just type a command similar to the following (replace the IP address range with addresses appropriate for your network):

```
nmap -O -sS 192.168.0.2-10
```

Here's a typical output listing from that command:

```
Starting nmap 3.50 ( http://www.insecure.org/nmap/ ) at 2004-04-14 21:01 EDT
Interesting ports on 192.168.0.2:
(The 1654 ports scanned but not shown below are in state: closed)
PORT     STATE SERVICE
135/tcp  open  msrpc
139/tcp  open  netbios-ssn
445/tcp  open  microsoft-ds
1025/tcp open  NFS-or-IIS
5000/tcp open  UPnP
Device type: general purpose
Running: Microsoft Windows 95/98/ME|NT/2K/XP
OS details: Microsoft Windows Millennium Edition (Me), Windows 2000 Professional
 or Advanced Server, or Windows XP
```

```
Interesting ports on 192.168.0.6:
(The 1654 ports scanned but not shown below are in state: closed)
PORT      STATE SERVICE
21/tcp    open  ftp
22/tcp    open  ssh
23/tcp    open  telnet
111/tcp   open  rpcbind
32771/tcp open  sometimes-rpc5
Device type: general purpose
Running: Linux 2.4.X|2.5.X
OS details: Linux 2.5.25 - 2.5.70 or Gentoo 1.2 Linux 2.4.19 rc1-rc7)
Uptime 5.015 days (since Wed Apr 10 20:41:00 2004)
<<Lines deleted...>>
Nmap run completed -- 9 IP addresses (3 hosts up) scanned in 167.191 seconds
```

As you can see, `nmap` displays the names of the open ports and hazards a guess at the operating system name and version number.

## Nessus

The Nessus Security Scanner is a modular security auditing tool that uses plugins written in the Nessus scripting language to test for a wide variety of network vulnerabilities. Nessus uses a client-server software architecture with a server called `nessusd` and a client called `nessus`.

Before you try to install Nessus, you must install the `sharutils` RPM. That package includes the `uudecode` utility that the Nessus installation script needs. The `sharutils` package isn't installed with any of the standard package groups, so you have to install it yourself.

To install `sharutils`, mount the companion DVD and install it with the following commands:

```
cd /mnt/cdrom/Fedora/RPMS
rpm -ivh sharutils*.rpm
```

To download and install Nessus, follow these steps:

1. **Read the instructions at** `www.nessus.org/download.html`**. Then follow the link to the package you want to download. Follow the instructions and download the files** `nessus-installer.sh` **and** MD5**.**

2. **Type the following command to install Nessus (you must have the development tools, including the GIMP Toolkit, installed):**

   ```
   sh nessus-installer.sh
   ```

   Respond to the prompts from the installer script to finish the installation. You can usually press Enter to accept the default choices.

After the installation is complete, follow these steps to use Nessus:

1. **Log in as** root **and type the following command to create the Nessus SSL certificate used for secure communication between the Nessus client and the Nessus server:**

   ```
   nessus-mkcert
   ```

2. **Provide the requested information to complete the certificate generation process.**

3. **Create a** nessusd **account with the following command:**

   ```
   nessus-adduser
   ```

4. **When prompted, enter your username, password, and any rules (press Ctrl+D if you don't know what rules to enter). Then press the Y key.**

5. **If you want to, you can configure** nessusd **by editing the configuration file** /usr/local/etc/nessus/nessusd.conf.

   If you want to try out Nessus, you can proceed with the default configuration file.

6. **Start the Nessus server with this command:**

   ```
   nessusd -D
   ```

7. **Run the Nessus client by typing the following command in a terminal window:**

   ```
   nessus
   ```

   The Nessus Setup window appears.

8. **Type a** nessusd **username and password and then click the Log In button (shown in Figure 4-1).**

9. **When Nessus displays the certificate used to establish the secure connection and asks if you accept it, click Yes.**

   After the client connects to the server, the Log In button changes to Log Out, and a Connected label appears at its left.

10. **On the Target Selection tab, enter a range of IP addresses to scan all hosts in a network.**

    For example, to scan the first eight hosts in a private network 192.168.0.0, I enter the address as:

    ```
    192.168.0.0/29
    ```

11. **Click Start the Scan.**

    Nessus starts scanning the IP addresses and checks for many different vulnerabilities. Progress bars show the status of the scan (see Figure 4-2).

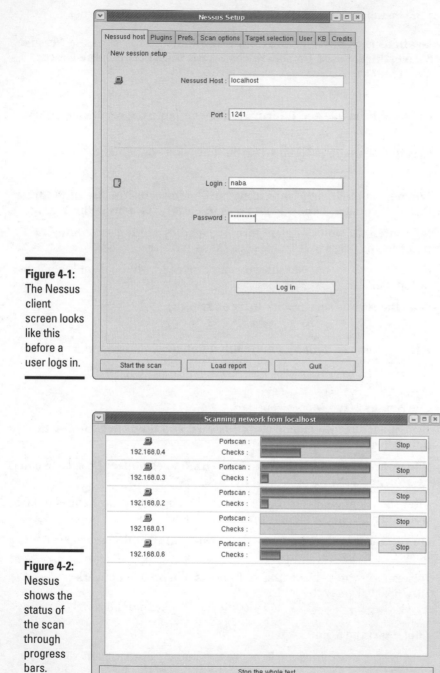

**Figure 4-1:**
The Nessus
client
screen looks
like this
before a
user logs in.

**Figure 4-2:**
Nessus
shows the
status of
the scan
through
progress
bars.

After Nessus completes the vulnerability scan of the hosts, it displays the result in a nice combination of graphical and text formats (see Figure 4-3). The report is interactive — you can select a host address to view the report on that host, and you can drill down on a specific vulnerability (including the CVE number that identifies the vulnerability).

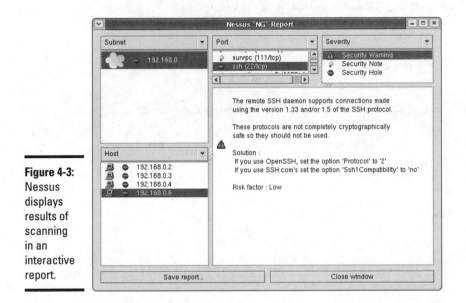

**Figure 4-3:** Nessus displays results of scanning in an interactive report.

# SAINT

Security Administrator's Integrated Network Tool (SAINT) scans hosts for a variety of security vulnerabilities. For the vulnerabilities it finds, SAINT shows the Common Vulnerabilities and Exposures (CVE) identifier. Older versions of SAINT are free, but the latest version is available only to those who purchase SAINTWriter or SAINTexpress.

You can download a restricted (limited to scanning two hosts only) 15-day trial version of SAINT from www.saintcorporation.com/products/download.html and see what it can do. You can decide whether to buy the full version or not.

I don't describe the steps for downloading and installing the trial version. You can find the instructions on the page from which you download the free trial version of SAINT.

## SARA

Security Auditor's Research Assistant (SARA) is a vulnerability-scanning tool based on SAINT. SARA scans for known vulnerabilities, including those in the CVE list and the SANS Top 20 List (`www.sans.org/top20/`).

To try out SARA, download the latest version of SARA from `www-arc.com/sara/downloads/`. After downloading the compressed `tar` file, build and install the software using these steps:

1. **Unpack the `tar` file with the following command:**

   ```
   tar zxvf sara*
   ```

2. **To configure SARA, type the following commands:**

   ```
   cd sara*
   ./configure
   ```

3. **To build the software, type**

   ```
   make
   ```

After SARA is built, run it with the following command:

```
./sara
```

SARA starts a Web browser and displays its user interface in the Web browser.

You can perform various tasks by clicking the links along the left side of the Web browser. For example, to perform a vulnerability scan, click the Target Selection link. SARA brings up a form where you can provide information about hosts and networks to scan. You can also specify the scanning level — anywhere from light to extreme.

After filling in the information, click the Start the Scan button at the bottom of the form. SARA starts to perform the vulnerability scan. During the scan, SARA displays a data-collection page that indicates progress of the scan.

After the scan is complete, you can proceed to the data analysis and view the vulnerability information.

# Book VIII

# Internet Servers

The 5th Wave          By Rich Tennant

"I'm sorry, but 'Arf', 'Bark', and 'Woof'
are already registered domain names.
How about 'Oink', 'Quack', or 'Moo'?"

# Contents at a Glance

**Chapter 1: Managing the Servers** ....................................................................597

**Chapter 2: Running the Apache Web Server**.................................................615

**Chapter 3: Setting Up the FTP Server** ............................................................639

**Chapter 4: Serving Up Mail and News** .........................................................647

**Chapter 5: Setting Up DNS**................................................................................675

**Chapter 6: Running Samba and NFS** .............................................................695

# Chapter 1: Managing the Servers

## In This Chapter

✔ **Understanding Internet services**

✔ **Controlling servers through** `xinetd`

✔ **Using** `chkconfig` **to manage servers**

✔ **Using the service-configuration utility**

The Internet is a world of clients and servers. Clients make requests to servers, and servers respond to the requests. For example, your Web browser is a client that downloads information from Web servers and displays it to you. Of course, the clients and servers are computer programs that run on a wide variety of computers. A Fedora Core system is an ideal system to run a wide variety of servers from a Web server to a Windows file and print server. In this chapter, I provide an overview of a typical Internet service, its client/server architecture, and how to manage the servers in Fedora Core. You can use the information in this chapter to manage any server running on your Fedora Core system.

## Understanding Internet Services

*Internet services* are network applications designed to deliver information from one system to another. By design, each Internet service is implemented in two parts — a *server* that provides information, and one or more *clients* that request information.

Such *client/server* architecture is the most common way to build distributed information systems. The clients and servers are computer programs that run on these computers and communicate through the network. The neat part is that you can be running a client at your desktop computer and access information from a server running on a computer anywhere in the world (as long as it's on the Internet).

The Web itself, e-mail, and FTP (File Transfer Protocol) are examples of Internet services that use the client/server model. For example, when you use the Web, you use the Web-browser client to download and view Web pages from the Web server.

Client/server architecture requires clients to communicate with the servers. That's where the *Transmission Control Protocol/Internet Protocol* — TCP/IP — comes in. TCP/IP provides a standard way for clients and servers to exchange packets of data. In the next few sections, I explain how TCP/IP-based services communicate.

## TCP/IP and sockets

Client/server applications such as the Web and FTP use TCP/IP for data transfers between client and server. These Internet applications typically use TCP/IP communications using the *Berkeley Sockets interface* (so named because the socket interface was introduced in Berkeley UNIX around 1982). The sockets interface is nothing physical — it's simply some computer code that a computer programmer can use to create applications that can communicate with other applications on the Internet.

Even if you don't write network applications using sockets, you may have to use or set up many network applications. Knowledge of sockets can help you understand how network-based applications work, which in turn helps you find and correct any problems with these applications.

### Socket definition

Network applications use sockets to communicate over a TCP/IP network A *socket* represents one end-point of a connection. Because a socket is bi-directional, data can be sent as well as received through it. A socket has three attributes:

✦ The *network address* (the IP address) of the system

✦ The *port number,* identifying the process (a process is a computer program running on a computer) that exchanges data through the socket

✦ The *type of socket,* identifying the protocol for data exchange

Essentially, the IP address identifies a computer (host) on the network; the port number identifies a process (server) on the node; and the socket type determines the manner in which data is exchanged — through a connection-oriented (stream) or connectionless (datagram) protocol.

### Connection-oriented protocols

The socket type indicates the protocol being used to communicate through the socket. A connection-oriented protocol works like a normal phone conversation. When you want to talk to your friend, you have to dial your friend's phone number and establish a connection before you can have a conversation. In the same way, connection-oriented data exchange requires both the sending and receiving processes to establish a connection before data exchange can begin.

In the TCP/IP protocol suite, TCP — *Transmission Control Protocol* — supports a connection-oriented data transfer between two processes running on two computers on the Internet. TCP provides reliable two-way data exchange between processes.

As the name TCP/IP suggests, TCP relies on IP — *Internet Protocol* — for delivery of packets. IP does not guarantee delivery of packets, nor does it deliver packets in any particular sequence. IP does, however, efficiently move packets from one network to another. TCP is responsible for arranging the packets in the proper sequence, detecting whether errors have occurred, and requesting retransmission of packets in case of an error.

TCP is useful for applications intended to exchange large amounts of data at a time. In addition, applications that need reliable data exchange use TCP. (For example, FTP uses TCP to transfer files.)

In the sockets model, a socket that uses TCP is referred to as a *stream socket*.

### Connectionless protocols

A *connectionless* data-exchange protocol does not require the sender and receiver to explicitly establish a connection. It's like shouting to your friend in a crowded room — you can't be sure that your friend hears you.

In the TCP/IP protocol suite, the *User Datagram Protocol* (UDP) provides connectionless service for sending and receiving packets known as *datagrams*. Unlike TCP, UDP does not guarantee that datagrams ever reach their intended destination. Nor does UDP ensure that datagrams are delivered in the order they are sent.

UDP is used by applications that exchange small amounts of data at a time, or by applications that don't need the reliability and sequencing of data delivery. For example, SNMP (*Simple Network Management Protocol*) uses UDP to transfer data.

In the sockets model, a socket that uses UDP is referred to as a *datagram socket*.

### Sockets and the client/server model

Two sockets are needed to complete a communication path. When two processes communicate, they use the client/server model to establish the connection. Figure 1-1 illustrates the concept. The server application listens on a specific port on the system — the server is completely identified by the IP address of the system where it runs and the port number where it listens for connections. The client initiates a connection from any available port and tries to connect to the server (identified by the IP address and port number). When the connection is established, the client and the server can exchange data according to their own protocol.

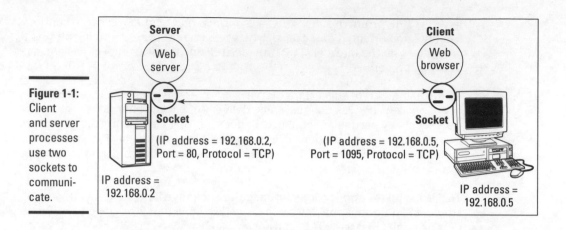

**Figure 1-1:**
Client
and server
processes
use two
sockets to
communi-
cate.

The sequence of events in socket-based data exchanges depends on whether the transfer is connection-oriented (TCP) or connectionless (UDP).

For a connection-oriented data transfer using sockets, the server "listens" on a specific port, waiting for clients to request connection. Data transfer begins only after a connection is established.

For connectionless data transfers, the server waits for a datagram to arrive at a specified port. The client does not wait to establish a connection; it simply sends a datagram to the server.

Regardless of whether it's a server or a client, each application first creates a socket. Then it *associates* (binds) the socket with the local computer's IP address and a port number. The IP address identifies the machine (where the application is running), and the port number identifies the application using the socket.

Servers typically listen to a well-known port number so clients can connect to that port to access the server. For a client application, the process of binding a socket to the IP address and port is the same as that for a server, but the client can use 0 as the port number — the sockets library automatically uses an unused port number for the client.

For a connection-oriented stream socket, the communicating client and server applications have to establish a connection. The exact steps for establishing a connection depend on whether the application is a server or a client.

In the client/server model, the server has to be up and running before the client can run. After creating a socket and binding the socket to a port, the server application sets up a queue of connections, which determines how many clients can connect to the server. Typically, a server listens to anywhere from one to five connections. However, the size of the listen queue is one of the parameters you can adjust (especially for a Web server) to ensure that the server responds to as many clients as possible. After setting up the listen queue, the server waits for a connection from a client.

Establishing the connection from the client side is somewhat simpler. After creating a socket and binding the socket to an IP address, the client establishes a connection with the server. To make the connection, the client must know the host name or IP address of the server, as well as the port on which the server accepts connection. All Internet services have well-known standard port numbers.

After a client establishes a connection to a server via a connection-oriented stream socket, the client and server can exchange data by calling the appropriate sockets' API functions. Like a conversation between two persons, the server and client alternately send and receive data — the meaning of the data depends on the message protocol the server and clients use. Usually, a server is designed for a specific task; inherent in that design is a message protocol that the server and clients use to exchange necessary data. For example, the Web server and the Web browser (client) communicate using the HTTP (HyperText Transfer Protocol).

## Internet services and port numbers

The TCP/IP protocol suite is the *lingua franca* of the Internet because the Internet services "speak" TCP/IP. These services make the Internet tick by making possible the transfer of mail, news, and Web pages. Each Internet service has its own protocol that relies on TCP/IP for the actual transfer of the information. Each service also has one or more assigned port numbers that it uses to do whatever it's designed to do. Here are some well-known Internet services and their associated protocols:

✦ **DHCP (Dynamic Host Configuration Protocol)** is for dynamically configuring TCP/IP network parameters on a computer. DHCP is primarily used to assign dynamic IP addresses and other networking information such as name server, default gateway, domain names that are needed to configure TCP/IP networks. The DHCP server listens on port 67.

✦ **FTP (File Transfer Protocol)** is used to transfer files between computers on the Internet. FTP uses two ports — data is transferred on port 20; control information is exchanged on port 21.

✦ **HTTP (HyperText Transfer Protocol)** is for sending documents from one system to another. HTTP is the underlying protocol of the Web. By default, the Web server and client communicate on port 80.

✦ **SMTP (Simple Mail Transfer Protocol)** is for exchanging e-mail messages between systems. SMTP uses port 25 for information exchange.

**Book VIII
Chapter 1**

Managing the
Servers

✦ **NNTP (Network News Transfer Protocol)** is for distribution of news articles in a store-and-forward fashion across the Internet. NNTP uses port 119.

✦ **SSH (Secure Shell)** is a protocol for secure remote login and other secure network services over an insecure network. SSH uses port 22.

✦ **TELNET** enables a user on one system to log in to another system on the Internet (the user must provide a valid user ID and password to log in to the remote system). TELNET uses port 23 by default. However, the TELNET client can connect to any specified port.

✦ **NFS (Network File System)** is for sharing files among computers. NFS uses Sun's Remote Procedure Call (RPC) facility, which exchanges information through port 111.

✦ **NTP (Network Time Protocol)** is used by client computers to synchronize the system time with that on a server (one with a more accurate clock). NTP uses port 123.

✦ **SNMP (Simple Network Management Protocol)** is for managing all types of network devices on the Internet. Like FTP, SNMP uses two ports: 161 and 162.

✦ **TFTP (Trivial File Transfer Protocol)** is for transferring files from one system to another (typically used by X terminals and diskless workstations to download boot files from another host on the network). TFTP data transfer takes place on port 69.

Each service is provided by a *server process* — a computer program that runs on a system awaiting client requests that arrive at the well-known port associated with its service. Thus the Web server expects client requests at port 80, the standard port for HTTP service.

The /etc/services text file on your Fedora Core system stores the association between a service name and a port number (as well as a protocol). Here is a small subset of entries in the /etc/services file from a Fedora Core system:

```
ftp-data    20/tcp
ftp         21/tcp
ssh         22/tcp              # SSH Remote Login Protocol
ssh         22/udp              # SSH Remote Login Protocol
telnet      23/tcp
smtp        25/tcp      mail
time        37/tcp      timserver
time        37/udp      timserver
rlp         39/udp      resource    # resource location
nameserver  42/udp      name        # IEN 116
whois       43/tcp      nicname
```

A quick look through the entries in the /etc/services file shows the breadth of networking services available under TCP/IP.

**Note:** Port number 80 is designated for Web service. In other words, if you set up a Web server on your system, that server listens to port 80. By the way, IANA — the Internet Assigned Numbers Authority (www.iana.org) — is the organization responsible for coordinating the assignment of port numbers below 1,024.

# Using the xinetd Super Server

The client/server architecture of Internet services requires that the server be up and running before a client makes a request for service. A simplistic idea would be to run all the servers all the time — impractical because each server process would use up system resources in the form of memory and processor time. Besides, you don't really need *all* the services up and ready at all times. A smart solution to this problem is to run a single server, xinetd, that listens to all the ports and then starts the appropriate server when a client request comes in. (The xinetd server is a replacement for an older server named inetd, offering improved access control and logging. The name xinetd stands for *extended* inetd.)

For example, when a client tries to connect to the TELNET port, xinetd starts the TELNET server and lets it communicate directly with the client (and the TELNET server exits when the client disconnects).

Because it starts various servers on demand, xinetd is known as the Internet super server. Typically, a UNIX system starts xinetd when the system boots. The xinetd server reads a configuration file named /etc/xinetd.conf at startup. This file tells xinetd which ports to listen to and what server to start for each port. The file can contain instructions that include other configuration files. In Fedora Core, the /etc/xinetd.conf file looks like the following:

```
# Simple configuration file for xinetd
#
# Some defaults, and include /etc/xinetd.d/

defaults
{
        instances               = 60
        log_type                = SYSLOG authpriv
        log_on_success          = HOST PID
        log_on_failure          = HOST
        cps                     = 25 30
}
includedir /etc/xinetd.d
```

Comment lines begin with the pound sign (#). The `defaults` block of attributes, enclosed in curly braces ({ . . . }), specifies default values for some attributes. These default values apply to all other services in the configuration file. The `instances` attribute is set to 60, which means, at most, 60 servers can be simultaneously active for any service.

The last line in the `/etc/xinetd.conf` file uses the `includedir` directive to include all files inside the `/etc/xinetd.d` directory, excluding files that begin with a period (.). The idea is that the `/etc/xinetd.d` directory contains all service-configuration files — one file for each type of service the `xinetd` server is expected to manage.

Here is the listing of files that appears when I type the `ls /etc/xinetd.d` command on a typical Fedora Core system (the exact content of the `/etc/xinetd.d` directory depend on the Internet services installed on your system):

```
chargen      cups-lpd  daytime-udp  echo-udp  ktalk  services  telnet  time-udp
chargen-udp  daytime   echo         finger    rsync  sgi_fam   time
```

Each of these files specifies the attributes for one service. For example, the following listing shows the contents of the `/etc/xinetd.d/telnet` file, which specifies the `xinetd` configuration for the TELNET service:

```
# description: The Telnet server serves Telnet sessions; it uses
#        unencrypted username/password pairs for authentication.
service telnet
{
        flags            = REUSE
        socket_type      = stream
        wait             = no
        user             = root
        server           = /usr/sbin/in.telnetd
        log_on_failure   += USERID
        disable          = yes
}
```

The filename (in this case, `telnet`) can be anything; what matters is the service name that appears next to the `service` keyword in the file. In this case, the line `service telnet` tells `xinetd` the name of the service. `xinetd` uses this name to look up the port number from the `/etc/services` file. To look for `telnet` in the `/etc/services` file, type the following command:

```
grep "^telnet" /etc/services
```

The command displays the following lines:

```
telnet          23/tcp
telnet          23/udp
telnets         992/tcp
telnets         992/udp
```

The first two lines of the listing that begin with `telnet` show that the port number of the TELNET service is 23. This number tells `xinetd` that any connection requests arriving at port 23 are meant for TELNET service. The configuration file `/etc/xinetd.d/telnet` then tells `xinetd` what to do to take care of these service requests.

The attributes in `/etc/xinetd.d/telnet`, enclosed in curly braces, have the following meanings:

- ✦ The `flags` attribute provides specific instructions about how to run the servers that `xinetd` starts. The `REUSE` flag means that the service is left running even if `xinetd` re-starts. *Note:* The `REUSE` flag is now implicitly assumed to be set for all services.

- ✦ The `socket_type` attribute is set to `stream`, which tells `xinetd` that the TELNET service uses a connection-oriented TCP socket to communicate with the client. For services that use the connectionless UDP sockets, this attribute is set to `dgram`.

- ✦ The `wait` attribute is set to `no`, which tells `xinetd` to start a new server for each request. If this attribute is set to `yes`, `xinetd` waits until the server exits before starting the server again.

- ✦ The `user` attribute provides the user ID that `xinetd` uses to run the server. In this case, the server runs the TELNET server as `root`.

- ✦ The `log_on_failure` attribute tells `xinetd` what information to log when it cannot start a server. In this case, the attribute is set to `HOST`, which means that if `xinetd` cannot start the TELNET service, it logs the name of the remote host that requested the service.

- ✦ The `server` attribute specifies the program to run for this service. In this case, `xinetd` runs the `/usr/sbin/in.telnetd` program to provide TELNET service.

- ✦ The `disable` attribute turns off the service if it's set to `yes`. By default, the `disable` attribute is set to `yes` and TELNET is turned off.

Browse through the files in the `/etc/xinetd.d` directory on your Fedora Core system to find out the kinds of services `xinetd` is set up to start. Some of these services, such as `finger`, provide information that intruders may use to break into your system. If they are not already disabled, you may want to turn off these services by placing the following line inside the curly braces that enclose all attributes:

```
disable       = yes
```

On the other hand, if you can't seem to connect to your Fedora Core system by using `telnet`, check the appropriate file in the `/etc/xinetd.d` directory

**Book VIII
Chapter 1**

**Managing the
Servers**

and make sure the `disable` attribute is set to `no`, or that line is *commented out* (changed from a line of code to a nonrunning comment by placing # at the beginning of the line).

When you make such a change to the `xinetd` configuration files, you must restart the `xinetd` server by typing the following command:

```
/etc/init.d/xinetd restart
```

If you want to type a little less, use the following command that does the exact same thing:

```
service xinetd restart
```

You can also use the `chkconfig` command to disable and enable services started by `xinetd`. For example, to enable the TELNET service, log in as `root` and type the following command:

```
chkconfig telnet on
```

To turn TELNET off again, type **chkconfig telnet off**.

# Running Standalone Servers

Starting servers through `xinetd` is a smart approach, but it's not efficient if a service has to be started very often. If the Web server were controlled by `xinetd`, you'd have a situation where that server is started often because every time a user clicks a link on a Web page, a request arrives for the Web service. For such high-demand services, starting the server in a standalone manner is best, to run as a *daemon* — a process that runs continuously and never dies. That means the server listens on the assigned port and whenever a request arrives, the server handles it by making a copy of itself. In this way, the server keeps running as long as the machine is running — in theory, forever. A more efficient strategy, used for Web servers, is to run multiple copies of the server and let each copy handle some of the incoming requests.

You can easily configure your Fedora Core system to start various standalone servers automatically. I show you how in this section.

## Starting and stopping servers manually

To start a service that's not running, use the server command. For example, if the Web server (`httpd`) isn't running, you can start it by running a special shell script with the following command:

```
/etc/init.d/httpd start
```

That command runs the /etc/init.d/httpd script with start as the argument. If the httpd server is already running and you want to stop it, run the same command with stop as the argument, like this:

```
/etc/init.d/httpd stop
```

To stop and start a server again, just use restart as the argument:

```
/etc/init.d/httpd restart
```

Fedora Core includes another script called service that does the same job, but is a bit easier to remember. Basically, you can strip off the /etc/init.d and replace it with service followed by a space. Thus, to start httpd, you type

```
service httpd start
```

What are all the services that you can start and stop? Well, the answer is in the files in /etc/init.d directory. To get a look at it, type the following command:

```
ls /etc/init.d
```

All the files you see listed in response to this command are the services installed on your Fedora Core system — and you can start and stop them as needed. For example, here's a typical list of services on a Fedora Core system:

| | | | | | |
|---|---|---|---|---|---|
| acpid | functions | lisa | portmap | single | winbind |
| aep1000 | gpm | messagebus | postgresql | smartd | xfs |
| anacron | halt | microcode_ctl | random | smb | xinetd |
| apmd | httpd | named | rawdevices | snmpd | ypbind |
| atd | innd | netfs | readahead | snmptrapd | yppasswdd |
| autofs | iptables | netplugd | readahead_early | squid | ypserv |
| bcm5820 | irda | network | rhnsd | sshd | ypxfrd |
| cpuspeed | irqbalance | nfs | rpcgssd | syslog | yum |
| crond | isdn | nfslock | rpcidmapd | tux | |
| cups | kdcrotate | nscd | rpcsvcgssd | udev | |
| dovecot | killall | ntpd | saslauthd | vncserver | |
| firstboot | kudzu | pcmcia | sendmail | vsftpd | |

That's over 65 services!

## Starting servers automatically at boot time

You can start, stop, and restart servers manually by using the scripts in the /etc/init.d directory, but you want some of the services to start as soon as you boot the Fedora Core system. You can configure servers to start automatically at boot time by using the chkconfig command or a graphical server-configuration utility.

## Using chkconfig command

The `chkconfig` program is a command-line utility for checking and updating the current setting of servers in Fedora Core. Various combinations of servers are set up to start automatically at different run levels. Each *run level* represents a system configuration in which a selected set of processes runs. You're usually concerned about run levels 3 and 5 because run level 3 is for text-mode login and run level 5 is for logging in through a graphical interface.

The `chkconfig` command is simple to use. For example, suppose you want to automatically start the `named` server at run levels 3 and 5. All you have to do is log in as `root` and type the following command at the shell prompt:

```
chkconfig --level 35 named on
```

To see the status of the `named` server, type the following command:

```
chkconfig --list named
```

You see a line of output similar to the following:

```
named   0:off  1:off  2:off  3:on   4:off  5:on   6:off
```

The output shows you the status of the named server at run levels 0 through 6. As you can see, `named` is set to run at run levels 3 and 5.

If you want to turn `named` off, you can do so with this command:

```
chkconfig --level 35 named off
```

You can use `chkconfig` to see the status of all services, including the ones started through `xinetd`. For example, you can view the status of all services by typing the following command:

```
chkconfig --list | more
```

Here's a typical output:

```
anacron         0:off  1:off  2:on   3:on   4:on   5:on   6:off
readahead_early 0:off  1:off  2:off  3:off  4:off  5:on   6:off
yum             0:off  1:off  2:off  3:off  4:off  5:off  6:off
aep1000         0:off  1:off  2:off  3:off  4:off  5:off  6:off
irqbalance      0:off  1:off  2:off  3:on   4:on   5:on   6:off
cups            0:off  1:off  2:on   3:on   4:on   5:on   6:off
acpid           0:off  1:off  2:off  3:on   4:on   5:on   6:off
udev            0:off  1:off  2:on   3:on   4:on   5:on   6:off
netfs           0:off  1:off  2:off  3:on   4:on   5:on   6:off
xinetd          0:off  1:off  2:off  3:on   4:on   5:on   6:off
bcm5820         0:off  1:off  2:off  3:off  4:off  5:off  6:off
messagebus      0:off  1:off  2:off  3:on   4:on   5:on   6:off
```

```
isdn         0:off   1:off   2:on    3:on    4:on    5:on    6:off
dovecot      0:off   1:off   2:off   3:off   4:off   5:off   6:off
network      0:off   1:off   2:on    3:on    4:on    5:on    6:off
tux          0:off   1:off   2:off   3:off   4:off   5:off   6:off
ypbind       0:off   1:off   2:off   3:off   4:off   5:off   6:off
ypserv       0:off   1:off   2:off   3:off   4:off   5:off   6:off
firstboot    0:off   1:off   2:off   3:on    4:off   5:on    6:off
... many lines of output deleted ...
```

The output shows the status of each service for each of the run levels from 0 through 6. For each run level, the service is either on or off. At the very end of the listing, `chkconfig` displays a list of the services that `xinetd` controls. Each `xinetd`-based service is also marked on or off, depending on whether or not `xinetd` is configured to start the service.

*Note:* You can typically configure services to run under `xinetd` or on a standalone basis. For example, prior to version 8.1, Red Hat Linux started the FTP service under control of `xinetd`. Starting with version Red Hat Linux 8.1 and in Fedora Core, however, the Very Secure FTP server (`vsftpd`) is set up as a standalone server. Nowadays, if you have to start the FTP service, type **service vsftpd start**. To start the FTP service automatically at boot time, type **chkconfig vsftpd on**.

### Using the service configuration utility

If you don't like typing the `chkconfig` commands, you can use a graphical service configuration utility program to configure the services. To run the service configuration utility, log in as `root` and choose Main Menu⇨System Settings⇨Server Settings⇨Services from the GNOME or KDE desktop. You can then turn services on or off from the Service Configuration window (as in Figure 1-2).

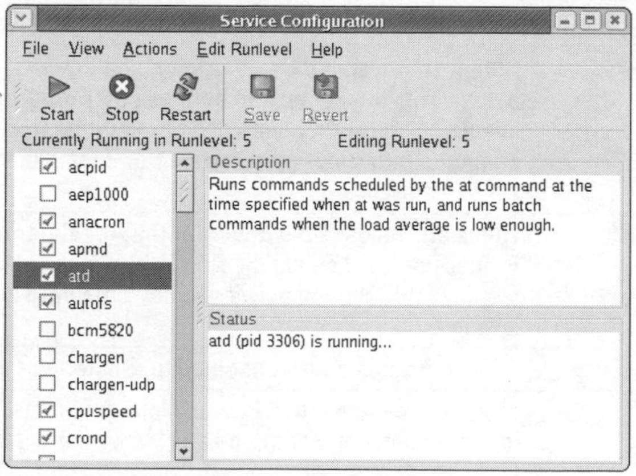

**Figure 1-2:** From the Service Configuration window, you can set services to start automatically at boot time.

The service configuration utility shows the names of services in a scrolling list. Each line in the list shows the name of a service with a box in front of the name. A check mark in the box indicates that the service is already selected to start at boot time for the current run level. When the dialog box first appears, many services are already selected.

You can scroll up and down the list and click the box to select or deselect a service. If you click the box, the check mark alternately turns on and off. To find out more about a service, click the service name and a brief description appears in the right-hand side of the window. For example, Figure 1-2 shows the help text for the `atd` service. Additionally, the utility also shows you whether the selected service is currently running or not.

After you select all the servers you want to start when the system boots, click Save on the toolbar to save the changes. Then choose File⇨Quit to exit.

By default, the service configuration utility configures the selected services for the current run level. That means if you're selecting services from the graphical desktop, the system is in run level 5 and the services you configure are set to start at run level 5. If you want to set up the services for a different level, select that run level from the Edit Runlevel menu.

Table 1-1 shows a list of the services, along with a brief description of each one. The first column shows the name of the service, which is the same as the name of the program that has to run to provide the service. You may not see all these services listed when you run the service configuration utility on your system because the exact list of services depends on what is installed on your Fedora Core system.

| Table 1-1 | Some Common Services in Fedora Core |
| --- | --- |
| *Service Name* | *Description* |
| acpid | Listens to Advanced Configuration and Power Interface (ACPI) events from the kernel and notifies other programs when such events occur. ACPI events can occur when the kernel puts the computer into a low-power state (for example, standby mode) to save energy. |
| aep1000 | Loads and unloads the driver for the Accelerated Encryption Processing card called the AEP1000, which can do encryption fast (use this service only if you have the card installed in your system). |
| anacron | Executes commands scheduled to run periodically. |
| apmd | Monitors the Advanced Power Management (APM) BIOS and logs the status of electric power (AC or battery backup). |
| atd | Runs commands scheduled by the at and cron commands. |

| Service Name | Description |
|---|---|
| autofs | Automatically mounts file systems (for example, when you insert a CD-ROM in the CD-ROM drive). |
| bcm5820 | Loads and unloads the driver for Broadcom's BCM5820 Cryptonet SSL (secure sockets layer) accelerator chip (use this service only if you have the hardware installed). |
| cpuspeed | Dynamically adjusts the CPU's frequency (the clock speed) and voltage to slow it down in order to conserve power and reduce heat. Controlling the CPU frequency can help increase a laptop computer's battery life and reduce the heat it generates. This daemon is configured through the configuration file /etc/cpuspeed.conf. |
| crond | Runs user-specified programs according to a periodic schedule the crontab command set. |
| cups | Runs the Common UNIX Printing System (CUPS) daemon (cupsd). |
| cups-lpd | Enables applications to use the legacy LPD (line printer daemon) protocol to communicate with CUPS. |
| finger | Answers finger protocol requests (for user information, such as login name and last login time). You have to enable xinetd for this service to run. |
| firstboot | Runs the first time you boot Fedora Core and enables you to set the date and time, create user accounts, and install other CD-ROMs. |
| gpm | Enables use of mouse in text-mode screens. |
| httpd | The Apache World Wide Web (WWW) server. |
| innd | The InterNetNews daemon — the Internet news server you can use to support local newsgroups on your system. |
| ipop3 | Allows remote POP3 (Post Office Protocol version 3) clients to download mail messages. You have to enable xinetd for this service to run. |
| iptables | Automates a packet-filtering firewall with iptables. |
| irda | Supports communications with IrDA-compliant infrared devices in Linux (IrDA is a standard for infrared wireless communication at speeds ranging from 2400bps to 4Mbps). |
| irqbalance | Distributes interrupts to the processors in a multiprocessor system so as to balance the load among the processors. |
| isdn | Starts and stops ISDN (Integrated Services Digital Network) services — a digital communication service over regular phone lines (enable only if you have ISDN service). |
| kudzu | Probes for new hardware and configures changed hardware. |

*(continued)*

**Book VIII
Chapter 1**

**Managing the
Servers**

**Table 1-1** *(continued)*

| Service Name | Description |
|---|---|
| lisa | Starts and stops the LAN Information Server (LISa) daemon that can display information about hosts in the local area network (LAN) by broadcasting on TCP port 7741. To find out more about LISa, visit `lisa-home.sourceforge.net`. |
| messagebus | Runs the D-BUS daemon that enables applications to receive notification of system events, such as the addition of a new hardware device. To find out more about D-BUS, see `www.freedesktop.org/software/dbus/`. |
| named | A server for the Domain Name System (DNS) that translates host names into IP addresses. You can run a copy on your system if you want. |
| netfs | Enables you to mount and unmount all network file systems (NFS, Samba, and Netware). |
| network | Enables you to activate or deactivate all network interfaces configured to start at system boot time. |
| nfs | Enables sharing of file systems specified in the `/etc/exports` file using the Network File System (NFS) protocol. |
| nfslock | Provides file-locking capability for file systems exported using the Network File System (NFS) protocol, so other systems (running NFS) can share files from your system. |
| ntpd | The server for Network Time Protocol version 4 (NTPv4) that is used for synchronizing clocks on computers in a network. |
| pcmcia | Provides support for PCMCIA devices. |
| portmap | Server used by any software that relies on Remote Procedure Calls (RPC). For example, NFS requires the `portmap` service. |
| postgresql | Starts or stops the PostgreSQL server that handles database requests. (PostgreSQL is a free database that comes with Fedora Core.) |
| random | Server needed to generate high-quality random numbers on the Fedora Core system. |
| rawdevices | Assigns raw devices to block devices (needed for applications such as Oracle). |
| readahead | Loads into memory programs used during startup before they are needed. This service makes the system start up faster. |
| rhnsd | Periodically connects to the Red Hat Network Services servers to check for updates and notifications. |
| rpcgssd | Server that manages the Generic Security Service (GSS) for NFS version 4 clients and provides security for protocols that use Remote Procedure Call (RPC). |
| rpcidmapd | Server that maps user name to user ID and group ID numbers. This is needed to support NFS version 4. |

| Service Name | Description |
|---|---|
| rpcsvcgssd | Server that manages security for NFS version 4 servers and provides security for RPC-based protocols such as NFS. |
| rsync | Server that supports remote copying of files. You have to enable xinetd for this service to run. |
| saslauthd | Supports authentication using the Cyrus-SASL (Simple Authentication and Security Layer) software. |
| sendmail | Moves mail messages from one machine to another. Start this service if you want to send mail from your Fedora Core system. If you don't plan to use your Fedora Core system as a mail server, don't start the sendmail server because it can slow down the booting process and consume unnecessary resources. |
| services | Lists active services that are being managed by xinetd. This server requires xinetd to run. |
| sgi_fam | Implements a file alternation monitor (FAM) that can be used to get reports when files change. |
| smartd | Monitors the Self-Monitoring, Analysis and Reporting Technology (SMART) system built into many ATA, IDE, and SCSI-3 hard drives. This daemon can monitor the reliability of the hard drive and predict drive failures, and can perform various self-tests of the drives. |
| smb | Starts and stops the Samba smbd and nmbd services that support LAN Manager services on a Fedora Core system. |
| snmpd | Simple Network Management Protocol (SNMP) service used for network-management functions. |
| snmptrapd | Receives and logs SNMP messages known as TRAP and INFORM messages. |
| squid | A caching server for Internet objects — anything that can be accessed through HTTP and FTP. |
| sshd | Server for the OpenSSH (Secure Shell) secure remote login facility. |
| syslog | Service used by many other programs (including other services) to log various error and status messages in a log file (usually, the /var/log/messages file). Always run this service. |
| telnet | Server that supports TELNET remote login sessions. You have to enable xinetd for this service to run. |
| tux | The kernel-based HTTP server. |
| udev | Manages device nodes dynamically. You can use it to manage the device files in the /dev directory by editing udev's configuration file /etc/udev/udev.conf. |

**Book VIII
Chapter 1**

**Managing the
Servers**

*(continued)*

**Table 1-1** *(continued)*

| Service Name | Description |
|---|---|
| vncserver | Starts and stops the Virtual Network Computing (VNC) desktop by running or stopping the X VNC server (Xvnc). By running the VNC server, you can remotely control a Fedora Core computer from any other computer on the network (you do need a VNC viewer on the computers from which you want to access the Fedora Core system's X display). |
| vsftpd | Very Secure FTP daemon for file transfers using the File Transfer Protocol (FTP). |
| winbind | Starts and stops the Samba winbindd server that provides a name-switch capability similar to that provided by the /etc/nsswitch.conf file. |
| xfs | Server that starts and stops the X Font Server. |
| xinetd | The Internet super server, a replacement for the older inetd. It starts other Internet services, such as TELNET and FTP, whenever they are needed. |
| ypbind | Service that runs on Network Information System (NIS) clients and binds the clients to a NIS domain. You don't have to start ypbind unless you're using NIS. |
| yppasswdd | Service needed for password changes in Network Information System (NIS). You don't have to start yppasswdd unless you're using NIS. |
| ypserv | The server for Network Information System (NIS). You don't have to start ypserv unless you're using NIS. |
| ypxfrd | A server that helps ypserv. Start this service only if you're using Network Information System (NIS). |
| yum | Runs Yum daily to update the software packages installed on your system. Yum is a program updater, like Up2date. |

# Chapter 2: Running the Apache Web Server

## In This Chapter

- ✔ Exploring HTTP
- ✔ Installing the Apache Web server
- ✔ Configuring the Apache Web server
- ✔ Supporting virtual hosts with the Apache Web server

The World Wide Web (*WWW* or the *Web*) has catapulted the Internet into the mainstream because Web browsers make browsing documents stored on various Internet hosts easy for users. Whether you run a small business or manage computer systems and networks for a large company, chances are good that you have to set up and maintain a Web server. Because it has built-in networking support, a Fedora Core PC makes an affordable Web server. This chapter describes how to configure the Apache Web server on a Fedora Core PC.

## Exploring HTTP

Web servers provide information using HTTP. Web servers are also known as *HTTP daemons* (because continuously running server processes are called daemons in UNIX) or *HTTPD* for short. The Web server program (such as the Apache Web server that comes with Fedora Core) is usually named `httpd`.

HTTP stands for *HyperText Transfer Protocol*. The *HyperText* part refers to the fact that Web pages include hypertext links. The *Transfer Protocol* part refers to the standard conventions for transferring a Web page across the network from one computer to another. Although you really don't have to understand HTTP to set up a Web server or use a Web browser, taking a look at its workings does help you understand how the Web works.

You can get a firsthand experience with HTTP by using the TELNET program to connect to the port where a Web server listens. On most systems, the Web server listens to port 80 and responds to any HTTP requests sent to that port. Therefore you can use the TELNET program to connect to port 80 of a system (if it has a Web server) and try some HTTP commands.

## Is HTTP an Internet standard?

Despite its widespread use in the Web since 1990, HTTP was not an Internet standard until fairly recently. All Internet standards are first distributed as a *Request for Comment* (RFC). The first HTTP-related RFC was RFC 1945, "HyperText Transfer Protocol — HTTP/1.0" (T. Berners-Lee, R. Fielding, and H. Frystyk, May 1996). However, RFC 1945 is considered an informational document, not a standard.

RFC 2616, "HyperText Transfer Protocol — HTTP/1.1" (R. Fielding, J. Gettys, J. Mogul, H.

Frystyk, L. Masinter, P. Leach, T. Berners-Lee, June 1999) is the Draft Internet standard for HTTP.

To read these RFCs, point your Web browser to either `www.apps.ietf.org/rfc/` or `www.faqs.org/rfcs/`.

To find out more about HTTP/1.1 and other Web-related standards, use a Web browser to access `www.w3.org/pub/WWW/Protocols/`.

To see an example of HTTP at work, follow these steps:

1. **Make sure your Fedora Core PC's connection to the Internet is up and running.**

   If you use PPP, for example, make sure you have established a connection. If you have a broadband cable or DSL connection, chances are your connection is always on.

2. **Type the following command:**

   ```
   telnet www.gao.gov 80
   ```

3. **After you see the `Connected...` message, type the following HTTP command and then press Enter twice:**

   ```
   GET / HTTP/1.0
   ```

   In response to this HTTP command, the Web server returns some useful information, followed by the contents of the default HTML file (usually called `index.html`).

The following is what I get when I try the `GET` command on the U. S. General Accounting Office's Web site:

```
Trying 161.203.16.2...
Connected to www.gao.gov.
Escape character is '^]'.
HTTP/1.1 200 OK
Date: Sat, 13 Mar 2004 21:14:42 GMT
Server: Apache
Connection: close
```

```
Content-Type: text/html

<!DOCTYPE HTML PUBLIC "-//W3C//DTD HTML 4.0 Transitional//EN"
    "http://www.w3.org/TR/REC-html40/loose.dtd">

<HTML>
<HEAD>
<TITLE>The United States General Accounting Office</TITLE>
...... (lines deleted)
</HEAD>

...... (lines deleted)

</BODY>
</html>
Connection closed by foreign host.
```

When you try this example with TELNET, you see exactly what the Web server sends back to the Web browser. The first few lines are administrative information for the browser. The server returns this information:

✦ A line that shows that the server uses HTTP protocol version 1.1 and a status code of 200 indicating success:

```
HTTP/1.1 200 OK
```

✦ The current date and time. A sample date and time string looks like this:

```
Date: Sat, 13 Mar 2004 21:14:42 GMT
```

✦ The name of the Web-server software. For example, for a site running the Apache Web server, the server returns the following string:

```
Server: Apache
```

The server suppresses the version number and other details so crackers cannot easily exploit known security holes in specific versions of Apache Web server.

✦ The type of document the Web server returns. For HTML documents, the content type is reported as follows:

```
Content-type: text/html
```

The document itself follows the administrative information. An HTML document has the following general layout:

```
<title>Document's title goes here</title>
<html>
<body optional attributes go here >
... The rest of the document goes here
</body>
</html>
```

You can identify this layout by looking through the listing that shows what the Web server returns in response to the GET command. Because the example uses a telnet command to get the document, you see the HTML content as lines of text. If you were to access the same Web site (www.gao.gov) with a Web browser (such as Mozilla), you see the page in its graphical form (as in Figure 2-1).

The example of HTTP commands shows the result of the GET command. GET is the most common HTTP command; it causes the server to return a specified HTML document.

The other two HTTP commands are HEAD and POST. The HEAD command is almost like GET: It causes the server to return everything in the document except the body. The POST command sends information to the server; it's up to the server to decide how to act on the information.

## Exploring the Apache Web Server

You probably already know how to use the Web, but you may not know how to set up a Web server so you, too, can provide information to the world through Web pages. To become an information provider on the Web, you have to run a Web server on your Fedora Core PC on the Internet. You also have to prepare the Web pages for your Web site — a task that may be more demanding than the Web server setup.

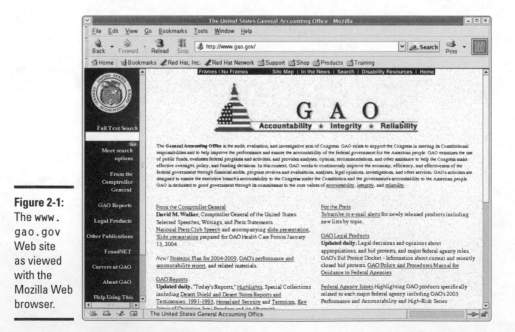

**Figure 2-1:** The www.gao.gov Web site as viewed with the Mozilla Web browser.

## Why is it called Apache?

According to the information about the Apache Web server project on www.apache.org/foundation/faq.html, the Apache group was formed in March 1995 by a number of people who provided patch files that had been written to fix bugs in NCSA HTTPD 1.3. The result after applying the patches to NCSA HTTPD was what they called *a patchy server* (that's how the name Apache came about). The Apache Group has now evolved into The Apache Software Foundation (ASF), a nonprofit corporation that was incorporated in Delaware, U.S.A., in June 1999. ASF has a number of other ongoing projects. You can read about these projects at www.apache.org. In particular, visit httpd.apache.org for more information about the Apache Web server project.

According to the April 2004 Netcraft Web Server Survey at news.netcraft.com/archives/web_server_survey.html, the Apache Web server is the most popular — 66.99 percent of the 49,750,568 sites reported using the Apache server. Microsoft Internet Information Server (IIS) is a distant second, with 21.49 percent of the sites.

Among the available Web servers, the Apache Web server is the most popular, and it comes with Fedora Core. The Apache Web server started out as an improved version of the NCSA HTTPD server but soon grew into a separate development effort. Like NCSA HTTPD, the Apache server is developed and maintained by a team of collaborators. Apache is freely available over the Internet.

## Installing the Apache Web server

Depending on the Fedora Core installation options, the Apache Web server may be already installed in your system. To find out whether it's installed, type the following command:

```
rpm -q httpd
```

If the Web server is installed, you see an output like this:

```
httpd-2.0.48-16.1
```

If you get a message that httpd is not installed, you can install it easily from this book's companion DVD-ROMs using these steps:

*1.* **Log in as** root **and insert the DVD-ROM into the DVD drive.**

If you're in the GNOME or KDE graphical desktop, the DVD is automatically mounted. If not, type the command **mount /dev/cdrom** to mount the DVD-ROM.

2. **Type the following commands to install the Apache Web server:**

```
cd /mnt/cdrom/Fedora/RPMS
rpm -ivh httpd*
```

That's it! You can now run the Apache Web server.

## Starting the Apache Web server

Even if the Apache Web server is installed, it may not be set up to start at boot time. If you want to try it out, you have to start the server. To do so, log in as root and type the following command:

```
service httpd start
```

To see whether the httpd process (httpd is the name of the Apache Web server program) is running, type the following command:

```
ps ax | grep httpd
```

The output shows a number of httpd processes. Running several Web server processes — one parent and several child processes — is a common approach so several HTTP requests can be handled efficiently by assigning each request to an httpd process.

If you can't find an httpd process, errors may be lurking in the Apache configuration file. If this is the case, some error messages appear and give you a clue about the cause of the error. You have to fix the problem in the configuration file and start the server again.

If the httpd processes are up and running, you can use the TELNET program to see if it works, but first you have to add a default home page in the /var/www/html directory. If you don't have time to prepare one, copy the Web page that's supposed to be sent out in case of errors. Here's the command you type (while logged in as root) to get it:

```
cp /var/www/error/noindex.html /var/www/html/index.html
```

Now you have a default home page and you can type the following command in a terminal window to check out if the Web server is working or not:

```
telnet localhost 80
```

After you get the Connected message, type

```
HEAD / HTTP/1.0
```

Then press Enter twice. You get a response that looks similar to the following (with different dates and numbers, of course):

```
HTTP/1.1 200 OK
Date: Sat, 13 Mar 2004 21:51:18 GMT
Server: Apache/2.0.48 (Fedora)
Last-Modified: Sat, 13 Mar 2004 21:51:08 GMT
ETag: "8c246-f30-3eec2b00"
Accept-Ranges: bytes
Content-Length: 3888
Connection: close
Content-Type: text/html; charset=UTF-8

Connection closed by foreign host.
```

The response shows some information about the Web server and the default home page. You can also check out the Web server by using a Web browser, such as Mozilla, running on your Fedora Core system. Use the URL `http://localhost/` and see what happens. You see a Web page with the title "Test Page for the Apache HTTP Server on Fedora Core."

If you want to start the Apache Web server automatically at boot time, type the following command to set it up:

```
chkconfig --levels 35 httpd on
```

# Configuring the Apache Web Server

By default, the Apache Web server software is configured to use the following files and directories:

✦ The Web server program — `httpd` — is installed in the `/usr/sbin` directory.

✦ The Apache Web server configuration file — `httpd.conf` — is located in the `/etc/httpd/conf` directory. The configuration file is a text file with directives that specify various aspects of the Web server. The `/etc/httpd/conf` directory also contains information about the Secure Sockets Layer (SSL) implementation needs. (The SSL implementation comes as part of the Apache Web server.)

✦ The Apache Web server is set up to serve the HTML documents from the `/var/www/html` directory. Therefore, place your Web pages in this directory.

✦ If you have any Common Gateway Interface (CGI) programs — programs the Web server can invoke to access other files and databases — place these in the `/var/www/cgi-bin/` directory.

✦ The /var/log/httpd directory is meant for Web server log files (access logs and error logs).

✦ The /etc/init.d/httpd script starts the httpd process as your Fedora Core system boots, provided you enable it by using the chkconfig command.

## Using Apache configuration tools

Fedora Core comes with a graphical configuration tool that you can use to configure the Apache Web server. To run this configuration tool, log in as root and choose Main Menu⊃System Settings⊃Server Settings⊃HTTP from the GNOME desktop. The Apache Configuration window appears (as in Figure 2-2).

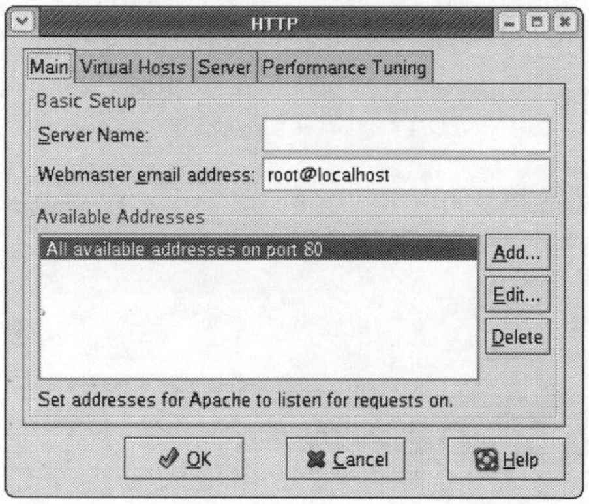

**Figure 2-2:** You can configure the Apache HTTP server from this configuration window.

The Apache Configuration window is organized into four tabs. You can set various options from each of these tabs:

✦ **Main:** From this tab, you can specify the IP addresses and port number where Apache expects requests for Web service. You can also set the e-mail address of the Webmaster.

✦ **Virtual Hosts:** Here you can set up virtual hosts. I discuss the options for virtual hosts later in this chapter. You can also edit the default settings that apply to all virtual hosts. Clicking the Edit Default Settings button on the Virtual Hosts tab brings up another window (shown in Figure 2-3) from which you can set a number of different options.

✦ **Server:** This tab has settings for the server such as the user and group names under which the HTTP server runs and the locations of the file where the process ID is stored.

✦ **Performance Tuning:** On this tab, you can set some parameters that control overall performance. You can set the maximum number of connections allowed, the timeout period for connections, and the maximum number of requests per connection.

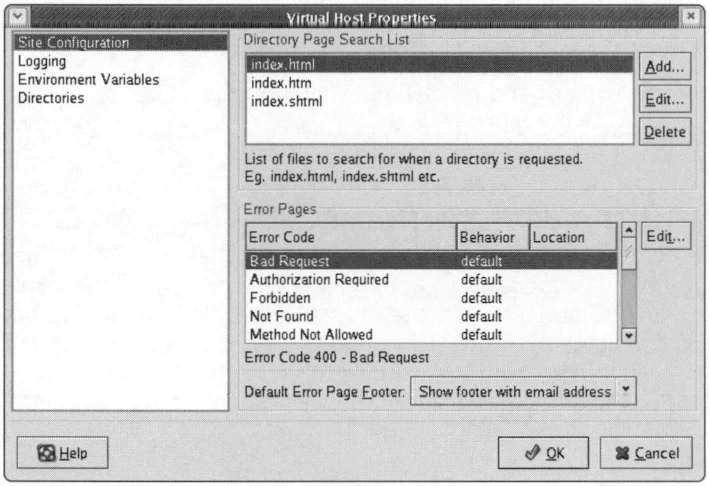

**Figure 2-3:**
You can configure the virtual host properties from this configuration window.

Initially the configuration window displays the default values from the configuration file /etc/httpd/conf/httpd.conf. After you make any changes, click the OK button. The configuration tool prompts you to ask whether you really want to save the changes and exit. If you do, click Yes and you are done.

When you configure the Apache HTTP server from this configuration tool, all you're doing is changing options and attributes stored in the /etc/httpd/conf/httpd.conf file. You can just as easily make the changes by editing the configuration file, which is a plain text file. In the next sections, I introduce you to some common configuration directives in the Apache configuration file.

## *Apache configuration files*

The Apache server's operation is controlled by the httpd.conf configuration file located in the /etc/httpd/conf directory. This file controls how the server runs, what documents it serves, and who can access these documents.

In the next few sections, I summarize key information about the httpd.conf configuration file. Typically, you don't have to change anything in the configuration files to run the Apache Web server. However, knowing the format of the configuration files and the meaning of the various keywords used in them is useful.

As you study the configuration files in the `/etc/httpd/conf` directory, keep these syntax rules in mind:

✦ Each configuration file is a text file that you can edit with your favorite text editor and view with the `more` command.

✦ All comment lines begin with a #.

✦ Each line can have only one directive.

✦ Extra spaces and blank lines are ignored.

✦ All entries, except pathnames and URLs, are case insensitive.

## *The httpd.conf configuration file*

The `/etc/httpd/conf/httpd.conf` file is the main HTTP-daemon configuration file — it includes directives that control how the Apache Web server runs. For example, the `httpd.conf` file specifies the port number the server uses, the name of the Web site, and the e-mail address to which mail is sent in case of any problems with the server. In addition, `httpd.conf` also includes information on where the Web pages are located and who can access what directories.

In the following sections, I present the Apache directives grouped in three separate categories: general HTTPD directives, resource-configuration directives, and access-control directives. Finally, I explain how virtual hosts can be set up in Apache Web server so a single Web server can handle Web requests sent to several IP addresses or host names.

To browse the Apache HTTPD documentation online, visit `httpd.apache.org/docs-2.0/`. Specifically, you can look up information on configuration directives at `httpd.apache.org/docs-2.0/mod/directives.html`.

### *General HTTPD directives*

Some interesting items from the `httpd.conf` file are

✦ `ServerName` specifies the host name of your Web site (of the form `www.your.domain`) and the port number where the Web server accepts connections. `ServerName` is used only when redirecting a Web page to another Web page. The name is a registered domain name other users can locate through their name servers. Here is an example:

```
ServerName  www.myhost.com:80
```

If you don't have a registered domain name, use the IP address of your Fedora Core system.

✦ ServerAdmin is the e-mail address that the Web server provides to clients in case any errors occur. The default value for ServerAdmin is root@ localhost. Set this address to a valid e-mail address that anyone on the Internet can use to report errors your Web site contains.

✦ Include loads more configuration directives from a specified file. For example, the default /etc/httpd/conf/httpd.conf file loads all the configuration files from the /etc/httpd/conf.d directory by using the following Include directive:

```
Include conf.d/*.conf
```

This command means that you can load another set of configurations by simply adding a file to the /etc/httpd/conf.d directory. In fact, that's the directory where you find the configuration files for various Apache HTTPD modules, such as Perl, PHP, and SSL. Study the configuration file in the /etc/httpd/conf.d directory to find out more about the total set of directives that affect the Apache Web server's behavior.

Many more directives control the way that the Apache Web server works. The following list summarizes some of the directives you can use in the httpd. conf file. You can leave most of these directives in their default settings, but knowing about them if you're maintaining a Web server is important.

✦ Listen *IP-Address:Port*: Forces the Web server to listen to a specific IP address and port number. By default, the Web server responds to all IP addresses associated with the host.

✦ User *name* [ *#id*]: Specifies the username (or ID) the HTTP daemon uses. You can leave this directive at the default setting (apache). If you specify a user ID, use a hash (#) prefix for the numeric ID.

✦ Group *name* [ *#id*]: Specifies the group name (or ID) of the HTTP daemon when running in stand-alone mode. The default group name is apache.

✦ ServerRoot *pathname*: Specifies the directory where the Web server is located. By default, the configuration and log files are expected to reside in subdirectories of this directory. In Fedora Core, ServerRoot is set to /etc/httpd.

✦ ServerName *www.company.com*:80: Sets the server's host name to *www.company.com* and the port number to 80. ServerName is used only when redirecting a Web page to another.

✦ ServerTokens Major|Minor|Min|Prod|OS|Full: Controls how much information is sent back to the client in the Server field of the header. Set the directive to Prod for a Server response that simply identifies the product name (in this case, Apache).

- ✦ StartServers *num*: Sets the number of child processes that start as soon as the Apache Web server runs. The default value is 8.

- ✦ MaxSpareServers *num*: Sets the desired maximum number of idle child-server processes (a child process is considered idle if it's not handling an HTTP request). The default value is 20.

- ✦ MinSpareServers *num*: Sets the desired minimum number of idle child server processes (a child process is considered idle if it's not handling an HTTP request). A new spare process is created every second if the number falls below this threshold. The default value is 5.

- ✦ Timeout *numsec*: Sets the number of seconds that the server waits for a client to send a query after the client establishes connection. The default Timeout is 300 seconds (five minutes).

- ✦ ErrorLog *filename*: Sets the file where httpd logs the errors it encounters. If the filename does not begin with a slash (/), the name is taken to be relative to ServerRoot. The default ErrorLog is /etc/httpd/logs/error_log, but /etc/httpd/logs is a symbolic link to the /var/log/httpd directory. Therefore the log files are in /var/log/.httpd directory. Typical error-log entries include events, such as server restarts, and any warning messages, such as the following:

    ```
    [Sat Mar 13 18:10:01 2004] [notice] Apache/2.0.48 (Fedora) configured --
        resuming normal operations
    [Sat Mar 13 18:10:37 2004] [error] [client 192.168.0.3] File does not
        exist: /var/www/html/book
    ```

- ✦ *TransferLog filename*: Sets the file where httpd records all client accesses (including failed accesses). The default TransferLog is /var/log/httpd/access_log. The following example shows how a typical access is recorded in this log file:

    ```
    192.168.0.3 - - [13/Mar/2004:18:10:23 -0500] "GET / HTTP/1.1" 200 3888 "-
        " "Mozilla/4.0 (compatible; MSIE 6.0; Windows NT 5.1; (R1 1.3); .NET
        CLR 1.1.4322)"
    192.168.0.3 - - [13/Mar/2004:18:10:23 -0500] "GET /icons/apache_pb2.gif
        HTTP/1.1" 200 2414 "http://192.168.0.6/" "Mozilla/4.0 (compatible;
        MSIE 6.0; Windows NT5.1; (R1 1.3); .NET CLR 1.1.4322)"
    192.168.0.3 - - [13/Mar/2004:18:10:23 -0500] "GET
        /icons/powered_by_fedora.png HTTP/1.1" 200 2243
        "http://192.168.0.6/" "Mozilla/4.0 (compatible; MSIE 6.0; Windows NT
        5.1; (R1 1.3); .NET CLR 1.1.4322)"
    ```

- ✦ LogFormat *formatstring formatname*: Specifies the format of log-file entries for the TransferLog. The CustomLog directive also uses this format to produce logs in a specific format.

- ✦ CustomLog *filename formatname*: Sets the name of the custom log file where httpd records all client accesses (including failed accesses) in a format specified by *formatname* (which you define using a LogFormat directive).

✦ **PidFile** *filename*: Sets the file where HTTPD stores its process ID. The default `PidFile` is `/var/run/httpd.pid`. You can use this information to kill or restart the HTTP daemon. The following example shows how to restart `httpd`:

```
kill -HUP 'cat /var/run/httpd.pid'
```

✦ **MaxClients** *num*: Sets the limit on the number of clients that can simultaneously connect to the server. The default value is 150. The value of `MaxClients` cannot be more than 256.

✦ **LoadModule** *module* `modules/modfile.so`: Loads a module that was built as a Dynamic Shared Object (DSO). You have to specify the module name and the module's object file. Because the order in which modules are loaded is important, leave these directives as they appear in the default configuration file. *Note:* The `mod_ssl` module provides support for encryption using the Secure Sockets Layer (SSL) protocol.

### Resource configuration directives

The resource configuration directives specify the location of the Web pages, as well as how to specify the data types of various files. To get started, you can leave the directives at their default settings. These are some of the resource configuration directives for the Apache Web server:

✦ **DocumentRoot** *pathname*: Specifies the directory where the HTTP server finds the Web pages. In Fedora Core, the default `DocumentRoot` is `/var/www/html`. If you place your HTML documents in another directory, set `DocumentRoot` to that directory.

✦ **UserDir** *dirname*: Specifies the subdirectory below a user's home directory where the HTTP server looks for Web pages when a username appears in the URL (in an URL such as `http://www.psn.net/~naba`, for example, which includes a username with a tilde prefix). By default, the `UserDir` feature is turned off by setting *dirname* to `disable`. If you want it enabled, you can set it to `public_html`, which means that a user's Web pages are in the `public_html` subdirectory of that user's home directory.

✦ **DirectoryIndex** *filename1 filename2 ...*: Indicates the server return default file or files when the client does not specify a document. The default `DirectoryIndex` is `index.html`. If `httpd` does not find this file, it returns an index (basically, a nice-looking listing of the files) of that directory, provided indexing is allowed for that directory.

✦ **AccessFileName** *filename*: Specifies the name of the file that may appear in each directory that contains documents and that indicates who has permission to access the contents of that directory. The default `AccessFileName` is `.htaccess`. The syntax of this file is the same as that of Apache access-control directives, which I discuss in the next section.

✦ **AddType** *type/subtype extension*: Associates a file extension with a MIME data type (of the form *type/subtype*, such as text/plain or image/gif). Thus, to have the server treat files with the .lst extension as plain-text files, specify the following:

```
AddType text/plain .lst
```

The default MIME types and extensions are listed in the /etc/mime. types file.

✦ **AddEncoding** *type extension*: Associates an encoding type with a file extension. To have the server mark files ending with .gz or .tgz as encoded with the x-gzip encoding method (the standard name for the GZIP encoding), specify the following:

```
AddEncoding x-gzip gz tgz
```

✦ **DefaultType** *type/subtype*: Specifies the MIME type that the server uses if it cannot determine the type from the file extension. If you don't specify DefaultType, HTTPD assumes the MIME type to be text/html. In the default httpd.conf file, DefaultType is specified as text/ plain.

✦ **Redirect** *requested-file actual-URL*: Specifies that any requests for *requested-file* be redirected to *actual-URL*.

✦ **Alias** *requested-dir actual-dir*: Specifies that the server use *actual-dir* to locate files in the *requested-dir* directory (in other words, *requested-dir* is an alias for *actual-dir*). To have requests for the /icons directory go to /var/www/icons, specify the following:

```
Alias /icons/ /var/www/icons/
```

✦ **ScriptAlias** *requested-dir actual-dir*: Specifies the real name of the directory where scripts for the Common Gateway Interface (CGI) are located. The default configuration file contains this directive:

```
ScriptAlias /cgi-bin/ "/var/www/cgi-bin/"
```

This directive means that when a Web browser requests a script, such as /cgi-bin/test-cgi, the HTTP server runs the script /var/www/ cgi-bin/test-cgi.

✦ **DefaultIcon** *iconfile*: Specifies the location of the default icon that the server uses for files that have no icon information. By default, DefaultIcon is /icons/unknown.gif.

✦ **ReadmeName** *filename*: Specifies the name of a README file whose contents are added to the end of an automatically generated directory listing. The default ReadmeName is README.

✦ **HeaderName** *filename*: Specifies the name a header file whose contents are prepended to an automatically generated directory listing. The default HeaderName is HEADER.

✦ `AddDescription "file description" filename`: Specifies that the *file description* string display next to the specified filename in the directory listing. You can use a wildcard, such as `*.html`, as the filename. For example, the following directive describes files ending with `.tgz` as GZIP compressed tar archives:

```
AddDescription "GZIP compressed tar archive" .tgz
```

✦ `AddIcon iconfile extension1 extension2 ...`: Associates an icon with one or more file extensions. The following directive associates the icon file `/icons/text.gif` with the file extension `.txt`:

```
AddIcon /icons/text.gif .txt
```

✦ `AddIconByType iconfile MIME-types`: Associates an icon with a group of file types specified as a wildcard form of MIME types (such as `text/*` or `image/*`). To associate an icon file of `/icons/text.gif` with all `text` types, specify the following:

```
AddIconByType (TXT,/icons/text.gif) text/*
```

This directive also tells the server to use `TXT` in place of the icon for clients that cannot accept images. (Browsers tell the server what types of data they can accept.)

✦ `AddIconByEncoding iconfile encoding1 encoding2 ...`: Specifies an icon to display for one or more encoding types (such as `x-compress` or `x-gzip`).

✦ `IndexIgnore filename1 filename2 ...`: Instructs the server to ignore the specified filenames (they typically contain wildcards) when preparing a directory listing. To leave out `README`, `HEADER`, and all files with names that begin with a period (.), a trailing tilde (~), or a trailing hash mark (#), specify the following:

```
IndexIgnore .??* *~ *# HEADER* README* RCS CVS *,v *,t
```

✦ `IndexOptions option1 option2 ...`: Indicates the options you want in the directory listing prepared by the server. Options can include one or more of the following:

- `FancyIndexing` turns on the fancy directory listing that includes filenames and icons representing the files' types, sizes, and last-modified dates.

- `IconHeight=N` specifies that icons are N pixels tall.

- `IconWidth=N` specifies that icons are N pixels wide.

- `NameWidth=N` makes the filename column N characters wide.

- `IconsAreLinks` makes the icons act like links.

- `ScanHTMLTitles` shows a description of HTML files.

- `SuppressHTMLPreamble` does not add a standard HTML preamble to the header file (specified by the `HeaderName` directive).

- `SuppressLastModified` stops display of the last date of modification.

- `SuppressSize` stops display of the file size.

- `SuppressDescription` stops display of any file description.

- `SuppressColumnSorting` stops the column headings from being links that enable sorting the columns.

✦ `ErrorDocument` *errortype* *filename*: Specifies a file the server sends when an error of a specific type occurs. You can also provide a text message for an error. Here are some examples:

```
ErrorDocument 403 "Sorry, no access to this directory"
ErrorDocument 403 /error/noindex.html
ErrorDocument 404 /cgi-bin/bad_link.pl
ErrorDocument 401 /new_subscriber.html
```

If you don't have the `ErrorDocument` directive, the server sends a built-in error message. The *errortype* can be one of the following `HTTP/1.1` error conditions (see RFC 2616 at `www.ietf.org/rfc/rfc2616.txt` or `www.faqs.org/rfcs/rfc2616.html` for more information):

- 400: Bad Request

- 401: Unauthorized

- 402: Payment Required

- 403: Forbidden

- 404: Not Found

- 405: Method Not Allowed

- 406: Not Acceptable

- 407: Proxy Authentication Required

- 408: Request Timeout

- 409: Conflict

- 410: Gone

- 411: Length Required

- 412: Precondition Failed

- 413: Request Entity Too Large

- 414: Request-URI Too Long

- 415: Unsupported Media Type

- 416: Requested Range Not Satisfiable

- 417: Expectation Failed

- 500: Internal Server Error

- 501: Not Implemented

- 502: Bad Gateway

- 503: Service Unavailable

- 504: Gateway Timeout

- 505: HTTP Version Not Supported

✦ `TypesConfig` *filename*: Specifies the file that contains the mapping of file extensions to MIME data types. (MIME stands for Multipurpose Internet Mail Extensions, a way to package attachments in a single message file.) The server reports these MIME types to clients. If you don't specify a `TypesConfig` directive, HTTPD assumes that the `TypesConfig` file is `/etc/mime.types`. The following are a few selected lines from the default `/etc/mime.types` file:

```
application/msword              doc
application/pdf                 pdf
application/postscript          ai eps ps
application/x-tcl               tcl
audio/mpeg                      mpga mp2 mp3
audio/x-pn-realaudio            ram rm
audio/x-wav                     wav
image/gif                       gif
image/jpeg                      jpeg jpg jpe
image/png                       png
text/html                       html htm
text/plain                      asc txt
video/mpeg                      mpeg mpg mpe
```

Each line shows the MIME type (such as `text/html`), followed by the file extensions for that type (`html` or `htm`).

## Access-control directives

Access-control directives enable you to control who can access different directories in the system. These are the global access-configuration directives. You can also have another access-configuration file that uses a name specified by the `AccessFileName` directive in every directory from which the Apache Web server can serve documents. (That *per-directory* access-configuration file is named `.htaccess` by default.)

**Book VIII**
**Chapter 2**

**Running the Apache Web Server**

Stripped of most of its comment lines, the access-control directive has this format:

```
# First, we configure the "default" to be a
# very restrictive set of permissions.
<Directory />
    Options FollowSymLinks
    AllowOverride None
</Directory>

# The following directory name should
# match DocumentRoot in httpd.conf
<Directory /var/www/html>
    Options Indexes FollowSymLinks
    AllowOverride None
    order allow,deny
    allow from all
</Directory>

# The directory name should match the
# location of the cgi-bin directory
<Directory "/var/www/cgi-bin">
    AllowOverride None
    Options None
    Order allow,deny
    Allow from all
</Directory>
```

Access-control directives use a different syntax from the other Apache directives. The syntax is like that of HTML. Various access-control directives are enclosed within pairs of tags, such as `<Directory> ... </Directory>`.

The following list describes some of the access-control directives. In particular, notice the `AuthUserFile` directive; you can have password-based access control for specific directories.

✦ `Options opt1 opt2 ...:` Specifies the access-control options for the directory section in which this directive appears. The options can be one or more of the following:

- `None` disables all access-control features.
- `All` turns on all features for the directory.
- `FollowSymLinks` enables the server to follow symbolic links.
- `SymLinksIfOwnerMatch` follows symbolic links, only if the same user of the directory owns the linked directory.
- `ExecCGI` enables execution of CGI scripts in the directory.

- `Includes` enables server-side include files in this directory (the term *server-side include* refers to directives, placed in an HTML file, that the Web server processes before returning the results to the Web browser).

- `Indexes` enables clients to request indexes (directory listings) for the directory.

- `IncludesNOEXEC` disables the `#exec` command in server-side includes.

✦ `AllowOverride` *directive1 directive2* ...: Specifies which access-control directives can be overridden on a per-directory basis. The directive list can contain one or more of the following:

- `None` stops any directive from being overridden.

- `All` enables overriding of any directive on a per-directory basis.

- `Options` enables the use of the `Options` directive in the directory-level file.

- `FileInfo` enables the use of directives controlling document type, such as `AddType` and `AddEncoding`.

- `AuthConfig` enables the use of authorization directives, such as `AuthName`, `AuthType`, `AuthUserFile`, and `AuthGroupFile`.

- `Limit` enables the use of `Limit` directives (`allow`, `deny`, and `order`) in a directory's access-configuration file.

✦ `AuthName` *name*: Specifies the authorization name for a directory.

✦ `AuthType` *type*: Specifies the type of authorization to be used. The only supported authorization type is Basic.

✦ `AuthUserFile` *filename*: Specifies the file in which usernames and passwords are stored for authorization. For example, the following directive sets the authorization file to `/etc/httpd/conf/passwd`:

```
AuthUserFile /etc/httpd/conf/passwd
```

You have to create the authorization file with the `/usr/bin/htpasswd` support program. To create the authorization file and add the password for a user named `jdoe`, specify the following:

```
/usr/bin/htpasswd -c /etc/httpd/conf/passwd jdoe
```

When prompted for the password, enter the password and then confirm it by typing it again.

✦ `AuthGroupFile` *filename*: Specifies the file to consult for a list of user groups for authentication.

✦ `order` *ord*: Specifies the order in which two other directives — `allow` and `deny` — are evaluated. The order is one of the following:

- `deny,allow` causes the Web server to evaluate the `deny` directive before `allow`.

- `allow,deny` causes the Web server to evaluate the `allow` directive before `deny`.

- `mutual-failure` enables only hosts in the `allow` list.

✦ `deny from host1 host2...`: Specifies the hosts denied access.

✦ `allow from host1 host2...`: Specifies the hosts allowed access. To enable all hosts in a specific domain to access the Web documents in a directory, specify the following:

```
order deny,allow
allow from .nws.noaa.gov
```

✦ `require entity en1 en2...`: This directive specifies which users can access a directory. `entity` is one of the following:

- `user` enables only a list of named users.

- `group` enables only a list of named groups.

- `valid-user` enables all users listed in the `AuthUserFile` access to the directory (provided they enter the correct password).

## Virtual host setup

A useful feature of the Apache HTTP server is that it can handle virtual Web servers. *Virtual hosting* simply means that a single Web server can respond to many different IP addresses and serve Web pages from different directories, depending on the IP address. That means you can set up a single Web server to respond to both `www.big.org` and `www.tiny.com` and serve a unique home page for each host name. A server with this capability is known as a *multi-homed* Web server, a *virtual* Web server, or a server with *virtual host support*.

As you might guess, Internet Service Providers (ISPs) use the virtual host feature of Apache Web server to offer virtual Web sites to their customers. You need the following to support virtual hosts:

✦ The Web server must be able to respond to multiple IP addresses (each with a unique domain name) and must enable you to specify document directories, log files, and other configuration items for each IP address.

✦ The host system must be able to associate multiple IP addresses with a single physical network interface. Fedora Core can do so.

✦ Each domain name associated with the IP address must be a unique, registered domain name with proper DNS entries.

For the latest information on how to set up virtual hosts in an Apache HTTP server, consult the following URL:

```
http://httpd.apache.org/docs-2.0/vhosts
```

The Apache HTTP server can respond to different host names with different home pages. You have two options when supporting virtual hosts:

+ **Run multiple copies of the** `httpd` **program, one for each IP address:** In this case, you create a separate copy of the `httpd.conf` configuration file for each host and use the `Listen` directive to make the server respond to a specific IP address.

+ **Run a single copy of the** `httpd` **program with a single** `httpd.conf` **file:** In the configuration file, set `Listen` to a port number only (so the server responds to any IP address associated with the host), and use the `VirtualHost` directive to configure the server for each virtual host.

Run multiple HTTP daemons only if you don't expect heavy traffic on your system; the system may not able to respond well because of the overhead associated with running multiple daemons. However, you may need multiple HTTP daemons if each virtual host has a unique configuration need for the following directives:

+ `UserId` and `GroupId` (the user and group ID for the HTTP daemon)

+ `ServerRoot` (the `root` directory of the server)

+ `TypesConfig` (the MIME type configuration file)

For a site with heavy traffic, configure the Web server so a single HTTP daemon can serve multiple virtual hosts. Of course, this recommendation implies that there is only one configuration file. In that configuration file, use the `VirtualHost` directive to configure each virtual host.

Most ISPs use the `VirtualHost` capability of Apache HTTP server to provide virtual Web sites to their customers. Unless you pay for a dedicated Web host, you typically get a virtual site where you have your own domain name, but share the server and the actual host with many other customers.

The syntax of the `VirtualHost` directive is as follows:

```
<VirtualHost hostaddr>
    ... directives that apply to this host
    ...
</VirtualHost>
```

With this syntax, you use `<VirtualHost>` and `</VirtualHost>` to enclose a group of directives that applies only to the particular virtual host identified by the *hostaddr* parameter. The *hostaddr* can be an IP address or the fully qualified domain name of the virtual host.

You can place almost any Apache directives within the `<VirtualHost>` block. At a minimum, Webmasters include the following directives in the `<VirtualHost>` block:

✦ `DocumentRoot`, which specifies where this virtual host's documents reside

✦ `Servername`, which identifies the server to the outside world (this name is a registered domain name DNS supports)

✦ `ServerAdmin`, the e-mail address of this virtual host's Webmaster

✦ `Redirect`, which specifies any URLs to be redirected to other URLs

✦ `ErrorLog`, which specifies the file where errors related to this virtual host are to be logged

✦ `CustomLog`, which specifies the file where accesses to this virtual host are logged

When the server receives a request for a document in a particular virtual host's `DocumentRoot` directory, it uses the configuration parameters within that server's `<VirtualHost>` block to handle that request.

Here is a typical example of a `<VirtualHost>` directive that sets up the virtual host `www.lnbsoft.com`:

```
<VirtualHost www.lnbsoft.com>
    DocumentRoot    /home/naba/httpd/htdocs
    ServerName    www.lnbsoft.com
    ServerAdmin    webmaster@lnbsoft.com
    ScriptAlias    /cgi-bin/    /home/naba/httpd/cgi-bin/
    ErrorLog /home/naba/httpd/logs/error_log
    CustomLog    /home/naba/httpd/logs/access_log common
</VirtualHost>
```

Here the name `common` in the `CustomLog` directive refers to the name of a format defined earlier in the `httpd.conf` file by the `LogFormat` directive, as follows:

```
LogFormat "%h %l %u %t \"%r\" %>s %b" common
```

This format string for the log produces lines in the log file that looks like this:

```
dial236.dc.psn.net - - [13/Jul/2003:18:09:00 -0500] "GET /
   HTTP/1.0" 200 1243
```

The format string contains two letter tokens that start with a percent sign (%). The meaning of these tokens is shown in Table 2-1.

| Table 2-1 | LogFormat Tokens |
|---|---|
| *Token* | *Meaning* |
| %b | The number of bytes sent to the client, excluding header information |
| %h | The host name of the client machine |
| %l | The identity of the user, if available |
| %r | The HTTP request from the client (for example, GET / HTTP/1.0) |
| %s | The server response code from the Web server |
| %t | The current local date and time |
| %u | The username the user supplies (only when access-control rules require username/password authentication) |

**Book VIII
Chapter 2**

**Running the Apache
Web Server**

# Chapter 3: Setting Up the FTP Server

## In This Chapter

- ✔ Installing the FTP server
- ✔ Configuring the FTP server
- ✔ Setting up anonymous FTP

*F*ile Transfer Protocol (FTP) is a popular Internet service for transferring files from one system to another. *Anonymous FTP* is another popular Internet service for distributing files. The neat thing about anonymous FTP is that if a remote system supports anonymous FTP, anyone can use FTP with the `anonymous` user ID and can download files from that system. Although anonymous FTP is useful for distributing data, it poses a security risk if it's not set up properly.

Fedora Core comes with several FTP clients and the "very secure" FTP daemon (`vsftpd`), written by Chris Evans. Fedora Core also includes an RPM called `anonftp` that sets up the files you need to support anonymous FTP. In this chapter, I show you how to configure the FTP server through text configuration files and how to control access to the FTP server. I also describe anonymous FTP — how it's set up and how to ensure that it's secure.

## Installing the FTP Server

During Fedora Core installation, you have the option to install the FTP server software. To check if the FTP server is already installed, type the following command:

```
rpm -q vsftpd
```

If the software is indeed installed, you see an output similar to the following:

```
vsftpd-1.2.1-2
```

If you get a message saying that the package isn't installed, you can easily install it from the companion DVD-ROM. To install the RPM files for FTP, log in as `root` and place the DVD-ROM in the DVD-ROM drive. If you're using the GNOME or KDE desktop, the DVD-ROM mounts automatically. If not, type the following command to mount the DVD-ROM:

```
mount /mnt/cdrom
```

Then type the following command to change the directory:

```
cd /mnt/cdrom/Fedora/RPMS
```

This command is how you find the RPM files for FTP. You can install the FTP server (which includes the anonymous FTP setup) with the following RPM command:

```
rpm -ivh vsftpd*
```

# Configuring the FTP Server

Fedora Core comes with the very secure FTP daemon (`vsftpd`), written by Chris Evans. The executable file for `vsftpd` is `/usr/sbin/vsftpd`, and it uses a number of configuration files in the `/etc` and `/etc/vsftpd` directories. By default, the `vsftpd` server is disabled — and if you want to use the FTP server, first you have to enable it. In this section, I show you how.

The `vsftpd` server is configured to run stand-alone and an initialization script (or *initscript*) — `/etc/init.d/vsftpd` — starts and stops the server. To start the `vsftpd` server, log in as `root` and type the following command:

```
service vsftpd start
```

You can also type the following command as `root` to turn `vsftpd` on so it starts at system startup:

```
chkconfig --level 35 vsftpd on
```

After you start the `vsftpd` server, the default settings are all you need to begin using the server. That's because other FTP clients can now connect and request files from your FTP server. However, you need to know about the configuration files in case you have to customize them some other time.

## vsftpd configuration files

The `vsftpd` server consults a number of configuration files located in the `/etc` and `/etc/vsftpd` directories. These directories control many aspects of the FTP server such as whether it runs stand-alone, who can download files, and whether to allow anonymous FTP. The key configuration files for vsftpd are the following:

+ /etc/vsftpd/vsftpd.conf controls how the vsftpd server works (for example, whether it allows anonymous logins, allows file uploads, and so on).

+ /etc/vsftpd.ftpusers lists names of users who cannot access the FTP server.

+ /etc/vsftpd.user_list lists names of users who are denied access (not even prompted for password). However, if the userlist_deny option is set to NO in /etc/vsftpd/vsftpd.conf, these users are allowed to access the FTP server.

You can usually leave most of these configuration files with their default settings. However, just in case you have to change something to make vsftpd suit your needs, I explain the configuration files briefly in the next few sections.

## /etc/vsftpd/vsftpd.conf file

To find out what you can have in the /etc/vsftpd/vsftpd.conf file and how these lines affect the vsftpd server's operation, start by looking at the /etc/vsftpd/vsftpd.conf file that's installed by default in Fedora Core. The comments in this file tell you what each option does.

By default, vsftpd allows almost nothing. By editing the options in /etc/vsftpd/vsftpd.conf, you can loosen the restrictions so users can use FTP. You can decide how loose the settings are.

Here are some of the options you can set in /etc/vsftpd/vsftpd.conf:

+ anon_mkdir_write_enable=YES enables anonymous FTP users to create new directories. This option is risky and you may want to set it to NO, even if you allow anonymous users to upload files.

+ anon_upload_enable=YES means anonymous FTP users can upload files. This option takes effect only if write_enable is already set to YES and the directory has write permissions for everyone. ***Remember:*** Allowing anonymous users to write on your system can be very risky because someone could fill up the disk or use your disk for their personal storage.

+ anonymous_enable=YES enables *anonymous FTP* (users can log in with the username anonymous and provide their e-mail address as a password). Comment out this line if you don't want anonymous FTP.

**Book VIII
Chapter 3**

**Setting Up the
FTP Server**

✦ `ascii_download_enable=YES` enables file downloads in ASCII mode. Unfortunately, a malicious remote user can issue the `SIZE` command with the name of a huge file and essentially cause the FTP server to waste huge amounts of resources opening that file and determining its size. This technique is used in a Denial of Service attack (as mentioned later in this section).

✦ `ascii_upload_enable=YES` enables file uploads in ASCII mode (for text files).

✦ `async_abor_enable=YES` causes `vsftpd` to recognize `ABOR` (abort) requests that arrive at any time. You may have to enable it to allow older FTP clients to work with `vsftpd`.

✦ `banned_email_file=/etc/vsftpd.banned_emails` specifies the file with the list of banned e-mail addresses (used only if `deny_email_enable` is set to `YES`).

✦ `chown_uploads=YES` causes uploaded anonymous files to be owned by a different user specified by the `chown_username` option. Don't enable this option unless absolutely necessary — and don't specify `root` as the `chown_username` (that's a disaster just waiting to happen).

✦ `chown_username=name` specifies the username that owns files uploaded by anonymous FTP users.

✦ `chroot_list_enable=YES` causes `vsftpd` to confine all users except those on a list specified by the `chroot_list_file` to their home directories when they log in for FTP service. This option prevents these users from getting to any other files besides what's in their home directories.

✦ `chroot_list_file=/etc/vsftpd.chroot_list` is the list of users who are either confined to their home directories or not, depending on the setting of `chroot_local_user`.

✦ `connect_from_port_20=YES` causes `vsftpd` to make sure that data transfers occur through port 20 (the FTP data port).

✦ `data_connection_timeout=120` is the time in seconds after which an inactive data connection is timed out.

✦ `deny_email_enable=YES` causes `vsftpd` to check a list of banned e-mail addresses and deny access to anyone who tries to log in anonymously with a banned e-mail address as password.

✦ `dirmessage_enable=YES` causes `vsftpd` to display messages when FTP users change to certain directories.

✦ `ftpd_banner=Welcome to my FTP service` sets the banner that `vsftpd` displays when a user logs in. You can change the message to anything you want.

✦ `idle_session_timeout=600` is the time (in seconds) after which an idle session (refers to the situation where someone connects and does not do anything) times out and `vsftpd` logs the user out.

✦ `listen=YES` causes `vsftpd` to listen for connection requests and, consequently, run in stand-alone mode. Set this option to `NO` if you want to run `vsftpd` under `xinetd`.

✦ `local_enable=YES` causes `vsftpd` to grant local users access to FTP.

✦ `local_umask=022` means whatever files FTP writes have a permission of 644 (read access for everyone, but write access for owner only). You can set it to any file permission mask setting you want. For example, if you want no permissions for anyone but the owner, change this option to 077.

✦ `ls_recurse_enable=YES` enables FTP users to recursively traverse directories by using the `ls -R` command.

✦ `nopriv_user=ftp` identifies an unprivileged user account that the FTP server can use.

✦ `pam_service_name=vsftpd` is the name of the Pluggable Authentication Module (PAM) configuration file that is used when `vsftpd` must authenticate a user. By default, the PAM configuration files are in the `/etc/pam.d` directory. That means `vsftpd`'s PAM configuration file is `/etc/pam.d/vsftpd`.

✦ `tcp_wrappers=YES` enables support for access control through TCP wrapper that consults the files `/etc/hosts.allow` and `/etc/hosts.deny` (for more information about TCP wrapper, see Book VII, Chapter 3).

✦ `userlist_deny=YES` causes `vsftpd` to deny access to the users listed in the `/etc/vsftpd.user_list` file. These users are not even prompted for a password.

✦ `write_enable=YES` causes `vsftpd` to allow file uploads to the host.

✦ `xferlog_enable=YES` turns on the logging of file downloads and uploads (always a good idea, but takes disk space).

✦ `xferlog_file=/var/log/vsftpd.log` specifies the full pathname of the `vsftpd` log file. The default is `/var/log/vsftpd.log`.

✦ `xferlog_std_format=YES` causes `vsftpd` to generate log files in a standard format used by other FTP daemons.

## /etc/vsftpd.ftpusers file

The `vsftpd` server uses the *Pluggable Authentication Module* (PAM) to authenticate users when they try to log in (just as the normal login process uses PAM to do the job). The PAM configuration file for `vsftpd` is `/etc/pam.d/vsftpd`. That PAM configuration file refers to `/etc/vsftpd.ftpusers` like this:

```
auth    required  /lib/security/pam_listfile.so item=user sense=deny
     file=/etc/vsftpd.ftpusers onerr=succeed
```

This command basically says that anyone listed in the /etc/vsftpd. ftpusers is denied login. The default /etc/vsftpd.ftpusers file contains the following list of users:

```
root
bin
daemon
adm
lp
sync
shutdown
halt
mail
news
uucp
operator
games
nobody
```

### /etc/vsftpd.user_list file

If the userlist_deny option is set to YES, vsftpd does not allow users listed in the /etc/vsftpd.user_list file any access to FTP services. It does not even prompt them for a password. However, if userlist_deny is set to NO, the meaning is reversed and these users are the only ones allowed access (but the PAM configuration still denies anyone on the /etc/vsftpd. ftpusers list).

## Setting Up Secure Anonymous FTP

Anonymous FTP refers to the use of the username anonymous, which anyone can use with FTP to transfer files from a system. Anonymous FTP is a common way to share files on the Internet.

If you have used anonymous FTP to download files from Internet sites, you already know the convenience of that service. Anonymous FTP makes information available to anyone on the Internet. If you have a new Fedora Core application that you want to share with the world, set up anonymous FTP on your Fedora Core PC and place the software in an appropriate directory. After that, all you have to do is announce to the world (probably through a posting in the comp.os.linux.announce newsgroup) that you have a new program available. Now anyone can get the software from your system at his or her convenience.

Even if you run a for-profit business, you can use anonymous FTP to support your customers. If you sell a hardware or software product, you may want to provide technical information or software "fixes" through anonymous FTP.

Unfortunately, the convenience of anonymous FTP comes at a price. If you don't configure the anonymous FTP service properly, intruders and pranksters may gain access to your system. Some intruders may simply use your system's disk as a temporary holding place for various files; others may fill your disk with junk files, effectively making your system inoperable (this sort of attack is called a *Denial of Service* attack). At the other extreme, an intruder may gain user-level (or, worse, `root`-level) access to your system and do much more damage. The default anonymous FTP setup in Fedora Core employs the necessary security precautions.

# Trying Anonymous FTP

To see anonymous FTP in action, try accessing your system by using an FTP client. For example, in the following sample session, I accessed the FTP server from a terminal window on the same system (my input appears in boldface):

```
ftp localhost
Connected to localhost (127.0.0.1).
220 (vsFTPd 1.2.1)
Name (localhost:naba): anonymous
331 Please specify the password.
Password:        <-- I can type anything as password
230 Login successful. Have fun.
Remote system type is UNIX.
Using binary mode to transfer files.
ftp> ls -l
227 Entering Passive Mode (127,0,0,1,169,190)
150 Here comes the directory listing.
drwxr-xr-x    2 0        0            4096 Jun 06 04:36 pub
226 Directory send OK.
ftp> bye
221 Goodbye.
```

When you successfully log in for anonymous FTP, you access the home directory of the user named `ftp` (the default directory is `/var/ftp`). Place the publicly accessible files — the ones you want to enable others to download from your system — in the `/var/ftp/pub` directory.

## Key features of anonymous FTP

The key features of an anonymous FTP setup are as follows:

✦ A user named `ftp` whose home directory is `/var/ftp`. The user does not have a shell assigned. Here is what you get when you search for `ftp` in the `/etc/passwd` file:

```
grep ftp /etc/passwd
```

The output is something like this:

```
ftp:x:14:50:FTP User:/var/ftp:/sbin/nologin
```

The x in the second field means that no one can log in with the user-name ftp.

✦ Here is the full permission setting and owner information for the /var/ftp directory:

```
drwxr-xr-x    3 root     root      4096 Jun 22 12:10 ftp
```

As this line shows, the /var/ftp directory is owned by root, and the permission is set to 755 (only root can read, write and execute; every-one else can only read and execute).

✦ You can view the contents of the /var/ftp directory with the ls -la command. The result is as follows:

```
total 12
drwxr-xr-x    3 root     root      4096 Jun 22 12:10 .
drwxr-xr-x   21 root     root      4096 Jun 22 12:10 ..
drwxr-xr-x    2 root     root      4096 Jun  6 00:36 pub
```

✦ The pub directory is where you place any files you want to enable others to download from your system through anonymous FTP.

# Chapter 4: Serving Up Mail and News

## In This Chapter

✔ **Installing and using** `sendmail`

✔ **Testing mail delivery manually**

✔ **Configuring** `sendmail`

✔ **Installing the InterNetNews (INN) server**

✔ **Configuring and starting INN**

✔ **Setting up local newsgroups**

*E*lectronic mail (e-mail) is one of the popular services available on Internet hosts. E-mail software comes in two parts: a mail-transport agent (MTA), which physically sends and receives mail messages; and a mail-user agent (MUA), which reads messages and prepares new messages. In this chapter, I describe the e-mail service and show you how to configure the `sendmail` server on a Fedora Core PC.

Internet newsgroups provide another convenient way, besides e-mail, to discuss various topics and to share your knowledge with others. Fedora Core comes with the software you need to read newsgroups and to set up your own system as a news server. In this chapter, I describe how to configure and run the InterNetNews server, a popular news server. I also show you how to set up local newsgroups for your corporate intranet (or even your home network).

## Installing the Mail Server

If you install the mail server software during Fedora Core installation, you don't have to do much more to begin using the mail service. To see whether the mail server is already installed, type the following command:

```
rpm -q sendmail
```

You're all set if the response looks like this:

```
sendmail-8.12.11-3.2.1
```

This output says that `sendmail` version 8.12.11 is installed on the system.

If the output message tells you that `sendmail` isn't installed, you can use the Red Hat Package Manager (RPM) to install the individual packages needed for running and configuring `sendmail`. To install the RPM files for `sendmail`, log in as `root` and insert the DVD-ROM in the DVD-ROM drive. If you're using GNOME or KDE, the DVD-ROM automatically mounts. Otherwise, type the following command to mount the DVD-ROM:

```
mount /mnt/cdrom
```

Then type the following commands to install the `sendmail` files:

```
cd /mnt/cdrom/Fedora/RPMS
rpm -ivh sendmail*
```

This command installs two packages:

✦ `sendmail`: A complex mail transport agent (MTA)

✦ `sendmail-cf`: Configuration files for `sendmail`

## *Using sendmail*

To set up your system as a mail server, you must configure the `sendmail` mail-transport agent properly. `sendmail` has the reputation of being a complex but complete mail-delivery system. Just one look at `sendmail`'s configuration file, `/etc/mail/sendmail.cf`, can convince you that `sendmail` is indeed complex. Luckily, you don't have to be an expert on the `sendmail` configuration file. All you need is one of the predefined configuration files — like the one that's installed on your system — to use `sendmail`.

Your system already has a working `sendmail` configuration file — `/etc/mail/sendmail.cf`. The default file assumes you have an Internet connection and a name server. Provided you have an Internet connection and your system has an official domain name, you can send and receive e-mail from your Fedora Core PC.

To ensure that mail delivery works correctly, your system's name must match the system name your ISP has assigned to you. Although you can give your system any host name you want, other systems can successfully deliver mail to your system only if your system's name is in the ISP's name server.

## A mail-delivery test

To try out the `sendmail` mail-transfer agent, you can use the `mail` command to compose and send a mail message to any user account on your Fedora Core system. For example, here's how I send myself a message using the `mail` command:

```
mail naba
Subject: Testing e-mail
This is from my Fedora Core system.
.
Cc: Press Ctrl+D
```

The `mail` command is a simple mail-user agent. In the preceding example, I specify the addressee — naba@comcast.net — in the command line. The `mail` program prompts for a subject line. Following the subject, I enter my message and end it with a line that contains only a period. When prompted for a Cc:, I press Ctrl+D. After I end the message, the mail-user agent passes the message to `sendmail` — the mail-transport agent — for delivery to the specified address. `sendmail` delivers the mail message immediately. To verify the delivery of mail, I run the `mail` command again and read the message.

Thus, the initial `sendmail` configuration file that comes with Fedora Core is adequate for sending and receiving e-mail, at least within your Fedora Core system. External mail delivery also works, provided your Fedora Core system has an Internet connection and a registered domain name.

If you have an ISP account that provides your Fedora Core system with a dynamic IP address, you have to use mail clients such as Evolution or Mozilla Mail that contact your ISP's mail server to deliver outbound e-mail.

## The mail-delivery mechanism

On an Internet host, the `sendmail` mail-transport agent delivers mail using the Simple Mail Transfer Protocol (SMTP). SMTP-based mail-transport agents listen to the TCP port 25 and use a small set of text commands to exchange information with other mail-transport agents. In fact, SMTP commands are simple enough that you can use them manually from a terminal to send a mail message. The following example shows how I use SMTP commands to send a mail message to my account on the Fedora Core PC from a `telnet` session running on the same system:

```
telnet localhost 25
Trying 127.0.0.1...
Connected to localhost.
Escape character is '^]'.
220 localhost.localdomain ESMTP Sendmail 8.12.11/8.12.11; Sun, 14 Mar 2004
    15:14:38 -0500
```

```
help
214-2.0.0 This is sendmail version 8.12.9
214-2.0.0 Topics:
214-2.0.0       HELO    EHLO    MAIL    RCPT    DATA
214-2.0.0       RSET    NOOP    QUIT    HELP    VRFY
214-2.0.0       EXPN    VERB    ETRN    DSN     AUTH
214-2.0.0       STARTTLS
214-2.0.0 For more info use "HELP <topic>".
214-2.0.0 To report bugs in the implementation send email to
214-2.0.0       sendmail-bugs@sendmail.org.
214-2.0.0 For local information send email to Postmaster at your site.
214 2.0.0 End of HELP info
HELP DATA
214-2.0.0 DATA
214-2.0.0       Following text is collected as the message.
214-2.0.0       End with a single dot.
214 2.0.0 End of HELP info
HELO localhost
250 localhost.localdomain Hello localhost.localdomain [127.0.0.1], pleased to
    meet you
MAIL FROM: naba
553 5.5.4 naba... Domain name required for sender address naba
MAIL FROM: naba@localhost
250 2.1.0 naba@localhost... Sender ok
RCPT TO: naba
250 2.1.5 naba... Recipient ok
DATA
354 Enter mail, end with "." on a line by itself
Testing... 1 2 3
Sending mail by telnet to port 25
.
250 2.0.0 h6FNMOLw002082 Message accepted for delivery
quit
221 2.0.0 localhost.localdomain closing connection
Connection closed by foreign host.
```

The `telnet` command opens a TELNET session to port 25 — the port on which `sendmail` expects SMTP commands. The `sendmail` process on the Fedora Core system immediately replies with an announcement.

I type `HELP` to view a list of SMTP commands. To get help on a specific command, I can type `HELP commandname`. The listing shows the help information `sendmail` prints when I type `HELP DATA`.

I type `HELO localhost` to initiate a session with the host. The `sendmail` process replies with a greeting. To send the mail message, I start with the `MAIL FROM:` command that specifies the sender of the message. (I enter the username on the system from which I am sending the message.) `sendmail` requires a domain name along with the user name.

Next, I use the `RCPT TO:` command to specify the recipient of the message. If I want to send the message to several recipients, all I have to do is provide each recipient's address with the `RCPT TO:` command.

To enter the mail message, I use the DATA command. In response to the DATA command, sendmail displays an instruction that I have to end the message with a period on a line by itself. I enter the message and end it with a single period on a separate line. The sendmail process displays a message indicating that the message is accepted for delivery. Finally, I quit the sendmail session with the QUIT command.

Afterward, I log in to my Fedora Core system and check mail with the mail command. The following is the session with the mail command when I display the mail message I sent through the sample SMTP session with sendmail:

```
mail
Mail version 8.1 6/6/93.  Type ? for help.
"/var/spool/mail/naba": 1 message 1 new
>N  1 naba@localhost.local  Sun Mar 14 15:16  12/479
& 1
Message 1:
From naba@localhost.localdomain  Sun Mar 14 15:16:31 2004
Date: Sun, 14 Mar 2004 15:14:38  0500
From: Naba Barkakati <naba@localhost.localdomain>

Testing... 1 2 3
Sending mail by telnet to port 25

& q
Saved 1 message in mbox
```

As this example shows, the SMTP commands are simple enough for humans to understand. This example helps you understand how a mail-transfer agent uses SMTP to transfer mail on the Internet. Of course, e-mail programs usually automate this whole process — and so does the sendmail program (through settings in the sendmail configuration file /etc/mail/sendmail.cf).

## *The sendmail configuration file*

You don't have to understand everything in the sendmail configuration file, /etc/mail/sendmail.cf, but you need to know how that file is created. That way, you can make minor changes if necessary and regenerate the /etc/mail/sendmail.cf file.

Before you can regenerate the sendmail.cf file, you have to install the sendmail-cf package. To check whether the sendmail-cf package is installed, type

```
rpm -q sendmail-cf
```

If the command doesn't print the name of the `sendmail-cf` package, you have to install the package. This RPM file is in the DVD-ROM bundled with this book. To install that package, log in as `root` and insert the DVD-ROM into the DVD-ROM drive. In GNOME or KDE, the DVD-ROM mounts automatically. Otherwise, you can mount the DVD-ROM with the following command:

```
mount /mnt/cdrom
```

Then install the package by typing the following commands:

```
cd /mnt/cdrom/Fedora/RPMS
rpm -ivh sendmail-cf*
```

The `sendmail-cf` package installs in the `/usr/share/sendmail-cf` directory all the files needed to generate a new `sendmail.cf` configuration file. As I explain in the next few sections, the `sendmail.cf` file is generated from a number of m4 *macro files* (text files in which each line eventually expands to multiple lines that mean something to some program). These macro files are organized into a number of subdirectories in the `/usr/share/sendmail-cf` directory. You can read the `README` file in `/usr/share/sendmail-cf` to find out more about the creation of `sendmail` configuration files.

Now that you've taken care of the prerequisites, you can find out how to regenerate the `sendmail.cf` file.

### m4 macro processor

The m4 macro processor generates the `sendmail.cf` configuration file, which comes with the `sendmail` package in Fedora Core. The main macro file, `sendmail.mc`, is included with the `sendmail` package, but that file needs other m4 macro files that are in the `sendmail-cf` package.

So what's a macro? A *macro* is basically a symbolic name for code that handles some action, usually in a shorthand form that substitutes for a long string of characters. A *macro processor* such as m4 usually reads its input file and copies it to the output, processing the macros along the way. The processing of a macro generally involves performing some action and generating some output. Because a macro generates a lot more text in the output than merely the macro's name, the processing of macros is referred to as *macro expansion*.

The m4 macro processor is *stream-based*. That means it copies the input characters to the output while it's busy expanding any macros. The m4 macro processor does not have any concept of lines, so it copies newline characters (that mark the end of a line) to the output. That's why you see the word `dnl` in most m4 macro files; `dnl` is an m4 macro that stands for "delete through newline." The `dnl` macro deletes all characters starting at the `dnl` up to and including the next newline character. The newline characters in the output don't cause any harm; they merely create unnecessary blank lines. The `sendmail` macro package uses `dnl` to avoid such blank lines in the output configuration file. Because `dnl` basically means delete everything up to the end of the line, m4 macro files also use `dnl` as the prefix for comment lines.

To see a very simple use of m4, consider the following m4 macro file that defines two macros — `hello` and `bye` — and uses them in a form letter:

```
dnl  #############################################################
dnl  #   File: ex.m4
dnl  #   A simple example of m4 macros
dnl  #############################################################
define('hello', 'Dear Sir/Madam')dnl
define('bye',
'Sincerely,


Customer Service')dnl
dnl Now type the letter and use the macros
hello,

This is to inform you that we received your recent inquiry.
We will respond to your question soon.

bye
```

Type this text (using your favorite text editor) and save it in a file named `ex.m4`. You can name a macro file anything you like, but using the `.m4` extension for m4 macro files is customary.

Before you process the macro file by using m4, note the following key points about the example:

✦ Use the `dnl` macro to start all the comment lines (for example, the first four lines in the example).

✦ End each macro definition with the `dnl` macro. Otherwise, when m4 processes the macro file, it produces a blank line for each macro definition.

✦ Use the built-in m4 command `define` to define a new macro. The macro name and the value are both enclosed between a pair of left and right quotes (' . . . '). Note that you cannot use the plain single quote to enclose the macro name and definition.

Now process the macro file `ex.m4` by typing the following command:

```
m4 ex.m4
```

m4 processes the macros and displays the following output:

```
Dear Sir/Madam,

This is to inform you that we received your recent inquiry.
We will respond to your question soon.

Sincerely,


Customer Service
```

Sounds just like a typical customer service form letter, doesn't it?

If you compare the output with the `ex.m4` file, you see that m4 prints the form letter on standard output, expanding the macros `hello` and `bye` into their defined values. If you want to save the form letter in a file called `letter`, use the shell's output redirection feature, like this:

```
m4 ex.m4 > letter
```

What if you want to use the word `hello` or `bye` in the letter without expanding them? You can do so by enclosing these macros in a pair of quotes (`'...'`). You have to do so for other predefined m4 macros, such as `define`. To use define as a plain word, not as a macro to expand, type **'define'**.

### sendmail.mc file

The simple example in the preceding section gives you an idea of how m4 macros are defined and used to create configuration files such as the `sendmail.cf` file. You find many complex macros stored in files in the `/usr/share/sendmail-cf` directory. A top-level macro file, `sendmail.mc`, described later in this section, brings in these macro files with the `include` macro (used to copy a file into the input stream).

By defining its own set of high-level macros in files located in the `/usr/share/sendmail-cf` directory, `sendmail` essentially creates its own macro language. The `sendmail` macro files use the `.mc` extension. The primary `sendmail` macro file you configure is `sendmail.mc`, located in the `/etc/mail` directory.

Unlike the `/etc/mail/sendmail.cf` file, the `/etc/mail/sendmail.mc` file is short and easier to work with. Here is the full listing of the `/etc/mail/sendmail.mc` file that comes with Fedora Core:

```
divert(-1)dnl
dnl #
dnl # This is the sendmail macro config file for m4. If you make changes to
dnl # /etc/mail/sendmail.mc, you will need to regenerate the
```

```
dnl # /etc/mail/sendmail.cf file by confirming that the sendmail-cf package is
dnl # installed and then performing a
dnl #
dnl #      make -C /etc/mail
dnl #
include('/usr/share/sendmail-cf/m4/cf.m4')dnl
VERSIONID('setup for Red Hat Linux')dnl
OSTYPE('linux')dnl
dnl #
dnl # default logging level is 9, you might want to set it higher to
dnl # debug the configuration
dnl #
dnl define('confLOG_LEVEL', '9')dnl
dnl #
dnl # Uncomment and edit the following line if your outgoing mail needs to
dnl # be sent out through an external mail server:
dnl #
dnl define('SMART_HOST','smtp.your.provider')
dnl #
define('confDEF_USER_ID',''8:12'')dnl
dnl define('confAUTO_REBUILD')dnl
define('confTO_CONNECT', '1m')dnl
define('confTRY_NULL_MX_LIST',true)dnl
define('confDONT_PROBE_INTERFACES',true)dnl
define('PROCMAIL_MAILER_PATH','/usr/bin/procmail')dnl
define('ALIAS_FILE', '/etc/aliases')dnl
define('STATUS_FILE', '/var/log/mail/statistics')dnl
define('UUCP_MAILER_MAX', '2000000')dnl
define('confUSERDB_SPEC', '/etc/mail/userdb.db')dnl
define('confPRIVACY_FLAGS', 'authwarnings,novrfy,noexpn,restrictqrun')dnl
define('confAUTH_OPTIONS', 'A')dnl
dnl #
dnl # The following allows relaying if the user authenticates, and disallows
dnl # plaintext authentication (PLAIN/LOGIN) on non-TLS links
dnl #
dnl define('confAUTH_OPTIONS', 'A p')dnl
dnl #
dnl # PLAIN is the preferred plaintext authentication method and used by
dnl # Mozilla Mail and Evolution, though Outlook Express and other MUAs do
dnl # use LOGIN. Other mechanisms should be used if the connection is not
dnl # guaranteed secure.
dnl # Please remember that saslauthd needs to be running for AUTH.
dnl #
dnl TRUST_AUTH_MECH('EXTERNAL DIGEST-MD5 CRAM-MD5 LOGIN PLAIN')dnl
dnl define('confAUTH_MECHANISMS', 'EXTERNAL GSSAPI DIGEST-MD5 CRAM-MD5 LOGIN PLA
IN')dnl
dnl #
dnl # Rudimentary information on creating certificates for sendmail TLS:
dnl #      make -C /usr/share/ssl/certs usage
dnl # or use the included makecert.sh script
dnl #
define('CERT_DIR','/etc/mail/certs')
define('confCACERT_PATH','CERT_DIR')
define('confCACERT','CERT_DIR/cacert.pem')
define('confSERVER_CERT','CERT_DIR/cert.pem')
define('confSERVER_KEY','CERT_DIR/key.pem')
define('confCLIENT_CERT','CERT_DIR/cert.pem')
define('confCLIENT_KEY','CERT_DIR/key.pem')
dnl #
dnl # This allows sendmail to use a keyfile that is shared with OpenLDAP's
dnl # slapd, which requires the file to be readable by group ldap
dnl #
```

```
dnl define('confDONT_BLAME_SENDMAIL','groupreadablekeyfile')dnl
dnl #
dnl define('confTO_QUEUEWARN', '4h')dnl
dnl define('confTO_QUEUERETURN', '5d')dnl
dnl define('confQUEUE_LA', '12')dnl
dnl define('confREFUSE_LA', '18')dnl
define('confTO_IDENT', '0')dnl
dnl FEATURE(delay_checks)dnl
FEATURE('no_default_msa','dnl')dnl
FEATURE('smrsh','/usr/sbin/smrsh')dnl
FEATURE('mailertable','hash -o /etc/mail/mailertable.db')dnl
FEATURE('virtusertable','hash -o /etc/mail/virtusertable.db')dnl
FEATURE(redirect)dnl
FEATURE(always_add_domain)dnl
FEATURE(use_cw_file)dnl
FEATURE(use_ct_file)dnl
dnl #
dnl # The -t option will retry delivery if e.g. the user runs over his quota.
dnl #
FEATURE(local_procmail,'','procmail -t -Y -a $h -d $u')dnl
FEATURE('access_db','hash -T<TMPF> -o /etc/mail/access.db')dnl
FEATURE('blacklist_recipients')dnl
EXPOSED_USER('root')dnl
dnl #
dnl # The following causes sendmail to only listen on the IPv4 loopback address
dnl # 127.0.0.1 and not on any other network devices. Remove the loopback
dnl # address restriction to accept email from the internet or intranet.
dnl #
DAEMON_OPTIONS('Port=smtp,Addr=127.0.0.1, Name=MTA')dnl
dnl #
dnl # The following causes sendmail to additionally listen to port 587 for
dnl # mail from MUAs that authenticate. Roaming users who can't reach their
dnl # preferred sendmail daemon due to port 25 being blocked or redirected find
dnl # this useful.
dnl #
dnl DAEMON_OPTIONS('Port=submission, Name=MSA, M=Ea')dnl
dnl #
dnl # The following causes sendmail to additionally listen to port 465, but
dnl # starting immediately in TLS mode upon connecting. Port 25 or 587 followed
dnl # by STARTTLS is preferred, but roaming clients using Outlook Express can't
dnl # do STARTTLS on ports other than 25. Mozilla Mail can ONLY use STARTTLS
dnl # and doesn't support the deprecated smtps; Evolution <1.1.1 uses smtps
dnl # when SSL is enabled-- STARTTLS support is available in version 1.1.1.
dnl #
dnl # For this to work your OpenSSL certificates must be configured.
dnl #
dnl DAEMON_OPTIONS('Port=smtps, Name=TLSMTA, M=s')dnl
dnl #
dnl # The following causes sendmail to additionally listen on the IPv6 loopback
dnl # device. Remove the loopback address restriction listen to the network.
dnl #
dnl DAEMON_OPTIONS('port=smtp,Addr=::1, Name=MTA-v6, Family=inet6')dnl
dnl #
dnl # enable both ipv6 and ipv4 in sendmail:
dnl #
dnl DAEMON_OPTIONS('Name=MTA-v4, Family=inet, Name=MTA-v6, Family=inet6')
dnl #
dnl # We strongly recommend not accepting unresolvable domains if you want to
dnl # protect yourself from spam. However, the laptop and users on computers
dnl # that do not have 24x7 DNS do need this.
dnl #
```

```
FEATURE('accept_unresolvable_domains')dnl
dnl #
dnl FEATURE('relay_based_on_MX')dnl
dnl #
dnl # Also accept email sent to "localhost.localdomain" as local email.
dnl #
LOCAL_DOMAIN('localhost.localdomain')dnl
dnl #
dnl # The following example makes mail from this host and any additional
dnl # specified domains appear to be sent from mydomain.com
dnl #
dnl MASQUERADE_AS('mydomain.com')dnl
dnl #
dnl # masquerade not just the headers, but the envelope as well
dnl #
dnl FEATURE(masquerade_envelope)dnl
dnl #
dnl # masquerade not just @mydomainalias.com, but @*.mydomainalias.com as well
dnl #
dnl FEATURE(masquerade_entire_domain)dnl
dnl #
dnl MASQUERADE_DOMAIN(localhost)dnl
dnl MASQUERADE_DOMAIN(localhost.localdomain)dnl
dnl MASQUERADE_DOMAIN(mydomainalias.com)dnl
dnl MASQUERADE_DOMAIN(mydomain.lan)dnl
MAILER(smtp)dnl
MAILER(procmail)dnl
```

If you make changes to the /etc/mail/sendmail.mc file, you must generate the /etc/mail/sendmail.cf file by running the sendmail.mc file through the m4 macro processor with the following command (you have to log in as root):

```
m4 /etc/mail/sendmail.mc > /etc/mail/sendmail.cf
```

The comments also tell you that you need the sendmail-cf package to process this file.

From the previous section's description of m4 macros, you can see that the sendmail.mc file uses define to create new macros. You can also see the liberal use of dnl to avoid inserting too many blank lines into the output.

The other uppercase words (such as OSTYPE, FEATURE, and MAILER) are sendmail macros. These are defined in the .m4 files located in the subdirectories of the /usr/share/sendmail-cf directory and are incorporated into the sendmail.mc file with the following include macro:

```
include('/usr/share/sendmail-cf/m4/cf.m4')dnl
```

The /usr/share/sendmail-cf/m4/cf.m4 file, in turn, includes the cfhead. m4 file, which includes other m4 files, and so on. The net effect is that, as the m4 macro processor processes the sendmail.mc file, the macro processor incorporates many m4 files from various subdirectories of /usr/share/ sendmail-cf.

**Book VIII
Chapter 4**

**Serving Up
Mail and News**

Here are some key points to note about the `/etc/mail/sendmail.mc` file:

✦ `VERSIONID('setup for Red Hat Linux')` macro inserts the version information enclosed in quotes into the output.

✦ `OSTYPE('linux')` specifies Linux as the operating system. You have to specify this macro early to ensure proper configuration.

Placing this macro right after the `VERSIONID` macro is customary.

✦ `MAILER(smtp)` describes the mailer. According to instructions in the `/usr/share/sendmail-cf/README` file, `MAILER` declarations are always placed at the end of the `sendmail.mc` file, and `MAILER(smtp)` always precedes `MAILER(procmail)`. The mailer `smtp` refers to the SMTP mailer.

✦ `FEATURE` macros request various special features. For example, `FEATURE('blacklist_recipients')` turns on the capability to block incoming mail for certain usernames, hosts, or addresses. The specification for what mail to allow or refuse is placed in the access database (`/etc/mail/access.db` file). You also need the `FEATURE('access_db')` macro to turn on the access database.

✦ `MASQUERADE_AS('mydomain.com')` causes `sendmail` to label outgoing mail as having come from the host `mydomain.com` (replace with your domain name). The idea is for a large organization to set up a single `sendmail` server that handles the mail for many subdomains and makes everything appear to come from a single domain (for example, mail from many departments in a University appear to come from the University's main domain name).

✦ `MASQUERADE_DOMAIN(subdomain.mydomain.com)` instructs `sendmail` to send mail from an address such as `user@subdomain.mydomain.com` as having originated from the same username at the domain specified by the `MASQUERADE_AS` macro.

The `sendmail` macros such as `FEATURE` and `MAILER` are described in the `/usr/share/sendmail-cf/README` file. Consult that file to find out more about the `sendmail` macros before you make changes to the `sendmail.mc` file.

Typically, you have to add your system's host name in the last line of the `/etc/mail/sendmail.mc` file. Follow these steps to add the host name:

*1.* **If the host name is** `mycompany.com`, **edit the** `Cw` **line in** `/etc/mail/sendmail.mc` **as follows:**

```
Cwlocalhost.localdomain mycompany.com mycompany
```

2. **Rebuild the** `/etc/mail/sendmail.cf` **file with this command:**

```
m4 /etc/mail/sendmail.mc > /etc/mail/sendmail.cf
```

3. **Restart** `sendmail` **with the following command:**

```
service sendmail restart
```

## sendmail.cf file syntax

The `sendmail.cf` file's syntax is designed to be easy to parse by the `sendmail` program because `sendmail` reads this file whenever it starts. Human readability was not a primary consideration when the file's syntax was designed. Still, with a little explanation, you can understand the meaning of the control lines in `sendmail.cf`.

Each `sendmail` control line begins with a single-letter operator that defines the meaning of the rest of the line. A line that begins with a space or a tab is considered a continuation of the previous line. Blank lines and lines beginning with a pound sign (#) are comments.

Often, no space is between the single-letter operator and the arguments that follow the operator, which makes the lines even harder to understand. For example, `sendmail.cf` uses the concept of a *class* — essentially a collection of phrases. You can define a class named P and add the phrase REDIRECT to that class with the following control line:

```
CPREDIRECT
```

Because everything is jumbled together, the command is hard to decipher. On the other hand, to define a class named Accept and set it to the values OK and RELAY, write the following:

```
C{Accept}OK RELAY
```

This command may be slightly easier to understand because the delimiters (such as the class name, Accept) are enclosed in curly braces.

Other — more recent — control lines are even easier to understand. For example, the line

```
O HelpFile=/etc/mail/helpfile
```

defines the option HelpFile as the filename `/etc/mail/helpfile`. That file contains help information `sendmail` uses when it receives a HELP command.

**Book VIII
Chapter 4**

**Serving Up
Mail and News**

Table 4-1 summarizes the one-letter control operators used in `sendmail.cf`. Each entry also shows an example of that operator. This table helps you understand some of the lines in `sendmail.cf`.

| Table 4-1 | Control Operators Used in sendmail.cf |
|---|---|
| *Operator* | *Description* |
| C | Defines a class; a variable (think of it as a set) that can contain several values. For example, `Cwlocalhost` adds the name `localhost` to the class `w`. |
| D | Defines a macro, a name associated with a single value. For example, `DnMAILER-DAEMON` defines the macro `n` as `MAILER-DAEMON`. |
| F | Defines a class that's been read from a file. For example, `Fw/etc/mail/local-host-names` reads the names of hosts from the file `/etc/mail/local-host-names` and adds them to the class `w`. |
| H | Defines the format of header lines that `sendmail` inserts into a message. For example, `H?P?Return-Path: <$g>` defines the `Return-Path:` field of the header. |
| K | Defines a map (a key-value pair database). For example, `Karith arith` defines the map named `arith` as the compiled-in map of the same name. |
| M | Specifies a mailer. The following lines define the `procmail` mailer: `Mprocmail,P=/usr/bin/procmail,F=DFMSPhnu9,S=EnvFromSMTP/HdrFromSMTP,R=EnvToSMTP/HdrFromSMTP,T=DNS/RFC822/X-Unix,A=procmail -Y -m $h $f $u`. |
| O | Assigns a value to an option. For example, `O AliasFile=/etc/aliases` defines the `AliasFile` option to `/etc/aliases`, which is the name of the `sendmail` alias file. |
| P | Defines values for the precedence field. For example, `Pjunk=-100` sets to `-100` the precedence of messages marked with the header field `Precedence: junk`. |
| R | Defines a rule (a rule has a left-hand side and a right-hand side; if input matches the left-hand side, the right-hand side replaces it — this rule is called *rewriting*). For example, the rewriting rule `R$* ; $1` strips trailing semicolons. |
| S | Labels a ruleset you can start defining with subsequent R control lines. For example, `Scanonify=3` labels the next ruleset as `canonify` or ruleset 3. |
| T | Adds a username to the trusted class (class `t`). For example, `Troot` adds `root` to the class of trusted users. |
| V | Defines the major version number of the configuration file. For example, `V10/Berkeley` defines the version number as 10. |

## Other sendmail files

The /etc/mail directory contains other files that sendmail uses. These files are referenced in the sendmail configuration file, /etc/mail/sendmail.cf. For example, here's how you can search for the /etc/mail string in the /etc/mail/sendmail.cf file:

```
grep "\/etc\/mail" /etc/mail/sendmail.cf
```

Here's what the grep command displays as a result of the search on my Fedora Core system:

```
Fw/etc/mail/local-host-names
FR-o /etc/mail/relay-domains
Kmailertable hash -o /etc/mail/mailertable.db
Kvirtuser hash -o /etc/mail/virtusertable.db
Kaccess hash -T<TMPF> -o /etc/mail/access.db
#O ErrorHeader=/etc/mail/error-header
O HelpFile=/etc/mail/helpfile
O UserDatabaseSpec=/etc/mail/userdb.db
#O ServiceSwitchFile=/etc/mail/service.switch
#O DefaultAuthInfo=/etc/mail/default-auth-info
O CACertPath=/etc/mail/certs
O CACertFile=/etc/mail/certs/cacert.pem
O ServerCertFile=/etc/mail/certs/cert.pem
O ServerKeyFile-/etc/mail/certs/key.pem
O ClientCertFile=/etc/mail/certs/cert.pem
O ClientKeyFile=/etc/mail/certs/key.pem
Ft/etc/mail/trusted-users
```

You can ignore the lines that begin with a hash mark or number sign (#) because sendmail treats those lines as comments. The other lines are sendmail control lines that refer to other files in the /etc/mail directory.

Here's what some of these sendmail files are supposed to contain (note that not all of these files have to be present in your /etc/mail directory and even when present, some files may be empty):

✦ **/etc/mail/access**: Names and/or IP addresses of hosts allowed to send mail (useful in stopping *spam* — unwanted e-mail)

✦ **/etc/mail/access.db**: Access database generated from /etc/mail/access file

✦ **/etc/mail/helpfile**: Help information for SMTP commands

✦ **/etc/mail/local-host-names**: Names by which this host is known

**Book VIII Chapter 4**

**Serving Up Mail and News**

✦ `/etc/mail/mailertable`: Mailer table used to override how mail is routed (for example, the entry `comcast.net smtp:smtp.comcast.net` tells `sendmail` that mail addressed to `comcast.net` addressed has to be sent to `smtp.comcast.net`)

✦ `/etc/mail/relay-domains`: Hosts that permit relaying

✦ `/etc/mail/trusted-users`: List of users allowed to send mail using other user's names without a warning

✦ `/etc/mail/userdb.db`: User database file containing information about each user's login name and real name

✦ `/etc/mail/virtusertable`: Database of users with virtual-domain addresses hosted on this system

The remaining `sendmail` files in the `/etc/mail` directory — `/etc/mail/certs` and the files with the `.pem` extension — are meant for use supporting privacy enhanced mail (PEM) in `sendmail` by using the STARTTLS extension to SMTP. The STARTTLS extension uses TLS (more commonly known as SSL) to authenticate the sender and encrypt mail. RFC 2487 describes STARTTLS (this RFC is available online at `ietf.org/rfc/rfc2487.txt`).

If you edit the `/etc/mail/mailertable` file, you have to type the following command before the changes take effect:

```
makemap hash /etc/mail/mailertable < /etc/mail/mailertable
```

Here is an easier way to make sure that you rebuild everything necessary after making any changes — just type the following commands while logged in as root:

```
cd /etc/mail
make
```

## The .forward file

Users can redirect their own mail by placing a `.forward` file in their home directory. The `.forward` file is a plain-text file with a comma-separated list of mail addresses. Any mail sent to the user is then forwarded to these addresses. If the `.forward` file contains a single address, all e-mail for that user is redirected to that single e-mail address. For example, suppose a `.forward` file containing the following line is placed in the home directory of a user named `emily`:

```
ashley
```

This line causes `sendmail` to automatically send all e-mail addressed to `emily` to the username `ashley` on the same system. User `emily` does not receive mail at all.

You can also forward mail to a username on another system by listing a complete e-mail address. For example, I added a `.forward` file with the following line to send my messages (addressed to my username, `naba`) to the mail address `naba@comcast.net`:

```
naba@comcast.net
```

Now suppose I want to keep a copy of the message on the original system, in addition to forwarding to the address `naba@comcast.net`. I can do so by adding the following line to the `.forward` file:

```
naba@comcast.net, naba\
```

I simply append my username and end the line with a backslash. The backslash (\) at the end of the line stops `sendmail` from repeatedly forwarding the message (because when a copy is sent to my username on the system, `sendmail` processes my `.forward` file again — the backslash tells `sendmail` not to forward the message repeatedly).

## Invoking procmail in the .forward file

An interesting use of the `.forward` file is to run `procmail` to handle some mail messages automatically. For example, suppose you want to delete any e-mail message that comes from an address containing the string `mailing_list`. Here's what you do to achieve that:

1. **Create a `.forward` file in your home directory and place the following line in it:**

   ```
   "| /usr/bin/procmail"
   ```

   This line causes `sendmail` to run the external program `/usr/bin/procmail` and to send the e-mail messages to the input stream of that program.

2. **Create a text file named `.procmailrc` in your home directory and place the following lines in that file:**

   ```
   # Delete mail from an address that contains
      mailing_list:0
   * ^From:.*mailing_list
   /dev/null
   ```

3. **Log in as** `root` **and set up a symbolic link in** `/etc/smrsh` **to the** `/usr/bin/procmail` **program with the following command:**

```
ln -s /usr/bin/procmail /etc/smrsh/procmail
```

This step is necessary because `sendmail` uses the SendMail Restricted Shell — `smrsh` — to run external programs. Instead of running `/usr/bin/procmail`, `smrsh` runs `/etc/smrsh/procmail`. That's why you need the symbolic link. This link is a security feature of `sendmail` that controls what external programs it can run.

That's it! Now, if you receive any messages from an address containing `mailing_list`, the message is deleted.

With `procmail`, you can perform other chores, such as automatically storing messages in a file or forwarding messages to others. All you have to do is create an appropriate `.procmailrc` file in your home directory. To find out more about `procmail`, type **man procmail**. To see examples of `.procmailrc`, type **man procmailex**.

## *The sendmail alias file*

In addition to the `sendmail.cf` file, `sendmail` also consults an alias file named `/etc/aliases` to convert a name into an address. The location of the alias file appears in the `sendmail` configuration file.

Each *alias* is typically a shorter name for an e-mail address. The system administrator uses the `sendmail` alias file to forward mail, to create mailing lists (a single alias that identifies several users), or to refer to a user by several different names. For example, here are some typical aliases:

```
barkakati: naba
naba: naba@lnbsoft
all: naba, leha, ivy, emily, ashley
```

The first line says that mail addressed to `barkakati` is delivered to the user named `naba` on the local system. The second line indicates that mail for `naba` really is sent to the username `naba` on the `lnbsoft` system. The last line defines `all` as the alias for the five users `naba`, `leha`, `ivy`, `emily`, and `ashley`. That means mail sent to `all` goes to these five users.

After defining any new aliases in the `/etc/aliases` file, you must log in as `root` and make the new alias active by typing the following command:

```
sendmail -bi
```

# Installing the News Server

If you install the news server during Fedora Core installation, you don't have to do much more to begin using the news services. Otherwise, you can use the Red Hat Package Manager (RPM) to install the InterNetNews (INN) — a TCP/IP-based news server.

To check whether INN is already installed, type the following command:

```
rpm -q inn
```

If INN is installed, you see a line similar to this:

```
inn-2.3.5-8
```

If you get a message saying the package isn't installed, you can install it manually from the companion DVD-ROM. Log in as `root` and insert the DVD-ROM into the DVD-ROM drive. If you're using GNOME or KDE desktop, the DVD-ROM mounts automatically. Otherwise, type the following command to mount it:

```
mount /mnt/cdrom
```

Then type the following commands to install INN:

```
cd /mnt/cdrom/Fedora/RPMS
rpm -ivh inn-*
```

# Configuring and Starting the INN Server

Much of the *InterNetNews* (INN) software, bundled with Fedora Core, is ready to go as soon as you install the RPM. All you need is to brush up a bit on the various components of INN, edit the configuration files, and start `innd` — the INN server. By the way, sometimes I refer to the INN server as the *news server*.

If you want to support a selection of Internet newsgroups, you also have to arrange for a *news feed* — the source from which your news server gets the newsgroup articles. Typically, you can get a news feed from an ISP, but the ISP charges an additional monthly fee to cover the cost of resources required to provide the feed. You need the name of the upstream server that provides the news feed, and you have to provide that server with your server's name and the newsgroups you want to receive.

Depending on the newsgroups you want to receive and the number of days you want to retain articles, you have to set aside appropriate disk space to hold the articles. The newsgroups are stored in a directory hierarchy (based on the newsgroup names) in the `/var/spool/news` directory of your system. If you're setting up a news server, you may want to devote a large disk partition to the `/var/spool/news` directory.

In your news server's configuration files, enter the name of the server providing the news feed. At the same time, add to the configuration files the names of any downstream news servers (if any) that receive news feeds from your server. Then you can start the news server and wait for news to arrive. Monitor the log files to ensure that the news articles sort and store properly in the `/var/spool/news` directory on your system.

When you have news up and running, you must run news maintenance and cleanup scripts by running the `cron` jobs. On Fedora Core, a `cron` job is already set up to run the `/usr/bin/news.daily` script to perform the news maintenance tasks.

In the following sections, I introduce you to INN setup, but you can find out more about INN from the Internet Software Consortium (ISC), a nonprofit corporation dedicated to developing and maintaining open source Internet software, such as BIND (an implementation of Domain Name System), DHCP (Dynamic Host Configuration Protocol), and INN. Rich Salz originally wrote INN; ISC took over the development of INN in 1996. You can find out more about INN and can access other resources at ISC's INN Web page at `www.isc.org/products/INN`.

## InterNetNews components

INN includes several programs that deliver and manage newsgroups. It also includes a number of files that control how the INN programs work. The most important INN programs are the following:

✦ `innd`: The news server. It runs as *a daemon* — a background process that keeps itself running to provide a specific service — and listens on the NNTP port (TCP port 119). The `innd` server accepts connections from other feed sites, as well as from local newsreader clients, but it hands off local connections to the `nnrpd`.

✦ `nnrpd`: A special server invoked by `innd` to handle requests from local newsreader clients.

✦ `expire`: Removes old articles based on the specifications in the text file `/etc/news/expire.ctl`.

✦ nntpsend: Invokes the innxmit program to send news articles to a remote site by using NNTP. The configuration file /etc/news/nntpsend.ctl controls the nntpsend program.

✦ ctlinnd: Enables you to control the innd server interactively. The ctlinnd program can send messages to the control channel of the innd server.

The other vital components of INN are the control files. Most of these files are in the /etc/news directory of your Fedora Core system, although a few are in the /var/lib/news directory. Between those two directories, you have more than 30 INN control files. Some important files include the following:

✦ /etc/news/inn.conf: Specifies configuration data for the innd server. (To view online help for this file, type **man inn.conf**.)

✦ /etc/news/newsfeeds: Specifies what articles to feed downstream to other news servers. (The file is complicated, but you can get help by typing **man newsfeeds**.)

✦ /etc/news/incoming.conf: Lists the names and addresses of hosts that provide news feeds to this server. (To view online help for this file, type **man incoming.conf**.)

✦ /etc/news/storage.conf: Specifies the storage methods to be used when storing news articles. (To view online help for this file, type **man storage.conf**.)

✦ /etc/news/expire.ctl: Controls expiration of articles, on a per-newsgroup level, if desired. (To view online help for this file, type **man expire.ctl**.)

✦ /var/lib/news/active: Lists all active newsgroups, showing the oldest and newest article number for each, and each newsgroup's posting status. (To view online help for this file, type **man active**.)

✦ /var/lib/news/newsgroups: Lists newsgroups, with a brief description of each.

✦ /etc/news/readers.conf: Specifies hosts and users that are permitted to read news from this news server and post news to newsgroups. The default file allows only the localhost to read news; you have to edit it if you want to allow other hosts in your local area network to read news. (To view online help for this file, type **man readers.conf**.)

In the next few sections, I describe how to set up some of the important control files.

**Book VIII
Chapter 4**

**Serving Up
Mail and News**

## the inn.conf file

This file holds configuration data for all INN programs — which makes it the most important file. Each line of the file has the value of a parameter in the following format:

```
parameter:     value
```

Depending on the parameter, the value is a string, a number, or `true` or `false`. As in many other configuration files, comment lines begin with a number or pound sign (#).

Most of the parameters in the default `inn.conf` file in the `/etc/news` directory do not require changes. You may want to edit one or more of the parameters shown in Table 4-2.

| Table 4-2 | Configuration Parameters in /etc/news/inn.conf |
|-----------|------------------------------------------------|
| *Parameter Name* | *Description* |
| `mta` | Set this parameter to the command used to start the mail transfer agent that is used by `innd` to transfer messages. The default is to use `sendmail`. |
| `organization` | Set this parameter to the name of your organization in the way you want it to appear in the `Organization:` header of all news articles posted from your system. Users may override this parameter by defining the `ORGANIZATION` environment variable. |
| `ovmethod` | Sets the type of overview storage method (the *overview* is an index of news articles in the newsgroup). The default method is `tradindexed`, which is fast for reading news, but slow for storing news items. |
| `pathhost` | Set this parameter to the name of your news server as you want it to appear in the `Path` header of all postings that go through your server. If `pathhost` isn't defined, the fully qualified domain name of your system is used. |
| `pathnews` | Set this parameter to the full pathname of the directory that contains INN binaries and libraries. In Fedora Core, `pathnews` is set to `/usr/lib/news`. |
| `domain` | Set this parameter to the domain name for your server. |
| `allownewnews` | Set this parameter to `true` if you want INN to support the `NEWNEWS` command from newsreaders. In the past, this option was set to `false` because the `NEWNEWS` command used to reduce the server's performance, but nowadays the default is set to `true`. |

| Parameter Name | Description |
|---|---|
| hiscachesize | Set this parameter to the size in kilobytes that you want INN to use for caching recently received message IDs that are kept in memory to speed history lookups. This cache is only used for incoming feeds and a small cache can hold quite a few history file entries. The default setting of 0 disables history caching. If you have more than one incoming feed, you may want to set this parameter to a value of 256 (for 256KB). |
| innflags | Set this parameter to any flags you want to pass to the INN server process when it starts up. |

### The newsfeeds file

The newsfeeds file specifies how incoming news articles are redistributed to other servers and to INN processes. If you provide news feeds to other servers, you have to list these news feeds in this file. (You also must have an entry labeled ME, which serves a special purpose that I explain later in this section.)

The newsfeeds file contains a series of entries, one for each feed. Each feed entry has the following format:

```
site[/exclude,exclude...]\
     :pattern,pattern...[/distrib,distrib...]\
     :flag,flag...\
     :param
```

Each entry has four fields separated by colons (:). Usually, the entries span multiple lines and a backslash (\) at the end of the line is used to continue a line to the next. Here's what the four fields mean:

✦ The first field, *site*, is the name of the feed. Each name must be unique, and for feeds to other news servers, the name is set to the host name of the remote server. Following the name is an optional slash and an exclude list (*/exclude,exclude...*) consisting of a list of names. If any of the names in this list appear in the Path line of an article, that article isn't forwarded to the feed. You can use an exclude list if you don't want to receive articles from a specific source.

✦ The second field consists of a comma-separated list of newsgroup patterns, such as *,@alt.binaries.warez.*,!control*,!local*, followed by an optional distribution list. The distribution list is a list of comma-separated keywords, with each keyword specifying a specific set of sites to which the articles are distributed. The newsgroup patterns essentially define a subscription list of sites that receive this news feed. An asterisk matches all newsgroups. A pattern beginning with an @

Book VIII
Chapter 4

Serving Up
Mail and News

causes newsgroups matching that pattern to be dropped. A pattern that begins with an exclamation mark (!) means the matching newsgroups are not sent. By the way, the simple pattern-matching syntax used in INN configuration files is referred to as a *wildmat* pattern.

✦ The third field is a comma-separated list of *flags* — fields that determine the feed-entry type and set certain parameters for the entry. You see numerous flags; type **man newsfeeds** and read the man page for more information about the flags.

✦ The fourth field is for parameters whose values depend on the settings in the third field. Typically, this field contains names of files or external programs that the INN server uses. You can find more about this field from the `newsfeeds` man page.

Now that you know the layout of the `/etc/news/newsfeeds` file, you can study that file as an example. The default file contains many sample feed entries, but only two are commented out:

✦ `ME` is a special feed entry that's always required. It serves two purposes. First, the newsgroup patterns listed in this entry are preprended to all newsgroup patterns in all other entries. Second, the `ME` entry's distribution list determines what distributions your server accepts from remote sites.

✦ The `controlchan` feed entry is used to set up INN so an external program is used to handle control messages (these messages are used to create new newsgroups and remove groups). For example, the following `controlchan` entry specifies the external program `/usr/lib/news/bin/controlchan` to handle all control messages, except `cancel` messages (meant for canceling an article):

```
controlchan!\
        :!*,control,control.*,!control.cancel\
        :Tc,Wnsm:/usr/lib/news/bin/controlchan
```

In addition to these feed entries, you add entries for any actual sites to which your news server provides news feed. Such entries have the format

```
feedme.domain.com\
                :!junk,!control/!foo\
                :Tm:innfeed!
```

where `feedme.domain.com` is the fully qualified domain name of the site to which your system sends news articles.

## The incoming.conf file

The `incoming.conf` file describes which hosts are allowed to connect to your host to feed articles. For a single feed, you can add an entry like

```
peer mybuddy {
    hostname: a-feed-site.domain.com
}
```

where *mybuddy* is a label for the peer and *a-feed-site.domain.com* identifies the site that feeds your site.

Keep in mind that simply adding a site's name in the incoming.conf file
does not cause that remote site to start feeding your site news — it simply
enables your server to accept news articles from the remote site. At the
remote site, your buddy has to configure his or her server to send articles
to your site.

## The readers.conf file

This file specifies the host names or IP addresses from which newsreader
clients (such as Mozilla) can retrieve newsgroups from your server. For
example, the following readers.conf file allows *read access* and *post access*
(meaning you can submit articles) from localhost and any from host in
the network 192.168.0.0:

```
auth "localhost" {
    hosts: "localhost, 127.0.0.1, stdin"
    default: "<localhost>"
}
access "localhost" {
    users: "<localhost>"
    newsgroups: "*"
    access: RPA
}
auth "localnet" {
    hosts: 192.168.0.0/24
    default: "<localnet>"
}
access "localnet" {
    users: "<localnet>"
    newsgroups: "*"
    access: RPA
}
```

## InterNetNews startup

In addition to the configuration files, you also have to initiate cron jobs that
perform periodic maintenance of the news server. In Fedora Core, these
cron jobs are already set up. Therefore, you're now ready to start the INN
server — innd.

Before you start innd, you must run makehistory and makedbz to initialize
and rebuild the INN history database. Type **man makehistory** and **man
makedbz** to find more about these commands. Type the following commands

to create an initial history database, associated indexes, and set the owner-ships and permissions of some files:

```
/usr/lib/news/bin/makehistory -b -f history -O -l 30000 -I
cd /var/lib/news
/usr/lib/news/bin/makedbz -s 'wc -l < history' -f history
chown news.news *
chown news.news /var/spool/news/overview/group.index
chmod 664 /var/spool/news/overview/group.index
```

As with any other servers in Fedora Core, to start innd, log in as root and type the following command:

```
service innd start
```

To ensure that innd starts at boot time, type the following command:

```
chkconfig --level 35 innd on
```

If you change any configuration file (such as inn.conf or newsfeeds), restart the innd server with the following command:

```
service innd restart
```

Type **ps ax** to see if the innd process is up and running. If all goes well, you see two processes, such as the following, listed in the output of the ps ax command:

```
23789 ?     S    0:00 /usr/lib/news/bin/innd -p4
23794 ?     S    0:00 /usr/bin/perl /usr/lib/news/bin/controlchan
```

The /var/log/spooler file contains all status and error messages from innd. Type the following command to see the last few messages in that file:

```
tail /var/log/spooler
```

## Setting Up Local Newsgroups

If you want to use newsgroups as a way to share information within your company, you can set up a hierarchy of local newsgroups. Then you can use these newsgroups to create virtual communities within your company, where people with shared interests can informally discuss issues and exchange knowledge.

## Defining a newsgroup hierarchy

The first task is to define a hierarchy of newsgroups and decide what each newsgroup will discuss. For example, if your company name is XYZ Corporation, here's a partial hierarchy of newsgroups you might define:

✦ `xyz.general`: General items about XYZ Corporation

✦ `xyz.weekly.news`: Weekly news

✦ `xyz.weekly.menu`: The weekly cafeteria menu and any discussions about it

✦ `xyz.forsale`: A listing of items offered for sale by employees

✦ `xyz.jobs`: Job openings at XYZ Corporation

✦ `xyz.wanted`: Wanted (help, items to buy, and so on) postings by employees

✦ `xyz.technical.hardware`: Technical discussions about hardware

✦ `xyz.technical.software`: Technical discussions about software

## Updating configuration files

Here are the steps you follow to update the configuration files for your local newsgroups and then restart the news server:

*1.* **Add descriptive entries for each of these newsgroups to the** `/var/lib/news/newsgroups` **file.**

Here are the entries from the default `/var/lib/news/newsgroups` file:

```
control         Various control messages (no posting).
control.cancel  Cancel messages (no posting).
control.checkgroups  Hierarchy check control messages (no posting).
control.newgroup  Newsgroup creation control messages (no posting).
control.rmgroup  Newsgroup removal control messages (no posting).
junk            Unfiled articles (no posting).
```

Add to this file a line for each local newsgroup — type its name, followed by a brief description. For example, here's what you might add for the `xyz.general` newsgroup:

```
xyz.general     General items about XYZ Corporation
```

*2.* **Edit the** `ME` **entry in the** `/etc/news/newsfeeds` **file and add the phrase** `,!xyz.*` **to the comma-separated list of newsgroup patterns.**

This step ensures that your local newsgroups are not distributed outside your site.

3. **Add a storage method to be used for the local newsgroups.**

   For example, you can add the following lines in `/etc/news/storage.conf` to define the storage method for the new `xyz` hierarchy of newsgroups (change `xyz` to whatever you name your local newsgroups):

   ```
   method tradspool {
       class: 1
       newsgroups: xyz.*
   }
   ```

4. **To make these changes effective, restart the news server with the command:**

   ```
   service innd restart
   ```

## Adding the newsgroups

The final step is to add the newsgroups. After you update the configuration files and have `innd` running, adding a local newsgroup is easy. Log in as `root` and use `ctlinnd` to perform this task. For example, here's how you add a newsgroup named `xyz.general`:

```
/usr/lib/news/bin/ctlinnd newgroup xyz.general
```

That's it! That command adds the `xyz.general` newsgroup to your site. If you use the traditional storage method, the `innd` server creates the directory `/var/spool/news/articles/xyz/general` and stores articles for that newsgroup in that directory (this happens the first time someone posts a news article to that newsgroup).

After you create all the local newsgroups, users from your intranet can post news articles and read articles in the local newsgroups. If they have problems accessing the newsgroups, make sure that the `/etc/news/readers.conf` file contains the IP addresses or names of the hosts that have access to the `innd` server.

## Testing your newsgroups

For example, I added a newsgroup named `local.news` on an INN server running on my Fedora Core system by using the instructions explained in the previous sections. Then I start Mozilla on another Fedora Core system on the LAN and set up a new news account with the news server set to my INN server. Next, I access the local.news newsgroup by typing **news:local.news** as the URL. Try it! I bet you'll like it.

# Chapter 5: Setting Up DNS

## In This Chapter

✓ Understanding DNS

✓ Learning about BIND

✓ Configuring DNS

✓ Setting up a caching name server

✓ Configuring a primary name server

*Domain Name System* (DNS) is an Internet service that converts a fully qualified domain name, such as www.redhat.com, into its corresponding IP address, such as 216.148.218.195. You can think of DNS as the directory of Internet hosts — DNS is the reason why you can use easy-to-remember host names even though TCP/IP requires numeric IP addresses for data transfers. DNS is basically a hierarchy of distributed DNS servers. In this chapter, I provide an overview of DNS and show you how to set up a caching DNS server on your Fedora Core system.

*Network Information System* (NIS) is another client/server service designed to manage information shared among several host computers on a network. Typically, NIS maintains a common set of user accounts and other system files on a UNIX or Linux system for a group of hosts on a local-area network (LAN). This service, among others, enables a user to log in on all hosts with the same username and password. This chapter briefly describes the NIS client and server software, and I show you how to use them on a Fedora Core system.

## Understanding Domain Name System (DNS)

In TCP/IP networks, each network interface (for example, an Ethernet card or a dial-up modem connection) is identified by an IP address. Because IP addresses are hard to remember, an easy-to-remember name is assigned to the IP address — much like the way a name goes with a telephone number. For example, instead of having to remember that the IP address of Red Hat's Web server is 216.148.218.195, you can simply refer to that host by its name, www.redhat.com. When you type www.redhat.com as the URL in a Web browser, the name www.redhat.com is translated into its corresponding IP address. This is where the concept of DNS comes in.

## What is DNS?

Domain Name System is a distributed, hierarchical database that holds information about computers on the Internet. That information includes host name, IP address, and mail-routing specifications. Because this information resides in many DNS hosts on the Internet; DNS is called a *distributed* database. The primary job of DNS is to associate host names to IP addresses and vice versa.

In ARPANET — the precursor to today's Internet — the list of host names and corresponding IP addresses was maintained in a text file named HOSTS. TXT, which was managed centrally and periodically distributed to every host on the network. As the number of hosts grew, this static host table quickly became unreasonable to maintain. DNS was proposed by Paul Mockapetris to alleviate the problems of a static host table. As formally documented in Request for Comment (RFC) 882 and 883 (published in November 1983, see www.faqs.org/rfcs/rfc882.html and www.faqs.org/rfcs/rfc883.html), the original DNS introduced two key concepts:

✦ Use of hierarchical domain names, such as www.ee.umd.edu and www.redhat.com

✦ Distributed responsibility for managing the host database by using DNS servers throughout the Internet

Today, DNS is an Internet standard documented in RFCs 1034 and 1035. The standard has been updated and extended by several other RFCs — 1101, 1183, 1348, 1876, 1982, 1996, 2065, 2181, 2136, 2137, 2308, 2535, 2845, and 2931. The earlier updates define data encoding, whereas later ones focus on improving DNS security. To read these and other RFCs online, visit the RFC page at the Internet Engineering Task Force (IETF) Web site:

www.ietf.org/rfc.html

DNS defines the following:

✦ A hierarchical domain-naming system for hosts

✦ A distributed database that associates every domain name with an IP address

✦ Library routines (resolvers) that network applications can use to query the distributed DNS database (this library is called the *resolver library*)

✦ A protocol for DNS clients and servers to exchange information about names and IP addresses

Nowadays, all hosts on the Internet rely on DNS to access various Internet services on remote hosts. As you may know from personal experience, when you obtain Internet access from an Internet Service Provider (ISP), your ISP provides you with the IP addresses of *name servers* — the DNS servers your system accesses whenever host names are mapped to IP addresses.

If you have a small LAN, you may decide to run a DNS server on one of the hosts or to use the name servers provided by the ISP. For medium-sized networks with several subnets, you can run a DNS server on each subnet to provide efficient DNS lookups. On a large corporate network, the corporate domain (such as `microsoft.com`) is further subdivided into a hierarchy of subdomains; several DNS servers may be used in each subdomain.

In the following sections, I provide an overview of the hierarchical domain-naming convention and describe BIND — the DNS software used on most UNIX systems, including Fedora Core.

## Learning hierarchical domain names

DNS uses a hierarchical tree of domains to organize the *namespace* — the entire set of names. Each higher-level domain has authority over its lower-level subdomains. Each domain represents a distinct block of the namespace and is managed by a single administrative authority. Figure 5-1 illustrates the hierarchical organization of the DNS namespace.

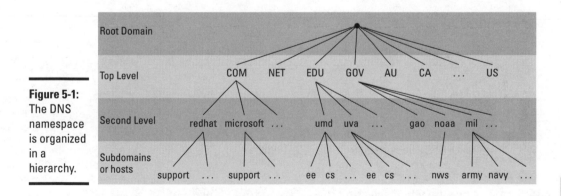

**Figure 5-1:** The DNS namespace is organized in a hierarchy.

The root of the tree is called the *root domain* and is represented by a single dot (.). The top-level, or root-level, domains come next. The top-level domains are further divided into second-level domains, which, in turn, can be broken into further subdomains.

The top-level domains are relatively fixed and include well-known domains such as `COM`, `NET`, `ORG`, `EDU`, `GOV`, and `MIL`. These are the commonly used top-level domains in the United States. These top-level domains came about as the Internet came to widespread use in the early 1990s.

Another set of top-level domain names is for the countries. These domain names use the two-letter country codes assigned by the International Organization for Standardization (abbreviated as ISO, see `www.iso.ch`). For example, the top-level country code domain for the United States is US. In the United States, many local governments and organizations use the US domain. For example, `mcps.k12.md.us` is the domain name of the Montgomery County Public Schools in the state of Maryland, USA.

The *fully qualified domain name* (FQDN) is constructed by stringing together the subdomain names, from lower- to higher-level, using dots (`.`) as separators. For example, `REDHAT.COM` is a fully qualified domain name; so is `EE.UMD.EDU`. Note that each of these may also refer to a specific host computer. Figure 5-2 illustrates the components of a fully qualified domain name.

**Figure 5-2:**
A fully qualified domain name has a hierarchy of components.

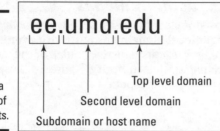

Domain names are case-insensitive. Therefore, as far as DNS is concerned, the domains `UMD.EDU` and `umd.edu` both represent University of Maryland's domain. The norm, however, is to type domain names in all lowercase.

## *Exploring Berkeley Internet Name Domain (BIND)*

Most UNIX systems, including Fedora Core, come with the BIND system — a well-known implementation of DNS. The BIND software is installed during Fedora Core installation, as long as you select the DNS Name Server package group when selecting the packages for installation.

To see which version of BIND is installed on your Fedora Core system, type the following command:

```
rpm -q bind
```

If BIND is installed, this command displays a line similar to the following with the version number of the RPM file:

```
bind-9.2.3-8.1
```

As this output shows, BIND Version 9.2.3 is installed on my system.

BIND includes three major components:

+ The `named` daemon — the name server — that responds to queries about host names and IP addresses

+ A resolver library that applications can use to resolve host names into IP addresses (and vice versa)

+ Command-line DNS utility programs (DNS clients), such as `dig` (Domain Internet Groper) and `host` that users can use to query DNS

I describe these components of BIND in the next few sections. In later sections, I explain how to configure the resolver and the name server.

### named — the BIND name server

The `named` daemon is the name server that responds to queries about host names and IP addresses. Based on the configuration files and the local DNS database, `named` either provides answers to queries or asks other servers and caches their responses. The `named` server also performs a function referred to as *zone transfer*, which involves copying data among the name servers in a domain.

The name server operates in one of three modes:

+ **Primary or Master:** In this case, the name server keeps the master copy of the domain's data on disk. One primary server is for each domain or subdomain.

+ **Secondary or Slave:** A secondary name server copies its domain's data from the primary server using a zone transfer operation. You can have one or more secondary name servers for a domain.

+ **Caching:** A *caching name server* loads the addresses of a few authoritative servers for the root domain, and gets all domain data by caching responses to queries it has resolved by contacting other name servers. Primary and secondary servers also cache responses.

A *name server* can be authoritative or not, depending on what information it's providing. As the term implies, the response from an authoritative name server is supposed to be accurate. The primary and secondary name servers are authoritative for their own domains, but they are not authoritative for responses provided from cached information.

Caching name servers are never authoritative because all their responses come from cached information.

**Book VIII
Chapter 5**

**Setting Up DNS**

To run a name server on your Fedora Core system, you have to run `named` with the appropriate configuration files. Later in this chapter, you find out about the configuration files and data files that control how the name server operates.

### Resolver library

Finding an IP address for a host name is referred to as *resolving the host name*. Network-aware applications, such as a Web browser or an FTP client, use a *resolver library* to perform the conversion from the name to an IP address. Depending on the settings in the `/etc/host.conf` file, the resolver library consults the `/etc/hosts` file or makes a DNS query to resolve a host name to its IP address. The resolver library queries the name servers listed in the `/etc/resolv.conf` file.

You don't have to know much about the resolver library unless you're writing network-aware applications. To run Internet services properly, all you have to know is how to configure the resolver. Later in this chapter, I show you how to configure the server and other aspects of DNS.

### DNS utility programs

You can use the DNS utility programs — `dig` and `host` — to try out DNS from the shell prompt interactively. These utility programs are DNS clients. You can use them to query the DNS database and debug any name server you may set up on your system. By default, these programs query the name server listed in your system's `/etc/resolv.conf` file.

You can use `dig`, the Domain Internet Groper program, to look up IP addresses for a domain name or vice versa. For example, to look up the IP address of `ftp.redhat.com`, type

```
dig ftp.redhat.com
```

`dig` prints the results of the DNS query in great detail. Look in the part of the output labeled `ANSWER SECTION:` for the result. For example, here's what that section looks like for this sample query:

```
;; ANSWER SECTION:
ftp.redhat.com.          300     IN      A       209.132.176.30
ftp.redhat.com.          300     IN      A       66.187.224.51
```

This output means that the name `ftp.redhat.com` refers to both IP addresses — `209.132.176.30` and `66.187.224.51`.

*Reverse lookups* (finding host names for IP addresses) are also easy with `dig`. For example, to find the host name corresponding to the IP address 209.132.176.30, type the following:

```
dig -x 209.132.176.30
```

Again, the answer appears in the ANSWER SECTION of the output, which, for this example, looks like this:

```
;; ANSWER SECTION:
30.176.132.209.in-addr.arpa.. 600 IN      PTR      ftp.redhat.com.
```

In this case, the host name corresponding to the IP address 209.132.176.30 happens to be `ftp.redhat.com`.

You can also query DNS by using the `host` program. The `host` program produces output in a compact format. For example, here's a typical use of `host` to look up an IP address for a host name:

```
host www.gao.gov
```

This command generates the following one-liner:

```
www.gao.gov has address 161.203.16.2
```

By default, `host` prints the IP address and any *MX record* (these records list the names of mail handlers for the host).

For a reverse lookup, use the `-t ptr` option, along with the IP address as an argument, like this:

```
host -t ptr 161.203.16.2
```

Here's the relay from `host`:

```
2.16.203.161.in-addr.arpa domain name pointer www.gao.gov.
```

In this case, `host` prints the PTR record (from the DNS database) that shows the host name corresponding to the IP address.

You can also try other types of records, such as CNAME (for canonical name), as follows:

```
host -t cname www.ee.umd.edu
```

**Book VIII Chapter 5**

**Setting Up DNS**

The response from host says

```
www.ee.umd.edu is an alias for edison.eng.umd.edu.
```

This output indicates that the *canonical name* (or alias) for www.ee.umd.edu is edison.eng.umd.edu.

# Configuring DNS

You configure DNS by using a number of configuration files. The exact set of files depends on whether or not you're running a name server and, if so, the type of name server — caching or primary. Some configuration files are needed whether you run a name server or not.

## Configuring the resolver

You don't need a name server running on your system to use the DNS clients (dig and host). You can use them to query your domain's name server. Typically, your ISP provides you with this information. You have to list the IP addresses of these name servers in the /etc/resolv.conf file — the resolver library reads this file to determine how to resolve host names. The format of this file is

```
domain your-domain.com
search your-domain.com
nameserver A.B.C.D
nameserver X.Y.Z.W
```

where A.B.C.D and X.Y.Z.W are the IP addresses (dot-separated numeric addresses, such as 192.168.0.1) of the primary and secondary name servers your ISP provides you.

The domain line lists the local domain name. The search line specifies the domains on which a host name is searched first (usually, you put your own domain in the search line). The domain listed on the search line is appended to any host name before the resolver library tries to resolve it. For example, if you look for a host named mailhost, the resolver library first tries mailhost.your-domain.com; if that fails, it tries mailhost. The search line applies to any host name you try to access. For example, if you're trying to access www.redhat.com, the resolver first tries www.redhat.com.your-domain.com and then www.redhat.com.

Another important configuration file is /etc/host.conf — this file tells the resolver what to do when attempting to resolve a host name. A typical /etc/host/conf file contains the following line:

```
order hosts,bind
```

This command tells the resolver to consult the `/etc/hosts` file first and, if that fails, to query the name server listed in the `/etc/resolv.conf` file. The `/etc/hosts` file usually lists any local host names and their IP addresses. Here's a typical line from the `/etc/hosts` file:

```
127.0.0.1    lnbp200  localhost.localdomain  localhost
```

This line says that the IP address `127.0.0.1` is assigned to the host names `lnbp200`, `localhost.localdomain`, and `localhost`.

In the latest version of the Linux kernel that uses GNU C Library version 2 (glibc 2) or later, the name service switch (NSS) file, `/etc/nsswitch.conf`, controls how services such as the resolver library, NIS, NIS+, and local files such as `/etc/hosts` and `/etc/shadow` interact. For example, the following `hosts` entry in the `/etc/nsswitch.conf` file specifies that the resolver library first try the `/etc/hosts` file, then try NIS+, and finally try DNS:

```
hosts:       files nisplus dns
```

To find more about the `/etc/nsswitch.conf` file and what it does, type **info libc "Name Service Switch"** in a terminal window.

## Configuring a caching name server

A simple, but useful, name server is one that finds answers to host-name queries by using other name servers and then remembers the answer (by saving it in a cache) the next time you need it. This caching name server can shorten the time it takes to access hosts you have accessed recently; the answer is already in the cache.

When you install the DNS Name Server package group during Fedora Core installation, the configuration files for a caching name server are also installed. That means you can start running the caching name server without much work on your part. This section describes the configuration files and what you have to do to start the caching name server.

### the /etc/named.conf file

The first configuration file you need is `/etc/named.conf`. The `named` server reads this configuration file when it starts. You already have this file if you installed the DNS Name Server during Fedora Core installation. Here's what the default `/etc/named/conf` file contains:

```
// generated by named-bootconf.pl

options {
    directory "/var/named";
    /*
     * If there is a firewall between you and nameservers you want
     * to talk to, you might need to uncomment the query-source
```

```
    * directive below. Previous versions of BIND always asked
    * questions using port 53, but BIND 8.1 uses an unprivileged
    * port by default.
    */
   // query-source address * port 53;
};

//
// a caching only nameserver config
//
controls {
    inet 127.0.0.1 allow { localhost; } keys { rndckey; };
};
zone "." IN {
    type hint;
    file "named.ca";
};

zone "localhost" IN {
    type master;
    file "localhost.zone";
    allow-update { none; };
};

zone "0.0.127.in-addr.arpa" IN {
    type master;
    file "named.local";
    allow-update { none; };
};

include "/etc/rndc.key";
```

Comments are C-style (/* ... */) or C++-style (starts with //). The file contains block statements enclosed in curly braces ({...}) and terminated by a semicolon (;). A block statement, in turn, contains other statements, each ending with a semicolon.

This /etc/named.conf file begins with an options block statement with a number of option statements. The directory option statement tells named where to look for all other files that appear on file lines in the configuration file. In this case, named looks for the files in the /var/named directory.

The controls statement in /etc/named.conf contains security information so the rndc command can connect to the named service at port 953 and interact with named. In this case, the controls statement contains the following line:

```
inet 127.0.0.1 allow { localhost; } keys { rndckey; };
```

This command says rndc can connect from localhost with the key named rndc (the file /etc/rndc.key defines the key and the encryption algorithm to be used).

The rndc (remote name daemon control) utility is a successor to the older ndc (for *name daemon controller*) utility used to control the named server by sending it messages over a special control channel, a TCP port where named listens for messages. The rndc utility uses a cryptographic key to authenticate itself to the named server. The named server has the same cryptographic key so it can decode the authentication information sent by rndc.

After the options statement, the /etc/named.conf file contains several zone statements, each enclosed in curly braces and terminated by a semicolon. Each zone statement defines a zone. The first zone is named . (root zone); it's a hint zone that specifies the root name servers.

The next two zone statements in /etc/named.conf are master zones. The syntax for a *master zone statement* for an Internet class zone (indicated by the IN keyword) is as follows:

```
zone "zone-name" IN {
        type master;
        file "zone-file";
        [...other optional statements...]
};
```

The zone-name is the name of the zone, and zone-file is the zone file that contains the resource records (RR) — the database entries — for that zone. I describe zone file formats and resource record formats in the next two sections.

### Zone file formats

The zone file typically starts with a number of directives, each of which begins with a dollar sign ($) followed by a keyword. Two commonly used directives are $TTL and $ORIGIN.

For example, the line

```
$TTL    86400
```

uses the $TTL directive to set the default Time To Live (TTL) for subsequent records with undefined TTLs. The value is in seconds, and the valid TTLs are in the range 0 to 2147483647 seconds. In this case, the directive sets the default TTL as 86400 seconds (or one day).

The $ORIGIN directive sets the domain name that is appended to any unqualified records. For example, the following $ORIGIN directive sets the domain name to localhost:

```
$ORIGIN localhost.
```

If there is no $ORIGIN directive, the initial $ORIGIN is the same as the zone name that comes after the zone keyword in the /etc/named.conf file.

After the directives, the zone file contains one or more resource records. These records follow a specific format, which I outline in the next section.

### Resource record (RR) formats

You have to understand the format of the resource records before you can understand and intelligently work with zone files. Each resource record has the following format (the optional fields are shown in square brackets):

```
[domain] [ttl] [class] type data [;comment]
```

The fields are separated by tabs or spaces and may contain some special characters, such as an @ symbol for the domain and a semicolon (;) to indicate the start of a comment.

The first field, which must begin at the first character of the line, identifies the domain. You can use the @ symbol to use the current $ORIGIN for the domain name for this record. If you have multiple records for the same domain name, leave the first field blank.

The optional ttl field specifies the Time To Live — the duration for which the data can be cached and considered valid. You can specify the duration in one of the following formats:

✦ *N*, where *N* is a number meaning *N* seconds

✦ *N*W, where *N* is a number meaning *N* weeks

✦ *N*D, where *N* is a number meaning *N* days

✦ *N*H, where *N* is a number meaning *N* hours

✦ *N*M, where *N* is a number meaning *N* minutes

✦ *N*S, where *N* is a number meaning *N* seconds

The letters W, D, H, M, and S can also be in lowercase. Thus, you can write 86400 or 1D (or 1d) to indicate a duration of one day. You can also combine these to specify more precise durations, such as 5w6d16h to indicate 5 weeks, 6 days, and 16 hours.

The class field specifies the network type. The most commonly used value for this field is IN for Internet.

Next in the resource record is the type field, which denotes the type of record (such as SOA, NS, A, or PTR). Table 5-1 lists the DNS resource record types. The data field comes next, and it depends on the type field.

**Table 5-1**                                 **DNS Resource Record Types**

| Type | Name | Description |
|------|------|-------------|
| SOA | Start of Authority | Indicates that all subsequent records are authoritative for this zone. |
| NS | Name Server | Identifies authoritative name servers for a zone. |
| A | Address | Specifies the IP address corresponding to a host name. |
| PTR | Pointer | Specifies the name corresponding to an address (used for reverse mapping — converting an IP address to a host name). |
| MX | Mail Exchanger | Identifies the host that accepts mail meant for a domain (used to route e-mail). |
| CNAME | Canonical Name | Defines the nickname or alias for a host name. |
| KEY | Public Key | Stores a public key associated with a DNS name. |
| CERT | Digital Certificate | Holds a digital certificate. |
| HINFO | Host Info | Identifies the hardware and operating system for a host. |
| RP | Responsible Person | Provides the name of a technical contact for a domain. |
| SRV | Services | Lists well-known network services provided by the domain. |
| TXT | Text | Used to include comments and other information in the DNS database. |

Read the resource records, at least the ones of type SOA, NS, A, PTR, and MX, which are some of the most commonly used. Next, I briefly describe these records, illustrating each record type through an example.

A typical SOA record has the following format:

```
@       1D IN SOA       @ root (
                        42              ; serial
                        3H              ; refresh -- 3 hours
                        15M             ; retry -- 15 minutes
                        1W              ; expiry -- 1 week
                        1D )            ; minimum -- 1 day
```

The first field specifies the domain as an @, which means the current domain (by default, the zone name, as shown in the /etc/named.conf file). The next field specifies a TTL of one day for this record. The class field is set to IN, which means the record is for Internet. The type field specifies the record type as SOA. The rest of the fields constitute the data for the SOA record.

**Book VIII
Chapter 5**

**Setting Up DNS**

The data includes the name of the primary name server (in this case, @, or the current domain), the e-mail address of the technical contact, and five different times enclosed in parentheses.

The NS record specifies the authoritative name servers for a zone. A typical NS record looks like the following:

```
.          3600000  IN  NS     A.ROOT-SERVERS.NET.
```

In this case, the NS record lists the authoritative name server for the root zone (notice that the name of the first field is a single dot). The Time-To-Live field specifies the record to be valid for 1,000 hours (3600000 seconds). The class is IN, for Internet; and the record type is NS. The final field lists the name of the name server (A.ROOT-SERVERS.NET.), which ends with a dot.

An A record specifies the address corresponding to a name. For example, the following A record shows the address of A.ROOT-SERVERS.NET. as 198.41.0.4:

```
A.ROOT-SERVERS.NET.      3600000       A       198.41.0.4
```

In this case, the network class isn't specified because the field is optional, and the default is IN.

PTR records are used for reverse mapping — converting an address to a name. Consider the following example:

```
1        IN      PTR      localhost.
```

This record comes from a file for a zone named 0.0.127.in-addr.arpa. Therefore, this record says that the name associated with the address 127.0.0.1 is localhost.

An MX record specifies the name of a host that accepts mail on behalf of a specific domain. For example, here's a typical MX record:

```
naba    IN    MX    10    mailhub.lnbsoft.com.
```

This record says that mail addressed to the host named naba in the current domain is sent to mailhub.lnbsoft.com (this host is called a mail exchanger). The number 10 is the preference value. For a list of multiple MX records with different preference values, the ones with lower preference values are tried first.

Armed with this bit of information about resource records, you can go through the zone files for the caching name server.

### The /var/named/named.ca file

Information about the thirteen root name servers is in the file `/var/named/named.ca`, as specified in the zone statement for the root zone in the `/etc/named.conf` file. The following listing shows the `/var/named/named.ca` file from a Fedora Core system:

```
;       This file holds the information on root name servers needed to
;       initialize cache of Internet domain name servers
;       (e.g. reference this file in the "cache  .  <file>"
;       configuration file of BIND domain name servers).
;
;       This file is made available by InterNIC
;       under anonymous FTP as
;           file                /domain/named.cache
;           on server           FTP.INTERNIC.NET
;       -OR-                    RS.INTERNIC.NET
;
;       last update:    Jan 29, 2004
;       related version of root zone:   2004012900
;
;
; formerly NS.INTERNIC.NET
;
.                       3600000 IN  NS      A.ROOT-SERVERS.NET.
A.ROOT-SERVERS.NET.     3600000     A       198.41.0.4
;
; formerly NS1.ISI.EDU
;
.                       3600000     NS      B.ROOT-SERVERS.NET.
B.ROOT-SERVERS.NET.     3600000     A       192.228.79.201
;
; formerly C.PSI.NET
;
.                       3600000     NS      C.ROOT-SERVERS.NET.
C.ROOT-SERVERS.NET.     3600000     A       192.33.4.12
;
; formerly TERP.UMD.EDU
;
.                       3600000     NS      D.ROOT-SERVERS.NET.
D.ROOT-SERVERS.NET.     3600000     A       128.8.10.90
;
; formerly NS.NASA.GOV
;
.                       3600000     NS      E.ROOT-SERVERS.NET.
E.ROOT-SERVERS.NET.     3600000     A       192.203.230.10
;
; formerly NS.ISC.ORG
;
.                       3600000     NS      F.ROOT-SERVERS.NET.
F.ROOT-SERVERS.NET.     3600000     A       192.5.5.241
;
; formerly NS.NIC.DDN.MIL
;
.                       3600000     NS      G.ROOT-SERVERS.NET.
G.ROOT-SERVERS.NET.     3600000     A       192.112.36.4
;
; formerly AOS.ARL.ARMY.MIL
;
.                       3600000     NS      H.ROOT-SERVERS.NET.
H.ROOT-SERVERS.NET.     3600000     A       128.63.2.53
```

**Book VIII
Chapter 5**

**Setting Up DNS**

```
;
; formerly NIC.NORDU.NET
;
.                               3600000    NS    I.ROOT-SERVERS.NET.
I.ROOT-SERVERS.NET.             3600000    A     192.36.148.17
;
; operated by VeriSign, Inc.
;
.                               3600000    NS    J.ROOT-SERVERS.NET.
J.ROOT-SERVERS.NET.             3600000    A     192.58.128.30
;
; operated by RIPE NCC
;
.                               3600000    NS    K.ROOT-SERVERS.NET.
K.ROOT-SERVERS.NET.             3600000    A     193.0.14.129
;
; operated by ICANN
;
.                               3600000    NS    L.ROOT-SERVERS.NET.
L.ROOT-SERVERS.NET.             3600000    A     198.32.64.12
;
; operated by WIDE
;
.                               3600000    NS    M.ROOT-SERVERS.NET.
M.ROOT-SERVERS.NET.             3600000    A     202.12.27.33
; End of File
```

This file contains NS and A resource records that specify the names of authoritative name servers and their addresses for the root zone (indicated by the . in the first field of each NS record).

The comment lines in the file begin with a semicolon. These comments give you hints about the location of the root name servers. There are 13 root name servers for the Internet; most root servers are located in the United States. This file is a necessity for any name server because the name server has to be able to reach at least one root name server.

### The /var/named/localhost.zone file

The /etc/named.conf file includes a zone statement for the localhost zone that specifies the zone file as localhost.zone. That file is located in the /var/named directory of your Fedora Core system. Here's a listing of what the /var/named/localhost.zone file contains:

```
$TTL    86400
$ORIGIN localhost.
@               1D IN SOA       @ root (
                                42              ; serial (d. adams)
                                3H              ; refresh
                                15M             ; retry
                                1W              ; expiry
                                1D )            ; minimum

                1D IN NS        @
                1D IN A         127.0.0.1
```

This zone file starts with a $TTL directive that sets the default TTL to one day (86400 seconds) for subsequent records with undefined TTLs. Next, a $ORIGIN directive sets the domain name to localhost.

After these two directives, the /var/named/localhost.zone file contains three resource records (RRs): an SOA record, an NS record, and an A record. The SOA and the NS record specify localhost as the primary authoritative name server for the zone. The A record specifies the address of localhost as 127.0.0.1.

### The /var/named/named.local file

The third zone statement in the /etc/named.conf file specifies a reverse-mapping zone named 0.0.127.in-addr.arpa. For this zone, the zone file is /var/named/named.local, which contains the following:

```
$TTL    86400
@       IN      SOA     localhost. root.localhost. (
                                1997022700 ; Serial
                                28800      ; Refresh
                                14400      ; Retry
                                3600000    ; Expire
                                86400 )    ; Minimum
        IN      NS      localhost.

1       IN      PTR     localhost.
```

The SOA and NS records specify localhost as the primary name server.

The SOA record also shows root.localhost. as the e-mail address of the technical contact for the domain. Note that the DNS zone files use a user. host. (notice the ending period) format for the e-mail address. When sending any e-mail to the contact, you have to replace the first dot with an @ and remove the final dot.

### Caching name server: startup and test

Now that you studied the configuration files for the caching name server, you can start the name server and see it in operation. To start the name server, log in as root and type the following command in a terminal window:

```
service named start
```

This command starts named — the name-server daemon.

To ensure that the named server starts every time you reboot the system, type the following command while logged in as root:

```
chkconfig --level 35 named on
```

The `named` server writes diagnostic log messages in the `/var/log/messages` file. After you start `named`, you can check the log messages by opening `/var/log/messages` in a text editor. If no error messages are from `named`, you can proceed to test the name server.

Before you try the caching name server, you have to specify that name server as your primary one. To do so, make sure that the first line in the `/etc/resolv.conf` file is the following:

```
nameserver 127.0.0.1
```

Now you can use `host` to test the name server. For example, to look up the IP address of `www.gao.gov` by using the caching name server on `localhost`, type the following command:

```
host www.gao.gov localhost
```

Here's the resulting output from the `host` command:

```
Using domain server:
Name: localhost
Address: 127.0.0.1#53
Aliases:
www.gao.gov. has address 161.203.16.2
```

As the output shows, the `host` command uses `localhost` as the DNS server and returns the IP address of `www.gao.gov`. If you get an output similar to this output, the caching name server is up and running.

## Configuring a primary name server

The best way to configure a primary name server is to start by configuring a caching name server (as explained in the previous sections). Then, add master zones for the domains for which you want this name server to be the primary name server. For example, suppose I want to define a primary name server for the `naba.net` domain. Here are the steps I go through to configure that primary name server (after I log in as `root`):

1.  **Add the following zone statements to `/etc/named.conf` file:**

    ```
    zone "naba.net" IN {
        type master;
        file "naba.zone";
    };
    zone "0.168.192.in-addr.arpa" IN {
        type master;
        file "0.168.192.zone";
    };
    ```

2. **Create the zone file** /var/named/naba.zone **with the following lines in it:**

```
$TTL       86400
$ORIGIN naba.net.
@             1D IN SOA        @ root.naba.net (
                              100              ; serial
                              3H               ; refresh
                              15M              ; retry
                              1W               ; expiry
                              1D )             ; minimum

              1D IN NS         @
              1D IN A          192.168.0.7

wxp     IN     A     192.168.0.2
```

3. **Create the zone file** /var/named/0.168.192.zone **with the following lines in it:**

```
$TTL       86400
; Remember zone name is: 0.168.192.in-addr.arpa
@          IN      SOA       naba.net. root.naba.net  (
                              1          ; Serial
                              28800      ; Refresh
                              14400      ; Retry
                              3600000    ; Expire
                              86400 )    ; Minimum
           IN      NS        naba.net.

7          IN      PTR       naba.net.
2          IN      PTR       wxp.naba.net.
```

4. **To test the new configuration, restart the** named **server with the following command:**

```
service named restart
```

5. **Use** dig **or** host **to query the DNS server.**

For example, here's how I use host to check the address of the host wxp.naba.net at the DNS server running on localhost:

```
host wxp.naba.net localhost
```

This command results in the following output:

```
Using domain server:
Name: localhost
Address: 127.0.0.1#53
Aliases:

wxp.naba.net has address 192.168.0.2
```

If you want to use `dig` to check the DNS server, type the following command:

```
dig @localhost wxp.naba.net
```

That `@localhost` part specifies the DNS server that `dig` contacts.

When you successfully use `dig` to contact a DNS server, you can get a bit fancier with what you ask that server to do. Here, for example, is the command I type to try a reverse lookup with the IP address `192.168.0.2`:

```
host 192.168.0.2 localhost
```

This command displays the following output:

```
Using domain server:
Name: localhost
Address: 127.0.0.1#53
Aliases:

2.0.168.192.in-addr.arpa domain name pointer wxp.naba.net
```

# Chapter 6: Running Samba and NFS

## In This Chapter

✔ **Sharing files with NFS**

✔ **Using the NFS Server Configuration tool**

✔ **Installing and configuring Samba**

✔ **Setting up a Windows server using Samba**

*I*f your local area network is like many others, it needs the capability to share files between systems that run Linux and other systems that don't. Thus Fedora Core includes two prominent file-sharing services:

✦ **Network File System (NFS)** is for sharing files with other UNIX systems (or PCs with NFS client software)

✦ **Samba** is for file sharing and print sharing with Windows systems.

In this chapter, I describe how to share files using both NFS and Samba.

## Sharing Files with NFS

Sharing files through NFS is simple and involves two basic steps:

✦ On the Fedora Core system that runs the NFS server, you export (share) one or more directories by listing them in the /etc/exports file and by running the exportfs command. In addition, you must run the NFS server by logging in as root and typing the command **service nfs start**.

✦ On each client system, you use the mount command to mount the directories that your server has exported.

The only problem in using NFS is that each client system must support it. Microsoft Windows doesn't come with NFS. That means you have to buy NFS software separately if you want to share files by using NFS. However, using NFS if all systems on your LAN run Linux (or other variants of UNIX with built-in NFS support) makes sense.

*Note:* NFS has security vulnerabilities. Do not set up NFS on systems directly connected to the Internet.

In the next few sections, I walk you through NFS setup, using an example of two Fedora Core PCs on a LAN.

## Exporting a file system with NFS

Start with the server system that exports — makes available to the client systems — the contents of a directory. On the server, you must run the NFS service and also designate one or more file systems to export — made available to the client systems.

To export a file system, you have to add an appropriate entry to the /etc/ exports file. For example, suppose you want to export the /home directory and you want to enable the host named LNBP75 to mount this file system for read and write operations. You can do so by adding the following entry to the /etc/exports file:

```
/home LNBP75(rw,sync)
```

If you want to give access to all hosts on a LAN such as 192.168.0.0, you could change this line to

```
/home 192.168.0.0/24(rw,sync)
```

Every line in the /etc/exports file has this general format:

```
directory    host1(options)  host2(options)  ...
```

The first field is the directory being shared via NFS, followed by one or more fields that specify which hosts can mount that directory remotely and a number of options within parentheses. You can specify the hosts with names or IP addresses, including ranges of addresses.

The options within parentheses denote the kind of access each host is granted and how user and group IDs from the server are mapped to ID the client (for example, if a file is owned by root on the server, what owner is that on the client?). Within the parentheses, commas separate the options. For example, if a host is allowed both read and write access — and all IDs are to be mapped to the anonymous user (by default this is the user named nobody) — then the options look like this:

```
(rw,all_squash)
```

Table 6-1 shows the options you can use in the /etc/exports file. You find two types of options — general options and user ID mapping options.

| Table 6-1 | Options in /etc/exports |
|-----------|-------------------------|
| *This Option* | *Does the Following* |
| **General Options** | |
| secure | Allows connections only from ports 1024 or lower (default). |
| insecure | Allows connections from 1024 or higher. |
| ro | Allows read-only access (default). |
| rw | Allows both read and write access. |
| sync | Performs write operations (writing information to the disk) when requested (by default). |
| async | Performs write operations when the server is ready. |
| no_wdelay | Performs write operations immediately. |
| wdelay | Waits a bit to see whether related write requests arrive, and then performs them together (by default). |
| hide | Hides an exported directory that's a subdirectory of another exported directory (by default). |
| no_hide | Behaves exactly the opposite of hide. |
| subtree_check | Performs subtree checking, which involves checking parent directories of an exported subdirectory whenever a file is accessed (by default). |
| no_subtree_check | Turns off subtree checking (opposite of subtree_check). |
| insecure_locks | Allows insecure file locking. |
| **User ID Mapping Options** | |
| all_squash | Maps all user IDs and group IDs to the anonymous user on the client. |
| no_all_squash | Maps remote user and group IDs to similar IDs on the client (by default). |
| root_squash | Maps remote root user to the anonymous user on the client (by default). |
| no_root_squash | Maps remote root user to the local root user. |
| anonuid=UID | Sets the user ID of anonymous user to be used for the all_squash and root_squash options. |
| anongid=GID | Sets the group ID of anonymous user to be used for the all_squash and root_squash options. |

After adding the entry in the /etc/exports file, manually export the file system by typing the following command in a terminal window:

```
exportfs -a
```

This command exports all file systems defined in the /etc/exports file.

**Book VIII
Chapter 6**

**Running
Samba and NFS**

Now you can start the NFS server processes. To do so, log in as `root` and type the following command in a terminal window:

```
service nfs start
```

If you want the NFS server to start when the system boots, type the following command to turn it on:

```
chkconfig --level 35 nfs on
```

When the NFS service is up, the server side of NFS is ready. Now you can try to mount the exported file system from a client system, and access the exported file system as needed.

If you ever make any changes to the exported file systems listed in the `/etc/exports` file, remember to restart the NFS service. To do so, log in as `root` and type the following command in a terminal window:

```
service nfs restart
```

## Mounting an NFS file system

To access an exported NFS file system on a client system, you have to mount that file system on a mount point. The *mount point* is nothing more than a local directory. For example, suppose you want to access the `/home` directory exported from the server named `LNBP200` at the local directory `/mnt/lnbp200` on the client system. To do so, follow these steps:

1. **Log in as `root` and create the directory with this command:**

   ```
   mkdir /mnt/lnbp200
   ```

2. **Type the following command to mount the directory from the remote system (`LNBP200`) on the local directory `/mnt/lnbp200`:**

   ```
   mount lnbp200:/home /mnt/lnbp200
   ```

After these steps, you can view and access exported files from the local directory `/mnt/lnbp200`.

To confirm that the NFS file system is indeed mounted, log in as `root` on the client system and type **mount** in a terminal window. You see a line similar to the following about the NFS file system:

```
lnbp200:/home/public on /mnt/lnbp200 type nfs (rw,addr=192.168.0.4)
```

## Using the NFS Server Configuration tool

Fedora Core comes with a graphical NFS Server Configuration tool that makes configuring and starting the NFS server easy. To configure the NFS server using this tool, follow these steps:

1. **Log in as** root **and choose Main Menu⇨System Settings⇨ Server Settings⇨NFS from the GNOME or KDE desktop.**

   The NFS Server Configuration window appears.

2. **Click Add on the toolbar.**

   The Add NFS Share dialog box appears.

3. **Add the directories you want to share via NFS.**

   Start by specifying the directory, who has access to it (the hosts or IP addresses), and what type of access (read-only or read-write). Figure 6-1 shows the settings for the /home directory being shared with read-write access with all hosts in the 192.168.0.0 network.

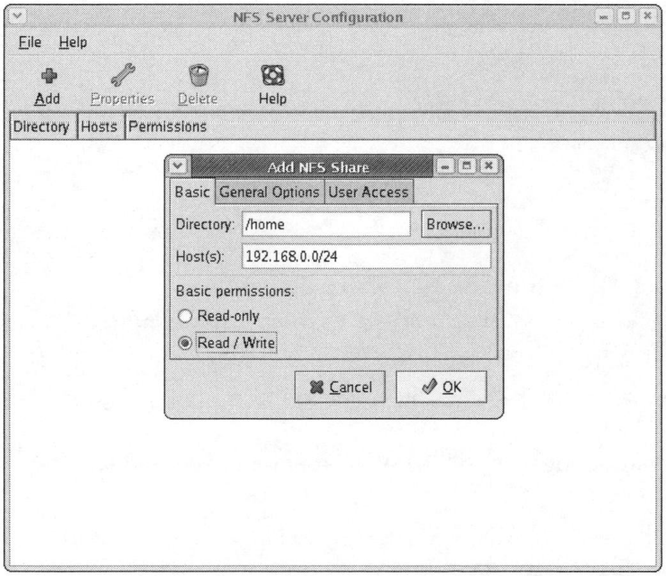

**Figure 6-1:** Specify the share directory and basic permissions from this dialog box.

**Book VIII Chapter 6**

**Running Samba and NFS**

4. **Click the General Options tab in the Add NFS Share dialog box and set the options you want (as shown in Figure 6-2).**

   These options correspond to the options listed in the General Options section of Table 6-1.

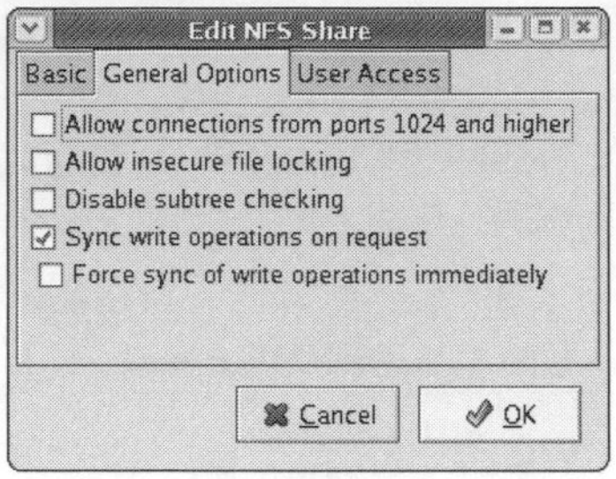

**Figure 6-2:**
Specify the general options for an NFS share from this dialog box.

**5.** **Click the User Access tab in the Add NFS Share dialog box and set the options you want (see Figure 6-3).**

These options correspond to the options listed in the User ID Mapping Options section of Table 6-1.

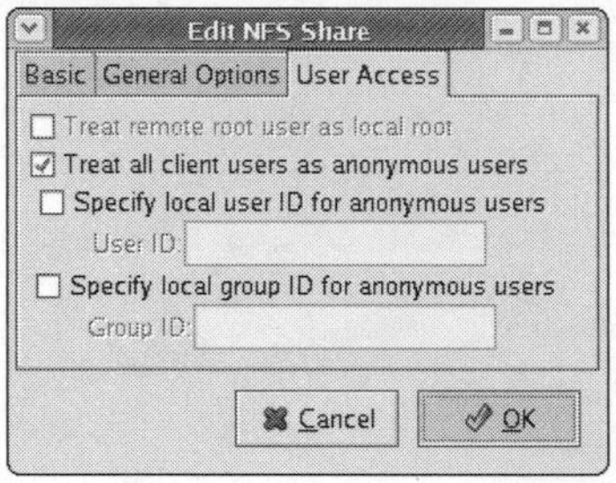

**Figure 6-3:**
Specify the user access options for an NFS share from this dialog box.

**6.** **Click OK in the Add NFS Share dialog box.**

The NFS Configuration tool saves the settings in the /etc/exports file and starts the NFS server.

**7.** **Choose File⇨Quit to exit the NFS Configuration tool.**

After completing these steps, you can mount the NFS shares on other hosts in your network.

## Setting Up a Windows Server Using Samba

If you rely on Windows for file sharing and print sharing, you probably use Windows in your servers and clients. If so, you can still move to a Fedora Core PC as your server without losing Windows file- and print-sharing capabilities; you can set up Fedora Core as a Windows server. When you install Fedora Core from this book's companion DVD-ROM, you also get a chance to install the Samba software package, which performs that setup. All you have to do is select the Windows File Server package group during installation.

After you install and configure Samba on your Fedora Core PC, your client PCs — even if they're running the old Windows for Workgroups operating system or the more recent Windows 95/98/NT/2000/XP versions — can access shared disks and printers on the Fedora Core PC. To do so, they use the Server Message Block (SMB) protocol, the underlying protocol in Windows file and print sharing.

With the Samba package installed, you can make your Fedora Core PC a Windows client, which means that the Fedora Core PC can access the disks and printers that a Windows server manages.

The Samba software package has these major components:

✦ /etc/samba/smb.conf: The Samba configuration file the SMB server uses.

✦ /etc/samba/smbusers: This Samba configuration file shows the Samba user names corresponding to usernames on the local Fedora Core PC.

✦ nmbd: The NetBIOS name server, which clients use to look up servers. (NetBIOS stands for Network Basic Input/Output System — an interface that applications use to communicate with network transports, such as TCP/IP.)

✦ nmblookup: This command returns the IP address of a Windows PC identified by its NetBIOS name.

✦ smbadduser: This program adds users to the SMB password file.

✦ smbcacls: This program manipulates Windows NT access control lists (ACLs) on shared files.

✦ smbclient: The Windows client, which runs on Linux and allows Linux to access the files and printer on any Windows server.

✦ smbcontrol: This program sends messages to the smbd, nmbd, or winbindd processes.

✦ smbd: The SMB server, which accepts connections from Windows clients and provides file- and print-sharing services.

✦ smbmount: This program mounts a Samba share directory on a Fedora Core PC.

✦ smbpasswd: This program changes the password for an SMB user.

✦ smbprint: This script enables printing on a printer on a SMB server.

✦ smbstatus: This command lists the current SMB connections for the local host.

**Book VIII Chapter 6**

**Running Samba and NFS**

✦ `smbtar:` This program backs up SMB shares directly to tape drives on the Fedora Core system.

✦ `smbumount:` This program unmounts a currently mounted Samba share directory.

✦ `testparm:` This program ensures that the Samba configuration file is correct.

✦ `winbindd:` This server resolves names from Windows NT servers.

In the following sections, I describe how to install Samba from the companion DVD-ROM and how to print from the Fedora Core PC to a shared printer on a Windows PC.

## *Checking whether Samba is installed*

Check whether Samba is installed by typing the following command in a terminal window:

```
rpm -q samba
```

If you see an output similar to the following, Samba is already installed on your system:

```
samba-3.0.2a-1.1
```

If you get a message saying that the package isn't installed, follow these steps to install Samba from this book's companion DVD-ROM:

*1.* **Log in as `root` and insert the DVD-ROM into the drive. If you're using GNOME or KDE, the DVD-ROM automatically mounts. If not, type the following command to mount the DVD-ROM:**

```
mount /mnt/cdrom
```

*2.* **Change the directory to the DVD-ROM — specifically to the directory where the Red Hat Package Manager (RPM) packages are located — with the following command:**

```
cd /mnt/cdrom/Fedora/RPMS
```

*3.* **Use the following `rpm` command to install Samba:**

```
rpm -ivh samba*
```

If Samba is already installed, this command returns an error message. Otherwise, the `rpm` command installs Samba on your system by copying various files to their appropriate locations.

After installing the Samba software, you have to configure Samba before you can use it.

## Configuring Samba

To set up the Windows file-sharing and print-sharing services, use the graphical Samba Server Configuration tool following these steps:

1. **Select Main Menu⇨System Settings⇨Server Settings⇨Samba.**

   If you are not logged in as root, enter the root password when prompted for it. Then the Samba Server Configuration window appears.

2. **Click the Add button.**

   The Create Samba Share dialog box appears.

3. **Enter the name of the directory to share or click Browse and select a directory. The directory must already exist. Also select the permission — either read-only or both read and write (see Figure 6-4).**

   Figure 6-4 shows a typical example that shares the /home/public directory. If the directory does not exist, you can create the directory by logging in as root and typing **mkdir /home/public** in a terminal window.

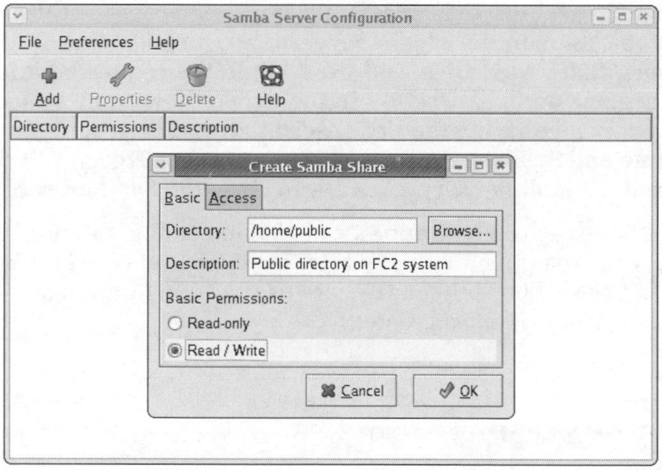

**Figure 6-4:**
Enter information about the directory you want to share.

4. **Click the Access tab in the Create Samba Share dialog box. Then type in the users who need access to the shared directory or click the Allow Access to Everyone radio button. Then click OK.**

   The Samba Server Configuration tool creates the Samba share by adding entries in the configuration file /etc/samba/smb.conf.

5. **To set the Samba server's workgroup name, select Preferences⇨ Server Settings in the Samba Server Configuration tool. Then enter the same workgroup name as your Windows network on the Basic tab of the Server Settings dialog box (see Figure 6-5).**

6. **On the Security tab of the Server Settings dialog box, select the name of guest user, if you want one, and select the authentication mode. If you set the authentication mode as User, users can log in with a user-name and password to access the Samba share.**

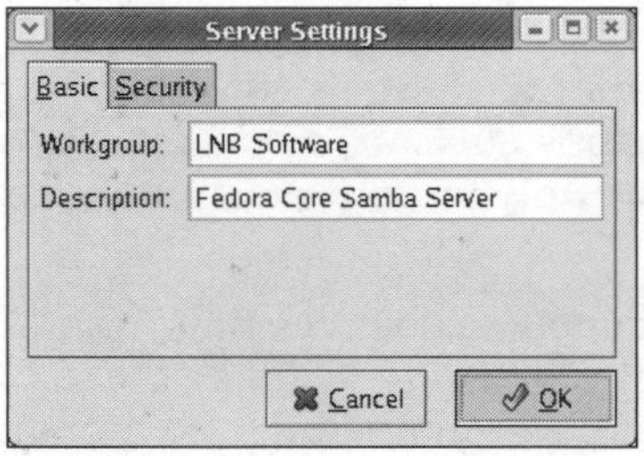

**Figure 6-5:** Enter the name of your workgroup and a description.

7. **To add users who can access the Samba share, select Preferences⇨ Samba Users in the Samba Server Configuration tool. In the Samba Users dialog box, click Add User. Fill in the requested information — username and password — in the Create New Samba User dialog box. Start by identifying the Unix username and then set a Samba user-name and Samba password for that user (see Figure 6-6). When you are done adding users, click OK to close the Samba Users dialog box.**

This steps creates the appropriate Samba configuration files in the /etc/samba directory and starts the Samba service. In particular, the file /etc/samba/smb.conf contains the configuration details for the Samba share you just created.

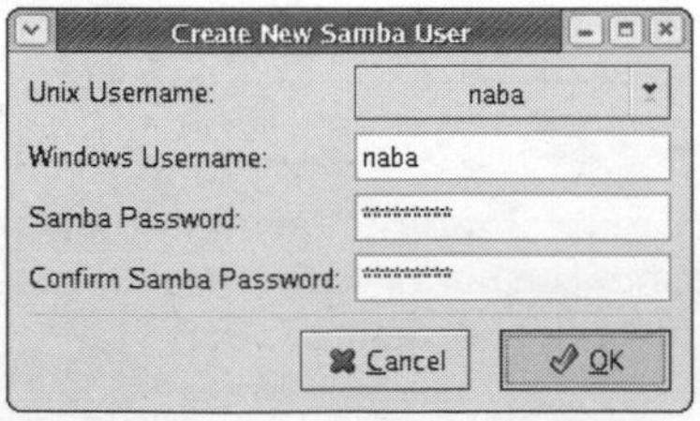

**Figure 6-6:** Add information about users who can access the Samba share.

After adding a Samba share, type the following command in a terminal window to verify that the Samba configuration file is okay:

```
testparm
```

If the command says that it loaded the files okay, you're all set to go. The `testparm` command also displays the contents of the Samba configuration file.

To start the SMB services automatically when the system reboots, type the following command:

```
chkconfig --level 35 smb on
```

## Trying out Samba

You can now try to access the Samba server on the Fedora Core system from one of the Windows systems on the LAN. Double-click the Network Neighborhood icon on the Windows 95/98/ME desktop. On Windows XP, choose Start⇨My Network Places and then click View Workgroup Computers. All the computers on the same workgroup are shown.

As you can see from the label (see Figure 6-7), the selected icon represents a Fedora Core system running Samba.

**Figure 6-7:**
You can view the Fedora Core Samba server from Windows XP.

When you see the Samba server, you can open it by double-clicking the icon. You are prompted for your Samba username and the Samba password and, after you enter that information correctly, you can access the folders and printers (if any) on the Samba share. For example, Figure 6-8 shows the shared resources on my Samba server running on Fedora. As you can see, there are

**Book VIII Chapter 6**

**Running Samba and NFS**

two shared folders — one is my home directory and the other is the public share that I had created with the Samba Server Configuration tool. You can then open these folders to explore the contents of the directories further.

**Figure 6-8:**
Shared
resources
on a Fedora
Samba
server, as
viewed from
Windows
XP.

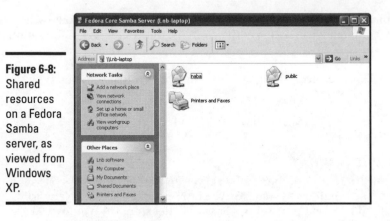

# Book IX

# Programming

THE GREAT THING ABOUT OBJECT-ORIENTED PROGRAMMING IS, IT'S MADE SOFTWARE DEVELOPMENT AS EASY AS PUTTING ONE FOOT IN FRONT OF THE OTHER.

# Contents at a Glance

Chapter 1: Fedora Core Programming Essentials ...........................................................709

Chapter 2: Programming in C ...................................................................................735

Chapter 3: Writing Shell Scripts ..............................................................................767

Chapter 4: Programming in Perl ..............................................................................779

# Chapter 1: Fedora Core Programming Essentials

## In This Chapter

✔ **Learning programming**

✔ **Exploring the software development tools in Fedora Core**

✔ **Compiling and linking programs with GCC**

✔ **Learning to use** make

✔ **Debugging programs with** gdb

✔ **Understanding the implications of GNU, GPL, and LGPL**

Your Fedora Core system comes loaded with all the tools you need to develop software. In particular, it has all the GNU software-development tools, such as GCC (C and C++ compiler), GNU make, and the GNU debugger. In this chapter, I introduce you to programming, describe these software-development tools, and show you how to use them. Although I use examples in the C and C++ programming languages, the focus is not on showing how to program in those languages, but to show how to use various software-development tools (such as compilers, make, and debugger).

I also briefly explain how the Free Software Foundation's GNU Public License (GPL) may affect any plans you might have to develop Linux software. You need to know this because you use GNU tools and GNU libraries to develop software in Linux.

## Learning Programming

If you've written computer programs in any programming language, you can start writing programs on your Fedora Core system very quickly. If you've never written a computer program, however, you need two basic resources before you get into it: a look at the basics of programming, and a quick review of computers and the major parts that make them up. In this section, I give you an overview of computer programming — just enough to get you going.

## A simplified view of a computer

Before you get a feel for computer programming, you need to understand where computer programs fit into the rest of your computer. Figure 1-1 shows a simplified view of a computer, highlighting the major parts that are important to a programmer.

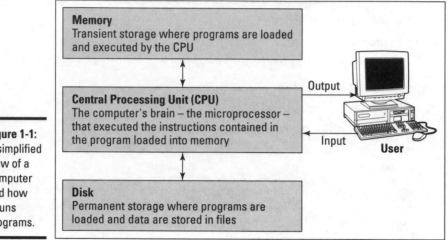

**Figure 1-1:** A simplified view of a computer and how it runs programs.

At the heart of a computer is the *central processing unit* (CPU) that performs the instructions contained in a computer program. The specific piece of hardware that does the job (which its makers call a *microprocessor* and the rest of us call a *chip*) varies by system: In a Pentium PC, it's a Pentium; in a Sun SPARC workstation, it's a SPARC chip; in an HP UNIX workstation, it's a PA-RISC chip. These microprocessors have different capabilities but the same mission: Tell the computer what to do.

Random Access Memory (RAM), or just *memory,* serves as the storage for computer programs while the CPU executes them. If a program works on some data, that data is also stored in the memory. The contents of the memory are not permanent; they go away (never to return) when the computer is shut down or when a program is no longer running.

The *hard disk,* or *disk,* serves as the permanent storage space for computer programs and data. The disk is organized into files, which are in turn organized in hierarchical directories and subdirectories (somewhat like organizing paper folders into the drawers in a file cabinet). Each file is essentially a block of storage capable of holding a variety of information. For example, a file may be a human-readable text file — or it may be a collection of computer instructions that makes sense only to the CPU. When you create computer programs, you work a lot with files.

For a programmer, the other two important items are the *input* and *output* — the way a program gets input from the user and displays output to the user. The user provides input through the keyboard and output appears on the monitor. However, a program may also accept input from a file and send output to a file.

## Role of the operating system

The operating system is a special collection of computer programs whose primary purpose is to load and run other programs. The operating system also acts as an interface between the software and the hardware. All operating systems include one or more command processors (called *shells* in Fedora Core) that allow users to type commands and perform tasks such as running a program or printing a file. Most operating systems also include a graphical user interface (such as GNOME and KDE in Fedora Core) that allows the user to perform most tasks by clicking on-screen icons. Fedora Core, Windows (whether the NT, 2000, or XP version), and various versions of UNIX, including Linux, are examples of operating systems.

It's the operating system that gives a computer its personality. For example, you can run Windows 2000 or Windows XP on a PC. On that same PC, you can also install and run Fedora Core. That means, depending on the operating system installed on it, the selfsame PC could be a Windows 2000, Windows XP, or a Fedora Core system.

Computer programs are built *on top of* the operating system. That means a computer program must make use of the capabilities that the operating system includes. For example, computer programs read and write files by using built-in capabilities of the operating system. (And if the operating system can't make coffee, no program can tell it to and still expect positive results.)

Although the details vary, most operating systems support a number of similar concepts. As a programmer, you need to be familiar with the following handful of concepts:

✦ A *process* is a computer program that is currently running in the computer. Most operating systems allow multiple processes to run simultaneously.

✦ A *command processor,* or *shell,* is a special program that allows the user to type commands and perform various tasks, such as run any program, look at a host of files, or print a file. In Windows 2000 or Windows XP, you can type commands in a Command Prompt window.

✦ The term *command line* refers to the commands that a user types to the command processor. Usually a command line contains a command and one or more *options* — the command is the first word in the line and the rest are the options (specific behaviors demanded of the computer).

✦ *Environment variables* are essentially text strings with a name. For example, the PATH environment variable refers to a string that contains the names of directories. Operating systems use environment variables to provide useful information to processes. To see a list of environment variables in a Windows 2000 or Windows XP system, type **SET** in the Command Prompt window. In Fedora Core, you can type **printenv** to see the environment variables.

## Basics of computer programming

A *computer program* is a sequence of instructions for performing a specific task like adding two numbers or searching for some text in a file. Consequently, computer programming involves *creating* that list of instructions, telling the computer how to complete a specific task. The exact instructions depend on the programming language that you use. For most programming languages, you have to go through the following steps to create a computer program:

1. Use a text editor to type in the sequence of commands from the programming language.

   This sequence of commands accomplishes your task. This human-readable version of the program is called the *source file* or *source code*. You can create the source file using any application (such as a word processor) that can save a document in plain text form.

   Always save your source code as plain text (the filename depends on the type of programming language). Word processors can sometimes put extra instructions in their documents that tell the computer to display the text in a particular font or other format. Trust me, your program is much better off without such stuff.

2. Use a *compiler* program to convert that text file — the source code — from human-readable form into machine-readable *object code*.

   Typically, this step also combines several object code files into a single machine-readable computer program, something that the computer can actually run.

3. Use a special program called a *debugger* to track down any errors and find which lines in the source file might have caused the errors.

4. Go back to Step 1 and use the text editor to fix the errors and repeat the rest of the steps.

These steps are referred to as the *Edit-Compile-Debug cycle* of programming because most programmers have to repeat this sequence several times before a program works correctly.

In addition to knowing the basic programming steps, you also need to be familiar with the following terms and concepts:

✦ *Variables* are used to store different types of data. You can think of each variable as being a placeholder for data — kind of like a mailbox, with a name and room to store data. The content of the variable is its value.

✦ *Expressions* combine variables by using operators. An expression may add several variables; another may extract a part of a string.

✦ *Statements* perform some action, such as assigning a value to a variable or printing a string.

✦ *Flow-control statements* allow statements to execute in various orders, depending on the value of some expression. Typically, flow-control statements include `for`, `do-while`, `while`, and `if-then-else` statements.

✦ *Functions* (also called subroutines or routines) allow you to group several statements and give them a name. This feature allows you to execute the same set of statements by invoking the function that represents those statements. Typically, a programming language provides many predefined functions to perform tasks such as opening (and reading from) a file.

# Exploring the Software Development Tools in Fedora Core

Fedora Core includes these traditional UNIX software-development tools:

✦ Text editors such as `vi` and `emacs` for editing the source code. (To find out more about `vi`, see Book II, Chapter 5.)

✦ A C compiler for compiling and linking programs written in C — the programming language of choice for writing UNIX applications (though nowadays many programmers are turning to C++ and Java). Fedora Core includes the GNU C and C++ compilers. Originally, the GNU C Compiler was known as GCC — which now stands for *GNU Compiler Collection* (see a description at `gcc.gnu.org`).

✦ The GNU `make` utility for automating the software *build process* — the process of combining object modules into an executable or a library.

✦ A debugger for debugging programs. Fedora Core includes the GNU debugger `gdb`.

✦ A version-control system to keep track of various revisions of a source file. Linux comes with RCS (Revision Control System) and CVS (Concurrent Versions System). Nowadays most open-source projects use CVS as their version-control system.

These tools install automatically if you select the Development Tools when you install Fedora Core from this book's companion DVD-ROM. In the next few sections, I briefly describe how to use these software-development tools to write applications for Fedora Core.

# GNU C and C++ compilers

The most important software-development tool in Fedora Core is GCC — the GNU C and C++ compiler. In fact, GCC can compile three languages: C, C++, and Objective-C (a language that adds object-oriented programming capabilities to C). You use the same gcc command to compile and link both C and C++ source files. The GCC compiler supports ANSI standard C, making it easy to port any ANSI C program to Linux. In addition, if you've ever used a C compiler on other UNIX systems, you're right at home with GCC.

## Using GCC

Use the gcc command to invoke GCC. By default, when you use the gcc command on a source file, GCC preprocesses, compiles, and links to create an executable file. However, you can use GCC options to stop this process at an intermediate stage. For example, you might invoke gcc by using the -c option to compile a source file and to generate an object file, but not to perform the link step.

Using GCC to compile and link a few C source files is very simple. Suppose you want to compile and link a simple program made up of two source files. I use the following program source for this task; it's stored in the file area.c, and it's the main program that computes the area of a circle whose radius is specified through the command line:

```
#include <stdio.h>
#include <stdlib.h>

/* Function prototype */
double area_of_circle(double r);

int main(int argc, char **argv)
{
  if(argc < 2)
  {
    printf("Usage: %s radius\n", argv[0]);
    exit(1);
  }
  else
  {
    double radius = atof(argv[1]);
    double area = area_of_circle(radius);
    printf("Area of circle with radius %f = %f\n",
        radius, area);
  }
  return 0;
}
```

You need another file that actually computes the area of a circle. Here's the listing for the file circle.c, where I define a function that computes the area of a circle:

```
#include <math.h>

#define SQUARE(x) ((x)*(x))

double area_of_circle(double r)
{
   return 4.0 * M_PI * SQUARE(r);
}
```

For such a simple program, of course, I could have placed everything in a single file, but I needed this contrived example to show you how to handle multiple files.

To compile these two files and to create an executable file named area, you use this command:

```
gcc -o area area.c circle.c
```

This invocation of GCC uses the -o option to specify the name of the executable file. (If you don't specify the name of an output file with the -o option, GCC saves the executable code in a file named a.out.)

If you have too many source files to compile and link, you can compile the files individually and generate *object files* (that have the .o extension). That way, when you change a source file, you need to compile only that file — you just link the compiled file to all the object files. The following commands show how to separate the compile and link steps for the sample program:

```
gcc -c area.c
gcc -c circle.c
gcc -o area area.o circle.o
```

The first two commands run gcc with the -c option compiling the source files. The third gcc command links the object files into an executable named area.

In case you are curious, here's how you run the area program (to compute the area of a circle with a radius of 1):

```
./area 1
```

The program generates the following output:

```
Area of circle with radius 1.000000 = 12.566371
```

Incidentally, you have to add the ./ prefix to the program's name (area) only if the current directory is not in the PATH environment variable. You do no harm in adding the prefix, even if your PATH contains the current directory.

### Compiling C++ programs

GNU CC is a combined C and C++ compiler, so the gcc command also can compile C++ source files. GCC uses the file extension to determine whether a file is C or C++. C files have a lowercase .c extension, whereas C++ files end with .C or .cpp.

Although the gcc command can compile a C++ file, that command does not automatically link with various class libraries that C++ programs typically require. That's why compiling and linking a C++ program by using the g++ command is easy, which, in turn, runs gcc with appropriate options.

Suppose you want to compile the following simple C++ program stored in a file named hello.C (using an uppercase C extension for C++ source files is customary):

```
#include <iostream>

int main()
{
  using namespace std;
  cout << "Hello from Fedora Core!" << endl;
}
```

To compile and link this program into an executable program named hello, use this command:

```
g++ -o hello hello.C
```

The command creates the hello executable, which you can run as follows:

```
./hello
```

The program displays the following output:

```
Hello from Fedora Core!
```

A host of GCC options controls various aspects of compiling C and C++ programs.

## Exploring GCC options

Here is the basic syntax of the `gcc` command:

```
gcc options filenames
```

Each option starts with a hyphen (-) and usually has a long name, such as `-funsigned-char` or `-finline-functions`. Many commonly used options are short, however, such as `-c`, to compile only, and `-g`, to generate debugging information (needed to debug the program by using the GNU debugger, `gdb`).

You can view a summary of all GCC options by typing the following command in a terminal window:

```
man gcc
```

Then you can browse through the commonly used GCC options. Usually, you don't have to provide GCC options explicitly because the default settings are fine for most applications. Table 1-1 lists some of the GCC options you may use.

| Table 1-1 | Commonly Used GCC Options |
|---|---|
| **Option** | **Meaning** |
| `-ansi` | Support ANSI standard C (ISO C89) syntax only. (This option disables some GNU C-specific features, such as the `asm` and `typeof` keywords.) |
| `-c` | Compile and generate object file only. |
| `-DMACRO` | Define the macro with the string `"1"` as its value. |
| `-DMACRO=DEFN` | Define the macro as `DEFN` where `DEFN` is some text string. |
| `-E` | Run only the C preprocessor. |
| `-fallow-single-precision` | Perform all math operations in single precision. |
| `-fpcc-struct-return` | Return all `struct` and `union` values in memory, rather than return in registers. (Returning values this way is less efficient, but at least it's compatible with other compilers.) |
| `-fPIC` | Generate position-independent code (PIC) suitable for use in a shared library. |
| `-freg-struct-return` | When possible, return `struct` and `union` values in registers. |
| `-g` | Generate debugging information. (The GNU debugger can use this information.) |

*(continued)*

**Table 1-1** *(continued)*

| Option | Meaning |
|--------|---------|
| -I *DIRECTORY* | Search the specified directory for files you include by using the #include preprocessor directive. |
| -L *DIRECTORY* | Search the specified directory for libraries. |
| -l *LIBRARY* | Search the specified library when linking. |
| -mcpu=*cputype* | Optimize code for a specific processor. (*cputype* can take many different values — some common ones are i386, i486, i586, and i686.) |
| -o *FILE* | Generate the specified output file (used to designate the name of an executable file). |
| -O0 | Do not optimize. |
| -O or -O1 | Optimize the generated code. |
| -O2 | Optimize even more. |
| -O3 | Perform optimizations beyond those done for -O2. |
| -Os | Optimize for size (to reduce the total amount of code). |
| -pedantic | Generate errors if any non-ANSI standard extensions are used. |
| -pg | Add extra code to the program so that, when run, it generates information the gprof program can use to display timing details for various parts of the program. |
| -shared | Generate a shared object file (typically used to create a shared library). |
| -U*MACRO* | Undefine the specified macro. |
| -v | Display the version number of GCC. |
| -w | Don't generate any warning messages. |
| -Wl,*OPTION* | Pass the *OPTION* string (containing multiple comma-separated options) to the linker. To create a shared library named libXXX.so.1, for example, use the following flag: -Wl,-soname,libXXX.so.1 |

## The GNU make utility

When an application is made up of more than a few source files, compiling and linking the files by manually typing the gcc command can get very tiresome. Also, you do not want to compile every file whenever you change something in a single source file. These situations are where the GNU make utility comes to your rescue.

The make utility works by reading and interpreting a *makefile* — a text file that describes which files are required to build a particular program, as well as how to compile and link the files to build the program. Whenever you change one or more files, `make` determines which files to recompile — and issues the appropriate commands for compiling those files and rebuilding the program.

### Makefile names

By default, GNU `make` looks for a makefile that has one of the following names, in the order shown:

✦ `GNUmakefile`

✦ `makefile`

✦ `Makefile`

In UNIX systems, using `Makefile` as the name of the makefile is customary because it appears near the beginning of directory listings where the upper-case names appear before the lowercase names.

When you download software from the Internet, you usually find a `Makefile`, together with the source files. To build the software, you have only to type **make** at the shell prompt and `make` takes care of all the steps necessary to build the software.

If your makefile doesn't have a standard name (such as `Makefile`), you have to use the `-f` option with `make` to specify the makefile's name. If your makefile is called `myprogram.mak`, for example, you have to run `make` using the following command line:

```
make -f myprogram.mak
```

### The makefile

For a program made up of several source and header files, the makefile specifies the following:

✦ The items that `make` creates — usually the object files and the executable. Using the term *target* to refer to any item that `make` has to create is common.

✦ The files or other actions required to create the target.

✦ Which commands to execute to create each target.

Suppose you have a C++ source file named `form.C` that contains the following preprocessor directive:

```
#include "form.h"  // Include header file
```

The object file `form.o` clearly depends on the source file `form.C` and the header file `form.h`. In addition to these dependencies, you must specify how `make` converts the `form.C` file to the object file `form.o`. Suppose you want `make` to invoke g++ (because the source file is in C++) with these options:

✦ `-c` (compile only)

✦ `-g` (generate debugging information)

✦ `-O2` (optimize some)

In the makefile, you can express these options with the following rule:

```
# This a comment in the makefile
# The following lines indicate how form.o depends
# form.C and form.h and how to create form.o.

form.o: form.C form.h
        g++ -c -g -O2 form.C
```

In this example, the first noncomment line shows `form.o` as the target and `form.C` and `form.h` as the dependent files.

The line following the dependency indicates how to build the target from its dependents. This line must start with a tab.

The benefit of using `make` is that it prevents unnecessary compilations. After all, you can run g++ (or gcc) from a shell script to compile and link all the files that make up your application, but the shell script compiles everything, even if the compilations are unnecessary. GNU `make`, on the other hand, builds a target only if one or more of its dependents have changed since the last time the target was built. `make` verifies this change by examining the time of the last modification of the target and the dependents.

`make` treats the target as the name of a goal to be achieved; the target doesn't have to be a file. You can have a rule such as this one:

```
clean:
        rm -f *.o
```

This rule specifies an abstract target named `clean` that doesn't depend on anything. This dependency statement says that to create the target `clean`, GNU `make` invokes the command `rm -f *.o`, which deletes all files that have the `.o` extension (namely the object files). Thus, the net effect of creating the target named `clean` is to delete the object files.

## Variables (or macros)

In addition to the basic capability of building targets from dependents, GNU `make` includes many nice features that make expressing the dependencies and rules for building a target from its dependents easy for you. If you need to compile a large number of C++ files by using GCC with the same options, for example, typing the options for each file is tedious. You can avoid this repetitive task by defining a variable or macro in `make` as follows:

```
# Define macros for name of compiler
CXX= g++

# Define a macro for the GCC flags
CXXFLAGS= -O2 -g -mcpu=i686

# A rule for building an object file
form.o: form.C form.h
        $(CXX) -c $(CXXFLAGS) form.C
```

In this example, `CXX` and `CXXFLAGS` are `make` variables. (GNU `make` prefers to call them *variables,* but most UNIX `make` utilities call them *macros.*)

To use a variable anywhere in the makefile, start with a dollar sign ($) followed by the variable within parentheses. GNU `make` replaces all occurrences of a variable with its definition; thus it replaces all occurrences of `$(CXXFLAGS)` with the string `-O2 -g -mcpu=i686`.

GNU `make` has several predefined variables that have special meanings. Table 1-2 lists these variables. In addition to the variables listed in Table 1-2, GNU `make` considers all environment variables (such as `PATH` and `HOME`) to be predefined variables as well.

| Table 1-2 | Some Predefined Variables in GNU make |
|-----------|----------------------------------------|
| *Variable* | *Meaning* |
| `$%` | Member name for targets that are archives. If the target is `libDisp.a(image.o)`, for example, `$%` is `image.o`, and `$@` is `libDisp.a`. |
| `$*` | Name of the target file without the extension. |
| `$+` | Names of all dependent files with duplicate dependencies, listed in their order of occurrence. |
| `$<` | The name of the first dependent file. |
| `$?` | Names of all dependent files (with spaces between the names) that are newer than the target. |
| `$@` | Complete name of the target. |

*(continued)*

**Table 1-2** *(continued)*

| Variable | Meaning |
|---|---|
| $^ | Names of all dependent files, with spaces between the names. Duplicates are removed from the dependent filenames. |
| AR | Name of the archive-maintaining program (Default value: ar). |
| ARFLAGS | Flags for the archive-maintaining program (Default value: rv). |
| AS | Name of the assembler program that converts the assembly language to object code (Default value: as). |
| ASFLAGS | Flags for the assembler. |
| CC | Name of the C compiler (Default value: cc). |
| CFLAGS | Flags that are passed to the C compiler. |
| CO | Name of the program that extracts a file from RCS (Default value: co). |
| COFLAGS | Flags for the RCS co program. |
| CPP | Name of the C preprocessor (Default value: $(CC) -E). |
| CPPFLAGS | Flags for the C preprocessor. |
| CXX | Name of the C++ compiler (Default value: g++). |
| CXXFLAGS | Flags that are passed to the C++ compiler. |
| FC | Name of the FORTRAN compiler (Default value: f77). |
| FFLAGS | Flags for the FORTRAN compiler. |
| LDFLAGS | Flags for the compiler when it is supposed to invoke the linker ld. |
| RM | Name of the command to delete a file (Default value: rm -f). |

### A sample makefile

You can write a makefile easily if you use the predefined variables of GNU make and its built-in rules. Consider, for example, a makefile that creates the executable xdraw from three C source files (xdraw.c, xviewobj.c, and shapes.c) and two header files (xdraw.h and shapes.h). Assume that each source file includes one of the header files. Given these facts, here is what a sample makefile may look like:

```
###############################################################
# Sample makefile
# Comments start with '#'
#
###############################################################

# Use standard variables to define compile and link flags

CFLAGS= -g -02
# Define the target "all"
```

```
all: xdraw

OBJS=xdraw.o xviewobj.o shapes.o

xdraw: $(OBJS)

# Object files
xdraw.o: Makefile xdraw.c xdraw.h

xviewobj.o: Makefile xviewobj.c xdraw.h

shapes.o: Makefile shapes.c shapes.h
```

This makefile relies on GNU make's implicit rules. The conversion of .c files to .o files uses the built-in rule. Defining the variable CFLAGS passes the flags to the C compiler.

The target named all is defined as the first target for a reason — if you run GNU make without specifying any targets in the command line (see the make syntax described in the following section), the command builds the first target it finds in the makefile. By defining the first target all as xdraw, you can ensure that make builds this executable file, even if you do not explicitly specify it as a target. UNIX programmers traditionally use all as the name of the first target, but the target's name is immaterial; what matters is that it is the first target in the makefile.

### How to run make

Typically, you run make by simply typing the following command at the shell prompt:

```
make
```

When run this way, GNU make looks for a file named GNUmakefile, makefile, or Makefile — in that order. If make finds one of these makefiles, it builds the first target specified in that makefile. However, if make does not find an appropriate makefile, it displays the following error message and then exits:

```
make: *** No targets specified and no makefile found.  Stop.
```

If your makefile happens to have a different name from the default names, you have to use the -f option to specify the makefile. The syntax of the make command with this option looks like this:

```
make -f filename
```

where *filename* is the name of the makefile.

Even when you have a makefile with a default name such as `Makefile`, you may want to build a specific target out of several targets defined in the makefile. In that case, you have to use the following syntax when you run `make`:

```
make target
```

For example, if the makefile contains the target named `clean`, you can build that target with this command:

```
make clean
```

Another special syntax overrides the value of a `make` variable. For example, GNU `make` uses the `CFLAGS` variable to hold the flags used when compiling C files. You can override the value of this variable when you invoke `make`. Here is an example of how you can define `CFLAGS` as the option `-g -02`:

```
make CFLAGS="-g -02"
```

In addition to these options, GNU `make` accepts several other command-line options. Table 1-3 lists the GNU `make` options.

| **Table 1-3** | **Options for GNU make** |
|---|---|
| *Option* | *Meaning* |
| `-b` | Ignore but accept for compatibility with other versions of `make`. |
| `-C DIR` | Change to the specified directory before reading the makefile. |
| `-d` | Print debugging information. |
| `-e` | Allow environment variables to override definitions of similarly named variables in the makefile. |
| `-f FILE` | Read *FILE* as the makefile. |
| `-h` | Display the list of `make` options. |
| `-i` | Ignore all errors in commands executed when building a target. |
| `-I DIR` | Search specified directory for included makefiles (the capability to include a file in a makefile is unique to GNU `make`). |
| `-j NUM` | Specify the number of commands that `make` can run simultaneously. |
| `-k` | Continue to build unrelated targets, even if an error occurs when building one of the targets. |
| `-l LOAD` | Don't start a new job if load average is at least *LOAD* (a floating-point number). |
| `-m` | Ignore but accept for compatibility with other versions of `make`. |
| `-n` | Print the commands to execute, but do not execute them. |
| `-o FILE` | Do not rebuild the file named *FILE*, even if it is older than its dependents. |

| Option | Meaning |
|--------|---------|
| -p | Display the make database of variables and implicit rules. |
| -q | Don't run anything, but return 0 (zero) if all targets are up to date; return 1 if anything needs updating; and 2 if an error occurs. |
| -r | Get rid of all built-in rules. |
| -R | Get rid of all built-in variables and rules. |
| -s | Work silently (without displaying the commands as they execute). |
| -t | Change the timestamp of the files. |
| -v | Display the version number of make and a copyright notice. |
| -w | Display the name of the working directory before and after processing the makefile. |
| -W FILE | Assume that the specified file has been modified (used with -n to see what happens if you modify that file). |

## The GNU debugger

Although make automates the process of building a program, that part of programming is the least of your worries when a program doesn't work correctly or when a program suddenly quits with an error message. You need a debugger to find the cause of program errors. Fedora Core includes gdb — the versatile GNU debugger with a command-line interface.

Like any debugger, gdb lets you perform typical debugging tasks, such as the following:

+ Set the breakpoint so the program stops at a specified line.
+ Watch the values of variables in the program.
+ Step through the program one line at a time.
+ Change variables in an attempt to fix errors.

The gdb debugger can debug C and C++ programs.

### Preparing to debug a program

If you want to debug a program by using gdb, you have to ensure that the compiler generates and places debugging information in the executable. The debugging information contains the names of variables in your program and the mapping of addresses in the executable file to lines of code in the source file. gdb needs this information to perform its functions, such as stopping after executing a specified line of source code.

To ensure that the executable is properly prepared for debugging, use the -g option with GCC. You can do this task by defining the variable CFLAGS in the makefile as

```
CFLAGS= -g
```

### Running gdb

The most common way to debug a program is to run gdb by using the following command:

```
gdb progname
```

*progname* is the name of the program's executable file. After it runs, gdb displays the following message and prompts you for a command:

```
GNU gdb Red Hat Linux (6.0post-0.20031117.7rh)
Copyright 2003 Free Software Foundation, Inc.
GDB is free software, covered by the GNU General Public License, and you are
welcome to change it and/or distribute copies of it under certain conditions.
Type "show copying" to see the conditions.
There is absolutely no warranty for GDB.  Type "show warranty" for details.
This GDB was configured as "i386-redhat-linux-gnu".
(gdb)
```

You can type gdb commands at the (gdb) prompt. One useful command is help — it displays a list of commands as the next listing shows:

```
(gdb) help
List of classes of commands:

aliases -- Aliases of other commands
breakpoints -- Making program stop at certain points
data -- Examining data
files -- Specifying and examining files
internals -- Maintenance commands
obscure -- Obscure features
running -- Running the program
stack -- Examining the stack
status -- Status inquiries
support -- Support facilities
tracepoints -- Tracing of program execution without stopping the program
user-defined -- User-defined commands

Type "help" followed by a class name for a list of commands in that class.
Type "help" followed by command name for full documentation.
Command name abbreviations are allowed if unambiguous.
(gdb)
```

To quit gdb, type **q** and then press Enter.

gdb has a large number of commands, but you need only a few to find the cause of an error quickly. Table 1-4 lists the commonly used gdb commands.

| Table 1-4 | Commonly Used gdb Commands |
| --- | --- |
| *This Command* | *Does the Following* |
| break *NUM* | Sets a *breakpoint* at the specified line number (the debugger stops at breakpoints). |
| bt | Displays a trace of all stack frames. (This command shows you the sequence of function calls so far.) |
| clear *FILENAME:NUM* | Deletes the breakpoint at a specific line in a source file. For example, clear xdraw.c:8 clears the breakpoint at line 8 of file xdraw.c. |
| continue | Continues running the program being debugged. (Use this command after the program stops due to a signal or breakpoint.) |
| display *EXPR* | Displays the value of expression (consisting of variables defined in the program) each time the program stops. |
| file *FILE* | Loads a specified executable file for debugging. |
| help *NAME* | Displays help on the command named *NAME*. |
| info break | Displays a list of current breakpoints, including information on how many times each breakpoint is reached. |
| info files | Displays detailed information about the file being debugged. |
| info func | Displays all function names. |
| info local | Displays information about local variables of the current function. |
| info prog | Displays the execution status of the program being debugged. |
| info var | Displays all global and static variable names. |
| kill | Ends the program you're debugging. |
| list | Lists a section of the source code. |
| make | Runs the make utility to rebuild the executable without leaving gdb. |
| next | Advances one line of source code in the current function without stepping into other functions. |
| print EXPR | Shows the value of the expression *EXPR*. |
| quit | Quits gdb. |
| run | Starts running the currently loaded executable. |
| set variable *VAR=VALUE* | Sets the value of the variable *VAR* to *VALUE*. |
| shell *CMD* | Executes a UNIX command *CMD* without leaving gdb. |
| step | Advances one line in the current function, stepping into other functions, if any. |

*(continued)*

**Table 1-4** *(continued)*

| This Command | Does the Following |
|---|---|
| watch *VAR* | Shows the value of the variable named *VAR* whenever the value changes. |
| where | Displays the call sequence. Use this command to locate where your program died. |
| x/*F ADDR* | Examines the contents of the memory location at address *ADDR* in the format specified by the letter *F*, which can be o (octal); x (hex); d (decimal); u (unsigned decimal); t (binary); f (float); a (address); i (instruction); c (char); or s (string). You can append a letter indicating the size of data type to the format letter. Size letters are b (byte); h (halfword, 2 bytes), w (word, 4 bytes); and g (giant, 8 bytes). Typically, *ADDR* is the name of a variable or pointer. |

### Finding bugs by using gdb

To understand how you can find bugs by using gdb, you need to see an example. The procedure is easiest to show with a simple example, so I start with a rather contrived program that contains a typical bug.

The following is the contrived program, which I store in the file dbgtst.c:

```
#include <stdio.h>

static char buf[256];
void read_input(char *s);

int main(void)
{
  char *input = NULL; /* Just a pointer, no storage for
            string */

  read_input(input);

/* Process command. */
  printf("You typed: %s\n", input);

/* ... */
  return 0;
}

void read_input(char *s)
{
  printf("Command: ");
  gets(s);
}
```

This program's `main` function calls the `read_input` function to get a line of input from the user. The `read_input` function expects a character array in which it returns what the user types. In this example, however, `main` calls `read_input` with an uninitialized pointer — that's the bug in this simple program.

Build the program by using `gcc` with the `-g` option:

```
gcc -g -o dbgtst dbgtst.c
```

Ignore the warning message about the `gets` function being dangerous; I'm trying to use the shortcoming of that function to show how you can use `gdb` to track down errors.

To see the problem with this program, run it and type **test** at the `Command:` prompt:

```
./dbgtst
Command: test
Segmentation fault
```

The program dies after displaying the `Segmentation fault` message. For such a small program as this one, you can probably find the cause by examining the source code. In a real-world application, however, you may not immediately know what causes the error. That's when you have to use `gdb` to find the cause of the problem.

To use `gdb` to locate a bug, follow these steps:

1. **Load the program under** `gdb`. **To load a program named** `dbgtst` **in** `gdb`, **type the following:**

    ```
    gdb dbgtst
    ```

2. **Start executing the program under** `gdb` **by typing the** `run` **command. When the program prompts for input, type some input text.**

    The program fails as it did previously. Here's what happens with the `dbgtst` program:

    ```
    (gdb) run
    Starting program: /home/naba/rhls4e/dbgtst
    Command: test

    Program received signal SIGSEGV, Segmentation fault.
    0x00b6a4f6 in gets () from /lib/tls/libc.so.6
    (gdb)
    ```

3. **Use the** `where` **command to determine where the program died.**

   For the `dbgtst` program, this command yields this output:

   ```
   (gdb) where
   #0  0x00b6a4f6 in gets () from /lib/tls/libc.so.6
   #1  0x080483dc in read_input (s=0x0) at dbgtst.c:22
   #2  0x0804839e in main () at dbgtst.c:10
   (gdb)
   ```

   The output shows the sequence of function calls. Function call #0 — the most recent one — is to a C library function, `gets`. The `gets` call originates in the `read_input` function (at line 22 of the file `dbgtst.c`), which in turn is called from the `main` function at line 10 of the `dbgtst.c` file.

4. **Use the** `list` **command to inspect the lines of suspect source code.**

   In `dbgtst`, you may start with line 22 of `dbgtst.c` file, as follows:

   ```
   (gdb) list dbgtst.c:22
   17        }
   18
   19        void read_input(char *s)
   20        {
   21          printf("Command: ");
   22          gets(s);
   23        }
   24
   (gdb)
   ```

   After looking at this listing, you can tell that the problem may be the way `read_input` is called. Then you list the lines around line 10 in `dbgtst.c` (where the `read_input` call originates):

   ```
   (gdb) list dbgtst.c:10
   5
   6         int main(void)
   7         {
   8          char *input = NULL; /* Just a pointer, no
       storage for string */
   9
   10         read_input(input);
   11
   12       /* Process command. */
   13         printf("You typed: %s\n", input);
   14
   (gdb)
   ```

   At this point, you can narrow the problem to the variable named `input`. That variable is an array, not a `NULL` (which means zero) pointer.

## Fixing bugs in gdb

Sometimes you can fix a bug directly in `gdb`. For the example program in the preceding section, you can try this fix immediately after the program dies after displaying an error message. Because the example is contrived, I have an extra buffer named buf defined in the dbgtst program, as follows:

```
static char buf[256];
```

I can fix the problem of the uninitialized pointer by setting the variable input to buf. The following session with gdb corrects the problem of the uninitialized pointer (this example picks up immediately after the program runs and dies, due to the segmentation fault):

```
(gdb) file dbgtst
A program is being debugged already.  Kill it? (y or n) y

Load new symbol table from "dbgtst"? (y or n) y
Reading symbols from dbgtst...
done.
(gdb) list
1       #include <stdio.h>
2
3       static char buf[256];
4       void read_input(char *s);
5
6       int main(void)
7       {
8         char *input = NULL; /* Just a pointer, no storage
           for string */
9
10        read_input(input);
(gdb) break 9
Breakpoint 1 at 0x8048393: file dbgtst.c, line 9.
(gdb) run
Starting program: /home/naba/code/dbgtst

Breakpoint 1, main () at dbgtst.c:10
10        read_input(input);
(gdb) set var input=buf
(gdb) cont
Continuing.
Command: test
You typed: test

Program exited normally.
(gdb)q
```

As the previous listing shows, if I stop the program just before read_input is called and set the variable named input to buf (which is a valid array of characters), the rest of the program runs fine.

After finding a fix that works in gdb, you can make the necessary changes to the source files and make the fix permanent.

# Understanding the Implications of GNU Licenses

You have to pay a price for the bounty of Linux — to protect its developers and users, Linux is distributed under the GNU GPL (General Public License), which stipulates the distribution of the source code.

The GPL does not mean, however, that you cannot write commercial software for Linux that you want to distribute (either for free or for a price) in binary form only. You can follow all the rules and still sell your Linux applications in binary form.

When writing applications for Linux, be aware of two licenses:

✦ The GNU General Public License (GPL), which governs many Linux programs, including the Linux kernel and GCC

✦ The GNU Library General Public License (LGPL), which covers many Linux libraries

The following sections provide an overview of these licenses and some suggestions on how to meet their requirements. Because I am not a lawyer, however, don't take anything in this book as legal advice. The full text for these licenses is in text files on your Fedora Core system; show these licenses to your legal counsel for a full interpretation and an assessment of applicability to your business.

## The GNU General Public License

The text of the GNU General Public License (GPL) is in a file named `COPYING` in various directories in your Fedora Core system. For example, type the following commands to read the GPL:

```
cd /usr/share/doc/gdb*
more COPYING
```

The GPL has nothing to do with whether you charge for the software or distribute it for free; its thrust is to keep the software free for all users. GPL requires that the software is distributed in source-code form and by stipulating that any user can copy and distribute the software in source-code form to anyone else. In addition, everyone is reminded that the software comes with absolutely no warranty.

The software that the GPL covers is not in the public domain. Software covered by GPL is always copyrighted and the GPL spells out the restrictions on the software's copying and distribution. From a user's point of view, of course, GPL's restrictions are not really restrictions; the restrictions are really benefits because the user is guaranteed access to the source code.

If your application uses parts of any software the GPL covers, your application is considered a *derived work,* which means that your application is also covered by the GPL, and you must distribute the source code to your application.

Although the GPL covers the Linux kernel, the GPL does not cover your applications that use the kernel services through system calls. Those applications are considered normal use of the kernel.

If you plan to distribute your application in binary form (as most commercial software is distributed), you must make sure your application does not use any parts of any software the GPL covers. Your application may end up using parts of other software when it calls functions in a library. Most libraries, however, are covered by a different GNU license, which I describe in the next section.

You have to watch out for only a few library and utility programs the GPL covers. The GNU dbm (gdbm) database library is one of the prominent libraries GPL covers. The GNU bison parser-generator tool is another utility the GPL covers. If you allow bison to generate code, the GPL covers that code.

Other alternatives for the GNU dbm and GNU bison are not covered by GPL. For a database library, you can use the Berkeley database library db in place of gdbm. For a parser-generator, you may use yacc instead of bison.

## The GNU Library General Public License

The text of the GNU Library General Public License (LGPL) is in a file named COPYING.LIB. If you have the kernel source installed, a copy of COPYING.LIB file is in one of the source directories. To locate a copy of the COPYING.LIB file on your Fedora Core system, type the following command in a terminal window:

```
find /usr/share/doc -name "COPYING*" -print
```

This command lists all occurrences of COPYING and COPYING.LIB in your system. The COPYING file contains the GPL, whereas COPYING.LIB has the LGPL.

The LGPL is intended to allow use of libraries in your applications, even if you do not distribute source code for your application. The LGPL stipulates, however, that users must have access to the source code of the library you use and that users can make use of modified versions of those libraries.

The LGPL covers most Linux libraries, including the C library (libc.a). Thus, when you build your application on Fedora Core by using the GCC compiler, your application links with code from one or more libraries the LGPL covers. If you want to distribute your application in binary form only, you need to pay attention to LGPL.

One way to meet the intent of the LGPL is to provide the object code for your application and a makefile that relinks your object files with any updated Linux libraries the LGPL covers.

A better way to satisfy the LGPL is to use *dynamic linking,* in which your application and the library are separate entities, even though your application calls functions in the library when it runs. With dynamic linking, users immediately get the benefit of any updates to the libraries without ever having to relink the application.

# Chapter 2: Programming in C

## In This Chapter

↦ Learning the basics of C programming

↦ Learning the features of the C programming language

↦ Taking stock of the standard C library

↦ Using shared libraries in Linux applications

The composition of the C programming language — a sparse core with a large support library — makes it an ideal language for developing software. The core offers a good selection of data types and control structures while all additional tasks, including input and output (I/O), math computations, and access to peripheral devices are relegated to a library of functions. Basically, C allows you to get to anything you want in a system. That means you can write anything from device drivers to graphical applications in C. In this chapter, I introduce you to C programming. I also briefly explain the importance of shared libraries and how to create one in Fedora Core using the C programming language.

## The Structure of a C Program

A typical C program is organized into one or more source files, or modules (see Figure 2-1). Each file has a similar structure with comments, preprocessor directives, declarations of variables and functions, and their definitions. You usually place each group of related variables and functions in a single source file.

Some files are simply a set of declarations that are used in other files through the #include directive of the C preprocessor. These files are usually referred to as *header files* and have names ending with the .h extension. In Figure 2-1, the file shapes.h is a header file that declares common data structures and functions for the program. Another file, shapes.c, defines the functions. A third file, shapetest.c, implements the main function — the execution of a C program begins in this function. These files with names ending in .c are the source files where you define the functions needed by your program. Although Figure 2-1 shows only one function in each source file, in typical programs many functions are in a source file.

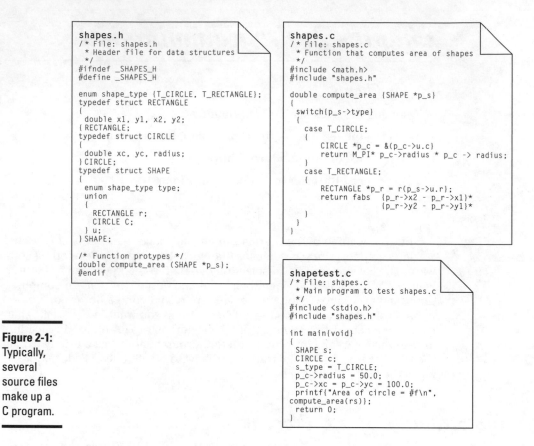

```
shapes.h
/* File: shapes.h
 * Header file for data structures
 */
#ifndef _SHAPES_H
#define _SHAPES_H

enum shape_type {T_CIRCLE, T_RECTANGLE};
typedef struct RECTANGLE
{
  double x1, y1, x2, y2;
{ RECTANGLE;
typedef struct CIRCLE
{
  double xc, yc, radius;
} CIRCLE;
typedef struct SHAPE
{
  enum shape_type type;
  union
  {
    RECTANGLE r;
    CIRCLE C;
  } u;
} SHAPE;

/* Function protypes */
double compute_area (SHAPE *p_s};
#endif
```

```
shapes.c
/* File: shapes.c
 * Function that computes area of shapes
 */
#include <math.h>
#include "shapes.h"

double compute_area {SHAPE *p_s}
{
  switch(p_s->type}
  {
    case T_CIRCLE:
    {
        CIRCLE *p_c = &(p_c->u.c}
        return M_PI* p_c->radius * p_c -> radius;
    }
    case T_RECTANGLE:
    {
        RECTANGLE *p_r = r(p_s->u.r};
        return fabs   {p_r->x2 - p_r->x1}*
                      {p_r->y2 - p_r->y1}*
    }
  }
}
```

```
shapetest.c
/* File: shapes.c
 * Main program to test shapes.c
 */
#include <stdio.h>
#include "shapes.h"

int main{void}
{
  SHAPE s;
  CIRCLE c;
  s_type = T_CIRCLE;
  p_c->radius = 50.0;
  p_c->xc = p_c->yc = 100.0;
  printf("Area of circle = #f\n",
compute_area(rs)};
  return 0;
}
```

**Figure 2-1:**
Typically,
several
source files
make up a
C program.

To create an executable program, you must compile and link the source files. The exact steps for building programs from C source files depend on the compiler and the operating system. For example, in Fedora Core, you can compile and link the files shown in Figure 2-1 with the following command:

```
gcc -o shapetest shapetest.c shapes.c
```

This command creates an executable file named `shapetest`. You can then run that file with the command

```
./shapetest
```

Here is the output the program displays:

```
Area of circle = 7853.981634
```

## Declaration versus definition

A *declaration* determines how the program interprets a symbol. A *definition*, on the other hand, actually creates a variable or a function. Definitions cause the compiler to set aside storage for data or code, but declarations do not. For example,

```
Int x, y, z;
```

is a definition of three distinct integer variables, but

```
Extern int x, y, z;
```

is a declaration, indicating that the three integer variables are defined in another source file.

---

Within each source file, the components of the program are laid out in a standard manner. As the files illustrated in Figure 2-1 show, the typical components of a C source file follow a certain order if you scroll down through them on-screen:

*1.* The file starts with some comments that describe the purpose of the module and provide some other pertinent information, such as the name of the author and revision dates. In C, comments start with /* and end with */.

*2.* Commands for the preprocessor, known as *preprocessor directives,* follow the comments. The first few directives typically are for including header files and defining constants.

*3.* Declarations of variables and functions that are visible throughout the file come next. In other words, the names of these variables and functions may be used in any of the functions in this file. Here, you also define variables needed within the file.

*4.* The rest of the file includes definitions of functions. Inside a function's body, you can define variables that are local to the function and that exist only while the function's code is being executed.

## Preprocessor Directives

*Preprocessing* refers to the first step in translating or compiling a C file into machine instructions. The preprocessor processes the source file and acts on certain commands (called *preprocessor directives*) embedded in the program. These directives begin with the hash mark (#) followed by a keyword. Usually the compiler automatically invokes the preprocessor before beginning compilation, but most compilers give you the option of invoking the preprocessor alone. You can utilize three major capabilities of the preprocessor to make your programs modular, more readable, and easier to customize:

✦ You can use the #include directive to insert the contents of a file into your program. With this directive, you can place common declarations in one location and use them in all source files through file inclusion. The result is a reduced risk of mismatches between declarations of variables and functions in separate program modules.

✦ Through the #define directive, you can define macros that enable you to replace one string with another. You can use the #define directive to give meaningful names to numeric constants, thus improving the readability of your source files.

✦ With directives such as #if, #ifdef, #else, and #endif, you can compile only selected portions of your program. You can use this feature to write source files with code for two or more systems, but compile only those parts that apply to the computer system on which you compile the program. With this strategy, you can maintain multiple versions of a program using a single set of source files.

## Including files

You can write modular programs by exploiting the #include directive. This directive is possible because the C preprocessor enables you to keep commonly used declarations in a single file that you can insert in other source files as needed. ANSI C supports three forms of the #include directive. As a C programmer, you need to be familiar with the first two forms:

```
#include <stdio.h>
#include "shapes.h"
```

You use the first form of #include to read the contents of a file — in this case, the standard C header file stdio.h from the default location where all the header files reside. Put the filename within double quotes when the file (for example, shapes.h) is in the current directory. The exact conventions for locating the included files depend on the compiler.

## Defining macros

A *macro* is essentially a short name for a reusable block of C code. The code can be as simple as a numerical constant or as complicated as many lines of detailed C code. The idea is that after you define a macro, you can use that macro wherever you want to use that code in your program. When the source file is preprocessed, every occurrence of a macro's name is replaced with its definition.

A common use of macros is to define a symbolic name for a numerical constant and then use the symbol instead of the numbers in your program. A macro improves the readability of the source code; with a descriptive name, you aren't left guessing why a particular number is being used in the program. You can define such macros in a straightforward manner using the #define directive. Here are some examples:

```
#define PI          3.14159
#define GRAV_ACC    9.80665
#define BUFSIZE     512
```

After these symbols are defined, you can use PI, GRAV_ACC, and BUFSIZE instead of the numerical constants throughout the source file.

Macros, however, can do much more than simply replace a symbol for a constant or some block of code. A macro can accept a parameter and replace each occurrence of that parameter with the provided value when the macro is used in a program. Thus, the code that results from the expansion of a macro can change depending on the parameter you use when running the macro. For example, here is a macro that accepts a parameter and expands to an expression designed to calculate the square of the parameter:

```
#define square(x) ((x)*(x))
```

If you use square(z) in your program, it becomes ((z)*(z)) after the source file is preprocessed. In effect, this macro is equivalent to a function that computes the square of its arguments — except you don't call a function. Instead, the expression generated by the macro is placed directly in the source file.

### Conditional directives

You can use the conditional directives, such as #if, #ifdef, #ifndef, #else, #elif, and #endif, to control which parts of a source file are compiled and under what conditions. With this feature, you maintain a single set of source files that can be selectively compiled with different compilers and in different environments. (Another common use is to insert printf statements for debugging that are compiled only if a symbol named DEBUG is defined.) Conditional directives start with #if, #ifdef, or #ifndef — and may be followed by any number of #elif directives (or by none at all). Next comes an optional #else, followed by an #endif directive that marks the end of that conditional block. Here are some common ways of using conditional directives.

To include a header file only once, you can use the following:

```
#ifndef _ _PROJECT_H
#define _ _PROJECT_H
/*  Declarations to be included once */
/* ... */

#endif
```

The following prints a diagnostic message during debugging (when the symbol DEBUG is defined):

```
#ifdef DEBUG
    printf("In read_file: bytes_read = %d\n", bytes_read);
#endif
```

The following example shows how you can include a different header file depending on the type of system for which the program is being compiled. To selectively include a header file, you can use the following:

```
#if CPU_TYPE == I386
    #include <i386\sysdef.h>
#elif CPU_TYPE == M68K
    #include <m68k\sysdef.h>
#else
    #error Unknown CPU type.
#endif
```

The #error directive is used to display error messages during preprocessing.

### Other directives

Several other preprocessor directives perform miscellaneous tasks. For example, you can use the #undef directive to remove the current definition of a symbol. The #pragma directive is another special purpose directive that you can use to convey information to the C compiler. You can use pragma to access the special features of a compiler — and those vary from one compiler to another.

C compilers provide several predefined macros (see Table 2-1). Of these, the macros, _ _FILE_ _ and _ _LINE_ _, respectively refer to the current source filename and the current line number being processed. You can use the #line directive to change these. For example, to set _ _FILE_ _ to "file_io.c" and _ _LINE_ _ to 100, you say:

```
#line 100 "file_io.c"
```

| Table 2-1 | Predefined Macros in C |
|-----------|------------------------|
| *Macro* | *Definition* |
| _ _DATE_ _ | This string contains the date when you invoke the C compiler. It is of the form MMM DD YYYY (for example, Oct 26 2002). |
| _ _FILE_ _ | This macro expands to a string containing the name of the source file. |
| _ _LINE_ _ | This macro is a decimal integer with a value equal to the line number within the current source file. |

| Macro | Definition |
|---|---|
| _ _STDC_ _ | This macro expands to the decimal constant 1 to indicate that the C compiler conforms to the ANSI standard. |
| _ _TIME_ _ | This string displays the time when you started compiling the source file. It is of the form HH:MM:SS (for example, 21:59:45). |

# Declaration and Definition of Variables

In C, you must either define or declare all variables and functions before you use them. The definition of a variable specifies three things:

✦ Its *visibility,* which indicates exactly where the variable can be used. (Is it defined for all files in a program, the current file, or only in a function?)

✦ Its *lifetime,* which determines whether the variable exists temporarily (for example, a local variable in a function) or permanently (as long as the program is running).

✦ Its *type* (and, in some cases, its *initial value*). For example, an integer variable x initialized to 1 is defined this way:

```
int  x = 1;
```

If you're using a variable defined in another source file, you declare the variable with an extern keyword, like this:

```
extern int message_count;
```

You must define this variable without the extern qualifier in at least one source file. When the program is built, the linker resolves all references to the message_count variable and ensures that they all use the same variable.

## Basic data types

C has four basic data types: char and int are for storing characters and integers, and float and double are for floating-point numbers. You can define variables for these basic data types in a straightforward manner:

```
char    c;
int     i, j, bufsize;
float   volts;
double  mean, variance;
```

You can expand the basic data types into a much larger set by using the long, short, and unsigned qualifiers as prefixes. The long and short qualifiers are size modifiers. For example, a long int is at least 4 bytes long, whereas a `short int` has a minimum size of only 2 bytes. The size of an `int` is system dependent, but it definitely is at least as large as a `short`.

The `unsigned` qualifier is reserved for `int` and `char` types only. Normally, each one of these types holds negative as well as positive values. This qualifier is the default signed form of these data types. You can use the `unsigned` qualifier when you want the variable to hold positive values only. Here are some examples of using the `short`, `long`, and `unsigned` qualifiers:

```
unsigned char mode_select, printer_status;
short      record_number; /* Same as "short int"     */
long       offset;     /* Same as "long int"       */
unsigned    i, j, msg_id; /* Same as "unsigned int"     */
unsigned short width, height; /* Same as "unsigned short int" */
unsigned long file_pos;    /* Same as "unsigned long int" */
long double  result;
```

When the `short`, `long`, and `unsigned` qualifiers are used with `int` types, you can drop the `int` from the declaration. You can also extend the `double` data type with a `long` prefix.

GCC comes with the predefined header files — `limits.h` and `float.h` — that define exact sizes of the various data types — and ranges of values — in those header files. You can examine these files in the `/usr/include` directory of your Fedora Core system to determine the sizes of the basic data types that the GCC compiler supports.

## Enumerations

You can use the `enum` data type to define your own enumerated list — a fixed set of named integer constants. For example, you can declare a Boolean data type named `BOOLEAN` by using `enum` as follows:

```
/* Declare an enumerated type named BOOLEAN */
    enum BOOLEAN {false = 0, true = 1, stop = 0, go = 1,
                    off = 0, on = 1};
```

```
/* Define a BOOLEAN called "status" and initialize it */
    enum BOOLEAN status = stop;
```

This example first declares `BOOLEAN` to be an enumerated type. The list within the braces shows the enumeration constants that are valid values of an `enum BOOLEAN` variable. You can initialize each constant to a value of your choice, and several constants can use the same value. In this example, the constants `false`, `stop`, and `off` are set to 0, while `true`, `go`, and `on` are initialized to 1. The example then defines an enumerated `BOOLEAN` variable named `status`, which is initially set to the constant `stop`.

# Structures, Unions, and Bit Fields

Use struct to group related data items together, and refer to that group by a name. For example, the declaration of a structure to hold variables of a queue may look like this:

```
/* Declare a structure */
struct QUEUE
{
    int   count;     /* Number of items in queue     */
    int   front;     /* Index of first item in queue */
    int   rear;      /* Index of last item in queue  */
    int   elemsize;  /* Size of each element of data */
    int   maxsize;   /* Maximum capacity of queue    */
    char *data;      /* Pointer to queued data       */
};

/* Define two queues */
struct QUEUE rcv_q, xmit_q;
```

The elements inside the QUEUE structure are called its *members*. You can access these members by using the member selection operator (.). For instance, rcv_q.count refers to the count member of the rcv_q structure.

A union is like a struct, but instead of grouping related data items together (as struct does), a union allocates storage for several data items starting at the same location. Thus, all members of a union share the same storage location. You can use unions to view the same data item in different ways. Suppose you are using a compiler that supports 4-byte long numbers, and you want to access the 4 individual bytes of a single long integer. Here is a union that lets you accomplish just that:

```
union
{
    long  file_type;
    char  bytes[4];
} header_id;
```

With this definition, header_id.file_type refers to the long integer, while header_id.bytes[0] is the first byte of that long integer.

## Arrays

An *array* is a collection of one or more identical data items. You can declare arrays of any type of data, including structures and types defined by typedef. For example, to define an array of 80 characters, you write the following:

```
char    string[80];
```

The characters in the string array occupy successive storage locations, beginning with location 0. Thus in this example, string[0] refers to the first character in this array, while string[79] refers to the last one. You can define arrays of other data types and structures similarly:

```
struct Customer          /* Declare a structure     */
{
  int id;
  char first_name[40];
  char last_name[40];
};

struct Customer customers[100]; /* Define array of structures */
int        index[64];   /* An array of 64 integers  */
```

You can also define multidimensional arrays. For example, to represent an 80-column-by-25-line text-display screen, you can use a two-dimensional array as follows:

```
unsigned char text_screen[25][80];
```

Each item of text_screen is an array of 80 unsigned chars, and text_screen contains 25 such arrays. In other words, the two-dimensional array is stored by laying out one row after another in memory. You can use expressions such as text_screen[0][0] to refer to the first character in the first row and text_screen[24][79] to refer to the last character of the last row of the display screen. Higher-dimensional arrays are defined similarly:

```
float coords[3][2][5];
```

This example defines coords as a three-dimensional array of three data items: Each item is an array of two arrays, each of which, in turn, is an array of five float variables. Thus, you interpret a multidimensional array as an "array of arrays."

## Pointers

A *pointer* is a variable that can hold the address of any type of data except a bit field. For example, if p_i is a pointer to an integer variable, you can define and use it as follows:

```
/* Define an int pointer and an integer */
   int *p_i, count;

/* Set pointer to the address of the integer "count" */
   p_i = &count;
```

In this case, the compiler allocates storage for an int variable count and a pointer to an integer p_i. The number of bytes necessary to represent a pointer depends on the underlying system's addressing scheme.

Don't use a pointer until it contains the address of a valid object.

The example shows p_i being initialized to the address of the integer variable count using the & operator, which provides the address of a variable. After p_i is initialized, you can refer to the value of count with the expression *p_i, which is read as "the contents of the object with its address in p_i."

Pointers are useful in many situations; an important one is the dynamic allocation of memory. The standard C libraries include functions such as malloc and calloc, which you can call to allocate storage for arrays of objects. After allocating memory, these functions return the starting address of the block of memory. Because this address is the only way to reach that memory, you must store it in a variable capable of holding an address — a pointer.

Suppose you allocated memory for an array of 50 integers and saved the returned address in p_i. Now you can treat this block of memory as an array of 50 integers with the name p_i. Thus, you can refer to the last element in the array as p_i[49], which is equivalent to *(p_i+49). Similarly, C treats the name of an array as a pointer to the first element of the array. The difference between the name of an array and a pointer variable is that the name of the array is a constant without any explicit storage necessary to hold the address of the array's first element. The pointer, on the other hand, is an actual storage location capable of holding the address of any data.

In addition to storing the address of dynamically allocated memory, pointers are also commonly used as arguments to functions. When a C function is called, all of its arguments are passed by value — that is, the function gets a copy of each argument, not the original variables appearing in the argument list of the function call. Thus, a C function cannot alter the value of its arguments. Pointers provide a way out. To change the value of a variable in a function, you can pass a pointer to the variable; the function can alter the value through the pointer.

## Type definitions

Through the typedef keyword, C provides you with a convenient way of assigning a new name to an existing data type. You can use the typedef facility to give meaningful names to data types used in a particular application. For example, a graphics application might declare a data type named Point as follows:

```
/* Declare a Point data type */
    typedef struct Point
    {
        short x;
        short y;
```

```
    } Point;

/* Declare PointPtr to be pointer to Point types */
    typedef Point *P_PointPtr;

/* Define some instances of these types
 * and initialize them */
    Point     a = {0, 0};
    PointPtr  p_a = &a;
```

As shown by the Point and PointPtr types, you can use typedef to declare complex data types conveniently.

## Type qualifiers: const and volatile

Two type qualifiers, const and volatile, work this way in a declaration:

✦ The const qualifier in a declaration tells the compiler that the program must not modify the particular data object. The compiler must not generate code that might alter the contents of the location where that data item is stored.

✦ The volatile qualifier specifies that factors beyond the program's control may change the value of a variable.

You can use both const and volatile keywords on a single data item to mean that, although your program must not modify the item, some other process may alter it. The const and volatile keywords always qualify the item that immediately follows (to the right). The information provided by the const and the volatile qualifiers is supposed to help the compiler optimize the code it generates. For example, suppose the variable block_size is declared and initialized as follows:

```
const int block_size = 512;
```

In this case, the compiler does not need to generate code to load the value of block_size from memory. Instead, it can use the value 512 wherever your program uses block_size. Now suppose you add volatile to the declaration and change the declaration to

```
volatile const int block_size = 512;
```

This declaration says that some external process can change the contents of block_size. Therefore, the compiler cannot optimize away any reference to block_size. You may need to use such declarations when referring to an I/O port or video memory because these locations can be changed by factors beyond your program's control.

# *Expressions*

An *expression* is a combination of variables, function calls, and operators that results in a single value. For example, here is an expression with a value that is the number of bytes needed to store the *null-terminated string* str (that is, an array of char data types with a zero byte at the end):

```
(strlen(str) * sizeof(char) + 1)
```

This expression involves a function call — strlen(str) — and the multiplication (*), addition (+), and sizeof operators.

C has a large number of operators that are an important part of expressions. Table 2-2 provides a summary of the operators in C.

| Table 2-2 | Summary of C Operators | |
|---|---|---|
| *Name of Operator* | *Syntax* | *Result* |
| *Arithmetic Operators* | | |
| Addition | x+y | Adds x and y. |
| Subtraction | x-y | Subtracts y from x. |
| Multiplication | x*y | Multiplies x and y. |
| Division | x/y | Divides x by y. |
| Remainder | x%y | Computes the remainder that results from dividing x by y. |
| Preincrement | ++x | Increments x before use. |
| Postincrement | x++ | Increments x after use. |
| Predecrement | --x | Decrements x before use. |
| Postdecrement | x-- | Decrements x after use. |
| Minus | -x | Negates the value of x. |
| Plus | +x | Maintains the value of x unchanged. |
| *Relational and Logical Operators* | | |
| Greater than | x>y | Value is 1 if x exceeds y; otherwise, value is 0. |
| Greater than or equal to | x>=y | Value is 1 if x exceeds or equals y; otherwise, value is 0. |
| Less than | x<y | Value is 1 if y exceeds x; otherwise, value is 0. |
| Less than or equal to | x<=y | Value is 1 if y exceeds or equals x; otherwise, value is 0. |

*(continued)*

**Table 2-2** *(continued)*

| Name of Operator | Syntax | Result |
|---|---|---|
| **Relational and Logical Operators** | | |
| Equal to | x==y | Value is 1 if x equals y; otherwise, value is 0. |
| Not equal to | x!=y | Value is 1 if x and y are unequal; otherwise, value is 0. |
| Logical NOT | !x | Value is 1 if x is 0; otherwise, value is 0. |
| Logical AND | x&&y | Value is 0 if either x or y is 0. |
| Logical OR | x\|\|y | Value is 0 if both x and y are 0. |
| **Assignment Operators** | | |
| Assignment | x=y | Places the value of y into x. |
| Compound Assignment | x O=y | Equivalent to x = x O y, where O is one of the following operators: +, -, *, /, %, <<, >, &, ^, or \|. |
| **Data Access and Size Operators** | | |
| Subscript | x[y] | Selects the *y*-th element of array x. |
| Member selection | x.y | Selects member y of structure (or union) x. |
| Member selection | x->y | Selects the member named y from a structure or union with x as its address. |
| Indirection | *x | Contents of the location with x as its address. |
| Address of | &x | Address of the data object named x. |
| Size of | sizeof(x) | Size (in bytes) of the data object named x. |
| **Bitwise Operators** | | |
| Bitwise NOT | ~x | Changes all 1s to 0s and 0s to 1s. |
| Bitwise AND | x&y | Result is the bitwise AND of x and y. |
| Bitwise OR | x\|y | Result is the bitwise OR of x and y. |
| Bitwise exclusive OR | x^y | Result contains 1s where corresponding bits of x and y differ. |
| Left shift | x<<y | Shifts the bits of x to the left by y bit positions. Fills 0s in the vacated bit positions. |
| Right shift | x>y | Shifts the bits of x to the right by y bit positions. Fills 0s in the vacated bit positions. |

| Name of Operator | Syntax | Result |
|---|---|---|
| **Miscellaneous Operators** | | |
| Function call | x(y) | Result is the value returned (if any) by function x, which is called with argument y. |
| Type cast | (type)x | Converts the value of x to the type named in parentheses. |
| Conditional | z?x:y | If z is not 0, evaluates x; otherwise, evaluates y. |
| Comma | x,y | Evaluates x first and then y. |

# Operator Precedence

Typical C expressions consist of several operands and operators. When writing complicated expressions, you must be aware of the order in which the compiler evaluates the operators. For example, suppose a program uses an array of pointers to integers defined as follows:

```
typedef int *IntPtr;/* Use typedef to simplify declarations*/
IntPtr  iptr[10];   /* An array of 10 pointers to int       */
```

Now suppose that you encounter the expression *iptr[4]. Does it refer to the value of the int with the address in iptr[4], or is this the fifth element from the location with the address in iptr? What you really need to know is whether the compiler is evaluates the subscript operator ([]) before the indirection operator (*) — or does it work the other way around? To answer questions such as these, you need to know the *precedence* — the order in which the program applies the operators.

Table 2-3 summarizes C's precedence rules. The table shows the operators in order of decreasing precedence. The operators with highest precedence — those applied first — are shown first. The table also shows *associativity* — the order in which operators at the same level are evaluated.

| Table 2-3 | Precedence and Associativity of C Operators | | |
|---|---|---|---|
| **Operator Group** | **Operator Name** | **Notation** | **Associativity** |
| Postfix | Subscript | x[y] | Left to right |
| | Function call | x(y) | |
| | Member selection | x.y | |
| | Member selection | x->y | |

*(continued)*

**Table 2-3** *(continued)*

| Operator Group | Operator Name | Notation | Associativity |
|---|---|---|---|
| Unary | Postincrement | `x++` | Right to left |
| | Postdecrement | `x--` | |
| | Preincrement | `++x` | |
| | Predecrement | `--x` | |
| | Address of | `&x` | |
| | Indirection | `*x` | |
| | Plus | `+x` | |
| | Minus | `-x` | |
| | Bitwise NOT | `~x` | |
| | Logical NOT | `!x` | |
| | Sizeof | `sizeof x` | |
| | Type cast | `(type)x` | |
| Multiplicative | Multiply | `x*y` | Left to right |
| | Divide | `x/y` | |
| | Remainder | `x%y` | |
| Additive | Add | `x+y` | Left to right |
| | Subtract | `x-y` | |
| Shift | Left shift | `x<<y` | Left to right |
| | Right shift | `x>y` | |
| Relational | Greater than | `x>y` | Left to right |
| | Greater than or equal to | `x>=y` | |
| | Less than | `x<y` | |
| | Less than or equal to | `x<=y` | |
| Equality | Equal to | `x==y` | Left to right |
| | Not equal to | `x!=y` | |
| Bitwise | Bitwise AND | `x&y` | Left to right |
| | Bitwise exclusive OR | `x^y` | |
| | Bitwise OR | `x|y` | |
| Logical | Logical AND | `x&&y` | Left to right |
| | Logical OR | `x||y` | |
| Conditional | Conditional | `z?x:y` | Right to left |
| Assignment | Assignment | `x=y` | Right to left |
| | Multiply assign | `x *= y` | |
| | Divide assign | `x /= y` | |

| Operator Group | Operator Name | Notation | Associativity |
|---|---|---|---|
| | Remainder assign | x %= y | |
| | Add assign | x += y | |
| | Subtract assign | x -= y | |
| | Left shift assign | x <<= y | |
| | Right shift assign | x >= y | |
| | Bitwise AND assign | x &= y | |
| | Bitwise XOR assign | x ^= y | |
| | Bitwise OR assign | x |= y | |
| Comma | Comma | x , y | Left to right |

Getting back to the question of interpreting *iptr[4], a quick look at Table 2-3 tells you that the [] operator has precedence over the * operator. Thus, when the compiler processes the expression *iptr[4], it evaluates iptr[4] first, and then it applies the indirection operator, resulting in the value of the int with the address in iptr[4].

# Statements

You use statements to represent the actions C functions perform and to control the flow of execution in the C program. A *statement* consists of keywords, expressions, and other statements. Each statement ends with a semicolon (;).

A special type of statement — the *compound statement* — is a group of statements enclosed in a pair of braces ({ . . . }). The body of a function is a compound statement. Such compound statements (also known as *blocks*) can contain local variables.

In the following sections — which are alphabetically arranged — I briefly describe the types of statements available in C.

## The break statement

You use the break statement to jump to the statement following the innermost do, for, switch, or while statement. It is also used to exit from a switch statement. Here is an example that uses break to exit a for loop:

```
for(i = 0; i < ncommands; i++)
{
    if(strcmp(input, commands[i]) == 0) break;
}
```

## The case statement

The case statement marks labels in a switch statement. Here is an example (here interrupt_id is an integer variable):

```
switch (interrupt_id)
{
    case XMIT_RDY:
        transmit();
        break;

    case RCV_RDY:
        receive();
        break;
}
```

## A compound statement or block

A *compound statement* or block is a group of declarations followed by statements, all enclosed in a pair of braces ({ . . . }). Typical compound statements are the body of a function and the block of code following an if statement. In the following example, everything that appears within the braces — the declarations and the statements — constitute a compound statement:

```
if(theEvent.xexpose.count == 0)
{
    int i;
/* Clear the window and draw the figures
 * in the "figures" array
 */
    XClearWindow(theDisplay, dWin);
    if(numfigures > 0)
        for(i=0; i<numfigures; i++)
            draw_figure(theDisplay, dWin, theGC, i);
}
```

## The continue statement

The continue statement begins the next iteration of the innermost do, for, or while statement in which it appears. You can use continue when you want to skip the execution of the loop. For example, to add the numbers from 1 to 10, excluding 5, you can use a for loop that skips the body when the loop index (i) is 5:

```
for(i=0, sum=0; i <= 10, i++)
{
    if(i == 5) continue;    /* Exclude 5 */
    sum += i;
}
```

## The default label

You use default as the label in a switch statement to mark code that executes when none of the case labels match the switch expression.

## The do statement

The do statement, together with while, forms iterative loops with the following structure:

```
do
  statement
  while(expression);
```

*statement* (usually a compound statement) executes until the *expression* in the while statement evaluates to 0. The expression is evaluated after each execution of the statement — thus a do-while block *always executes at least once*. For example, to add the numbers from 1 to 10, you can use the following do statement:

```
sum = 0;
do
{
    sum += i;
    i++;
}
while(i <= 10);
```

## Expression statements

Expression statements are evaluated for their side effects. Some typical uses of expression statements include calling a function, incrementing a variable, and assigning a value to a variable. Here are some examples:

```
printf("Hello, World!\n");
i++;
num_bytes = length * sizeof(char);
```

## The for statement

Use the for statement to execute a statement any number of times (basing that number on the value of an expression). The syntax is as follows:

```
for (expr_1; expr_2; expr_3) statement
```

The *expr_1* is evaluated once at the beginning of the loop, and the statement executes until the expression *expr_2* evaluates to 0. The third expression, *expr_3*, is evaluated after each execution of the statement. All three expressions are optional and the value of *expr_2* is assumed to be 1 if it is omitted. Here is an example that uses a `for` loop to add the numbers from 1 to 10:

```
for(i=0, sum=0; i <= 10; sum += i, i++);
```

In this example, the actual work of adding the numbers is done in the third expression, and the statement controlled by the `for` loop is a `null` statement (a lone `;`).

## The *goto* statement

The `goto` statement transfers control to a statement label. Here is an example that prompts the user for a value and repeats the request if the value is not acceptable:

```
ReEnter:
    printf("Enter offset: ");
    scanf(" %d", &offset);
    if(offset < 0 || offset > MAX_OFFSET)
    {
        printf("Bad offset: %d Please reenter:\n",
            offset);
        goto ReEnter;
    }
```

## The *if* statement

You can use the `if` statement to test an expression and execute a statement only when the expression is not zero. An `if` statement takes the following form:

```
if ( expression )  statement
```

The statement following the `if` statement executes only if the expression in parentheses evaluates to a non-zero value. That statement is usually a compound statement. Here is an example:

```
if(mem_left < threshold)
{
    Message("Low on memory! Close some windows.\n");
}
```

## The *if-else* statement

The `if-else` statement is a form of the `if` statement coupled with an `else` clause. The statement has the syntax

```
if ( expression )
    statement_1
```

```
else
    statement_2
```

*statement_1* executes if the *expression* within the parentheses is not zero. Otherwise, *statement_2* executes. Here is an example that uses if and else to pick the smaller of two variables:

```
if ( a <= b)
    smaller = a;
else
    smaller = b;
```

## The null statement

The null statement, represented by a solitary semicolon, does nothing. You use null statements in loops when all processing is done in the loop expressions rather than in the body of the loop. For example, to locate the zero byte marking the end of a string, you may use the following:

```
char str[80] = "Test";
int i;

for (i=0; str[i] != '\0'; i++)
                            ;  /* Null statement */
```

## The return statement

The return statement stops executing the current function and returns control to the calling function. The syntax is

```
return expression;
```

where the value of the *expression* is returned as the value of the function. For a function that does not return a value, use the return statement without the expression as follows:

```
return;
```

## The switch statement

The switch statement performs a multiple branch, depending on the value of an expression. It has the following syntax:

```
switch (expression)
{
    case value1:
        statement_1
```

```
        break;
case value2:
        statement_2
        break;

                .
                .
                .

default:
        statement_default
}
```

If the *expression* being tested by switch evaluates to *value1*, *statement_1* executes. If the expression is equal to *value2*, *statement_2* executes. The value is compared with each case label and the statement following the matching label executes. If the value does not match any of the case labels, the block *statement_default* following the default label executes. Each statement ends with a break statement that separates the code of one case label from another. Here is a switch statement that calls different routines depending on the value of an integer variable named command:

```
switch (command)
{
    case 'q':
        quit_app(0);

        case 'c':
        connect();
        break;

    case 's':
        set_params();
        break;

    case '?':
    case 'H':
        print_help();
        break;

    default:
        printf("Unknown command!\n");
}
```

## The while statement

The while statement is used in the form

```
while (expression) statement
```

The *statement* executes until the *expression* evaluates to 0. A while statement evaluates the expression before each execution of the statement. Thus, a while loop executes the statement zero or more times. Here is a while statement for copying one array to another:

```
i = length;
while (i >= 0)   /* Copy one array to another */
{
     array2[i] = array1[i];
     i--;
}
```

# Functions

A *function* is a collection of declarations and statements. As such, functions are the building blocks of C programs. Each C program has at least one function — the *main function,* where the execution of a C program begins. The C library contains mostly functions, although it contains quite a few macros as well.

## Function prototypes

In C, you must declare a function before using it. The function declaration tells the compiler the type of value that the function returns and the number and type of arguments it takes. Declare a function as a complete *function prototype,* showing the return type as well as a list of arguments. The calloc function in the C library returns a void pointer and accepts two arguments, each of type size_t, which is an unsigned integer type of sufficient size to hold the value of the sizeof operator. Thus the function prototype for calloc is the following:

```
void *calloc(size_t, size_t);
```

This prototype shows the type of each argument in the argument list. You can also include an identifier for each argument. In that case, you write the prototype as follows:

```
void *calloc(size_t num_elements, size_t elem_size);
```

Here the prototype looks exactly like the first line in the definition of the function, except you stop short of defining the function and end the line with a semicolon. With well-chosen names for arguments, this form of prototype can provide a lot of information about the function's use. For example, one look at the prototype of calloc tells you that its first argument is the number of elements to allocate, and the second argument is the size of each element.

Prototypes also help the compiler check function arguments and generate code that may use a faster mechanism for passing arguments. From the prototype, the compiler can determine the exact number and type of arguments to expect. Therefore, the prototype enables the compiler to catch any mistakes you might make when calling a function, such as passing the wrong number of arguments (when the function takes a fixed number of arguments) or passing a wrong type of argument to a function.

## The void type

What do you do when a function doesn't return anything nor accept any parameters? To handle these cases, C provides the `void` type, which is useful for declaring functions that return nothing and for describing pointers that can point to any type of data. For example, you can use the `void` return type to declare a function such as `exit` that does not return anything:

```
void exit(int status);
```

On the other hand, if a function doesn't accept any formal parameters, its list of arguments is represented by a `void`:

```
FILE *tmpfile(void);
```

The `void` pointer is useful for functions that work with blocks of memory. For example, when you request a certain number of bytes from the memory allocation routine `malloc`, you can use these locations to store any data that fits the space. In this case, the address of the first location of the allocated block of memory is returned as a `void` pointer. Thus, the prototype of `malloc` is written as follows:

```
void *malloc(size_t numbytes);
```

## Functions with a variable number of arguments

If a function accepts a variable number of arguments, you can indicate this by using an ellipsis (. . .) in place of the argument list; however, you must provide at least one argument before the ellipsis. A good example of such functions is the `printf` family of functions defined in the header file `stdio.h`. The prototypes of these functions are as follows:

```
int fprintf(FILE *stream, const char *format, ...);
int printf(const char *format, ...);
int sprintf(char *buffer, const char *format, ...);
```

## The C Library

The ANSI and ISO standards for C define all aspects of C — the language, the preprocessor, and the library. The prototypes of the functions in the library, as well as all necessary data structures and preprocessor constants, are defined in a set of standard header files. Table 2-4 lists the standard header files, including a summary of their contents.

If you're going to write applications in C, you have to become familiar with many of the standard libraries because that's where much of C's programming prowess lies. If you are writing graphical applications, you also must be familiar with other libraries such as the GIMP toolkit.

| Table 2-4 | Standard Header Files in C |
|-----------|----------------------------|
| *Header File* | *Purpose* |
| `<assert.h>` | Defines the `assert` macro. Used for program diagnostics. |
| `<ctype.h>` | Declares functions for classifying and converting characters. |
| `<errno.h>` | Defines macros for error conditions, `EDOM` and `ERANGE`, and the integer variable `errno` where library functions return an error code. |
| `<float.h>` | Defines a range of values that can be stored in floating-point types. |
| `<iso646.h>` | Defines a number of macros that are helpful when writing C programs in non-English languages that may use character combinations such as & and ~ for other purposes. |
| `<limits.h>` | Defines the limiting values of all integer data types. |
| `<locale.h>` | Declares the `lconv` structure and the functions necessary for customizing a C program to a particular locale. |
| `<math.h>` | Declares common mathematical functions and the `HUGE_VAL` macro. |
| `<setjmp.h>` | Defines the `setjmp` and `longjmp` functions that can transfer control from one function to another without relying on normal function calls and returns. Also defines the `jmp_buf` data type used by `setjmp` and `longjmp`. |
| `<signal.h>` | Defines symbols and routines necessary for handling exceptional conditions. |
| `<stdarg.h>` | Defines macros that provide access to the unnamed arguments in a function that accepts a varying number of arguments. |
| `<stddef.h>` | Defines the standard data types `ptrdiff_t`, `size_t`, `wchar_t`; the symbol `NULL`; and the macro `offsetof`. |
| `<stdio.h>` | Declares the functions and data types necessary for input and output operations. Defines macros such as `BUFSIZ`, `EOF`, `SEEK_CUR`, `SEEK_END`, and `SEEK_SET`. |
| `<stdlib.h>` | Declares many utility functions, such as the string conversion routines, random number generator, memory allocation routines, and process control routines (such as `abort`, `exit`, and `system`). |

*(continued)*

**Table 2-4 (continued)**

| Header File | Purpose |
| --- | --- |
| `<string.h>` | Declares the string manipulation routines such as `strcmp` and `strcpy`. |
| `<time.h>` | Defines data types and declares functions that manipulate time. Defines the types `clock_t` and `time_t` and the `tm` data structure. |
| `<wchar.h>` | Defines data types and declares functions for working with wide character data types (`wchar_t`). |
| `<wctype.h>` | Defines data types and declares functions for classifying and converting wide character data types (`wchar_t`). |

# Shared Libraries in Linux Applications

Most Linux programs use shared libraries. At a minimum, most C programs use the C shared library `libc.so.X`, wherein *X* is a version number. Using shared libraries is desirable because many executable programs can share the same shared library — you need only one copy of the shared library loaded into memory. Also, the *dynamic linking* (wherein a program loads code modules and links with them at runtime) is becoming increasingly popular because it enables an application to load blocks of code only when needed, thus reducing the memory requirement of the application.

When a program uses one or more shared libraries, you need the program's executable file, as well as all the shared libraries, to run the program. In other words, your program doesn't run if all shared libraries are not available on a system.

If you sell an application that uses shared libraries, make sure all necessary shared libraries are distributed with your software.

The subject of shared libraries is of interest to Linux programmers because use of shared libraries reduces the size of executables. In this section I briefly describe how to create and use a shared library in a sample program.

## Examining shared libraries that a program uses

Use the `ldd` utility to determine which shared libraries an executable program needs. Type the following `ldd` command to see the shared libraries used by a program (that was stored by GCC in the default file named `a.out`):

```
ldd a.out
```

Here is what `ldd` reports for a typical C program:

```
libc.so.6 => /lib/tls/libc.so.6 (0x00b0a000)
/lib/ld-linux.so.2 => /lib/ld-linux.so.2 (0x00af1000)
```

A more complex program, such as the GIMP (an Adobe Photoshop-like program) uses many more shared libraries. To view its shared library needs, type the following command:

```
ldd /usr/bin/gimp
```

Here's the list displayed on my Fedora Core system:

```
libgimpwidgets-1.3.so.26 => /usr/lib/libgimpwidgets-1.3.so.26 (0x03783000)
libgimpcolor-1.3.so.26 => /usr/lib/libgimpcolor-1.3.so.26 (0x001ce000)
libgimpmodule-1.3.so.26 => /usr/lib/libgimpmodule-1.3.so.26 (0x001d8000)
libgimpbase-1.3.so.26 => /usr/lib/libgimpbase-1.3.so.26 (0x001a1000)
libgimpthumb-1.3.so.26 => /usr/lib/libgimpthumb-1.3.so.26 (0x00d8e000)
libgimpmath-1.3.so.26 => /usr/lib/libgimpmath-1.3.so.26 (0x00d87000)
libgtk-x11-2.0.so.0 => /usr/lib/libgtk-x11-2.0.so.0 (0x00448000)
libgdk-x11-2.0.so.0 => /usr/lib/libgdk-x11-2.0.so.0 (0x00762000)
libatk-1.0.so.0 => /usr/lib/libatk-1.0.so.0 (0x0073f000)
libgdk_pixbuf-2.0.so.0 => /usr/lib/libgdk_pixbuf-2.0.so.0 (0x003d5000)
libm.so.6 => /lib/tls/libm.so.6 (0x00c46000)
libXcursor.so.1 => /usr/X11R6/lib/libXcursor.so.1 (0x00191000)
libpangoxft-1.0.so.0 => /usr/lib/libpangoxft-1.0.so.0 (0x0075b000)
libpangox-1.0.so.0 => /usr/lib/libpangox-1.0.so.0 (0x00731000)
libart_lgpl_2.so.2 => /usr/lib/libart_lgpl_2.so.2 (0x003bd000)
libpangoft2-1.0.so.0 => /usr/lib/libpangoft2-1.0.so.0 (0x003ec000)
libpango-1.0.so.0 => /usr/lib/libpango-1.0.so.0 (0x00412000)
libgobject-2.0.so.0 => /usr/lib/libgobject-2.0.so.0 (0x002aa000)
libgmodule-2.0.so.0 => /usr/lib/libgmodule-2.0.so.0 (0x002e7000)
libdl.so.2 => /lib/libdl.so.2 (0x00c6b000)
libglib-2.0.so.0 => /usr/lib/libglib-2.0.so.0 (0x001f5000)
libfontconfig.so.1 => /usr/lib/libfontconfig.so.1 (0x00168000)
libfreetype.so.6 => /usr/lib/libfreetype.so.6 (0x00101000)
libz.so.1 => /usr/lib/libz.so.1 (0x00d61000)
libpthread.so.0 => /lib/tls/libpthread.so.0 (0x00d74000)
libc.so.6 => /lib/tls/libc.so.6 (0x00b0a000)
libX11.so.6 => /usr/X11R6/lib/libX11.so.6 (0x00c71000)
libXrandr.so.2 => /usr/X11R6/lib/libXrandr.so.2 (0x0019c000)
libXi.so.6 => /usr/X11R6/lib/libXi.so.6 (0x003b3000)
libXext.so.6 => /usr/X11R6/lib/libXext.so.6 (0x00d51000)
libXft.so.2 => /usr/X11R6/lib/libXft.so.2 (0x00dcb000)
libXrender.so.1 => /usr/X11R6/lib/libXrender.so.1 (0x00df4000)
/lib/ld-linux.so.2 => /lib/ld-linux.so.2 (0x00af1000)
libexpat.so.0 => /usr/lib/libexpat.so.0 (0x00da9000)
```

In this case, the program uses quite a few shared libraries, including the X11 library (`libX11.so.6`), the GIMP toolkit (`libgtk-x11-2.0.so.0`), the General Drawing Kit (GDK) library (`libgdk-x11-2.0.so.0`), the Math library (`libm.so.6`), and the C library (`libc.so.6`).

Almost any Linux application requires shared libraries to run.

## Creating a shared library

Creating a shared library for your own application is fairly simple. Suppose you want to implement an object in the form of a shared library (think of an object as a bunch of code and data). A set of functions in the shared library represents the object's interfaces. To use the object, you load its shared library and invoke its interface functions. (I show you how to load a library in the following section.)

Here is the C source code for this simple object, implemented as a shared library (you might also call it a *dynamically linked library*) — save this code in a file named `dynobj.c`:

```c
/*------------------------------------------------------*/
/* File: dynobj.c
 *
 * Demonstrate use of dynamic linking.
 * Pretend this is an object that can be created by calling
 * init and destroyed by calling destroy.
 */
#include <stdio.h>
#include <stdlib.h>
#include <string.h>

/* Data structure for this object */
typedef struct OBJDATA
{
  char *name;
  int version;
} OBJDATA;

/*------------------------------------------------------*/
/* init
 *
 * Initialize object (allocate storage).
 *
 */
void* init(char *name)
{
  OBJDATA *data = (OBJDATA*)calloc(1, sizeof(OBJDATA));
  if(name)
    data->name = malloc(strlen(name)+1);
  strcpy(data->name, name);

  printf("Created: %s\n", name);

  return data;
}
/*------------------------------------------------------*/
```

```
/* s h o w
 *
 * Show the object.
 *
 */
void show(void *data)
{
  OBJDATA *d = (OBJDATA*)data;
  printf("show: %s\n", d->name);
}
/*----------------------------------------------------------*/
/* d e s t r o y
 *
 * Destroy the object (free all storage).
 *
 */
void destroy(void *data)
{
  OBJDATA *d = (OBJDATA*)data;
  if(d)
  {
    if(d->name)
    {
      printf("Destroying: %s\n", d->name);
      free(d->name);
    }
    free(d);
  }
}
```

The object offers three interface functions:

+ init to allocate any necessary storage and initialize the object

+ show to display the object (here, it simply prints a message)

+ destroy to free any storage

To build the shared library named libdobj.so, follow these steps:

*1.* **Compile all source files with the** -fPIC **flag. In this case, compile the**
dynobj.c **file by using this command:**

```
gcc -fPIC -c dynobj.c
```

*2.* **Link the objects into a shared library with the** -shared **flag and provide appropriate flags for the linker. To create the shared library
named** libdobj.so.1, **use the following:**

```
gcc -shared -Wl,-soname,libdobj.so.1 -o libdobj.so.1.0
  dynobj.o
```

3. **Set up a sequence of symbolic links so that programs using the shared library can refer to it with a standard name.**

   For the sample library, the standard name is `libdobj.so`, and the following commands set up the symbolic links:

   ```
   ln -sf libdobj.so.1.0 libdobj.so.1
   ln -sf libdobj.so.1 libdobj.so
   ```

4. **When you test the shared library, define and export the** `LD_LIBRARY_PATH` **environment variable by using the following command:**

   ```
   export LD_LIBRARY_PATH=`pwd`:$LD_LIBRARY_PATH
   ```

After you test the shared library and are satisfied that the library works, copy it to a standard location, such as `/usr/local/lib`, and run the `ldconfig` utility to update the link between `libdobj.so.1` and `libdobj.so.1.0`. These are the commands you use to install your shared library for everyone's use (you have to be `root` to perform these steps):

```
cp libdobj.so.1.0 /usr/local/lib
/sbin/ldconfig
cd /usr/local/lib
ln -s libdobj.so.1 libdobj.so
```

## *Dynamically loading a shared library*

Loading a shared library in your program and using the functions within the shared library is simple. In this section, I demonstrate the way you do this action. The header file `<dlfcn.h>` (that's a standard header file in Linux) declares the functions for loading and using a shared library. Four functions are declared in the file `dlfcn.h` for dynamic loading:

✦ `void *dlopen(const char *filename, int flag);`: Loads the shared library specified by the filename and returns a handle for the library. The flag can be `RTD_LAZY` (resolve undefined symbols as the library's code executes); or `RTD_NOW` (resolve all undefined symbols before `dlopen` returns and fail if all symbols are not defined). If `dlopen` fails, it returns `NULL`.

✦ `const char *dlerror (void);`: If `dlopen` fails, call `dlerror` to get a string that contains a description of the error.

✦ `void *dlsym (void *handle, char *symbol);`: Returns the address of the specified symbol (function name) from the shared library identified by the handle (that was returned by `dlopen`).

✦ `int dlclose (void *handle);`: Unloads the shared library if no one else is using it.

When you use any of these functions, include the header file `dlfcn.h` with this preprocessor directive:

```
#include <dlfcn.h>
```

Finally, here is a simple test program — `dltest.c` — that shows how to load and use the object defined in the shared library `libdobj.so`, which you create in the preceding section:

```
/*--------------------------------------------------------*/
/* File: dltest.c
 *
 * Test dynamic linking.
 *
 */
#include <dlfcn.h>   /* For the dynamic loading functions */
#include <stdio.h>

int main(void)
{
  void *dlobj;
  void * (*init_call)(char *name);
  void (*show_call)(void *data);
  void (*destroy_call)(void *data);

/* Open the shared library and set up the function pointers
   */
  if(dlobj = dlopen("libdobj.so.1",RTLD_LAZY))
  {
    void *data;

    init_call=dlsym(dlobj,"init");
    show_call=dlsym(dlobj,"show");
    destroy_call=dlsym(dlobj,"destroy");

/* Call the object interfaces */
    data = (*init_call)("Test Object");
    (*show_call)(data);
    (*destroy_call)(data);
  }
  return 0;
}
```

The program is straightforward: It loads the shared library, gets the pointers to the functions in the library, and calls the functions through the pointers.

You can compile and link this program in the usual way, but you must link with the `-ldl` option so you can use the functions declared in `dlfcn.h`. Here is how you build the program `dltest`:

```
gcc -o dltest dltest.c -ldl
```

To see the program in action, run dltest by typing the following command:

```
./dltest
```

It displays the following lines of output:

```
Created: Test Object
show: Test Object
Destroying: Test Object
```

Although this sample program is not exciting, you now have a sample program that uses a shared library.

To see the benefit of using a shared library, return to the preceding section and make some changes in the shared library source file — dynobj.c. For example, you could print some other message in a function so you can easily tell that you have made some change. Rebuild the shared library alone. Then run dltest again. The resulting output shows the effect of the changes you make in the shared library, which means you can update the shared library independently of the application.

*Note:* A change in a shared library can affect many applications installed on your system. Therefore, be careful when making changes to *any* shared library. By the same token, shared libraries can be a security risk if someone manages to replace one with some malicious code.

# Chapter 3: Writing Shell Scripts

## In This Chapter

- ✔ Trying out simple shell scripts
- ✔ Learning the basics of shell scripting
- ✔ Exploring Bash's built-in commands

Linux gives you many small and specialized commands, along with the plumbing necessary to connect these commands. By *plumbing,* I mean the way in which one command's output can be used as a second command's input. Bash (short for Bourne Again SHell) — the default shell in Fedora Core — provides this plumbing in the form of I/O redirection and pipes. Bash also includes features such as the `if` statement that you can use to run commands only when a specific condition is true and the `for` statement that repeats commands a specified number of times. You can use these features of Bash when writing programs called *shell scripts*.

In this chapter, I show you how to write simple *shell scripts* — task-oriented collections of shell commands stored in a file. Shell scripts are used to automate various tasks. For example, when your Fedora Core system boots, many shell scripts stored in various subdirectories in the `/etc` directory (for example, `/etc/init.d`) perform many initialization tasks.

## Trying Out Simple Shell Scripts

If you are not a programmer, you may feel apprehensive about programming. But shell *scripting* (or programming) can be as simple as storing a few commands in a file. In fact, you can have a useful shell program that has a single command.

While writing this book, for example, I captured screens from the X Window System and used the screen shots in figures. I used the X screen-capture program, `xwd`, to store the screen images in the X Window Dump (XWD) format. The book's production team, however, wanted the screen shots in TIFF format. Therefore, I used the Portable Bitmap (PBM) toolkit to convert the XWD images to TIFF format. To convert each file, I've run two programs and deleted a temporary file, as follows:

```
xwdtopnm < file.xwd > file.pnm
pnmtotiff < file.pnm > file.tif
rm file.pnm
```

These commands assume that the xwdtopnm and pnmtotiff programs are in the /usr/bin directory — one of the directories listed in the PATH environment variable. By the way, xwdtopnm and pnmtotiff are two programs in the PBM toolkit.

After converting a few XWD files to TIFF format, I get tired of typing the same sequence of commands for each file, so I prepare a file named totif and save the following lines in it:

```
#!/bin/sh
xwdtopnm < $1.xwd > $1.pnm
pnmtotiff < $1.pnm > $1.tif
rm $1.pnm
```

Then I make the file executable by using this command:

```
chmod +x totif
```

The chmod command enables you to change the permission settings of a file. One of those settings determines whether the file is executable. The +x option means you want to mark the file as executable. You do have to mark it that way because Bash runs only executable files.

Now when I want to convert the file figure1.xwd to figure1.tif, I can do so by typing the following command:

```
./totif figure1
```

The ./ prefix indicates that the totif file is in the current directory — you don't need the ./ prefix if the PATH environment variable includes the current directory. The totif file is a shell script (also called a *shell program*). When you run this shell program with the command totif figure1, the shell substitutes figure1 for each occurrence of $1 (note that $1 refers to the first option that the user types on the command used to execute the script).

Shell scripts are popular among system administrators. If you are a system administrator, you can build a collection of custom shell scripts that help you automate tasks you perform often. If a disk seems to be getting full, for example, you may want to find all files that exceed some size (say, 1MB) and that have not been accessed in the past 30 days. In addition, you may want to send an e-mail message to all users who have large files, requesting that they archive and clean up those files. You can perform all these tasks with a shell script. You might start with the following find command to identify large files:

```
find / -type f -atime +30 -size +1000k -exec ls -l {} \; > /tmp/largefiles
```

This command creates a file named `/tmp/largefiles`, which contains detailed information about old files taking up too much space. After you get a list of the files, you can use a few other Linux commands — such as `sort`, `cut`, and `sed` — to prepare and send mail messages to users who have large files to clean up. Instead of typing all these commands manually, place them in a file and create a shell script. That, in a nutshell, is the essence of shell scripts — to gather shell commands in a file so you can easily perform repetitive system-administration tasks.

Just as most Linux commands accept command-line options, a Bash script also accepts command-line options. Inside the script, you can refer to the options as $1, $2, and so on. The special name $0 refers to the name of the script itself.

Here's a typical Bash script that accepts arguments:

```
#!/bin/sh
echo "This script's name is: $0"
echo Argument 1: $1
echo Argument 2: $2
```

The first line runs the `/bin/sh` program, which subsequently processes the rest of the lines in the script. The name `/bin/sh` traditionally refers to the Bourne shell — the first UNIX shell. In Fedora Core, `/bin/sh` is a symbolic link to `/bin/bash`, which is the executable program for Bash.

Save this simple script in a file named `simple`, and make that file executable with the following command:

```
chmod +x simple
```

Now run the script as follows:

```
./simple
```

It displays the following output:

```
This script's name is: ./simple
Argument 1:
Argument 2:
```

The first line shows the script's name. Because you have run the script without arguments, the script displays no values for the arguments.

Now try running the script with a few arguments, like this:

```
./simple "This is one argument" second-argument third
```

This time the script displays more output:

```
This script's name is: ./simple
Argument 1: This is one argument
Argument 2: second-argument
```

As the output shows, the shell treats the entire string within the double quotation marks as a single argument. Otherwise, the shell uses spaces as separators between arguments on the command line.

This sample script ignores the third argument because the script is designed to print only the first two arguments. The script ignores all arguments after the first two.

# Learning the Basics of Shell Scripting

Like any programming language, the Bash shell supports the following features:

+ Variables that store values, including special built-in variables for accessing command-line arguments passed to a shell script and other special values

+ The capability to evaluate expressions

+ Control structures that enable you to loop over several shell commands or to execute some commands conditionally

+ The capability to define functions that can be called in many places within a script. Bash also includes many built-in commands that you can use in any script.

In the next few sections, I illustrate some of these programming features through simple examples. (I'm assuming that you're already running Bash, in which case you can try the examples by typing them at the shell prompt in a terminal window.)

## Storing stuff

You define variables in Bash just as you define environment variables. Thus, you may define a variable as follows:

```
count=12  # note no embedded spaces allowed
```

To use a variable's value, prefix the variable's name with a dollar sign ($). For example, $PATH is the value of the variable PATH (this variable is the famous PATH environment variable that lists all the directories that Bash searches when trying to locate an executable file). To display the value of the variable count, use the following command:

```
echo $count
```

Bash has some special variables for accessing command-line arguments. In a shell script, $0 refers to the name of the shell script. The variables $1, $2, and so on refer to the command-line arguments. The variable $* stores all the command-line arguments as a single variable, and $? contains the exit status of the last command the shell executes.

From a Bash script, you can prompt the user for input and use the read command to read the input into a variable. Here is an example:

```
echo -n "Enter value: "
read value
echo "You entered: $value"
```

When this script runs, the read value command causes Bash to read whatever you type at the keyboard.

*Note:* The -n option prevents the echo command from automatically adding a new line at the end of the string that it displays.

## Calling shell functions

You can group a number of shell commands that you use consistently into a *function* and assign it a name. Later, you can execute that group of commands by using the single name assigned to the function. Here is a simple script that illustrates the syntax of shell functions:

```
#!/bin/sh

hello() {
        echo -n "Hello, "
        echo $1 $2
}

hello Jane Doe
```

When you run this script, it displays the following output:

```
Hello, Jane Doe
```

This script defines a shell function named hello. The function expects two arguments. In the body of the function, these arguments are referenced by $1 and $2. The function definition begins with hello() — the name of the function, followed by parentheses. The body of the function is enclosed in curly braces — { . . . }. In this case, the body uses the echo command to display a line of text.

The last line of the example shows how a shell function is called with arguments. In this case, the hello function is being called with two arguments: Jane and Doe. The hello function takes these two arguments and prints out a line that says Hello, Jane Doe.

## Controlling the flow

In Bash scripts, you can control the flow of execution — the order in which the commands are executed — by using special commands such as if, case, for, and while. These control statements use the exit status of a command to decide what to do next. When any command executes, it returns an exit status — a numeric value that indicates whether or not the command has succeeded. By convention, an exit status of zero means the command has succeeded. (Yes, you read it right: Zero indicates success!) A nonzero exit status indicates that something has gone wrong with the command.

For example, suppose you want to make a backup copy of a file before editing it with the vi editor. More importantly, you want to avoid editing the file if a backup can't be made. Here's a Bash script that takes care of this task:

```
#!/bin/sh
if cp "$1" "#$1"
then
    vi "$1"
else
    echo "Failed to create backup copy"
fi
```

This script illustrates the syntax of the if-then-else structure and shows how the exit status of the cp command is used by the if command to determine the next action. If cp returns zero, the script uses vi to edit the file; otherwise, the script displays an error message and exits. By the way, the script saves the backup in a file whose name is the same as that of the original, except for a hash mark (#) added at the beginning of the filename.

Don't forget the final fi that terminates the if command. Forgetting fi is a common source of errors in Bash scripts.

You can use the test command to evaluate any expression and to use the expression's value as the exit status of the command. Suppose you want a script that edits a file only if it already exists. Using test, you can write such a script as follows:

```
#!/bin/sh
if test -f "$1"
```

```
then
    vi "$1"
else
    echo "No such file"
fi
```

A shorter form of the `test` command is to place the expression in square brackets ([...]). Using this shorthand notation, you can rewrite the preceding script like this:

```
#!/bin/sh
if [ -f "$1" ]
then
    vi "$1"
else
    echo "No such file"
fi
```

*Note:* You must have spaces around the two square brackets.

Another common control structure is the `for` loop. The following script adds the numbers 1 through 10:

```
#!/bin/sh
sum=0
for i in 1 2 3 4 5 6 7 8 9 10
do
    sum=`expr $sum + $i`
done
echo "Sum = $sum"
```

This example also illustrates the use of the `expr` command to evaluate an expression.

The `case` statement is used to execute a group of commands based on the value of a variable. For example, consider the following script, based on the `confirm()` function in the `/etc/init.d/functions` file in your Fedora Core system:

```
#!/bin/sh
echo -n "What should I do -- (Y)es/(N)o/(C)ontinue? [Y] "
read answer
case $answer in
    y|Y|"")
      echo "YES"
    ;;
    c|C)
      echo "CONTINUE"
    ;;
    n|N)
```

```
      echo "NO"
   ;;
   *)
      echo "UNKNOWN"
   ;;
esac
```

Save this code in a file named `confirm` and type **chmod +x confirm** to make it executable. Then try it out like this:

```
./confirm
```

When the script prompts you, type one of the characters **y**, **n**, or **c** and then press Enter. The script displays `YES`, `NO`, or `CONTINUE`. For example, here's what happens when I type **c** (and then press Enter):

```
What should I do -- (Y)es/(N)o/(C)ontinue? [Y] c
CONTINUE
```

The script displays a prompt and reads the input you type. Your input is stored in a variable named `answer`. Then the `case` statement executes a block of code based on the value of the answer variable. For example, when I type **c**, the following block of commands execute:

```
   c|C)
      echo "CONTINUE"
   ;;
```

The `echo` command causes the script to display `CONTINUE`.

From this example, you can see that the general syntax of the `case` command is as follows:

```
case $variable in
    value1 | value2)
    command1
    command2
    ...other commands...
    ;;

    value3)
    command3
    command4
    ...other commands...
    ;;
esac
```

Essentially, the `case` command begins with the word `case` and ends with `esac`. Separate blocks of code are enclosed between the values of the variable, followed by a closing parenthesis and terminated by a pair of semicolons ( ; ; ).

## Exploring Bash's built-in commands

Bash has more than 50 built-in commands, including common commands such as `cd` and `pwd`, as well as many others that are used infrequently. You can use these built-in commands in any Bash script or at the shell prompt. Table 3-1 describes most of the Bash built-in commands and their arguments. After looking through this information, type **help *cmd*** to read more about a specific built-in command. For example, to find out more about the built-in command `test`, type the following:

```
help test
```

Doing so displays the following information on my Fedora Core system:

```
test: test [expr]
    Exits with a status of 0 (true) or 1 (false) depending on
    the evaluation of EXPR. Expressions may be unary or binary. Unary
    expressions are often used to examine the status of a file. There
    are string operators as well, and numeric comparison operators.

    File operators:

      -a FILE      True if file exists.
      -b FILE      True if file is block special.
      -c FILE      True if file is character special.
      -d FILE      True if file is a directory.
      -e FILE      True if file exists.
      -f FILE      True if file exists and is a regular file.
      -g FILE      True if file is set-group-id.
      -h FILE      True if file is a symbolic link.
      -L FILE      True if file is a symbolic link.
      -k FILE      True if file has its 'sticky' bit set.
      -p FILE      True if file is a named pipe.
      -r FILE      True if file is readable by you.
      -s FILE      True if file exists and is not empty.
      -S FILE      True if file is a socket.
      -t FD        True if FD is opened on a terminal.
      -u FILE      True if the file is set-user-id.
      -w FILE      True if the file is writable by you.
      -x FILE      True if the file is executable by you.
      -O FILE      True if the file is effectively owned by you.
      -G FILE      True if the file is effectively owned by your group.
    (... Lines deleted ...)
```

Where necessary, the online help from the `help` command includes a considerable amount of detail.

Some external programs may have the same name as Bash built-in commands. If you want to run any such external program, you have to specify explicitly the full pathname of that program. Otherwise, Bash executes the built-in command of the same name.

| Table 3-1 | Summary of Built-In Commands in Bash Shell |
|---|---|
| *This Function* | *Does the Following* |
| `. filename [arguments]` | Reads and executes commands from the specified file using the optional arguments (works the same way as the `source` command). |
| `: [arguments]` | Expands the arguments but does not process them. |
| `[ expr ]` | Evaluates the expression `expr` and returns zero status if `expr` is true. |
| `alias [name[=value] ...]` | Defines an alias. |
| `bg [job]` | Puts the specified job in the background. If no job is specified, it puts the currently executing command in the background. |
| `bind [-m keymap] [-lvd] [-q name]` | Binds a key sequence to a macro. |
| `break [n]` | Exits from a `for`, `while`, or `until` loop. If *n* is specified, the *n*-th enclosing loop is exited. |
| `builtin builtin_command [arguments]` | Executes a shell built-in command. |
| `cd [dir]` | Changes the current directory to dir. |
| `command [-pVv] cmd [arg ...]` | Runs the command `cmd` with the specified arguments (ignoring any shell function named `cmd`). |
| `continue [n]` | Starts the next iteration of the `for`, `while`, or `until` loop. If *n* is specified, the next iteration of the *n*-th enclosing loop is started. |
| `declare [-frxi] [name[=value]]` | Declares a variable with the specified name and, optionally, assigns it a value. |
| `dirs [-l] [+/-n]` | Displays the list of currently remembered directories. |
| `echo [-neE] [arg ...]` | Displays the arguments on standard output. |
| `enable [-n] [-all] [name ...]` | Enables or disables the specified built-in commands. |
| `eval [arg ...]` | Concatenates the arguments and executes them as a command. |
| `exec [command [arguments]]` | Replaces the current instance of the shell with a new process that runs the specified command. |
| `exit [n]` | Exits the shell with the status code *n*. |

| This Function | Does the Following |
|---|---|
| `export [-nf] [name[=word]] ...` | Defines a specified environment variable and exports it to future processes. |
| `fc -s [pat=rep] [cmd]` | Re-executes the command after replacing the pattern *pat* with *rep*. |
| `fg [jobspec]` | Puts the specified job in the foreground. If no job is specified, it puts the most recent job in the foreground. |
| `getopts optstring name [args]` | Gets optional parameters (which are called in shell scripts to extract arguments from the command line). |
| `hash [-r] [name]` | Remembers the full pathname of a specified command. |
| `help [cmd ...]` | Displays help information for specified built-in commands. |
| `history [n]` | Displays past commands or past *n* commands, if you specify a number *n*. |
| `jobs [-lnp] [ jobspec ... ]` | Lists currently active jobs. |
| `kill [-s sigspec \| -sigspec] [pid \| jobspec] ...let arg [arg ...]` | Evaluates each argument and returns 1 if the last *arg* is 0. |
| `local [name[=value] ...]` | Creates a local variable with the specified name and value (used in shell functions). |
| `logout` | Exits a login shell. |
| `popd [+/-n]` | Removes entries from the directory stack. |
| `pushd [dir]` | Adds a specified directory to the top of the directory stack. |
| `pwd` | Prints the full pathname of the current working directory. |
| `read [-r] [name ...]` | Reads a line from standard input and parses it. |
| `readonly [-f] [name ...]` | Marks the specified variables as read-only, so that the variables cannot be changed later. |
| `return [n]` | Exits the shell function with the return value *n*. |
| `set [--abefhkmnptuvxldCHP] [-o option] [arg ...]` | Sets various flags. |
| `shift [n]` | Makes the *n+1* argument $1, the *n+2* argument $2, and so on. |
| `source filename [arguments]` | Reads and executes commands from a file. |
| `suspend [-f]` | Stops execution until a `SIGCONT` signal is received. |

*(continued)*

**Table 3-1** *(continued)*

| This Function | Does the Following |
|---|---|
| test expr | Evaluates the expression expr and returns zero if expr is true. |
| times | Prints the accumulated user and system times for processes run from the shell. |
| trap [-l] [cmd] [sigspec] | Executes cmd when the signal sigspec is received. |
| type [-all] [-type \| -path] name [name ...] | Indicates how the shell interprets each name. |
| ulimit [-SHacdfmstpnuv [limit]] | Controls resources available to the shell. |
| umask [-S] [mode] | Sets the file creation mask — the default permission for files. |
| unalias [-a] [name ...] | Undefines a specified alias. |
| unset [-fv] [name ...] | Removes the definition of specified variables. |
| wait [n] | Waits for a specified process to terminate. |

# Chapter 4: Programming in Perl

## In This Chapter

✔ **Writing your first Perl program**

✔ **Getting an overview of Perl**

✔ **Understanding Perl packages and modules**

✔ **Using objects in Perl**

*W*hen it comes to writing scripts, the Perl language is very popular among system administrators, especially on UNIX and Linux systems. System administrators use Perl to automate routine system administration tasks such as looking for old files that could be archived and deleted to free up disk space.

Perl is a scripting language, which means that you do not have to compile and link a *Perl script* (a text file containing Perl commands). Instead, an interpreter executes the Perl script. This capability makes writing and testing Perl scripts easy because you do not have to go through the typical edit-compile-link cycles to write Perl programs.

Besides ease of programming, another reason for Perl's popularity is that Perl is distributed freely and is available for a wide variety of computer systems, including Fedora Core and many others such as UNIX, Windows 95/98/NT/2000/XP, and Apple Macintosh.

In this chapter, I introduce you to Perl scripting.

## Understanding Perl

Officially Perl stands for *Practical Extraction Report Language*, but Larry Wall, the creator of Perl, says people often refer to Perl as *Pathologically Eclectic Rubbish Lister*. As these names suggest, Perl was originally designed to extract information from text files and generate reports.

Perl began life in 1986 as a system administration tool created by Larry Wall. Over time, Perl grew by accretion of many new features and functions. The latest version — Perl 5.8 — supports object-oriented programming and allows anyone to extend Perl by adding new modules in a specified format.

True to its origin as a system-administration tool, Perl has been popular with UNIX system administrators for many years. More recently, when the World Wide Web (or Web for short) became popular and the need for Common Gateway Interface (CGI) programs arose, Perl became the natural choice for those already familiar with the language. The recent surge in Perl's popularity is primarily due to the use of Perl in writing CGI programs for the Web. Of course, as people pay more attention to Perl, they discover that Perl is useful for much more than CGI programming. That, in turn, has made Perl even more popular among users.

Perl is available on a wide variety of computer systems because, like the Linux operating system, Perl can be distributed freely.

If you are familiar with shell programming or the C programming language, you can pick up Perl quickly. If you have never programmed, becoming proficient in Perl may take a while. I encourage you to start with a small subset of Perl's features and to ignore anything you don't immediately understand. Then, slowly add Perl features to your repertoire.

## Determining Whether You Have Perl

Before you proceed with the Perl tutorial, check whether you have the `perl` program installed on your Fedora Core system. Type the following command:

```
which perl
```

The `which` command tells you whether it finds a specified program in the directories listed in the PATH environment variable. If `perl` is installed, you see the following output:

```
/usr/bin/perl
```

If the `which` command complains that no such program exists in the current PATH, that doesn't necessarily mean you don't have `perl` installed; it may mean simply that you don't have the `/usr/bin` directory in PATH. Ensure that `/usr/bin` is in PATH; check by typing the following command:

```
echo $PATH
```

See if the output lists the `/usr/bin` directory. If `/usr/bin` is not in PATH, use the following command to redefine PATH:

```
export PATH=$PATH:/usr/bin
```

Now, try the `which perl` command again. If you still get an error, you may not have installed Perl. You can install Perl from the companion DVD-ROM by performing the following steps:

1. **Log in as** `root`.

2. **Insert the companion DVD-ROM in the DVD-ROM drive. If you are working in the GNOME or KDE graphical environment, the DVD-ROM mounts automatically. Otherwise, mount the DVD-ROM by typing the following command:**

   ```
   mount /mnt/cdrom
   ```

3. **Type the following command to change the directory to the location of the Red Hat packages:**

   ```
   cd /mnt/cdrom/Fedora/RPMS
   ```

4. **Type the following** `rpm` **(Red Hat Package Manager) command to install Perl:**

   ```
   rpm -ivh perl*
   ```

After you install Perl on your system, type the following command to see its version number:

```
perl -v
```

Here is typical output from that command:

```
This is perl, v5.8.3 built for i386-linux-thread-multi

Copyright 1987-2003, Larry Wall

Perl may be copied only under the terms of either the Artistic License or the
GNU General Public License, which may be found in the Perl 5 source kit.

Complete documentation for Perl, including FAQ lists, should be found on
this system using 'man perl' or 'perldoc perl'.  If you have access to the
Internet, point your browser at http://www.perl.com/, the Perl Home Page.
```

This output tells you that you have Perl Version 5.8, patch Level 3, and that Larry Wall, the originator of Perl, holds the copyright. (Remember, however, that Perl is distributed freely under the GNU General Public License.)

You can get the latest version of Perl by pointing your World Wide Web browser to the Comprehensive Perl Archive Network (CPAN). The following address connects you to the CPAN site nearest to you:

```
www.perl.com/CPAN/
```

# Writing Your First Perl Script

Perl has many features of C, and, as you may know, most books on C start with an example program that displays `Hello, World!` on your terminal. Because Perl is an interpreted language, you can accomplish this task directly from the command line. If you enter

```
perl -e 'print "Hello, World!\n";'
```

Perl responds with the following:

```
Hello, World!
```

This command uses the `-e` option of the `perl` program to pass the Perl program as a command-line argument to the Perl interpreter. In this case, the following line constitutes the Perl program:

```
print "Hello, World!\n";
```

To convert this line to a Perl script, simply place the line in a file, and start the file with a directive to run the `perl` program (as you do in shell scripts, when you place a line such as `#!/bin/sh` to run the shell to process the script).

To try this Perl script, follow these steps:

1. **Use a text editor to type and save the following lines in the file named** `hello.pl`**:**

   ```
   #!/usr/bin/perl
   # This is a comment.
   print "Hello, World!\n";
   ```

2. **Make the** `hello.pl` **file executable by using the following command:**

   ```
   chmod +x hello.pl
   ```

3. **Run the Perl script by typing the following at the shell prompt:**

   ```
   ./hello.pl
   ```

   It displays the following output:

   ```
   Hello, World!
   ```

That's it! You have written and tried your first Perl script.

Notice that the first line of a Perl script starts with `#!`, followed by the full pathname of the `perl` program. If the first line of a script starts with `#!`, the shell simply strips off the `#!`, appends the script file's name to the end, and runs the script. Thus, if the script file is named `hello.pl` and the first line is `#!/usr/bin/perl`, the shell executes the following command:

```
/usr/bin/perl hello.pl
```

# Getting an Overview of Perl

Most programming languages, including Perl, have some common features:

✦ **Variables** store different types of data. You can think of each variable as a placeholder for data — kind of like a mailbox, with a name and room to store data. The content of the variable is its value.

✦ **Expressions** combine variables by using operators. One expression may add several variables; another might extract a part of a string.

✦ **Statements** perform some action, such as assigning a value to a variable or printing a string.

✦ **Flow-control statements** enable statements to execute in various orders, depending on the value of some expression. Typically, flow-control statements include for, do-while, while, and if-then-else statements.

✦ **Functions** (also called *subroutines* or *routines*) enable you to group several statements and give them a name. Using this feature, you can execute the same set of statements by invoking the function that represents those statements. Typically, a programming language provides some predefined functions.

✦ **Packages *and* modules** that enable you to organize a set of related Perl subroutines that are designed to be reusable. (Modules were introduced in Perl 5.)

In the next few sections, I provide an overview of these major features of Perl and illustrate the features through simple examples.

## Basic Perl syntax

Perl is free-form, like C. There are no constraints on the exact placement of any keyword. Often, Perl programs are stored in files with names that end in .pl, but there is no restriction on the filenames you use.

As in C, each Perl statement ends with a semicolon (;). A hash mark or pound sign (#) marks the start of a comment; the perl program disregards the rest of the line beginning with the hash mark.

Groups of Perl statements are enclosed in braces ({ . . . }). This feature also is similar in C.

## Variables

You don't have to declare Perl variables before using them, as you do in the C programming language. You can recognize a variable in a Perl script easily because each variable name begins with a special character: an at symbol (@), a dollar sign ($), or a percent sign (%). These special characters denote the variable's type. The three variable types are as follows:

✦ **Scalar variables** represent the basic data types: integer, floating-point number, and string. A dollar sign ($) precedes a scalar variable. Following are some examples:

```
$maxlines = 256;
$title = "Fedora Core All-in-One Desk Reference";
```

✦ **Array variables** are collections of scalar variables. An array variable has an at symbol (@) as a prefix. Thus, the following are arrays:

```
@pages = (62, 26, 22, 24);
@commands = (" start", "stop", "draw", "exit");
```

✦ **Associative arrays** are collections of key-value pairs, in which each key is a string and the value is any scalar variable. A percent-sign (%) prefix indicates an associative array. You can use associative arrays to associate a name with a value. You may store the amount of disk space each user occupies in an associative array, such as the following:

```
%disk_usage = ("root", 147178, "naba", 28547,
               "emily", 55, "ashley", 40);
```

Because each variable type has a special character prefix, you can use the same name for different variable types. Thus, %disk_usage, @disk_usage, and $disk_usage can appear within the same Perl program.

### Scalars

A *scalar variable* can store a single value, such as a number or a text string. Scalar variables are the basic data type in Perl. Each scalar's name begins with a dollar sign ($). Typically, you start using a scalar with an assignment statement that initializes it. You even can use a variable without initializing it; the default value for numbers is zero, and the default value of a string is an empty string. If you want to see whether a scalar is defined, use the defined function as follows:

```
print "Name undefined!\n" if !(defined $name);
```

The expression (defined $name) is 1 if $name is defined. You can "undefine" a variable by using the undef function. You can undefine $name, for example, as follows:

```
undef $name;
```

Variables are evaluated according to context. Following is a script that initializes and prints a few variables:

```
#!/usr/bin/perl
$title = "Fedora Core All-in-One Desk Reference";
$count1 = 650;
$count2 = 238;

$total = $count1 + $count2;

print "Title: $title -- $total pages\n";
```

When you run the preceding Perl program, it produces the following output:

```
Title: Fedora Core All-in-One Desk Reference -- 888 pages
```

As the Perl statements show, when the two numeric variables are added, their numeric values are used; but when the $total variable prints, its string representation displays.

Another interesting aspect of Perl is that it evaluates all variables in a string within double quotation marks ("..."). However, if you write a string inside single quotation marks ('...'), Perl leaves that string untouched. If you write

```
 print 'Title: $title -- $total pages\n';
```

with single quotes instead of double quotes, Perl displays

```
Title: $title -- $total pages\n
```

and does not generate a new line.

A useful Perl variable is $_ (the dollar sign followed by the underscore character). This special variable is known as the *default argument*. The Perl interpreter determines the value of $_ depending on the context. When the Perl interpreter reads input from the standard input, $_ holds the current input line; when the interpreter is searching for a specific pattern of text, $_ holds the default search pattern.

## Arrays

In Perl, an *array* is a collection of scalars. The array name begins with an at symbol (@). As in C, array subscripts start at zero. You can access the elements of an array with an index. Perl allocates space for arrays dynamically.

Consider the following simple script:

```
#!/usr/bin/perl
@commands = ("start", "stop", "draw" , "exit");

$numcmd = @commands;
print "There are $numcmd commands.\n";
print "The first command is: $commands[0]\n";
```

When you run the script, it produces the following output:

```
There are 4 commands.
The first command is: start
```

As you can see, equating a scalar to the array sets the scalar to the number of elements in the array. The first element of the @commands array is referenced as $commands[0] because the index starts at zero. Thus the fourth element in the @commands array is $commands[3].

Two special scalars are related to an array. The $[ variable is one of them, and it's the current base index (the starting index), which is zero by default. The other scalar is $#*arrayname* (in which *arrayname* is the name of an array variable), which has the last array index as the value. Thus, for the @commands array, $#commands is 3.

You can print an entire array with a simple print statement like this:

```
print "@commands\n";
```

When Perl executes this statement, it displays the following output:

```
start stop draw exit
```

### Associative arrays

*Associative array* variables, which are declared with a percent-sign (%) prefix, are unique features of Perl. Using associative arrays, you can index an array with a string, such as a name. A good example of an associative array is the %ENV array that Perl automatically defines for you. In Perl, %ENV is the array of environment variables you can access by using the environment variable name as an index. The following Perl statement prints the current PATH environment variable:

```
print "PATH = $ENV{PATH}\n";
```

When Perl executes this statement, it prints the current setting of PATH. In contrast to indexing regular arrays, you have to use braces to index an associative array.

Perl has many built-in functions — such as delete, each, keys, and values — that enable you to access and manipulate associative arrays.

### Predefined variables in Perl

Perl has several predefined variables that contain useful information you may need in a Perl script. Following are a few important predefined variables.

+ @ARGV is an array of strings that contains the command-line options to the script. The first option is $ARGV[0], the second one is $ARGV[1], and so on.

+ %ENV is an associative array that contains the environment variables. You can access this array by using the environment variable name as a key. Thus $ENV{HOME} is the home directory, and $ENV{PATH} is the current search path that the shell uses to locate commands.

+ $_ is the default argument for many functions. If you see a Perl function used without any argument, the function probably is expecting its argument to be contained in the $_ variable.

+ @_ is the list of arguments passed to a subroutine.

+ $0 is the name of the file containing the Perl program.

+ $^V is the version number of Perl you are using (for example, if you use Perl Version 5.8.3, $^V is v5.8.3).

+ $< is the user ID (an identifying number) of the user running the script.

+ $$ is the script's process ID.

+ $? is the status the last system call has returned.

## Operators and expressions

*Operators* are used to combine and compare Perl variables. Typical mathematical operators are addition (+), subtraction (-), multiplication (*), and division (/). Perl and C provide nearly the same set of operators. When you use operators to combine variables, you end up with expressions. Each expression has a value.

Here are some typical Perl expressions:

```
error < 0
$count == 10
$count + $i
$users[$i]
```

These expressions are examples of the comparison operator (the first two lines), the arithmetic operator, and the array-index operator.

In Perl, don't use the == operator to determine whether two strings match; the == operator works only with numbers. To test the equality of strings, Perl includes the FORTRAN-style eq operator. Use eq to see whether two strings are identical, as follows:

```
if ($input eq "stop") { exit; }
```

Other FORTRAN-style, string-comparison operators include ne (inequality), lt (less than), gt (greater than), le (less than or equal), and ge (greater than or equal to). Also, you can use the cmp operator to compare two strings. The return value is –1, 0, or 1, depending on whether the first string is less than, equal to, or greater than the second string.

Perl also provides the following unique operators. C lacks an exponentiation operator, which FORTRAN includes; Perl uses ** as the exponentiation operator. Thus, you can write the following code in Perl:

```
$x = 2;
$y = 3;
$z = $x**$y;  # z should be 8 (2 raised to the power 3)
$y **= 2; # y is now 9 (3 raised to the power 2)
```

You can initialize an array to null by using () — the null-list operator — as follows:

```
@commands = ();
```

The dot operator (.) enables you to concatenate two strings, as follows:

```
$part1 = "Hello, ";
$part2 = "World!";
$message = $part1.$part2;  # Now $message = "Hello, World!"
```

The repetition operator, denoted by x=, is interesting and quite useful. You can use the x= operator to repeat a string a specified number of times. Suppose you want to initialize a string to 65 asterisks (*). The following example shows how you can initialize the string with the x= operator:

```
$marker = "*";
$marker x= 65;  # Now $marker is a string of 65 asterisks
```

Another powerful operator in Perl is range, which is represented by two periods (..). You can initialize an array easily by using the range operator. Following are some examples:

```
@numerals = (0..9); # @numerals = 0, 1, 2, 3, 4, 5, 6, 7, 8 , 9
@alphabet = ('A'..'Z'); # @alphabet = capital letters A through Z
```

## Regular expressions

If you have used any UNIX or Linux system for a while, you probably know about the grep command, which enables you to search files for a pattern of strings. Following is a typical use of grep:

```
cd /usr/src/linux*/drivers/cdrom
grep "[bB]laster"  *.c
```

The preceding grep command finds all occurrences of blaster and Blaster in the files with names ending in .c.

The grep command's "[bB]laster" argument is known as a *regular expression,* a pattern that matches a set of strings. You construct a regular expression with a small set of operators and rules that resemble the ones for writing arithmetic expressions. A list of characters inside brackets ([...]), for example, matches any single character in the list. Thus, the regular expression "[bB]laster" is a set of two strings, as follows:

```
blaster    Blaster
```

Perl supports regular expressions, just as the grep command does. Many other Fedora Core programs, such as the vi editor and sed (the stream editor), also support regular expressions. The purpose of a regular expression is to search for a pattern of strings in a file. That's why editors support regular expressions.

You can construct and use complex regular expressions in Perl. The rules for these regular expressions are fairly simple. Essentially, the regular expression is a sequence of characters in which some characters have special meaning. Table 4-1 summarizes the basic rules for interpreting the characters used to construct a regular expression.

| Table 4-1 | Rules for Interpreting Regular Expression Characters |
|---|---|
| *Expression* | *Meaning* |
| . | Matches any single character except a newline. |
| x* | Matches zero or more occurrences of the character x. |
| x+ | Matches one or more occurrences of the character x. |
| x? | Matches zero or one occurrence of the character x. |
| [...] | Matches any of the characters inside the brackets. |
| x{n} | Matches exactly n occurrences of the character x. |
| x{n,} | Matches n or more occurrences of the character x. |
| x{,m} | Matches zero or, at most, m occurrences of the character x. |

*(continued)*

**Table 4-1** *(continued)*

| Expression | Meaning |
|---|---|
| x{n,m} | Matches at least n occurrences, but no more than m occurrences of the character x. |
| $ | Matches the end of a line. |
| \0 | Matches a null character. |
| \b | Matches a backspace. |
| \B | Matches any character not at the beginning or end of a word. |
| \b | Matches the beginning or end of a word — when not inside brackets. |
| \cX | Matches Ctrl-X (where X is any alphabetic character). |
| \d | Matches a single digit. |
| \D | Matches a nondigit character. |
| \f | Matches a form feed. |
| \n | Matches a newline (line-feed) character. |
| \ooo | Matches the octal value specified by the digits ooo (where each o is a digit between 0 and 7). |
| \r | Matches a carriage return. |
| \S | Matches a nonwhite space character. |
| \s | Matches a white space character (space, tab, or newline). |
| \t | Matches a tab. |
| \W | Matches a nonalphanumeric character. |
| \w | Matches an alphanumeric character. |
| \xhh | Matches the hexadecimal value specified by the digits hh (where each h is a digit between 0 and f). |
| ^ | Matches the beginning of a line. |

If you want to match one of the characters $, |, *, ^, [, ], \, and /, you have to place a backslash before the character you want to match. Thus you type these characters as \$, \|, \*, \^, \[, \], \\, and \/. Regular expressions often look confusing because of the preponderance of strange character sequences and the generous sprinkling of backslashes. As with anything else, however, you can start slowly and use only a few of the features in the beginning.

So far, I have summarized the syntax of regular expressions. But I haven't yet shown how to use regular expressions in Perl. Typically, you place a regular expression within a pair of slashes and use the match (=~) or not-match (!~) operators to test a string. You can write a Perl script that performs the same search as the one done with grep earlier in this section. Follow these steps to complete this task:

1. **Use a text editor to type and save the following script in a file named** lookup:

   ```
   #!/usr/bin/perl

   while (<STDIN>)
   {
        if ( $_ =~ /[bB]laster/ ) { print $_; }
   }
   ```

2. **Make the** lookup **file executable by using the following command:**

   ```
   chmod +x lookup
   ```

3. **Try the script by using the following command:**

   ```
   cat /usr/src/linux*/drivers/cdrom/sbpcd.c | ./lookup
   ```

   In this case, the `cat` command feeds the contents of a specific file (which, as you know from the `grep` example, contains some lines with the regular expression) to the `lookup` script. The script simply applies Perl's regular expression-match operator (=~) and prints any matching line. The output is similar to what the `grep` command displays with the following command:

   ```
   grep "[bB]laster"  /usr/src/linux*/drivers/cdrom/sbpcd.c
   ```

The `$_` variable in the `lookout` script needs some explanation. The `<STDIN>` expression gets a line from the standard input and, by default, stores that line in the `$_` variable. Inside the `while` loop, the regular expression is matched against the `$_` string. The following single Perl statement completes the lookup script's work:

```
if ( $_ =~ /[bB]laster/ ) { print $_; }
```

This example illustrates how you might use a regular expression to search for occurrences of strings in a file.

After you use regular expressions for a while, you can better appreciate their power. The trick is to find the regular expression that performs the task you want. For example, here is a search that looks for all lines that begin with exactly seven spaces and end with a closing parenthesis:

```
while (<STDIN>)
{
    if ( $_ =~ /\)\n/ && $_ =~ /^ {7}\S/ )  { print $_; }
}
```

## Flow-control statements

So far, you have seen Perl statements intended to execute in a serial fashion, one after another. Perl also includes statements that enable you to control the flow of execution of the statements. You already have seen the `if` statement and a `while` loop. Perl includes a complete set of flow-control statements just like those in C, but with a few extra features.

In Perl, all conditional statements take the following form:

```
conditional-statement
{ Perl code to execute if conditional is true }
```

Notice that you must enclose within braces ({ . . . }) the code that follows the conditional statement. The conditional statement checks the value of an expression to determine whether to execute the code within the braces. In Perl, as in C, any nonzero value is considered logically true, whereas a zero value is false.

Next I briefly describe the syntax of the major conditional statements in Perl.

### if and unless

The Perl `if` statement resembles the C `if` statement. For example, an `if` statement may check a count to see whether the count exceeds a threshold, as follows:

```
if ( $count > 25 ) { print "Too many errors!\n"; }
```

You can add an `else` clause to the `if` statement, like this:

```
if ($user eq "root")
{
    print "Starting simulation...\n";
}
else
{
    print "Sorry $user, you must be \"root\" to run this
            program.\n";
    exit;
}
```

If you know C, you can see that Perl's syntax looks quite a bit like that in C. Conditionals with the `if` statement can have zero or more `elsif` clauses to account for more alternatives, as in the following:

```
print "Enter version number:"; # prompt user for version number
$os_version = <STDIN>;     # read from standard input
chop $os_version; # get rid of the newline at the end of the line
# Check version number
if ($os_version >= 10 ) { print "No upgrade necessary\n";}
elsif ($os_version >= 6 && $os_version < 9)
                { print "Standard upgrade\n";}
elsif ($os_version > 3 && $os_version < 6) { print "Reinstall\n";}
else { print "Sorry, cannot upgrade\n";}
```

The unless statement is unique to Perl. This statement has the same form as if, including the use of elsif and else clauses. The difference is that unless executes its statement block only if the condition is false. You can, for example, use unless in the following code:

```perl
unless ($user eq "root")
{
    print "You must be \"root\" to run this program.\n";
    exit;
}
```

In this case, unless the string user is "root", the script exits.

### while

Use Perl's while statement for *looping* — the repetition of some processing until an existing condition becomes logically false. To read a line at a time from standard input and to process that line, you may use the following while loop:

```perl
while ($in = <STDIN>)
{
# Code to process the line
    print $in;
}
```

If you read from the standard input without any argument, Perl assigns the current line of standard input to the $_ variable. Thus, you can write the preceding while loop as follows:

```perl
while (<STDIN>)
{
# Code to process the line
    print $_;
}
```

Perl's while statements are more versatile than those of C because you can use almost anything as the condition to be tested. If you use an array as the condition, for example, the while loop executes until the array has no elements left, as in the following example:

```perl
# Assume @cmd arg has the current set of command arguments
while (@cmd arg)
{
    $arg = shift @cmd arg;  # this extracts one argument
# Code to process the current argument
    print $arg;
}
```

The `shift` function removes the first element of an array and returns that element.

You can skip to the end of a loop with the `next` keyword; the `last` keyword exits the loop. For example, the following `while` loop adds the numbers from 1 to 10, skipping 5:

```
while (1)
{
  $i++;
  if($i == 5) { next;} # Jump to the next iteration if $i is 5
  if($i > 10) { last;} # When $i exceeds 10, end the loop
  $sum += $i;        # Add the numbers
}
# At this point $sum should be 50
```

### for and foreach

Perl and C's `for` statements have similar syntax. Use the `for` statement to execute a statement any number of times, based on the value of an expression. The syntax is as follows:

```
for (expr_1; expr_2; expr_3) { statement block }
```

*expr_1* is evaluated one time, at the beginning of the loop; the statement block executes until *expr_2* evaluates to zero. The third expression, *expr_3*, is evaluated after each execution of the statement block. You can omit any of the expressions, but you must include the semicolons. In addition, the braces around the statement block are required. Following is an example that uses a `for` loop to add the numbers from 1 to 10:

```
for($i=0, $sum=0; $i <= 10; $sum += $i, $i++) {}
```

In this example, the actual work of adding the numbers is done in the third expression, and the statement the `for` loop controls is an empty block (`{}`).

The `foreach` statement is most appropriate for arrays. Following is the syntax:

```
foreach Variable (Array) { statement block }
```

The `foreach` statement assigns to *Variable* an element from the *Array* and executes the statement block. The `foreach` statement repeats this procedure until no array elements remain. The following `foreach` statement adds the numbers from 1 to 10:

```
foreach $i (1..10) { $sum += $i;}
```

Notice that I declare the array by using the range operator (..). You also can use a list of comma-separated items as the array.

If you omit the *Variable* in a `foreach` statement, Perl implicitly uses the `$_` variable to hold the current array element. Thus you can use the following:

```
foreach (1..10) { $sum += $_;}
```

### goto

The `goto` statement causes Perl to jump to a statement identified by a label. Here is an example that prompts the user for a value and repeats the request, if the value is not acceptable:

```
ReEnter:
print "Enter offset: ";
$offset = <STDIN>;
chop $offset;
unless ($offset > 0 && $offset < 512)
{
    print "Bad offset: $offset\n";
    goto ReEnter;
}
```

## Accessing Linux commands

You can execute any Linux command from Perl in several ways:

✦ Call the `system` function with a string that contains the Linux command you want to execute.

✦ Enclose a Linux command within backquotes (`), which also are known as *grave accents*. You can run a Linux command this way and capture its output.

✦ Call the `fork` function to copy the current script and process new commands in the child process. (If a process starts another process, the new one is known as a *child* process.)

✦ Call the `exec` function to overlay the current script with a new script or Linux command.

✦ Use `fork` and `exec` to provide shell-like behavior. (Monitor user input, and process each user-entered command through a child process.) In this section, I present a simple example of how to accomplish this task.

The simplest way to execute a Linux command in your script is to use the `system` function with the command in a string. After the system function returns, the exit code from the command is in the $? variable. You can easily write a simple Perl script that reads a string from the standard input and processes that string with the system function. Follow these steps:

1. **Use a text editor to enter and save the following script in a file named** rcmd.pl:

```
#!/usr/bin/perl
# Read user input and process command

$prompt = "Command (\"exit\" to quit): ";
print $prompt;

while (<STDIN>)
{
    chop;
    if ($_ eq "exit") { exit 0;}

# Execute command by calling system
    system $_;
    unless ($? == 0) {print "Error executing: $_\n";}
    print $prompt;
}
```

2. **Make the** rcmd.pl **file executable by using the following command:**

```
chmod +x rcmd.pl
```

3. **Run the script by typing** ./rcmd.pl **at the shell prompt.**

Here's a sample output from the rcmd.pl script (the output depends on what commands you enter):

```
Command ("exit" to quit): ps
  PID TTY          TIME CMD
 3128 pts/2     00:00:00 bash
 3314 pts/2     00:00:00 rcmd.pl
 3315 pts/2     00:00:00 ps
Command ("exit" to quit): exit
```

You can also run Linux commands by using fork and exec in your Perl script. Following is an example script — psh.pl — that uses fork and exec to execute commands the user enters:

```
#!/usr/bin/perl

# This is a simple script that uses "fork" and "exec" to
# run a command entered by the user

$prompt = "Command (\"exit\" to quit): ";
print $prompt;

while (<STDIN>)
{
```

```
chop;      # remove trailing newline
if($_ eq "exit") { exit 0;}

$status = fork;
if($status)
{
# In parent... wait for child process to finish...
    wait;
    print $prompt;
    next;
}
else
{
    exec $_;
}
}
```

The following sample output shows how the `psh.pl` script executes the `ps` command:

```
Command ("exit" to quit): ps
  PID TTY          TIME CMD
 3128 pts/2    00:00:00 bash
 3321 pts/2    00:00:00 psh.pl
 3322 pts/2    00:00:00 ps
Command ("exit" to quit): exit
```

Shells (such as Bash) use the `fork` and `exec` combination to run commands.

## File access

You may have noticed the `<STDIN>` expression in various examples in this chapter. That's Perl's way of reading from a file. In Perl, a *file handle,* also known as an *identifier,* gives a file a distinct identity while it's being read. Usually, file handles are in uppercase characters. `STDIN` is a predefined file handle that denotes the standard input — by default, the keyboard. `STDOUT` and `STDERR` are the other two predefined file handles. `STDOUT` is used for printing to the terminal, and `STDERR` is used for printing error messages.

To read from a file, write the file handle inside angle brackets (`<>`). Thus, `<STDIN>` reads a line from the standard input.

You can open other files by using the `open` function. The following example shows you how to open the `/etc/passwd` file for reading and how to display the lines in that file:

```
open (PWDFILE, "/etc/passwd"); # PWDFILE is the file handle
while (<PWDFILE>) { print $_;} # By default, input line is in $_
close PWDFILE;         # Close the file
```

By default, the open function opens a file for reading. You can add special characters at the beginning of the filename to indicate other types of access. A < prefix opens the file for writing, whereas a > prefix opens a file for appending. Following is a short script that reads the /etc/passwd file and creates a new file, named output, with a list of all users who lack shells (the password entries for these users have : at the end of each line):

```
#!/usr/bin/perl
# Read /etc/passwd and create list of users without any shell

open (PWDFILE, "/etc/passwd");
open (RESULT, ">output");    # open file for writing

while (<PWDFILE>)
{
    if ($_ =~ /:\n/) {print RESULT $_;}
}

close PWDFILE;
close RESULT;
```

After you execute this script, you find a file named output in the current directory. Here's what the output file contains when I run this script on a Fedora Core system:

```
news:x:9:13:news:/etc/news:
```

## Filename with pipe prefix

One interesting filename prefix is the *pipe character* — the vertical bar (|). If you call open with a filename that begins with |, the rest of the filename is treated as a command. The Perl interpreter executes the command, and you can use print calls to send input to this command. The following Perl script sends a mail message to a list of users by using the mail command:

```
#!/usr/bin/perl
# Send mail to a list of users

foreach ("root", "naba")
{
  open (MAILPIPE, "| mail -s Greetings $_");
  print MAILPIPE "Remember to send in your weekly report today!\n";
  close MAILPIPE;
}
```

If a filename ends with a pipe character (|), that filename executes as a command; you can read that command's output with the angle brackets (<...>), as shown in the following example:

```
open (PSPIPE, "ps ax |");
while (<PSPIPE>)
{
```

```
# Process the output of the ps command
# This example simply echoes each line
    print $_;
}
```

## Subroutines

Although Perl includes a large assortment of built-in functions, you can add your own code modules in the form of *subroutines*. In fact, Perl comes with a large set of these programs-within-programs. Here's a simple script that illustrates the syntax of subroutines in Perl:

```
#!/usr/bin/perl
sub hello
{
# Make local copies of the arguments from the @_ array
    local ($first,$last) = @_;

    print "Hello, $first $last\n";
}

$a = Jane;
$b = Doe;

&hello($a, $b);        # Call the subroutine
```

When you run the preceding script, it displays the following output:

```
Hello, Jane Doe
```

Note the following points about subroutines:

✦ The subroutine receives its arguments in the array @_ (the at symbol, followed by an underscore character).

✦ Variables used in subroutines are global by default. Use the `local` function to create a local set of variables.

✦ Call a subroutine by placing an ampersand (&) before its name. Thus, the subroutine `hello` is called by typing &hello.

If you want, you can put a subroutine in its own file. The `hello` subroutine, for example, can reside in a file named `hello.pl`. When you place a subroutine in a file, remember to add a return value at the end of the file — just type 1; at the end to return 1. Thus, the `hello.pl` file appears as follows:

```
sub hello
{
# Make local copies of the arguments from the @_ array
    local ($first,$last) = @_;
```

```
        print "Hello, $first $last\n";
}
1;      # return value
```

Then, you have to write the script that uses the `hello` subroutine, as follows:

```
#!/usr/bin/perl
require 'hello.pl';  # include the file with the subroutine

$a = Jane;
$b = Doe;

&hello($a, $b);      # Call the subroutine
```

This script uses the require function to include the `hello.pl` file that contains the definition of the `hello` subroutine.

### Built-in functions in Perl

Perl has nearly 200 built-in functions (also referred to as *Perl functions*), including functions that resemble the ones in the C Run-Time Library, as well as functions that access the operating system. You really need to go through the list of functions to appreciate the breadth of capabilities available in Perl. I don't have enough space in this book to cover these functions, but you can find out about the Perl built-in functions by pointing your Web browser to the following address:

```
www.perldoc.com/perl5.8.0/pod/perlfunc.html
```

This address connects you to the Perl 5.8.0 documentation page so you can get an overview of the Perl built-in functions. On that page, click a function's name to view more detailed information about that function.

You can also read the Perl function manual on your Fedora Core system by typing the following command in a terminal window:

```
man perlfunc
```

This command displays the text `man` page for the functions. (I think you'll find the Web-based documentation much easier to use.)

## Understanding Perl Packages and Modules

A *Perl package* is a way to group together data and subroutines. Essentially, it's a way to use variable and subroutine names without conflicting with any names used in other parts of a program. The concept of a package existed in Perl since version 4.

The package provides a way to control the *namespace* — a term that refers to the collection of variable and subroutine names. Although you may not be aware of this, when you write a Perl program, it automatically belongs to a package named `main`. Besides `main`, other Perl packages are in the Perl library (in the `/usr/lib/perl5/X.Y.Z` directory of your Fedora Core system where `X.Y.Z` is the version number of Perl such as `5.8.3`), and you can define your own package, as well.

Perl *modules* are packages that follow specific guidelines.

## Perl packages

You can think of a Perl package as a convenient way to organize a set of related Perl subroutines. Another benefit is that variable and subroutine names defined in a package do not conflict with names used elsewhere in the program. Thus, a variable named `$count` in one package remains unique to that package and does not conflict with a `$count` used elsewhere in a Perl program.

A Perl package is in a single file. The `package` statement is used at the beginning of the file to declare the file as a package and to give the package a name. For example, the file `timelocal.pl` defines a number of subroutines and variables in a package named `timelocal`. (Note that the Time::Local module supercedes the `timelocal.pl` file.) The `timelocal.pl` file has the following `package` statement in various places:

```
package timelocal;
```

The effect of this package declaration is that all subsequent variable names and subroutine names are considered to be in the `timelocal` package. You can put such a package statement at the beginning of the file that implements the package.

What if you are implementing a package and you need to refer to a subroutine or variable in another package? As you might guess, all you need to do is specify both the package name and the variable (or subroutine) name. Perl provides the following syntax for referring to a variable in another package:

```
$Package::Variable
```

Here *Package* is the name of the package, and *Variable* is the name of the variable in that package. If you omit the package name, Perl assumes you're referring to a variable in the `main` package.

To use a package in your program, you can simply call the `require` function with the package filename as an argument. For example, a package named ctime is defined in the file ctime.pl. That package includes the ctime subroutine that converts a binary time into a string. The following simple program uses the ctime package from the ctime.pl file:

```
#!/usr/bin/perl -w

# Use the ctime package defined in ctime.pl file
require 'ctime.pl';

# Call the ctime subroutine
$time = ctime(time());

# Print the time string
print $time;
```

As you can see, this program uses the require function to bring the ctime.pl file into the program. When you run this program, it prints the current date and time formatted, as shown in the following sample output:

```
Sat Jan 24 16:40:17 2004
```

Note that the first line of this script uses the -w option. That option causes the Perl interpreter to print warning messages about any bad constructs in the Perl script. Including the -w option on the line that invokes the Perl interpreter is a good idea.

If you want to check the syntax of a Perl program without actually running it, run the Perl interpreter with the -c option, like this (*filename* is the name of the Perl program whose syntax you want to check):

```
perl -c filename
```

## Perl modules

Perl 5 took the concept of a package one step further and introduced the *module,* a package that follows certain guidelines and is designed to be reusable. Each module is a package that is defined in a file with the same name as the package but with a .pm extension. Each Perl object is implemented as a module. For example, the CGI object (for use in Web servers) is implemented as the CGI module, stored in the file named CGI.pm.

Nowadays Perl comes with many modules. You find these modules in the /usr/lib/perl5/X.Y.Z directory where X.Y.Z is the Perl version number. For Perl Version 5.8.3, the Perl modules are in the /usr/lib/perl5/5.8.3 directory. Look for files with names that end in .pm (which stands for *Perl module*).

## Using a module

You can call the `require` function or the `use` function to include a Perl module in your program. For example, a Perl module named `Cwd` (defined, as expected, in the `Cwd.pm` file) provides a `getcwd` subroutine that returns the current directory. You can call the `require` function to include the `Cwd` module and call `getcwd` as follows:

```
require Cwd;  # You do not need the full file name
$curdir = Cwd::getcwd();
print "Current directory = $curdir\n";
```

The first line brings the `Cwd.pm` file into this program — you do not have to specify the full filename; the `require` function automatically appends `.pm` to the module's name to figure out which file to include. The second line shows how you call a subroutine from the `Cwd` module. When you use `require` to include a module, you must invoke each subroutine with the *Module::subroutine* format.

If you rewrite this example program with the `use` function in place of `require`, it takes the following form:

```
use Cwd;
$curdir = getcwd(); # no need for Cwd:: prefix
print "Current directory = $curdir\n";
```

The most significant difference is that you no longer need to qualify a sub-routine name with the module name prefix (such as `Cwd::`).

You can call either `require` or `use` to include a module in your program. Just remember the following nuances when you use these functions:

✦ When you include a module by calling `require`, the module is included only when the `require` function is invoked as the program runs. You must use the *Module::subroutine* syntax to invoke any subroutines from a module you include with the require function.

✦ When you include a module by calling `use`, the module is included in the program as soon as the `use` statement is processed. Thus, you can invoke subroutines and variables from the module as if they are part of your program. You do not need to qualify subroutine and variable names with a *Module::* prefix.

You may want to stick to the `use` *Module;* syntax to include modules in your program because this syntax lets you use a simpler syntax when you call subroutines from the module.

# Using Objects in Perl

An *object* is a data structure together with the functions that operate on that data. Each object is an instance of a class that defines the object's type. For example, a rectangle class may have the four corners of the rectangle as data; functions such as one that computes the rectangle's area; and another that draws the rectangle. Then, each rectangle object can be an *instance* of the rectangle *class,* with different coordinates for each of the four corners. In this sense, an object is an instance of a class.

The functions (or subroutines) that implement the operations on an object's data are known as *methods*. That's terminology borrowed from Smalltalk, one of the earliest object-oriented programming languages.

Classes also suggest the notion of inheritance. You can define a new class of objects by extending the data or methods (or both) of an existing class. A common use of inheritance is to express the IS A relationship among various classes of objects. Consider, for example, the geometric shapes. Because a circle IS A shape and a rectangle IS A shape, you can say that the circle and rectangle classes inherit from the shape class. In this case, the shape class is called a parent class or base class.

The basic idea behind *object-oriented programming* is that you can package the data and the associated methods (subroutines) of an object so they work like a *black box* — input generates output, without your having to specify every detail of how to get the job done. Programmers access the object only through advertised methods, without having to know the inner workings of the methods. Typically, a programmer can create an object, invoke its methods to get or set attributes (that's another name for the object's data), and destroy the object. In this section, I show you how to use objects in Perl. With this knowledge in hand, you can exploit objects as building blocks for your Perl programs.

# Understanding Perl Objects

Perl implements objects by using modules, which package data and subroutines in a file. Perl presents the following simple model of objects:

✦ An *object* is denoted by a reference (objects are implemented as references to a hash).

✦ A *class* is a Perl module that provides the methods to work with the object.

✦ A *method* is a Perl subroutine that expects the object reference as the first argument.

Object implementers have to follow certain rules and provide certain methods in a module that represents a class. However, you really don't need to know much about an object's implementation to use it in your Perl program. For practical purposes, all you need to know are the steps you have to follow when you use an object.

## Creating and accessing Perl objects

An especially useful Perl object is the Shell object, which is implemented by the Perl module Shell.pm. That module comes with the Perl distribution and is in the /usr/lib/perl5/5.8.3 directory (for Perl Version 5.8.3).

As the name implies, the Shell object is meant for running shell commands from within Perl scripts. You can create a Shell object and have it execute commands.

To use the Shell object, follow these general steps:

1. **Place the following line to include the Shell module in your program:**

   ```
   use Shell;
   ```

   You must include this line before you create a Shell object.

2. **To create a Shell object, use the following syntax:**

   ```
   my $sh = Shell->new;
   ```

   where $sh is the reference to the Shell object.

3. **Run Linux commands by using the Shell object and capture any outputs by saving to an appropriate variable. For example, to save the directory listing of the /usr/lib/perl5/5.8.0 directory in an array named @modules, write the following:**

   ```
   @modules = $sh->ls("/usr/lib/perl5/5.8.3/*.pm");
   ```

   Then you can work with this array of Perl module filenames (that's what *.pm files are) any way you want. For example, to simply go through the array and print each string out, use the following while loop:

   ```
   while(@modules)
   {
     $mod = shift @modules;
     # Do whatever you want with the module name
     print $mod;
   }
   ```

How do you know which methods to call and in what order to call them? You have to read the object's documentation before you can use the object. The method names and the sequences of method invocation depend on what the object does.

## Using the English module

Perl includes several special variables with strange names, such as $_ (for the default argument) and $! (for error messages corresponding to the last error). When you read a program, guessing what a special variable means can be difficult. The result is that you may end up avoiding a special variable that could be useful in your program.

As a helpful gesture, Perl 5 provides the English module (English.pm), which enables you to use understandable names for various special variables in Perl. To use the English module, include the following line in your Perl program:

```
use English;
```

After that, you can refer to $_ as $ARG and $! as $ERRNO. (These "English" names can still be a bit cryptic, but they're definitely better than the punctuation marks.)

The following program uses the English module — and prints a few interesting variables:

```
#!/usr/bin/perl -w
# File: english.pl

use English;
print "Perl executable = $EXECUTABLE_NAME\n";
print "Script name = $PROGRAM_NAME\n";
```

Run this script with the following command:

```
./english.pl
```

When I run this script on Fedora Core, here's what I get as output:

```
Perl executable = /usr/bin/perl
Script name = ./english.pl
```

The English module is handy because it lets you write Perl scripts in which you can refer to special variables by meaningful names. To find out more about the Perl special variables and their English names, type **man perlvar** in a terminal window — or, better yet, point your Web browser to

```
www.perldoc.com/perl5.8.0/pod/perlvar.html
```

# Appendix: About the DVD

## In This Appendix

✓ System requirements

✓ DVD installation instructions

✓ What you can find on the DVD

✓ Troubleshooting

**M**ake sure that your computer meets the minimum system requirements shown in the following list. If your computer doesn't match up to most of these requirements, you may have problems using the software and files on the DVD.

✦ A PC with processor running at 400 MHz or faster for graphical installation

✦ At least 192MB of total RAM installed on your computer for graphical installation (256MB recommended)

✦ At least 520MB free space on your hard disk for a minimal installation; 5GB of free space recommended if you plan to install most packages so that you can try out everything covered in this book

✦ A DVD-ROM drive (if you have only a CD-ROM drive, use the included coupon to order Fedora Core on CD-ROMs or download and burn your own CDs — see Book I, Chapter 5 for instructions)

✦ A graphics card and a monitor capable of displaying at least 256 colors

✦ A sound card

✦ Ethernet network interface card (NIC) or modem with a speed of at least 56 Kbps

## DVD Installation Instructions

Installing Fedora Core from the DVD is easy as long as you can boot your PC from the DVD-ROM drive.

To install Fedora Core from the companion DVD, follow these steps. (For the latest and greatest information, please refer to the README file located at the root of the DVD-ROM.)

1. **Gather information about your PC's hardware, such as graphics card, network card, and SCSI card, before you install Fedora Core.**

2. **Use a partitioning program such as PartitionMagic or the FIPS program to create room on your hard disk for Fedora Core.**

   Skip this step if you plan to use Fedora Core as the sole operating system on your PC or if you plan to install it on an empty second hard disk.

3. **Boot your PC with the DVD.**

   This step automatically runs the Fedora Core installation program. From this point on, respond to the questions and choices in a number of windows as the Fedora Core installation program takes you through the steps. Here are some of the key installation steps:

   - Identify any SCSI adapters installed on your PC.

   - Prepare the hard disk partitions for Fedora Core. If you have created space by reducing the size of an existing Windows partition, this step enables you to create the partitions for Fedora Core.

   - Configure the Ethernet network, if any. You may have to specify parameters, such as the IP address and host name for your Fedora Core system.

   - Specify the local time zone and set the root password.

   - Install a boot loader program on your hard disk so that you can boot Fedora Core when you power up your PC after shutting it down.

   - Select the specific software packages that you want to install, such as the X Window System and the GNOME or KDE graphical desktop.

To install specific packages from the DVD to your hard drive, follow these steps:

1. **Log in as** root.

2. **Insert the DVD into your computer's DVD-ROM drive.**

3. **If you are using GNOME or KDE GUI, wait for the DVD to mount. Otherwise, open a terminal window and at the command prompt type**

   ```
   mount /mnt/cdrom
   ```

4. **Choose Main Menu⇨System Settings⇨Add/Remove Applications.**

The Add and Remove Software utility starts and gathers information about the status of packages installed on your system. After it sorts through the information about all the installed packages, the utility displays a list of all the packages.

5. **To install any uninstalled package, select the package.**

6. **Click Update to Install the selected package.**

7. **To remove the DVD from your DVD-ROM drive, type the following command at the command prompt:**

```
umount /mnt/cdrom
```

# What You Can Find on the DVD

This section provides a summary of the software and other goodies you find on the DVD. If you need help with installing the items provided on the DVD, refer to the installation instructions in the preceding section.

*Shareware programs* are fully functional, free, trial versions of copyrighted programs. If you like particular programs, register with their authors for a nominal fee and receive licenses, enhanced versions, and technical support.

*Freeware programs* are free, copyrighted games, applications, and utilities. You can copy them to as many PCs as you like — for free — but they offer no tech support.

*GNU software* is governed by its own license, which is included in the folder of the GNU software. There are no restrictions on distribution of GNU software. See the GNU license at the root of the DVD for details.

*Trial*, *demo*, or *evaluation* versions of software are usually limited by time or functionality (such as not letting you save a project after you create it).

You can find the following software on the DVD (for info on the directory organization of a DVD, refer to the README file located at the root of the DVD-ROM):

✦ Linux kernel 2.6.5 with driver modules for major PC hardware configurations, including IDE/EIDE and SCSI drives, PCMCIA devices, CD drives and DVD drives

✦ A complete set of installation and configuration tools for setting up devices and services

✦ A graphical user interface based on the X.Org X11 6.7.0 package, with GNOME 2.6 and KDE 3.2.2 graphical desktops

- ✦ Full TCP/IP networking for Internet, LANs, and intranets

- ✦ Tools for connecting your PC to your Internet Service Provider (ISP) using PPP, DSL, or dial-up serial communications programs

- ✦ A complete suite of Internet applications, including electronic mail (`sendmail`, `mail`), news (INN), TELNET, FTP, DNS, and NFS

- ✦ Evolution 1.4.6 e-mail and calendar application

- ✦ OpenOffice.org 1.1.1 office suite with word processor, spreadsheet, presentation software, and more

- ✦ Apache Web server 2.0.49, to turn your PC into a Web server; and Mozilla 1.6, to surf the Net

- ✦ Samba 3.0.3 LAN Manager software for Microsoft Windows connectivity

- ✦ Several text editors (for example, GNU Emacs 21.3; `vim`)

- ✦ Graphics and image manipulation software, such as The GIMP, Xfig, Gnuplot, Ghostscript, Ghostview, and ImageMagick

- ✦ Programming languages (GNU C and C++ 3.3, Perl 5.8.3, Tcl/Tk 8.4.5, Python 2.3.3, GNU AWK 3.1.3) and software development tools (GNU Debugger 6.0, CVS 1.11, RCS 5.7, GNU Bison 1.875, flex 2.5.4a, TIFF, and JPEG libraries)

- ✦ Support for industry standard Executable and Linking Format (ELF) and Intel Binary Compatibility Specification (iBCS)

- ✦ A complete suite of standard UNIX utilities from the GNU project

- ✦ Tools to access and use DOS files and applications (`mtools` 3.9.9)

- ✦ Text formatting and typesetting software (`groff`, TeX, and LaTeX)

## Troubleshooting

If you have difficulty installing or using the materials on the companion DVD, consult the detailed installation and troubleshooting instructions in Book I.

If you still have trouble with the DVD-ROM, please call the Wiley Product Technical Support phone number: (800) 762-2974. Outside the United States, call 1(317) 572-3994. You can also contact Wiley Product Technical Support through the Internet at `www.wiley.com/techsupport`. Wiley Publishing will provide technical support only for installation and other general quality control items; for technical support on the applications themselves, consult the program's vendor or author.

To place additional orders or to request information about other Wiley products, please call (800) 225-5945.

# Index

## Numbers & Symbols

* (asterisks) as command wildcards, 140–141
[ ] (brackets) as command wildcards, 140–141
! (exclamation points) in repeating commands, 142
? (question marks) as command wildcards, 140–141
10BaseT Ethernet, 301–302, 305–306. *See also* Ethernet
802.11x. *See* wireless Ethernet

## A

A (Address) resource records, 687, 688
absolute pathnames, 158
access points, 310
access-control directives in httpd.conf, 631–634
accounts. *See* users
ad-hoc mode in wireless Ethernet, 308
Add New Device Type window, 313–315
Add NFS Share dialog box, 699–700
Add and Remove Packages utility, 72–74

addresses, e-mail, 338, 664. *See also* IP addresses; Web site addresses
AIM (AOL Instant Messenger). *See* IM
Anaconda program, 11, 23, 31
analog signals, 274
anonymous FTP. *See* FTP
Anyware Office application, 173–174
a.out format, 503
Apache Web server. *See also* HTTP; Internet servers
  configuring
    default configuration, 621–622
    HTTP configuration tool, 622–623
    HTTP servers, 623
    performance tuning, 623
    virtual hosts, 622, 623
  configuring using httpd.conf files
    access-control directives, 631–634
    defined, 624
    general directives, 624–627
    LogFormat directive tokens, 636–637
    online documentation on, 624
    overview, 623–624
    resource configuration directives, 627–631
    virtual hosts, 634–637

  defined, 21, 618–619
  HTTP and, 615–618
  httpd daemon server, 615, 635
  installing, 619–620
  online resources, 619
  overview, 615
  starting, 620–621
  vulnerabilities, 581
  Web servers, defined, 352, 355–356, 615
applets on GUI desktop panels, 116
application development. *See* building; programming
application gateways, 570–571. *See also* proxy servers
Application layer in TCP/IP, 296
applications. *See* Fedora Core 2 applications; managing
archiving files commands, 145
*area* (of a circle) program, 715–716
arguments
  in Bash shell, 96, 136–137
  in C programming, 745, 758
  default, in Perl, 785
  in shell scripting, 769–772
Arkeia backup utility, 447
ARPA (Advanced Research Projects Agency), 297
ARPANET, 676

array variables in Perl, 784, 785–786

arrays in C, 743–744, 745

ASCII-armored format, 551

ASF (Apache Software Foundation), 619

Aspell tool, 170, 175–176

associative arrays in Perl, 784, 786–787

asterisks (*) as command wildcards, 140–141

Asymmetric DSL (Digital Subscriber Line), 275–276

at command, 419–421

AT Modem Cable, 287

ATA (AT Attachment), 33

ATAPI (AT Attachment Packet Interface), 504–506

atd daemon server, 419

attachments, e-mail, 214, 339

audio CDs. *See also* CD-ROMs; sound
  creating WAV files from, 188
  finding WAV files, 187
  playing, 186–187
  recording, 191–192

audio, MP3, 189

authentication, PAP/CHAP, 293–294

auto-completing shell commands, 140

auto-handling mail, 663–664

auto-starting servers, 403, 607–614

Autoconf software, 18

Automake software, 17. *See also* make

automated backups, 451–452

automating tasks. *See* macros; programming

AutoPilot in Calc, Function, 239, 245–246

AutoPilot in Impress, 253–254

## *B*

backgrounds in GNOME, 85–87, 125–126

backgrounds in KDE, 93–94, 133–134

backing up/restoring. *See* managing file systems

base stations, 310

Bash shell. *See* shells

bastion hosts. *See* hosts

Bc software, 17

Berkeley database library, 733

Berkeley Sockets interface, 598

Berners-Lee, T., 616

/bin directory, 155, 439

BIND (Berkeley Internet Name Domain). *See* DNS

Binutils software, 17

bison tool, 733

bit buckets, 139

BitTorrent. *See also* Fedora Core 2 installation
  defined, 99
  downloading Fedora Core via, 101–102
  downloading/installing, 100–101
  joining, 100
  opening TCP ports used by, 101

black box, 804

block devices, 481, 503–504

blocks, statement, 751, 752

BogoMIPS, 76, 416

bookmark fields, inserting, 234

boot commands, kernel, 62–64

boot disks, installer, 32

boot file permission settings, 583

boot loaders, 47–48, 75. *See also* GRUB

boot messages, 76

/boot directory, 155, 407, 439, 583

booting. *See also* Fedora Core 2 boot process
  defined, 75
  rebooting, 517
  rebuilt Linux kernels, 515–517
  turning off SELinux during, 513

brackets [ ] as command wildcards, 140–141

break statements, 751

Bricklin, Dan, 237

BrightStor ARCserve Backup for Linux, 447

browsers. *See* Web browsers

BRU backup utility, 447

buffer overflow problem, 544

buffers, 204

building software. *See also* programming; rebuilding
  PostgreSQL databases, 179–180

software packages from source files. *See also* managing applications
downloading source files, 469–470
GNU GPLs and, 471
and installing, 472
overview, 469
RPM packages, 474
and running, 473
steps in, 471–473
warning, 472
built-in. *See also* predefined
built-in Bash commands, 775–778
built-in firewall, 571–575
built-in Perl functions, 800
bus options, 502–503
bytes, 104

# C

.c extension, 716, 735
C language. *See* programming in C
cable modem. *See* Internet connections
Cable/DSL routers, 279, 283, 305. *See also* NAT
caching name servers. *See* DNS
cal command, 148
calculating data. *See* OpenOffice.org Calc
calculator tools in GUI desktops, 170, 172–173
calibrating delay loops, 77
case statements, 752, 773–775
cat command, 137, 151
cd command, 158–159

CD-ROMs. *See also* DVD; X-CD-Roast
audio, creating WAV files from, 188
audio, playing, 186–187
burning
    backup files onto, 445
    using Cdrecord command, 170
    Fedora Core onto, 103–104
    using GNOME Nautilus shell, 120–121
    using X-CD-Roast, 188–193
drive requirements, 33
free CD database, 186, 191
installing during firstboot, 78–79
Linux file system and, 153–154, 440–441
managing, 25–26, 71–72
mounting
    defined, 440–441
    from GUI desktops, 25–26, 71–72
    using mount command, 166–167, 441–443
saving files received on, 214
unmounting, 167, 442
central processing units (CPUs), 9–10, 33, 710
CGI (Common Gateway Interface), 621, 780
CHAP (Challenge Handshake Authentication Protocol), 293, 294
character devices, 481, 508–509

charting data. *See* OpenOffice.org Calc
charts in Impress presentations, 257–258, 259
chgrp command, 434
chips, 710
chkconfig command
    auto-starting servers at startup, 403, 607–609
    defined, 608
    disabling standalone servers, 558
    turning xinetd services on/off, 559–560, 606
    viewing lists of servers, 403
chmod command, 152, 162–163, 541–542, 768
chown command, 163, 434–435
chsh command, 136
classes of objects, 804
classes in sendmail.cf, 659
client/server architecture, 597–598
CMTS (Cable Modem Termination System), 280, 281
CNAME (Canonical Name) resource records, 681–682, 687
code maturity level options, 501
colon (:) command mode in vi editor, 206–207, 208
color backgrounds in GNOME, 85–86
color backgrounds in KDE, 93
command interpreters, 95. *See also* shells

command-line interface
arguments, 96, 136–137
command lines, 96, 136, 711
defined, 16
using FTP from, 387–390
commands. *See also* Linux commands; Linux file system
for adding user accounts, 428–429
in ed text editor, 203–204
gpg, 550–554
iptables, 571, 573–575
kernel boot commands, 62–64
for managing file systems, 456–460
for managing Loadable Driver Modules, 483–485
mount, 166–167, 441–443
mtools, 456–460
r commands, 561, 581
rpm commands, 461–469
SMTP commands, 649–651
tar
backing up/restoring files, 447–449, 451
defined, 19, 27, 145
unpacking source files, 469–470
in vi text editor, 207–209
wildcards for, 140–141
commenting out, 606
Common Gateway Interface (CGI), 621, 780
compiler programs, 712
compound statements/ blocks, 751, 752
compressed tarballs, 469

compressing files commands, 145
computer programming. *See* building; programming
computer security audits. *See* security audits
computers, 710–711
concatenate, 162, 541
Concurrent Versions System (CVS), 22, 713
conditional directives, 738, 739–740. *See also* flow-control statements
configuration files. *See* system configuration
Configure Network Settings window, 313, 315
configure shell script, 472
Configure Wireless Connection window, 313, 314
const type qualifier, 746
contexts of files, security, 15
contiguous, 34
continue statements, 752
Control Center in GNOME, 125
Control Center in KDE, 92–93, 132–134
converting file formats, 767–768
copying files, 163–164
Coreutils software, 17
cp command, 163–164
Cpio software, 17
.cpp extension, 716
CPUs (central processing units), 9–10, 33, 502, 710
crackers, 521
Create New Samba User dialog box, 704

Create New User dialog box, 69–70, 427
Create Samba Share dialog box, 703
Create Wireless Device window, 315
cron maintenance jobs, 666, 671
crontab command, 421–424, 451–452
cross-reference fields, 234, 235
CrossOver Office application, 173, 174–175
CSMA/CD (Carrier-Sense Multiple Access/ Collision Detection) protocol, 300–301
CTAR backup utility, 447
ctlinnd program, 667, 674
Ctrl+Alt+Del, 35
CUPS (Common UNIX Printing System), 489
cupsd daemon server, 491
cursor movement commands in vi editor, 206, 208
customizing GNOME desktop, 84–88, 124–127
customizing KDE desktop, 92–94, 132–134
CVE (Common Vulnerabilities and Exposures) list, 580
CVS (Concurrent Versions System), 22, 713

## D

daemon servers. *See also* Internet servers; servers
atd, 119
cupsd, 491
daemon process, 606
defined, 615
Line Printer Daemon, 581
listed, 610–614
named, 679–680. *See also* DNS
DARPA (Defense Advanced Research Projects Agency), 297
database applications. *See* MySQL; PostgreSQL
datagrams, 599. *See also* packets
date and time, setting, 76, 77, 146, 147–148
db Berkeley database library, 733
debugger programs, 712. *See also* programming
declaring/defining variables. *See* variables
default Apache Web server configuration, 621–622
default arguments in Perl, 785
default labels in switch statements, 753
default Linux kernel settings, 498
default shells, changing, 136
default umask permissions, 542–543
defragmenting hard disks, 34–36

delay loops, calibrating, 77
deleting. *See also* removing
directories, 165
files, 164
hidden files, 35–36
slides, 255
text characters, 150
user accounts, 71, 428–429
derived works, 733
Desktop Background Preferences dialog box, 85–87
Desktop Wallpaper Preferences dialog box, 125–126
desktops. *See* GNOME; KDE
/dev directory, 155, 439
device driver options, 503. *See also* managing devices
df command, 167–168, 414
DHCP (Dynamic Host Configuration Protocol). *See also* TCP/IP
defined, 298, 601
in network configuration, 49–50
port number, 601
Dia drawing program, 170
dial-up networking. *See* Internet connections
dictionary tool, 170
Diff software, 17
dig (Domain Internet Groper) utility, 680–681, 694
digital camera (gtkam) application, 171, 183–186
digital data, 274

digital signatures, 548–549, 553
Digital Subscriber Line. *See* Internet connections
directories. *See also* Linux file system
/boot, 155, 407, 439, 583
/etc/X11, 159–162
appending to PATH, 433
defined, 122, 153
links to files in, 160–161
directory paths in URLs, 355
directory security. *See* securing hosts
disks. *See* CD; DVD; floppy; hard disks; Zip
display setup during firstboot, 77–78. *See also* monitors
distributed databases, 676. *See also* DNS
DLLs (dynamically linked libraries). *See* shared libraries
DMZs (demilitarized zones), 569
DNS (Domain Name System)
BIND system
caching name servers, 679
command-line utilities, 679, 680–682
named daemon server, 679–680
overview, 679
primary name servers, 679
resolver libraries, 676, 679, 680
secondary name servers, 679

DNS (Domain Name System)
BIND system *(continued)*
seeing installed versions
of, 678
vulnerabilities, 581
configuring
overview, 682
primary name servers,
692–694
resolver libraries,
682–683
configuring caching name
servers
in /etc/named.conf,
683–685
in /var/named/
localhost.zone,
690–691
in /var/named/
named.ca, 689–690
in /var/named/named.
local, 691
overview, 683
resource record formats,
686–688
startup, 691–692
and testing, 692
zone file formats,
685–686
defined, 675, 676
dig utility, 680–681, 694
DNS name servers
defined, 676–677
name daemon
controllers, 684–685
named daemon server,
679–680
overview, 675
running, 680
domain names
case in, 678
fully qualified domain
names, 678

hierarchy, 677–678
namespace, 677
root domains, 677
second-level domains,
677, 678
subdomains or host
names, 675, 677, 678
top-level domains,
677–678
host utility, 680, 681–682,
693–694
IP addresses and, 290,
675–677
resource record types,
681, 687–688
reverse lookups, 681–682
RFCs on, 676
vulnerabilities, 581
do-while statements, 753
DOCSIS (Data Over Cable
Service Interface), 281
documentation online,
23–24
documents. *See* OpenOffice.
org Writer
domain names in URLs, 355
domains in SELinux, 15
DoS (Denial of Service)
attacks, 521, 524,
642, 645
DOS file system. *See*
managing file systems
dotted-decimal notation,
297–298
downstream data, 281
Draw Functions toolbar, 231
drawing. *See* OpenOffice.
org Draw
DSL. *See* Internet
connections
DSL/Cable routers, 279, 283,
305. *See also* NAT

du command, 168, 414–415
dual-homed hosts. *See also*
hosts; securing
networks
as bastion hosts, 567, 569
defined, 567–568
with proxy services,
564, 568
warning, 568
DVD-ROM in book
contents, 809–810
copying, 11
installing Fedora Core
from, 807–809
installing RPMs from. *See
also* RPM
Apache httpd Web
server, 619–620
FTP vsftpd server,
639–640
gftp RPM, 384
INN news server, 665
kernel-source RPM,
466, 496
Perl language, 781
python-2 RPM, 100
using rpm command,
466–467
Samba software, 702
sendmail server,
647–648
sendmail-cf, 651–652
sharutils RPM, 590
source RPMs, 474
xcdroast RPM, 189
xmms RPM, 187
overview, 4
system requirements for,
807
troubleshooting, 810
viewing RPM listings, 463

DVD-ROMs. *See also*
    CD-ROMs
  burning Fedora Core onto,
      104–107
  Cdrecord and, 170
  drive requirements, 33
  mounting
    defined, 440–441
    from GUI desktops,
        25–26, 71–72
    using `mount` command,
        166–167, 441–443
  saving files received on,
      214
  unmounting, 167, 442
dynamic linking, 734, 760
dynamically linked
    libraries. *See* shared
    libraries

# E

e-mail. *See also* IM; Internet
    services; newsgroups;
    `sendmail`
  addresses, 338
  attachments, 214, 339
  defined, 337
  Fedora Core mail clients
    defined, 340
    KMail, 340
    Mozilla Mail, 340,
        344–349
    overview, 337
    Ximian Evolution,
        340–344
  HTML messages, 339
  mail-transport agents,
      338–339, 647
  mail-user agents, 338–339,
      340, 647

`mailto://` URL, 354
Mozilla Mail client
  composing/sending
      messages, 348–349
  defined, 340, 344
  main window, 346–347
  managing mail in folders,
      347–348
  new account setup,
      345–346, 376
  overview, 21, 271
  sending to lists using Perl,
      798–799
  warning, 339
Ximian Evolution client
  defined, 340
  help, 344
  main window, 342–344
  setting up, 340–342
editing. *See also* text editors
  documents in Writer,
      221–224
  system configuration files,
      406
  user accounts, 71, 428, 429
  Web pages, 366
802.11x. *See* wireless
    Ethernet
EISA (Extended Industry
    Standard Architecture)
    buses, 502
ELF (Executable and
    Linkable Format), 503
`#else` directives, 738,
    739–740
`else/elseif` clauses,
    792–793
`emacs` text editor, 17, 23
encryption. *See also*
    securing hosts
  MD5 encryption, 537–538

public-key encryption
  defined, 547–548
  in digital signing,
      548–549
  in OpenSSH protocol,
      561–563
  in wireless Ethernet LANs,
      312, 317
`#endif` directives, 738,
    739–740
English module for Perl
    variables, 806
Enhanced IDE support
    option, 505–506
enumerations, 742
`env` command, 431–432
environment variables. *See
    also* variables
  defined, 712
  defining in Bash shell,
      432–433
  in GNU `make` utility, 721
  listed, 433
  `PATH`
    appending directories
        to, 433
    defined, 770–771
    defining, 432
    finding files in, 432, 780
Epiphany Web browser, 357
errors. *See also*
    troubleshooting
  saving error messages,
      139
  in shell scripting, 772
  signal 11 error, 61
`/etc` files. *See* system
    configuration; TCP/IP
Ethereal packet-sniffing
    tool, 328

Ethernet cables
in 10BaseT Ethernet LANs, 301–302, 306
in cable modem connections, 284
defined, 301
in DSL connections, 278–279
Ethernet frames/packets, 301
Ethernet hubs
in 10BaseT Ethernet LANs, 301–302, 305–306
in cable modem connections, 283–284
in DSL connections, 278–279
Ethernet LANs (local area networks). *See also* TCP/IP; wireless
10BaseT Ethernet LANs, 301–302, 305–306
benefits, 299–300
connecting to Internet, 305–306
defined, 299
Ethernet cables, 301–302, 306
Ethernet cards, 299, 301–302, 306, 481
Ethernet hubs, 301–302, 305–306
how Ethernet works, 300–301
NAT routers in, 278–279, 283–284, 305–306
overview, 295
TCP/IP protocols in
configuring, 302–305
four-layer model, 295–297

the Internet and, 297
IP addresses, 297–298
overview, 295
services/port numbers, 298–299, 601–603
Evans, Chris, 639
exclamation points (!) in repeating commands, 142
exclusive-OR operations, 309
exec-shield feature, 544–545
executable file formats, 503
executable, making files, 768
*expire* program, 666
expressions. *See also* programming
in C
defined, 747
examples, 753
operator precedence, 749–751
operators in, 747–749
defined, 713
in Perl
defined, 783
grep command and, 789, 791
operators in, 787–788
regular expressions, 789–791
warning, 788
EXT3 file system for Linux, 485

**F**

fdiv (floating point division) bug, 416

Fedora Core. *See also* Linux kernel; Web site addresses
defined, 11–12
version 1, 13, 32
version numbers, 12–13
Fedora Core 2. *See also* GNOME; KDE; shells
accessing Windows from. *See* Samba
adding user accounts, 69–70
editing user accounts, 71, 428, 429
getting started with, 28–29
LogWatch monitoring system, 556
mail clients. *See also* Mozilla; Ximian
defined, 340
KMail, 340
Mozilla Mail, 340, 344–349
overview, 337
Ximian Evolution, 340–344
new features
GNU software, 16–19
graphical applications, 20
GUI desktops, 19–20
Internet servers, 21–22
Internet services, 21
office applications, 20
online documentation, 23–24
overview, 1
software-development tools, 22–23
TCP/IP protocols, 20–21
release date, 13
shell, 94–95
shutting down, 98

software-development.
*See* building;
programming;
rebuilding
warning, 98
what it helps you manage
CDs/DVDs, 25–26, 71–72
file systems/sharing, 27
floppy disks/Zip
drives, 26
networks, 27
peripheral devices, 26
system hardware, 25
Fedora Core 2 applications.
*See also* managing;
RPM
for graphics and imaging.
*See also* GIMP
The Gimp, 193–196
GNOME Ghostview, 171,
196–197
listed, 171
Internet applications, 171
multimedia applications
burning CDs, 188–193
digital cameras, 183–186
overview, 170–171, 183
playing audio CDs,
186–187
playing sound files,
187–188
MySQL database, 170, 176
office applications. *See
also* OpenOffice
aspell checker, 170,
175–176
calculators, 170, 172–173
Dia drawing program,
170
dictionary, 170

OpenOffice.org, 170,
171–172
overview, 20
office applications,
commercial
Anyware Office, 173–174
CrossOver Office, 173,
174–175
overview, 173
StarOffice, 174
overview, 169
PostgreSQL database
adding users, 177–178
creating empty
databases in, 180
creating tables in, 181
defined, 170, 176
designing, 179
inserting records, 182
installing, 177
interactive terminal,
180–181
online documentation,
183
querying, 182–183
starting, 177
steps in building,
179–180
Fedora Core 2 boot process.
*See also* boot; system
administration
/etc/inittab file in,
398–401
auto-starting servers, 403
booting for first time
boot messages, 76
date/time setup, 76, 77
display setup, 77–78
installing additional CDs,
78–79
logging in, 79–80
overview, 75–76

running firstboot, 76–80
running firstboot
again, 79
troubleshooting, 59
user account setup,
77 78
warning, 77
changing run levels,
400–401
GUI startup, 404–406
init process, 397–399
overview, 397
run levels in, 398–399
starting/stopping servers
manually, 402–403
startup scripts, 401–402
troubleshooting, 328
Fedora Core 2 installation
BitTorrent, defined, 99
downloading BitTorrent,
100–101
downloading Fedora
Core, 101–102
joining BitTorrent, 100
opening TCP ports, 101
burning onto CDs,
103–104
burning onto DVDs,
104–107
configuring
overview, 28–29
printers, 64–68
sound cards, 68
configuring key systems
boot loaders, 47–48
firewalls/SELinux, 50–51
language support, 51
networks, 48–50
overview, 47
root passwords, 52–53
time zones, 51–52
getting help, 32

Fedora Core 2 installation
   *(continued)*
   hardware requirements,
      33–34
   installation steps, 31–33
   making space for
      defragmenting hard
         disks, 34–36
      deleting hidden files,
         35–36
      overview, 34
      resizing/splitting
         partitions, 36–39
      warnings, 35, 36, 37, 39
   over networks via FTP,
      107–108
   overview, 28, 31
   RPM packages, 72–74
   selecting
      installation type, 41, 43
      keyboard/monitor type,
         41, 42
      package groups, 53–55
      partitioning strategies,
         43–46
   starting, 39–40
   troubleshooting
      boot process, 59, 328
      failure to start, 58,
         59, 77
      kernel boot commands,
         62–64
      `linux noprobe`
         command, 58–59
      overview, 57, 61
      by reconfiguring X, 59–61
      signal 11 error, 61
      text-mode installation,
         58
      undetected hardware, 58
   warnings, 43, 46
Fielding, R., 616

fields, inserting in
      documents, 233–235
file ownership. *See also*
      permissions
   auditing security of,
      582–584
   changing, 162–163,
      434–435, 541
file security. *See* securing
      hosts
file systems. *See also* Linux
      file system; managing
      file systems
   defined, 153
   EXT3 system, 485
   supported by Linux,
      511–513
   sysfs system, 14, 482
File Transfer Protocol.
      *See* FTP
filenames in URLs, 355
files
   accessing in Perl,
      797–799
   converting file formats,
      767–768
   deleting hidden files,
      35–36
   file handles in Perl, 797
   finding with Linux
      commands, 143–144,
      165–166
   making executable, 768
finding
   bugs, 728–730
   files in `PATH` variable, 432,
      780
   Usenet newsgroups,
      380–381
   WAV files, 187
Findutils software, 17
Finger software, 17

fingerprint, 537, 548, 552
FIPS (First Nondestructive
      Interactive Partition
      Splitting Program),
      36–39
firewalls. *See also* securing
      networks
   application gateways
      (proxy servers) and,
      570–571
   configuring security levels
      in cable modem
         connections, 283
      in DSL connections, 278
      overview, 27, 50–51
   defined, 522, 563–564
   types of
      dual-homed host with
         proxy services, 564,
         567–568, 570–571
      overview, 564–565
      perimeter network with
         bastion hosts, 565,
         568–570
      screening router with
         packet filtering, 564,
         565–567
   warning, 568
Firewire (IEEE 1394)
   support options, 506
firstboot. *See* Fedora Core 2
      boot process
FLAC (Free Lossless Audio
      Codec), 187
flags in INN configuration
      files, 670
floating point division
      (`fdiv`) bug, 416
floppy disks
   as backup media, 446–449
   DOS floppies
      formatting, 459–460
      mounting, 453–456

unmounting, 454, 455
Linux file system and,
  153–154, 440–441
mounting, 26, 167, 394,
  440–441
saving files received on,
  214
flow-control statements.
  *See also* conditional
  directives; statements
defined, 713
in Perl. *See also*
  programming in Perl
  defined, 783
  else/elseif clauses,
    792–793
  for loops, 794
  foreach statements,
    794–795
  goto statements, 795
  if statements, 791, 792
  overview, 791–792
  unless statements, 793
  while loops, 791,
    793–794
in shell scripts
  case statements,
    773–775
  defined, 713, 772
  for loops, 773
  if statements, 772–773
for loops, 753–754, 773,
  794
foreach statements,
  794–795
formatting data in Calc,
  241–244
formatting DOS floppies,
  459–460
FQDNs (fully qualified
  domain names), 678
frames in Ethernet, 301

frames in page layouts, 229
freeware programs, 809
Frystyk, H., 616
FSF (Free Software
  Foundation), 16
FTP (File Transfer Protocol).
  *See also* Internet
  services
anonymous FTP
  defined, 639, 644
  enabling, 641
  key features of, 645–646
  risks, 641, 645
  securing, 645
  trying, 645
command-line FTP client,
  387–390
configuring vsftpd server
  in /etc/vsftpd/
    vsftpd.conf, 641–643
  in /etc/vsftpd.
    ftpusers, 643–644
  in /etc/vsftpd.
    user_list, 644
  in configuration files,
    640–644
  to start, 640
defined, 298, 383, 601
ftp:// URL, 354, 386–387
graphical FTP clients
  gFTP, 384–385
  Mozilla Web browser,
    386
  overview, 383–384
  warning, 386
  Web browsers as,
    385–387
installing vsftpd server,
  639–640
port numbers, 601
vulnerabilities, 581

fully qualified domain
  names (FQDNs), 678
Function AutoPilot in Calc,
  239, 245–246
functions. *See also*
  programming
in C
  changing value of
    variables in, 745
  defined, 757
  function prototypes,
    757–758
  main function, 757
  overview, 737
  pointers as arguments
    to, 745
  with variable numbers of
    arguments, 758
  void type, 758
defined, 713
in Perl
  built-in functions, 800
  defined, 783–784
  open, 797–799
  require, 801–802, 803
  subroutines, 799–800
  undef, 784
  use, 803
in shell scripts, 771–772

## G

g++ compiler. *See*
  programming
Gaim instant messaging
  client, 171, 340,
  349–350. *See also* IM
Gallery, 232, 240, 262
Gawk software, 17
GB (megabyte), 104
gcc compiler. *See*
  programming

gcj Java compiler, 22

gdb debugger. *See*
programming

gdbm database library, 18,
733

GET command in HTTP,
616–618

Gettext software, 18

Gettys, J., 616

GFTP application, 171

GGV (GNOME Ghostview)
software, 18, 171,
196–197

The GIMP (GNU Image
Manipulation Program).
*See also* graphics;
images
defined, 193
installing, 194
main window, 194–195
opening image files in, 195
overview, 18, 20, 171
resources, 196
shared library use, 761
starting, 194

G.lite ADSL, 276

GMT (Greenwich Mean
Time), 51

GNOME (GNU Object Model
Environment) desktop.
*See also* KDE
Add/Remove Packages,
72–74
backgrounds, 85–87,
125–126
calculator, 172–173
CD Player, 186–187
Control Center, 125
customizing, 84–88,
124–127
defined, 18, 20, 81–82, 119
gdm login session
manager, 404–406

icon pop-up menus,
113–114
logging in, 120
logging out, 88
Main Menu button, 83–85,
116–119
using Nautilus shell
burning data CDs,
120–121
defined, 120
navigation windows,
121–124
object windows, 120
warning, 124
online help, 23–24
overview, 19–20, 81, 111
panel, 82–85, 112, 114–116
pop-up menus, 112–113
Preferences window, 125
Service Configuration
utility, 609–614
Start Here window,
124–125
System Logs utility,
555–556
System Monitor, 411–412
text editor, 199–200
themes, 87–88
User Manager, 69–70,
426–428
warning, 81
Web browser, 357
Web site address, 119

GNU (GNU's Not UNIX)
Project, 16

GNU Image Manipulation
Program. *See* GIMP

GNU licenses
derived works and, 733
GNU GPL, 11, 16, 471,
732–733
GNU LGPL, 733–734

overview, 732
warnings, 732, 733

GNU software packages,
16–19. *See also*
programming

goto statements, 754, 795

GPG or GnuPG (GNU
Privacy Guard), 475,
527. *See also* securing
hosts

gprof profiling utility, 22

GQView application, 171

graphical FTP clients
gFTP, 384–385
Mozilla Web browser,
386
overview, 383–384
warning, 386
Web browsers as,
385–387

graphical user interfaces.
*See* GNOME; KDE

graphics. *See also* images;
OpenOffice.org Draw
adding to documents,
231–233
adding to presentations,
257–259
vector graphics, 262

graphics/imaging
applications. *See also*
Fedora Core 2
applications; The
Gimp
The Gimp, 193–196
GNOME Ghostview,
196–197
listed/defined, 171

greeter (login) screens, 405

grep command, 96, 137,
148, 789, 791

grep software package, 18

Groff software, 18

groups. *See* users
GRUB (GRand Unified
    Bootloader)
  defined, 47–48
  forgotten passwords and,
    396–397
  setting to boot new
    kernels, 515–517
GTK+ software, 18
gtkam application, 171,
    183–184
GUI desktops. *See* GNOME;
    KDE
Gzip software, 18

## H

.h extension, 735
handouts for presentations,
    256, 260
hard disks
  checking space usage,
    167–168
  defined, 710
  defragmenting, 34–36
  deleting hidden files, 35–36
  drive requirements, 33
  Linux file system and,
    153–154, 440–441
  monitoring, 414–415
  partitioning
    mounting DOS
      partitions, 452–453, 455
    overview, 32, 33
    resizing/splitting
      partitions, 36–39
    selecting strategies for,
      43–46
hardware. *See also* hard
    disks; system
    administration
  defined, 9–10
  Linux 2.6 support, 13

requirements, 33–34
  system hardware, 25
  undetected,
    troubleshooting, 58
  in wireless Ethernet,
    310–312
hash, 548
hdparm program, 414
HEAD command in HTTP,
    618
head end, 281
header files. *See also*
    programming in C
  C library of, 759–760
  defined, 735
  GCC predefined header
    files, 742
  including once, 739
  including selectively, 740
help. *See also* Web site
    addresses
  in Mozilla Composer, 338
  online documentation
    Apache Web server, 624
    Fedora Core, 23–24
    overview, 23–24
    PostgreSQL database,
      183
  online help
    in GNOME/KDE
      desktops, 23–24
    with installing Fedora
      Core, 32
    Linux commands for
      getting, 143
    in *vi* text editor, 206
    in Ximian Evolution, 344
    in OpenOffice.org Writer,
      218, 219
hexadecimal digits, 312
hidden files, deleting, 35–36
home pages. *See* Web pages
/home directory, 155, 439

host names, in DNS, 675,
    677, 678
host utility, 680, 681–682,
    693–694
hosts. *See also* securing
    hosts; security audits
  bastion hosts, perimeter
    networks with, 565,
    568–570
  dual-homed hosts
    as bastion hosts, 567, 569
    defined, 567–568
    with proxy services, 564,
      568
    warning, 568
  host names, defined,
    79–80
  host names in DNS, 675,
    677, 678
  security issues, 527, 568
  troubleshooting
    connections to, 325
  virtual hosts in Apache,
    622, 623, 634–637
hot plug devices, 26, 486
HTML (Hypertext Markup
    Language). *See also*
    Web, the
  creating Web pages with
    Mozilla Composer
    balloon help, 368
    changing views, 368
    editing existing pages,
      366
    <HTML> Source view,
      369
    HTML tags view, 369–370
    inserting images,
      367–368
    Normal view, 369
    overview, 364, 366
    Preview, 369

HTML *(continued)*
  creating Web pages in text
    editors, 364–366
  HTML anchors in URLs,
    355
  HTML e-mail messages,
    339
  overview, 352
HTTP (Hypertext Transfer
    Protocol). *See also*
    TCP/IP
  configuration tool,
    622–623
  defined, 299, 601, 615
  GET command, 616–618
  HEAD command, 618
  http:// URL, 354
  httpd server. *See* Apache
  Internet standard for, 616
  overview, 352
  port number, 601
  POST command, 618
  TELNET example, 615–618
https:// URL, 354, 360
hung GUIs, 135
hypertext links, 353

# 1

I/O (input/output)
  defined, 710, 711
  I/O redirection of shell
    commands, 138–139
  Network Input/Output
    System, 701
  port addresses, 287
I20 device support options,
    507
I2C protocol support
    options, 509
IA-32 architecture, 10

IANA (Internet Assigned
    Numbers Authority),
    603
IC (Integrity Check) fields,
    309
ICAT Metabase index, 580
ICMP (Internet Control
    Message Protocol),
    325
icon pop-up menus in GUI
    desktops, 113–114
IDE (integrated drive
    electronics) controllers,
    33, 505–506
idle sessions, 643
IEEE 1394 (Firewire)
    support, 506
IEEE 802.11x. *See* wireless
    Ethernet
IEEE (Institute of Electrical
    and Electronics
    Engineers), 301
IETF (Internet Engineering
    Task Force), 298
#if directives, 738, 739–740
if statements, 754,
    772–773, 791, 792
IM (instant messaging). *See
    also* e-mail
  defined, 337
  Fedora Core IM clients
    Gaim, 171, 340, 349–350
    Kit, 340
    overview, 337
images. *See also* graphics;
    OpenOffice.org Impress
  converting file formats,
    767–768
  inserting in Web pages,
    367–368
  ISO images, 103
  raster images, 262

incremental backups, 451
Indent software, 18
inetd server. *See* xinetd
infrastructure mode in
    wireless Ethernet,
    308
init command, 400–401
init process, 397–399
initrd file, 514–515
INN (InterNetNews) server.
    *See also* Internet
    services; newsgroups;
    NNTP
  components
    configuration files,
      667–671
    ctlinnd program, 667,
      674
    expire program, 666
    innd daemon server, 21,
      665, 666
    nnrpd local server, 666
    nntpsend program, 667
  configuration files
    incoming.conf, 667,
      670–671
    inn.conf, 667, 668–669
    newsfeeds, 667, 669–670
    overview, 665, 667
    readers.conf, 667, 671
  cron maintenance jobs,
    666, 671
  installing, 665
  local newsgroup setup
    adding newsgroups, 674
    newsgroup hierarchy,
      673
    overview, 672
    testing newsgroups, 674
    updating config files,
      673–674
  news feed setup, 665–666

resources on, 666
starting, 665, 671–672
input/output. *See* I/O
in.telnetd server, 22. *See
also* TELNET
Internet. *See also* Web
applications, 171
defined, 272
TCP/IP protocols and,
297
Internet Assigned Numbers
Authority (IANA), 603
Internet Configuration
Wizard, 27, 290–292
Internet connections. *See
also* Ethernet; wireless
via cable modem
in 10BaseT Ethernet
LANs, 305–306
configuring firewalls, 283
defined, 273, 279–280
versus dial-up and DSL,
273–274
downstream data, 281
Ethernet cables, 284
Ethernet hubs, 283–284
how it works, 280–281
NAT routers, 283–284
setting up, 282–284
sharing connections,
283–284
upstream data, 281
warning, 283
via dial-up networking
connecting modems,
286–288
defined, 273
versus DSL and cable,
273–274
internal/external
modems, 287

Minicom program and,
289–291
modem requirements, 34
PAP/CHAP
authentication, 293–294
PPP connections, 285,
290–294
versus serial
communication,
284–285
serial port detection, 288
serial-port device names,
287–288
setup overview, 285
TCP/IP protocols in, 285
testing modems, 289–290
winmodems
(softmodems), 286
via Digital Subscriber Line
in 10BaseT Ethernet
LANs, 305–306
Asymmetric DSL,
275–276
caveat, 272–273
configuring firewalls, 278
defined, 272, 274
versus dial-up and cable,
273–274
DSL modems, 274–275,
277–279
Ethernet hubs/cables,
278–279
how it works, 274–275
ISDN DSL, 276
local loops, 274, 275
microfilters, 277, 278
NAT routers, 278–279
PPPoE protocol, 279
setting up, 276–279
Symmetric DSL, 276
warnings, 275, 278
overview, 271

Internet Protocol. *See* IP
Internet servers. *See also*
daemon; DNS; servers
defined, 21–22, 602
httpd daemon, 615, 635.
*See also* Apache
innd daemon, 21, 365, 666
in.telnetd daemon, 22,
586
proxy servers, 564, 568,
570–571
sendmail server. *See*
sendmail
server process, 299, 602
sshd daemon, 22
standalone servers
auditing security of, 587
auto-starting, 403,
607–614
configuring with
chkconfig command,
607–609
configuring in graphical
utility, 609–614
defined, 606
disabling, 558
starting/stopping
manually, 402–403,
606–607
warning, 610
vsftpd daemon, 21, 639.
*See also* FTP
Web servers, 21, 352,
355–356, 615
xinetd daemon
/etc/xinetd.conf file,
559–561, 603–606
auditing services started
by, 585–586
configuring to disable
services, 558–561
defined, 603

Internet services. *See also*
  securing networks
defined, 21, 271–272, 597
file-sharing services. *See*
  NFS; Samba
file-transfer services. *See*
  FTP; TFTP
listed/defined, 610–614
mail services. *See* e-mail;
  `sendmail`
news services. *See* INN;
  newsgroups
overview, 557
remote access services,
  21, 271. *See also* SSH
TCP/IP and. *See also*
  TCP/IP
  client/server
    architecture, 597–598,
    599–601
  connection-oriented
    protocols, 598–599,
    600–601
  connectionless
    protocols, 599, 600
  defined, 598
  services/port numbers,
    298–299, 601–603
  sockets, 598, 599–601
  warnings, 557, 560
Web services, 21, 271. *See*
  *also* Web browsers;
  Web servers
internetworking, 297
IP addresses. *See also* DNS
  binding sockets to,
    600–601
  in configuring TCP/IP
    networks, 304–305
  defined, 297–298
  DNS and, 290, 675–677
  multihomed addresses,
    321

in packet filtering, 565–567
in PAP/CHAP
  authentication, 294
setting up, 49–50, 290, 292
spoofing, 567
IP (Internet Protocol), 272,
  599. *See also* TCP/IP
IP routing/forwarding, 567
`ipconfig` command,
  323–324
IPng (Internet Protocol
  Next Generation), 298
IPP (Internet Printing
  Protocol), 489
IPv6 (Internet Protocol
  version 6), 298
IRQs (interrupt request
  numbers), 287
ISA (Industry Standard
  Architecture) buses,
  502
ISBN (International
  Standard Book
  Number), 179
ISC (Internet Software
  Consortium), 666
ISDN (Integrated Services
  Digital Network) DSL,
  276
ISDN subsystem options,
  508
ISO (International
  Organization for
  Standardization), 678
ISO images, 103
IV (Initialization Vector),
  309

*J*

job-scheduling. *See* system
  administration

*K*

KB (kilobyte), 104
Kbps (kilobits per second),
  272, 276
KDE (K Desktop
  Environment). *See also*
  GNOME
backgrounds, 93–94,
  133–134
calculator, 173
CD player, 186
Control Center, 92–93,
  132–134
customizing, 92–94,
  132–134
defined, 88–89, 127
desktop pop-up menus,
  112–113
icon pop-up menus,
  113–114
`kdm` login display
  manager, 404
Kmail client, 171, 340
Konqueror feature
  defined, 128, 357
  as file manager, 72,
    128–132
  as Web browser, 132
logging in to, 89–90,
  127–128
logging out of, 94
Main Menu button, 90–91,
  116–117, 119
online help, 23–24
overview, 19–20, 81, 111
panel, 90–92, 112, 114–116
Service Configuration
  utility, 609–614
text editor, 200
warning, 131
Web site address, 89

kernel hacking options, 513. *See also* Linux kernel

keyboards, 33, 41, 42

keychain storage devices, 487–488

kill command, 147

Kimball, Spencer, 194

Kmail application, 171, 340

.ko extension, 14

Konqueror feature. *See also* KDE; Web browsers
defined, 128, 357
as file manager, 72, 128–132
as Web browser, 132

KsCD application, 170

Ksnapshot application, 171

kudzu utility, 443, 487

Kview application, 171

## L

language support, foreign, 51

LANs. *See* Ethernet LANs

launcher applets, GNOME, 83

layers in Impress presentations, 255–256

layouts in Impress, slide, 253–254

layouts in Writer, page, 228–231

ldd utility, 760–761

Leach, P., 616

Less software, 18

LGPL (Library General Public License), GNU, 733–734

/lib directory, 155, 439

Libpng software, 18

libraries. *See also* shared libraries
database libraries, 18, 733
DNS resolver libraries, 676, 679, 680, 682–683
Libpng image library, 18
of header files, 759–760
SANE library, 171

LILO (Linux Loader), installing, 47–48

Line Printer Daemon (LPD), 581

linking device drivers into kernel, 497

linking, dynamic, 734, 760. *See also* shared libraries

links
to directory files, 160–161
hypertext links, 353
symbolic links, 161

Linksys LNE100TX Fast Ethernet Adapters, 34

Linux. *See also* Red Hat; Web site addresses
commercial backup tools for, 447
compatibility, 10
Conexant driver, 286
distributions, 9–11
EXT3 file system for, 485
Linux-related newsgroups, 374–375
operating system, 10–11. *See also* Linux kernel

Linux commands. *See also* commands; Linux file system; shells
Bash shell and, 95
for date and time, 146
defined, 142–143

executing in Perl scripts, 795–797
for getting online help, 143
kernel boot commands, 62–64
for making commands easier, 143
for managing processes, 145
for managing users, 145
trying in shell, 96–97

Linux file system. *See also* managing file systems
/etc/fstab file and, 442–443
defined, 153–154, 437–438
directory hierarchy, 154, 155, 438–440
drive letters and, 153
filenames, 154, 155
locating files, 154–155
mounting storage devices on, 440–443
navigating with Linux commands. *See also* Linux commands
archiving/compressing files, 145
changing permissions/ owners, 162–163
checking disk-space usage, 167–168
commands, listed, 143–146
copying files, 163–164
deleting directories, 165
deleting files, 164
directory listings, 159–162
directory navigation, 158–159

Linux file system (*continued*)
   finding files, 143–144,
      165–166
   making directories,
      164–165
   managing the file
      system, 145–146
   managing files/
      directories, 143,
      163–165
   mounting CDs/DVDs,
      166–167, 440–443
   moving files, 164
   overview, 143–146,
      157–158
   processing files, 144
   unmounting CDs/DVDs,
      167, 442
   viewing permissions, 161
   warning, 164
   overview, 153
   pathnames, 154–155, 439
   root directory, 153–156,
      439
   subdirectories, 156–157,
      440
   top-level directories,
      155–156, 439
Linux kernel. *See also*
      rebuilding
   boot commands, 62–64
   booting, 75–76
   defined, 10–11
   exec-shield feature,
      544–545
   file systems supported by,
      511–513
   upgrading, 493, 494–495
   version 2.6 improvements
      computer hardware
         support, 13
      device handling, 14–15,
         482

   mandatory access
      control, 15
   overview, 13
   scalability, 13–14
   version numbers, 12
linux noprobe command,
      58–59
Linux Security Module
      (LSM), 15
load averages, 410
Loadable Driver Modules,
      managing, 482–485
loadable module support
      options, 501
local loops in DSL, 274, 275
locate command, 166
log files, monitoring,
      554–556
LogFormat directive
      tokens, 636–637
logging in
   to Firstboot, 79–80
   to GNOME desktop, 120
   to KDE desktop, 89–90,
      127–128
   securing remote logins,
      561–563
logging out of GNOME, 88
logging out of KDE, 94
LogWatch software, 556
LONE-TAR backup utility,
      447
loops
   calibrating delay
      loops, 77
   for loops, 753–754, 773,
      794
   local loops in DSL, 275
   looping, defined, 793
   while loops, 756–757, 791,
      793–794
/lost+found directory,
      155

lp command, 489–490
LPD (Line Printer Daemon),
      581
lpq command, 490
lpstat command, 491
ls command
   in combining shell
      commands, 138
   getting directory listings,
      159–162
lsmod command,
      483–485
LSM (Linux Security
      Module), 15

## M

.m4 extension, 653
macros. *See also*
      programming
   defined, 652, 738
   defining
      in C, 739
      in GNU make, 721
      in sendmail, 652–654,
         657
   m4 macro processor, 18,
      652–654
   macro expansion, 652
   predefined macros
      in C, 740–741
      in GNU make, 721–722
      in sendmail, 654–660
   stream-based processing,
      652
Magicdev utility, 71
mail merges in Writer, 215.
      *See also* e-mail
mailto:// URL, 354
main function in C, 757
Main Menu buttons in
      GNOME, 83–85,
      116–119

Main Menu buttons in KDE, 90–91, 116–117, 119

major device numbers, 480–481

`make config` command, 498

`make menuconfig` command, 498

`make` utility. *See* programming

`make xconfig` command, 498, 499–513. *See also* rebuilding

`man` command, 23

managed mode in wireless Ethernet, 308

managing. *See also* system administration

managing applications. *See also* Fedora Core 2 applications

building software from source files

downloading source files, 469–470

GNU GPLs and, 471

and installing, 472

overview, 469

RPM packages, 474

and running, 473

steps in, 471–473

warning, 472

overview, 461

RPM files. *See also* RPM

defined, 461

installing, 466–467

querying RPM databases, 463–466

removing, 467

using `rpm` commands, 461–469

updating with Up2date, 474–475, 476

updating with Yum, 475–477

upgrading, 467–468

verifying, 468–469

viewing RPM filenames, 462–463

warning, 468

managing devices. *See also* mounting

block devices, 481

character devices, 481

device drivers

configuring options for, 503

defined, 479–480

linking into kernel, 497

device files, 480–481

device numbers, 480–481

in Linux kernel 2.6, 14–15, 482

Loadable Driver Modules

`/etc/modprobe.conf` and, 485–486

with commands, 483–485

defined, 482

loading, 483–485

unloading, 483, 485

network devices, 481

overview, 26, 479

print queues

canceling print jobs, 490–491

checking with `lpq` command, 490

checking printers with `lpstat`, 491

enabling/disabling, 491–492

printing with `lp` command, 489–490

spooling print jobs, 488–489

USB devices, 486–488

managing file systems

accessing DOS/Windows file system

converting DOS filenames to Linux, 453

formatting DOS floppies, 459–460

mounting DOS floppies, 453–456

mounting DOS partitions, 452–453, 455

mounting NTFS partitions, 455

`mtools` commands, 456–460

overview, 452

unmounting DOS floppies, 454, 455

backing up and restoring files

automated backups, 451–452

using commercial utilities, 447

incremental backups, 451

multi-volume archives, 449–450

onto CDs, 445

onto floppy disks, 446–449

onto tape drives, 446, 450–451

onto Zip disks, 446

overview, 445

managing file systems
  *(continued)*
  selecting strategies/
    media, 445–446
  single-volume archives,
    447–449
  using tar command,
    447–449, 451
  Linux file system. *See also*
    Linux file system;
    mounting
  /etc/fstab file and,
    442–443
  defined, 437–438
  directory hierarchy,
    438–440
  mounting storage
    devices on, 440–443
  overview, 27, 437
  sharing files with NFS. *See
    also* NFS
  configuring NFS servers,
    699–700
  exporting file systems
    with NFS, 444,
    696–698
  mounting NFS file
    systems, 445, 698
  NFS, defined, 299, 602,
    695
  overview, 443–444, 695
  warning, 696
managing users. *See also*
  root; users
  /etc/passwd file and,
    429–430
  adding user accounts,
    425–429
  file ownership, 434–435
  forgotten root
    passwords, 396–397
  groups, 430–431

Linux commands for, 145
  overview, 425
  user environments,
    431–433
Masinter, L., 616
master documents in
  Writer, 235–236
master name servers, 679,
  692–694
master notes/handouts for
  presentations, 256, 260
master slides in
  presentations, 255
Mattis, Peter, 194
Mbps (megabits per
  second), 272
MBR (Master Boot
  Record), 48
MBs (megabytes), 104
.mc extension, 654
MCA (Micro Channel
  Architecture) buses,
  502
MD5 encryption, 537–538
members in C structures,
  743
memory. *See* RAM
Metcalf, Robert M., 300
MFM (Modified Frequency
  Modulation), 504–505
mice
  bus support for, 509
  compatibility with Fedora
    Core, 33
  long-clicking, 264–265
microfilters in DSL, 277, 278
microprocessors, 710
Microsoft Office. *See*
  OpenOffice.org
Microsoft Word, 213–214,
  215. *See also*
  OpenOffice.org Writer

Minicom program, 289–291
minor device numbers,
  480–481
MIPS (millions of
  instructions per
  second), 77
mkdir command, 164–165
mkinitrd command, 514
/mnt directory, 155, 439
mobile stations, 310
Mockapetris, Paul, 676
modems. *See* Internet
  connections
Modify Slide dialog box, 253
modprobe command,
  485–486
modular kernels, 497
modules, Perl, 783, 801,
  802–803, 804
Mogul, J., 616
monitoring log files. *See*
  securing hosts
monitoring performance.
  *See* system
  administration
monitors, 34, 41, 42. *See
  also* display
monolithic kernels, 497
more command, 97, 142,
  148–149
mounting file systems. *See
  also* file systems;
  managing file systems
  /etc/fstab file and,
    442–443
  CDs/DVDs, 25–26, 71–72,
    166–167, 440–442
  defined, 26, 440–441
  DOS disk partitions,
    452–453, 455
  DOS floppy disks, 453–456
  floppy disks, 26, 167, 394,
    440–441

from GNOME/KDE
desktops, 25–26, 71–72
keychain devices, 488
using mount command,
166–167, 441–443
mount points, 167, 698
NFS file systems, 445
NTFS partitions, 455
unmounting
CDs/DVDs, 167, 442
DOS floppies, 454, 455
keychain devices, 488
Zip disks, 26
mouse. *See* mice
moving files, 164
Mozilla Navigator. *See also*
Web browsers
changing home pages, 361
changing themes, 361–363
creating HTML Web pages
with Mozilla Composer
balloon help, 368
changing views, 368
editing existing pages,
366
<HTML> Source view,
369
HTML tags view, 369–370
inserting images,
367–368
Normal view, 369
overview, 364, 366
Preview, 369
defined, 171, 357
as graphical FTP client,
386
Mozilla Mail
composing/sending
messages, 348–349
defined, 340, 344
main window, 346–347

managing mail in folders,
347–348
new account setup,
345–346, 376
Mozilla Mail newsreader
new account setup,
376–377
posting news, 379–380
subscribing to
newsgroups, 377–379
Preferences window,
361–363
starting, 357
surfing the Net, 363
user interface
menus, 360–361
overview, 357–358
status bar, 359–360
toolbars, 358–359
viewing HTML files in, 365
Web site address, 171
MS-DOS versus Bash shell,
136, 151
MS-DOS/Windows file
system. *See* managing
file systems
MTAs (mail-transport
agents), 338–339
mtools commands, 18,
456–460
MUAs (mail-user agents),
338–339, 340
multi-homed Web servers,
634. *See also* virtual
hosts
multihomed IP addresses,
321
multimedia applications.
*See also* Fedora Core 2
applications
burning CDs, 188–193
using digital cameras,
183–186

overview, 170–171, 183
playing audio CDs,
186–187
playing sound files,
187–188
multimedia device options,
509
mv command, 164
MX (Mail Exchanger)
resource records, 681,
687, 688
MySQL database, 170, 176

## N

name servers. *See* DNS
name service switch (NSS),
323, 683
namespace, 677
NAT (Network Address
Translation) routers.
*See also* Ethernet
defined, 278, 283
in Ethernet LANs,
278–279, 283–284,
305–306
in wireless Ethernet LANs,
311
Nautilus shell in GNOME.
*See also* GNOME; shells
burning data CDs, 120–121
defined, 120
navigation windows,
121–124
object windows, 120
warning, 124
Navigation toolbar in
Mozilla, 358, 359
navigation windows in
Nautilus shell,
121–124
Navigator in Calc, 240

Ncurses software, 18

ndc (name daemon controller), 685

Nessus security-testing tool, 590–593

NetBIOS (Network Input/Output System), 701. *See also* I/O

netstat command, 325–326

network addresses. *See* IP addresses

network cards, 34

Network Configuration screen in installer, 27, 48–50

Network Configuration tool
configuring dial-up networks, 292–293
configuring TCP/IP on Ethernet LANs, 303–305
configuring wireless Ethernet LANs, 315–316
overview, 27

network devices. *See* managing devices

Network File System. *See* NFS

Network layer in TCP/IP, 296

network management. *See* TCP/IP

Network News Transfer Protocol. *See* NNTP

network protocols, 20–21, 354–355. *See also* TCP/IP

Network Time Protocol (NTP), 602

networking support options, 507–508

networks, local area. *See* Ethernet; wireless

news server. *See* INN

News Transfer Protocol. *See* NNTP

newsgroups
categories, 373–374
defined, 371–372
hierarchy, 372–373
Linux-related groups, 374–375
names, 372–373
overview, 21, 272
posting news, 379–380
reading
from ISPs, 375–378
from public news servers, 375
from Web browsers, 380–381
searching for, 380–381
on security, 532
subscribing to, 377–379
Usenet newsgroups, 371–372, 380–381

NFS (Network File System). *See also* Internet services; managing file systems
defined, 299, 602, 695
port number, 602
sharing files with
configuring NFS servers, 699–700
exporting file systems with NFS, 444, 696–698
mounting NFS file systems, 445, 698
overview, 443–444, 695
warning, 696

NIS (Network Information System), 675

NIS and NIS+ (network information services), 323

NIST (National Institute of Standards and Technology), 580

nmap security-testing tool, 589–590

nnrpd local news server, 666

NNTP (Network News Transfer Protocol). *See also* INN
defined, 299
innd server and, 21
news:// URL, 355
overview, 372
port number, 602

nntpsend program, 667

NS (Name Server) resource records, 687, 688

NSS (name service switch), 323, 683

NTFS (NT File System) partitions, 455

NTP (Network Time Protocol), 602

null statements, 755

null-terminated strings in C, 747

## O

.o extension, 715

object code, 712

object files, 715

object model, 127

object-oriented programming, 804

objects, defined, 15, 804

objects, using in Perl, 804–805

OFDM (orthogonal frequency-division multiplexing), 308

office applications. *See also* Fedora Core 2 applications; OpenOffice
aspell checker, 170, 175–176
calculators, 170, 172–173
commercially available for Linux
Anyware Office, 173–174
CrossOver Office, 173, 174–175
overview, 173
StarOffice, 174
Dia drawing program, 170
dictionary, 170
Microsoft Word, 213–214, 215
overview, 20
OLE (Object Linking and Embedding), 228
online documentation
Apache Web server, 624
Fedora Core, 23–24
overview, 23–24
PostgreSQL database, 183
online help. *See also* help; Web site addresses
in GNOME/KDE desktops, 23–24
with installing Fedora Core, 32
Linux commands for getting, 143
in vi text editor, 206
in Ximian Evolution, 344
OpenOffice.org applications, 170, 171–172. *See also* Fedora Core 2 applications

OpenOffice.org Calc
defined, 237
Function AutoPilot, 239, 245–246
main window, 239–240
preparing spreadsheets
calculating/charting data, 244–247
creating scenarios, 244–245, 247
entering/formatting data, 241–244
overview, 241
and printing to PDF files, 242
and sharing, 242
setting up, 240–241
starting, 238
tasks you can do with, 237–238
VisiCalc and, 237
OpenOffice.org Draw
configuring options, 264
defined, 261
long-clicking the mouse, 264–265
main window, 262–264
starting, 262
tasks, how to do, 265–267
tasks you can do with, 261–262
OpenOffice.org Impress
defined, 249
main window, 251–253
PowerPoint and, 249
preparing presentations
adding graphics/effects, 257–259
configuring options, 252–253

creating with AutoPilot, 253–254
creating from Writer documents, 254
deleting slides, 255
and delivering, 260
inserting charts, 257–258, 259
using layers, 255–256
master notes/handouts, 256, 260
master slides, 255
rearranging slides, 255
slide layouts, 253–254
tasks in, how to do, 256–257
starting, 250–251
tasks you can do with, 249–250
OpenOffice.org Writer
defined, 213
help, 218, 219
main window, 216–218
Microsoft Word and, 213–214, 215
preparing documents
creating graphics, 231, 232
and creating presentations from, 254
editing, 221–224
existing documents, 217
inserting fields, 233–235
inserting graphics, 232–233
large/master documents, 235–236
layouts, 228–231
overview, 221
styles, 224–225, 227–228

OpenOffice.org Writer
*(continued)*
templates,
225–227
tracking/reviewing
changes, 221, 223
saving files from others,
214
setting options,
218–221
starting, 216
tasks you can do with,
215–216
warning, 213
OpenSSH protocol, 561–563.
*See also* SSH
operating systems. *See also*
Linux kernel
defined, 10, 711
Linux operating system,
10–11
role in programming,
711–712
updating, 582
operators in C
programming, 747–751
operators in Perl scripting,
787–788
operators in `sendmail`,
control, 659–660
`/opt` directory, 155, 439
options, command line,
711
ownership of files, 162–163,
434–435, 541

## *P*

package groups, RPM, 73
packages, Perl, 783, 800–802

packet-filtering firewalls.
*See also* firewalls;
securing networks
enabling/disabling, 572
using `iptables`
commands, 571,
573–575
overview, 571–572
with screening routers,
564, 565–567
warning, 574
packet-sniffing tools,
327–328, 589
packets, Ethernet, 301. *See
also* datagrams
PAE (Physical Address
Extension), 13
page layouts in Writer,
228–231
Pager applet, GNOME, 83
PAMs (Pluggable
Authentication
Modules), 538–540,
643–644
Pan newsreader, 375
panels
defined, 112, 114
on GNOME desktop,
82–85, 115–116
on KDE desktop, 90–92,
115–116
PAP (Password
Authentication
Protocol), 293–294
parallel port options, 503
PartitionMagic, 36, 37
partitions. *See* hard disks
passwords. *See also*
securing hosts
auditing security of,
584–585
changing, 540

root, restoring forgotten,
396–397
setting root passwords,
52–53
vulnerabilities, 581
Patch software, 18
`PATH` environment variable.
*See also* variables
appending directories to,
433
defined, 770–771
defining, 432
finding files in, 432, 780
pathnames, 154–155, 158,
439
paths in URLs, directory,
355
PBM (Portable Bitmap)
toolkit, 767–768
PCI (Peripheral Component
Interconnect) buses,
502
PCMCIA (Personal
Computer Memory
Card International
Association) buses,
502–503
PDF files
exporting Impress
presentations to, 260
.pdf extension, 196
printing Calc
spreadsheets to, 242
printing Writer documents
to, 216
viewing with GGV, 18, 171,
196–197
.pem extension, 662
penetration testing,
network, 588
performance. *See* system
administration

perimeter networks with bastion hosts, 565, 568–570

peripheral devices. *See* managing devices

Perl. *See* programming in Perl

permissions. *See also* securing hosts

default umask permissions, 542–543

to files

auditing security of, 582–584

changing, 162–163, 541–542

viewing, 161, 540–541

setuid permission risks, 543–544

Personal toolbar in Mozilla, 358–359

physical consoles, 135

Physical layer in TCP/IP, 296

Pick a Color dialog box, 86

PID (process identification) numbers, 147, 398

PIM (personal information manager). *See* Ximian

ping command, 325

pipes (vertical bars) in script commands, 138, 798–799

.pl extension, 783

Plug-and-Play (PnP) options, 503

plug-ins, 116

Pluggable Authentication Modules (PAMs), 538–540, 643–644

.pm extension, 802

Pointer (PTR) resource records, 681, 687, 688

pointers in C, 744–745

POP (Post Office Protocol), 296

pop-up menus in GUI desktops, 112–114

port numbers, 298–299, 598, 600–603

port scanner tools, 588, 589–590

Portable Bitmap (PBM) toolkit, 767–768

ports in URLs, 355

PostgreSQL database. *See also* Fedora Core 2 applications

adding users, 177–178

creating empty databases, 180

creating tables, 181

defined, 170, 176

designing, 179

inserting records, 182

installing, 177

interactive terminal, 180–181

online documentation, 183

querying, 182–183

starting, 177

steps in building, 179–180

PostScript viewer tool. *See* GGV

power management options, 502

PowerPoint, 249. *See also* OpenOffice.org Impress

PPP (Point-to-Point Protocol), 285, 290–294, 481

PPPoE (PPP over Ethernet) protocol, 279

precedence of operators in C, 749–751

predefined. *See also* built-in

predefined GCC header files, 742

predefined macros

in C, 740–741

in GNU make, 721–722

in sendmail, 654–660

predefined Perl file handles, 797

predefined Perl variables, 787

Preferences windows, 125, 361–363

preprocessor directives. *See also* programming in C

#define directive, 738, 739

#include directive, 738

conditional directives, 738, 739–740

defined, 737

other directives, 740–741

presentations. *See* OpenOffice.org Impress

primary name servers, 679, 692–694

print queues. *See also* managing devices

canceling print jobs, 490–491

checking with lpq command, 490

checking printers with lpstat, 491

enabling/disabling, 491–492

printing with lp command, 489–490

spooling print jobs, 488–489

printers, configuring, 64–68
printers, USB, 487
printing Calc spreadsheets
   to PDF files, 242
printing Writer documents
   to PDF files, 216
processes
   /proc file system, 156,
      415–418
   defined, 598, 711
   Linux commands for
      managing, 145
   managing in Bash shell,
      147
processing text files. *See*
   *also* shells
   counting words/lines, 149
   deleting characters, 150
   overview, 144, 148–149
   sorting, 150
   splitting, 150–151
   substituting characters,
      150
processors (CPUs), 9–10,
   33, 502, 710
procmail, invoking,
   663–664
programming. *See also*
   building; macros;
   rebuilding
   build process, 713
   computer programs,
      defined, 712
   computers and, 710–711
   Edit-Compile-Debug cycle
      in, 712
   Fedora Core software-
      development tools.
      *See also* vi
     defined, 22–23, 713
     emacs text editor, 17, 23

GNU gcc C/C++
   compilers, 22, 713,
   714–718
GNU gcj Java
   compiler, 22
GNU gdb debugger, 22,
   713, 725–731
GNU gprof profiling
   utility, 22
GNU make utility, 22, 713,
   718–725
installing, 472, 713
overview, 709, 713
with GNU C/C++ compilers
C++ programs, 716
C programs, 714–716
defined, 22, 713, 714
gcc command options,
   717–718
gcc versus g++
   commands, 716
predefined header files,
   742
with GNU gdb debugger
defined, 18, 22, 713, 725
finding bugs, 728–730
fixing bugs, 730–731
gdb commands, 726–728
preparing to use,
   725–726
running, 726
GNU licenses and
  derived works and, 733
General Public License,
  732–733
Library General Public
  License, 733–734
overview, 732
warnings, 732, 733
with GNU make utility
command options,
  724–725

defined, 18, 713, 718–719
versus gcc or g++, 718,
  720, 721
macros, 721–722
makefiles, 718–720,
  723–724
overview, 471–472, 513
running, 723–724
targets, 719, 720
warning, 720
writing makefiles,
  722–723
operating system role in,
  711–712
overview, 709
steps in, 712
terminology, 710–712, 713
programming in C
comments, 737
declaring/defining
  variables
arrays, 743–744, 745
const type qualifier, 746
data types, 741–742,
  745–746
defined, 737
enumerations, 742
expressions, 713,
  747–749
overview, 741
pointers, 744–745
structures, 743
type definitions, 745–746
unions, 743
variables, defined, 713
volatile type qualifier,
  746
defined, 735
functions
changing value of
  variables in, 745
defined, 713, 757

function prototypes, 757–758

main function, 757

overview, 737

pointers as arguments to, 745

with variable numbers of arguments, 758

void type, 758

header files

C library of, 759–760

defined, 735

GCC predefined header files, 742

including once, 739

including selectively, 740

including modular files, 738

macros

defined, 738

defining, 739

predefined macros, 740–741

members, 743

null-terminated strings, 747

operators

associativity of, 749–751

listed/defined, 747–749

precedence of, 749–751

preprocessor directives

#define directive, 738, 739

#include directive, 738

conditional directives, 738, 739–740

defined, 737

other directives, 740–741

shared libraries

C shared library, 760, 761

creating, 762–764

defined, 760

dynamic allocation of memory, 745

dynamic linking, 734, 760, 762

dynamically loading, 764–766

viewing program use of, 760–761

warning, 766

source files structure, 735–737

statements

break statements, 751

case statements, 752

compound statements/blocks, 751, 752

continue statements, 752

default labels in, 753

defined, 713, 751

do-while statements, 753

expressions statements, 753

for statements, 753–754

goto statements, 754

if statements, 754

if-else statements, 754–755

null statements, 755

return statements, 755

switch statements, 753, 755–756

while statements, 756–757

programming in Perl

to access files, 797–799

basic Perl syntax, 783

checking if Perl installed, 780–781

defined, 23, 779–780

to execute Linux commands, 795–797

expressions

defined, 783

grep command and, 789, 791

operators in, 787–788

regular expressions, 789–791

warning, 788

flow-control statements

defined, 783

else/elseif clauses, 792–793

for statements, 794

foreach statements, 794–795

goto statements, 795

if statements, 791, 792

overview, 791–792

unless statements, 793

while loops, 791, 793–794

functions

built-in functions, 800

defined, 783

defined, 784

open, 797–799

require, 801–802, 803

subroutines, 799–800

undef, 784

use, 803

using objects, 804–805

Perl modules, 783, 801, 802–803, 804

Perl packages, 783, 800–802

pipes (vertical bars) in, 798–799

predefined file handles, 797

to send mail messages, 798–799

statements, 783

trying out, 782–783

programming in Perl
*(continued)*
variables
array variables, 784,
785–786
associative arrays, 784,
786–787
default arguments, 785
defined, 783
English module for, 806
predefined variables, 787
scalar variables, 784–785
viewing Perl version
numbers, 781
programming shell scripts.
*See also* shells, Bash
with arguments, 769–772
to automate tasks,
768–769
Bash shell features for,
767, 770
built-in Bash commands
and, 775–778
to convert file formats,
767–768
defined, 95, 151–152, 767
errors in, 772
flow-control statements
case statements,
773–775
defined, 713, 772
for loops, 773
if statements, 772–773
functions, 771–772
for storing user input,
770–771
variables, 770–771
warning, 776
protocols. *See* network
protocols; TCP/IP

proxy servers, 564, 568,
570–571
ps ax command, 97, 147,
149
.ps extension, 196
pseudorandom bits, 309
PTR (Pointer) resource
records, 681, 687, 688
public-key encryption. *See
also* encryption
defined, 547–548
in digital signing, 548–549
in OpenSSH protocol,
561–563
Python programming
language, 23

## *Q–R*

question marks (?) as
command wildcards,
140–141
r commands, 561
RAM (Random Access
Memory)
creating RAM disk files,
514–515
defined, 25, 710
requirements, 33
raster images, 262
RCS (Revision Control
System), 19, 22, 713
rebooting system, 517
rebuilding Linux kernel. *See
also* Linux kernel
and configured modules
using make, 513
configuring options for
ATA/ATAPI/MFM/RLL
support, 504–506
block devices, 503–504

busses, 502–503
character devices,
508–509
code maturity levels, 501
using default settings,
498
device drivers, 503
enhanced IDE support,
505–506
executable file formats,
503
file systems, 511–513
I20 device support, 507
I2C protocol support,
509
IEEE 1394 (Firewire)
support, 506
ISDN subsystem, 508
kernel hacking, 513
loadable module
support, 501
using make config, 498
using make menuconfig,
498
using make xconfig,
498, 499–513
multimedia devices, 509
networking support,
507–508
parallel port support,
503
Plug-and-Play support,
503
power management
options, 502
processor type/features,
502
SCSI device support, 506
security, 513
sound, 509
telephony support, 508

USB support, 510–511
warning, 501
creating initial RAM disk
files, 514–515
defined, 496
installing configured
modules, 514
installing kernel-source
RPMs, 496
linking device drivers into
kernel, 497
monolithic versus
modular kernels, 497
overview, 493
phases in, 497
proving new kernel
running, 517
reasons for, 496
rebooting system after,
517
and setting GRUB to boot,
515–517
warning, 517
recurring jobs, 421–424
Red Hat Enterprise Linux
(RHEL) product line,
1, 12
Red Hat home page, 359
Red Hat Linux product line,
1, 9. *See also* Fedora
Core; Linux
Red Hat mailing lists, 32
Red Hat Package Manager.
*See* RPM
redlining, 221
regular expressions in Perl,
789–791
relational databases, 176
relative directory names,
158
remote access services, 21,
272. *See also* SSH

removing RPM files. *See
also* deleting
using Add/Remove
Packages, 72–74
using `rpm` commands, 467
using Yum, 475, 476
repeating shell commands,
142
resolver libraries in DNS,
676, 679, 680, 682–683
resource configuration
directives in
`httpd.conf`, 627–631
resource records (RRs),
681, 686–688
restoring files. *See*
managing file systems
`return` statements, 755
reverse lookups, 681–682
Revision Control System
(RCS), 19, 22, 713
rewriting rule, 660
RFCs (Request for
Comments)
1321, 537
2487, 662
2616, 630
on DNS, 676
on HTTP, 616
RHEL (Red Hat Enterprise
Linux), 1, 12
Rhythmbox application,
170
ripping music, 188–189
RJ-45 jacks, 278
RLL (Run Length Limited),
504–505
`rm` command, 164
`rmdir` command, 165
`rndc` (remote name
daemon control),
684–685

root directory, 153–156, 439
root domains, 677
`root` superusers. *See also*
users
adding, 425
defined, 52
forgotten passwords,
restoring, 396–397
gaining privileges of, 69,
146, 395–396
setting passwords, 52–53
warning, 81
`route` command, 324–325
route spoofing/attacks, 564,
567
routers, screening, 564,
565–567. *See also* NAT
routines. *See* functions
RPC (Remote Procedure
Calls), 581
RPM (Red Hat Package
Manager) files
building from source files,
474
defined, 72, 461, 494
installing. *See also* DVD
using Add/Remove
Packages, 72–74
kernel RPMs, 494–496
operating-system
updates, 582
using `rpm` commands,
466–467, 582
source RPMs, 474
using Up2date, 474–475
using Yum, 475–477
managing with `rpm`
commands
installing RPMs, 466–467
overview, 461–462
querying RPM
databases, 463–466

RPM (Red Hat Package
    Manager) files *(continued)*
  upgrading RPMs,
    467–468
  verifying RPMs, 468–469
  viewing RPM filenames,
    462–463
  warning, 468
removing
  using Add/Remove
    Packages, 72–74
  using rpm commands,
    467
  using Yum, 475, 476
updating with Up2date,
    474–475, 476
updating with Yum,
    475–477
RRs (resource records),
    681, 686–688
Run Length Limited (RLL),
    504–505
run levels
  changing with init
    command, 400–401
  defined, 398–399
  reviewing with chkconfig
    command, 587, 608–609
rwx permissions, 161

### S

SAINT (Security
    Administrator's
    Integrated Network
    Tool), 593
Salz, Rich, 666
Samba software package
  checking if installed, 702
  components, 701–702
  configuring, 703–705

defined, 27, 695, 700–701
trying out, 705–706
SANE (Scanner Access Now
    Easy) library, 171
SANS/FBI Top 20
    vulnerabilities, 580–581
SARA (Security Auditor's
    Research Assistant),
    594
saving
  command output, 139
  error messages, 139
  files gotten from others,
    214
  text editing changes, 203,
    207
/sbin directory, 156, 439
scalar variables, 784–785
scanners, USB, 487
scenarios in Calc, 244–245,
    247
Schaefer, Arno, 37
scheduling jobs. *See* system
    administration
screening routers, 564,
    565–567
scripting. *See* programming
    in Perl; programming
    shell
SCSI (Small Computer
    System Interface)
    controllers, 33, 34, 506
searching. *See* finding
second-level DNS domains,
    677, 678
secondary DNS servers, 679
Secure Shell protocol.
    *See* SSH
Secure Sockets Layer (SSL)
    protocol, 354, 360

securing hosts. *See also*
    encryption; security
    audits; SELinux
  defined, 535
  using GnuPG
    decrypting documents,
      554
    defined, 547
    digital signatures and,
      548–549
    encrypting documents,
      553–554
    exchanging keys,
      551–552
    generating key pairs,
      550–551
    gpg command, 550–554
    public-key encryption
      and, 547–549
    signing files, 553
    warning, 552
  installing system updates,
    535–536
  issues in, 527
  monitoring log files
    using LogWatch, 556
    using System Logs,
      555–556
    using Tripwire, 554
  protecting files/
    directories
    from buffer overflow, 544
    changing ownerships,
      541
    changing permissions,
      541–542
    using default umask
      permissions, 542–543
    using exec-shield
      feature, 544–545
    overview, 540

`setuid` permission risks, 543–544

viewing ownerships/ permissions, 540–541

securing passwords

/etc/passwd file and, 536

using MD5 encryption, 537–538

using pluggable authentication modules, 538–540

using shadow passwords, 536–537

using SELinux, 545–547

securing networks. *See also* security audits

with built-in packet- filtering firewall enabling/disabling, 572

using `iptables` commands, 571, 573–575

overview, 571–572

warning, 574

using firewalls

application gateways and, 570–571

defined, 522, 563–564

dual-homed host with proxy services, 564, 567–568, 570–571

perimeter network with bastion hosts, 565, 568–570

screening router with packet filtering, 564, 565–567

types of, 564–571

warning, 568

Internet services

configuring `xinetd` to disable, 558–561

disabling standalone servers, 558

overview, 557

warnings, 557, 560

issues in, 528

overview, 557

remote logins, 561–563

security

establishing security frameworks

business requirements, 523

defined, 522–523

risk analysis, 524–525

security management, 526

security policy, 522–523, 525–526

security solutions (mitigation), 526

news/alerts/updates on, 532–533

overview, 521–522

securing Linux

host security issues, 527

network security issues, 528

options for, 513

overview, 527

terminology, 529

threats

Denial of Service attacks, 521, 524, 642, 645

information disclosure, 524

IP spoofing, 567

route spoofing, 564

unauthorized access, 524

updates, 533

vulnerabilities

in anonymous FTP, 641, 645

buffer overflow, 544

listed, 524–525

logins on dual-homed hosts, 568

of Internet servers, 557

open ports, 588

overview, 524

tools to scan for, 588–589, 590–594

in UNIX systems, 581

security audits, computer

benefits, 578

defined, 577

host reviews. *See also* securing hosts

file ownership/ permissions, 582–584

incident response policy, 585

operating-system updates, 582

overview, 582

password security, 584–585

host/network test methodology, 579–580

network reviews. *See also* securing networks

overview, 585

penetration testing, 588

services started by `xinetd` server, 585–586

standalone servers, 587

nontechnical aspects of, 578

reasons for, 578

security testing tools

Nessus, 590–593

`nmap`, 589–590

security audits, computer
*(continued)*
overview, 588–589
port scanners, 588, 589–590
SAINT, 593
SARA, 594
vulnerability scanners, 588–589, 590–594
technical aspects of, 579
vulnerabilities, 580–581
Security Level Configuration tool, 572
security policy, 15
Sed software, 19
Select Device Type window, 313
Select Wireless Device window, 313–314
SELinux (Security Enhanced Linux). *See also* securing hosts
/selinux directory, 156, 439
configuring options, 50–51, 513
defined, 15
securing hosts, 545–547
turning off during booting, 513
sendmail server. *See also* e-mail; Internet services
configuration files
/etc/aliases file, 664
/etc/mail string, 661–662
auto-handling mail, 663–664
control operators, 659–660
converting names to addresses, 664

.forward file, 662–663
installing, 651–652
invoking procmail in .forward, 663–664
m4 macro processor and, 652–654
macro files, 652, 654–659
overview, 648, 651
syntax, 659–660
defined, 21
installing, 647–648, 651–652
sending mail using mail command, 649
sending mail using SMTP commands, 649–651
verifying delivery with mail, 649, 651
vulnerabilities, 581
serial communication, 284–285
serial port detection, 288
serial-port device names, 287–288
Server Message Block (SMB) protocol, 701–702
Server Settings dialog box, 704
server-side include files, 633
servers. *See also* daemon; Internet servers
auto-starting, 403
client/server architecture, 597–598
server processes, 299
starting/stopping manually, 402–403
Service Configuration utility, 609–614
sessions, 81

setuid permission risks, 543–544
sgi-fam server, 586
SGML (Standard Generalized Markup Language), 119
shadow passwords, 536–537
shared libraries. *See also* libraries; programming in C
C shared library, 760, 761
creating, 762–764
defined, 23, 760
dynamic linking, 734, 760, 762
dynamically loading, 764–766
viewing program use of, 760–761
warning, 766
shareware programs, 809
sharing
cable modem connections, 283–284
Calc spreadsheets, 242
files with NFS
configuring NFS servers, 699–700
exporting file systems with NFS, 444, 696–698
mounting NFS file systems, 445, 698
NFS, defined, 299, 602, 695
overview, 443–444, 695
warning, 696
Impress presentations, 260
information on Internet, 272
Writer documents, 216

Sharutils software, 19
shells
  Bash shell. *See also*
    programming shell
    scripts
  defined, 17, 95, 136
  versus MS-DOS, 136, 151
  starting, 95
  writing shell scripts, 95,
    151–152
  Bash shell commands
  auto-completing, 140
  built-in commands,
    775–778
  combining, 138
  getting input from files,
    138
  history, 142
  I/O redirection of,
    138–139
  and Linux commands,
    96–97, 142–151
  repeating, 142
  saving error messages,
    139
  saving output, 139
  shortcuts, 140–142
  syntax of, 95–96, 136–138
  wildcards, 140–141
  C Shell, 136
  changing default shells,
    136
  defined, 16, 95, 136, 711
  using Linux commands in.
    *See also* Linux file
    system
  to become root user,
    146
  for date/time, 147–148
  defined, 142–143
  listed, 143–146
  for managing processes,
    145, 147

  for processing files, 144,
    148–151
  trying out, 96–97
Nautilus shell in GNOME
  burning data CDs,
    120–121
  defined, 120
  navigation windows,
    121–124
  object windows, 120
  warning, 124
opening terminal
  consoles, 95, 135
opening virtual consoles,
  135–136
overview, 94
processing text files
  counting words/lines,
    149
  deleting characters, 150
  overview, 144, 148–149
  sorting, 150
  splitting, 150–151
  substituting characters,
    150
shutting down Fedora
  Core, 98
signal 11 error, 61
signatures, digital, 548–549,
  553
slave name servers, 679
slide shows. *See*
  OpenOffice.org Impress
SMB (Server Message
  Block) protocol,
  701–702
SMBus (System
  Management Bus)
  protocol, 509
SMTP (Simple Mail Transfer
  Protocol), 299, 601, 662
snail mail, 227

sniffing tools, packet,
  327–328, 589
SNMP (Simple Network
  Management Protocol)
  defined, 299, 602
  overview, 599
  port number, 602
  vulnerabilities, 581
SOA (Start of Authority)
  resource records,
  687–688
softmodems, 286
software, 9–10
software development. *See*
  building; programming;
  rebuilding
sort command, 150
sound cards. *See also* audio
  configuring, 26, 68, 509
  requirements, 34
  testing, 26
source code, 11, 712. *See*
  *also* building;
  programming
source RPMs (SRPMS),
  installing, 474
special effects in
  presentations, 257–259
split command, 150
spoofing threats, 564, 567
spooling print jobs,
  488–489
spreadsheets. *See*
  OpenOffice.org Calc
SSH (Secure Shell)
  protocol. *See also*
  Internet services
  defined, 299, 602
  OpenSSH, 561–563
  port number, 602
  sshd daemon server, 22
  vulnerabilities, 581

SSL (Secure Sockets Layer) protocol, 354, 360
Stallman, Richard, 16
standalone servers. *See* Internet servers
StarOffice application, 174
Start Here window in GNOME, 124–125
STARTTLS extension to SMTP, 662
startup scripts, 401–402
statements in C. *See also* programming in C
`break` statements, 751
`case` statements, 752
compound statements/blocks, 751, 752
`continue` statements, 752
`default` labels in, 753
defined, 713, 751
`do-while` statements, 753
expression statements, 753
`for` loops, 753–754
`goto` statements, 754
`if` statements, 754
`if-else` statements, 754–755
`null` statements, 755
`return` statements, 755
`switch` statements, 753, 755–756
`while` loops, 756–757
statements in Perl. *See also* programming in Perl
defined, 783
flow-control statements. *See also* flow-control statements
defined, 783
`else`/`elseif` clauses, 792–793

`for` loops, 794
`foreach` statements, 794–795
`goto` statements, 795
`if` statements, 791, 792
overview, 791–792
`unless` statements, 793
`while` loops, 791, 793–794
statistical attacks, 309
storage media. *See* CD; DVD; floppy; hard disks; keychain; Zip
storing user input via scripts, 770–771
stream cipher algorithm, 309
stream sockets, 599
stream-based macro processors, 652
structures in C, 743
.stw extension, 225
styles in Writer, 224–225, 227–228
Stylist window in Calc, 240
Stylist window in Draw, 262, 265
`su` command, 146, 395
subarchitectures, 13
subdomains in DNS, 677, 678
subroutines. *See* functions
Subscribe dialog box, 377
subscribing to mailing lists, 533
subscribing to newsgroups, 377–379
Subversion utility, 22
swapping in hard drives, 414
`switch` statements, 753, 755–756

.sxc extension, 238
.sxi extension, 249
.sxw extension, 217
symbolic links, 161
Symmetric DSL (Digital Subscriber Line), 276
symmetric encryption, 554
/sys directory, 156
sysfs file system, 14, 482
system administration. *See also* Linux kernel; managing
using /proc file system, 156, 415–418
becoming `root` user, 395–396
configuration files, 406–408
defined, 25, 393
Fedora Core boot process. *See also* boot
/etc/inittab file in, 398–401
auto-starting servers, 403
changing run levels, 400–401
GUI startup, 404–406
`init` process, 397–399
overview, 397
run levels in, 398–399
starting/stopping servers manually, 402–403
startup scripts, 401–402
monitoring performance
GNOME System Monitor, 411–412
and hard disk usage, 414–415
overview, 408–409
`top` utility, 409–411

`uptime` command, 412
`vmstat` utility, 413–414
Perl scripts, 779–780
scheduling jobs
  one-time jobs, 419–421
  overview, 418
  recurring jobs, 421–424
system administrators,
  393
tasks in, 393–395
warnings, 397, 416
system configuration files.
  *See also* TCP/IP
`.config`, 498
`/etc` directory, defined,
  155, 439
`/etc/exports`, 696–698,
  699–700
`/etc/fstab`, 442–443
`/etc/grub.conf`,
  515–517
`/etc/httpd/conf`, 621,
  623–634
`/etc/mail/sendmail.cf`
  `/etc/aliases` file, 664
  auto-handling mail,
    663–664
  control operators,
    659–660
  converting names into
    addresses, 664
  file syntax, 659–660
  `.forward` file, 662–663
  installing, 651–652
  invoking `procmail` in
    `.forward` file, 663–664
  m4 macro processor
    and, 652–654
  overview, 648, 651
  searching for `/etc/mail`
    string, 661–662
  `sendmail.mc` macro
    files, 652, 654–659

`/etc/modprobe.conf`,
  485–486
`/etc/mtools.conf`,
  456–457
`/etc/named.conf`,
  683–685
`/etc/nsswitch.conf`,
  683
in `/etc/pam.d`, 538–540
`/etc/resolv.conf`,
  682–683
`/etc/services`, 602–603
`/etc/shadow`, 536–537
`/etc/syslog.conf`, 555
`/etc/udev/udev`, 14, 482
`/etc/X11`, 159–162
`/etc/xinetd.conf`,
  559–561, 603–606
for DNS caching servers,
  683–685
editing, 406
for FTP server
  `/etc/vsftpd/vsftpd.`
    `conf`, 641–643
  `/etc/vsftpd.`
    `ftpusers`, 643–644
  `/etc/vsftpd.`
    `user_list`, 644
  overview, 640–641
for INN news server,
  667–671
listed, 406–408
for OpenSSH, 562
password ownership/
  permissions, 585
permission settings for,
  583–584
for Samba, 701
for TCP/IP, 319–323, 328
System Logs utility, 555–556

### T

tape drives, 446, 450–451
`tar` (tape archiver)
  program
  backing up/restoring files,
    447–449, 451
  defined, 19, 27, 145
  unpacking source files,
    469–470
tasks. *See* system
  administration
Tcl (Tool Command
  Language), 23
TCP (Transmission Control
  Protocol), 296, 599
TCP wrappers, 560
TCP/IP network
  management. *See also*
  Ethernet; wireless
overview, 319
TCP/IP configuration files
  `/etc/host.allow`,
    321–322
  `/etc/host.conf`,
    320–321
  `/etc/host.deny`, 322
  `/etc/hosts`, 320
  `/etc/networks`, 320
  `/etc/nsswitch.conf`,
    323
  `/etc/resolv.conf`, 321
  `/etc/sysconfig/`
    `network`, 328
  overview, 319
troubleshooting
  host connections with
    `ping`, 325
  IP routing tables with
    `route`, 324–325
  network interfaces with
    `ipconfig`, 323–324
  network startup at boot
    time, 328

TCP/IP network *(continued)*
  network status with
    *netstat*, 325–326
  with packet-sniffing
    tools, 327–328, 589
TCP/IP protocol suite. *See
    also* Internet
    services; IP
  Application layer. *See also*
    FTP; HTTP; TELNET
    defined, 295–296
    Post Office Protocol, 296
    Simple Mail Transfer
      Protocol, 299, 601, 662
  client/server model, 598,
    599–601
  configuring on Ethernet
    LANs, 302–305
  in dial-up networking, 285
  the Internet and, 297
  Network layer, 295–296
  overview, 20–21, 295, 598
  Physical layer, 295–296
  port numbers, 298–299,
    598, 599–603
  protocols
    connection-oriented
      protocols, 598–599,
      600–601
    connectionless
      protocols, 599, 600
    listed/defined, 298–299,
      601–602
  sockets, 598, 599–601
  Transport layer
    defined, 296
    overview, 295
    Transmission Control
      Protocol, 296, 599, 600
    User Datagram Protocol,
      296, 599
tcpdump command, 327

tearoff menus, 265
telephony support options,
  508
TELNET protocol. *See also*
    Internet services;
    TCP/IP
  defined, 299, 602
  example of HTTP use,
    615–618
  port number, 602
  proxy services, 571
  telnet server, 22, 586
  viewing on/off status,
    586
  xinetd configuration for,
    604–606
templates in Writer,
  document, 225–227
10BaseT Ethernet, 301–302,
  305–306. *See also*
  Ethernet
testing. *See also* security
    audits
  dial-up modems, 289–290
  DNS caching servers, 692
  newsgroup setup, 674
  sound cards, 26
Texinfo software, 19
text editors
  creating HTML Web pages
    in, 364–366
  ed
    command mode, 201, 203
    commands, listed,
      203–204
    defined, 17
    editing files, 201–203
    overview, 200–201
    saving changes/quitting,
      203
    text-input mode, 201, 203
  emacs, 17, 23

in GNOME GUI, 199–200
  in KDE GUI, 200
  vi
    colon (:) command
      mode, 206–207, 208
    cursor movement
      commands, 206, 208
    defined, 204
    online help, 206
    overview, 200–201
    saving changes/quitting,
      207
    starting, 205
    text-editing commands,
      207–209
    text-input mode, 206, 207
    visual command mode,
      205, 207
text file processing. *See
    also* shells
  counting words/lines, 149
  deleting characters, 150
  overview, 144, 148–149
  sorting, 150
  splitting, 150–151
  substituting characters,
    150
text-mode installation, 58
TFTP (Trivial File Transfer
    Protocol), 299, 602
Theme Preferences dialog
    box, 88
themes
  changing in Mozilla,
    361–363
  defined, 87
  selecting for GNOME,
    87–88
thick/thin Ethernet cable,
  301
TIFF format, converting
    XWD to, 767–768

Time software, 19
time zones, 51–52
time/date tools, 76, 77, 146, 147–148
TKIP (Temporal Key-Integrity Protocol), 310
TLS. *See* SSL
/tmp directory, 156, 439
Tool Command Language (Tcl), 23
tooltips, 218
top utility, 409–411
torrents, 101
Torvalds, Linus, 10, 77
tr command, 150
trackers, 101
tracking changes in documents, 221, 223
Transport layer in TCP/IP, 296
Tripwire software, 554
troubleshooting
  buffer overflow, 544
  using DVD-ROM in book, 810
  Fedora Core installation
    hung boot process, 59
    kernel boot commands, 62–64
    linux noprobe command, 58–59
    overview, 57, 61
    by reconfiguring X, 59–61
    signal 11 error, 61
    text-mode installation, 58
    undetected hardware, 58
    X failure to start, 58, 59, 77
  hung GUIs, 135
  shell scripting errors, 772
  system hang on reboot, 517

TCP/IP networks
  host connections with ping, 325
  IP routing tables with route, 324–325
  network interfaces with ipconfig, 323–324
  network startup at boot time, 328
  network status with netstat, 325–326
  with packet-sniffing tools, 327–328, 589
TTL (Time To Live) values, 686
typedef keyword in C, 745–746

**U**

UART (universal asynchronous receiver/transmitter) chips, 288
udev program, 14, 482
UDP (User Datagram Protocol), 296, 599
umask command, 542–543
umount command, 167, 442, 454, 455
uname command, 96
unions in C, 743
UNIX-to-UNIX Copy Protocol (UUCP), 371–372
unless statements, 793
updating
  news server configuration, 673–674
  operating-systems, 582
  security, 533
upstream data, 281

uptime command, 96, 412
URLs (Uniform Resource Locators), 353–355
USB (Universal Serial Bus)
  configuring support for, 510–511
  defined, 510
  managing USB devices, 486–488
  USB Mass Storage, 184–186
Usenet newsgroups, 371–372, 380–381
user ID mapping options in /etc/exports, 697, 700
user input storage, scripting, 770–771
User Properties dialog box, 426–427
users, managing. *See also* managing; system administration
  changing file ownership, 434–435
  Linux commands for, 145
  overview, 425
  user accounts. *See also* root
    adding to PostgreSQL, 177–178
    adding via commands, 428–429
    adding via User Manager, 69–70, 426–428
    editing, 71, 428–429
    overview, 425
    password vulnerabilities, 581
    setting up in firstboot, 77–78
    viewing in /etc/passwd file, 429–430

users, managing *(continued)*
user environments,
431–433
user groups, 430–431
/usr/ directory, 156–157,
440, 561–562
UTC (Universal
Coordinated Time), 51
UUCP (UNIX-to-UNIX Copy
Protocol), 371–372

## V

/var/ directory
defined, 156
DNS caching server files,
689–691
log file permissions, 584
monitoring log files,
555–556
newsgroup files, 667
subdirectories, 157, 408,
440
variables
defined, 713
defining in GNU make
utility, 721–722
defining in shell scripts,
770–771
environment variables
defined, 712
defining in Bash shell,
432–433
in GNU make utility, 721
listed, 433
PATH environment
variable
appending directories to,
433
defined, 770–771
defining, 432
finding files in, 432, 780

variables in C. *See also*
programming in C
changing value of in
functions, 745
declaring/defining
arrays, 743–744, 745
const type qualifier, 746
data types, 741–742,
745–746
defined, 737
enumerations, 742
expressions, 713,
747–749
overview, 741
pointers, 744–745
structures, 743
type definitions,
745–746
unions, 743
volatile type qualifier,
746
variables in Perl
array variables, 784,
785–786
associative arrays, 784,
786–787
default arguments, 785
defined, 783
English module for, 806
predefined variables, 787
scalar variables, 784–785
vector graphics, 262
version-control systems, 22,
713
vertical bars (pipes) in
script commands, 138,
798–799
vi text editor. *See also* text
editors
colon (:) command mode,
206–207, 208
cursor movement
commands, 206, 208

defined, 204
online help, 206
overview, 200–201
saving changes/quitting,
207
starting, 205
text-editing commands,
207–209
text-input mode, 206, 207
visual command mode,
205, 207
video cards, 33
virtual consoles, 58
virtual hosts in Apache,
622, 623, 634–637
VisiCalc, 237
visual command mode in
vi editor, 205, 207
vmstat utility, 413–414
volatile type qualifier,
746
vsftpd server. *See* FTP

## W

Wall, Larry, 18, 779, 781
wallpaper
defined, 85
on GNOME desktops, 87,
125–126
on KDE desktops, 93–94
WAV files, 187, 188
wc command, 149
weather applet, GNOME, 83
Web, the. *See also* HTML;
Internet
defined, 351–353
HTML document format,
352
HTTP protocol, 352
hypertext links, 353
URLs, 353–355

Web browsers. *See also*
      Konqueror; Mozilla
   defined, 351, 352, 355–356
   Epiphany, 357
   as graphical FTP clients,
      385–387
   Konqueror, 132, 357
   Mozilla Navigator, 357–363
   reading newsgroups on,
      380–381
Web pages
   changing home pages in
      Mozilla, 361
   creating in HTML
      inserting images,
         367–368
      with Mozilla Composer,
         364, 366–370
      overview, 364
      using text editors,
         364–366
   home pages, defined, 357
Web servers, 352, 355–356,
      615. *See also* Apache;
      Internet servers
Web services, 21, 271. *See
      also* Internet services;
      Web browsers; Web
servers
Web site addresses. *See
      also* help
   Adobe Reader, 216, 242,
      260
   Anywhere Desktop for
      Linux, 20
   Apache Web server, 619
   Applixware Office, 174
   Aspell, 170
   backup utilities, 447
   bandwidth speed test, 281
   Cdrecord, 170
   computer vulnerabilities,
      580

CPAN, 781
CrossOver Office, 20, 175
Dia, 170
DSL availability, 275, 277
DSL distance limits, 273
Epiphany, 357
Ethereal, 328
Fedora Core
   applications, 170–171
   home page, 5
   mailing lists, 32
   mirror sites, 494
   security updates, 533
free CD database, 186, 191
Gaim, 171
GAO, 357–358
The GIMP, 196
GNOME desktop, 119
GNOME Ghostview, 171
GNU Compiler Collection,
      713
GNU Project, 16
Google, 32, 363
Google Groups, 381
gPhoto, 184
GQView, 171
Gtkam, 171
HTTP/1.1 standard, 616
IANA, 603
Internal Revenue Service,
      132
iptables commands, 574
ISO, 678
Java 2 SDK, 433
KDE desktop, 89
Kmail, 171
Linux
   Conexant driver, 286
   IEEE 1394 peripherals,
      506
   IPv6, 298
   kernel versions, 12

   Online Web, 28
   Winmodem Support, 286
MD5 algorithm, 537
MLA style template, 225
Mozilla, 171
MySQL, 170
Netcraft Web Server
      Survey, 619
news servers, 375, 666
newsgroup categories, 374
nmap tool, 589
OpenOffice, 170
OpenSSH, 561
Perl
   built-in functions, 800
   latest versions, 781
   special variables, 806
PostgreSQL, 183
PowerQuest's
      PartitionMagic, 36
Red Hat home page, 359
Red Hat mailing lists, 32
RFCs
   1321, 537
   2487, 662
   2616, 630
   on DNS, 676
   on HTTP, 616
Rhythmbox, 170
SAINT, 593
SARA, 594
security alerts/updates,
      532–533
security tools, 588
SELinux, 15, 513
signal 11 problem, 61
StarOffice, 20, 174
themes, 362
Tripwire, 554
UNIX vulnerabilities, 581
Usenet newsgroups,
      380–381
virtual hosts in Apache,
      635

Web site addresses
*(continued)*
VisiCalc, 237
Web-related standards,
616
Wi-Fi Alliance, 308
Wiley Tech Support, 810
Wine, 175
X-CD-Roast, 171
XFree86 Project, 19
Ximian Desktop 2, 111
Ximian Evolution, 171
XMMS, 171
X.Org Foundation, 19
Xsane, 171
Yahoo, 363
Yum, 476
WEP (Wired Equivalent
Privacy) problems, 309,
310
which command, 780–781
while loops, 756–757, 791,
793–794
Wi-Fi Alliance, 308, 310
Wi-Fi (Wireless Fidelity)
networks, 307
wildmat pattern in INN
configuration, 670
Wiley Product Technical
Support, 810
Windows client/server
setup. *See* Samba
Windows file system. *See*
managing file systems
Wine application, 175
winmodems, 286
wireless Ethernet LANs. *See
also* Ethernet; TCP/IP
access points, 312
ad-hoc mode, 308
configuring, 312–318

encryption, 312, 317
hardware setup, 310–312
IEEE 802.11x standards
for, 307–308, 310
infrastructure (managed)
mode, 308
overview, 307
WEP problems, 309, 310
Wi-Fi Alliance and, 308,
310
Wi-Fi networks and, 307
WPA standard for, 310
Word, Microsoft, 213–214,
215. *See also*
OpenOffice.org Writer
World Wide Web. *See* Web
WPA (Wi-Fi Protected
Access) standard, 310
Writer. *See* OpenOffice.org
Writer

## X–Y–Z

X Window System. *See also*
rebuilding
converting XWD files to
TIFF, 767–768
defined, 19
kernel configuration tool,
498, 499–513
reconfiguring, 59–61
troubleshooting failure to
start, 58, 59, 77
xdm login display
manager, 404
X-CD-Roast. *See also*
CD-ROMs
burning Fedora Core CDs,
103–104
defined, 171, 188–189
installing, 189

MP3 audio and, 189
recording audio CDs,
191–192
recording data CDs, 193
Setup window, 190–191
starting, 189–190
warning, 189
Web site address, 171
XFree86, 19
Ximian Evolution mail
client. *See also* e-mail
defined, 340
help, 344
main window, 342–344
setting up, 340–342
xinetd server. *See also*
Internet servers
/etc/xinetd.conf file,
559–561, 603–606
auditing services started
by, 585–586
configuring to disable
services, 558–561
defined, 603
XMMS (X Multimedia
System)
creating WAV files, 188
defined, 171, 187
installing, 187
MP3 files and, 188
rebuilding from source
files, 469–473
starting, 188
Web site address, 171
X.Org Foundation, 19
X.Org X11, 19
Xsane, 171
Yum (Yellow dog Updater,
Modified), 475–477
Zip disks, 214, 446
zone file formats, 685–686

# GNU General Public License

Version 2, June 1991
Copyright (C) 1989, 1991 Free Software Foundation, Inc.
59 Temple Place - Suite 330, Boston, MA 02111-1307, USA

## Preamble

The licenses for most software are designed to take away your freedom to share and change it. By contrast, the GNU General Public License is intended to guarantee your freedom to share and change free software—to make sure the software is free for all its users. This General Public License applies to most of the Free Software Foundation's software and to any other program whose authors commit to using it. (Some other Free Software Foundation software is covered by the GNU Library General Public License instead.) You can apply it to your programs, too.

When we speak of free software, we are referring to freedom, not price. Our General Public Licenses are designed to make sure that you have the freedom to distribute copies of free software (and charge for this service if you wish), that you receive source code or can get it if you want it, that you can change the software or use pieces of it in new free programs; and that you know you can do these things.

To protect your rights, we need to make restrictions that forbid anyone to deny you these rights or to ask you to surrender the rights. These restrictions translate to certain responsibilities for you if you distribute copies of the software, or if you modify it.

For example, if you distribute copies of such a program, whether gratis or for a fee, you must give the recipients all the rights that you have. You must make sure that they, too, receive or can get the source code. And you must show them these terms so they know their rights.

We protect your rights with two steps: (1) copyright the software, and (2) offer you this license which gives you legal permission to copy, distribute and/or modify the software.

Also, for each author's protection and ours, we want to make certain that everyone understands that there is no warranty for this free software. If the software is modified by someone else and passed on, we want its recipients to know that what they have is not the original, so that any problems introduced by others will not reflect on the original authors' reputations.

Finally, any free program is threatened constantly by software patents. We wish to avoid the danger that redistributors of a free program will individually obtain patent licenses, in effect making the program proprietary. To prevent this, we have made it clear that any patent must be licensed for everyone's free use or not licensed at all.

The precise terms and conditions for copying, distribution and modification follow.

# Terms and Conditions for Copying, Distribution and Modification

0.  This License applies to any program or other work which contains a notice placed by the copyright holder saying it may be distributed under the terms of this General Public License. The "Program", below, refers to any such program or work, and a "work based on the Program" means either the Program or any derivative work under copyright law: that is to say, a work containing the Program or a portion of it, either verbatim or with modifications and/or translated into another language. (Hereinafter, translation is included without limitation in the term "modification".) Each licensee is addressed as "you".

    Activities other than copying, distribution and modification are not covered by this License; they are outside its scope. The act of running the Program is not restricted, and the output from the Program is covered only if its contents constitute a work based on the Program (independent of having been made by running the Program). Whether that is true depends on what the Program does.

1.  You may copy and distribute verbatim copies of the Program's source code as you receive it, in any medium, provided that you conspicuously and appropriately publish on each copy an appropriate copyright notice and disclaimer of warranty; keep intact all the notices that refer to this License and to the absence of any warranty; and give any other recipients of the Program a copy of this License along with the Program.

    You may charge a fee for the physical act of transferring a copy, and you may at your option offer warranty protection in exchange for a fee.

2.  You may modify your copy or copies of the Program or any portion of it, thus forming a work based on the Program, and copy and distribute such modifications or work under the terms of Section 1 above, provided that you also meet all of these conditions:

    a)  You must cause the modified files to carry prominent notices stating that you changed the files and the date of any change.

    b)  You must cause any work that you distribute or publish, that in whole or in part contains or is derived from the Program or any part thereof, to be licensed as a whole at no charge to all third parties under the terms of this License.

    c)  If the modified program normally reads commands interactively when run, you must cause it, when started running for such interactive use in the most ordinary way, to print or display an announcement including an appropriate copyright notice and a notice that there is no warranty (or else, saying that you provide a warranty) and that users may redistribute the program under these conditions, and telling the user how to view a copy of this License. (Exception: if the Program itself is interactive but does not normally print such an announcement, your work based on the Program is not required to print an announcement.)

    These requirements apply to the modified work as a whole. If identifiable sections of that work are not derived from the Program, and can be reasonably considered independent and separate works in themselves, then this License, and its terms, do not apply to those sections when you distribute them as separate works. But when you distribute the same sections as part of a whole which is a work based on the Program, the distribution of the whole must be on the terms of this License, whose permissions for other licensees extend to the entire whole, and thus to each and every part regardless of who wrote it.

Thus, it is not the intent of this section to claim rights or contest your rights to work written entirely by you; rather, the intent is to exercise the right to control the distribution of derivative or collective works based on the Program.

In addition, mere aggregation of another work not based on the Program with the Program (or with a work based on the Program) on a volume of a storage or distribution medium does not bring the other work under the scope of this License.

3. You may copy and distribute the Program (or a work based on it, under Section 2) in object code or executable form under the terms of Sections 1 and 2 above provided that you also do one of the following:

   a) Accompany it with the complete corresponding machine-readable source code, which must be distributed under the terms of Sections 1 and 2 above on a medium customarily used for software interchange; or,

   b) Accompany it with a written offer, valid for at least three years, to give any third party, for a charge no more than your cost of physically performing source distribution, a complete machine-readable copy of the corresponding source code, to be distributed under the terms of Sections 1 and 2 above on a medium customarily used for software interchange; or,

   c) Accompany it with the information you received as to the offer to distribute corresponding source code. (This alternative is allowed only for noncommercial distribution and only if you received the program in object code or executable form with such an offer, in accord with Subsection b above.)

   The source code for a work means the preferred form of the work for making modifications to it. For an executable work, complete source code means all the source code for all modules it contains, plus any associated interface definition files, plus the scripts used to control compilation and installation of the executable. However, as a special exception, the source code distributed need not include anything that is normally distributed (in either source or binary form) with the major components (compiler, kernel, and so on) of the operating system on which the executable runs, unless that component itself accompanies the executable.

   If distribution of executable or object code is made by offering access to copy from a designated place, then offering equivalent access to copy the source code from the same place counts as distribution of the source code, even though third parties are not compelled to copy the source along with the object code.

4. You may not copy, modify, sublicense, or distribute the Program except as expressly provided under this License. Any attempt otherwise to copy, modify, sublicense or distribute the Program is void, and will automatically terminate your rights under this License. However, parties who have received copies, or rights, from you under this License will not have their licenses terminated so long as such parties remain in full compliance.

5. You are not required to accept this License, since you have not signed it. However, nothing else grants you permission to modify or distribute the Program or its derivative works. These actions are prohibited by law if you do not accept this License. Therefore, by modifying or distributing the Program (or any work based on the Program), you indicate your acceptance of this License to do so, and all its terms and conditions for copying, distributing or modifying the Program or works based on it.

6. Each time you redistribute the Program (or any work based on the Program), the recipient automatically receives a license from the original licensor to copy, distribute or modify the Program subject to these terms and conditions. You may not impose any further restrictions on the recipients' exercise of the rights granted herein. You are not responsible for enforcing compliance by third parties to this License.

7. If, as a consequence of a court judgment or allegation of patent infringement or for any other reason (not limited to patent issues), conditions are imposed on you (whether by court order, agreement or otherwise) that contradict the conditions of this License, they do not excuse you from the conditions of this License. If you cannot distribute so as to satisfy simultaneously your obligations under this License and any other pertinent obligations, then as a consequence you may not distribute the Program at all. For example, if a patent license would not permit royalty-free redistribution of the Program by all those who receive copies directly or indirectly through you, then the only way you could satisfy both it and this License would be to refrain entirely from distribution of the Program.

   If any portion of this section is held invalid or unenforceable under any particular circumstance, the balance of the section is intended to apply and the section as a whole is intended to apply in other circumstances.

   It is not the purpose of this section to induce you to infringe any patents or other property right claims or to contest validity of any such claims; this section has the sole purpose of protecting the integrity of the free software distribution system, which is implemented by public license practices. Many people have made generous contributions to the wide range of software distributed through that system in reliance on consistent application of that system; it is up to the author/donor to decide if he or she is willing to distribute software through any other system and a licensee cannot impose that choice.

   This section is intended to make thoroughly clear what is believed to be a consequence of the rest of this License.

8. If the distribution and/or use of the Program is restricted in certain countries either by patents or by copyrighted interfaces, the original copyright holder who places the Program under this License may add an explicit geographical distribution limitation excluding those countries, so that distribution is permitted only in or among countries not thus excluded. In such case, this License incorporates the limitation as if written in the body of this License.

9. The Free Software Foundation may publish revised and/or new versions of the General Public License from time to time. Such new versions will be similar in spirit to the present version, but may differ in detail to address new problems or concerns.

   Each version is given a distinguishing version number. If the Program specifies a version number of this License which applies to it and "any later version", you have the option of following the terms and conditions either of that version or of any later version published by the Free Software Foundation. If the Program does not specify a version number of this License, you may choose any version ever published by the Free Software Foundation.

10. If you wish to incorporate parts of the Program into other free programs whose distribution conditions are different, write to the author to ask for permission. For software which is copyrighted by the Free Software Foundation, write to the Free Software Foundation; we sometimes make exceptions for this. Our decision will be guided by the two goals of preserving the free status of all derivatives of our free software and of promoting the sharing and reuse of software generally.

# Wiley Publishing, Inc.
# Linux CD Mail-In Offer

If you do not have access to a PC with a DVD drive, we offer the complete set on CD-ROM for a nominal shipping-and-materials fee. If you would like the CDs sent to you, please follow the instructions below to order by phone, online, or mail.

For each ordering method, please use ISBN 0764577298 and Promo Code F2AIO when prompted. For orders shipping within the U.S., the cost is $13.50 (U.S. funds). For orders outside the U.S., the cost is $20.00 (U.S. funds).

Terms: Void where prohibited or restricted by law. Allow 2-4 weeks for delivery.

**To order by phone:**

1. Call toll free in the United States — 1-877-762-2974. International customers, dial 1-317-572-3994.

2. Give the operator the appropriate ISBN and Promo Code. Please have your credit card ready.

**To order online:**

1. Point your Web browser to www.wiley.com.

2. Use the Product Search feature to search for Linux Disk Multipack.

3. Place your order through the shopping cart using the appropriate ISBN and Promo Code.

**To order by mail:**

1. Complete the coupon below.

2. Include a check or money order for $13.50 (U.S. funds) for orders shipping within the U.S. or $20.00 (U.S. funds) for orders outside the U.S.

3. Send it to the address listed at the bottom of the coupon.

---

*Name* _____

*Company* _____

*Address* _____

*City* _____ *State* _____ *Postal Code* _____ *Country* _____

*E-mail* _____ *Telephone* _____

*Place where book was purchased* _____

❑ Check here to find out what we're up to by joining our e-mail list — a convenient way to receive news about our products and events as well as about special discount offers.

**Return this coupon with the appropriate U.S. funds to:**
Wiley Publishing, Inc.
Customer Care
**Linux Disk Multipack, 0764577298 Fulfillment Promo: F2AIO**
10475 Crosspoint Blvd.
Indianapolis, IN 46256

**Terms:** Wiley is not responsible for lost, stolen, late, or illegible orders. For questions regarding this fulfillment offer, please call us at 1-877-762-2974 or 1-317-572-3994.

# FOR DUMMIES®

## The easy way to get more done and have more fun

## PERSONAL FINANCE

0-7645-5231-7        0-7645-2431-3        0-7645-5331-3

**Also available:**

Estate Planning For Dummies
(0-7645-5501-4)
401(k)s For Dummies
(0-7645-5468-9)
Frugal Living For Dummies
(0-7645-5403-4)
Microsoft Money "X" For
Dummies
(0-7645-1689-2)
Mutual Funds For Dummies
(0-7645-5329-1)

Personal Bankruptcy For
Dummies
(0-7645-5498-0)
Quicken "X" For Dummies
(0-7645-1666-3)
Stock Investing For Dummies
(0-7645-5411-5)
Taxes For Dummies 2003
(0-7645-5475-1)

## BUSINESS & CAREERS

0-7645-5314-3        0-7645-5307-0        0-7645-5471-9

**Also available:**

Business Plans Kit For
Dummies
(0-7645-5365-8)
Consulting For Dummies
(0-7645-5034-9)
Cool Careers For Dummies
(0-7645-5345-3)
Human Resources Kit For
Dummies
(0-7645-5131-0)
Managing For Dummies
(1-5688-4858-7)

QuickBooks All-in-One Desk
Reference For Dummies
(0-7645-1963-8)
Selling For Dummies
(0-7645-5363-1)
Small Business Kit For
Dummies
(0-7645-5093-4)
Starting an eBay Business For
Dummies
(0-7645-1547-0)

## HEALTH, SPORTS & FITNESS

0-7645-5167-1        0-7645-5146-9        0-7645-5154-X

**Also available:**

Controlling Cholesterol For
Dummies
(0-7645-5440-9)
Dieting For Dummies
(0-7645-5126-4)
High Blood Pressure For
Dummies
(0-7645-5424-7)
Martial Arts For Dummies
(0-7645-5358-5)
Menopause For Dummies
(0-7645-5458-1)

Nutrition For Dummies
(0-7645-5180-9)
Power Yoga For Dummies
(0-7645-5342-9)
Thyroid For Dummies
(0-7645-5385-2)
Weight Training For Dummies
(0-7645-5168-X)
Yoga For Dummies
(0-7645-5117-5)

**Available wherever books are sold.**

WILEY

# FOR DUMMIES®

## A world of resources to help you grow

# FOR DUMMIES®

## Plain-English solutions for everyday challenges

## COMPUTER BASICS

0-7645-0838-5          0-7645-1663-9          0-7645-1548-9

**Also available:**

PCs All-in-One Desk Reference For Dummies (0-7645-0791-5)

Pocket PC For Dummies (0-7645-1640-X)

Treo and Visor For Dummies (0-7645-1673-6)

Troubleshooting Your PC For Dummies (0-7645-1669-8)

Upgrading & Fixing PCs For Dummies (0-7645-1665-5)

Windows XP For Dummies (0-7645-0893-8)

Windows XP For Dummies Quick Reference (0-7645-0897-0)

## BUSINESS SOFTWARE

0-7645-0822-9          0-7645-0839-3          0-7645-0819-9

**Also available:**

Excel Data Analysis For Dummies (0-7645-1661-2)

Excel 2002 All-in-One Desk Reference For Dummies (0-7645-1794-5)

Excel 2002 For Dummies Quick Reference (0-7645-0829-6)

GoldMine "X" For Dummies (0-7645-0845-8)

Microsoft CRM For Dummies (0-7645-1698-1)

Microsoft Project 2002 For Dummies (0-7645-1628-0)

Office XP For Dummies (0-7645-0830-X)

Outlook 2002 For Dummies (0-7645-0828-8)

## Get smart! Visit www.dummies.com

- **Find listings of even more *For Dummies* titles**
- **Browse online articles**
- **Sign up for Dummies eTips™**
- **Check out *For Dummies* fitness videos and other products**
- **Order from our online bookstore**

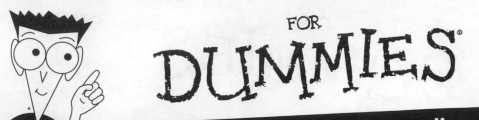

# FOR DUMMIES®

**Helping you expand your horizons and realize your potential**

## INTERNET

**0-7645-0894-6**

**0-7645-1659-0**

**0-7645-1642-6**

## DIGITAL MEDIA

**0-7645-1664-7**

**0-7645-1675-2**

**0-7645-0806-7**

## GRAPHICS

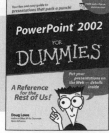

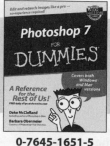

**0-7645-0817-2**

**0-7645-1651-5**

**0-7645-0895-4**

# FOR DUMMIES®

## The advice and explanations you need to succeed

---

## SELF-HELP, SPIRITUALITY & RELIGION

**Sex For Dummies**
0-7645-5302-X

**Parenting For Dummies**
0-7645-5418-2

**Religion For Dummies**
0-7645-5264-3

**Also available:**

The Bible For Dummies
(0-7645-5296-1)

Buddhism For Dummies
(0-7645-5359-3)

Christian Prayer For Dummies
(0-7645-5500-6)

Dating For Dummies
(0-7645-5072-1)

Judaism For Dummies
(0-7645-5299-6)

Potty Training For Dummies
(0-7645-5417-4)

Pregnancy For Dummies
(0-7645-5074-8)

Rekindling Romance For Dummies
(0-7645-5303-8)

Spirituality For Dummies
(0-7645-5298-8)

Weddings For Dummies
(0-7645-5055-1)

---

## PETS

**Puppies For Dummies**
0-7645-5255-4

**Dog Training For Dummies**
0-7645-5286-4

**Cats For Dummies**
0-7645-5275-9

**Also available:**

Labrador Retrievers For Dummies
(0-7645-5281-3)

Aquariums For Dummies
(0-7645-5156-6)

Birds For Dummies
(0-7645-5139-6)

Dogs For Dummies
(0-7645-5274-0)

Ferrets For Dummies
(0-7645-5259-7)

German Shepherds For Dummies
(0-7645-5280-5)

Golden Retrievers For Dummies
(0-7645-5267-8)

Horses For Dummies
(0-7645-5138-8)

Jack Russell Terriers For Dummies
(0-7645-5268-6)

Puppies Raising & Training Diary For Dummies
(0-7645-0876-8)

---

## EDUCATION & TEST PREPARATION

**Spanish For Dummies**
0-7645-5194-9

**Algebra For Dummies**
0-7645-5325-9

**The ACT For Dummies**
0-7645-5210-4

**Also available:**

Chemistry For Dummies
(0-7645-5430-1)

English Grammar For Dummies
(0-7645-5322-4)

French For Dummies
(0-7645-5193-0)

The GMAT For Dummies
(0-7645-5251-1)

Inglés Para Dummies
(0-7645-5427-1)

Italian For Dummies
(0-7645-5196-5)

Research Papers For Dummies
(0-7645-5426-3)

The SAT I For Dummies
(0-7645-5472-7)

U.S. History For Dummies
(0-7645-5249-X)

World History For Dummies
(0-7645-5242-2)

---

**Available wherever books are sold. Go to www.dummies.com or call 1-877-762-2974 to order direct.**